explorer

Dubai
Residents' Guide

there's more to life...
ask**explorer**.com

Go knowing
www.crownrelo.com/uae

Valuable cargo

It's important to choose someone who'll take extra care of the most precious things.

Crown service offerings include:
- International & Domestic Shipments
- Storage, Airfreight
- Transit Insurance
- Immigration & Legalization
- Home Search
- School Search

Tel: +971 4 230 5300
dubai@crownrelo.com

CROWN
RELOCATIONS

INTERNATIONALLY ACCREDITED HEALTHCARE ON YOUR DOORSTEP

MEDICLINIC MIDDLE EAST OPERATES:

- Mediclinic Welcare Hospital
- Mediclinic Dubai Mall
- Mediclinic Meadows
- Mediclinic Mirdif
- Mediclinic Beach Road

- Mediclinic City Hospital
- Mediclinic Ibn Battuta
- Mediclinic Arabian Ranches
- Mediclinic Al Qusais
- Mediclinic Al Sufouh

EXPERTISE YOU CAN TRUST.

UAE • SOUTH AFRICA • NAMIBIA • SWITZERLAND
www.mediclinic.ae

MOH 2722-2-10-27-1-14 *Ad approval covers facility in UAE only*

ميديكلينيك
MEDICLINIC

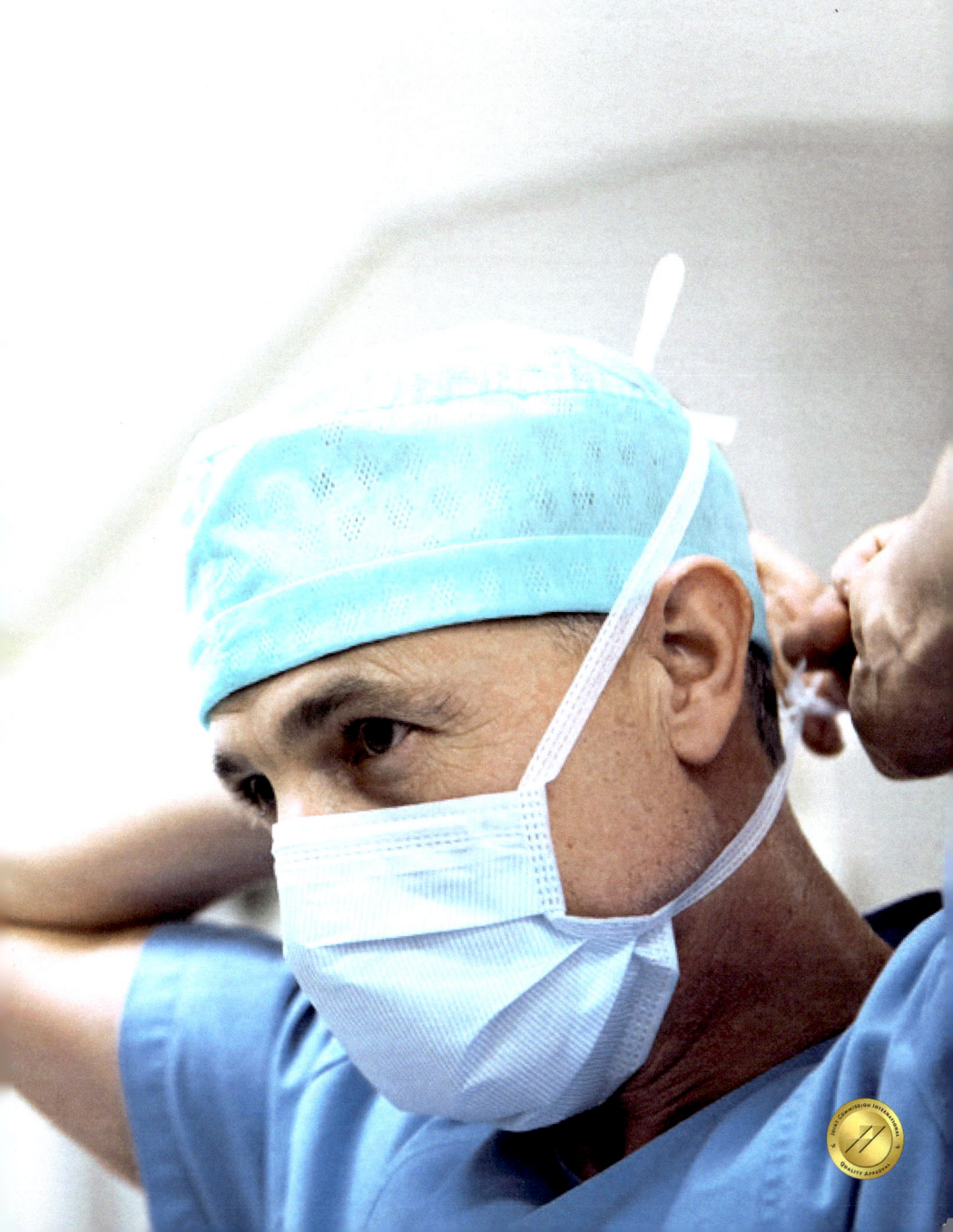

www.golfandshootingshj.com

PRACTICE TARGET SHOOTING WITH REAL GUNS & REAL BULLETS

OR SWING INTO OUR INDOOR & OUTDOOR ARCHERY RANGES

نادي الشارقة للجولف والرماية
SHARJAH GOLF & SHOOTING CLUB

For Bookings, Contact:
+971 6 548 7777
+971 50 475 8871

PAINTBALL
@ SHARJAH PAINTBALL PARK

WHEN WAS THE LAST TIME YOU HAD PURE FUN?

- **2 INDOOR FIELDS**
- **3 OUTDOOR FIELDS**
- **LARGEST IN THE MIDDLE EAST**
- **STATE-OF-THE-ART GUNS & GEAR**
- **5 STAR CHANGING & WASHROOMS**
- **EXCITING BIRTHDAY PARTY VENUE**
- **CLASSIC TEAM BUILDING EXERCISE**
- **FUN ZONE FOR THE ENTIRE FAMILY**

Sharjah Paintball Park

www.paintballuae.com

BOOKINGS
050 203 22 88

Golf & Shooting Club, PO Box 12, Sharjah, UAE
paintball@golfandshootingshj.com

Dubai Duty Free

Stylish designer bags
Irresistible fragrances
Glamorous sunglasses
One way to have it all

TRAVEL LIGHT
Shop at Dubai Duty Free

www.dubaidutyfree.com

Full of surprises.

YAS ISLAND

ACTIVITIES, EVENTS, DINING,
ACCOMMODATION AND SO MUCH MORE...

CHOOSING WHAT TO DO IS A PUZZLE!

FERRARI WORLD ABU DHABI

The world's first indoor Ferrari branded theme park, featuring its record breaking roller coaster, Formula Rossa which speeds up to 240 kmph.

UNIQUE WATER ADVENTURES AT YAS WATERWORLD

The largest Emirati themed waterpark in the UAE and the world's first aqua park with a rollercoaster ride.

YAS LINKS GOLF COURSE

The first championship links course in the UAE designed by Kyle Phillips, a world leading golf course designer.

ROOMS WITH ISLAND VIEW

Yas Island offers a great range of accommodation (from affordable to luxury) with Yas Viceroy and six centralized Yas Plaza hotels, all hosting gourmet restaurants, entertainment, fitness and wellness venues.

PURE RELAXATION – YAS BEACH

Let your soul wander, swim, paddle board, or kayak away on the shores of Yas Island's exclusive beach.

HOME TO THE FORMULA 1™ ETIHAD AIRWAYS ABU DHABI GRAND PRIX

Drive a Formula Yas 3000 or Aston Martin GT4 on the same circuit as the pros. – You can!

NEED A CLUE?
FIND US AT

FACEBOOK.COM/YASISLAND @YASISLAND YASISLANDAE

YAS ISLAND.AE

TIME TO REFRESH YOUR WORLD.

Get a fresh take on life and discover a different Dubai with Wild Wadi's splashy attractions and sunny surprises. Exciting rides and even more exciting adventures await you at the wildest park in town!

www.wildwadi.com | Call: +971 4 348 4444

JUMEIRAH GROUP

Jumeirah Hotel guests can access the park with compliments of the Jumeirah Group

Wild Wadi WATERPARK

LIFE. REFRESHED.

Jumeirah Sceirah | Master Blaster | Tunnel of Doom | Flowriders | Lazy River | Wave Pool | Flood River | Children's Play Structure | Family Rides

A DIVISION OF LANDMARK RETAIL LTD.

Mint three-seater
Dhs 2,450

No two homes will be the same.

You are like no one else. Shouldn't your home be too? That's why, we offer the widest selection of furniture and home furnishings at Home Centre. Choose from 228 sofas, 245 lamps, 101 beds, 54 dining sets and unlimited other home ideas. Make your home like no other.

homecentre

shukran

800 MYHOME
694663

UAE - Dubai, Abu Dhabi, Sharjah, Fujairah, Al Ain, Ras Al Khaimah
UAE | Saudi Arabia | Kuwait | Bahrain | Qatar | Oman | Jordan | Egypt | Lebanon | India | www.homecentrestores.com | /homecentrestores

مجموعة صالح بن لاحج
SALEH BIN LAHEJ GROUP
★ ★ ★ ★ ★
قطاع الضيافة
HOSPITALITY DIVISION

" Saleh Bin Lahej Group - Hospitality Division houses the best restaurant brands in the Middle East, connecting with a diverse range of consumers across a broad spectrum of cuisine offerings in its constant pursuit to *Serving You a World of Taste.*

Chili's

BLACK CANYON
Good Food for Good Health and Good Life

ROMANO'S Macaroni GRILL

El Chico Since 1940
MEXICAN RESTAURANT

The PIZZA Company

Cantina LAREDO
gourmet mexican food

FAMOUS FOR Steak 'n Shake STEAKBURGERS

SILVER FOX
PRIME STEAKS . SEAFOOD . LOBSTER

Dubai . Abu Dhabi . Sharjah
Ras Al Khaimah . Al Ain . Fujairah

600 56 1112
www.salehbinlahejgroup.com

an 'out of the world'
experience awaits...

For the latest updates f t **Dreamland Aqua Park**
Umm Al Quwain, Etihad Road E11 through Mohammad Bin Zayed Road (E311)
or Emirates Road (E611), Exit 103, Tel: 06 7681888
Fridays and Public Holidays are reserved for families, pre-booked groups or special pass holders

DREAMLAND AQUA PARK

www.dreamlanduae.com

AFRICAN + EASTERN STORES ARE ALL OVER TOWN!

With 13 conveniently-located African + Eastern stores all across the city, you will always find one in your neighbourhood.

And where there's African + Eastern, there's always an extensive portfolio of labels across ales, grape, malt and more from all over the world. Visit your nearest neighbourhood store for all the brands you love.

For more information call us on **800 CHEERS** (243377) or ask our staff in-store.

Al Wasl Road* · Arabian Ranches* · Bur Dubai* · Burj Views* · Deira* · Dubai Marina Mall*
Dubai Marina Walk* · Green Community** · Jumeirah* · Karama · Le Méridien Dubai** · Mirdif · TECOM*

*Stores also open on Fridays from 2:00pm - 9:00pm
**Stores open Saturday to Thursday from 2:00pm - 9:00pm

african + eastern
INSPIRING GREAT BLENDS

www.africaneastern.com

BRINGING HOME VALUE
SINCE 1975

OVER 50 SOFA SETS,
OVER 35 BEDROOM SETS,
OVER 30 DINING SETS

DISPLAYED AT OUR
MEGA STORE ON
SHEIKH ZAYED RD.
DUBAI, TEL: 04 3389690

Dubai Mega Store: Sheikh Zayed Road (Before Oasis Centre). Tel: 04 3389690
Sharjah Showroom: Al Qasimia Street. Tel: 06 5663777

0% installment plan available*
Conditions apply

Emirates NBD | NBAD

united furniture
surprisingly affordable since 1975

Sofas | Dinings | Bedrooms | Kids | Accessories

/unitedfurn   /ufuae   www.unitedfurnitureco.com

ADVENTURELAND

Premier indoor theme park in the region

GO WILD
TWIST AND SHOUT

25 world-class thrills & first-time attractions in the region!
• Indoor Electric Go-Karts • Motocoaster • Sidewinder • Drop & Twist • Rollercoaster • Family Train • Multi-level Soft Play and more!

ADVENTURELAND is at First Level, Sahara Centre
Dubai-Sharjah Road, Sharjah, U.A.E | Tel. 06-5319668
www.adventureland-sharjah.com

Follow us on /adventurelanduae and @adventureland1

A BOLD JOURNEY.
ONE THAT STARTED GENERATIONS AGO.

ALL NEW
2014 CTS

Take the road less travelled with the Cadillac CTS. Its state of the art technologies and optimized safety embrace every challenge and risk. Its standard 2.0L Turbo with 272hp (net) and 3.6L V6 with 321hp (net) perform better than ever. And with standard Brembo brakes, CUE with 12.3" genuine material and available 8-speed automatic transmission and reconfigurable digital instrument cluster, we're still paving the way forward to standout on the road today.

CADILLAC PREMIUM CARE PROGRAM
- Complimentary service and maintenance for 4 years / 100,000 km
- Resale Value Guarantee*
- Warranty for 4 years / 100,000 km
- Regional roadside assistance for 4 years*
- Courtesy transportation*

* Terms and conditions apply.

cadillacarabia.com Facebook.com/CadillacArabia Twitter.com/CadillacArabia

KSA, Al Jomaih Automotive, Toll Free 800 244 2000. **UAE**, Liberty Abu Dhabi Automobiles Co. L.L.C, Abu Dhabi, Liberty Automobiles Co. L.L.C, Dubai, Toll Free 800 Liberty (5423789). **Qatar**, Mannai Trading Co. W.L.L, Doha, Tel: (974) 455 8877, Wakra, Tel: (974) 448 3666, Umm Al Afai, Tel: (974) 490 1086. **Kuwait**, Yusuf A. Alghanim & Sons W.L.L, Kuwait, Tel: (965) 2475 4400 **Oman**, Oman Trading Establishment L.L.C, Muscat, Tel: (968) 245 02870. **Bahrain**, National Motor Company, Sitra, Tel: (973) 174 57212. **Lebanon**, Impex, Beirut, Tel: (961) 1 615 715. **Jordan**, Abukhader Automotive, Amman, Tel: (962) 6 580 3600.

Cadillac

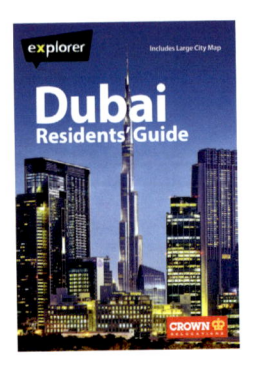

Dubai Residents' Guide 2014/18th Edition
First Published 1996
2nd Edition 1997
3rd Edition 1998
4th Edition 2000
5th Edition 2001
6th Edition 2002
7th Edition 2003
8th Edition 2004
9th Edition 2005
10th Edition 2006
11th Edition 2007
12th Edition 2008
13th Edition 2009
14th Edition 2010
15th Edition 2011
16th Edition 2012
17th Edition 2013
18th Edition 2014   ISBN 978-9948-20-261-5

Copyright © Explorer Group Ltd, 1996, 1997, 1998, 2000, 2001, 2002, 2003, 2004, 2005, 2006, 2007, 2008, 2009, 2010, 2011, 2012, 2013, 2014.
All rights reserved.

Front Cover Photograph – Burj Khalifa – Pete Maloney

Explorer Publishing & Distribution
PO Box 34275, Dubai
United Arab Emirates
Phone   +971 (0)4 340 8805
Fax   +971 (0)4 340 8806
Email   info@askexplorer.com
Web   askexplorer.com

While every effort and care has been made to ensure the accuracy of the information contained in this publication, the publisher cannot accept responsibility for any errors or omissions it may contain.
No part of this publication may be reproduced, stored in a retrieval system, or transmitted, in any form or by any means, electronic, mechanical, photocopying, recording or otherwise, without the prior permission in writing of the publisher.

Welcome...

...to the new look Dubai Residents' Guide. This 18th anniversary edition gets straight to the crucial information you need to know about moving to, living in and enjoying life in this fascinating emirate. From red-tape procedures to schools, restaurants and things to see and do, it's all covered here.

Dubai is a modern, thriving metropolis – one that is constantly growing and changing. We can only fit so much exhaustive information onto these pages, so to keep abreast of the latest news, as well as reviews on the newest restaurants, information on upcoming events and updates to UAE laws, make askexplorer.com your online companion while in Dubai.

Finally, don't forget that Explorer publishes hundreds of maps and activity guides that help you to extract the most from life in the UAE. Discover more at askexplorer.com/shop.

In your hands, in the glovebox, in your rucksack; on your laptop, tablet or smartphone. Wherever you're going and whatever you're doing, be sure to take us with you.

There's more to life...
The Explorer Team

We'd love to hear from you, whether you make a great insider discovery or want to share your views about this or any of our products. Fill in our reader survey at askexplorer.com/feedback – and get 20% off your next online purchase.

askexplorer.com

CONTENTS

THE UAE — 1

The UAE Today	2

Country Profile — 3
Capital	3
Population	3
Area	3
Flag	3
Currency	3
Time Zone	3
Country Code	4
Business Hours	4

Geography — 4
Weather	4

History — 6

Government — 8
Key Government Figures	8

Economy — 8
Dubai	12
Trade	12
Tourism	12
International Relations	13

Environment — 13
Flora & Fauna	13
Wildlife	14
Sustainability	14
Recycling	15

Culture & Lifestyle — 16
Culture	16
Language	16
Religion	16
Basic Arabic	17
National Dress	18
Food & Drink	18

Crime — 20
Laws To Know	20
The Legal System	22
Police	22

Local Media — 23
Internet	23
Useful Apps	23
Useful Websites	24
Radio	24
Newspapers	24
Television	24

UAE Calendar — 26
Public Holidays	26
Events & Exhibitions	26

LIVING IN DUBAI — 31

City Profile — 33

Before You Arrive — 33
Checklist	33

When You Arrive — 34
Checklist	34
Visit Visa	34
Residence Visas	36
Employment Visa	36
Family Visa	40
Domestic Worker Visa	40
Medical Test	42
Health Card	43
Resident Identity Card	43
Driving Licence	44
Liquor Licence	44
Temporary Accommodation	46

Settling In — 48
National Groups	48
Social Networks	48
Places Of Worship	49

Before You Leave — 49
Cancelling Visas	49

Housing — 50

Accommodation — 51
When You Arrive	51
Apartments	51
Villas	51
Home Address	51
RERA	52
Real Estate Agents	52
Renting A Home	52
Tenancy Contract	54
Buying A Home	56
Real Estate Law	58
Mortgages	59
Purchase Costs	60
Buying Process	60
Selling A Home	60

Residential Areas — 64
Marsa Dubai & JBR	65
Palm Jumeirah	66
Jumeira	68
Emirates Living	70
Downtown Dubai	72
Al Barsha	74
Discovery Gardens	76
Dubailand	77
Old Dubai	80
Mirdif	81

Setting Up Home — 82
Moving Services	83
Furnishing Accommodation	84
Utilities & Services	86
Telecommunications	88
Postal Services	89
Television	90
Maids & Cleaners	90
Home Improvements	91
Gardens	92
Home Insurance	93

Getting Around — 94
Dubai Road Network	95
Driving in Dubai	96
Parking	96
Road Tolls	97
Traffic Offences	97
Breakdowns	98
Traffic Accidents	98
Petrol Stations	99
Learning To Drive	99
Hiring A Car	99
Buying A Car	100
Insurance	104
Registering A Vehicle	104
Vehicle Repairs	104
Cycling	106
Walking	106
Public Transport	109
Air Travel	111
The Future	112

Finance — 114
Main Banks	114
Online Banking	115
Cheques	115
Financial Planning	115
Tax	118
Offshore Accounts	118

Health — 120
Government Healthcare	121
Private Healthcare	121
Accidents & Emergencies	121
General Medical Care	122
Government Hospitals	124

xxii Dubai Explorer

CONTENTS

Private Hospitals	124
Specialist Hospitals & Clinics	128
Maternity	130
Obstetrics & Gynaecology	132
Orthopaedics	134
Paediatrics	134
Physiotherapy	135
Pharmacies	136
Medication	136
Dentists	138
Opticians	139
Alternative Therapies	140
Cosmetic Treatment & Surgery	140
Nutritionists & Slimming	142
Counselling & Therapy	143

Family & Parenting — 144
Marriage	144
Family Law	146
Death	147
Having A Baby	148
From Bump To Birth	150
Adoption	151
Single Parents	151
Mother & Baby Groups	151
Hiring A Nanny	151
Activities For Kids	152

Pets — 158
Moving Your Pet	158
Buying A Pet	158
Vaccinations & Registration	160
Taking Your Pet Home	160
Vets, Kennels & Boarding	160

Fitness — 164
Gyms & Fitness Clubs	164
Yoga & Pilates	165
Personal Training	166

Well-being — 168
Beauty Salons & Nail Bars	168
Hairdressers	169
Spas	170

Clubs & Groups — 178
Sport	179
Hobbies	194

WORKING IN DUBAI — 205

Employment — 207
Getting Started	207
Permit To Work	208
Employment Contracts	208
UAE Labour Law	210

Free Zones — 212
Freelance Work	213
Part-time Work	214

Business — 214
Business Culture	214
Networking & Events	216

Starting A Business — 216

Voluntary & Charity Work — 218
Environmental Groups	219

EDUCATION — 223

Nurseries — 225
International	225
Early Years Foundation Stage	225
Montessori	229

Selecting A School — 230
Curriculum	230
KHDA Rankings	231
School Fees	231
School Transport	232

Primary & Secondary Schools — 232
American Curriculum	233
English National Curriculum	234
International Baccalaureate Programme	243
Special Needs Education	245
After-School Activities	246

Universities & Colleges — 247
International Universities	248
Public Universities	250
Institutes & Colleges	252
Language Courses	254

THINGS TO SEE & DO — 257

Places Of Interest — 259
Deira & The Creek	259
Downtown Dubai	260
Marsa Dubai	261
Jumeira	262
Palm Jumeirah	263

Art & Culture — 266
Art Galleries	266
Heritage Sites	268
Museums	272

Attractions — 273
Amusement Centres	273
Theme Parks	274
Water Parks	274
Wildlife & Sealife	276

Parks & Beaches — 278
Beaches	278
Beach Clubs	280
Parks	281

Sports & Leisure — 283
Archery	283
Bowling	283
Golf	284
Ice Skating	288
Karting	288
Mini Golf	288
Motorsports	290
Multi-sports	290
Shooting & Paintballing	290
Skateparks	292
Skiing	292
Skydiving	292

Activities — 294
Biking	294
Boating	294
Camping	295
Caving	296
Climbing	296
Desert Activities	298
Diving	299
Hiking	302
Off-roading	303
Water Activities	304

Tours — 307
Bus	307
Desert & Mountain	307
Boat	310
Aerial Tours	312

Hotels — 313
Staycations	313
Visitors In Town?	314

CONTENTS

SHOPPING — 323

Second-hand — 374
Soft Furnishings — 374
Souvenirs — 375
Sports & Outdoor Equipment — 376
Textiles, Tailoring & Repairs — 379
Weddings — 380

Need to know — 325
How To Pay — 325
Shopping Events — 325
Online Shopping — 326
Deliveries & Shipping — 326
Refunds, Exchanges & Consumer Rights — 326

Shopping Districts — 328
Al Barsha — 328
Al Qouz — 329
Bur Dubai — 329
Deira — 330
Downtown Dubai — 330
Dubailand — 330
Marsa Dubai — 331
Jumeira & Umm Suqeim — 331
Mirdif — 333
Satwa — 333
Out Of Town — 333

Places To Shop — 334
Department Stores — 334
Hypermarkets — 336
Convenience Stores — 336
Supermarkets — 337
Delis & Health Foods — 337
Farm Shops — 338
Markets — 340
Souks — 344
Shopping Malls — 346

Buyers' Guide — 352
Alcohol — 353
Arts & Crafts — 353
Books, Music & DVDs — 354
Camera Equipment — 358
Car Accessories — 358
Clothing & Shoes — 359
Electrical Goods — 359
Furniture & Homewares — 360
Gardens & Pools — 364
Hardware & DIY — 365
Jewellery — 365
Kids — 366
Mother & Baby — 368
Musical Instruments — 369
Parties — 370
Perfumes & Cosmetics — 372
Pets — 372

GOING OUT — 383

Restaurants — 385
Alfresco — 390
Waterfront — 392
Brunch — 394
Celebrity Chef — 396
Cheap & Cheerful — 398
Family Friendly — 400
Hidden Gems — 402
Informal — 404
Live Music — 407
Quick Bites — 408
Romantic — 409
Showstopper — 411
Taste Of Home — 412

Cafes — 416
Breakfast — 416
Coffee Mornings — 417
Working Lunch — 418
Afternoon Tea — 419
Family Friendly — 420

Bars, Pubs & Clubs — 422
Beach Bars & Sundowners — 422
Cocktails — 424
Pubs — 425
Rooftop — 428
Showstopper — 430
Wine Bars & Cigar Lounges — 431
Nightclubs — 433

Entertainment — 435
Cabaret — 435
Cinema — 435
Comedy — 436
Live Music — 436
Theatre — 438

Staying In — 439
Home Delivery — 439
Parties — 439

OUT OF THE CITY — 443

Abu Dhabi — 445
Attractions — 445
Hotels — 448

Al Ain — 452
Attractions — 452
Hotels — 453

Al Gharbia — 454
Hotels — 456

Ajman — 457
Attractions — 457
Hotels — 457

Fujairah — 458
Attractions — 459
Hotels — 460

Ras Al Khaimah — 460
Attractions — 460
Hotels — 465

Sharjah — 468
Attractions — 468
Hotels — 471

Umm Al Quwain — 471
Attractions — 471
Hotels — 472

Oman — 472
Musandam — 472
Muscat — 473
Salalah — 474
Western Hajar — 476

Qatar — 476
Attractions — 476
Hotels — 478

INDEX — 482

NEED A DOCTOR?

800 DOCTOR
A Doctor At Your Doorstep In One Hour

CALL 800 DOCTOR
(800 3 6 2 8 6 7)

SERVICES

- Doctors On Call
- Nursing Care
- Physiotherapy
- Laboratory Tests

Home | Hotel | Office

24/7/365

Managed by
LIFELINE HOSPITAL

part of **LIFELINE HEALTHCARE**

MOH NO: 385-2-02-09-03-2014

www.lifeline.ae

seawings.ae

SEE DUBAI AS NEVER BEFORE

Get a bird's eye view of Dubai as you soar across clear blue skies and glittering coastline onboard the Seawings™ seaplane.

Hold your breath as you witness present day wonders – Palm Jumeirah, The World Islands, Burj Al Arab, Burj Khalifa, the historic Dubai Creek, bustling Port Rashid and more. It's a view that will be remembered for a lifetime!

Call For Reservations
☎ **+971 4 8070708**
or email reservations@seawings.ae

Seawings LLC, Dubai, UAE © Copyright 2014. All rights reserved.

tripadvisor Read Seawings customer reviews on Tripadvisor
Follow *Seawings Dubai* on Facebook and Twitter.

seawings
Seaplane Tours

THE UAE

Country Profile	**3**
Geography	**4**
History	**6**
Government	**8**
Economy	**8**
Environment	**13**
Culture & Lifestyle	**16**
Crime & The Law	**20**
Local Media	**23**
UAE Calendar	**26**

THE UAE

From the rugged northern mountains, to the vast interior deserts, the UAE has an astounding amount of cultural and physical diversity across its seven emirates.

Marsa Dubai with its iconic skyscrapers

The United Arab Emirates (UAE) comprises seven emirates: Abu Dhabi, Ajman, Dubai, Fujairah, Ras Al Khaimah, Sharjah and Umm Al Quwain. Located in the heart of the Middle East, its rise from a quiet strategic trading destination to a regional and global economic powerhouse is nothing short of remarkable – and makes it one of the most exciting places to live.

The UAE Today

While its culture is still rooted in Islamic tradition, the UAE is also one of the most cosmopolitan countries in the Middle East.

The country has a bold vision for its future and is working towards becoming a first-choice destination for tourism, finance, industry and trade. This makes it a vibrant and opportunity-filled place to live in and work. Trade and commerce are still the cornerstones of the economy, with the traditional manufacturing and distribution industries now joined by finance, construction, media, IT and telecom businesses. With so many world-class hotels, and leisure and entertainment options, the UAE is becoming a popular tourist destination too. Similarly, people from over 150 nations now call the UAE home as they bring their skills and manpower to help in the country's plan; and many expats find the country so welcoming that it becomes difficult to leave.

Sunshine and tax-free salaries may be why expats come, but what keeps them here is the ability to mix with other cultures, live in a liberal Middle Eastern country, and enjoy the sort of lifestyle they would be hard-pressed to find at home.

THE UAE
COUNTRY PROFILE

COUNTRY PROFILE

If you're looking to move to the UAE, live here already or are just visiting, there are a number of things that are useful to know. This section highlights some of those facts and figures that can help you make your way in the UAE, or, at the very least, arm you with some good ammunition for a quiz night.

Capital

The capital city of the UAE is Abu Dhabi, a large part of which is actually an island linked to the mainland by bridges. The city is part of the largest emirate and is continuing to grow at a significant rate. To the east of the main Abu Dhabi island an area of land between Khalifa City and Shakhbout City has been designated as Zayed City, or the Capital District. While still largely a huge patch of sand, the key initiative is for the Capital District to become the seat of power and government for the whole of the UAE. It will accommodate federal ministries as well as foreign embassies and help to reinforce the cultural diversity of the UAE. More details can be found in the Abu Dhabi Vision 2030 Plan, which outlines the city's plans to grow and diversify over the next 15 or so years.

Be Happy
Good news for UAE residents. A 2013 report by UN Sustainable Development Solutions Network ranked the country as the 14th happiest country in the world, higher than the USA, the UK, Germany and Japan. The World Happiness Report also rates the UAE as the happiest Arab country in the world.

Population

The UAE population has grown rapidly in recent years as expat arrivals, robust economic expansion and high birth rates have continued to push up the total number. According to the World Bank, the UAE's population was just 322,439, a year after the country was formed, in 1972.

By 2002, 30 years later, that had ballooned by 10 times to just over 3.2 million. After 40 years, population has now grown by over 28 times the 1972 figure, currently recorded at around 9.2 million. Compared to just 10 years previously, that's a 185% increase.

Unsurprisingly the vast majority of this growth has come from foreign workers moving to the country, the local population now accounts for just 15%. However, aside from the huge number of Indians settling in the UAE, Emirati nationals still make up the largest ethnic group and have considerable influence.

Area

The total land area of the UAE is approximately 83,600sq km, with around 1,318km of coastline. Dubai accounts for a huge 4,114sq km of that total. While not particularly mountainous, the highest named point is Jebel Yibir at 1,572m, 'jebel' meaning mountain or hill in Arabic. The UAE's coordinates are 24°00'North 54°00'East.

Flag

The UAE flag incorporates the Pan-Arab colours of green, white, black and red, symbolising Arabian unity. It was adopted on 2 December 1971 as the official flag of the country. Interestingly, each of the seven emirates aside from Fujairah also has its own flag, all of which use just red and white.

Currency

The monetary unit is the dirham (Dhs.), which is divided into 100 fils. The currency is also referred to as AED (Arab Emirate Dirham). On notes, all denominations are marked in both Arabic and English, although coin values are shown only in Arabic. Notes come in denominations of Dhs.5 (brown), Dhs.10 (green), Dhs.20 (light blue), Dhs.50 (purple), Dhs.100 (pink), Dhs.200 (yellowy-brown), Dhs.500 (blue) and Dhs.1,000 (browny-purple). Watch your Dhs.200 notes though, they can be mistaken for a Dhs.5 note if you're in a hurry.

All coins are silver in colour, with a total of six in circulation, but you typically only come across the three largest denominations: Dhs.1, 50 fils and 25 fils. The dirham has been pegged to the US dollar since 1980, at a mid-rate of $1 to Dhs.3.6725.

Time Zone

The UAE is four hours ahead of the UTC (Universal Coordinated Time, formerly known as GMT). Clocks are not altered for daylight saving in the summer, so when Europe and North America gain an hour in spring, the time in the UAE stays the same resulting in a shorter three hours time difference. Time differences between

askexplorer.com

3

THE UAE
GEOGRAPHY

the UAE and some cities around the world (not allowing for any daylight savings in those cities) are: Bangkok +3; Hong Kong +4; London -4; Los Angeles -12; Moscow -1; New York -9; Sydney +6; and Tokyo +5.

Country Code

The international dialling code for the UAE is +971. Each city also has its own dialling code, which is the first digit (or two digits in some cases) that you dial when calling. These are: 2, Abu Dhabi; 6, Ajman; 3, Al Ain; 58, Aweer; 6, Dhayd; 9, Dibba; 4, Dubai; 6, Falaj-Al-Moalla; 9, Fujairah; 48, Khawaneej; 7, Ras Al Khaimah; 6, Sharjah; 88, Tarif; 6, Umm Al Quwain.

Business Hours

The UAE working week is from Sunday to Thursday. Friday is the Islamic holy day and therefore a universal day off for offices and schools, so the two-day weekend spans Friday and Saturday. Some companies still require a six-day working week from their staff, while others operate on a five-and-a-half-day system. Consumer demand means that the hospitality and retail industries are open seven days a week.

Larger shops and shopping centres are generally open throughout the day and into the evening until around 10pm or midnight. Traditional shops and street retailers often operate under split shift timings, closing for three or four hours in the afternoon. Some food outlets and petrol stations are open for 24 hours a day.

Ramadan Hours

According to UAE labour laws, all companies are obliged to shorten the working day by two hours during the holy month of Ramadan. This is to assist Muslim employees who are fasting but the law also technically applies to non-Muslims. In reality, many international companies don't follow this principle, so it's a bonus if an expat is allowed to work Ramadan hours. Many schools, shops and businesses do change their hours during Ramadan, often opening later in the day and staying open until midnight or even 1am. The city's shisha cafes and some restaurants stay open until the early hours.

If you're working in the UAE, 8am to 5pm or 9am to 6pm with an hour for lunch are normal shifts in the private sector. It is common for working hours in the UAE to be longer than in other countries when working for a private company.

Most government offices are open from 7.30am to 2.30pm, Sunday to Thursday. Embassies and consulates operate similar hours, but may designate specific times and days for certain tasks (such as passport applications), so it's best to call before you go. All will have an emergency number on their answering service, website or on their office door during times they are closed.

GEOGRAPHY

Located in the heart of the Middle East, the UAE borders Saudi Arabia and the Sultanate of Oman, with coastlines on both the Arabian Gulf and the Gulf of Oman. The country comprises seven emirates: Abu Dhabi, Ajman, Dubai, Fujairah, Ras Al Khaimah, Sharjah and Umm Al Quwain. Abu Dhabi is by far the largest emirate, occupying over 80% of the country; the emirate of Dubai is second largest, although Abu Dhabi and Dubai have similar population sizes.

The country is perhaps best known for the modern, rapidly expanding metropolises of Abu Dhabi and Dubai, but visitors may be surprised by the variety of landscapes when they venture beyond the cities. The coast is littered with coral reefs and more than 200 islands, most of which are uninhabited. The interior of the country is characterised by *sabkha* (salt flats), stretches of gravel plain, and vast areas of sand desert. To the east rise the Hajar Mountains ('*hajar*' is Arabic for 'rock') which, lying close to the Gulf of Oman, form a backbone through the country, from the Musandam Peninsula in the north, through the eastern UAE and into Oman.

Weather

The UAE only really experiences two seasons: hot and hotter. Without a doubt the best time to live, and visit, the country is from October to April, when it's mostly blue skies and temperatures of 10°C (50°F) to 24°C (75°F). Every day in the winter is a sunny reminder of why you chose to live here – tepid sea water to swim in, cloudless skies to sunbathe under, and warm, comfortable evenings for alfresco dining.

However, during the summer months (between June and September), be prepared for triple-digit temperatures and high humidity levels. Thermometers range from 41°C (106°F) up to a scorching 48°C (118°) in August. Yes, it's undeniably hot, but the UAE is well and truly geared up for it with AC in every mall, restaurant, office and even bus shelters, to keep sweaty brows at bay.

HOME OF WORLD RECORDS

There's barely a week goes by when something from the UAE doesn't claim to be the world's biggest, tallest, fastest or most expensive; and even then you can be sure there are plans to go bigger, taller, faster or even more costly. While it may look like showy extravagance, it's actually a smart way to get this relatively new country on the map and make it a must-visit destination for tourists and a more attractive proposition to foreign companies looking to invest. For residents though, the 100 and more entries by the UAE in the Guinness World Records 2014 mean a seemingly endless list of things to see or do while living in the country.

Fastest rollercoaster made from steel – Formula Rossa, Ferrari World, Abu Dhabi
Most environmentally friendly city – Masdar City, Abu Dhabi
Tallest man-made structure on land – Burj Khalifa, Dubai
Largest shopping centre – The Dubai Mall, Dubai
Longest driverless metro – Dubai Metro, Dubai
Tallest residential building – Princess Tower, Dubai
Furthest leaning man-made tower – Hyatt Capital Gate, Abu Dhabi
Largest automated car park – Emirates Financial Towers, Dubai
Largest firework display – New Year's Eve 2013, Palm Jumeirah and The World, Dubai

THE UAE
HISTORY

Humidity is usually between 50% and 60%, and, when combined with high summer temperatures, can be a little uncomfortable to endure. Many expats escape the suffocating heat during the summer and head home for an extended holiday.

Leave those umbrellas and wellies at home, as rainfall is almost non-existent – just 25 days per year – and when it does fall it is rarely for long periods. So, there's more than enough good weather to brag about to those back home.

HISTORY

As a country, the UAE is still young having only formed in 1971 when unifying the different emirates was seen as a progressive move to enhance security and influence in the area. However, the region has a long history before that.

Much of the early existence is closely linked to the arrival and development of Islam in the greater Middle East. Islam developed in modern-day Saudi Arabia at the beginning of the seventh century AD with the revelations of the Quran being received by the Prophet Muhammad. Military conquests of the Middle East and North Africa enabled the Arab empire to spread the teachings of Islam from Mecca and Medina to the local Bedouin tribes inhabiting the surrounding areas.

Periods of dominance from other empires followed over the centuries, with the Turks, Mongols and Ottomans exerting their influence over the region. In the early 19th century the British and Portuguese dipped their oars into Arabian waters, attracted by the area's strategic position between Europe and India and the desire to quash the rise of piracy in the local waters. By 1820, the British had flexed their naval muscle in the region and a general treaty was agreed by the local rulers, denouncing piracy. The following years witnessed a series of maritime truces, with the emirates accepting British protection in 1892. In Europe, the area became known as the Trucial Coast, a name it retained until the departure of the British in 1971, the same year the UAE was established.

British Withdrawal
When Britain announced plans for its withdrawal in 1968, the ruling sheikhs of Bahrain, Qatar and the Trucial Coast realised that they would have a stronger voice in the Middle East by uniting forces as a single state. Negotiations collapsed when Bahrain and Qatar chose independence; however, in 1971, the federation of the United Arab Emirates was born from the Trucial Coast, with Ras Al Khaimah joining in 1972 to establish the UAE we know today.

Under the agreement, the individual emirates retained a certain amount of autonomy, with Abu Dhabi and Dubai providing the most input into the federation. The leaders of the new federation elected the ruler of Abu Dhabi, His Highness Sheikh Zayed bin Sultan Al Nahyan, to be the president of the newly founded country. The well-liked and highly respected Sheikh held the position until he passed on 2 November 2004. The eponymous Sheikh Zayed Grand Mosque in Abu Dhabi was his final place of rest, his mausoleum complete when the mosque opened in 2007. The mosque itself was his great vision and was intended to unite not just the UAE but the wider Arab populace. His eldest son, His Highness Sheikh Khalifa bin Zayed Al Nahyan, was elected to take over the presidency and oversaw the final few years of the mosque's fantastic construction.

In 1958, huge oil reserves were discovered in Abu Dhabi. The discovery dramatically transformed the emirate. In 1966, oil was also found in Dubai, by then already a relatively wealthy trading centre. Dubai's ruler at the time, the late Sheikh Rashid bin Saeed Al Maktoum, ensured that the emirate's oil revenues were used to develop an economic and social infrastructure to secure the emirate's future, which is the basis of today's modern society. His forward-thinking work was continued through the reign of his son and successor, Sheikh Maktoum bin Rashid Al Maktoum and by the present ruler, Sheikh Mohammed bin Rashid Al Maktoum.

Dhows on the creek at Deira

Dubai Explorer

THE UAE
UAE TIMELINE

UAE TIMELINE

The UAE's history is both rich and colourful, from the arrival and development of Islam in the greater Middle East region to the radical changes resulting from the discovery of oil to the formation of the federation of the United Arab Emirates.

Stone Age	Modern human settlement in the UAE dates back to ca. 7,000BC
Bronze Age	Archaeological evidence of human settlements; the domestication of the camel boosts trade
Iron Age	The invention of *falaj*, an irrigation technology, takes place somewhere between 1,300-300BC
630	Envoys from the Prophet Muhammad arrive, heralding the conversion of local people to Islam
1761	The Baniyas tribe discovers fresh water in Abu Dhabi and settles on the island; leading to the construction of Qasr Al Hosn
1790s	The pearl trade is booming off the coast of Abu Dhabi
1835	Maritime Truce signed between the Trucial States and Britain
1930s	The first oil concession in Abu Dhabi is granted to Trucial Coast Oil Development Company
1950s	Oil is discovered in the UAE, exports begin in 1962
1966	Sheikh Zayed bin Sultan Al Nahyan becomes ruler of Abu Dhabi
1971	Britain withdraws from the Gulf and the UAE is established, with Sheikh Zayed bin Sultan Al Nahyan of Abu Dhabi as the leader; the UAE joins the Arab League
1972	Ras Al Khaimah joins the UAE
1973	The UAE launches a single currency, the UAE dirham
1981	The Gulf Cooperation Council (GCC) is formed, with the UAE as a founding member
1985	Emirates Airline is founded
1999	The doors of the Burj Al Arab, the tallest hotel in the world, open for the first time in Dubai
2001	Construction starts on Dubai's Palm Jumeirah
2003	Etihad Airways is founded
2004	Sheikh Zayed bin Sultan Al Nahyan dies and is succeeded as leader of the UAE by his son, Sheikh Khalifa bin Zayed Al Nahyan
2005	Emirates Palace, billed as the world's most expensive hotel, opens to the public
2007	Sheikh Zayed Mosque, the eighth largest mosque in the world, opens during Ramadan. Work also begins on Yas Island and Saadiyat Island
2008	In the wake of a global economic crisis, much of the UAE's property market crashes
2009	Abu Dhabi hosts its inaugural Formula 1 Grand Prix at Yas Marina Circuit; the Sheikh Khalifa Bridge opens, linking the new areas of Abu Dhabi directly to the corniche; Dubai Metro, the region's first public mass-transit system, is launched
2010	The tallest building in the world, the Burj Khalifa, opens in Dubai; Ferrari World Abu Dhabi, the world's largest indoor theme park, opens
2011	The first hotels on Saadiyat Island open their doors to the public; Capital Gate, the world's 'most leaning' tower also opens in Abu Dhabi
2012	Yas Waterworld is completed
2013	Dubai wins the bid to host the World Expo 2020

THE UAE
GOVERNMENT

GOVERNMENT

The UAE is a federation of seven emirates, each with its own ruler, rules and regulations. The Supreme Council of Rulers – made up of the hereditary rulers of the emirates – is the top policy-making body in the UAE, responsible for laws governing education, defence, foreign affairs, communications and development, and for ratifying federal rules. Each emirate has one single vote, and the rulers of Dubai and Abu Dhabi have the power of veto over decisions.

The current President of the UAE is the ruler of Abu Dhabi, Sheikh Khalifa bin Zayed Al Nahyan, who took over the post in November 2004 from his late father, Sheikh Zayed bin Sultan Al Nahyan. The Vice President of the UAE is Sheikh Mohammed bin Rashid Al Maktoum, ruler of Dubai. Both members are elected by the Supreme Council for a five-year term, and are often re-elected time after time.

The UAE's Prime Minister, currently Sheikh Mohammed bin Rashid Al Maktoum, is appointed by the President and chairs the Council of Ministers, which meets once a week in Abu Dhabi to oversee the development and implementation of federal policy across all portfolios of government.

The Federal National Council (FNC) is a consultative assembly of 40 representatives, half of whom are elected. The Council monitors and debates government policy but has no power of veto. The last election was in 2011, and one-fifth of its members are currently women.

Key Government Figures

His Highness Sheikh Khalifa bin Zayed Al Nahyan, the President of the UAE and ruler of Abu Dhabi, has guided the country, and especially Abu Dhabi, through a period of astonishing growth. With his focus on the continuing development of the country's infrastructure, economic health and cultural contributions, he has laid the foundations for a prosperous UAE.

Sheikh Khalifa has always been generous with Abu Dhabi's oil wealth, ensuring other emirates within the country aren't left behind. In 2009, Abu Dhabi gave a US$10 billion loan to Dubai at the height of the financial crisis. The Burj Khalifa in Dubai, the world's tallest building, is named after Sheikh Khalifa.

The Abu Dhabi ruler is well known for his philanthropic commitments, particularly through the Khalifa Bin Zayed Al Nahyan Foundation, which focuses on providing support to the health and education sectors on a domestic, regional and global scale.

Sheikh Mohammed bin Rashid Al Maktoum is the Prime Minister and Vice President of the United Arab Emirates, and ruler of Dubai and is often considered the driving force behind Dubai's exponential growth, pioneering Free Trade Zones, such as Dubai Media City, offering tax exemptions which have attracted foreign companies to set up in the emirate, helping Dubai's economy flourish and reducing its reliance on oil-based industries. He has overseen the development of numerous landmark projects in Dubai including Palm Jumeirah, the 'seven-star' Burj Al Arab hotel and the Burj Khalifa. Find Sheikh Mohammed on Facebook at Facebook.com/HHSheikhMohammed. His brother, Sheikh Hamdan bin Rashid Al Maktoum, is the UAE Minister of Finance and Industry.

Emirs Or Sheikhs?
While the term emirate comes from the ruling title of 'emir', the rulers of the UAE are called 'sheikhs'. You may associate terms like 'sultan' with the Middle East, but this is a title given to rulers of sultanates.

ECONOMY

The UAE is considered the second richest Arab country, after Qatar, on a GDP per capita basis. Globally that equates to being the eighth richest country in the world. With just under 10% of the world's proven oil reserves (most of it within Abu Dhabi emirate) and the seventh largest proven natural gas reserves, hydrocarbon exports still play a large part in the country's wealth.

Since the financial crisis of 2009, which hit Dubai particularly hard, the UAE's perceived safe haven status amid regional political and social unrest has supported growing economic confidence. At an estimated $284.4 billion in 2013, the UAE economy is the second largest in the Gulf, after Saudi Arabia. In the Where-To-Be-Born Index, 2013 (which highlights the countries where new babies could expect the highest quality of life) the UAE came a respectable 17th, the highest ranking Arab country and just behind the United States and Germany.

While there are still issues such as readdressing the post-financial crisis increases in public spending, reducing energy subsidies and the challenge for Dubai to service its large debts, the outlook looks positive.

THE UAE
ECONOMY

Deira skyline

Successful economic diversification means that the UAE's wealth is no longer solely reliant on oil revenue; just 25% of GDP is based on oil and gas output now.

In mid-2013, the International Monetary Fund (IMF) forecast that the UAE's non-oil sector would accelerate by 4.3%, up from 3.5% on the previous year. This was supported by a recovery in construction and real estate, as well as ongoing growth in tourism-orientated sectors. The government aims to boost growth by creating jobs, lowering the costs of running businesses and by attracting more foreign investment.

Earning Potential

However, while the UAE GDP per capita income stands at around Dhs.183,000 ($49,800) this figure includes all sections of the community and the average labourer, of whom there are many, can expect to earn as little as Dhs.600 ($165) per month. Even before the financial crisis, the salaries for most job types were dropping too. Aside from highly skilled professionals, the average expat coming to work in the UAE shouldn't expect to automatically be on a huge salary.

While the unemployment level of the national population in the UAE is lower than that of many other Arab states, there are still a significant number of Emiratis out of work (over 20% according to some reports). This is partly due to a preference for public sector work and partly because of qualifications not matching the skills required for the roles available in the private sector. However, the government is trying to reverse this scenario and reduce unemployment in the local sector with a 'Nationalisation' or 'Emiratisation' programme.

Jobseekers searching for vacant positions and average salary details in Dubai are advised to do their research first via one of the many recruitment agencies based here. For an idea of what you can expect to earn (in a variety of roles) try charterhouseme.ae for further details.

World Expo 2020 Dubai

In November 2013, Dubai won the bid to host the World Expo 2020. Fireworks erupted from the Burj Khalifa and the ruler of Dubai promised that the city would 'astonish the world.'

What is the Expo?
Every five years and for a period of six months, World Expos attract millions of visitors. Also known as the World's Fair, it is an event that has been around for over 150 years. It is similar to the Olympic Games, except that instead of sports, it's about science, technology, culture and economics. The World Expo is effectively the largest mix of trade exhibitions or world fairs and is not by any means a new concept, with the first noted World Expo being hosted in London in 1851. Indeed, previous Expos have yielded legacies such as the Eiffel Tower, the telephone, ice cream and Heinz tomato ketchup.

Plans and development
While the majority of the design and construction of the Expo site is still in its infancy, organisers have reported that the site for the World Expo 2020 Dubai will be at Dubai Trade Center – Jabel Ali: a 438 hectare site on the south western edge of Dubai which is set to be one of the largest ever developed for a World Expo. Equidistant from the centres of Abu Dhabi and Dubai, the site is located next to the new Al Maktoum International Airport and also located in close proximity to Jebel Ali Port, the third busiest port in the world.

The theme for World Expo 2020 Dubai is Connecting Minds, Creating the Future – a nod to the importance of fostering partnerships and innovation to build a sustainable world today and in the future. Designed by architectural firm HOK, the sprawling new district features three main pavilions designed to symbolise opportunity, sustainability and mobility with 'innovation pods' and 'best practice areas' in each thematic zone. Different areas will be linked by walkways that are inspired by the layout of a traditional Arabic souk but their construction is set to be futuristic. A photovoltaic fabric structure is said to cover the walkways acting as a solar-powered sun shade capable of absorbing energy and supplying half the Expo's power requirements. At night, the fabric will act as a canvas for light displays and digital projections. At the core of the site there's said to be an open plaza called Al Wasl which is Arabic for 'the connection' – again in keeping with Dubai's Connecting Minds, Creating the Future theme – that will act as the central souk.

The plan for what to do with the site when the Expo closes is currently a hot topic for discussion. Recent news suggests that the organisers have agreed to combine the three major pavilions – the Welcome Pavilion, the Innovation Pavilion and the UAE's Pavilion – and transform them into one structure: the Museum of the Future.

The region's first
World Expo 2020 Dubai is the first to be held in the MENASA (Middle East, North Africa and South Asia) region. As the global community faces ever more complex and increasingly interconnected challenges, the links between people, societies and ideas have never been more important. The Expo promises to be a platform for connectivity to help pioneer new partnerships for growth and sustainability for the future. It was reported that the last Expo held in Shanghai in 2010 received over 73 million visitors from 250 countries. The site that showcased this phenomenon measured a massive 5.28sq km, and a new record attendance for a single day was set with more than 1.03 million people visiting the site. These numbers, by any standard, are hugely impressive, and an indicator of how important for the local economy the winning vote is to Dubai – especially when you consider the reported profits reached in excess of US$157 million for the Expo alone.

It is already predicted that there will be an influx to the region of 25 million visitors going through the turnstiles in Dubai. The knock-on effect is a predicted 277,000 jobs created for the region and a huge boost not only to the ensuing job market, but for the infrastructure of Dubai. With Al Maktoum International Airport's ambitious plans to overtake the likes of London Heathrow in the coming years, and its central location here in the Middle East, it is easy to see why this is the perfect platform and opportunity in which to raise the bar.

For updated information on news and events for the Expo, check out expo2020dubai.ae.

The Burj Al Arab hotel celebrates the Expo 2020 win

THE UAE
ECONOMY

Dubai

The pace of economic growth in Dubai over the last 20 years has been incredible. Trade alone has grown at more than 9% per annum over the past 10 years and the population has doubled since 1990.

Over the last decade, legislation and government institutions have been honed to reduce bureaucracy and create a constructive business environment. Free zones, such as Internet City, Media City and Healthcare City, offer financial incentives to encourage international business; they have flourished and multiplied and multi-billion dollar mega project proposals such as the three Palm Island projects, Dubai Sports City and Burj Khalifa, were the result of the government's active promotion of investment in Dubai.

According to the International Monetary Fund (IMF) the UAE's economy grew 3.8% in 2012 and by a further 3.1% in 2013. Inflation was just 1.6% in 2013 and is predicted to hold steady at 1.9% in 2014. The outlook is positive: the IMF has projected steady economic growth through to 2016.

Really Tax Free?
Do taxes exist in the UAE? Yes and no. You don't pay income or sales tax, except when you purchase alcohol from a licensed liquor store – when you'll be hit with a steep 30% tax. The main tax that you will come across is the municipality tax of 5% on rent and 10% on food, beverages and rooms in hotels. The rest are hidden taxes in the form of 'fees', such as your car registration renewal, visa/permit fees and Dubai's Salik (road toll).

Bolstering feelings of confidence in economic recovery, many construction projects that had been put on hold are resuming, such as the Palm Deira along with several residential and commercial buildings.

On a less positive note for renters, the property market is now booming with Dubai rents having increased 30% over the year from July 2012-2013 – and there's no sign of this trend slowing.

All in all, the UAE is still one of the world's richest countries on a per capita basis. With its sizeable government-led projects and ongoing expansion plans, Dubai is well placed to continue growing as a global hub and tourist destination.

Trade

Strategically the UAE has always been well-placed geographically, but with a trade policy based on economic openness and liberalisation the country continues to flourish. With flexible and investor-friendly laws, availability of raw materials and funds, tax exemptions and low tariffs, the climate in the UAE is an ideal one for foreign investment. Non-oil exports have grown significantly with a particular emphasis on re-exports; the World Trade Organisation (WTO) ranked the UAE as the 20th largest exporter in the world back in 2011 (14th if trade between European Union members was discounted).

Roughly 60% of exports are manufactured goods, fuels and mining products; India, Iran, Iraq, Switzerland and the European Union (EU) being the main recipients. Meanwhile over $200 billion of merchandise is imported into the country every year, mainly coming from the EU, India, China, USA and Japan. Main imports include: pearls and other precious metals and stones, machinery, vehicles, base metals and chemicals.

Tourism

The UAE is well ahead of many other countries in the Middle East in terms of travel and tourism. Boosting tourism plays a central part in the government's economic diversification plan and is a major force behind the array of record-breaking infrastructure and hospitality developments of recent times. Dubai is perhaps the most famous tourist destination in the UAE, with over 570 hotels and attractions such as the man-made Palm Jumeirah island, the Burj Al Arab hotel and an ever-growing marina area. Meanwhile, in the Downtown area records are set: the Burj Khalifa, the world's tallest building, towers over the world's largest dancing fountain and nearby is the world's

Burj Al Arab

largest mall, The Dubai Mall. Inside, visitors can even visit the world's largest sweet shop.

The development of these high-end tourist amenities and visitor attractions, in conjunction with an aggressive overseas marketing campaign, means that Dubai's popularity as a holiday destination continues to increase. It is striving to reach its target of 20 million visitors a year by 2020 – a goal that will surely be boosted following the emirate's winning bid to host the 2020 World Expo.

Visitor numbers to Dubai increased by 9.3% in 2012, with the city welcoming more than 10 million visitors over a one year period for the first time in its history. In the first nine months of 2013, Dubai welcomed over 7.9 million visitors, with the latest figures showing a 9.8% increase in visitor numbers year-on-year.

Annual passengers through Dubai International Airport – now ranked the world's second busiest in terms of international traffic – reached 60,384,407 in 2013 to November, up 13.2% from 2012. The 2013 passenger traffic exceeded Dubai Airports' forecast at the start of the year by more than 1 million passengers. Passenger numbers are projected to reach 98 million by 2020. Dubai World Central – Al Maktoum International Airport opened in 2010, in the south of Dubai, near to the Jabel Ali industrial area. It opened for passenger services in the second half of 2013, and will eventually become the world's largest airport, with a capacity of 160 million passengers and 12 million tonnes of cargo per year.

International Relations

The UAE remains open in its foreign relations and firmly supports Arab unity. Sheikh Khalifa bin Zayed Al Nahyan is very generous with the country's wealth when it comes to helping Arab nations and communities that are in need of aid.

The UAE became a member of the United Nations and the Arab League in 1971. It is a member of the International Monetary Fund (IMF), the Organisation of Petroleum Exporting Countries (OPEC), the World Trade Organisation (WTO) and other international Arab organisations. It is also a member of the Arab Gulf Cooperation Council (AGCC, also known as the GCC), whose members are Bahrain, Kuwait, Oman, Qatar and Saudi Arabia.

All major embassies and consulates are represented either in Abu Dhabi or in Dubai, or both. In general, most of the embassies are based in Abu Dhabi as this is the nation's capital. However, for many expats all their bureaucratic dealings (passport renewals, birth registration and the like) will be met via a trip to their home-country consulate. Most of the main consulates are located in the same area, off Al Seef Road, in Bur Dubai, beside Dubai Creek.

ENVIRONMENT

The UAE has environmental issues that can't be ignored thanks to a hot climate, a scarcity of natural drinking water and a growing population. Being a relatively wealthy country with high demands means that the average person in the UAE is consuming more than the country can produce on its own. The ecological footprint in the UAE, according to the WWF's Living Planet Report 2012, is 8.44 global hectares (gha). Meanwhile the capacity of the land to produce useful biological material and absorb waste created by humans is just 0.64gha. Globally, the UAE has the third largest deficit between these two figures, meaning a continued reliance on imports which could lead to problems in the future.

Couple that to being one of the largest consumers of water on the planet with a large population of expats, who are less likely to invest time into conservation than locals or long-term residents, and the situation needs addressing. Fortunately the government is conscious of this and has agencies set up across the emirates to help tackle the issues.

Flora & Fauna

The region has about 3,500 native plants, which is perhaps surprising considering the high salinity of the soil and the harsh environment. The most famous is, of course, the date palm, which is also the most flourishing of the indigenous flora. In mountainous regions, flat-topped acacia trees and wild grasses create scenery similar to that of an African savannah. The deserts are unexpectedly green in places, even during the dry summer months, but it takes an experienced botanist to get the most out of the area.

Indigenous fauna include the Arabian leopard and the Arabian oryx, but sightings are extremely rare. Realistically, the only large animals you will see are camels and goats (often roaming dangerously close to the roads). Other desert life includes sand cats, sand foxes, desert hares, gerbils, hedgehogs, geckos and snakes. Studies have shown that the number of bird species is rising each year, due in part to concentrated greening efforts. This is most apparent in parks, especially in spring and autumn, as the country is on the migratory route between central Asia and east Africa.

Off the coast of the UAE, the seas contain a rich abundance of marine life, including tropical fish, jellyfish, coral, dugong ('sea cows') and sharks. Eight

THE UAE
ENVIRONMENT

species of whale and seven species of dolphin have been recorded in UAE waters. Various breeds of turtle, including loggerhead, green and hawksbill, are also indigenous with sightings off the east coast by Snoopy Island and Khor Kalba not uncommon.

Wildlife

A number of indigenous animals have been hunted to the edge of extinction in the past, including the Arabian oryx (a large antelope) and houbara bustard (a large bird and popular quarry for falconers). Meanwhile, others have found their habitats disappearing. The survival or continued protection of these animals has been mainly thanks to government activities. Even back in 1968, the late Sheikh Zayed ordered the capture of the four remaining Arabian oryx in the wild to initiate a captive breeding programme at Al Ain Zoo. After the development of Sir Bani Yas Island, he also started another captive breeding programme for the oryx, where they are today flourishing. In 2007 a release programme began for the Arabian oryx in the emirate of Abu Dhabi, with 100 animals being released into the wild.

Al Ain Zoo continues to be instrumental in conserving species, while the Breeding Centre for Endangered Arabian Wildlife at Sharjah Desert Park, has been particularly successful breeding the endangered Arabian leopard. The International Fund for Houbara Conservation (IFHC) has also become a world authority on understanding and protecting the bird so integrated in the UAE's cultural past.

Similarly agencies like the Environmental Agency Abu Dhabi (ead.ae) and Emirates Wildlife Society, a national environmental NGO that operates in association with the WWF, work tirelessly to ensure the conservation of native and migrating animals and their habitats. Projects on Saadiyat Island in Abu Dhabi have helped protect nests of rare hawksbill turtles.

Meanwhile, tagging of passing dugong have helped to keep their migratory routes safe, and specific protection has been given to breeding colonies of the rare Socotra cormorant on the islands of Marawah and Al Yasat. Internationally, the UAE-based Mohammed bin Zayed Species Conservation Fund has donated over Dhs.33 million to help safeguard the threatened flora and fauna of the world.

My Environment, My Country
In 2013 the UAE re-launched its My environment, My country initiative in schools. Following success in the previous year, it aims to inspire children to protect the natural world, focussing on the concepts and challenges faced by the UAE.

Dubai's Emirates Marine Environmental Group (EMEG), the Environmental Agency Abu Dhabi (ead.ae) and Emirates Wildlife Society, a national environmental NGO that operates in association with the WWF, work tirelessly to ensure the conservation of native and migrating animals, as well as their environments. Meanwhile, the Dubai Turtle Rehabilitation Project is dedicated to protecting the critically endangered native hawksbill turtle. Vulnerable turtles are brought to Dubai's Wildlife Protection Office and rehabilitated at the Burj Al Arab Aquarium; the project was established by the Jumeirah Group, who tag and monitor the turtles online at seaturtle.org.

Sustainability

From the outside, the UAE looks totally unsustainable. Huge petrol use, massive energy consumption (for all that air conditioning) and seemingly unending generation of waste; it all looks like an environmental headache. Rapid growth has probably necessitated much of this but the UAE government is keen to spread the message of sustainability. In fact, the late president of the UAE, Sheikh Zayed, was a passionate environmentalist and much of what happens now is part of his legacy. There is a realisation about the energy and water issues in the UAE; generating energy requires water, and producing water (through desalination) requires energy. The government is active in finding ways to use less of both through increased efficiency. As part of the continuing work to solve the issues, the International Water Summit is taking place in Abu Dhabi this year during the Abu Dhabi Sustainability Week.

In Abu Dhabi, Masdar City is a leading light, aiming to become a zero carbon, zero waste city by 2025. The first phase is already complete, with the eco-friendly buildings using 65% less energy than the average building in the city. Masdar also opened the world's largest solar thermal energy plant in 2013. The Abu Dhabi project creates 10% of the world's solar thermal energy (where mirrors heat a boiler full of steam which then generates turbines), enough to power 20,000 homes in the UAE.

Dubai's Expo Legacy
Meanwhile, as sustainability – lasting sources of energy and water – is one of the three themes of the World Expo 2020 Dubai (the other two being mobility and opportunity), the emirate can expect some noticeable changes during the next six years in the build-up to the event. Green plans for the future include solar-powered street lamps in parks, more green building codes and conversion efforts to shift to an efficient lighting system.

THE UAE
ENVIRONMENT

Heroes Of The UAE

This environmentally friendly initiative, jointly developed by The Emirates Wildlife Society in association with the Worldwide Fund for Nature (EWS-WWF) and The Environment Agency-Abu Dhabi, provides a go-to resource for individuals, schools and businesses to find out how to save energy and water, and reduce the UAE's carbon footprint – which currently has the highest per capita ecological footprint on earth – with virtual calculators, tips and information. As part of its commitment to the Heroes of the UAE campaign, the Abu Dhabi government has launched a programme to fit Watersavers in every tap, in every single home and place of work in the emirate.

Solar Heaters A Must-Have

Although the UAE still has a long way to go to reduce its ecological footprint, it's refreshing to see that measures are being taken. Since 2012, any developer submitting plans for a new build has to integrate solar water heaters that provide for at least 75% of the building's hot water needs and 50% of any swimming pool heating, or Dubai Municipality will refuse to grant a building licence.

Recycling

Recycling is a relatively new concept in the UAE, with just over 20% of all non-hazardous waste being recycled. While the importance of reducing waste through the three 'R's (reduce, reuse, recycle) is being taught throughout the country, different emirates are finding different solutions. In Abu Dhabi, the Centre of Waste Management has already taken many initiatives. Just a few years ago around 60% of waste from construction was going to landfill, roughly 3.5 million tonnes. This is now re-used in road construction, footpaths, playgrounds and sports areas.

Domestically, there can be some confusion about recycling. Even amongst expats, what seems obviously recyclable might be quite different in the UAE compared to your home country. However, UAE residents are becoming more proactive. The Emirates Environmental Group has reported a large increase in recycling drives from schools, corporate and community groups, which collect paper, plastic, glass, aluminium and toner cartridges. Mobile phones, broken computers and all kinds of electronic equipment can be recycled through Enviroserve (enviroserve.ae) or at your nearest Plug-ins store (800 758 4467).

A few of Dubai's residential areas now have an official recycling collection service for glass, paper, cans and plastic bottles (800 732 9353, zenath.com). If your area doesn't have a recycling scheme, it can involve rather a lot of administrative wrangling with the developer or community management company, but it's worth bringing the issue to the attention of your residents' committee to build support and put pressure on the developers.

In the meantime, there are now a lot of recycling bins dotted around Dubai. The municipality has installed recycling bins for paper, glass and plastic at petrol stations and bus stops, while you'll find recycling bins for everything from plastic bottles to shoes and clothing outside the UAE's bigger supermarkets. In addition, large cages for collecting recyclable materials have been installed on Al Wasl Road near Safa Park, at Mirdif Recycling Centre and on the service road near to the Shangri-La on Sheikh Zayed Road. Keep your eyes peeled – your nearest bins won't be far away.

In line with many countries, plastic bags have been phased out across supermarkets and stores in the UAE. Early 2013 statistics show that residents were using a whopping 11 billion plastic bags annually – but that figure is slowly dropping, thankfully. While Abu Dhabi's Environment Agency recently introduced an app to teach youngsters in the UAE about biodiversity and protecting their environment, another app has been designed in Dubai to promote and prioritise recycling. A new smartphone introduced by Union Paper Mills aims to ease recycling for residents. The app called 'Reyoutilizer' allows households and small companies to book the collection of recyclables such as paper, plastic and aluminium cans from their premises. The app can be downloaded for free by iPhone and Android users.

Recycling bins

THE UAE
CULTURE & LIFESTYLE

CULTURE & LIFESTYLE

The UAE manages what some Arab countries fail to achieve; a healthy balance between western influences and eastern traditions. It is still a country very much rooted in Islamic culture; however, the country's effort to become modern and cosmopolitan is highlighted by an open-minded and liberal outlook.

Culture

Islam is an integral part of UAE life and to followers it is more than just a religion; it's a way of life that governs even everyday events, from what to wear to what to eat and drink. However, the UAE is progressively tolerant and welcoming; foreigners are free to practise their own religion, alcohol is served in hotels and the dress code is fairly liberal. Women face little discrimination and, contrary to the policies of neighbouring Saudi Arabia, are able to drive and walk around uncovered and unescorted.

The UAE has changed dramatically over the last 30 years, fuelled by economic prosperity that has made mega malls, towering skyscrapers and expensive 4WDs the norm. Yet the country is also keen to safeguard its heritage, with active promotion of cultural and sporting events that represent their traditions, such as falconry, camel racing and traditional dhow sailing. Arabic culture in poetry, dancing, songs, art and craftsmanship is encouraged too. Traditional virtues of courtesy and hospitality are also highly prized, although you may not always find this extended to the highways.

The Sheikh Mohammed Centre for Cultural Understanding (cultures.ae) near Dubai Creek actively promotes awareness of the local culture through various events and talks. Its motto, Open Doors, Open Minds, signifies a free and safe space to discuss sensitive topics openly and honestly. You can share a traditional meal with the hosts, learn about Muslim culture and ask questions that perhaps you were too nervous to ask before.

Language

Arabic is the official language of the UAE. However English is so widely used in all areas of life, including in business, that you might live here for years without needing to learn a single word of Arabic. Most road signs, shop signs and restaurant menus display both English and Arabic. That's not to say that learning a few words or phrases isn't a good idea, though. Arabic isn't the easiest language to pick up, or to pronounce, but if you can throw in a couple of words here and there, you're more likely to receive a warmer welcome or at least a smile – even if your pronunciation is terrible. Expats make up the vast majority of the UAE (around 80%, with the majority from India, Pakistan and Bangladesh) so you can expect to hear languages like Hindi, Malayalam and Urdu.

Religion

Islam is the official religion of the UAE, and is widely practised throughout the country. The Islamic holy day is Friday. The basis of Islam is the belief that there is only one God and that the Prophet Muhammad is his messenger. The faith shares a common ancestry with Christianity and many of the prophets before Muhammad can be found in Christian as well as Muslim writings. There are five pillars of Islam that all Muslims must follow: the Profession of Faith, Prayer, Charity, Fasting and Pilgrimage. Every Muslim is expected, at least once in his or her lifetime, to make the pilgrimage (Hajj) to the holy city of Mecca (also spelt Makkah) in Saudi Arabia.

Arabic Family Names

Arabic names have a formal structure that traditionally indicates the person's family and tribe. Names are usually taken from an important person in the Quran or from the tribe. This is followed by the word bin (son of) for a boy or bint (daughter of) for a girl, and then the name of the child's father. The last name indicates the person's tribe or family. For prominent families, this has Al, the Arabic word for 'the', immediately before it. For instance, the President of the UAE is His Highness Sheikh Khalifa bin Zayed Al Nahyan. When women get married, they do not change their name.

Muslims are required to pray five times a day (facing Mecca), and times vary according to the sun. Most people pray at a mosque, but it's not unusual to see people kneeling by the side of the road if they are not near a place of worship. It is considered impolite to stare at people praying or to walk over prayer mats. The modern-day call to prayer, transmitted through loudspeakers on the minarets, ensures that everyone knows it's time to pray.

Islam is the principle religion, but the UAE is tolerant of other denominations; the ruling family has, in the past, donated land for the building of churches. There is a vibrant Christian community in Dubai and there is even a Hindu temple.

BASIC ARABIC

General
Yes	na'am
No	la
Please	min fadlak (m) min fadlik (f)
Thank you	shukran
Please (in offering)	tafaddal (m) tafaddali (f)
Praise be to God	al-hamdu l-illah
God willing	in shaa'a l-laah

Greetings
Greeting (peace be upon you)	as-salaamu alaykom
Greeting (in reply)	wa alaykom is salaam
Good morning	sabah il-khayr
Good morning (in reply)	sabah in-nuwr
Good evening	masa il-khayr
Good evening (in reply)	masa in-nuwr
Hello	marhaba
Hello (in reply)	marhabtayn
How are you?	kayf haalak (m)/kayf haalik (f)
Fine, thank you	zayn, shukran (m) zayna, shukran (f)
Welcome	ahlan wa sahlan
Welcome (in reply)	ahlan fiyk (m)/ahlan fiyki (f)
Goodbye	ma is-salaama

Introductions
My name is...	ismiy...
What is your name?	shuw ismak (m)/shuw ismik (f)
Where are you from?	min wayn inta (m)/min wayn inti (f)
I am from…	anaa min...
America	ameriki
Britain	braitani
Europe	oropi
India	hindi

Questions
How many/much?	kam?
Where?	wayn?
When?	mataa?
Which?	ayy?
How?	kayf?
What?	shuw?
Why?	laysh?
Who?	miyn?
To/for	ila
In/at	fee
From	min
And	wa
Also	kamaan
There isn't	maa fee

Driving
Is this the road to...?	hadaa al tariyq ila...
Stop	kuf
Right	yamiyn
Left	yassar
Straight ahead	siydaa
North	shamaal
South	januwb
East	sharq
West	garb
Turning	mafraq
First	awwal
Second	thaaniy
Road	tariyq
Street	shaaria
Roundabout	duwwaar
Traffic light signal	ishaara
Close to	qarib min
Petrol station	mahattat betrol
Sea/beach	il bahar
Mountain/s	jabal/jibaal
Desert	al sahraa
Airport	mataar
Hotel	funduq
Restaurant	mata'am
Slow down	schway schway

Accidents & Emergencies
Police	al shurtaa
Permit/licence	rukhsaa
Accident	haadith
Papers	waraq
Insurance	ta'miyn
Sorry	aasif (m)/aasifa (f)

Numbers
Zero	sifr
One	waahad
Two	ithnayn
Three	thalatha
Four	arba'a
Five	khamsa
Six	sitta
Seven	saba'a
Eight	thamaanya
Nine	tiss'a
Ten	ashara
Hundred	miya
Thousand	alf
Million	million

THE UAE
CULTURE & LIFESTYLE

National Dress

Emiratis generally wear traditional dress in public, although many will dress in more western clothes if travelling abroad. For men, traditional dress means a *dishdasha* or *khandura*; a white, full length shirt dress, which is worn with a white or red checked headdress, known as *gutra* or *sifrah*. This is secured with a black chord (*agal*). Sheikhs and important businessmen may also wear a thin black or brown robe (known as a *bisht*), over their *dishdasha* at important events, which is equivalent to a dinner jacket in western culture. In public, women wear the black *abaya*; a long, loose black robe that covers their normal clothes, plus a headscarf called a *sheyla*.

The abaya is often of sheer, flowing fabric and may be open at the front. Some women also wear a thin black veil hiding their face, and gloves. Older women sometimes still wear a leather mask, known as a *burkha*, which covers the nose, brow and cheekbones. Underneath, women traditionally wear a long tunic over loose, flowing trousers (*sirwal*), which are often heavily embroidered and fitted at wrists and ankles. However, these are used more by the older generation and modern women will often wear the latest fashions under their *abayas*. At the beach, it's not unusual to see Muslim women in special bathing costumes that keep their legs, arms, bodies and heads covered, with only their faces, hands and feet on show.

Food & Drink

The cultural diversity of the population is reflected in the vast range of culinary delights available in the country. Anything from Mexican and Asian fusion to an English roast dinner is available. Most of the popular restaurants are in hotels, where alcoholic drinks are also served. Some of the tastiest food can be found in the small streetside cafeterias, where two people can often feast on less than Dhs.50. Fast food fans searching for the familiar will also find McDonalds, Burger King, KFC and Subway – the latter three all offering home delivery.

When it comes to food shopping, there are a number of supermarkets that stock many international brands. French chain Carrefour is one of the largest with a huge selection, while LuLu Hypermarket and Co-op stores offer similar choice and are popular with those on a budget. Spinneys, Abela and Waitrose are more expensive but sell an excellent range of British, South African and American food.

Eat Like The Locals

While modern Arabic cuisine comes from a blend of Moroccan, Tunisian, Iranian and Egyptian cooking styles, the term invariably refers to Lebanese food.

Aside from mezze, it's fairly reliant on meat, often lamb, beef or fish cooked over a charcoal grill. Meals generally end with nutty Lebanese sweets and are accompanied by a variety of fresh fruit juices.
Shawarma: lamb or chicken sliced from a spit and served in a pita bread with salad and tahina
Falafel: mashed chickpeas and sesame seeds, rolled into balls and deep fried
Mezze: a selection of dishes served with Arabic bread, a green salad and pickles
Hummus: a creamy dip made from ground chickpeas, tahina, olive oil and garlic
Tabouleh: finely chopped parsley, mint and cracked wheat salad
Fatoush: lettuce and tomato with small pieces of fried Arabic bread
Fattayer: small pastries filled with cottage cheese and spinach
Khouzi: whole lamb served on a bed of rice, mixed with nuts, a popular Ramadan feast
Kibbeh: deep fried mince, pine nuts and bulgur
Baklava: filo pastry layered with honey and pistachio nuts
Umm Ali: a dessert with layers of milk, bread, raisins and nuts

Emirati Specialities

Camel is eaten, but as they are highly prized for their milk and load-carrying ability, camel meat is usually saved for special occasions. You can however pick up a pint of camel milk in most supermarkets, and the odd bar of camel-milk chocolate.

Dates are more of a staple having been cultivated in the region for around 5,000 years, and it's said that in some countries the Bedouin way of life was sustained primarily by dates and camel milk up until as recently as the mid-20th century. Dates are also a bit of a super food, high in energy but low in fat, so make a great cheap and healthy snack. Just five dates per day provide enough nutrition for one recommended daily portion of fruit or vegetables.

Pork

Pork is taboo in Islam. Muslims should not eat, prepare or even serve pork. In order for a restaurant to serve pork on its menu, it should have a separate fridge, preparation equipment and cooking area. It also needs a specific licence. In restaurants where bacon appears on a menu, you will usually be served beef or veal bacon. Supermarkets that sell pork are also required to do so from a separate area clearly labelled for 'non-Muslims'. These are more common in areas with high expat concentrations. Outlets of Spinneys, Choithrams and Park n Shop all have pork sections within their stores. As pork is not locally produced you

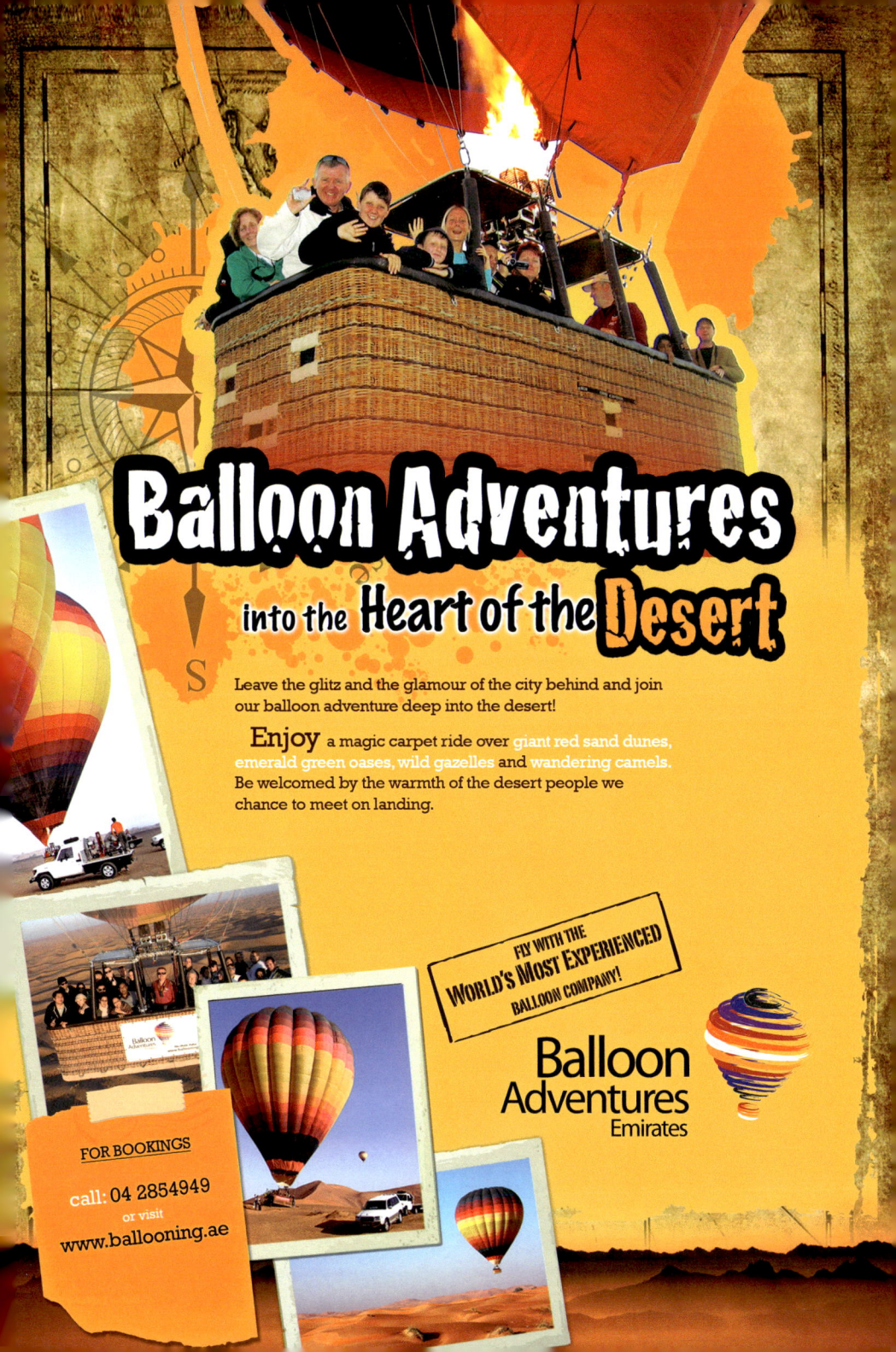

Balloon Adventures
into the Heart of the Desert

Leave the glitz and the glamour of the city behind and join our balloon adventure deep into the desert!

Enjoy a magic carpet ride over giant red sand dunes, emerald green oases, wild gazelles and wandering camels. Be welcomed by the warmth of the desert people we chance to meet on landing.

FLY WITH THE WORLD'S MOST EXPERIENCED BALLOON COMPANY!

Balloon Adventures Emirates

FOR BOOKINGS
call: 04 2854949
or visit
www.ballooning.ae

THE UAE
CRIME

will find that it's more expensive than other meats. All meat products for Muslim consumption have to be halal, which refers to the method of slaughter.

Alcohol

Alcohol is widely available in hotels plus a few leisure clubs, such as golf clubs and sports clubs, and the very occasional non-hotel bar/restaurant. During Ramadan, alcohol is only served after sunset, and there are 'dry' nights before certain public holidays. Officially you need a liquor licence to buy, transport or even consume alcohol, whether at home or at a hotel; you must also be a non-Muslim resident. Alcohol is sold at specially-licensed stores across the UAE. Sharjah is the only dry state in the UAE, and alcohol is not sold or served in any hotels there. If drinking, always be mindful that you are in a Muslim country; drunken behaviour is not tolerated, neither is drink-driving. See also the Living In and Shopping chapters.

Shisha

Also known as hookah pipes, hubbly bubbly or nagile, smoking the traditional shisha (water pipe) is a popular pastime throughout the Middle East. Shisha pipes can be smoked with a variety of flavours, such as strawberry, grape, mint or apple. Unlike a normal cigarette or cigar, the smoke is softened by the water, although it still causes smoking-related health problems (1g of shisha smoke has 100 times the tar content of a cigarette). Smoking shisha is an enjoyable experience but it's wise not to make it a habit. During Ramadan, when Iftar tents are erected throughout cities, shisha smoking is particularly popular.

Shisha pipes

CRIME

While crime figures aren't officially released, the UAE is known for having a low crime rate. Serious crimes like rape and murder are infrequent and unlikely to affect the quality of life of the average expat. The most common reason for expats getting on the wrong side of the law is often alcohol. In the UAE there is a zero-tolerance policy on drinking and driving; if you are arrested for this, the usual penalty is a minimum 30 days in prison. Being drunk and disorderly in public is also something that can land you in trouble.

Some stories about expats finding themselves on the wrong side of the law have gained international news coverage, and their seemingly harsh punishments do very little to appease concerned foreigners looking to relocate to the country. However, so long as you respect the UAE's laws, religion and cultural differences and act like a civilised human being, you'll be unlikely to land yourself in any kind of trouble.

Laws To Know

Get a liquor licence If you buy alcohol outside of a hotel you're required to have a liquor licence.
Don't live as an unmarried couple Men and women unrelated to each other cannot live together. You'd be unlucky to be pulled up for disregarding this law though.
Don't get pregnant out of wedlock At some point any hospital will ask to see your marriage certificate during the nine months up to birth. If you're unmarried and pregnant you may have issues registering the birth and may also be in hot water for non-marital sex.
Don't have one for the road The UAE has a zero tolerance approach to drink driving. There is no safe limit.
Illegal meds Some over-the-counter medicines from your home country may be illegal here. The Ministry of Health's website moh.gov.ae has a list of approved drugs.
Respect Ramadan Eating, drinking, smoking and even chewing gum in public during the daylight hours of Ramadan is illegal. You need to wait until *Iftar* (breaking of the fast) to eat, drink or smoke in public.
Don't phone while driving It's completely illegal to use your phone without a hands-free device, despite being one of the most flouted laws in history.
Get your Resident ID All expats must have a national identity card. Visit eida.gov.ae for details.
Don't bounce cheques Passing bad cheques is taken seriously in the UAE, resulting in fines or imprisonment.
Look before lighting up Smoking is illegal in many public areas such as shopping malls.

20   Dubai Explorer

Dos & Don'ts

You'll find that, in general, people in the UAE are patient when it comes to cultural etiquette and are keen to explain their customs to you. However, there are a few cultural dos and don'ts that you should be aware of to avoid causing offence or landing yourself in trouble with the law.

PDAs
Public displays of affection are a no-no in the UAE and anything more than an innocent peck on the cheek will at best earn you disapproving looks from passers-by.

Appropriate attire
Beach wear on the beach is fine, but in public, dress should be more conservative. Covering shoulders and knees is a safe bet if you are unsure. It's wise for women to carry a pashmina so they can cover up when necessary. That said, pretty much anything goes when out at bars and clubs.

Arabic coffee
If you're offered traditional Arabic coffee (*kahwa*) during a meeting it is polite to drink some. Cups should be taken in the right hand, and if there is a waiter there to replenish your cup, the signal to say you have had enough is to gently shake the cup from side to side.

Business etiquette
Introductions and small talk usually start a business meeting, with exchanging of business cards. Treat a received card with respect, like it's an extension of the person who gave it. Being late for a meeting is considered bad manners, but punctuality doesn't mean it will start at the appointed time or be uninterrupted.

Home values
When visiting an Emirati house it is customary to remove your shoes. Traditionally men and women dine separately and meals are eaten sat on floor cushions. Be careful when sitting not to point your feet at anyone or show the soles of your feet. Try everything offered at the meal, but if not sure you'll like something, just take a small amount. If you invite a Muslim to your home, offering pork or alcohol may cause offence.

Meeting people
While warm greetings and long handshakes are common, if you are meeting someone of the opposite sex a handshake may not always be welcome. It's best to wait until they first offer their hand. It's polite to send greetings to a person's family, but can be considered rude to enquire directly about someone's wife, sister or daughter. The customary nose kiss greeting used between men in the Gulf region shouldn't be attempted either.

Photography
Like anywhere in the Arab world, it is courteous to ask permission before photographing people, particularly women. Photographs of government and military buildings shouldn't be taken, especially if there are 'no photography' signs. Unwitting tourists have found themselves in deep trouble for this before.

Out on the town
Dubai has a good variety of nightlife and alcohol is widely available in the city's hotel bars, pubs and clubs (see Going Out section). Remember, however, that you're in a Muslim country and drunken or lewd behaviour in not only disrespectful but can lead to arrest and detention.

Tipping
Tipping is not compulsory, but tipping for good service is common, normally around 10% of your bill. For valet-parking at hotels a Dhs.5 tip is average. Taxi fares are often rounded up to include a tip, but not if the driving standards were poor. Many restaurants include a 10% service charge although it's unclear how much will find its way into your waiter's pocket, so some people add a little extra.

THE UAE
CRIME

The Legal System

The legal system in the UAE is a mix of Shariah (Islamic) and conventional laws, implemented by the Federal Judiciary. In comparison to Saudi Arabia and other Arab nations, the laws in the UAE are more liberal, but it is a Muslim country and so more conservative than some western countries. All emirates have Courts of First Instance and Courts of Appeal, either federal or local, in addition to the Shariah Courts which mainly deal with matters of personal status involving Muslims, such as marriage, divorce and inheritance.

Keep Calm

It pays to keep your calm if involved in any altercation; obscene gestures or profane language, even on the phone, are bad news. Physically or verbally abuse anyone so that it causes them harm, and you may end up in prison, unless the victim chooses to drop the charges.

Police

Dubai Police are generally calm and helpful – if you stay on the right side of the law. The police have a visible presence in the city, albeit not as prominent as in other large cities; you can recognise the police by their green army-style uniform and green and white saloon cars or 4WDs. You are most likely to be stopped for a traffic offence; you must always carry your driving licence and vehicle registration – failure to do so could result in a fine. If you are stopped by the police, it is important to appear helpful and co-operative at all times. Even if you are positive you are in the right, arguing your case aggressively or being impolite could land you in further trouble. If you are being charged with a very serious offence it is advisable to contact your embassy for more advice.

In an effort to better serve Dubai's visitors, the Dubai Police has launched the Department for Tourist Security. It acts as a liaison between you and Dubai Police, although in general police officers are extremely helpful. Its website (dubaipolice.gov.ae) is easy to navigate, helpful and has extensive information on policies and procedures. For assistance, call the toll free number (800 4438). This is a non-emergency number that you can call for information about the Dubai Police, its services and the locations of stations.

There is a hotline for people suffering problems at the beach such as sexual harassment (04 266 1228). However, for other emergency services call 999 for the police or ambulance and 997 for the fire department.

If You're Arrested

You'll first be taken to a police station and, if applicable, a court date will be set. Get arrested on a Thursday evening though and you'll be in the cell all weekend until the courts reopen; if it's a holiday (such as Eid) you could be there for longer. If the offence is a minor one, you may get bail; the police will keep your passport and often the passport of another UAE resident who is willing to vouch for you. If you don't get bail you'll be held in the police cell until the hearing.

All court proceedings are in Arabic so you'll need to hire a translator. If sentenced, you'll go straight from court to jail.

If you're in trouble with the law it's advisable to contact your embassy as soon as possible. They won't be able to pay your legal fees, secure bail, act as lawyers or get you released, but they can liaise with family, offer advice on procedures and provide you with a list of translators and lawyers.

Victim Support

Women and children who are victims of domestic violence can contact the Family Development Foundation (fdf.ae) for counselling and advice. The UAE Red Crescent runs women's shelters in Dubai, victims of sexual abuse can contact the National Committee to Combat Human Trafficking (nccht.gov.ae) for information on support services in the UAE, and Dubai Police (dubaipolice.gov.ae) also offers support for child victims of abuse.

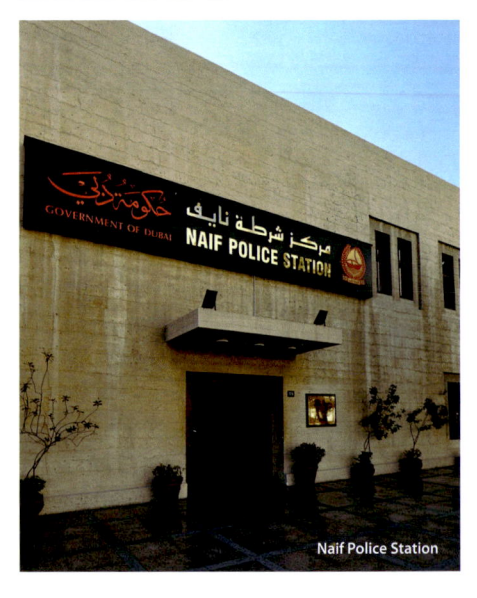

Naif Police Station

THE UAE
LOCAL MEDIA

LOCAL MEDIA

Media is one particular area that has boomed in the UAE. Expats from around the world have been recruited to voice the radio, write the newspapers and magazines, and film the TV shows. The idea is that their knowledge from more established media markets can be passed on to Emiratis and help local media to flourish further. The upshot of this is that there are many decent local media products available in the UAE now.

Censorship

International magazines are available in bookshops and supermarkets, at inflated prices. All titles are examined and, where necessary, censored to ensure that they don't offend the country's moral codes. You'll find much the same is true of the many international films and TV shows available in the UAE.

Internet

Around 85% of the UAE's population is online, reflecting how easy it is to get connected in the larger cities. Internet offerings might not be quite as quick as in areas like the US or Europe, but the UAE still ranks near the top for connectivity.

There are some things that expats need to remember though, particularly the despised proxy that blocks access to any site deemed offensive. What is or isn't offensive is up to the Telecommunication Regulatory Authority (TRA) which supposedly applies the same rules to both Etisalat and du subscribers, the two main providers.

Living in a Muslim community that means sites containing pornography (or explicit images) or dubious religious content will be blocked. Sites that offer online dating, gambling or drugs, and, oddly, some photo-sharing websites are also out of bounds. Of course, you can access these sites with the help of a proxy blocker (VPN), but then you're technically breaking the law.

Internet Entertainment

While satellite and digital TV or local radio were the only options to expats missing programmes from home, the internet now makes viewing and listening to favourites easy. Radio stations aren't blocked online, but you may need a VPN to access sources like Netflix. If you're using a tablet like an iPad, then cables can be bought to link it to your TV so you can even view it on a larger screen.

Similarly, despite VoIP (Voice over Internet Protocol) access having been blocked for a long time, regulators finally authorised it in 2010, but only to the four existing licence-holders; Etisalat, du and the satellite firms Yahsat and Thuraya. That meant making international calls through the internet was still effectively banned as authorised VoIP services weren't available from these companies. In 2013, both Etisalat and du lifted the ban on downloading the popular Skype service though, perhaps realising that the loss in revenue from calls could be made up by increased data use from customers.

It is shrouded in some confusion though, as Skype calls to mobile or landline phones still don't tend to work without a proxy blocker (such as VPN mentioned above). However, Skype or Google Chat can both be used well when communicating from computer to computer. The growth and popularity of the smartphone market here has also opened up a whole new world of communications for people and there are range of messaging apps enabling you to keep in touch with friends and family back home.

USEFUL APPS

Food On Click	Order takeaway from a selection of hundreds of eateries
The Dubai Mall	GPS app to help you find your way around the world's largest mall
Salik	Keep up-to-date on your Salik toll charges (the Dubai road toll system)
UAE Business	Guide to registration, licensing and costs for free zones and the mainland across UAE
UAE Off-Road	Choose from a selection of off-road routes and follow the interactive GPS coordinates
Abu Dhabi Map	A handy interactive map that offers detailed descriptions for POI and landmarks
Dubai Map	Navigate the city like a local with this handy and interactive map app

THE UAE
LOCAL MEDIA

Radio

The UAE has a number of commercial radio stations that broadcast in a wide range of languages. The leading English stations operate 24 hours a day.

Your digital or satellite TV may offer various radio channels as well as music television like MTV and VH1. Internet radio is the other and possibly most comprehensive option, with most of your favourite channels from home available on the web.

BBC World Service: MW at 1413 and 639 kHz, *bbc.co.uk/worldservice/schedules/010116_meast.shtml*
Channel 4 104.8FM: contemporary music for a younger audience, 104.8FM Nr Al Nasr Cinema, Zabeel Rd, Ajman, 06 06 746 1 444, *channel4FM.com*
Coast 103.2FM: middle of the road tunes and classic hits throughout the day, 103.2FM Nr Al Nasr Cinema, Zabeel Rd, Ajman, 06 600 55 1622, *1032thecoast.com*
Dubai 92: music, competitions and popular DJs on 92.00FM, BS16 Bldg, Dubai, 04 435 4700, *dubai92.com*
Dubai Eye 103.8: quality talk radio, 103.8FM. BS16 Bldg, Dubai, 04 435 4700, *dubaieye1038.com*
Radio 1: hit music broadcast across the country, 104.1FM Gulf News, Dubai, 04 406 2677, *gulfnews.com/radio1*
Radio 2: contemporary music for the UAE, 99.3FM Gulf News, Dubai, 04 406 2683, *gulfnews.com/radio2*
Virgin Radio 104.4: hit music along the lines of Virgin Radio in other cities, 104.4FM Dubai, 04 435 4700, *virginradiodubai.com*

Newspapers

There's no shortage of reading material for expats, with a number of daily English language broadsheets. Abu Dhabi's The National is very popular, being one of the first to deliver real journalism in the region, but Gulf News, Khaleej Times and Gulf Today are all readily available. Most supermarkets will also have some foreign newspapers if you're missing a tabloid from home. Around Dubai you can also find 7Days daily tabloid newspaper and various magazines with events and news of the city. The UAE also has its own versions of many popular international magazines, like Esquire, Ok!, Hello, Grazia, Good Housekeeping, Men's Fitness and Stuff. Keep an eye out for expat titles like Connector, as well as for listings magazines like Time Out and What's On.

Television

Satellite or cable TV is a staple in most expat homes – although a bit hit and miss compared to international standards. Some shows are aired just a few days later than they are in the US or UK, while others are delayed by a few months. OSN (osn.com) offers a range of TV packages, although the free-to-air channels such as Dubai One, Fox Movies and MBC are improving year on year. If you have digital or satellite TV then you probably have internet access, which is another route to take for watching your favourite programmes.

USEFUL WEBSITES

Dubai	7days.ae	Free and popular national daily newspaper
	definitelydubai.com	UAE Government official tourism site
	dha.gov.ae	Dubai Health Authority: numbers and e-services
	dm.gov.ae	Dubai Municipality
	dubaipolice.gov.ae	Dubai Police Headquarters
	dubaitourism.ae	Department of Tourism & Commerce Marketing
	dubizzle.com	Dubai's largest website for classifieds and community
UAE Information	ameinfo.com	Middle East business news
	expatwoman.com	Living in UAE from a woman's perspective
	government.ae	UAE government website
	gulfnews.com	Local newspaper
	khaleejtimes.com	Local newspaper
	propertyfinder.ae	Rental and sales property portal
	sheikhmohammed.co.ae	Info on Sheikh Mohammed bin Rashid Al Maktoum
	sheikhzayed.com	Dedicated to the life of the late UAE President
	thenational.ae	National newspaper
	uae4kidz.biz	Great site for kids' info
	uaeinteract.com	UAE National Media Council

UAE NATIONAL DAY

Every 2 December, the country turns green, black, red and white all over. In fact, the flag becomes as ubiquitous as traffic jams as residents throughout the emirates celebrate the birth of the UAE. Cars, trucks and taxis are decorated with flags and pictures of the country's rulers to show their patriotism. And, especially along the Beach Road, in public parks, bands and folklore exhibitions entertain the crowds. The National Day Downtown Dubai Parade features floats, balloons, performers, horses, camels and music groups. It wouldn't be a celebration without spectacular fireworks and, as the city is illuminated, it's almost impossible not to feel patriotic.

Traditional Arabic dhows

THE UAE
UAE CALENDAR

UAE CALENDAR

The Islamic calendar starts from the year 622AD, the year of the Prophet Muhammad's migration (*Hijra*) from Mecca to Al Madinah. Hence the Islamic year is called the *Hijra* year and dates are followed by AH (AH stands from *Anno Hegirae*, meaning 'after the year of the *Hijra*').

Public Holidays

During the year there are holidays on set dates, such as National Day every December 2nd. Other Islamic holidays are based on the sighting of the moon and therefore the dates vary. Often this can mean confirmation of a holiday less the 24 hours before it is due, something most companies will inform employees about via email when it is announced.

The main Muslim festivals during the year are *Eid Al Fitr* (the festival of the breaking of the fast, which marks the end of Ramadan) and *Eid Al Adha* (the festival of sacrifice, which marks the end of the pilgrimage to Mecca). *Mawlid Al Nabee* is the holiday celebrating the Prophet Muhammad's birthday, and *Lailat Al Mi'raj* celebrates the Prophet's ascension into heaven. See below for holiday dates for your diary.

2014-2015

The list below of public holidays applies mainly to the public sector; if you work in the private sector you may get fewer days holiday per year as the days called off will be at your company's discretion. National Day, which celebrates the foundation of the federation of the United Arab Emirates in 1971, is one day for private sector workers but two days for the public sector. The day is a huge day of patriotic celebration throughout the UAE with plenty of flag flying and many buildings are adorned in the flag's vibrant colours.

New Year	1 Jan 2014 (fixed)
Mawlid Al Nabee	12 Jan 2014 (moon)
Lailat Al Mi'raj	26 May 2014 (moon)
Eid Al Fitr (3 days)	28 July 2014 (moon)
Arafat Day	3 Oct 2014 (moon)
Eid Al Adha (3 days)	4 Oct 2014 (moon)
Islamic New Year	25 Oct 2014 (moon)
UAE National Day (1 or 2 days)	2 Dec 2014 (fixed)
New Year	1 Jan 2015 (fixed)
Mawlid Al Nabee	3 Jan 2015 (moon)
Lailat Al Mi'raj	15 May 2015 (moon)

Events & Exhibitions

Dubai Shopping Festival January-February
04 445 5642
dubaievents.ae
Established in 1996, the Dubai Shopping Festival is a great time to be in the city, with bargains galore for shoppers as well as many activities organised in malls across the city. Film festivals, special events for youngsters, impressive street displays, night fireworks, and international fashion shows, provide some of the cultural and entertainment programmes on offer. The prize draws held in participating malls are popular.

Omega Dubai Desert Classic January-February
Emirates Golf Club Al Thanyah 3 04 380 2112
dubaidesertclassic.com
Map **1 M6** Metro **Nakheel**
This longstanding PGA European Tour fixture has been won in the past by golfing legends such as Ernie Els and Tiger Woods, and is a popular event among Dubai's golfing community.

Standard Chartered Dubai Marathon January
Umm Suqeim Rd 04 433 5669
dubaimarathon.org
Map **1 R6** Metro **Mall of the Emirates**
This event attracts all types of runners, from those aiming to fundraise or work off that festive tummy in the 10km road race or 3km charity run, to dedicated pavement pounders and several of the biggest names in long distance running who tackle the full 42km.

Standard Chartered Dubai Marathon

THE UAE
UAE CALENDAR

Dubai Duty Free Tennis Championships > p.viii
February-March
The Aviation Club Al Garhoud 04 282 4122
dubaidutyfreetennischampionships.com
Map **2 M8** Metro **GGICO**

Firmly established on the ATP and WTP circuit, the $2 million tournament attracts the world's top men's and women's seeds. Tickets for the semis and finals sell out in advance, but you can often buy tickets to the opening matches just days before at reasonable prices.

Dubai Polo Gold Cup
February-March
Dubai Polo & Equestrian Club Al Hebiah 2
04 343 7877
dubaipologoldcup.com
Map **1 N13** Metro **Dubai Internet City**

Some of the world's best polo teams and players compete for the Silver Cup and Gold Cup in this prestigious and international week-long tournament.

Emirates Airline Dubai Jazz Festival
February
Festival Park Al Kheeran 04 391 1196
dubaijazzfest.com
Map **2 M10** Metro **Emirates**

The Jazz Festival, which celebrated its 11th year in 2013, attracts artists from all around the world to a stunning but chilled setting near Festival City. Courtney Pine, John Legend, James Blunt and David Gray have all performed in previous years.

Wild Wadi's Swim Burj Al Arab
February
Burj Al Arab Umm Suqeim 3 04 2911 0661
swimburjalarab.com
Map **1 S4** Metro **First Gulf Bank**

A charity swimming race on an 800m route around the island on which the spectacular Burj Al Arab hotel sits. Both competitive swimmers and fundraisers can take part. All proceeds go to Medecins Sans Frontieres. There is also a non-competitive social swim.

Abu Dhabi Desert Challenge
March
Empty Quarter Liwa
abudhabidesertchallenge.com

Prestigious annual international event, running for five days around Liwa, in the vast Rub al Khali desert. It's the season-opening round of the FIA Cross Country Rally World Cup and the FIM Cross Country Rallies World Championship.

Art Dubai
March
Madinat Jumeirah Al Sufouh 1 04 384 2000
artdubai.ae
Map **1 R5** Metro **Mall of the Emirates**

An international art exhibition that sees visits from dozens of international galleries. Running alongside it is the Global Art Forum lecture and discussion board programme, plus art prizes including a people's choice award and the $1 million Abraaj Capital Art Prize.

Dubai International Boat Show
March
Dubai International Marine Club Marsa Dubai
04 308 6430
boatshowdubai.com
Map **1 M5** Metro **Nakheel**

You don't need to have big bucks to enjoy the Boat Show. The largest marine industry exhibition in the Middle East showcases yachts and boats from both local and international builders, together with the latest innovations in marine equipment and accessories.

Dubai World Cup
March
Meydan Racecourse Nadd Al Shiba 1 04 327 0077
dubaiworldcup.com
Map **2 E10** Metro **Business Bay**

The world's richest horse race takes place at the state-of-the-art Meydan race course. The huge prize fund (last year's was over $27 million), a buzzing, vibrant atmosphere, and the star-studded entertainment line-up ensure that the Dubai World Cup is one of the year's big social occasions.

Emirates Airline Festival Of Literature
March
InterContinental Dubai Festival City 04 353 4002
emirateslitfest.com
Map **2 L9** Metro **Emirates**

This event draws a host of celebrated literary greats to take part in lectures, debates and panels. Past speakers have included Kate Adie, Alexander McCall

Dubai World Cup

askexplorer.com

27

THE UAE
UAE CALENDAR

Smith, Carol Ann Duffy, Michael Palin and Margaret Atwood. Join the festival reading group to swot up on the latest releases by speakers.

Dubai Festival City Dragon Boat Festival — April
Al Kheeran **050 763 4008**
dubaidragonboat.com
Map **2 M9** Metro **Emirates**
Open to social, school and corporate groups, this is a fun, competitive and sociable team building event.

International Property Show — April-May
Dubai International Convention & Exhibition Centre Trade Center 2 **04 392 3232**
internationalpropertyshow.ae
Map **2 H6** Metro **World Trade Centre**
Featuring everything to do with buying international property, this show is particularly popular among expats who are looking to invest overseas.

Terry Fox Run — April
Atlantis The Palm Nakhlat Jumeira
dubaiterryfoxrun.org
Map **1 N1** Metro **Nakheel**
Each year, thousands of individuals run, jog, walk, cycle and rollerblade their way around an 8.5km course to raise funds for cancer research programmes at approved institutions around the world. The run will be held at a new location for 2013, on the Palm Jumeirah (also known as Nakhlat Jumeira); another Terry Fox event is held in Ras Al Khaimah in March.

Dubai Summer Surprises — June-July
600 545 555
dubaievents.ae
Held in shopping malls around the city, with fun-packed, family-orientated activities and big shopping discounts, this is a popular event with Dubai residents and visitors looking to escape the summer heat.

Camel Racing — October-April
The Sevens Al Marmoom (and various location)
04 832 6526
This popular local sport is serious business, with racing camels changing hands for as much as Dhs.10 million. Races run October to March and admission is free.

GITEX Technology Week — October
Dubai International Convention & Exhibition Centre Trade Center 2
gitex.com
Map **2 H6** Metro **World Trade Centre**
Part of this five-day event is the renowned Gitex Shopper, where the public can snap up some great deals on the latest technology and gadgets, which are newly released at the exhibition.

Gulf Bike Week

Gulf Bike Week — October
Dubai Media City Ampitheatre Al Sufouh 2
04 435 6101
gulfbikeweek.com
Map **2 M5** Metro **Nakheel**
Over 50,000 visitors attended last year's event, enjoying stunt shows, motorbike displays, test rides and rock concerts, with previous acts including Nickelback, N.E.R.D and Megadeth. In 2013, the annual Gulf Bike Week returned to its original location in Dubai Media City from previously being held in Dubai Festival City.

DP World Tour Championship — November
Jumeirah Golf Estates Me'aisem 1
europeantour.com
Map **1 H9** Metro **Nakheel**
The world's best golfers congregate in Dubai for the final fixture of the PGA European Golf Tour and a shot at a share of the $8 million prize fund. One of Dubai's great spectator events attracting many of the world's top golfers, such as Henrik Stenson, 2013 champion.

Dubai Airshow — November
Dubai World Central Madinat Al Mataar **04 603 3300**
dubaiairshow.aero
Metro **Jebel Ali**
A five-day biennial event that has been attracting visitors for more than two decades. It began as the Arab Air Show in 1986 and today is a huge draw for all those interested in the aerospace sector, with more than 130 planes on display and spectacular aerial flybys. For the first time in 2013, the airshow moved to a new venue at Dubai World Central.

THE UAE
UAE CALENDAR

Dubai World Game Expo November
Dubai International Convention & Exhibition Centre Trade Center 2 **04 362 4717**
gameexpo.ae
Map **2 H6** Metro **World Trade Centre**
A calendar highlight for all gaming fans desperate to try out the latest software and hardware in the market; the expo also plays host to the Dubai World Game Championship.

Emirates Dubai Rugby Sevens November-December
The Sevens Al Marmoom **04 321 0008**
dubairugby7s.com
This is one of Dubai's biggest and most popular events, as over 130,000 spectators descend on The Sevens Stadium to watch top international teams compete for the coveted 7s trophy, as Gulf teams contest the local competitions. With friendly rivalry between competing nations and prizes for the best fancy dress, the party atmosphere carries on until the small hours.

Formula 1 Etihad Airways Abu Dhabi Grand Prix November
Yas Marina Circuit Abu Dhabi **02 659 9999**
yasmarinacircuit.com
Abu Dhabi always puts on a great show. As well as the on-track action, live music has been served up by the likes of Kanye West, Prince and Kings Of Leon, while free concerts, exhibitions and competitions are held for the public across the capital.

Powerboat Racing November-Feburary
Dubai International Marine Club Marsa Dubai Dubai **04 399 5777**
dimc.ae
Map **1 M5** Metro **Dubai Marina**
The UAE is very well established on the world championship powerboat racing circuit – in Dubai, DIMC have a busy annual calendar of both traditional dhow and full-throttle powerboat races.

UAE Horseracing November-March
04 327 0077
emiratesracing.com
All horseracing in Dubai has moved to the impressive Meydan City. Racing takes place at night under floodlights (see the website for race dates) with the winning horses, jockeys and trainers taking home prizes or cash. The season ends with the spectacular Dubai World Cup in March.

Whatever Floats Your Boat November
Festival Marina Al Kheeran **04 701 1059**
Map **2 L9** Metro **Creek**
This charity race invites schools and businesses to build boats from recycled materials to raise awareness of recycling and take part in a fun day on the water. For more info, email axelle.bouquet@ichdfc.ae.

Dubai International Film Festival December
04 363 3456
dubaifilmfest.com
A hotly anticipated annual event showcasing Hollywood and international arthouse films, as well as work from the Middle East region. Premieres are generally held at Madinat Jumeirah, while screenings take place in cinemas across the city. The red-carpet opening gala event has attracted Hollywood stars such as Cate Blanchett and Kevin Spacey. It's a great opportunity to catch non-mainstream films and do a bit of celeb spotting.

Mother, Baby & Child Show December
Dubai International Convention & Exhibition Centre Trade Center 2
motherbabyandchild.com
Map **2 J6** Metro **World Trade Centre**
Mums and kids will love this show, featuring exhibits by child-friendly companies and lots of entertainment for the little ones, plus endless samples and giveaways.

Sharmila Dance Gala December
Centrepoint Theatre, DUCTAC Mall of The Emirates, Dubai
Map **1 R6** Metro **Mall of the Emirates**
Over 160 renowned dancers come together for a dancing extravaganza, with Latino, Soul, Indian and hip-hop performances. The Stuttgart Ballet and talented local dance companies have performed here.

Rugby 7s

experience the
marhaba effect

When you arrive at a busy airport, you deserve a warm welcome.

We'll take care of you and your loved ones every step of the way as we help you glide through all the airport formalities getting you through to the arrival hall in no time.

Whatever your airline or class of travel, you'll always be welcome as a marhab customer where you can feel relaxed and pampered in our exclusive lounges, before take off or in transit.

Available in Dubai and Bahrain International Airports.
Visit marhabaservices.com for details.

marhaba

meet & greet | family packages | marhaba lounge | premium services | corporate services

LIVING IN DUBAI

Before You Arrive	33
Settling In	48
Before You Leave	49
Housing	50
Accommodation	51
Residential Areas	64
Setting Up Home	82
Getting Around	94
Finance	114
Health	120
Family & Parenting	144
Pets	158
Fitness	164
Well-being	168
Clubs & Groups	178

LIVING IN DUBAI

Deciding to move to Dubai is the first step, now discover all you need to know to start a new life in the sun.

Marsa Dubai

Dubai is for most people a wonderful place to live, with excellent career opportunities, a network of social contacts, unique activities and, apart from a few sweaty months in summer, brilliant weather. Most expats tell you their standard of living is better than it was back home, they travel more, spend more time with family, enjoy outdoor living and make more friends.

Erasing The Myths

Dubai does have a reputation for being bold and brash – it likes to have the biggest and best of everything – but there's far more to the city than that. Think of Dubai's showy attitude as the persona it likes to reveal to the rest of the world, while on the inside it can actually be quite down to earth. You just have to take time to get to know the city's personality. Yes, there are plenty of glitzy clubs and outrageously expensive restaurants, and people do dress up to the extreme, but there are also loads of low-key hidden corners, eclectic nightlife options and bars to satisfy the grungiest hippy.

The art and culture scene is growing, with new theatres, galleries and even Dubai's answer to jam sessions for aspiring musicians, as well as indie movie nights and artist groups. Life here is not just about showing off; it's not obligatory to get a flash 4WD and a Rolex, live on the Palm, and to dine in the Burj Khalifa every weekend.

Hopefully, this book, and this chapter in particular, will provide you with useful information about how to get settled in Dubai, deal with the paperwork, and eventually meet like-minded people.

LIVING IN DUBAI
CITY PROFILE

CITY PROFILE

There are certain descriptions of Dubai that are frequently used: pearl of the Gulf, sleepy fishing village transformed into modern metropolis, tax-free expat haven, headquarters of luxury living, and so on. There's more than a grain of truth in these cliches, but Dubai offers so much more.

On The Up
Living in Dubai is becoming more affordable, according to the 2013 Worldwide Cost Of Living survey. The emirate is ranked number 96 in the index – published by the Economist Intelligence Unit (EIU) – falling two places since 2012.

City Of Dreams
This chapter can help you, whether you are making the decision to move, if you've just arrived and don't know where to start, or if you find yourself faced with an overwhelming amount of red tape. Procedures and laws do change regularly, often in quite major ways. Changes are generally announced in newspapers, but they are often implemented quickly so it's a good idea to be prepared for the unexpected.

If you're still trying to make up your mind if Dubai is for you, then think about the sunny days, great shopping, outdoor living and tax-free salaries.

Economically, you'll probably find yourself slightly better off than back home, which is the draw for most expats. Prices have begun to climb again – especially rent – and salaries haven't climbed as much, but it's still affordable to live here, and if you're careful, you can also save some money each month.

The best way to make the move is to contact potential employers prior to your first visit and set up interviews and appointments to coincide with a short trip. Then head over and get a feel for the place whilst knocking a few job interviews on the head in the process. Dubai is an expensive to live without a job, so finding the right job should be your first priority. Plus, your employer is usually the one who sponsors you and thus gets you a residence visa – you can't live in Dubai long term without this visa.

Now that Dubai will be hosting the Expo 2020, new projects are popping up all over the city, and more tourists are being tempted to visit – by the year of the Expo, Dubai hopes to host 20 million visitors annually.

BEFORE YOU ARRIVE

There are several things you can do before arriving in Dubai to help you get prepared. Be sure to run through this checklist a few weeks ahead of your planned trip.

Checklist
- Qualification certificates and important documents attested (see below)
- Inform banks, building societies and the tax office about your move to Dubai
- Speak to your pension company to see if moving to Dubai affects your pension plan
- Research schools for children well in advance and get your child's name on the waiting list
- Get information about different neighbourhoods you might want to live in
- If accommodation is not provided by your employer, arrange temporary accommodation for when you arrive
- Bring at least 10 passport-sized photos with you for the visa applications
- Organise a shipping company to move your goods over, and bear in mind it can take two-three months

Attesting Certificates
To be accepted by the authorities here, your education certificates must be verified by a solicitor or public notary in your home country, then by your foreign office to verify the solicitor as bona fide, and finally by the UAE embassy. It's a good idea to have this done before you come to Dubai. There are private attestation companies in Dubai offering a verification service, but this is likely to take a minimum two weeks.

Customs
Before you fly into Dubai, be aware that several prescription medications are banned, especially anything containing codeine or temazepam. The UAE maintains a zero-tolerance policy on recreational drugs, and even microscopic amounts could land you in jail. Your bags will be scanned on arrival to ensure you have no offending magazines or DVDs. Each passenger is allowed to bring in 400 cigarettes, 2kg of loose tobacco or cigars worth up to Dhs.3,000. Non-Muslims are also allowed five bottles of wine, four bottles of liquor or 24 cans of beer and there is a value limit of Dhs.3,000 on gifts being brought into Dubai by travellers.

askexplorer.com 33

LIVING IN DUBAI
WHEN YOU ARRIVE

WHEN YOU ARRIVE

As you would expect during an international move to any new city, you're very likely to find a long 'to do' list waiting for you when you arrive in Dubai. You'll be doing a lot of driving around, form filling, and waiting in queues in government departments. Just keep your sense of humour handy, bear in mind that language barriers can sometimes delay things, and soon all the boring red tape will be a distant memory.

Tax-Free Shopping
Take this opportunity before you exit the airport to do any last-minute shopping at Dubai Duty Free (dubaidutyfree.com), located in Arrivals and Departures at Dubai International Airport, where you can purchase limited quantities of duty free goods such as cigarettes, cigars, tobacco, wine, spirits and perfumes.

Checklist
To get you started, here's a checklist of everything you need to do to become 'legal' in Dubai – and read on to find out exactly what to do to achieve each of the points below. Easy!
- Apply for a residence visa through your employer: you cannot live or work in Dubai without one
- Sponsor any family members who are not working for a residence visa: they also cannot live in Dubai without one
- Go for a medical test
- Apply for an Resident Identity Card: this is compulsory as part of the residence visa process
- Get a UAE driving licence: this is compulsory once you have a residence visa
- Apply for a liquor licence: this is compulsory if you plan to drink alcohol in Dubai
- Open a bank account

Arrive In Style
For a hassle-free arrival into Dubai you can book the Marhaba Meet & Greet Service (marhabaservices.com). You'll be met at arrivals before immigration, assisted through airport clearance and escorted with your baggage to the exit. A Gold package offers priority buggy car transfer, and the Family service is ideal for mothers travelling alone with children.

Visit Visa
Everyone entering the UAE needs a visit visa (also known as an entry permit) except for citizens of GCC countries; this must then be transferred to a residence visa if you plan to live and work here. The procedures for obtaining a visit visa vary depending on your nationality. Always check the regulations before travelling as details can change.

GCC citizens do not require a visa, while nationalities from 33 other countries can obtain a 30 day visa on arrival at no cost. The 30 day visa can be renewed for a further 30 days at a cost of Dhs.625, but it works out a lot cheaper to do a 'visa run' to the border of Oman, where you leave the country and re-enter on a new visit visa.

All other nationalities can apply for a visit visa in advance, sponsored by a hotel or tour operator, or by someone who is resident in Dubai. The fee is Dhs.620 for a 30 day visa, and Dhs.1,120 for 90 days. Also, a Dhs.1,000 deposit should be paid by a local sponsor and can be reimbursed after the visitor has left the country.

Expats resident in other GCC countries, who do not belong to one of the 33 visa-on-arrival nationalities, but who do meet certain criteria (professions such as managers, doctors and engineers), can get a non-renewable 30 day visa on arrival – check with your airline before flying.

All visitors to the UAE must have an eye scan upon arrival at immigration, except citizens of the GCC and anyone from the countries listed below.

Visa On Arrival
Citizens of the following countries receive an automatic visit visa on arrival: Andorra, Australia, Austria, Belgium, Brunei, Canada, Denmark, Finland, France, Germany, Greece, Hong Kong, Iceland, Ireland, Italy, Japan, Liechtenstein, Luxembourg, Malaysia, Monaco, the Netherlands, New Zealand, Norway, Portugal, San Marino, Singapore, South Korea, Spain, Sweden, Switzerland, United Kingdom, United States and Vatican City.

Business travellers can get multiple entry visas, which are issued by the General Directorate of Residency and Foreigners Affairs, the UAE's Consular offices abroad, or applied for after arrival on a visit visa. The visa is valid for 14 days at a time, for six months from the date of issue and costs Dhs.2,100. For an additional Dhs.200, a multiple-entry visa holder is eligible to use the airport e-Gates. Cruise tourists and property investors can also apply for a multi-entry permit; conditions apply and see the government website, dnrd.ae, for details.

Dubai Explorer

Being there, or being 'there'

Crown's people are always with you. Preparing you before you go, and helping you settle-in when you arrive.

Crown service offerings include:
- International & Domestic Shipments
- Storage, Airfreight
- Transit Insurance
- Immigration & Legalization
- Home Search
- School Search

Tel: +971 4 230 5300
dubai@crownrelo.com

Go knowing
www.crownrelo.com/uae

CROWN
RELOCATIONS

LIVING IN DUBAI
WHEN YOU ARRIVE

There are numerous companies that will arrange visas for you for a fee of up to Dhs.50, such as dnata. For further advice on visas, contact the government's toll free AMER service on 800 5111.

The General Directorate of Residency and Foreigners Affairs (GDRFA) is rolling out new technology that will enable visitors to apply for, cancel and renew a tourist visa through their smartphones – by the end of 2014.

Residence Visas

To live in Dubai, you need a residence visa, and there are three main types: employment, family and domestic worker. You either need to have a job in the UAE and be sponsored by an employer, or be married to, or related to (son/daughter) someone who has a job here and they will sponsor you. As part of any residence visa process you will need to take a medical test and apply for your Resident Identity Card (formerly known as the Emirates ID). Once you have your visa – and this process can be completed in less than a month if your employer is on the ball – you can legally live and work in the UAE. Well, for two years at least (or three years if working in some free zones and government jobs).

Once you initially enter the UAE, you have 60 days to complete the visa application process – but it's unlikely to take that long. While your visa is being processed you should be able to leave the country as long as you have the visit visa that was stamped in your passport when you first entered. Citizens of the visa on arrival countries may need to do a 'visa run' to get a new visit visa after 30 days.

The residence visa permits you to live anywhere in the UAE, and you can live and work in different emirates. It is valid for two or three years (depending on where you are working), after which you'll need to re-apply.

Visa renewal is a simpler procedure, usually looked after by your PRO, although you will need another medical. If you are out of the country for longer than six months, your residence visa will be cancelled

See Explorer's *Dubai How-To* guide and visit askexplorer.com for detailed step by step procedures for all residency applications, renewals and transfers.

Passport Photos
If you need passport photos (and you will need them) then you also need to know where to go. Grand Stores (grandstores.com) has branches throughout the city and can take your picture and provide the correct size photos. Look out for Kodak outlets in all shopping malls which can shoot a passport picture or print passport-sized photos from your own snaps.

Employment Visa

To work in the UAE you need to be under 65 years of age and pass the medical test. For those being sponsored by an employer for their residence visa, the majority of the legwork will be done by the company or their Public Relations Officer (PRO). Your company PRO will submit your medical certificate, passport, Resident ID application form, and attested education certificates to the General Directorate of Residency and Foreigners Affairs (GDRFA), and pay the required fees. At the same time, they will also apply for your labour card or free zone ID; the Ministry of Labour website (mol.go.ae) has a facility to check the status of your labour card application online. Your employer will typically start the visa application process during your probation period. They will also be responsible for renewing the card when needed.

Your residence visa will be valid for two or three years, and to renew it you will need to complete another medical and re-apply for both the visa and your Resident ID at the same time; once again your PRO will help with this.

Free Zones
If you are an employee of a company in a free zone, the free zone authority will process your residence visa directly through the GDRFA without having to get employment approval from the Ministry of Labour. This speeds up the process significantly, and visas can sometimes be granted in a matter of hours.

Labour Card
If you are sponsored by your employer, the company will apply for your labour card (or free zone ID), which is technically a permit to work. If you are on a family sponsorship and decide to work, your employer and not your visa sponsor, will need to apply for a labour card. You'll need to give your employer a No Objection Certificate (NOC) from your sponsor, your passport with residence visa, attested education certificates, passport photos, and a copy of your sponsor's passport. All labour cards must be renewed every two or three years in line with your residence visa; eventually, the Resident ID will replace this card.

PROs & NOCs
A PRO (Public Relations Officer) is the person in your company who liaises with various government departments and carries out admin procedures. The PRO will take care of all visa, residency, health card, and labour card applications.

An NOC (No Objection Certificate) is a letter stating that the person in question permits you to carry out a procedure. You'll need one of these in a variety of situations: your employer allowing you to switch jobs, or your own NOC permitting a family member to work.

10 REASONS TO LIVE HERE

Dubai is – simply put – a great place to live. Have a look at our top 10 reasons to live here.

1. **It's ready-made for outside living** Sunshine all year. There are more than 850 hectares of parks and in excess of 22,500 hectares of conservation areas. Nine Blue Flag beaches to lounge on.
2. **High standard of living** Spacious villa/apartment lifestyle, with private/shared pool in the garden Live-in nanny or maid an affordable option. Access to world-class restaurants, attractions and hotels.
3. **It's all about the money, money, money** Competitive, tax-free salaries. Expat packages including housing, education and health allowances, if you're lucky. Cheap-as-chips fuel.
4. **Very low crime rate** It's a safe place to live and raise a family.
5. **It's a melting pot of old and new** Middle Eastern traditions are well and truly alive in the local food, architecture, dress and museums. Where else can you watch camel racing and the international golf and tennis in one weekend?
6. **Access to world-class education** Highly rated public schools and universities.
7. **Developing arts and cultural centre** The region will be home to the Dubai Modern Art Museum and Opera House District – it doesn't get artier than that International superstars, the likes of Bruno Mars, The Killers and Florence and the Machine, come to town – and you can get tickets!
8. **Meet and work with many nationalities** Explore new cuisines and learn about different cultures.
9. **You're at the centre of everything – literally** It's only a 30 minute drive at most to any attraction, restaurant or beach from home. Dubai airports are less than a five-hour flight away from Goa, the Seychelles, parts of Africa and Europe, and the Maldives. Depending on the traffic, it's a one-hour drive to Abu Dhabi.
10. **It's the future** Forward-thinking companies. Fast-developing landscape. Growing economy.

Cost Of Living

Most expats find they enjoy a higher quality of living in Dubai than back home, but it's worth calculating how far that salary can take you.

Housing
Property prices and rents are on the increase, but you should still be able to keep the cost of your accommodation to a maximum of a third of your income. If you want to rent, as most expats initially do, spend a couple of months searching because you have to sift through some less desirable properties and prices before you find what you want. You'll need to search for newly advertised abodes on a daily basis to find the best deals because they get snapped up the same day (especially if you're looking to rent a room in a shared house). Be aware that many landlords ask for quarterly, half-yearly or annual rent up front – so you'll need some savings to get started. For a more detailed breakdown of property prices see the Housing section.

Transport costs
The good news is that taxis are dirt cheap and readily available. A 15 minute journey comes in at around Dhs.25. Likewise, the metro and buses are also affordable and you can expect to pay in the range of Dhs.2 and Dhs.7 for a single journey, depending on the distance travelled and the type of card purchased.

Special Deals
Residents soon learn that there are many ways to get discounts on everything from restaurant meals, to beauty treatments and holidays. There are several online companies offering special deals, such as groupon.ae and cobone.com as well as The Entertainer books full of vouchers, available to buy at most supermarkets and bookshops.

Food and drink
Depending on your tastes, eating out can be cheap as chips if you visit some of the authentic Indian eateries in Bur Dubai, or you can pay top dollar for a Michelin-star meal at a number of the city's poshest restaurants. Every weekend, many restaurants offer all you can eat and drink brunch for a fixed price, which is a good way to dine out cheaply as the best-priced deals begin at Dhs.150 per person. See the Going Out section for our pick of budget eateries.

As with restaurants, supermarkets also vary – the most affordable include stores such as Choithrams and LuLu, and the more upscale stores are Spinneys and Waitrose. Much of the fruit and veg have to be imported and so costs slightly more than back home, but other groceries are comparable in price what you are used to. A family of four will need about Dhs.2,400 to buy monthly groceries.

As alcohol is taxed it's advisable to set a budget for your social tipples because otherwise those nights on the town can end up putting a big hole in your pocket. Girls should look out for special 'ladies nights' where females get free or discounted drinks, while everyone should check which bar is holding a happy hour. Full price, it can cost as much as Dhs.50 for a pint of beer.

Petrol
An added bonus is that fuel is extremely affordable and it generally costs no more than Dhs.100 for a full tank in a mid-range family car. A Jeep Liberty 4WD costs about Dh.120 to fill up, a Mazda 2 hatchback about Dhs.60 – and don't forget to tip the petrol pump attendant.

Renting a car
Many new arrivals choose to rent a car, and it's worth haggling over prices as rental companies will negotiate. For an older saloon-type car you can find deals starting at Dhs.1,300 per month if you commit to six months or more. Renting a new family sized saloon will set you back about Dhs.1,800 monthly. Make sure you opt for the best insurance package you can to help put your mind at ease when you find new dents along the side from inconsiderate door-openers in neighbouring parking spaces.

Buying a car
If you've always dreamed of owning an expensive sports car or 4WD, living in the UAE might be your opportunity. Many expats find the cost of cars is much lower in the UAE than in their home country. Try test driving one of the latest sports models or 4WDs at one of the dealers or in the city centre. You'll also find good quality second-hand cars with low mileage being sold by expats who are packing up and moving on. Visit a dealer or check out the used vehicles for sale on websites such as dubizzle.com.

Maids and nannies
A maid may cost Dhs.1,600 to Dhs.3,000 a month plus a food, clothes and toiletries allowance. You'll also need to cover their flight home at least every two years, their annual visa costs and basic health insurance.

Education
For a good school you can expect to pay Dhs.25,000 plus per year for the nursery years, Dhs.30,000 and up for the middle primary years, and as much as Dhs.60,000 per year for secondary school. Ouch! On top of this you will usually need to pay around Dhs.500 to put your child's name on a school's waiting list, and a registration fee (around Dhs.2,000), which comes off the fees.

Health insurance
By 2016, all employers must provide employees with basic health insurance. However, you may want to pay extra for more comprehensive health insurance, with extra cover for dental, maternity etc. This can cost about Dhs.180 a month. Without insurance, a medical consultation will cost you around Dhs.150-300, a dental check-up Dhs.250, and a hip replacement Dhs.50,000.

Additional costs
Consider also the expense of travelling on your annual holidays and back home to visit family and friends. Most employers provide one flight per year back home for expat employees, but the whole family is not always covered. The good news is that Dubai is surrounded by countries where you can enjoy very cheap holidays, such as India, Sri Lanka or SE Asia.

Average Prices

Cappuccino (regular)	Dhs.15
Water (small bottle)	Dhs.1
Milk (regular, 1 litre)	Dhs.5.50
Glass of wine	Dhs.40
Pint of beer	Dhs.35
Eggs (12)	Dhs.9
Average monthly utility bills for one-bed apartment	Dhs.500
Taxi (5km trip)	Dhs.10
Monthly internet bill	Dhs.250
Monthly gym membership	Dhs.300
Cinema ticket	Dhs.40
Fuel	Dhs.1.72 per litre

Jumeirah Lakes Towers

LIVING IN DUBAI
WHEN YOU ARRIVE

Family Visa

If you have a UAE residence visa (employment) you should be able to sponsor your family members (wife, husband, children), allowing them to stay in the country as long as you are here. If the family member is already in the country on a visit visa you can still apply for their residency. You'll need to pay Dhs.680 to have the visa swapped. If the family member ends up getting a job, they don't need to change to employer sponsorship, but the company will need to apply for a labour card for them.

You will need a minimum monthly salary of Dhs.3,000 plus accommodation, or a minimum all-inclusive salary of Dhs.4,000. Only what is printed on your labour contract will be accepted as proof of your earnings, so make sure you're happy with this before starting the job.

Visa Procedures

Everything related to your visa is handled at the General Directorate of Residency and Foreigners Affairs (GDRFA), also known as the Department of Naturalisation and Residency Dubai – DNRD (dnrd.ae/en). There are GDRFA branches across Dubai in Umm Suqeim, Deira, Karama and Dubai International Airport (T3), and the HQ is in Al Jafiliya.

If that's all in place, you'll need to take your passport, the passports of the family member(s), their Resident ID application form certified by the EIDA, your labour contract, attested marriage and/or birth certificates for spouse/child, and their medical test results if over 18. You will also need copies of your Ejari-registered tenancy contract– see the Renting section in this chapter for further information – and a copy of a DEWA utilities bill (which covers your gas, electricity and water) in the sponsor's name. Take all documents to the Family Entry Permit counter at the General Directorate of Residency and Foreigners Affairs (GDRFA). Your company PRO may help, but in most cases you will need to do it (and pay for it) on your own.

The family member's passport with residence visa stamp can be collected within three to five days, or you can pay Dhs.15 to have it couriered to you. You will be responsible for renewing their visas; they will be valid for two or three years in line with your employment visa. If switching jobs, and therefore sponsorship, you can avoid having to cancel your spouse and/or children's visas by paying Dhs.5,000 to the GDRFA; this will be refunded once your new visa is issued.

Renewing a visa is a relatively simple process that requires another medical test. Expat residents in Dubai are now required to renew and show their Resident Identity Card for residence visa renewal. For further information on all procedures related to visas, see Explorer's *Dubai How-To* guide.

Sponsoring Your Husband

A working woman can sponsor her husband if she meets the minimum salary requirements; in this scenario, the spouse's visa must be renewed annually. If a husband sponsors his wife, the visa need only be renewed every two or three years, depending on whether he works in the private or public sector.

Older Children

For parents sponsoring children, difficulties arise when sons (not daughters) turn 18. Unless they are enrolled in full-time education at a recognised institution in the UAE, they must transfer their visa to an employer. Or, the parents can pay a one-off Dhs.5,000 deposit and apply for an annual visa, which must be renewed yearly and is valid until the son turns 21. Daughters can stay on their father's sponsorship until they marry.

Property Owners

Property owners and investors (and sometimes their family) can apply for a six-month multiple-entry permit, which is renewable for Dhs.2,000 provided the owner leaves and then re-enters the country. This is a permit, and doesn't give the holder as many rights as residency, such as being able to apply for a UAE driving licence, bank account etc. The property value must be a minimum of Dhs.1 million.

Sponsoring Your Parents

There are constraints when Dubai residents want to sponsor their parents – a new ruling at the end of 2013 states that individuals must earn a minimum monthly salary of Dhs.20,000 or Dhs.19,000 and live in a two-bedroom accommodation before they can sponsor their parents. The tenancy contract must be Ejari-registered, as must the proof of salary certificate (by the Ministry of Labour).

Upon applying to sponsor a parent a Dhs.2,000 deposit per parent is charged. In addition, you also need a letter stating that your parents are dependent on you and have no one at home to look after them, and this letter must be verified by the embassy in your home country. Contact the GDRFA for more information (dnrd.ae).

Domestic Worker Visa

It's not unusual in Dubai to have a live-in maid or nanny, and if you choose to do so you will need to organise and pay for her immigration, labour

Good guides can help before you go

Make sure you've got the local knowledge to settle in quicker.

Crown service offerings include:
- International & Domestic Shipments
- Storage, Airfreight
- Transit Insurance
- Immigration & Legalization
- Home Search
- School Search

Tel: +971 4 230 5300
dubai@crownrelo.com

Go knowing
www.crownrelo.com/uae

CROWN
RELOCATIONS

LIVING IN DUBAI
WHEN YOU ARRIVE

and health documents. She must be a national of Bangladesh, India, Ethiopia, Indonesia, Philippines or Sri Lanka, and be under 58 years.

To sponsor a domestic worker (a maid or a nanny) you must have a salary above Dhs.6,000 per month, and be able to provide the maid with housing and the usual benefits, including an airfare home at least once every two years. The process is very similar to sponsoring a family member, although you'll also be asked to sign a contract stating the domestic worker's salary (typically around Dhs1,600-2,500 per month). You will need copies of your Ejari-registered tenancy contract and a DEWA utilities bill. You will also need to apply for her Resident ID card, labour card and government health card (unless you choose to pay for private healthcare). The residence visa is then valid for one year, and allows a maid/nanny to legally live and work in Dubai. From 2016 however, all employers have to provide private health insurance under the new government scheme – Insurance System for Advancing Healthcare in Dubai (ISAHD – meaning 'happiness in Arabic).

There are additional costs involved – you have to pay a 'maid tax' of around Dhs.5,080 per year (to the GDRFA), as well as a refundable deposit of Dhs.2,030. The maid/nanny will need to pass a medical test, as well be tested for pregnancy. Additionally, there's a one-off Dhs.50 fee for a compulsory Hepatitis B vaccination. There will also be a small typing fee and Dhs.130 payment to have the employment contract attested if the maid is a private sector employee outside of a free zone.

See Explorer's *Dubai How-To* guide for a step-by-step guide to renewing, cancelling and transferring a domestic worker visa.

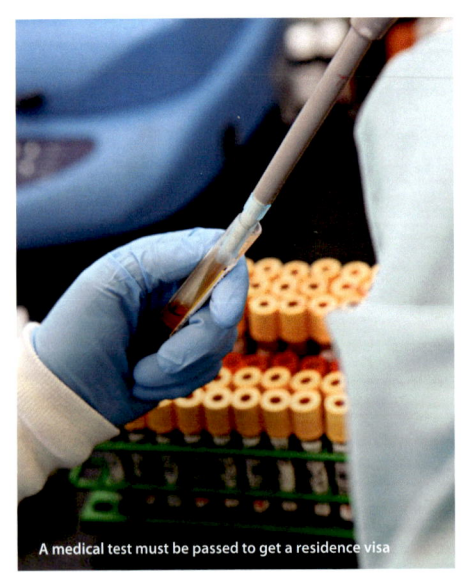

A medical test must be passed to get a residence visa

Medical Test

Any expat over the age of 18 must pass a medical test in order to get any type of residence visa. You will be tested for communicable diseases such as tuberculosis and HIV; if your tests are positive you will be deported to your home country. You will also need to have a chest x-ray to test for TB.

If you are sponsored by your employer, your PRO will arrange for you to take the medical test. Otherwise, it's up to you to get yourself to a Dubai Health Authority medical fitness centre with the following: test form completed in Arabic (there are typing offices near the medical centres that can do this for you for around Dhs.20), passport and visit visa, proof that your Resident ID Card application is underway, and the test fee of Dhs.250.

Once you have taken the required tests (expect to wait for around one to three hours, although you can pay Dhs.500 for a VIP/same-day service) you will be given a receipt, which will tell you when to collect your medical certificate (usually three days later).

See Dubai Health Authority (dha.gov.ae) for a full list of medical centres; some offer complete medical tests for all applicants, others are dedicated to female, executive employees or domestic workers. They also offer varying services: normal, 24 or 48 hours, and VIP. Free zones including JAFZA and DIFC have their own medical centres, as does Emirates airline.

Executive Medical Test

If you want to avoid the queues and are happy to splash that extra cash for convenience, visit Al Safa Health Centre. Arrive at 8am with your documents at the ready and there are hardly any queues. You'll be fast-tracked through the medical process and will be able to collect your medical forms that same afternoon. The executive medical test costs Dhs.690.

As with nannies and maids, all female domestic workers must also take a pregnancy test as part of the medical exam. Those working at nurseries, salons and health clubs, must also complete a course of Hepatitis B vaccinations, which costs Dhs.50; this is then valid for 10 years, so keep the certificate as proof.

You will need to take a medical test every two or three years depending on when you need to renew your residence visa; domestic workers must take the test annually in line with their visa.

You may find the government testing centres chaotic, which can be a little bit scary if this is your first experience of Dubai's healthcare system. Rest assured that, despite appearances, medical hygiene standards are followed and test results are processed efficiently. A good tip is to go wearing a plain, pale-coloured

LIVING IN DUBAI
WHEN YOU ARRIVE

T-shirt: this way you should not have to remove your clothes and wear a hospital gown (which may have been used by someone else before you) for your x-ray.

Online Applications

You can complete the necessary paperwork, submit required documents and pay the fees online at dha.gov.ae – a big time saver. To apply online you'll need a health card number; you can apply for a temporary one at dha.gov.ae if you don't already have one. After attending the DHA centre you will receive your test results via SMS, and then you just need to collect the test certificate. Once you have the results you will be able to proceed with the residence visa procedure.

Health Card

Once you have passed your medical test and obtained your residence visa, you are able to get a DHA health card. If you are not covered by a company or private medical insurance, it is advisable to apply for a health card as it entitles residents to low cost medical treatment at public hospitals and clinics. See Health, later in this chapter. The health card must be renewed each year (this can be done online at dha.gov.ae), but you only need to take a new medical test when your visa is up for renewal.

Digital Age
The Department of Health & Medical Services is embracing the digital age; online booking is now available at government health clinics and health cards can be renewed using the Express HC service. Register at dha.gov.ae to use these services.

Resident Identity Card

All expats living in Dubai need to register with the Emirates Identity Authority (EIDA) for a Resident Identity Card (previously called Emirates ID) before applying for their residence visa. Without a card you won't be able to complete the medical tests required for the visa. Additionally, if you fail to sign up you'll also face daily fines of Dhs.20, up to a total of Dhs.1,000.

Each card contains the holder's address, photo, date of birth and fingerprints, and is now an official source of identification in the UAE. It will eventually replace all other cards, such as health cards and labour cards, and can already be used at the e-Gate service at Dubai International Airport if the user pays the Dhs.150 activation fee. Great for frequent flyers!

UAE nationals must pay Dhs.100 for their ID cards; expat residents pay Dhs.100 per year of validity on their residence visa (two years on the visa equals Dhs.200), plus a small delivery fee. Children under the age of 15 also need one, but the fee is halved.

To register for your card, take your passport with your visit or residence visa, ID fee and a typing fee of Dhs.30 to an authorised typing centre, where your application will be filled in and translated into Arabic. Then, take the completed form to a registration centre, with your fee receipt, where you'll be fingerprinted and have your photo taken. You will then need your Resident ID application form, certified by the EIDA, to process your residence visa. Once your residence visa is approved and stamped you will receive a confirmation SMS that your Resident ID card is ready for collection; alternatively, it can be delivered to you (for an additional fee of Dhs.20).

A fast-track service at the Al Barsha centre allows applicants to obtain their Resident ID within just 24 hours.

For new residents this process is wrapped up in the visa application process and your company PRO will look after the whole process. If you're already a resident and need to apply, a list of registration centres and further details can be found at id.gov.ae. If you're registering yourself you'll need to take your passport to an authorised typing centre to get the forms processed. You'll then receive a SMS confirmation of your appointment to get your fingerprints and photograph taken (a step everyone must go through), then receive your ID card a few weeks later.

Apply Online
You can apply online at id.gov.ae and pay by credit card for first-time registration, renewals and replacement ID cards. This not only speeds up the process, it saves the need to visit a typing centre. If applying for a new card, you'll then be able to reserve an appointment to visit a Resident ID registration centre where your fingerprints and a photograph will be taken. Once it's time to renew your ID, you should be able to complete the entire process online. A list of authorised typing and registration centres, plus up-to-date information, can be found at id.gov.ae.

For a step-by-step guide to applying for or renewing a Resident ID, see Explorer's *Dubai How-To* guide.

Bank On It
Plans are in the pipeline for the Resident ID to be used as a bank card. The pilot phase with UAE Central Bank will be launched during the second quarter of 2014. If successful, bank cards will be integrated with ID cards, meaning that you can use them at ATMs. This service is optional for all Resident ID card holders.

LIVING IN DUBAI
WHEN YOU ARRIVE

Driving Licence

If you're in Dubai on a visit visa you can drive a rental car so long as you have a valid driving licence from your home country or an International Driving Permit (IDP). Once you have your residence visa, however, you must apply for a UAE driving licence (apart from GCC nationals who are allowed to drive on their existing GCC licences). This licence is then valid for 10 years. Many countries are given the option of an automatic licence transfer (see below). However, if you are not eligible, you will have to completely re-sit a theory and practical driving test. Obtaining a motorcycle licence follows the same procedure.

If you are a resident with a UAE driving licence and you cancel your visa and leave Dubai, and then return later on another visa, your UAE driving licence will still be valid (as long as it hasn't reached the expiry date on the licence).

Traffic Police
Traffic Police HQ: Al Quds St, Al Twar 1 (04 269 4444)
Bur Dubai Police Station: Nr Trade Centre Roundabout, Al Jafiliya (04 398 1111)
Al Quoz Police Station: Umm Suqeim St, Al Qouz Industrial 3 (04 347 2222)

Automatic Licence Transfer
Citizens with licences from the following countries are eligible for automatic driving licence transfers: Australia, Austria, Bahrain, Belgium, Canada, Denmark, Finland, France, Germany, Greece, Ireland, Italy, Japan, Kuwait, the Netherlands, New Zealand, Norway, Oman, Poland, Portugal, Qatar, Romania, Saudi Arabia, South Africa, South Korea, Spain, Sweden, Switzerland, Turkey, United Kingdom, United States.

Licence holders from some countries require translation or consulate letters: Canada, Greece, Cyprus, Poland, Turkey, Japan and South Korea.

You can read about the exact procedure to follow to get your UAE driving licence in Explorer's step-by-step *Dubai How-To* guide. In short, you need to take an eye test and submit the following documents to the Roads and Transport Authority (RTA): existing foreign licence, passport with residence visa, resident ID, No Objection Certificate (NOC) from your sponsor or employer, and Dhs.410. The licence is produced within minutes and is valid for 10 years.

Eye Test
To get a UAE driving licence, you'll need to take an eye test at an RTA/government-approved opticians. Just go to an optician and tell them you need the driving licence eye test; most will do it there and then for around Dhs.100. You'll need two passport photos. Once passed, you'll receive a stamped form that can be used in your licence application.

Online services
These opticians are approved to upload eye test results electronically to the RTA and renew driver licences: Barakat Optical, Grand Optics, Magrabi Optical, Yateem Optician and Al Jaber. Driving fines and fees can also be paid online, through the RTA call centre, or at an RTA office.

Liquor Licence

Dubai has a relatively liberal attitude towards alcohol. You can't buy alcohol in supermarkets, but you can buy it from licensed liquor shops for home consumption if you have a liquor licence. Independent restaurants cannot serve alcohol, but hotels, sports clubs and areas with special dispensation (Festival City and Wafi, for example) are permitted to serve alcoholic drinks in their bars and restaurants.

There's some confusion about what the legal situation really is, so let's clear a few things up. To drink in a bar or restaurant you need to be 21 or older. Visitors do not require a licence to drink alcohol, but they will not be able to buy it from licensed stores.

You need a liquor licence to buy alcohol from a liquor store in Dubai or Abu Dhabi. Residents can travel to other emirates and purchase alcohol without a liquor licence from licensed booze shops such as Barracuda Beach Resort in Umm Al Quwain or Al Hamra Cellar in Ras Al Khaimah, and can also purchase a limited amount at the airport Duty Free when passing through. However, you are legally required to have a licence in order to transport alcohol or consume it outside of licensed premises, such as at home. The reality is that it's very rare for people to be stopped and searched, and as long as you're driving carefully you should be OK. Have an accident though and it's likely to be a very different story.

The law states that UAE residents (i.e. anyone who has a visa) should be in possession of a liquor licence when drinking in licensed premises, such as bars, restaurants and clubs. In reality, it's unheard of for the police to enter a bar or sports event and check.

At home, as long as you're not throwing raucous parties and causing a drunken disturbance, it's unlikely that the police will call on you to justify that glass of red you sip with your dinner at the weekend.

Liquor Stores
There are two licensed liquor chains operating in Dubai: African + Eastern (africaneastern.com) and MMI (mmidubai.com), and you do need a licence to buy from these. They have branches throughout the city and, once you have your licence, you can buy

NEW TO DUBAI?

GET OFF TO AN EASY START BY APPLYING FOR YOUR BEVERAGE LICENCE WITH US!

Some things in life are sent to try us and make our life seem like hard work! We believe in making life EASY!

Whether you are applying for a new beverage licence or renewing your existing one, African + Eastern helps you get it done in **3 easy, hassle free steps!** Visit any one of our stores conveniently located all over Dubai to pick up an application form, get expert advice and have all your questions answered. **It's as EASY as that!**

If you have any queries, please ask our staff in-store or call **800 CHEERS** (243377)

Al Wasl Road* • Arabian Ranches* • Bur Dubai* • Burj Views* • Deira* • Dubai Marina Mall* • Dubai Marina Walk* • Green Community** • Jumeirah* • Karama • Le Méridien Dubai** • Mirdif • TECOM*

Stores also open on Fridays from 2:00pm - 9:00pm
**Green Community and Le Méridien Dubai stores open Saturday to Thursday from 2:00pm - 9:00pm

www.africaneastern.com

african+eastern

LIVING IN DUBAI
WHEN YOU ARRIVE

alcohol from any branch. They can work out expensive thanks to a 30% tax but the range and service is excellent. And they're extremely convenient. Plus, it's always better to be safe than sorry. You can also take advantage of special offers and events run by the liquor stores and even join the wine club.

Getting Your Licence

Applying for a liquor licence is straightforward, as long as you are non-Muslim and a resident of Dubai. The whole process can be carried out online at africaneastern.com or in any branch of MMI or African & Eastern. You must be 21 or older, in possession of a resident's visa, and earn more than Dhs.3,000 per month. You'll need to get the application form stamped by your employer, and then submit it along with a passport photo, copy of your passport with residence visa, copy of your Ejari-attested tenancy contract, (or a letter from your employer if you're in company accommodation), plus copies of your official Ministry of Labour contract in both Arabic and English, or salary certificate if you work in a free zone. The application costs Dhs.160, which the store typically gives you back in vouchers or credit.

If you want your spouse to use your liquor licence, you will need their photo, and a copy of their passport and residence visa.

The liquor licence, an easily identifiable red card, should be ready in around 10 days.

Using The Red Card

With your licence you get a monthly allowance, which is based on your salary and will be enough to keep one person in drinks for the month. However, you can't save up an unused allowance and use it the following month; so, for big parties, start to stock up a few months in advance. Alternatively, pay a visit to Barracuda or Al Hamra where you can buy in bulk.

Temporary Accommodation

When you first arrive in Dubai for work, usually your employer will have arranged accommodation for you for a week or more. If you find that you need more time to search for a home, then you may want to consider staying in a cheap hotel once you move out of the digs your company has paid for. Or perhaps you're just heading to Dubai for a look-see and need a good-value room to lay your head.

Al Bustan Residence Hotel Apartments Al Qusais 1, 04 263 0000, *al-bustan.com*
Al Waleed Palace Hotel Apartments Nr Lamcy Plaza, Oud Metha, 04 336 0004, *alwaleedhotels.com*
Arjaan By Rotana Dubai Media City Nr MBC, Media City, Al Sufouh 2, 04 436 0000, *rotana.com*
Ascott Park Place Dubai Shk Zayed Rd, Trade Center 1, 04 310 8555, *the-ascott.com*
Chelsea Tower Hotel Apartments Shk Zayed Rd, Trade Center 1, 04 343 4347, *chelseatowerdubai.com*
Dusit Residence Dubai Marina Marsa Dubai, 04 425 9999, *dusit.com*
Gloria Hotel Al Sufouh 2, 04 399 6666, *gloriahoteldubai.com*
Grand Belle Vue Hotel Nr Carrefour Express, TECOM, Al Thanyah 1, 04 449 9444, *bellevue-hotels.com*
Grand Hyatt Residence Shk Rashid Rd, Umm Hurair 2, 04 317 1234, *dubai.grand.hyatt.com*
JA Oasis Beach Tower The Walk at Jumeirah Beach Residence, JBR, Marsa Dubai, 04 8145 700, *jaresortshotels.com*
Lotus Hotel Apartments & Spa Marina Nr Trident Waterfront, Marsa Dubai, 04 440 2888, *lotus-hospitality.com*

Budget Hotels

Aside from the fancy hotels Dubai is famed for, there are plenty of alternative options where visitors can rest their heads. Radisson Blu (radissonblu.com), Rotana (rotana.com) and Holiday Inn (holidayinn.com) all have several outlets in Dubai. Al Barsha is home to a number of decent, less spectacular but well-priced hotels, while in Bur Dubai and Deira you'll find a number of places that offer good facilities and a central location, such as the Dhow Palace Hotel (dhowpalacedubai.com) and Park Regis Kris Kin Hotel (parkregishotels.com).

Guest houses are also becoming more popular in Dubai. While smaller in size, B&Bs offer a homely feel and are ideal for guests who want to see more of the 'real Dubai'. Located in residential areas, they won't have access to private beaches, but there is no shortage of good public beaches to enjoy. Some will have their own pool and benefit from intimate surroundings, while owners will be only too happy to give personal recommendations on what to see and do.

Villa 47 (04 286 8239, villa47.com) has only two guest rooms, but is located close to the airport in Garhoud. Other establishments that receive good reviews are The Jumeirah Garden Guesthouse – a villa that features 10 rooms, peaceful gardens and a good restaurant – book through the usual online portals.

Hotels & Serviced Apartments

Hotel apartments are expensive, but ideal if you need temporary, furnished accommodation. There's a large concentration in Bur Dubai, but more and more are cropping up around town, especially in Al Barsha. They can be rented on a daily, weekly, monthly or yearly basis. Water and electricity are also included in the rent.

explorer

there's more to life...

YOUR STEP-BY-STEP GUIDE FOR BATTLING BUREAUCRACY AND GETTING THINGS DONE

eBook available

Covering over 100 how-tos, including visas, vehicles, property, utilities and family matters

askexplorer.com/shop

askexplorer

Sponsored by:
axiommark

LIVING IN DUBAI
SETTLING IN

SETTLING IN

Jumeirah Lakes Towers

Relocating to a new country is a major upheaval, especially if your support network of family and friends is left behind. It's important to meet new people as soon as possible – start looking online for groups that share your interests before you arrive, and that way you can schedule to meet people as soon as you get here. Your new friends will be an invaluable source of information regarding the best restaurants, hairdressers, schools and more, and as they've already made the move themselves, they'll totally understand how it feels to be new in town. Dubai is a transient society, but consequently those who are here are more open and friendly. You'll find it easy to meet new people, and most likely many of them will end up as life-long friends.

National Groups

Dubai presents numerous opportunities to meet people from all over the world, but it's also important to have a network of friends from your own country. Sharing banter with someone from home is a good tonic for culture shock and will help you adapt quicker to your new environment. There are several groups formed by individual nationalities, where members enjoy reminiscing about home. Below are just a few of the nationality-based groups in Dubai:

Anza UAE: Australians and New Zealanders' social and community group with regular events. anzauae.org
BilgiDubai: A large, sociable network for the Turkish community, with regular activities and meet-ups. *anzauae.org*
Dubai Caledonian Society: A social network for Scottish expats with several annual events including the St Andrew's Ball in November and the Chieftain's Ball in May. *dubaicaledoniansociety.com*
Dubai Toastmasters Club: The Dubai branch of this worldwide, non-profit organisation provides a supportive environment that promotes self-confidence and personal growth. *http://7492.toastmastersclubs.org*
Dubai St George's Society: Serving the British expat community, the DSGS focuses mainly on fun and social activities, but also raises money for various charities. *dsgs.org*
South African Women's Association: SAWA is dedicated to bringing together South African women in Dubai through various networking and social events. *sawa-uae.org*

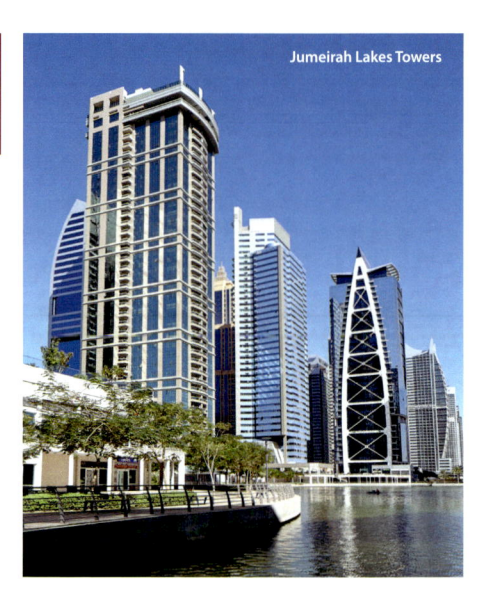

Social Networks

These social networking groups are great for meeting like-minded people in a friendly, social setting.

Ranches Ladies: A multinational ladies group which organises coffee mornings, social nights, activities and fundraising events. *arabianranchesladies.com*
Social Circles UAE: A well-organised social community that focuses on meeting new people and networking for business or pleasure. *socialcircles.me*
Speak Dating: Foreign language speakers can find 'language exchange' partners who help you practise your foreign language in return for you helping them to learn your native tongue. *shelter.ae*

Online forums

Websites like abudhabiwoman.com and expatwoman.com are great places for women to meet other women through the forums. You might also find job opportunities, chances for group days out and advice on problems you're encountering in the city. Expatwoman.com is like a permanent virtual coffee morning for women to chat about issues ranging from irritating husbands and cookery tips, to more serious problems. The group organises real life coffee mornings too, so be careful not to write anything derogatory about fellow members in case you meet them face-to-face.

meetup.com is a popular forum for finding friends with similar hobbies where you can arrange times for sessions in an easy-going manner, rather than having to stick to a rigid routine.

LIVING IN DUBAI
BEFORE YOU LEAVE

Places Of Worship

The UAE has a fairly liberal and welcoming attitude to other religions and, as a result, various places of worship also act as good community hubs, even if you're not a regular worshiper. In addition to the churches below, there is a Hindu temple complex in Bur Dubai, near Dubai Museum.

Christ Church Jebel Ali, christchurchjebelali.com
Dubai Evangelical Church Centre, deccc.com
Emirates Baptist Church International, ebci.org
Fellowship Of The Emirates, fellowshipoftheemirates.org
Holy Trinity Church Dubai, holytrinitychurchdubai.org
New Covenant Church Dubai, nccuae.org
St Francis of Assisi Church, stfrancisjebelali.ae
St Mary's Catholic Church Dubai, saintmarysdubai.com
Well Of Life Church Dubai, wolhome.com

BEFORE YOU LEAVE

If your time in Dubai has come to a close, there are a few things you should see to before leaving. To begin, get your electricity, water and other utilities disconnected. Most providers (DEWA, Etisalat, du) will need at least two days' notice to take a final reading and return any security deposits you have paid. You'll need to settle the final bill before you get your deposit, and make sure you keep hold of the original deposit receipt to smooth the process.

You'll also need to close any bank accounts you have here. Banks have been known to freeze an individual's account once they have been informed by the sponsor of a visa cancellation, or continue to charge you a monthly fee once you stop paying your salary into the account – bad news if you ever plan to return to the UAE.

Settle your debts – you can get into serious trouble if you try to leave the country without paying off all your loans and outstanding bills. You should also cancel all credit cards before you leave.

If you are leaving rented accommodation, make sure the place is spick and span so that you can reclaim your security deposit. The landlord may also require a clearance certificate from DEWA to prove you've paid all your bills, so leave enough time for the administration involved. If you own a property you may choose to either sell or rent out your home – see dubai.ae for more information.

Sell your car – but be prepared to take a financial knock if you need to offload it quickly with a dealer. Make sure you transfer ownership to the new owner and keep a copy of their new registration card; fail to do this and you will remain liable for any fines on the vehicle. It's also a good idea to cancel your Salik, although you won't be able to claim a refund on any credit not used.

Organise your shipping: give as much notice as possible to the shipping company. Sell the stuff you're not taking with you. Have a garage sale, list your items on dubizzle.com or expatwoman.com, or put photos up on supermarket noticeboards. Dubai Flea Market is a good option for last-minute clearouts.

If you're taking pets with you, you will need to make sure their vaccinations are up to date, particularly rabies. There are other procedures to be followed when exporting pets, and ideally you need around six months to prepare. If you can't take your pets with you, find them a new family home, ask friends and family, or advertise online – Dubai has a dreadful problem with abandoned pets.

If you're feeling overwhelmed, Crown Relocations (crownrelo.com) can assist with many aspects of these procedures.

Cancelling Visas

Different visa types require slightly different cancellation procedures. If your residence visa was sponsored by your employer, then they will be responsible for cancelling it once you cease to work for them. It's a simple process – you'll have to submit your passport and sometimes sign a document saying you've received all monies owed to you. You will also need to hand in your Resident ID.

The visa should only take about five days to be cancelled (longer during Ramadan), and your employer can pay to have the process fast-tracked if you need your passport back in a hurry.

Once the visa is cancelled you have 30 days before you have to leave the country – if you stay after this, you'll be fined at a rate of Dhs.25 per day for the first six months, Dhs.50 per day for the next six months, and Dhs.100 after that.

If you are in Dubai on a spousal visa and have separated, or need to leave, your husband or wife will need to help with the visa cancellation. If your spouse's company completed the paperwork, they will need your husband or wife to sign the cancellation papers.

You will also need to cancel your maid's visa, in which case, you must also arrange for her flight home. Alternatively, if she finds another employer in the emirate you can transfer the visa to her new sponsor. There is no notice period and you can cancel her visa at any time within the 12-month contract.

askexplorer.com

49

Luxury villas on the Palm Jumeirah

HOUSING

Housing is one of the great challenges about setting up in Dubai. Expat packages either include housing or an allowance to cover at least part of your accommodation costs, although the amounts are much smaller than in the boom days so it's likely that you'll need to top up from your own pocket to cover the rent or mortgage.

The first question to answer is: to rent or to buy? Most expats opt for renting as it gives you more flexibility, particularly when you first arrive in Dubai and are unsure of the best location to live in. Also, you need to have lived in Dubai for a minimum of six months before you can apply for a mortgage with a UAE bank, so your first year at least is likely to be in rented accommodation.

However, an increasing number of expats living in Dubai are now choosing to buy rather than rent property as they plan to put down longer term roots.

Unfortunately, the days of getting a 90% mortgage are over, and at the end of 2013 Central Bank announced a new ruling to cap mortgages. As restrictive as it sounds the good news for those wanting to buy a home is banks have dropped interest rates to attract borrowers.

Property Search

All your property questions are answered in this section, from which utilities you need to set up to some of the legalities regarding housing in the UAE. Like any major city, there is a varying scale of property: from labour camps for lower-paid workers and maid's rooms for domestic workers to modern high-rise apartments and spacious villas in affluent or up-and-coming areas across the emirate. And, whether you're single or moving here with a family in tow; whether you're living on a budget or got cash to splash, there is a place for you to call home.

ACCOMMODATION

When You Arrive

Apart from securing your new job, getting your accommodation satisfactorily sorted out is probably the most crucial factor in making your move to Dubai a success. Most expats will rent at first, although there are selected areas around the city where expats can buy property; this section covers the procedures and practicalities involved in both the rental and ownership markets.

Companies are legally obliged to provide employees with either accommodation or an accommodation allowance. This really varies as there are no official guidelines as to how much this should be. Some large organisations have complexes for employees, other companies have arrangements with particular developments and reserve a percentage of their properties for workers. It's worth checking your job offer though as often the housing allowance is included in your salary, so you won't get any additional help; your actual salary will only be a percentage of your monthly pay packet. You can use your housing allowance on either rent or a mortgage; if your company gives you the option of accommodation they may let you have the money to find your own place instead.

In previous years, Dubai has been home for many people working in Abu Dhabi; since 2013, however, public sector employees working in Abu Dhabi are now required by law to also live in the emirate, or forfeit their housing allowance.

Apartments

Apartments in Dubai are generally quite spacious, with everything from studios to seven bedrooms available. Master bedrooms in new builds can even come with an en-suite bathroom, walk-in wardrobe and lounge space. Newer apartments usually have central air conditioning, while older buildings can have noisier air conditioning (AC) units built into the walls. Some are linked up to district cooling, a system where all buildings in an area receive cold water from a central cooling plant. In this scenario, residents sign an agreement with the cooling company and pay monthly instalments. In winter, you won't need air conditioning much, so make sure it's possible to turn it off. Chilled water costs can creep up in the hotter months too.

Top of the range apartments generally come with white goods, have 24-hour security, covered parking (check if you get a space), a gym and a pool. Expats from some parts of the world tend to prefer villas to apartments, especially when they have families, but some of the facilities in the larger apartment complexes make for fun, comfortable and safe family living.

No Place To Park

Many apartments charge an additional rental fee for covered or underground parking. In some areas, this is essential, as finding parking outside your apartment can be nearly impossible, particularly if you live in the city centre, JBR or Marsa Dubai.

Villas

The villa lifestyle doesn't come cheap, and smart villas are snapped up pretty quickly. The good news is that if you look hard enough and use the grapevine, you might find the perfect villa that won't break the budget. Depending on the location, size and age of the property, it may be cheaper than some apartments, even if air-conditioning costs will be higher. Villas differ greatly in quality and facilities. Independent ones often have bigger gardens, while compound villas are usually newer and most have shared facilities like a pool or gym.

One Villa, One Family

Dubai bylaws prevent more than one family sharing a villa, although there are no restrictions on the number of members of the same family sharing. Children under 18 and maids are not included. The aim is to stop illegal villa sharing that can see dangerous overcrowding, as unauthorised partition walls turn a villa meant for a family to one housing up to 60 people in some cases.

Home Address

Traditionally, addresses in Dubai have not been as straightforward as you might be used to at home. Often your house would have two numbers, there's no postcode, and streets have traditionally only been labelled with numbers or letters – resulting in a dearth of streets with the exact same 'name', such as Street 1B.

Things are changing however. Dubai is introducing a new integrated address system, and the city has been divided into several districts, with each district further sub-divided into communities.

LIVING IN DUBAI
ACCOMMODATION

Communities include Burj Khalifa (including Downtown); Al Thanyah Third (including The Greens and The Gardens); and Marsa Dubai, which is the new name for Dubai Marina. The project will see more than 22,000 Dubai streets renamed over the next five years, so that each address will have a building number, street name and sector. So far 430 streets in the Jumeira and Umm Suqeim areas have been renamed with actual street names.

Many names used for Dubai roads reflect the heritage and culture; for example, Jumeira will have street names reflecting the marine environment like the names of fish, traditional boats and ships as well as other elements of the sea. Similarly, street names in the Financial District reflect various currencies.

In terms of giving directions to your abode, it's best to note nearby landmarks. When receiving post, many people rent a PO Box or use their company's address and PO Box, though this is slowly changing as the post office rolls out new services (see Postal Services).

RERA

When buying or selling a property, it is important to check that the real estate agent is registered with the government's Real Estate Regulatory Agency (RERA), which is there to safeguard and protect your rights.

An arm of the Dubai Land Department, the agency's responsibilities include the following: licensing all real estate activities; regulating and registering rental agreements, owners' associations, and real estate advertisements in the media; regulating and licensing real estate exhibitions; and publishing official research and studies for the sector.

Any potential property dispute can be taken to RERA; there are comprehensive rules on issues such as payments, escrow accounts and more. For more information, visit dubailand.gov.ae.

Real Estate Agents

Better Homes Jumeira 1, 600 522 212, *bhomes.com*
Deyaar > *p.53* Jumeira 1, 04 395 7700, *deyaar.ae*
Hamptons International > *p.57*
Emaar Business Park The Greens, Al Thanyah 3, 800 4267 8667, hamptons.ae
Landmark Properties
Best Homes Business Center Al Qouz 3, 04 350 2888, landmark-dubai.com
Pacific Ventures > *p.55* Bayswater Tower, Business Bay, 04 451 9771, *pacificworld.ae*
Premier Habitat Smart Heights Tower TECOM, Al Thanyah 1, 04 435 7433, *premierhabitat.com*
Propertyfinder Shatha Tower Media City, Al Sufouh 2, 04 454 8164, *propertyfinder.ae*

Renting A Home

Paying for rental accommodation in Dubai may be very different to what you're used to. Most landlords demand one cheque, and if you manage to negotiate two or three cheques expect to pay a slightly higher rent. Some landlords accept post-dated cheques that are cashed on their due date, while some employers will arrange to pay your rent payments directly from your salary, which can save a lot of hassle. Rental contracts are typically one year, and 90 days' notice must be given if you or the landlord want to cancel the contract rather than renew it. There is usually a fine of two months' rent if you break the lease early.

With a UAE residence visa you can rent a home in any emirate; the rapid increase in Dubai rents during 2013 has led to many expats seeking cheaper accommodation in the neighbouring emirate of Sharjah, although the downside to this are the hellish traffic jams if you commute.

Finding A Rental Home

Using a real estate agent is the easiest and often best option, although they will charge you for their services, usually around 5% of the annual rent, Dhs.5,000 or whichever is higher. Only ever deal with a RERA-registered broker or agent (see dubailand.ae for full list). All registered agents are given a Broker's Register card, with photo ID, which verifies that their office is licensed by RERA to manage, rent and sell real estate. If you do not use a registered agent, you will not be covered by the housing watchdog, RERA, or the Dubai Municipality's Rent Committee.

Alternatively, check out classified adverts in local newspapers or websites like dubizzle.com or propertyfinder.ae. It can also be useful to drive around the areas you fancy living in. Often there will be 'To Let' signs on vacant villas; if you like a certain complex ask the security guard if they know of any that are available.

Once you find a property, ask for proof of ownership of the property being rented out; a licensed agent will be able to present the owner's documents (including a copy of the landlord's passport and title deed). Also, always demand a receipt for any payments made by cash or cheque.

Rental Costs

Extra costs to be considered when renting a home are:
- Water and electricity deposit (Dhs.2,000 for villas, Dhs.1,000 for apartments) paid directly to Dubai Electricity & Water Authority (DEWA) and fully refundable on cancellation of the lease
- If your accommodation is in an area that uses district cooling, you will need to pay a deposit to the cooling company (usually Palm District Cooling, palmutilities.com). The deposit amount varies depending on the size and location of the property.

BE AT THE HEART OF DUBAI.

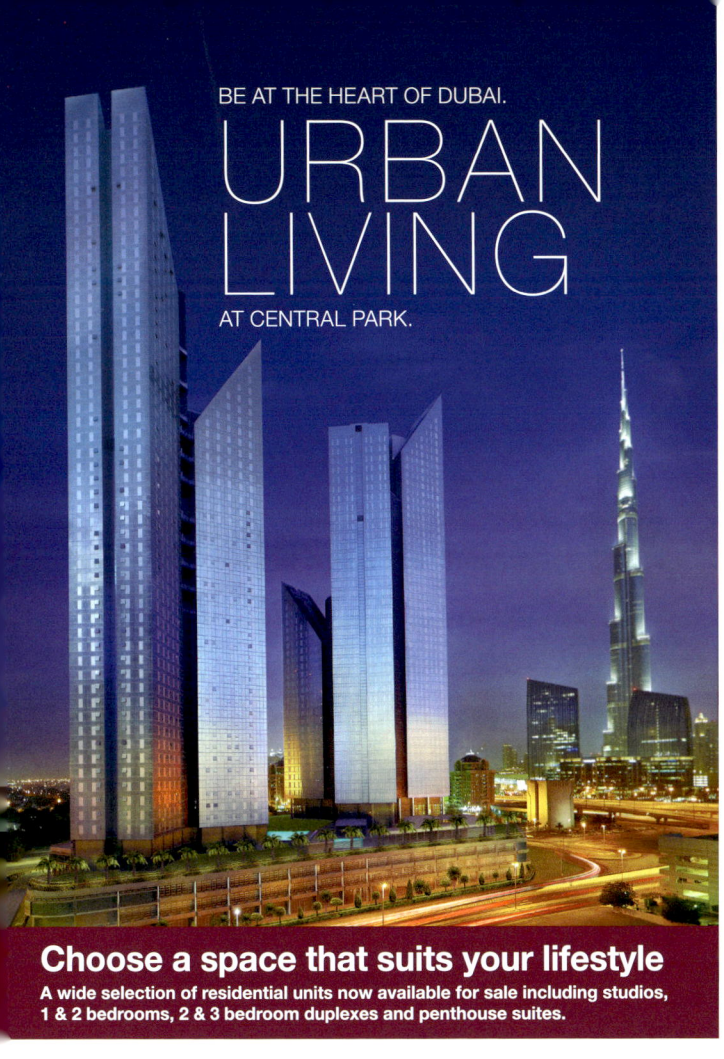

URBAN LIVING

AT CENTRAL PARK.

Choose a space that suits your lifestyle

A wide selection of residential units now available for sale including studios, 1 & 2 bedrooms, 2 & 3 bedroom duplexes and penthouse suites.

- The project represents a mix of residential, commercial & retail units
- Superior amenities at the Concourse Level, including swimming pool, gymnasium, kids play area, retail outlets, restaurants and coffee shops
- Direct access to retail, fine dining and more at DIFC
- Moments away from Burj Khalifa, Dubai Mall & other attractions
- Within a five-minute walk from Financial Centre metro station

For more information **call 800 339227**
or visit www.centralpark.ae

A joint venture between

DEYAAR

DUBAI PROPERTIES GROUP

CENTRAL PARK
AT DIFC

RESIDENCES

LIVING IN DUBAI
ACCOMMODATION

- Real estate commission is around 5% of annual rent and is a one-off payment
- Maintenance charges vary, but could be around 5% of annual rent, and are sometimes included
- A housing fee of 5% of your yearly rent is charged through your DEWA bill, spread across 12 months

If you're renting a villa, don't forget that you may have to maintain a garden and pay for extra water. It's worth asking the landlord what the average DEWA bills are for a particular property.

Renting A Room
When you first arrive, if you're alone, it works out cheaper just to rent a room because the rental payments are usually monthly (as opposed to quarterly, half-yearly or annually if you get your own place). In this scenario though, there is no guarantee that you will get a rental contract, which means that you can't get a liquor licence. The advantage is that you can usually leave your room with just one month's notice, so it gives you more flexibility. Also, the price will probably include all bills, so you can budget more easily knowing that your living costs are fixed.

Sharing
Let's clarify the issue of unrelated singles of the opposite sex sharing accommodation. There have been stories of people being evicted, but Dubai Municipality stated in the press at the time that the evictions were done to avoid overcrowding. Officially, under UAE law, it is illegal for unmarried or unrelated people of the opposite sex to live together. In reality, the police don't investigate who is living with whom unless they have need to visit you in relation to an official complaint. Do bear in mind that you are more likely to be frowned upon for sharing with someone of the opposite sex (who you are not married to or related to) if you're living in a family designated area such as Al Barsha or Jumeira where there is a high concentration of local families. Many expats share accommodation, but the issue should always be approached with caution.

Ejari
Meaning 'my rent' in Arabic, Ejari is an online system set up by RERA to oversee the rental market and its procedures. Its main purpose is to legalise the relationship between landlord and tenant, and all rental contracts must be registered with RERA, through Ejari.

Tenancy Contract
So, once you have found a property, you'll need to sign a tenancy contract and pay the 5% deposit required to secure the property; an official RERA template can be downloaded at ejari.ae, although your agent or landlord is ultimately responsible for this. Only a Dubai resident can sign a tenancy contract, so you cannot rent a property if you are still on a visit visa; however, by this stage you should have your residence visa stamped.

All tenancy/rental contracts must be registered through RERA's online Ejari service; this is required by law to safeguard the rights of both the tenant and the landlord. You will need an Ejari-registered contract in case you need to dispute a rent increase, eviction etc. For a lease to be registered with Ejari, the landlord must have an official title deed for the property – so always check this before handing over your deposit.

Once you have the keys to the property you can register the tenancy contract. Visit any Ejari typing centre with your tenancy contract (see ejari.ae for locations), Resident ID or passport copy for landlord, a copy of the security deposit receipt, and your Resident ID and passport. Pay the fee of Dhs.195 and your Ejari-registered contract (called a Tenancy Contract Registration Certificate) will be ready for collection within three days.

Your rental contract will cover the financial terms, the length of the rental and who is responsible for maintenance; since payments are usually made through post-dated cheques, make sure that payment terms are clearly stated. Before signing on the dotted line, you should also check the following:

- **Maintenance**: Some rents might be fully inclusive of all maintenance and repairs, while you could negotiate a much cheaper rent (particularly on older properties) if you agree to carry out any maintenance work

Many expats share villas

BURJ PACIFIC
AT THE HEART OF EXCLUSIVITY

1, 2 and 3 bedroom apartments with panoramic views

Three unique Duplex, Town-House Style Villas

Exclusive limited edition signature units

Designer's luxury interiors

5 minutes walk to Dubai Mall

PACIFIC
VENTURES فـنـتـشـرز
باسيفيك

📞 04-4519 771
pacificworld.ae

LIVING IN DUBAI
ACCOMMODATION

- **Utilities:** While not common, some landlords will include DEWA/utility expenses in the rent
- **Security deposit:** This can sometimes be negotiated, but Dhs.5,000 to Dhs.10,000 is standard
- **Parking:** Landlords do not have to provide parking, so check first if there is an additional fee for underground or covered parking
- **Home improvements:** Is DIY and decorating allowed in the property?
- **Pets:** Are they permitted and are there any restrictions on the type of pet? In some apartments, cats are permitted but dogs are not; there are seldom such restrictions in villas
- **Gardens:** If in a villa, are you responsible for the maintenance? This can become costly due to arid conditions and the amount of water needed. A well and pump can be installed for between Dhs.1,500 and Dhs.3,000, which may work out more cost effective in the long run

Once you have your tenancy contract, and only then, you will be able to apply for services, such as DEWA water and gas utilities, internet, and TV.

Renewals & Rent Rises

Rental contracts are valid for one year, after which they can be renewed for another year or terminated. A tenancy contract does not terminate automatically. Instead, it renews on the same terms until you or the landlord agree to change the terms or end it. If the landlord wants to evict you or increase the rent, he must give you 90 days' notice before the end of the contract; likewise, if you want to move out of the property you must give 90 days' notice. You will need to re-register your lease with Ejari when you renew your contract every year.

There are four circumstances under which a landlord can serve a notice for eviction on expiry of the tenancy contract: to demolish or add to the premises, making it unliveable; for repair or maintenance; to recover the premises for personal use or for a next of kin; or to sell the property.

Landlords can now raise rents annually based on prevailing market conditions, since the government removed the 5% rent cap at the end of 2013; landlords are able to increase rents by up to 20%, which overrides the previous 5% rental cap. There are restrictions though: the maximum increase is 10% if the property falls 21-30% below market rates and 15% if the property is 31-40% under average rents.

If your landlord does try to increase the rent unfairly then you can raise a dispute through the Dubai Municipality's Rent Committee (DMRC). Check the rent cap calculator at ejari.ae to receive the increase cap and average rental for your requested area and unit. If you, or the landlord, cannot reach an agreement either of you can take the case to the DMRC, whose decision is final and binding.

Buying A Home

The property market in Dubai grew at the fastest pace in the world in the year up to the end of June 2013, financed primarily from cash buyers. Mortgage lending is increasing though, and so buying a home is a viable option for well-paid expats planning to stay long-term or for those wanting to buy-to-let and make a return on their investment – especially as rents are rising each quarter. Interest rates on mortgages have dropped since 2010 from 9% to 4.5% per year, and banks are also offering incentives to would-be homeowners, such as discounts on processing and valuation fees, and reduced interest rates during the first year. Talk of another property bubble has been rejected by those in real estate, and the recent mortgage cap is an attempt to stabilise the market.

To buy a property in Dubai you need to have a UAE bank account, and have a 25% down payment/deposit (or 15% of the property value). Typically, you need to be salaried or self-employed with a minimum monthly salary of Dhs.15,000, and aged 21 or over; mortgages are available to both UAE and non-UAE residents.

For an in-depth step-by-step guide, see Explorer's *Dubai How-To* guide to buying and selling property in the UAE.

Freehold Or Leasehold?

Most property in Dubai available for purchase by expats is freehold. Maintenance fees are payable by the property owner and cover the cost to the developer of maintaining all the shared facilities. Fees are typically paid annually, though some developers will accept quarterly payments. If you buy leasehold your lease will stipulate who is responsible for maintenance and repairs, and any other conditions you should meet. There is also a small, annual ground rent fee payable to the owner of the land (the freeholder). Check that the seller is up to date on ground rent payments before you take over the contract.

House Hunting

The list of real estate agents earlier in this section is a great place to start, but it's often better to trawl through the property listings in *Gulf News* (gnads4u.com) or on dubizzle.com to find out which properties are listed with which agent. Always deal with a RERA-registered agent or broker. In general, expect to pay a flat fee of around 2-5% of the purchase price to the agent upon completion of sale.

One key point is that non-UAE nationals can only buy in specially designated areas for expatriate freehold or leasehold (typically 99 years) sales. Property in some areas is only available for purchase by Emiratis or GCC nationals; such areas include Jumeira, Umm Suqeim, Al Barsha and most parts of Old Dubai.

Thinking of buying or renting a new home in Dubai?

Call **800 Hamptons** or visit **hamptons.ae** to find your new home

It can take a lifetime to build a strong reputation and credibly call yourself an expert. We've spent more than 140 years developing our local and international knowledge and expertise to do just that. Our teams of highly qualified professionals have years of experience selling and renting thousands of properties and understand the local market. Contact Hamptons for the best advice on property.

Call **800 Hamptons** (800 4267 8667)
or email **enquiries@hamptons.ae**

hamptons.ae

HAMPTONS INTERNATIONAL
Your global property partner

UAE | UK | Saudi Arabia | Oman | India | Egypt | Morocco | Italy | Seychelles | Monaco

LIVING IN DUBAI
ACCOMMODATION

If you're buying a new development in an apartment building in Marsa Dubai, Jumeirah Lakes Towers (JLT) or Business Bay, be aware that many are built by sub-contractors and consequently the finished standard and management capability will vary. For peace of mind, stick with reputable companies.

You can choose to buy off-plan – though few UAE banks provide mortgages for this. This option means you get a good price for your property, but you have to be prepared for the possibility that the construction could be delayed, so check regularly on progress.

Likewise if you buy a completed property, the handover could be subject to delays due to rent or mortgage issues, which could delay your moving-in date. When buying or selling a property, always check that the real estate agent is registered with RERA, which is there to safeguard and protect your rights.

Developers

Arady Developers
SJ Tower, Shk Rashid Bin Saeed Al Maktoum St
Al Karamah, Abu Dhabi
02 447 2542
arady.com
With a sturdy reputation, Arady Developers is a Shariah-compliant investment company focused on real estate, real estate related investment and private equity. Their operations span the GCC, and they have several developments in Dubai.

Damac Properties
Executive Heights Bldg TECOM, Al Thanyah 1
04 373 1000
damacproperties.com
Map **1 N6** Metro **Dubai Internet City**
Develops apartment buildings and commercial office towers, including Ocean Heights, Marina Terrace and The Waves in Marsa Dubai, Palm Islands, and Lake View and Lake Terrace in Jumeirah Lakes Towers.

Dubai Properties Group
Vision Tower Business Bay **04 435 2117**
dubai-properties.ae
Map **2 E6** Metro **Business Bay**
Its flagship freehold properties are Jumeirah Beach Residence and Business Bay. It also has a big residential development called The Villa and is the master developer behind the Dubailand project.

Emaar Properties PJSC
Emaar Business Park The Greens, Al Thanyah 3
04 367 3333
emaar.com
Map **1 N5** Metro **Nakheel**
Emaar's flagship property is Burj Khalifa; its portfolio of freehold real estate projects includes: Marsa Dubai, Arabian Ranches, Emirates Living (The Views, The Meadows, The Springs, The Lakes and The Greens), Emaar Towers and Downtown Dubai (Burj Khalifa, Burj Residence, Burj Views, Old Town, South Ridge).

Nakheel Properties
Nr Knowledge Village Al Sufouh 2 **04 390 3333**
nakheel.com
Map **1 N5** Metro **Dubai Internet City**
Builds, sells and is responsible for maintaining several large developments, including: Palm Jumeirah, Jumeirah Islands, International City, Discovery Gardens, Jumeirah Village, Palm Jebel Ali, Palm Deira, The World and Al Furjan Community.

Meraas Development
Emaar, Downtown Dubai, Burj Khalifa, **04 511 4500**
meraas.com
Map **2 F6** Metro **Burj Khalifa/Dubai Mall**
Meraas has numerous projects in Dubai, including the hugely popular, low-rise Wasl Square development, which is made up of apartments and townhouses and is within walking distance of Safa Park. There's actually a waiting list to be able to rent a Wasl Square apartment.

Real Estate Law

The Real Estate Regulatory Authority (RERA) is a government organisation that, aside from setting the rental index, regulates the real estate market and aims to maintain healthy property investment in Dubai.

The agency's responsibilities include the following: licensing all real estate activities; regulating and registering owners' associations, and real estate advertisements in the media; regulating and licensing real estate exhibitions; and publishing official research and studies for the sector.

Any potential property dispute can be taken to RERA; there are comprehensive rules on issues such as payments, escrow accounts and more. To find out more about RERA, visit dubailand.gov.ae or call 04 222 1112.

Homeowners' Associations
Dubai Strata Law, better known locally as the Jointly Owned Property (JOP) Law, was implemented by RERA in Dubai in April 2007. This recognised Homeowners' Associations as democratic authorities, which enable people who own units in a development to decide the financial governance and service levels provided to the community's occupants. Dubai Strata Law is designed to remove ambiguities about who is responsible for common property management. It helps settle disputes over issues such as parking, pets that disturb neighbours, privacy and maintenance of common areas. There are numerous such associations registered with RERA, mostly in 'new' areas such

LIVING IN DUBAI
ACCOMMODATION

as Marsa Dubai, Jumeirah Lakes Towers and Palm Jumeirah. If you are thinking of buying property in Dubai, it's worth checking whether your chosen development offers a Homeowners' Association; it can provide you with an extra level of security.

Check out the government's official website for information on laws, fees and general facts related to property purchases in the emirate: dubailand.gov.ae (Dubai Land Department).

Mortgages

Before you go house hunting, it's advisable to get a mortgage in place, or pre-approval, so you're in a position to make an offer should you find the place of your dreams. A 10% deposit is required to secure a property and this could be money wasted should you then find nobody is willing to lend to you.

At the end of 2013, the UAE Central Bank announced a new ruling to cap mortgages (also known as home loans here). For properties valued at less than Dhs.5 million, expat first-time buyers can get a mortgage of 75%. For properties valued above Dhs.5 million, expats can only get a mortgage of 65%. Expats taking out a 'home loan' for a second, third, fourth or subsequent property will be able to get a 60% mortgage. Financing for off-plan property is restricted to 50% regardless of the value of the property or the nationality of the applicant.

A mortgage can be calculated on more than one salary, providing they are listed as co-borrowers in the loan contract. Central Bank rules also state that your monthly mortgage instalments and other debts should not consume more that 50% of your income. Expats may also find it more difficult to get a mortgage if they are single and have been here less than six months. If you have a family, a stable job and been in the country for a few years then they presume you are committed to the country and are happier to lend you money.

The amount financed by the lender also varies and depends on whether the property is a villa or an apartment, where they are and who built them. It's also worth noting that some banks and lenders will only provide mortgages for select developments. Additionally, they may also have different acceptance criteria and mortgage processes, which change frequently, so it's advisable to do your homework.

There are international names such as HSBC, Barclays, Standard Chartered and Citibank alongside local financial houses in Dubai, including Emirates NBD and Mashreq.

Fortunately, interest rates are currently much lower than the 9% highs of the pre-financial crisis era, with fixed rate deals available at around 3.99-4.99% depending on the term.

To help you get started, try some of the new price-compare websites such as Souqalmal.com or Moneycamel.com. Here you can compare rates from various national banks as well as international banks with UAE branches.

Lenders will only provide mortgages on a select number of developments, which varies from institution to institution. You'll probably be expected to take out a life insurance policy to cover the amount of the loan, and this should be done well in advance of the transfer date in order to avoid delays getting the mortgage though. Equity release and mortgage transfers have recently been introduced to the market, offering investors the opportunity to release equity and secure better rates. To combat price sensitive customers moving their loans, most banks have introduced exit fees but there are still completely flexible mortgages available. More recent innovations also include international mortgages, which offer loans in currency denominations other than dirhams. This offers clients the ability to structure their loan in a preferred currency, with the ability to switch if they choose to.

Islamic Mortgages

Shariah-compliant or Islamic mortgages are alternative financing options available to non-Muslims. The term 'home finance' is used as opposed to mortgage. Complying with Islamic beliefs, the bank purchases the asset on behalf of the buyer who then effectively leases it back from the institution at a marked-up price, but with zero interest. The bank owns the title deeds of the purchased property until the full amount is repaid.

Mortgage Application

The first step towards getting a mortgage is to get a pre-approval before beginning your property search – that way you can find out how much the banks are willing to lend you. The documents needed for this process are: the original and copies of your passport, six months of bank statements, salary confirmation from your employer and six months of salary slips.

The 'approval in principle' should come through in four working days. Generally, employed applicants will be able to borrow a higher percentage of their income than the self-employed. The amount is approximately 50% of disposable monthly income – and the calculations will take into account all your financial commitments. If you're able to pay a large deposit the terms are likely to improve. Mortgages are usually granted for 25 years and lenders will generally finance individuals up to 65 years of age.

The next step is for the lender to provide an unconditional approval on the basis that any conditions noted in the pre-approval are satisfied.

LIVING IN DUBAI
ACCOMMODATION

Purchase Costs

Make sure you budget for the additional costs associated with buying a house, as they can add up. The obligatory amounts equate to around 6% of the purchase price, not including any cash deposit.

Solicitor fees: By law there is no requirement to have a solicitor act for you when buying property in Dubai, but you may wish to employ legal help to see you through the process. Legal costs will vary depending on whose services you use.
Real estate agent/broker's fee: The flat fee to the agent is usually 2-5% of the purchase price, upon completion of sale.
Mortgage broker fee: Often 0.5% of the purchase price or a pre-determined flat fee.
Arrangement fee: Dhs.3,000, but can often be offset against the processing fee.
Processing fee: Often around 1.5% of purchase fee, but minimum amounts of around Dhs.3,000 are common.
Valuation fee: Expect to pay around Dhs.3,000.
Life and household insurance: Life insurance to the value of the property is mandatory for a mortgage. Shop around for the best deal.
Land registry: Payable to the Dubai Land Department (600 666 556, dubailand.gov.ae). The fee is 2% of the property value, plus a Dhs.10 surcharge, and establishes legal ownership of the property. The buyer also pays Dhs.250 fees (plus Dhs.10 surcharge) for the title deed and a Dhs.100 map issuance fee (plus Dhs.10 surcharge).

Buying Process

Once your offer has been accepted, a Sales & Purchase Agreement (SPA) will be drawn up by the real estate agency, which defines all the terms and conditions for the transfer of property. If you require a mortgage, the lender will issue an unconditional offer letter, which states the terms and conditions of the mortgage.

To process the mortgage, you need your passport plus copies, six months of bank statements, salary confirmation from your employer and six months of salary slips. Once the paperwork is signed and sent back to the lender, the settlement process begins. This is when the lender transfers the mortgage payment to either the seller or to the existing lender who has the first charge over the property. This usually occurs on the day of the transfer. Equal instalments are then taken from your bank every month. For the full transfer of ownership to take place, you will need to register the property and your mortgage with the Dubai Land Department. And then? Collect your keys and call the removal van.

Sales & Purchase Agreement

When you buy a property, a Sales & Purchase Agreement (SPA) will be drawn up by the real estate agency, which defines all the terms and conditions for the transfer or property. It is advisable to consult a lawyer so that you make sure you understand all the terms. When selling a property, you will need to provide this agreement, along with the title deeds, floorplans, location map and liability letter from the bank you have the mortgage with.

Land Registry

When you buy a property, in order for the full transfer of ownership to take place, you will need to register the property with the Dubai Land Department – the central agency for all transactional processes related to freehold and leasehold purchases.

This establishes legal ownership of the land or property, thus safeguarding the owner from future dispute, and provides the owner with the title deeds to their property or land. Fees levied by the Dubai Land Department are dependent on whether the property purchase is covered by a conventional mortgage, an Islamic (Shariah-compliant) mortgage or a cash purchase. All fees are payable by the buyer.

Fast-track service

Sign up to the e-Smart Travel Estate Pack (E-STEP) and the department will come to you, register your transaction and even issue the title deed – all in less than one hour. This service costs Dhs.4,000, and both the buyer and the seller need to be present at the same time.

Selling A Home

Selling a property in the UAE can be a simple process, but takes around six weeks to complete. Before putting up the 'For Sale' sign, sort out any maintenance issues and redecorate if needed. Then, you should market the property across a range of property websites. Most real estate agents can assist you with this by drawing floorplans, arranging viewings and giving you a free valuation based on market trends; you may also want to advertise the property on sites such as dubizzle.com.

Property transactions in Dubai can be viewed at their actual selling value on the Real Estate Regulatory Agency's (RERA) site, dubailand.gov.ae. Finding a good agent to help you sell your home is important, as private property sales here are rare. Agents can charge up to 2% of the property price to cover the costs of marketing your property. It shouldn't take long to find a buyer – Dubai's real estate market is the world's top performer according to a survey compiled by the Global Property Guide.

Rental & Property Prices

The price of renting and the cost of buying are hot topics for expats seeking a home in Dubai. It's no secret that the real estate sector is booming. Here's a look at the figures from the past year.

Popular Places
Leading real estate portal propertyfinder.ae announced at the end of 2013 that Marsa Dubai has held its position as the most-searched neighbourhood on the propertyfinder website since 2012. The price of rent in the area increased 36% over the course of 2013.

However, the nearby JLT development only saw a 6% increase in rental prices over the year.

Going up
The economic crisis is now a distant memory in Dubai. CBRE Middle East, a global commercial real estate advisor reports that Dubai continues to see strong economic growth and the total value of residential transactions reached Dhs.11.1 billion in Q3 of 2013. Figures show that roughly 75% of residential sales were cash transactions in 2013.

The rental market is booming too, and the average residential rentals grew by more than 30% in the 12 months preceding Q2 2013. CBRE reported that the residential sector is showing signs of overheating with lease and sale rates rising too quickly – significantly outpacing growth in wage levels. However, it is still possible to find affordable accommodation as rents have not reached extortionate highs.

Transport links
Proximity to metro stations and the soon-to-be-opened tram are factors that are affecting popularity – currently the tramline is still under construction, but once it is up and running in November 2014 it will provide a much-needed public transport link for residents on The Palm and JBR.

What you'll pay
If you're single and looking to rent a one-bedroom apartment in a central location such as Marsa Dubai, prices start at about Dhs.70,000 per year for an unfurnished place. To rent a three-bedroom villa prices start at around Dhs.220,000 annually for an unfurnished property somewhere a little further out such as Arabian Ranches.

The cost of renting a room in a central area or near the beach (in JBR for example) starts at around Dhs.5,000 per month for a furnished room with an en-suite bathroom.

Going down
Prices haven't gone up everywhere. Studios in Palm Jumeirah dropped in price by 7% in 2013. Though one-bedroom apartments saw a hike of 14% over the year, according to propertyfinder.ae, the property search portal.

Dubai Sports City has seen a 30% rise in rental prices over 2013, as the community becomes more developed.

Booming sales
The Expo 2020 win is expected to lead to a rise in asking price for both plots and ready villas/apartments in developments close to the Expo site and Jabal Ali area; rents have already seen an increase.

Buying an apartment in Dubai can cost from Dhs.850,000 for a 986 sq ft one-bedroom apartment near the beach in Marsa Dubai. A 1,900 sq ft three-bedroom villa with a garden about 15 minutes' drive from the beach in The Springs starts at approximately Dhs.1,900,000.

However, if you search further away from the seafront or in the Bur Dubai area and older parts of Dubai, the cost of renting and buying is less.

LIVING IN DUBAI
RESIDENTIAL AREAS MAP

Arabian Gulf

NAKHLAT JABAL ALI
NAKHLAT JUMEIRA
PALM JUMEIRAH
MENA JABAL ALI
JABAL ALI
2 JBR
1 MARSA DUBAI
AL SUFOUH
Jabal Ali Village
The Gardens
3 Jumeirah Lakes Towers
10 The Greens
15 Tecom
9 AL THANYAH
16 Discovery Gardens
8 Jumeirah Islands
Emirates Living
14 AL BARSHA
JABAL ALI INDUSTRIAL
17 Al Furjan
JABAL ALI INDUSTRIAL
AL KHAIL RD
24 Green Community
AL BARSHA SOUTH
SHK MOHD BIN ZAYED RD
DUBAI INVESTMENT PARK
International Media Production Zone (Impz)
19 Jumeirah Golf Estates
20 Dubai Sports City
AL HEBIA
21 Dubai MotorCity
22 Arabian Ranches

MADINAT AL MATAR
AL MAKTOUM INTERNATIONAL AIRPORT

EMIRATES RD E611

Area	No.	Page
Marsa Dubai	1	p.65
JBR	2	p.65
JLT	3	p.65
Palm Jumeirah (Nakhlat Jumeira)	4	p.66
Jumeira	5	p.68
Umm Suqeim	6	p.68
Satwa	7	p.68
Emirates Living	8	p.70
Jumeirah Islands	9	p.70
The Greens	10	p.70
Jumeirah Park	11	p.70
Downtown Dubai	12	p.72
Sheikh Zayed Road (in the Downtown area)	13	p.72
Al Barsha	14	p.74
TECOM	15	p.74
Discovery Gardens	16	p.76
Al Furjan	17	p.76
Dubailand	18	p.77
Jumeirah Golf Estates	19	p.77
Dubai Sports City	20	p.77
Dubai MotorCity	21	p.78
Arabian Ranches	22	p.78
The Villa	23	p.78
Green Community	24	p.78
Bur Dubai	25	p.80
Karama	26	p.80
Deira	27	p.80
Mirdif	28	p.81
Silicon Oasis	29	p.81

LIVING IN DUBAI
RESIDENTIAL AREAS MAP

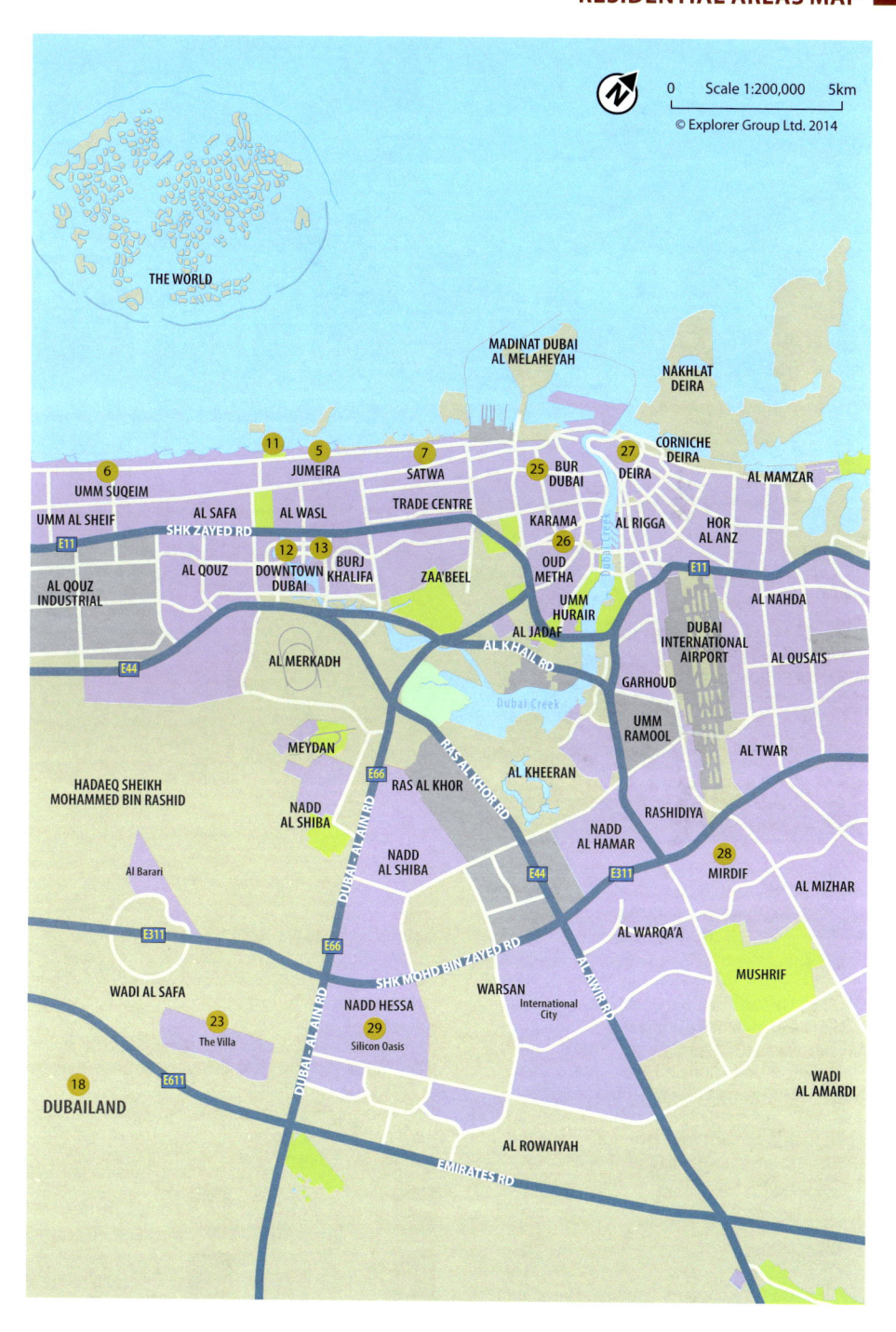

Lakeside villas at Jumeirah Islands

RESIDENTIAL AREAS

Dubai has plenty of residential areas to choose from, ranging from family villas, to snazzy high-rise apartments. More developments are springing up all the time and each, when finished, will have its own shops and restaurants, and usually, access to a school.

Some areas are more popular with local families, such as Al Warqa (south of Mirdif), or Al Sufouh (near Umm Suqeim) while others are so well-established that it's challenging to even find available accommodation, as is the case in Garhoud – although it benefits from being very near the airport and having a metro stop. The Gardens near Ibn Battuta Mall has virtually nothing available – the low-rise buildings here are set in an oasis of green and were snapped up long ago.

Select areas that appeal to you from our guide and then spend a few days driving to each place you are interested in – so you can see if the development is well established or still under construction, what facilities are there and what the traffic is like.

We've provided a price guide, with prices being for unfurnished properties – if you want to rent a furnished place, anticipate adding Dhs.10,000 or more a year to the rental price.

You'll find these icons (below) throughout the following section. They're a handy way to understand at a glance the main differences between housing developments in the same areas, or to quickly compare the dominant housing type in different areas of the city. Also see the Residential Areas Map for locations.

| By the beach | Family friendly |
| High-rise living | On a budget |

LIVING IN DUBAI
RESIDENTIAL AREAS

Marsa Dubai & JBR

Map **1 K5** Metro **Dubai Marina**

The high-rise apartment towers of Marsa Dubai and Jumeirah Beach Residence (JBR) are a popular choice for expats. The many hotels are home to numerous restaurants and bars and The Walk at JBR is packed every evening with people socialising and strolling. Roads in and out do get congested due to the construction of the new tram line, which is due to be completed in late 2014. The narrow road running alongside The Walk is where people come to cruise with their expensive cars, resulting in additional traffic at weekends and evenings.

Several new buildings are being constructed on the beach, which means that JBR residents do have to put up with construction noise and excess dust for the foreseeable future.

Much of the neighbourhood is walkable with easy access to amenities. If you have a car check if the property you want comes with a parking space.

Schools
None, but the Wellington International School and the International School of Choueifat in Al Sufouh are both just five minutes' drive away. There are a few nurseries in the marina.

Healthcare
Medcare Hospital near Al Safa Park has the closest emergency room. The Cedars Jebel Ali International Hospital offers 24-hour care. JBR has a medical centre and Al Sufouh and Knowledge Village also house medical and dental clinics.

Shops
Dubai Marina Mall – not huge, but has Waitrose and a number of high-street shops. Marina Walk has a Spinneys supermarket, a pharmacy, a bookshop, a florist and a liquor store, plus numerous ATMs. The Walk along JBR has clothing boutiques and furniture stores and the Mall of the Emirates and Ibn Battuta Mall are a short drive away.

Bars & Restaurants
The Walk below JBR is teeming with places to eat, many of which are open until the early hours. Marina Walk also has a number of popular restaurants, including The Rupee Room. The hotels along the beach all have bars and restaurants too, including the popular Mai Tai bar and Frankie's Italian restaurant at Oasis Beach Tower.

Attractions
Open sandy beach and marina. Currently under construction – the world's largest Ferris wheel and a beachfront shopping mall.

Marsa Dubai
Apartments here vary in quality. Most have a pool and amenities in the pedestrianised Marina Walk are a stone's throw away.

Annual rental prices: One-bedroom from Dhs.70,000. Three-bedroom from Dhs.140,000

JBR
JBR consists of several identical towers of around 40 storeys high, with communal pools, grassed areas and amenities. Most buildings are owned by expats.

Annual rental prices: One bedroom from Dhs.70,000. Three-bedroom from Dhs.135,000

Neighbouring Community: JLT
Jumeirah Lakes Towers (JLT) is comprised of 79 towers across Sheikh Zayed Road from the marina. There are lakes flanked by a promenade with cafes, shops and a park. Access to the area by car can be quite tedious due to the one-way system, but there are two adjacent metro stations. There is still some ongoing construction. Build quality is similar to Marsa Dubai.

Annual rental prices: One bedroom from Dhs.70,000. Three bedroom from Dhs.96,000.

Jumeirah Lakes Towers

askexplorer.com

65

LIVING IN DUBAI
RESIDENTIAL AREAS

Palm Jumeirah

Map **1 N1** Metro **Nakheel**

The Palm Jumeirah (also referred to by its Arabic name of Nakhlat Jumeira) is synonymous with Dubai's extravagance, and the rental prices on the man-made island match its reputation. In a recent survey, local estate agents said The Palm is one of the most sought-after areas for families due to its wide range of facilities and the fact it's away from the hustle and bustle.

There is a monorail system linking areas on The Palm and an extension linking the monorail to the metro is being constructed and should be functioning by the end of 2014.

Schools
Al Sufouh is 10-15 minutes' drive and has several popular expat schools.

Healthcare
Medical centres at JBR and Al Sufouh are within a 15 minute drive.

Shops
Construction is due to start on a huge mall, The Pointe, due to be completed by 2016. Dubai Marina Mall is a 15 minute drive.

Bars & Restaurants
Several high-class hotels are now open on the Palm including Sofitel The Palm, Atlantis and Rixos The Palm, all offering an array of superb restaurants and bars. There are also a few licensed restaurants and bars in the Shoreline Apartments on the trunk – The Palm is becoming a high-class hub for dining and partying. Also, the marina and Madinat Jumeirah are five minutes away by car.

Attractions
The Atlantis hotel houses several attractions including a waterpark and dolphinarium. This is also the home of the hugely popular Sandance festival, which sees world famous rock and dance groups perform on the adjacent beach.

The Palm has its own yacht marina, and the calm waters make it excellent for hiring watersports gear from the area's hotels – Stand-Up Paddleboarding (SUP) is becoming more and more popular here.

Palm Jumeirah
The trunk of the island is made up of large one to four-bedroom apartments, and a one-bedroom and the fronds are covered in nearly identical three to six-bedroom villas. Traffic onto the island isn't a problem (unless there's a large event) and there is plenty of parking underneath the apartment buildings and next to the villas.

Despite the Palm's obviously engineered shape when viewed from above, once you've got your feet planted on it, it doesn't appear quite so symmetrical.
Annual rental prices: One-bedroom from Dhs.95,000. Three-bedroom townhouse from Dhs 240,000.

Palm Jumeirah

Reliability	Speed	Ease
Comprehensive	Professional	Hassle-free

When it comes to relocation we tick all the right boxes.

Al-Futtaim logistics
An Al-Futtaim group company

P.O. Box 61450, Dubai, United Arab Emirates
Tel: +971 4 881 8288, Fax: +971 4 881 9157
Email: AFL.relocations@alfuttaim.ae

2020 READY

www.aflogistics.com

LIVING IN DUBAI
RESIDENTIAL AREAS

Jumeira

Map **2 G4** Metro **Business Bay**

The actual area of Jumeira occupies a prime nine-kilometre strip of coastline stretching south-west from the port area, but the name has been hijacked to such an extent that new residential and commercial developments bearing the Jumeira tag are cropping up for miles around. Even The Palm Jumeirah doesn't connect with Jumeira, but actually extends from the area of Al Sufouh. Jumeira itself is characterised by quiet streets lined with sophisticated villas, golden beaches, and good access to lots of shopping. Traffic and parking on the back streets is never a problem, but Al Wasl Road and Jumeira Road can get clogged during peak hours.

Within the same stretch of land between the beach and Sheikh Zayed Road are the areas of Al Wasl, Al Safa and Umm Suqeim. All these areas contain mostly villas and share the same facilities. Al Wasl and Al Safa are further from the beach, between Al Wasl Road and Sheikh Zayed Road.

Jumeirah or Jumeira?

According to the 'official' spelling used by Dubai Municipality, it's Jumeira, so that's what we use when referring to this area. However, many hotels, parks, clubs, schools, and residential developments have added an 'h' to the end, so don't be surprised if you see the two different spellings side by side throughout the book.

Schools

There are several schools including Jumeirah English Speaking School, Horizon School, Jumeirah College and GEMS Jumeirah Primary School, as well as an assortment of nurseries that includes Jumeirah International Nursery School and Blossom Village. The proximity to Sheikh Zayed Road makes GEMS Wellington International School a popular choice. The largest secondary school in Umm Suqeim is Emirates International School and the area is home to two Raffles International campuses.

Healthcare

Al Wasl Road and nearby Jumeira Road (Beach Road) have plenty of private medical centres, specialist doctors and dentists. The private Medcare Hospital near Safa Park has an emergency room, and the excellent value Iranian Hospital is just down Al Wasl Road towards Satwa.

Shops

Jumeira Road (also known as Beach Road) is home to art and fashion boutiques. For groceries, there are two Spinneys, a Union Co-op, two Choithrams and other supermarkets. There is also the popular Mercato Mall on Jumeira Road, along with several smaller shopping centres. Wasl Square, next to Safa Park, is a new retail hotspot with a variety of shops and eateries.

Bars & Restaurants

Jumeira Road hosts several independent restaurants and takeaways, as well as many fast food joints. The Jumeirah Beach Hotel and Madinat Jumeirah are both packed with impressive licensed restaurants and bars and the restaurant-filled hotels that line Sheikh Zayed Road are nearby as well.

Attractions

The city's most popular beaches are all within walking distance of Jumeira and Umm Suqeim. Safa Park and Jumeira Beach Park.

Jumeira

Jumeira villas still attract some of the highest rents in the city. There's a mixture of huge 'palaces', independent villas, and villas in compounds with shared facilities. You can pick up a cheaper rental if you are prepared to take care of the maintenance yourself.

Annual rental prices: Three-bedroom villa from Dhs.150,000.

Neighbouring Community: Satwa

Despite having large sections demolished for the now-on-hold Jumeirah Garden City project, Satwa is still a desirable place to live. The main 2nd December Street buzzes with pedestrians and is home to several of the city's favourite Arabic restaurants as well as plenty of fast food venues. There are a number of low-rise apartment blocks on 2nd December Street and Al Hudeiba Street (Plant Street), popular with singles looking for a vibrant area. There are also villas on the outskirts of the area, in Al Bada'a that are popular with families. Chelsea Plaza and Jumeirah Rotana have long been nightlife hubs and there are several three-star hotels in the area that are home to intimate licensed restaurants and bars.

Shoppers will be able to find everything they need along 2nd December Street and Plant Street, and supermarkets include two Carrefour Expresses and a Westzone. Traffic can be bad at rush hour and street parking is hard to come by, but it's an easy neighbourhood to walk around. Residents have easy access to the same facilities in the Jumeira area.

Annual rental prices: Two-bedroom apartment from Dhs.95,000. Three-bedroom villa from Dhs.170,000.

THINKING RELOCATION?
THINK SANTA FE.

"We make it easy"

SANTA FE
RELOCATION SERVICES

| Relocation | Storage | Moving | Lease Management |

Santa Fe Relocation Services
T: +971 4454 2724
T: 800 32800
F: +971 4454 2726
Email: info@santaferelo.ae
www.santaferelo.com

PROUDLY PART OF **SANTA FE** GROUP

LIVING IN DUBAI
RESIDENTIAL AREAS

Emirates Living

Map **1 L6** Metro **Nakheel**

Rated by property experts as one of the top five neighbourhoods to raise a family in Dubai, Emirates Living is a desirable address with a range of villa-style houses in The Springs, The Lakes, The Meadows and the exclusive Emirates Hills. Tree-lined streets and pathways, attractively landscaped lakes, gardens and recreation areas make it perfect for those who want to enjoy the peace and quiet of suburbia. Located between Sheikh Zayed Road and Al Khail Road, each individual zone of Emirates Living (for example Springs 6, Meadows 5) has its own gated security entrance. The gated-community feel runs throughout each neighbourhood, as kids play in the streets and parks, while adults jog the pavements. Traffic within each community is not a problem, though intersections near the highways can get busy at rush hour.

Of a similar style is the adjacent Jumeirah Islands community. There's a well-established community there (see Jumeirah Island Club page on Facebook) and good health and leisure facilities.

The nearby apartments at The Greens are convenient for those working in Media or Internet City, as there is a flyover connecting the two sides of Sheikh Zayed Road.

Schools

Waiting lists for a place in the most sought-after schools and nurseries are long, and it is best to sign up well in advance. Schools include Emirates International School in The Meadows, Dubai British School, Dubai International Academy in The Springs, and Dubai American Academy at the Emirates Living entrance near The Lakes. As for nurseries, Raffles International School (04 427 1200) operates several nurseries in The Springs, Springs Town Centre, Emirates Hills and The Lakes.

Healthcare

The Rosary Medical Centre is located at Springs Town Centre in Springs 7, while nearby facilities include a private medical centre in Al Barsha, Medical Specialist Centre (04 340 9495), the Cedars Jebel Ali International Hospital, and Mediclinic Al Sufouh in Knowledge Village (04 366 1030). There's also the Saudi German Hospital, close to The Greens.

Shops

There are supermarkets within the various compounds. There's a Choithrams at The Springs end, a large Spinneys at Springs Town Centre and a Spinneys Market in the Meadows. The Greens also has a Choithrams and a small shopping centre. There are also beauty salons, pharmacies and ATMs. Both Ibn Battuta and Mall of the Emirates are only 10 minutes away.

Bars & Restaurants

Fitness First in The Lakes has a licensed restaurant and bar, The Reform Club, and the Mongomerie Golf Club also has a licensed restaurant. Other than that, you'll have to venture to the marina or Al Barsha for a better selection of dining venues.

Attractions

The Montgomerie Golf Club, and three Fitness Firsts with outdoor pools at Lakes, Springs and Meadows.

Emirates Living

Generally, the style and quality of all houses in Emirates Living is good. The smallest villas available are located in The Springs, the larger properties are in The Meadows and Emirates Hills.
Annual rental prices: Two-bedroom townhouse from Dhs.115,000. Six-bedroom mansion from Dhs.350,000.

Neighbouring Community: Jumeirah Islands

Jumeirah Islands is made up of small artificial islands, each home to 16 villas, sitting in a man-made lake.
Annual rental prices: Four-bedroom villa is from Dhs.295,000.

Neighbouring Community: The Greens

The Greens offers a range of one to four-bedroom apartments, which are well appointed but a bit small for the money. There are small lakes and pathways lined with trees and flowers.
Annual rental prices: One-bedroom apartment from Dhs.80,000. Three-bedroom from Dhs.140,000.

Neighbouring Community: Jumeirah Park

Its prime location – next to Meadows, Lakes and Springs – is a draw. The three-, four- and five-bedroom villas are great for families. There's a children's day-care centre, play area, and kindergarten through to secondary school, as well as shops and restaurants.
Annual rental prices: Three-bedroom villa from Dhs.170,000.

LIVING IN DUBAI
RESIDENTIAL AREAS

Emirates Hills

View of JLT from Jumeirah Islands

Emirates Hills

LIVING IN DUBAI
RESIDENTIAL AREAS

Downtown Dubai

Map **2 F6** Metro **Burj Khalifa/Dubai Mall**
Downtown has a community feel: children's play areas, cafes and restaurants, souks and swimming pools. The wide promenades, Arabian passageways and palm-lined streets that link the different residential quarters encourage residents to get around on foot.

The adjacent Sheikh Zayed Road is Dubai's busiest motorway, but if traffic doesn't bother try the strip between Trade Centre Roundabout and Interchange One, which is home to some of Dubai's biggest towers.

Schools
There are nurseries (Old Town Nursery, Kangaroo Kids' and Cello Kids Club) but no schools in Downtown Dubai, but those in Jumeira and Al Qouz are close.

Healthcare
Apart from pharmacies dotted round the Old Town, The Dubai Mall and the Residences, there is the large Mediclinic Dubai Mall. The closest hospitals are Medcare Hospital (04 407 9100) in Al Safa and the Iranian Hospital (04 344 0250) on Al Wasl Road in Satwa. On Sheikh Zayed Road is also Al Zahra Medical Centre (04 331 5000) in Al Safa Tower.

Shops
Downtown Dubai is a shopper's dream with both The Dubai Mall and Souk Al Bahar within walking distance. Dubai Mall has a Waitrose and there are Spinneys stores and Al Maya outlets scattered around. Several banks are on the ground floor of Dubai Mall, along with pharmacies, money exchanges and opticians. Next to the mall, Souk Al Bahar houses boutique shops.

Sheikh Zayed Road also has Mazaya Centre and the supermarkets of Jumeira nearby. Both sides of Sheikh Zayed Road have pharmacies and smaller shops.

Bars & Restaurants
Souk Al Bahar is a nightlife hub with several licensed bars and restaurants. Dubai Mall has a few unlicensed restaurants along with two huge food courts. Also, there's the two Address hotels, home to Neos sky bar on the 63rd floor of the Downtown hotel, and Cabana, the funky pool bar at The Dubai Mall hotel.

Sheikh Zayed Road has plenty of takeaway restaurants and the strip is full of nightlife in the Shangri-La, Fairmont, Crowne Plaza and Towers Rotana.

Attractions
The Burj Khalifa is on your doorstep, as is Dubai Mall (with its aquarium) and the dancing fountains.

Downtown Dubai
The massive Downtown Dubai development is made up of high and low-rise residential units, with landmark buildings – The Address (Dubai Mall and Downtown), The Palace Hotel, Emaar Square and the Burj Khalifa – as the cornerstones. At one end, near to the Burj, are the Burj Residence towers, The Lofts and 8 Boulevard Walk, while at the opposite end, on the border with the Business Bay development, are the South Ridge and Burj Views high-rises. In between is the Arabian architecture of Old Town. There is plenty of parking within each of the residential complexes, and the Burj Khalifa/Dubai Mall Metro stop is walking distance from some apartments and a short feeder bus ride from the others.

Options range from tiny studios to expansive four-bedroom townhouses, and the finishing in most buildings is of a high spec. Most residential towers come with facilities including games rooms, libraries, barbecue areas, gyms, pools and sports courts.
Annual rental prices: One-bedroom from Dhs.90,000 in the Old Town or Dhs.160,000 in the Burj Khalifa.

Neighbouring Community: Sheikh Zayed Road
On the high-rise strip along Sheikh Zayed Road you'll find a mix of residential and commercial buildings alongside impressive hotels. It's a popular area.
Annual rental prices: One-bedroom from Dhs.85,000. Three-bedroom from Dhs.150,000.

LIVING IN DUBAI
RESIDENTIAL AREAS

Al Barsha

Map **1 Q6** Metro **Mall of the Emirates**

Al Barsha has two distinct zones. The main area offers large villas with big gardens popular with local families. Some of the older apartment blocks offer competitively priced options, while the new apartment blocks, closer to Mall of the Emirates, are popular with Media and Internet City workers.

New villas are being built on the other side of Al Khail Road (called Al Barsha South).

Schools
The Dubai American Academy and Al Mawakeb are located in Al Barsha, and Wellington International School, Dubai College and Jumeirah English Speaking School are nearby.

Healthcare
There is a GP and paediatrician at the Medical Specialist Centre (04 340 9495), in the Khoury Building near Sheikh Zayed Road, but the nearest emergency room is in the Medcare Hospital in Al Safa.

Shops
The nearby Mall of the Emirates has a Carrefour, a multi-screen cinema, and restaurants.

Bars & Restaurants
The Kempinski and Pullman hotels at Mall of the Emirates have licensed restaurants and bars, as do a handful of other business hotels nearby, plus Al Barsha is the other side of Sheikh Zayed Road from Madinat Jumeirah and a short drive from the marina.

Attractions
Mall of the Emirates and its indoor ski slope.

Al Barsha
Accommodation is mainly in the form of fairly new, three to five-bedroom villas. Around 75% of the houses are locally owned and inhabited. Al Barsha 1, near the Mall of the Emirates offers apartments.
Annual rental prices: Three-bedroom villa from Dhs.160,000.

Neighbouring Community: TECOM
TECOM is made up primarily of residential towers. There is still a lot of construction going on, and although the roads have all been finished, there are no pedestrian pavements. So, rents tend to be a bit cheaper than in neighbouring Al Barsha or The Greens.

The quality of apartments varies, and traffic in and out of the neighbourhood can get busy during peak hours. There is a Metro stop in front of the area, which is useful for anyone working on Sheikh Zayed Road, and there are small Geant and Park n Shop supermarkets, with the Choithrams and other amenities in The Greens just a stone's throw away. Nightlife destinations such as the marina and Al Sufouh are just across Sheikh Zayed Road and the Media Rotana in TECOM is home to local pub Nelson's.
Annual rental prices: Two-bedroom apartment from Dhs.100,000.

Up & Coming Areas
When buildings in brand new developments are completed, shops and services, and the gym and pool within the building, tend to follow a few steps behind. Until amenities are in place, prices are cheaper, and so while you may have to travel further for shops, chemists, schools and clinics, and you may find your balcony regularly inch-deep in construction dust, a brand new apartment can be a bargain.

Some up and coming areas include: Business Bay (particularly Executive Towers), Dubai Studio City, and The Crescent in International Media Production Zone. For a bargain new villa try The Plantation, Equestrian & Polo Club in Dubailand or one of Meydan City's developments, due to be completed in 2015. If you don't mind living on a building site with few facilities, you can pick up a bargain at the Mediterranean-themed Jumeirah Village. A one-bedroom apartment here starts at Dhs.45,000 (unfurnished).

Villa in Al Barsha

Dubai Explorer

Executive Relocations
MIDDLE EAST

CUSTOMISED MOBILITY SOLUTIONS
EXPATRIATION • REPATRIATION
www.executiverelocationsafrica.com

1. Visa, immigration and local registration assistance
2. Preview and area orientation, home finding and settling-in programmes
3. Helpline assistance and tenancy management
4. Departure services

EXECUTIVE RELOCATIONS IN THE MIDDLE EAST: Gladys Carmichael: +971 55 99 34 225

AGS
Worldwide movers, you deserve the best

- 40 years' experience 
- 128 locations in 80 countries

International removals and storage

AGS ABU DHABI
Tel: +971 2 5500917
Cheikh Diop: + 971 55 88 56 289

AGS DUBAI
Tel: +971 4 4541531
Muzamil Mohamed: +971 55 99 51 027

THE GLOBAL COMPACT — WE SUPPORT
IAM

Visit **www.agsmovers.com** to view our **128 locations worldwide**

LIVING IN DUBAI
RESIDENTIAL AREAS

Discovery Gardens

Map **1 H7** Metro **Nakheel**

Made up of clusters of Mediterranean style low-rise apartment blocks, Discovery Gardens is surprisingly green. Traffic bottlenecks can be a problem during rush hours, but there is plenty of parking around the buildings. There is also a Red Line Metro stop outside Ibn Battuta, but you need to take the F43 feeder bus to access it.

The neighbouring development Al Furjan is designed with families in mind.

Schools
Al Furjan has two schools. Jebel Ali Primary School and the Winchester School are both in the Jabal Ali vicinity approximately 15-20 minutes' drive away.

Healthcare
Discovery Gardens has the Aster Medical Centre. The Cedars Jebel Ali International Hospital is near to both Discovery Gardens and Al Furjan.

Shops
Although there aren't any major shops within the Discovery Gardens development, Ibn Battuta mall is conveniently close and contains a large Géant hypermarket. Al Furjan has the Village Centre with several shops and supermarkets.

Bars & Restaurants
Heading to Marsa Dubai and Al Barsha for a drink or a nice dinner isn't much of a hassle, and the Movenpick Ibn Battuta Gate Hotel is a welcome addition to the immediate area's dining and bar scene. Ibn Battuta Mall houses a cinema and several restaurants.

Attractions
Al Furjan has 50 hectares of park and outdoor spaces as well as cycling and jogging tracks.

Discovery Gardens
Rents tend to be lower here and apartments easy to come by. The buildings only contain studios and one-bedroom apartments. It's one of the few places where landlords will still accept quarterly rental payments as opposed to six months or a year upfront.
Annual rental prices: One-bedroom apartment from Dhs.55,000.

Neighbouring Community: Al Furjan
Al Furjan is a low-rise development with four communities of apartments, three- to six-bedroom villas and three-bedroom terraced houses. The whole area is designed to promote outdoor living.
It's a peaceful and pleasant area, but a little out of town and so is better for families and those seeking a peaceful existence.
Annual rental prices: Three-bedroom villa from Dhs.150,000.

Discovery Gardens

LIVING IN DUBAI
RESIDENTIAL AREAS

Dubailand

Dubailand is a vast development encompassing several varied communities within it. It stretches along Sheikh Mohammad Bin Zayed Road (formerly known as the Emirates Road) and will include sporting attractions as well as entertainment facilities, retail outlets and residential areas of villas and apartment blocks. Developments that are already built, or under construction are detailed below, but there are many more still to come.

Schools
Both JESS Arabian Ranches (jess.sch.ae) and the giant GEMS World Academy (04 373 6373) are a stone's throw away. The Jumeirah English Speaking School is in the Ranches, and there are options in Al Barsha and Emirates Living. Greenfield Community School and the International School of Choueifat are both in the nearby Dubai Investment Park, and Building Blocks Nursery in MotorCity takes infants and toddlers.

Healthcare
There's a Medicentre clinic (04 360 8866) in Uptown MotorCity, along with a couple of pharmacies. The Mediclinic Arabian Ranches (04 453 4020) offers general practice and a range of medical specialities. The nearest emergency room is Cedars Jebel Ali International Hospital.

Shops
MotorCity has a nice strip of cafes and shops, and Arabian Ranches has the Village Community Centre, which houses Le Marche supermarket, a chemist, liquor store and several cafes, restaurants and takeaways.

Bars & Restaurants
The Arabian Ranches Golf Course is home to a restaurant and bar. The licensed Dubai Polo & Equestrian Club are just a couple of minutes away from Arabian Ranches.

Attractions
Arabian Ranches Golf Course, The Els Club and Dubai Polo Club are all close at hand, plus it's just 20 minutes to Mall of the Emirates, Marsa Dubai and Madinat Jumeirah.

Jumeirah Golf Estates
Lots of people dream of living on a golf course. But now you can put on your Callaways, step out your front door and you're ready to sneak in a quick nine holes before dinner. Anyone looking to garner a slice of the residential golfing lifestyle could do a lot worse than moving into one of the villas at Jumeirah Golf Estates, home to the DP World Tour Championship.

Victory Heights

There are many things to love about living on a golf course: the stunning vistas, an expanse of manicured grass fairways, and unlimited access to first-class golf courses designed by the pros. There's a range of villa types, from four-bedrooms upwards, all oozing style and luxury. At the heart of this exclusive development is the Norman Country Club, with a leisure centre, bar and restaurants (including one by Jamie Oliver), tennis academy, lap pool and leisure lagoon.
Annual rental prices: Four-bedroom villa from Dhs.290,000.

Dubai Sports City
The world's first integrated sports city is not quite completed, but there are now a handful of occupied towers. The prices are competitive when you consider that facilities in each tower include underground parking, a gym, barbecue area, Jacuzzi, steam room and sauna, and free internet.
Annual rental prices: Two-bedroom apartment from Dhs.75,000. Four-bedroom townhouse from Dhs.180,000.

The area also includes the Victory Heights development – Spanish-style villas and townhouses all within a stone's throw of the Els Golf Club, and use of the same facilities as Dubai Sports City.

LIVING IN DUBAI
RESIDENTIAL AREAS

Dubai MotorCity
Built around the Dubai Autodrome, MotorCity has access to first-class race car action. The development is completed and consists of pretty, medium-rise apartments finished to a high standard with cobbled streets and a pleasing amount of greenery around.

The buildings have English-sounding names in the vein of 'Dickens Circus' and 'Sherlock House', which adds to the quaint feel of this community. A good array of services make it an attractive place to live for couples and singles after a slice of suburbia.

You may be able to hear the sound of cars racing around the Autodrome circuit if the wind is blowing towards the residential area though.

Annual rental prices: One-bedroom apartments from Dhs.65,000.

Arabian Ranches
The quiet, curving, grass-lined lanes of the Arabian Ranches development are home to several swimming pools, basketball and tennis courts, barbecue pits and grassy areas.

This is an all-villa project set among lush greenery, lakes and the Arabian Ranches Golf Course, with a range of luxury facilities that all add up to some pretty fine suburban living. It was one of the first freehold residential areas to be completed and there is certainly a homely and mature neighbourhood feel to the place. Most of the people who bought villas in the development still live in them, so finding one that suits your needs can be difficult.

Annual rental prices: Two-bedroom villa from Dhs.140,000.

The Villa
The Villa offers residents spacious villas – many with pools – meaning luxury living at an affordable price. Due to its location further out in Dubailand, and the lack of facilities as yet, most people who move here are large families looking for luxury and space. Prices are competitive, but be prepared to foot the bill for landscaping if you are the first to move in. For shops, schools and other amenities, Dubai Silicon Oasis, Dubai Autodrome, International Media Production Zone and Arabian Ranches are all only a short drive away.

Annual rental prices: Five-bedroom villa from Dhs.190,000.

Neighbouring Development: Green Community
An oasis of green in the desert, this modern and established development is good for families, and homes are hard to come by. The area is made up of high-quality villas with gardens, as well as spacious, low-rise apartment blocks set among small lakes and green parks. There's plenty of room for kids to play in and the place has quietly developed a strong community feel. It's a bit out of the city, but a good choice for people working in the Jebel Ali Free Zone. Its location away from the rest of Dubai means that taxis can be expensive for nights when the car needs to be left at home. However, the development of the site for the Expo 2020 is nearby and so access and facilities in the area are bound to improve over the coming years.

The original Green Community was so well received that the developer built a new phase – Green Community West. It's in the same style, with villas surrounded by greenery with meandering cobbles streets.

Schools: The Children's Garden (04 885 3484) offers a primary bilingual curriculum in English/German or English/French, and there are various primary and secondary schools in Emirates Living and Jabal Ali.

Healthcare: The private Green Community Medical Centre (04 885 3225) is upstairs in The Market, while the nearest government-run clinic is at Jabal Ali. For emergencies, the Cedars Jebel Ali International Hospital is nearest. For government A&E care, it's quite a trip to Rashid Hospital.

Shops: The area is serviced by The Market shopping centre, which houses a large Choithrams supermarket, as well as a jewellers, clothes shops, and home furnishing outlets. There's also a pharmacy, a florist, a dry cleaners, an optician, and a branch of ACE Hardware. If that's not enough, Ibn Battuta Mall is not far away.

Bars and restaurants: There are a few good licensed restaurants within the Courtyard by Marriott, and The Market is home to a number of coffee shops and good unlicensed restaurants. For a better selection, Marsa Dubai is about 15 minutes by car.

Attractions: The golf course at Jumeirah Golf Estates is nearby.

Annual rental prices: One-bedroom apartment from Dhs.65,000. Four-bedroom villa from Dhs.230,000.

LIVING IN DUBAI
RESIDENTIAL AREAS

The Villa

Arabian Ranches villas

Green Community

askexplorer.com 79

**LIVING IN DUBAI
RESIDENTIAL AREAS**

Old Dubai

Encompassing Bur Dubai, Deira and Karama, this older, traffic-laden area is a concrete jungle, with mid-size apartment blocks and virtually no green spaces. Newer apartments have excellent facilities, and the area is always humming with activity. The dense population means traffic and parking can be a problem, and it also means the streets are full of people. Women may get stared at in the street at night – but it's not dangerous.

Apartments in the BurJuman area, Bur Dubai

Schools
There's a wide choice of nurseries, and plenty of choice for schools nearby including the Dubai English Speaking School (DESS) in Oud Metha.

Healthcare
Bur Dubai and Karama have small medical centres. The emergency room at Rashid Hospital is near, as is the private American Hospital. Healthcare City, which has two hospitals and more than 100 outpatient medical centres, is a few minutes' drive.

Shops
The area has corner shops, supermarkets, banks and more as well as BurJuman Mall. The souk area of Bur Dubai and the markets in Karama are good for picking up funky gifts. Close to the bus station, there's the fish and fruit and vegetable markets. Karama Market sells imitation handbags and a wide range of goods.

Bars & Restaurants
There are great 'dive bars' around Khalid bin Al Waleed Road and for cheap eats, also check Al Rigga Street.

Attractions
There are some pleasant walking areas by the creek and along the corniche. Al Fahidi Historical Neighbourhood (formerly called Bastakiya), is the original old heart of Dubai with cafes and art galleries. Stroll around Zabeel Park in Karama with its lake and landscaped gardens, or Creek Park in Bur Dubai. BurJuman Mall is currently undergoing renovations and by the end of 2014 will feature a 14-screen VOX cinema and a Carrefour hypermarket.

Bur Dubai
The area is dominated by apartments in a mix of new and old medium-rise buildings. Some of the larger apartments are used as company flats.
Annual rental prices: Two-bedroom apartment from Dhs.70,000.

Deira
Deira is not very popular with expats in higher income brackets; the centre is densely built up with old apartments, but nearer the creek there are more modern apartments, many with spectacular views across the water. Rents are relatively low in some of the more built-up areas, while the creekside dwellings cost more. Not so good for cars, but easy to walk around.
Annual rental prices: Two-bedroom apartment from Dhs.60,000.

Karama
Mostly low-rise blocks with apartments ranging from studios to three-bedrooms. Karama has large Filipino and Indian communities, which means a great selection of affordable Eastern eateries on your doorstep.
Annual rental prices: Two-bedroom apartment from Dhs.75,000.

Falling Out Of Favour
Some areas are no longer as popular with expats. They are far from the centre, have a reputation for shoddy maintenance, or are looking a little jaded. International City, Qusais and districts neighbouring Bur Dubai tend to be eschewed by expats these days.

Mirdif

Map **2 Q 12** Metro **Rashidiya**

Mirdif is perceived to be a bit out in the sticks, but airport workers find it ideal. The development includes villas and newer buildings such as the Uptown Mirdiff complex, the upmarket Shorooq community villas and the low-cost Ghoroob apartments. There's everything you need within the area.

Schools

There is a choice of nurseries in Mirdif including Small Steps (04 288 3347), Super Kids and Emirates British Nursery. Uptown Primary is recommended. Other new schools include Star International School in Mirdif, the Sharjah American International School (04 280 1111) in Al Warqa, Royal Dubai School in Muhaisanah, and the American Academy in Al Mizhar.

Healthcare

Mediclinic Mirdif (04 288 1302) is in Uptown Mirdiff, as well as Drs Nicolas & Asp Dental Clinic (04 288 4411).

Shops

The Mirdif City Centre mall offers a central point for residents to shop. Small convenience stores are also scattered throughout the area along with all the other facilities you could need.

Bars & Restaurants

Though there are no licensed bars in the area (Festival City provides the nearest watering holes), there are plenty of dining options without booze.

Attractions

The massive Mirdif City Centre houses a cinema and Playnation, so there's plenty for the little ones. Further down Airport Road is the smaller Arabian Centre shopping mall which has a World Mart and a Cinecity cinema.

Mirdif

It's a great area for families and has developed into a bustling community with a well-established feel. Take your time with your search as the quality of the buildings varies greatly, and some areas are under the flight path to the airport.

Annual rental prices: One-bedroom apartment from Dhs.60,000. Three-bedroom villas from Dhs.95,000.

Out On A Limb

Silicon Oasis, off the Academic City Road, is a development containing hundreds of high-standard villas with gardens and apartment blocks. People say it's far out of town, although it is just a 10 minute drive from Mirdif. As new facilities open, it's starting to develop an identity and community feel.

The Outlet Mall is just a quick trip over the other side of the Dubai-Al Ain Road too. If you work locally, or are happy with a longer commute, you can find some bargains here, with two-bed apartments available for Dhs.65,000. For more information, see siliconoasis.org.

Mirdif

A furnished apartment in Dubai

SETTING UP HOME

Keys in hand and foot through the door; now the fun really begins. There's a fantastic selection of places that can supply furnishings for your new place and expats often find some unusual styles to try out that they can't get back home. However, there are familiar companies like IKEA, as well as many other furniture stores, that can give that modern feel to your new apartment or villa. See the Shopping chapter for more.

First Things First

For all the joy of moving in, there's also an array of phone calls to make and services to set up. Rarely does anything happen quickly or easily when it comes to this sort of thing, but being armed with the right information and approaching it all with a calm attitude can certainly help.

Don't forget that once you've moved in, the regular utility bills will need to be paid on time or you risk being cut off. No notice is given, you'll simply find your internet has stopped working or there's no water coming from the taps. Often you can get these reconnected quite quickly, but it can depend on the provider. Direct debits are only just starting to be employed in the country, so it can sometimes mean a one-off monthly payment and even a trip to a counter to pay the bill in person.

However, there isn't much else that you should be too worried about, aside from the slowness at which things can take to get done. For everything else, this chapter should point you in the right direction. Once you're settled in you'll find domestic life in Dubai is likely to be remarkably similar to the one that you left back at home. The dining, nightlife, sunshine and vast array of activities you'll be enjoying may be different, but you'll probably still find time to slouch on the sofa and catch up with your favourite TV shows.

LIVING IN DUBAI
SETTING UP HOME

Moving Services

If you're arriving with more than a suitcase, you'll need to send your belongings by air or by sea. Air freight is faster but more expensive. Sea freight takes longer but it's cheaper, and containers can hold a huge amount.

Most relocation companies will take care of the paperwork for you and also deal with the procedures at customs and so you don't need to be present when your goods arrive. Just be sure that you have booked and paid for a 'door-to-door' service and your boxes will be brought directly to your new home. Many companies specify that the quote they provide only covers your move to the first floor – the likelihood is in Dubai you could be on a much higher floor, but if there's elevator access then you shouldn't be charged any extra. Advise your security guard and check for any parking restrictions. One popular relocation company is Al Futtaim Logistics, who are specialists in international removals, with more than 80 years' experience.

Relocation Expertise
Map **2 N6**   Metro **Deira City Centre**

Crown Relocations is a global removal company that does far more than just physically moving your belongings. They offer storage facilities, pet relocations and maid and handyman services, as well as help with administrative procedures and advice on integrating into new cultures. Their 'settling in' service includes a preview trip, post-arrival orientations and repatriation services. Assistance doesn't stop there; they offer employment and family support services including education assistance and language training to help you make a positive start in your new country. See the listing to the right for their contact details.

If you have only paid for delivery of your belongings as far as Dubai customs, then you'll need to go to Cargo Village in Garhoud to collect air freight, or Jebel Ali Port to pick up sea freight. Take a copy of the inventory so you know what is in each box. And be patient.

Once at Cargo Village, head to the warehouse and fill out the customs information, and pay any applicable fees. You will then have to go across to Customs where you will pay any duty, plus a processing fee. Once this has been done, you can go back to the warehouse and collect your shipment. Before you can leave, you will have to head back over to Customs to have your goods x-rayed.

The process for sea freight is a little longer. Once your sea freight is ready for collection (you'll get a call or letter), go to the agent's office and pay the administration and handling charges. Keep these documents. The Bill of Lading number must be marked on all paperwork and entered into the customs computer system.

Then go to Dubai Customs House, on Al Mina Road. The staff are helpful and the procedure is straightforward. Ignore the touts outside. When the papers have been stamped and the Port Clearance received (there are fees) head to Jebel Ali Port.

Relocation & Removal Companies

Acorn Movers   04 323 6920, *acornmovers.com*
AGS Movers   **>** *p.75*   Jumeirah Business Centre, Al Thanyah 5, 04 454 1531, *agsmovers.com*
Al Futtaim Logistics   **>** *p.67*   Jabal Ali Port, Mena Jabal Ali, 04 881 8288, *aflogistics.com*
Allied Pickfords   One Business Bay, Jumeira 1, 04 818 0400, *alliedpickfords.com*
Crown Relocations   **>** *p.ii-iii, 35, 41, 85, 204, 237*   Dutco House, Al Itihad Rd, Port Saeed, 04 230 5300, *crownrelo.com*
Inchcape Shipping Services   Office Court Bldg, Oud Metha, 04 303 8500, *iss-shipping.com*
Interem   **>** *p.73*   Nr Lipton R/A 13, Jabal Ali Port, Mena Jabal Ali, 04 807 0584, *interem.ae*
Santa Fe Relocations   **>** *p.69*   Warsan Bldg, Al Thanyah 1, 04 454 2724, *santaferelo.com*
STORALL   Jabal Ali Ind. 1, 04 880 3644, *storall.ae*

Smooth Moves

- Get more than one quote – some companies will match lower quotes to get the job
- Make sure all items are covered by insurance
- Ensure you have a copy of the inventory and that each item is listed
- Don't be shy about requesting packers to repack items if you are not satisfied
- Take photos of the packing process to use for evidence if you need to make a claim
- Carry customs-restricted goods (DVDs, books) with you; it's easier to open a suitcase at the airport than empty a box outside in the sun

Local Move

If you are moving within Dubai and have valuable possessions, you can hire an insured company to do the packing and moving for you. If not, you may benefit from packing your belongings yourself and hiring an uninsured 'man with a van'. There are several trucks-for-hire companies in the city – just ask a friend or colleague. Make sure the driver is clear about where you are heading to and doesn't get lost.

Otherwise, go to large furniture places such as Dragon Mart or IKEA where these unlicensed movers often congregate. A quick drive through an industrial area such as Al Qouz will also turn up some results. The trucks will usually have a mobile number written on the side of the door. Call the number and try to negotiate a good price (usually around Dhs.60 an hour) for the truck, driver and moving labour.

askexplorer.com   83

LIVING IN DUBAI
SETTING UP HOME

Storage

Whether you're making the move to Dubai and haven't yet found the perfect home for all that furniture you've had shipped over, you've downsized a little and have possessions that simply won't fit between your current four walls, or you're moving on for a few months but don't want to take all your worldly goods with you quite yet, storage can be an excellent option. STORALL (storall.ae) based in Jabal Ali, for example, is a good facility with space rentable on a monthly basis and accessible seven days a week. Sentinel Storage (sentinelme.com) is another option, while the bigger removal and delivery firms may also be able to offer storage services.

Furnishing Accommodation

Most properties, including rentals (unless you're renting a room), come unfurnished, and don't even have basic white goods such as a cooker or fridge. Not all villas have fitted cupboards and wardrobes, although most apartments do. Dubai is home to a wide range of furniture shops offering different types of furnishings, from Swedish simplicity at IKEA and modern design at Home Centre and Dogtas (dogtasuae.com) to rich Indian teak at Marina Gulf Trading. Alternatively, head to one of the carpentry workshops on Naif Road or in Satwa.

Second-hand furniture is easy to come by thanks to the transitory nature of Dubai's population. You'll find small shops in Karama, Naif Road and Satwa and online classifieds should turn up good results. Try dubizzle.com, expatwoman.com, websouq.com or askexplorer.com. Or try supermarket noticeboards, or Dubai Flea Market (dubai-fleamarket.com). It's even possible to furnish an entire apartment in one fell swoop if you're lucky enough to find someone who is leaving in a hurry and selling everything they own – you could get everything from the cooker and fridge to the bedroom furniture at once.

See the Buyers' Guide for more information on where to buy furniture and white goods.

Renting furniture is an option worth considering. Indigo Living (indigo-living.com) provides rentals on a short and long-term basis – perfect for new arrivals and those who are in town on a short working contract.

Curtains & Blinds

Finding the right blinds or curtains can add a finishing touch to your room, ensure privacy if the house is overlooked, or stop you waking up with the sun. Some properties have windows built to standard sizes, which means you can buy ready-made options from shops such as IKEA and THE One. If these don't measure up, there are several companies that will tailor and install curtains and blinds to fit your property. Curtain specialist Dubai Blinds can bring swatches to your home to help you ensure the curtains or blinds match your decor, and they'll also take measurements for tailor-made finishes.

Swanky new curtains don't always come cheap though, so if you're looking for something more affordable, try your regular tailor, or look on community noticeboards for second-hand blinds or curtains that were made to fit the strange window sizes found in many freehold developments.

Interior Design

When you get your first place in Dubai, starting with an empty apartment can be a great opportunity to create a home from scratch. Whether you need help with choosing colours for the walls, decorative art to hang on them, or the furnishings throughout, there are an increasing number of specialists just a phone call away. A good interior designer will pick options that suit your lifestyle best, so it can be a good option to help you get settled, especially if you're busy with that new job.

3 Square 04 346 3872, *3squareinteriors.com*
Cecilia Clason 04 362 6261, *ceciliaclason.com*
Cottage Chic 04 437 0268, *cottagechic.ae*
Elan Interiors 04 338 7417, *elaninteriorsdubai.com*
Emirates Decor & Furniture Directory 04 267 4274, *emiratesdecor.com*
Indigo Living 04 339 7705, *indigo-living.com*
Jadis Interiors 04 347 4233, *jadisuae.com*
OX Interior Design 04 257 3300, *oxinterior.com*
WA International 04 266 3050, *wa-international.com*

Interior designers can add style

Think: Adventure!

We're with you all the way.

Crown service offerings include:
- International & Domestic Shipments
- Storage, Airfreight
- Transit Insurance
- Immigration & Legalization
- Home Search
- School Search

Tel: +971 4 230 5300
dubai@crownrelo.com

Go knowing
www.crownrelo.com/uae

CROWN
RELOCATIONS

LIVING IN DUBAI
SETTING UP HOME

Utilities & Services

Electricity & Water

Dubai Electricity and Water Authority (DEWA) provides electricity and water products and services for the entire emirate of Dubai. You can easily sign up for a new connection for your new premises at one of the 15 conveniently located DEWA customer care centres or online at dewa.gov.ae. A deposit (calculated based on supplied load), is required when you sign up for DEWA services; this will be refundable when you close your account and leave the property.

Standard DEWA charges are applicable as per its slab system with a fixed rate (fils per kWh and fils per gallon) in each slab, and rates will change based on your consumption. There will be an additional variable fuel surcharge of fils per kWh and fils per gallon, which will be added to the bill. For more information on the slab rate and other charges, visit dewa.gov.ae/tariff/newtariff.aspx.

Electricity

The electricity supply in Dubai is 220/240 volts and 50 cycles. The socket type is identical to the three-point UK system but most appliances here are sold with two-pin plugs. Adaptors can be bought from any grocery or hardware shop.

In line with global objectives to reduce greenhouse gas emissions, DEWA has an active campaign to encourage everyone to moderate their use of electricity and water (which will also help you save on bills). You'll find helpful advice and tips on the website, as well as a range of online services; for example, use the consumption calculator to help you manage and conserve your consumption. And, once you register, it's easy to pay your bills from your new home through one of DEWA's 20 payment methods.

Your DEWA bill also includes a housing charge from Dubai Municipality; this adds up to approximately 5% of the rental value of your property divided over the course of 12 months.

Failing to pay your DEWA bill by its due date will most likely result in the disconnection of your home's electricity and water services – often without warning; you will then have to pay a reconnection fee.

Clearance Certificate

In order to prove to your landlord that you have settled your DEWA account before moving out – or if you are looking to sell your own property – you need to obtain a clearance certificate from DEWA. This procedure is fairly simple and hassle-free, and you can obtain it the same day you disconnect your service.

Drinking Water

Bottled water is cheap, but most people end up buying a water cooler or pump (available from most large supermarkets), or leasing one from a water supplier and using the four or five-gallon bottles of purified water to drink at home. Prices vary per company; some charge a deposit of around Dhs.50 for each re-useable bottle, and then Dhs.7 per refill, while Masafi recycles its bottles rather than re-using them and charges Dhs.12 per new bottle. Companies will deliver the bottles straight to your door, and then collect your empties.

Al Shalal 800 4342, *alshalalwaters.com*
Culligan International Nr Federal Foods, Al Qouz Ind. 2, 800 4945, *culligan.com*
Desert Springs 800 6650, *desertspringswateruae.com*
Falcon Spring Drinking Water 04 396 6072, *falconspringwater.com*
Masafi Nr Dubai Garden Centre, Al Qouz Ind. 3, 04 3465 959, *masafi.com*
Nestle Waters Management & Technology Nr Wafi City, Healthcare City, Umm Hurair 2, 04 324 0800, *nestle-waters.com*
Oasis Water 600 522 261, *oasiscome2life.com*

Gas

There's no mains gas in Dubai, and individual gas canisters need to be purchased and attached to cookers. There are gas suppliers that will deliver the canisters and connect up the supply. Supply companies tend to slip stickers or flyers under doors on a regular basis and they're all essentially the same in terms of both service and price. A few of the largest companies include Al Fahidi Gas (04 351 6452), Oasis Gas (04 396 1812) and New City Gas (04 351 8282).

Gas bottles come in three sizes: most houses use the medium size, the small are better in apartments and the large are really only for industrial use – they are enormous. The canisters initially cost around Dhs.350 and refills are usually Dhs.75 (keep your receipt so that you can get some of your deposit back). There is usually a gas van operating around each area at all times; chances are that if you run out of gas in the middle of cooking your chips, one call to your local gas man and he can be with you in less than 20 minutes.

Sewerage

Much of Dubai now has mains sewers but there are areas where houses and apartment buildings are still serviced by septic tanks. These are emptied by municipality contractors, but should you have a problem, contact your landlord or local municipality office. All sewage has to be treated, hence the charges on the DEWA bill even for houses not on the main sewer network.

GOVERNMENT OF DUBAI

حكومة دبي

هيئة كهرباء ومياه دبي
Dubai Electricity & Water Authority

YOUR SMILE
DEFINES OUR SUCCESS

For years we have always been part of your life.
That is why no matter what time, day or night, we are always there to serve you better
for generations to come.

For generations to come

DEWA_OFFICIAL
DEWAOFFICIAL

CALL US 04 6019999
www.dewa.gov.ae

EXPO 2020
DUBAI, UNITED ARAB EMIRATES

Contact Us
customercare@dewa.gov.ae

e-Services
e-services.dewa.gov.ae

LIVING IN DUBAI
SETTING UP HOME

Rubbish Disposal
Dubai's per capita domestic waste rate is extremely high, with some estimates saying that each household generates over 1,000kg of rubbish per year – one of the worst offenders in the world. Fortunately, rubbish disposal is efficient, with municipality trucks driving around each area and emptying skips daily. Just empty your household bins into the skips (there is usually one on every street). If you don't have a skip on your street, then contact the municipality on 800 900 to request one. Certain areas, such as Emirates Living, have wheelie bins outside each house, where waste is regularly collected from. Recycling efforts are poor but slowly improving.

Telecommunications
There are two home phone providers in the UAE, Etisalat and du. Both are government-owned. The majority of homes in Dubai will have an Etisalat landline, but several new developments and du provides services to many Emaar and Nakheel properties, both business and residential (such as Marsa Dubai, Arabian Ranches, Emirates Living, the Greens/Springs/Lakes, and International City). Villas and apartments in these areas are equipped with multiple sockets for telephone, internet and TV signals. You can subscribe to du's call packages and internet services if you have an Etisalat landline (and vice versa), but you still have to pay the du (or Etisalat) line rental charge. Etisalat offers two landlines per property; installation of the second landline is free, you just pay the extra rental charges. du offers an unlimited number of landlines and extensions; each additional landline comes with a new subscription, a new phone number and a new handset. Additional extensions are added onto your existing landline subscription. Both Etisalat's Home Landline packages and du's Homephone packages include free local calls.

Additional Services
Etisalat's Najma 7 Services in 1 bundle includes call waiting, barring and forwarding and costs Dhs.50 installation, and Dhs.25 per month rental. du offers call barring for Dhs.50 (activation fee) plus Dhs.10 per month (rental).

Installing A Landline
To install a landline with Etisalat or du you must apply directly with a completed application form, the original and a copy of your passport and residence visa, and your Resident ID. Etisalat charges Dhs.180 for installation and Dhs.39 per month for line rental. du charges Dhs.200 for installation and Dhs.15 per month for line rental, as well as a Panasonic handset. (Anyone with an Etisalat landline can sign up to du's Homephone calls package, which costs Dhs.50 to activate). You will then be charged monthly for all calls to international and any mobile numbers. When applying, taking the number of the landline closest to your house can help pinpoint your location. The tariffs for international calls vary by country but there is some variation in peak timings, depending on country. For more information see etisalat.ae or du.ae.

Closing A Landline
A landline may be cancelled at any time, but it must be done in person at either an Etisalat or du office. You will be charged an early termination fee of Dhs.100 if you cancel within the first month.

Codes & prefixes

Abu Dhabi	02	Ajman	06
Al Ain	03	Dubai	04
Fujairah	09	Ras Al Khaimah	07
Sharjah	06	Umm Al Quwain	06
UAE Country Code	971		

Pre-paid Mobile
Mobile phone users can choose between du (prefix 055 and 052) and Etisalat (prefixes 050 or 056). Both providers offer monthly or pay-as-you-go packages.

Anyone visiting or living in Dubai, and above the age of 18, can apply for a pre-paid mobile phone account – you just need to buy a SIM card and then you can pay as you go by purchasing phone cards. Newcomers to Dubai and short-term visitors often opt for a pre-paid service: there are no monthly bills, you don't sign a contract, you can cancel at any time, and you do not need a residence visa. Etisalat's pre-paid Wasel card and du's Pay As You Go cards can be topped up with credit to use on calls, SMS and internet. Recharge cards are available in denominations ranging from Dhs.20-500 from fuel stations, supermarkets and electrical stores. You do not need to renew the line as long as you keep using it, and for du you get lifetime validity if you recharge the phone more than 20 times in four months.

Post-paid Mobile
Both companies also offer monthly post-paid services. To sign up for a post-paid plan through du or Etisalat, you will need to bring your passport and residence visa as well as either a UAE credit card, a recent utility bill with your physical address, your tenancy agreement, or a salary certificate that shows a minimum salary of Dhs.2,500 per month.

A new du post-paid line costs from Dhs.25 monthly plus a Dhs.125 connection fee, while an Etisalat line costs from Dhs.50 per month plus Dhs.125 connection fee (covered by a Dhs.125 welcome credit).

LIVING IN DUBAI
SETTING UP HOME

You can complete the application form online at shop.du.ae/en/mobilePlans or at etisalat.ae, or visit any phone outlet.

That's My Number

All mobile phone customers now have to register their SIM card with Etisalat or du. Wait until you receive an SMS asking you to register, then take along your Resident ID or a passport with your residency visa to the nearest service provider outlet. You have three months to register your details, after which any unregistered SIM cards will be cancelled. Registration is free and once only.

Mobile Services

Lost your mobile? For Etisalat, call 101, or for du call customer care on 055 567 8155 to temporarily disconnect your number (you will need to know your passport number for security). Your SIM card can be replaced and you can keep the same number, but you'll lose the numbers you had saved in your phone's memory. To replace a lost SIM card, du charges a flat rate of Dhs.55. Etisalat charges Dhs.25 to replace a lost SIM. You can also cancel your number permanently by simply filling out and submitting a cancellation form.

Etisalat and du launched a mobile phone number portability service at the end of 2013, which allows customers to switch between the two network operators while retaining their phone number. Enquiries about switching to du can be made on 800 242 643, and for Etisalat on 800 99.

Internet

Internet services in the UAE are provided by either Etisalat or du. You should note, however, that all internet usage, is regulated by the Telecommunications Regulatory Authority (TRA). This means that any sites that are deemed to be offensive, either religiously, culturally or politically, are blocked and can't be accessed.

Etisalat is the main Internet Service Provider (ISP), but du primarily serves the newly developed areas and free zones in the emirate. Currently, residents don't get to choose their service provider; rather you must go with whoever your home is pre-wired to, although there are plans to broaden the network to each ISP. Etisalat services range from a basic Al Shamil broadband connection to an eLife bundle that includes internet, TV and landline. For a 1mbps broadband connection with unlimited usage you pay a Dhs.199 installation fee plus Dhs.259 per month. Or, you can opt for an eLife landline, TV and internet bundle, which starts from Dhs.299 per month for 10mpbs plus Dhs.199 installation fee.

du services range from the Talk & Surf internet and landline packages to Talk, Surf and Watch packages, which also include digital TV. Packages range from 8mbps (Dhs.335 per month) to 100mbps (Dhs.810 per month). There is a Dhs.200 installation fee. You can also add on digital TV with packages starting from Dhs.279. Visit any Etisalat or du store to sign up and arrange for a home installation. The whole process takes at least one week.

Skype

Downloading voice over internet protocol (VoIP) services such as Skype can be difficult within the UAE due to the sites being blocked here. However, if you have downloaded it in a different country, or within an area where the restriction is lifted, such as in some free zones, it will work when calling another computer, but not when calling landlines or mobiles.

Wi-fi

When out and about, look out for Etisalat's wi-fi hotspots to get online. These are located all over town at various malls, cafes and restaurants and you can connect by purchasing a pre-paid card at the venue. See izone.ae for listings. Existing broadband customers can get a period of free time in these hotspots, depending on their package.

Postal Services

Previously, there was no postal delivery service to home addresses, and everyone had their mail delivered to a PO Box. In January 2012, Empost rolled out a new system that more closely resembles the traditional postal services in western countries. If you live in a villa, you can sign up to the My Home service which will see post delivered direct to your home three times a week – or six for an additional payment. My Building is the option for apartment residents, with post delivered to a PO Box in the lobby or basement. My Box sees your mail delivered to a PO Box at a post office, and finally there's My Zone, where post is delivered to local shelters that contain a large number of boxes, with the idea that you get a box close to your place of work or home. Visit empostuae.com for more details and rates. Alternatively, many people have personal mail delivered to their company's PO Box; this traditional method still works and, for many, may be the best option.

Letters and packages do occasionally go missing and, if the item has not been registered, there's little that you can do apart from wait – some turn up months after they are expected, although this happens less and less frequently.

Empost offers a courier service, while registered mail is a relatively inexpensive alternative and

LIVING IN DUBAI
SETTING UP HOME

can be tracked via a reference number. The major international courier services also deliver and have a presence in Dubai, including DHL (04 299 5333), FedEx (04 218 3860), UPS (800 4774) and Aramex (600 544 000). If you're expecting a package, ensure the person sending it has included your phone number, as that is often the only way for the courier to find your location.

Sending Gifts Home
If you would rather not chance the post, Gift Express provides a selection of gifts that can be sent to most countries (giftexpressinternational.com).

Television

There are a number of free television channels, but non-Arabic language channels are limited. Most expats opt for paid TV from one of the satellite services like Orbit Showtime Network (OSN), but if you don't fancy a satellite dish or your rental terms don't allow one, then Etisalat and du offer digital TV. Digital TV providers can also provide your broadband and landline phone services, with bundles offering various levels of broadband speed, call time and channel choice. It can get expensive for the best of each.

High Definition (HD) channels are now commonplace and there are plenty of the 'on demand' options available that many expats are used to. For example, OSN customers can purchase a Showbox (a recordable digital receiver) that allows them to pause live television and record favourite shows and they can also watch movies and series online through OSN Play, which is free to subscribers. Digital TV subscribers also get the benefits of recording and pausing live television. Etisalat is launching its eLife TV iPad App to let subscribers watch on their tablet via wi-fi or Etisalat's super-fast mobile internet.

Football Fans
If you're after English Premier League, Spanish La Liga, French Ligue 1, Italian Serie A or the UEFA Champion's League then you'll need to subscribe to Al Jazeera Sports package with access to channels +1 to +10. If you're an existing Etisalat or du subscriber you can do this through them for Dhs.58 or Dhs.70 respectively.

Free To View
Local free-to-air English language channels in Dubai include:
Dubai One: 24 hour entertainment specialising in various US series
MBC 4: primarily US series targeted at women
MBC Action: US action series, targeted at men
MBC Max: latest Hollywood films
MBC 2: mainly Western movies
City 7 TV: independent Dubai-based broadcaster. News, business, lifestyle, drama and comedy shows

Maids & Cleaners

Domestic Help
Domestic help is readily available in Dubai, both full and part-time. Legally, a live-in or out maid can only be employed by the individual who sponsors her and organises her residence visa, but in practice many maids take on extra cleaning or babysitting for other families; if you are caught you face a hefty fine and the maid may be deported. If you are looking for someone part-time, but want to stay within the law, there are many companies in Dubai that provide cleaners and maids on an hourly basis, and for around Dhs.35 per hour they'll take care of all your sweeping, mopping, dusting, washing, and ironing. Most companies stipulate a minimum number of hours, usually two or three per visit.

City Sky Maid Services Al Tayer Bldg, Al Wasl, 04 332 4600, *cityskymaid.com*
Dubai Carpet Cleaning G1 Deira Tower, Al Rigga, 04 221 9800, *dubai-carpet-cleaning.com*
Ecomaid Middle East Nr Mazaya Shopping Centre, Al Wasl, 04 388 1292, *ecomaidme.com*
Home Help Emirates Islamic Bank Bldg, Al Mankhool, 04 380 5111, *homehelp.ae*
Housekeeping Co 04 221 1996, *housekeepingco.com*
Howdra 04 238 0088, *howdra.ae*
Molly Maid Al Qouz 3, 04 339 7799, *mollymaidme.com*
Ready Maids Nasser Lootah Bldg, Umm Hurair 1, 04 396 6779, *readymaids.ae*

Laundry Services
Wall-to-wall carpets are rare in this part of the world, but many homes do sport loose rugs and carpets. When they're looking a bit grubby, the companies listed below can pay you a visit, give you a quote, and take the rugs away to be cleaned, returning them a couple of days later.

Alpha Cleaning Services 800 2737, *alphaserves.com*
Churchill Business Bay, 04 323 6863, *churchill-gulf.com*
Dubai Maids Jabal Ali Ind. 1, 04 880 4670, *dubai-maids.com*
Modern Cleaning Methods Nr Al Amani Spare Parts, Al Rashidiya, 04 285 1668, *modernmethodsco.com*

LIVING IN DUBAI
SETTING UP HOME

There are no self-service launderettes, but laundry shops are everywhere. Some of the largest chains in the city include Butler's (04 347 2106) and Champion Cleaners (04 366 3359). As well as dry cleaning and laundry, they all offer ironing services. If you have specific instructions, make sure these are noted when you drop off your laundry – creases in trousers are standard, so if you don't want them, speak up.

Compensation policies for lost or damaged items vary, but losses are rare, even in the places that look most disorganised. Large chains normally have a free pick-up and delivery service.

As a guide to prices, you can expect to pay around Dhs.19 for a shirt, Dhs.60 for a suit and Dhs.27 for a double quilt cover.

Home Improvements

Builders
Exact regulations are constantly changing when it comes to making alterations to your property, but so far they have always been extremely restrictive. In Nakheel and Emaar developments, for example, you are not allowed to build any higher than your perimeter wall.

To build an extension, you need to apply for permission via your master developer, and you then need to wait while they approve the plans. Following that, you have to pay a deposit of Dhs.5,000.

Once the works have begun, an inspector will make a site visit, and on completion of the building, a final assessment will be carried out. After this, your deposit will be returned if you have met all the guidelines. These guidelines are very stringent as developers seek to protect the look and feel of communities. They can determine the colour of the paint you may use on the exterior of your property and also the particular design and style of any doors, gates or decorative iron fencing.

All this may change though as the Planning & Engineering Department of Dubai Municipality is currently working to centralise all structural work carried out on residential buildings in Dubai, effectively taking the responsibility out of the hands of the developers. The anticipation is that when the new laws are passed, rules on extension plans and designs will be more lenient. See dm.gov.ae for more information.

If you are intending to make some structural changes to your property, you should always use a licensed and experienced contractor. There are a number of options, including Kalandoor Contracting (04 884 9426), Al Baraha Land Building Contracting and General Maintenance (04 272 2999), and Danube Buildmart (800 3131).

Interior Decorating
Once you own your property you are free to paint the inside in any style you choose. If you rent, the likelihood is that your landlord will not mind on the basis that he has your deposit, and will be happy to keep hold of it should you not leave the villa or apartment in its original state. Many Dubai landlords do not need much of a reason to hold back security deposits though, so it's worth checking and getting something in writing before you get the roller out.

An excellent range of paints can be found at Jotun Paints and ACE Hardware (800 275 223). Companies like Alpha Services (800 2737) offer painting services, and artists such as MacKenzie Art (mackenzieart.com, 04 341 9803) can be commissioned for children's murals and original artwork. The cost of internally painting a whole villa can vary between Dhs.3,000 and Dhs.8,000, depending on size.

Maintenance
Whether you're a homeowner or live in rental property, are responsible for your property's general maintenance or have an assigned company, housing in Dubai requires constant maintenance due to the climate. Air-conditioning units can be temperamental and need regular servicing, plumbing problems aren't uncommon, electrics can go haywire and creepy crawlies like to pay a visit.

Most homeowners and tenants employ the services of a maintenance company. Annual contracts don't come cheap, but the benefit is it will cover you for most of your maintenance needs. The contract should include regular scheduled servicing of

Apartments near Downtown

LIVING IN DUBAI
SETTING UP HOME

air-conditioning units and boilers, seasonal pest control protection, basic masonry works and 24 hour emergency call out services. Most companies offer extra services such as swimming pool maintenance and gardening for an add-on fee.

Contracts ideal for tenants that cover emergency call-outs only can start from Dhs.59 per month, or for more comprehensive cover, prices increase to Dhs.250 per month and up. Companies that offer maintenance services include Emrill (covering Emaar Properties, emrill.com), Howdra (howdra.ae), and Hitches & Glitches (hitchesandglitches.com); Green Facilities Management (green-fms.com) prides itself on its environmental and sustainability credentials, offers a 24/7 emergency call-out service, can assess your home for energy efficiency, and sources environmentally sound maintenance products. You'll also hear adverts on local radio stations for maintenance companies – as there are so many, prices should be competitive.

For more specialist services, try Under One Roof (04 323 2722, underoneroof.ae); Floorworld (800 35667, floorworld.ae) and Alomi Real Wood Flooring (04 885 8825, alomirealwoodflooringllc.ae).

Whichever community you live in, your developer will have standard rules and regulations relating to noise, parking, and general upkeep of your property. These will be detailed on the developer's website and local security guards perform regular checks. If you live in a villa, a dirty or messy garage may be frowned upon, and you could be fined for such things as parking on the street rather than in a designated bay, so it's worth making yourself aware of what is required of you as either a tenant or homeowner.

Gardens

For a city on the edge of the desert, Dubai boasts a surprising amount of lush greenery – but, with very little annual rainfall and rapidly diminishing groundwater, plenty of artificial hydration is required if you want to create your very own garden oasis. Gardens need watering twice a day ideally – as green can turn to brown within just a matter of days. You can install a timed irrigation system or employ the services of a gardener, while boring a well in your garden to access natural water supplies is also an option. For houses further in from the coast, you'll need to drill down approximately 25 metres before you hit groundwater, whereas houses in areas nearer to the coast, will access water after just a couple of metres. The level of salt in the water can vary considerably, and it is possible to pump the water into a mixed tank to desalinate it for your domestic use. The cost for drilling and finding should start from approximately Dhs.1,800 if you secure the expertise of any of the landscaping companies found in the Plant Street area of Satwa. Alternatively, opt for AstroTurf – all you need to do is hose it down every few weeks. You can buy AstroTurf in ACE Hardware (800 275 223), while Clearview (clearview.ae) and Cape Reed (capereed.com) both install fake lawns. Another option is to go for block paving or decking. You can purchase various qualities of decking in ACE Hardware.

Landscaping

To buy pot plants, trees and shrubs head to the Dubai Municipality Nursery in the Jadaf area, next

Al Barsha villas

LIVING IN DUBAI
SETTING UP HOME

to Business Bay Crossing. Prices are reasonable and discounts based on quantity will be given. Dubai Garden Centre (04 340 0006) sells pretty much everything you could ever need for your outdoor space; prices here are often at the higher end of the spectrum, but you can expect excellent service and expertise, as well as delivery for large orders. Plant Street in Satwa has a number of basic nurseries, but choice here can be limited.

Larger retailers such as Spinneys, Carrefour and IKEA sell plants, pots and smaller sized gardening implements, while ACE Hardware is a one-stop-shop for the outdoor enthusiast, selling everything from flora to furniture, tools to trees and plants to pergolas.

If you are buying a brand new house, the developers may have left you with no more than a sandpit plot, so you will need to start your garden from scratch, which can be somewhat challenging. Equally, landlords are not obliged to landscape the gardens of new villas before they rent them to you, so don't assume that the 'work in progress' you see upon viewing a property will be an outdoor oasis by the time you move in.

If the green-fingered DIY is not for you, Dubai Garden Centre offers a full landscaping service, while Royal Gardenscape (royalgardenscape.com) provides all you need in the way of paving and gravel. Plant Street is a great place to start for cheap labour and materials, while Terraverde (terraverde.ae), Toscana Landscaping & Pools (toscanalandscaping.com) and Bespoke Concept (bespokeconcept.com) all offer full service design and installation for gardens. For more information on garden furniture see Shopping.

Swimming Pools

A lot of properties in Dubai have private pools or access to a shared pool. If you don't have one in your villa, you can always pay to have one installed – but it doesn't come cheap. One option is to have a custom-made, free-form fibre glass and ceramic tiled pool fitted. As tough and durable as a concrete version, these are effectively portable. Delivery takes around four weeks, with an onsite installation period of approximately 10 days. Prices for such a pool start at around Dhs.110,000 including labour, pumps and filtration. Try Pools by Design (poolsdesign.net).

Aside from cleaning, your pool will also need the water to be changed and chemical levels balanced on a regular basis. Those Pool Guys (thosepoolguys.com), Al Wasel Swimming Pools Maintenance (alwaselswimmingpools.com) and Pools r Us (poolsrusdubai.com) are also well established in Dubai.

If you have a young family, then take a look at Aqua-Net (aquanet.ae), which creates custom safety netting that quickly and easily covers your pool.

Home Insurance

Crime and natural disasters are not generally a big concern for Dubai's residents – though the minor earth tremors of April 2013 did shake people up a bit, there was no substantial damage to property.

However, insuring your household goods against theft or damage is still wise. To create a policy, the insurance provider will need your home address, a list of household items and valuation, and invoices for anything worth more than Dhs.2,500. Cover usually includes theft, fire and storm damage. You can also insure personal items outside the home.

As a guideline you can expect to pay around Dhs.1,500 per 1.2 sq m for building insurance, Dhs.250 for up to Dhs.60,000 worth of home contents and Dhs.850 for up to Dhs.60,000 worth of personal possessions.

Established in 2001, Greenshield Insurance (greenshield.ae, 04 388 2200) offers some good insurance packages for your home (as well as medical, life, motor and travel insurance and more), and has a good reputation and high client retention rates of 98%. You can visit their website and submit an online query, or find their offices in Bur Dubai.

Animal lovers will also need to insure their pet(s). It's best to do so while he or she is still young and healthy, as prices can rise steeply over a certain age.

For peace of mind, register your home in the Dubai Police Home Security Programme, a free service that provides round-the-clock protection for houses while residents are away. Register at any Dubai Police station.

AFIA Insurance Brokerage Services LLC Kanoo Group Bldg, Al Karama, 04 337 9987, *afia.ae*
AXA Insurance (Gulf) > *p.105* Umm Hurair 2, 04 324 3434, *axa-gulf.com*
Emirates Insurance Company Al Ittihad St, Port Saeed, 04 294 2949, *eminsco.com*
Greenshield Insurance Brokers > *p.107, 119*
Al Musalla Towers, Al Hamriya, 04 388 2200, *greenshield.ae*
National General Insurance Co Al Ittihad Rd, Port Saeed, 04 222 2772, *ngi.ae*
Nexus Insurance Emaar Square, Burj Khalifa, 04 323 1111, *nexusadvice.com*
RSA Insurance Office Court Bldg, Oud Metha, 800 772, *rsadirect.ae*
Zurich Insurance 800 4560, *zurich.ae*

Additional Insurance

Insurance companies cover more than just your home – AXA, for example, also provides health insurance. There are even companies starting to provide pet insurance, such as Pet Secure, 04 252 2570, petsecure.ae.

Dubai road infrastructure

GETTING AROUND

Dubai is a city geared up for cars, and has a good and continuously improving infrastructure. With a grid-like street system it shouldn't take you too long to find your way around either. However, if you're planning on using satellite navigation systems they won't help you much due to a lack of official addresses in the city at the moment; so you'll have to get your Explorer map out if you get lost.

There are some good public transport options but most people travel by car, whether that's driving themselves or using the generally excellent and inexpensive taxi service. Getting behind the wheel of a car is probably the best way to get the measure of the city's numerous districts though.

Traffic during rush hours can get heavy, especially if there's even a minor accident, but you'll soon learn where the hotspots are and either avoid or leave for your destination at an appropriate time. There are other idiosyncrasies you'll find too; traffic lights spring up everywhere and you can find yourself sat at a red light in an empty building site for ages. You'll also encounter plenty of speed bumps, that even the largest 4WDs will take at crawling pace.

Other sights you may find unusual at first are the number of cars that pull over and stop on the hard shoulders of the highways. This is particularly obvious at sunset when some drivers will stop to answer the call to prayer by the side of the road. And once it's dark, watch out for workers who loiter by the side of roads waiting for lifts back to their camp. Sometimes they can be quite close to the road and difficult to spot. People sometimes try to cross highways on foot too.

While there are government guidelines on driving, don't count on other road users being aware of them or choosing to obey them. Cautious driving is the best approach to stay incident free.

LIVING IN DUBAI
GETTING AROUND

Dubai Road Network

When you arrive, the extensive, expanding network of roads can be intimidating, but once you find your bearings things become easier. The creek divides Bur Dubai (to the south) and Deira (to the north), and has five main crossing points: Shindagha Tunnel, Maktoum Bridge, Garhoud Bridge, Business Bay Bridge and the Floating Bridge. The Floating Bridge is due to be replaced by the Dubai 'Smile' Bridge in late 2014.

The main thoroughfare through the city is Sheikh Zayed Road, which runs from Sharjah, parallel to the sea, all the way to Abu Dhabi. Three bypass roads have been constructed inland towards the desert to ease the city's congestion problems. All run parallel to the coast and Sheikh Zayed Road.

Al Khail Road (E44) is the closest bypass to the coast and runs from Sports City to Ras Al Khor, where it turns east and heads towards Hatta and Oman. Sheikh Mohammed bin Zayed Road (E311), formerly Emirates Road, is the next furthest from the coast and connects Abu Dhabi directly to Sharjah and the northern emirates.

The Outer Ring Road (E611) sits outside of the E311 and runs roughly from the southern border of Dubai all the way to the Sharjah-Umm Al Quwain border, although it is still being expanded. There are also a few main east-west roads, including Umm Suqeim Road (D63), the Dubai-Al Ain Road (E66), Financial Centre Road (D71), and Muscat Street (D69). Despite all the road expansions, traffic is still a problem in Dubai, especially at the creek crossings.

Within the city, the roads in older parts of town, such as Bur Dubai and Deira, are smaller and more congested, while the road networks in newer developments such as Downtown Dubai tend to accommodate greater traffic flow.

Address System
As part of Dubai's new District Addressing project, which will cover the entire city by 2016, the city has been divided into several districts, and each district further sub-divided into communities. The project will see more than 22,000 Dubai streets renamed over the next two years, with the address system featuring the building number, street name, community and district. This replaces the rather confusing system of street numbers.

New districts to be aware of include Marsa Dubai, which is the new name for Dubai Marina; and Nakhlat Jumeira, which is the new name for Palm Jumeirah. 'Marsa' is Arabic for 'marina' and 'nakhlat' is Arabic for 'palm'. Another new district is Burj Khalifa, which includes the Downtown community (and of course, the Burj Khalifa building); and the old district Al Souk Al Kabeer, which includes Al Fahidi Historical Neighbourhood (formerly known as Bastakiya).

Although all roads in the city have an official name or number, several roads are referred to by a different moniker. For instance, Jumeira Road is often known as Beach Road, and Interchange One, on Sheikh Zayed Road, is invariably called Defence Roundabout. Dubai Municipality has started a more formal road-naming process to help eliminate confusion, and many of the city's main roads have been given the names of prominent Arab cities, such as Marrakech Road. Street signs now also include the direction of travel, so you know whether you are travelling north or south. This lack of consistency makes locating an address difficult. Companies often only list their building name, road and nearest landmark when writing their address. Explorer's *Dubai Street Atlas* features an index of over 13,000 roads and building. Also, you can search for a business, product or service on localsearch.ae, which lists information for around 110,000 companies such as telephone number, email and website address.

Finding Your Way Around
When you start driving it's pretty much a given that you'll need to schedule an extra 20 minutes for getting lost. Dubai is famed for its U-turns, which are used instead of allowing cars to turn across oncoming traffic. Many times you'll see the building you are aiming for, but will have to navigate a spaghetti-like tangle of roads to get to it – or drive for some distance in the opposite direction before you can link to the road that takes you to your destination. Once you get the hang of the thinking behind the road system it gets much easier, and once you have done a journey for the first time, repeating it is simple. Taxi drivers quite often get confused too – usually if they are new – so it's a good idea to have some specific directions or a simple map with you if you aren't sure how to get to your destination. When giving instructions to a taxi driver, remember that a traffic light is commonly referred to as a 'signal'.

Maps
With new roads popping up on a weekly basis, finding your way around Dubai can be difficult. Explorer produces several of the most up-to-date street maps available, including the fully indexed *Dubai Street Atlas* and the pocket-sized *Dubai Mini Map*. Newly released is the Dubai Map app, one of a series of GCC map apps.

Road Signs
Signposting in Dubai is generally good once you understand the system. Blue or green signs indicate the roads, exits or locations out of the city, and brown signs show heritage sites, places of interest and hospitals. Dubai's new signage system relies more heavily on street names and compass directions,

LIVING IN DUBAI
GETTING AROUND

compared to the older system which featured local area names. If the signage gets confusing, remember that Abu Dhabi is south of Dubai, Sharjah is north, the beach is to the west and the desert is to the east.

Driving in Dubai

While the infrastructure is superb, the general standard of driving is not. You'll see drivers displaying all manner of dangerous driving habits and, as a result, you must take extra care when driving. Once you're behind the wheel, it isn't as scary as it looks, and you'll soon learn to drive defensively and safely.

You drive on the right side of the road in Dubai, and you should overtake on the left – people often ignore this rule but if you are caught you could receive a fine. Speed limits are usually 60 to 80kph in town, while on main roads and roads to other emirates they are 100 to 120kph. The limit is clearly indicated on signs. Both fixed and movable radar traps, and Dubai Traffic Police, are there to catch the unwary violator. Be warned – you can be fined for gesticulating at another driver, and using the offensive middle finger can mean jail.

Automatic Licence Transfer
Citizens with licences from the following countries are eligible for automatic driving licence transfers: Australia, Austria, Belgium, Canada, Denmark, Finland, France, Germany, Greece, Ireland, Italy, Japan, Netherlands, New Zealand, Norway, Poland, South Africa, South Korea, Sweden, Switzerland, Turkey, United Kingdom and United States. Citizens of GCC countries do not need to apply for a licence transfer.

Roads & Transport Authority (RTA)
The RTA was launched by the government in 2005 and has taken over the responsibility for most procedures described in this chapter. Among other things the RTA deals with all transport and traffic projects in Dubai and enforcing transport legislation. The RTA is also a great source of information on Dubai's driving and licensing laws. Visit rta.ae for up-to-date information and all the latest traffic news.

Licence To Drive
Tourists can drive hire cars on their domestic licence or International Driving Permit. If you have a residence visa then you must have a UAE driving licence – it is illegal to drive without one. Some nationals qualify for an automatic licence transfer, so long as their original licence has not expired. See Getting Started. Always keep your driving licence in the vehicle, along with the vehicle registration card – you could be fined if stopped by the police otherwise.

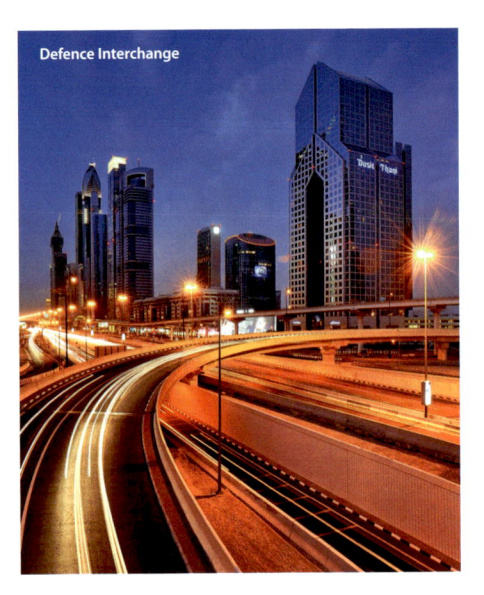

Defence Interchange

Parking

Most street parking in Dubai is now governed by parking meters. After feeding your coins into the machine, you get a ticket to display on your dashboard. The minimum fare is Dhs.2 for one hour. The price increases steeply the longer you park in a spot, so you'll pay Dhs.4 or Dhs.5 for two hours, Dhs.8 for three hours, and Dhs.11 for four hours (the maximum). Parking is free from 1pm to 4pm and 9pm to 8am daily, and on Fridays and public holidays.

Several areas support the mParking system (mpark.rta.ae), which allows drivers to pay parking tolls through SMS (non-Dubai registered vehicles must register online first). Areas where mParking is supported have an orange sign displaying the parking code and a guide on how to use the system. To use mParking, send an SMS to PARK (7275) with your car licence plate number (including the first letter), a space, the area parking code listed on the sign, a space, and the number of hours you wish to pay for (one to four). The system will then send you a confirmation SMS, and the parking fee plus a 30 fils service charge will be deducted from your Etisalat or du phone credit. Ten minutes before your time has expired, the system will send an SMS reminder and ask if you'd like to add more time. Commuters can also use their Nol Metro card to pay for parking at many machines, with the appropriate fee being deducted from the card's credit.

Parking at Dubai's shopping malls used to be mostly free, but since the opening of the metro several shopping centres that are adjacent or near to metro

96   Dubai Explorer

LIVING IN DUBAI
GETTING AROUND

stations have introduced parking charges for stays over a certain length of time. Both Mall of the Emirates and Deira City Centre have free parking for the first four hours, and then charges that rise steeply from Dhs.20 for four to five hours up to Dhs.150 for eight hours or over and Dhs.350 for overnight (Fridays and public holidays are free).

Disabled parking spaces do exist, though are sometimes taken by ignorant drivers who don't need the facility; however, police do monitor these spaces and hand out fines to offenders.

Pre-paid Parking

Pre-paid parking cards are divided into two sections A and B. An A-card holder has the right to park in all car parks. A B-card holder has the right to park only in B-marked car parks. Just take a copy of your car registration card to Al Twar Centre, Dubai Municipality – Al Karama branch, or the Dubai Roads and Transport Authority HQ, and pay the required fee – from Dhs.450 for three months. The card is not valid in car parks at Dubai International Airport, Dubai Media City and Dubai Internet City.

Road Tolls

Salik is an automated toll system for Dubai's roads. There are currently six gates: one at Garhoud Bridge, another on the Sheikh Zayed Road after Mall of the Emirates, one at Safa Park on Sheikh Zayed Road (between interchanges one and two), another on Maktoum Bridge, one on Al Ittihad Rd and another near Dubai Airport Tunnel.

The Maktoum Bridge crossing is free between 10pm and 6am Saturday to Thursday, and 10pm and 9am on Fridays, when the Floating Bridge is closed. There are no booths, and no need to stop as you drive through. Instead, drivers stick a tag to their windscreen, which is read by radio frequency as they pass through.

Salik Tag

Drivers must initially buy a 'welcome pack' costing Dhs.100: Dhs.50 for the tag and Dhs.50 credit. It costs Dhs.4 each time you pass a toll gate (rental car drivers can be charged Dhs.5), but if you travel between the Al Barsha toll gate and the Al Safa toll gate during one trip (and in the space of an hour) you will only be charged once. If your Salik card is out of credit you will be fined Dhs.50 for each gate you pass through.

The Salik system will send you an SMS when your account balance runs low or when you pass through a gate without any balance. The kit can be bought from Emarat, EPPCO, ENOC, and ADNOC petrol stations, Dubai Islamic Bank and Emirates NBD. For more information about the toll gates, visit the Salik website, salik.gov.ae, or call 800 72545 (800 SALIK). The Roads and Transport Authority (RTA) has proposed that the toll be increased to Dhs.5 in 2014, but the proposal has yet to be approved.

Traffic Offences

In an effort to help combat bad driving, the Dubai Police initiated a black points system to go along with the existing fines system. You are issued a certain number of black points against your licence according to the particular violation. For example, the fine for allowing a child under 10 years of age to sit in the front of a car is Dhs.400 and the driver will be given four black points. If you get 24 points you will lose your licence for a year, but any points you acquire will expire 12 months after they are issued.

The white points system came into operation in 2013, and it 'rewards' law-abiding drivers with one white point every month; motorists will be given incentives to collect white points, ranging from raffle prizes to exemption from traffic fines.

Check Online For Fines

You can check whether you have any outstanding traffic fines against your vehicle by entering your registration plate number at dubaipolice.gov.ae. There is no time limit to pay your fines – but you will have to pay them at the end of each year in order to re-register and insure your vehicle.

Bad drivers can choose to eradicate some of their black points by electing to take a driving course costing Dhs.200 per session (there are three sessions in a course). They can also cancel out black points by gaining white points in some cases.

Fines

Parking fines start at Dhs.200, and speeding fines start at Dhs.400 for driving up to 10kph over the speed limit and go up from there. Driving in a reckless manner or racing will earn you six points, as will parking in a handicapped zone or in front of a fire hydrant.

There are numerous speed cameras on Dubai's roads; drivers caught racing can face a fine of up to Dhs.2,000 as well as 12 black points and confiscation of their licence for 30 days. To see all the possible penalties for bad driving go to dubaitrafficfines.org or check dubaipolice.gov.ae for more information.

Be careful to avoid driving in the dedicated bus and taxi lanes, which have recently been added to some major roads. The lanes are clearly marked, and you are liable to a fine of Dhs.600 if you enter one without

LIVING IN DUBAI
GETTING AROUND

authorisation. The only exception is if you need to cross the lane to enter or exit the thoroughfare.

Average-speed and stopping-distance traps have recently been introduced to try to catch speeding drivers who only slow down when they see speed cameras, and to discourage tailgating. On-the-spot traffic fines for certain offences have been introduced, but in most cases you won't know you've received a fine until you check on the Dubai Police website or renew your vehicle registration.

Most fines are paid when you renew your annual car registration. However, parking tickets that appear on your windscreen must be paid within a week, or the fine increases.

Blood Money

By law, the family of a pedestrian killed in a road accident is entitled to Dhs.200,000 *diya* (blood) money. The money is usually paid by the insurance company unless there's any whiff of the driver having been under the influence of alcohol. However, an amendment to the law is being considered to put a stop to the terrible trend among desperate lower-income workers of killing themselves to provide for their family. This will mean blood money is not automatically due if the victim was walking across a road not intended for use by pedestrians, such as Sheikh Zayed Road.

Drinking & Driving

Dubai Police exercises a strict zero-tolerance policy on drinking and driving. If you get into an accident, whether it is your fault or not, and you fail a blood-alcohol test, you could find yourself spending a night in a cell before a trial in Dubai Courts, after which you'll most likely be jailed. In addition, your insurance is automatically void. Police have increased the number of random drink-driving checks.

Breakdowns

In the event of your vehicle breaking down, you will usually find that passing police cars will stop to help, or at least to check your documents. It's important that you keep water in your car at all times so you don't get dehydrated while waiting, especially during the hotter months. Dubai Traffic officers recommend, if possible, that you pull your car over to a safe spot. If you are on the hard shoulder of a highway you should pull your car as far away from the yellow line as possible and step away from the road until help arrives.

As an added safety measure, make sure you've got a red warning triangle and reflective jacket stored in your car, for use in case you have to stop by the side of the road.

Recovery Services

The Arabian Automobile Association – the AAA – (04 266 9989 or 800 4900, aaauae.com) offers a 24 hour roadside breakdown service for an annual charge. This includes help in minor mechanical repairs, battery boosting, or help if you run out of petrol, have a flat tyre or lock yourself out. Mashreq Bank Visa card holders receive free AAA membership. The more advanced service includes off-road recovery, vehicle registration and a rent-a-car service. Other breakdown services that will be able to help you out without membership include IATC (iatcuae.com), Dubai Auto Towing Services (04 359 4424) and AKT Recovery (04 263 6217). Some dealers and insurance companies offer a free breakdown and recovery service for the first few years after buying a new car. Be sure to ask the dealership about this option when purchasing a new car.

Traffic Accidents

If you are involved in an accident call 999. If the accident is minor and no one has been hurt you need to agree with the other driver where the blame lies and move your cars to the side of the road to avoid obstructing the flow of traffic. You can be fined Dhs.100 for failing to do so even if the accident wasn't your fault. If blame has been clearly decided and the accident is minor, the 999 dispatcher may ask you to drive yourself to the nearest Traffic Police station to fill out the necessary paperwork. The Dubai Police Information Line (800 7777, Arabic and English) gives the numbers of police stations around the emirate.

If blame cannot be decided without police intervention, an officer will be dispatched to assess the accident and apportion blame. The officer will then give you a copy of the accident report; if it is green then the other party is at fault but if it is pink then you are to blame for the accident and you will receive a Dhs.200 fine from the attending officer. You will need to submit the accident report to the insurance company in order to process the claim, or to the garage for repairs. Keep in mind that garages rarely repair vehicles without a police report.

Stray animals are something to avoid on desert roads. If the animal hits your vehicle and causes damage or injury, the animal's owner should pay compensation, but if you are found to have been speeding, you must compensate the animal's owner.

Be sure to keep your licence on you at all times. If you are pulled over by the police or are involved in an accident you'll need to show your driving licence or risk being fined. You will be given a grace period in which to present your licence at the police station; if you fail to do so, you risk having your car impounded and facing a court appearance.

LIVING IN DUBAI
GETTING AROUND

Petrol Stations

Petrol is subsidised in the UAE and generally inexpensive. Within Dubai, you will find Emarat, ENOC and EPPCO stations, and the price of unleaded petrol (around Dhs.1.75 per litre) is the same at all of them. The octane rating of unleaded petrol in the UAE is high – 'Special' is rated at 95 octane and 'Super' at 98 octane. Many of the stations have convenience stores and some have small cafes or fast food restaurants attached to them; Tim Hortons and Costa have opened at several fuel stations across the emirate.

Every station is manned by attendants who will pump your petrol for you, and often clean your windscreen too; it's commonplace to give them a Dhs.5 tip. Most petrol stations offer other services such as car washes, oil changes and even tyre replacement.

Some petrol stations only accept cash, though there is usually an ATM if you are caught short.

Learning To Drive

Emirates Driving Institute (EDI) is one choice of driving school. You do 40 lessons – each for 30 minutes in two blocks of two hours per week. So it should only take 10 weeks to complete your practical training.

You'll also need to attend eight one-hour lectures – the first two must be attended before you can begin your practical lessons – to prepare for the theory test. After 20 lessons there's also a parking test. After 36 lessons, you will have an assessment test which you need to pass before you can register for your final practical test. The final four lessons include highway training on Al Khail Road.

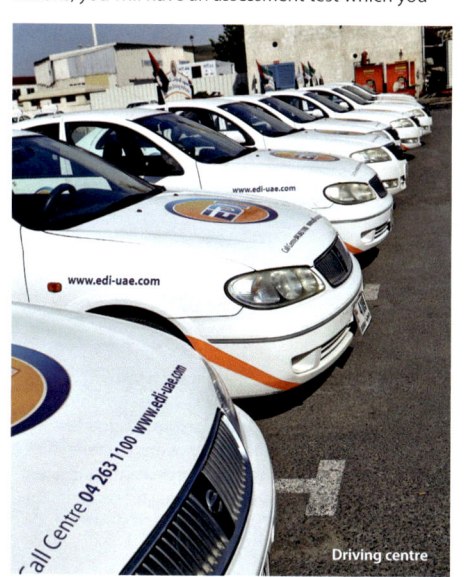

The final driving test should last around 20 minutes. There could be two or three passengers in the car – other students taking their tests too. After you've each had a turn behind the wheel, the instructor will take you all back to the centre and reveal who has passed.

Women learning to drive will be given a female instructor unless they specifically request a male, which they can do on the condition that they produce an NOC and pay a Dhs.10 fee. Regardless of the instructor you have for your 40 lessons, women will have a female instructor for their parking, assessment and final tests.

If you fail the test, you'll have to take another set of lessons before you can take the test again.

Pre-booked Driving Lessons

Some driving schools insist that you pay for a set of pre-booked lessons. The package can include 40 lessons and cost up to Dhs.3,000, although the cost can be paid in instalments. Lessons usually last 30 minutes and must be taken on consecutive days.
Al Ahli Driving Center Nr Atlas Marine Services, Al Qouz Ind. 4, 04 341 1500, *alahlidubai.ae*
Belhasa Driving Center Nr Latifa Hospital, Sama Al Jadaf, Al Jadaf, 04 324 3535, *bdc.ae*
Dubai Driving Center Nr Dubai Dry Docks, Al Qouz Ind. 4, 04 345 5855, *dubaidrivingcenter.net*
Emirates Driving Institute Nr Al Bustan Centre, Al Qusais 1, 04 263 1100, *edi-uae.com*
Galadari Motor Driving Center Amman St, Al Qusais Ind. 4, 04 267 6166, *gmdc.ae*

Hiring A Car

New arrivals to Dubai often find that they have no other option than to hire a vehicle until their residence visa goes though. Most leasing companies include the following in their rates: registration, maintenance, replacement, 24 hour assistance and insurance. All the main car rental companies, plus a few extra, can be found in Dubai.

It is best to shop around as the rates vary considerably. The larger, reputable firms generally have more reliable vehicles and a greater capacity to help in an emergency (an important factor when dealing with the aftermath of an accident). Find out which car hire agent your company uses, as you might qualify for a corporate rate. Most rental companies will keep track of how many times you pass through Salik gates and charge you at the end of the month, along with a Salik service charge.

Leasing is generally weekly, monthly or yearly. Monthly lease prices start at around Dhs.1,800 for

Driving centre

LIVING IN DUBAI
GETTING AROUND

a small vehicle such as a Toyota Yaris, and go up from there. As the lease period increases, the price decreases, so if you're considering keeping the car for a long period, it may not work out that much more expensive than buying.

Before you take possession of your leased car, check for any dents or bumps. To hire any vehicle you will need to provide a passport copy, credit card and a valid driving licence. Those with a residence visa must have a UAE driving licence to drive a hired car, while those on a visit visa can use a licence from their home country as long as it is at least one year old. Comprehensive insurance is essential; make sure that it includes personal accident coverage, and perhaps Oman cover if you're planning on exploring.

Car Hire Companies

Autolease Rent A Car Nr Millennium Airport Hotel, Al Garhoud, 04 282 6565, *autolease-uae.com*
Avis Al Maktoum Rd, Al Rigga, 04 295 7121, *avisuae.ae*
Bettercar Rentals Damascus Rd, Al Qusais Ind. 1, 04 258 6331, *bettercardubai.com*
Budget Car & Van Rental UAE > *p.101* Lehbab Rd, Dubai Investment Park 2, 800 2722, *budget-uae.com*
Diamondlease Car Rental Kharbash Bldg, Trade Center 1, 04 885 2677, *diamondlease.com*
DRC Rent A Car Shk Zayed Rd, Al Qouz Ind. 1, 04 338 9070, *discountcardubai.com*
Dubai Exotic Limo Nr Chili's Restaurant, Al Rigga, 04 286 8635, *dubaiexoticlimo.com*
Euroline Rent A Car 052 999 5355, *euroline-rent.com*
EuroStar Rent A Car Al Wuheida Rd, Hor Al Anz East, 04 266 1117, *eurostarrental.com*
Green Car Rental Dubai World Trade Centre, Trade Center 1, 04 358 8488, *greencardubai.com*
Hertz UAE Airport Rd, Umm Ramoul, 800 43789, *hertzuae.com*
Shift Car Rental & Leasing Al Qouz Ind. 1, 04 3393 722, *shiftleasing.com*

Buying A Car

Aside from the horrendous traffic, the UAE is a motorist's dream. Petrol is cheap, big engines are considered cool and the wide motorways stretching across the country are perfect for weekend drives.

Most of the major car makes are available through franchised dealerships in Dubai, especially big Japanese and American brands. New vehicles are surprisingly affordable too. A new BMW 3-series in Dubai is likely to cost around 20% less than the same car in the UK.

There is a large second-hand car market in the UAE. Dealers are scattered around town but good areas to start are Sheikh Zayed Road and Warsan, behind Ras Al Khor. Expect to pay a premium of between Dhs.5,000 and Dhs.10,000 for buying through a dealer (as opposed to buying from a private seller), since they also offer a limited warranty, insurance, finance and vehicle registration.

The Al Awir complex houses several smaller used-car dealers and it's easy to spend a whole day walking around the lots speaking with salesmen. Al Awir is also the location for Golden Bell Auctions (goldenbellauctions.com), with sales held each Wednesday evening. All cars up for auction have to undergo a test at the nearby Eppco Tasjeel garage, and all outstanding fines will have been cleared. There's a Traffic Department office on the site so buyers can register their new vehicles on the spot.

For private sales, check the classifieds in *Gulf News* and *Khaleej Times* and supermarket noticeboards. Online sites such as dubizzle.com and expat forums such as expatwoman.com are also useful.

Tinted Windows

Currently, the government allows you to avoid the sun somewhat by tinting your vehicle's windows up to 30%. Some areas have facilities where you can get your car windows tinted but don't get carried away – remember to stick to the limit. Random checks take place and fines are handed out to those caught in the dark. Tinting in Sharjah is allowed for a fee of Dhs.100 and Ajman residents may tint for Dhs.200 per annum, but only if they are women. Company cars are banned from having tinted windows.

Second-hand Sales

As well as getting the vehicle tested, check that the engine plate number on the car corresponds with that given on the vehicle registration card. Also, check with the Dubai Traffic Police that the vehicle is neither stolen nor has any fines; visit dubaipolice.gov.ae.

After you have purchased the vehicle, you will need to insure it, then transfer ownership/vehicle registration, and purchase a Salik tag, if required.

Transferring Ownership

If you buy a second-hand vehicle, you will need to transfer ownership to your name. If you fail to do this, you are liable to pay a Dhs.3,000 fine by Dubai Police. You will need to collect an application form from the Traffic Police and submit it, along with a no objection certificate from the finance company (if using one), the original licence plates, the previous owner's valid registration card, your new insurance certificate, your UAE driving licence and Dhs.100 transfer fee. The previous owner must also be present to sign the form. The new registration card will then be issued within five to 10 minutes.

Going places in the UAE?

When it comes to getting more value for your money, there's just one name – Budget. Whether it is short-term rental, lease or international reservations, you can be assured of the quality of service that has earned us the vote as 'Best Car Rental Company in the Middle East'.

For Reservations:

Toll-free: **800 2722 (24 Hrs.)**
Abu Dhabi: +971 2 443 8430
Al Ain: +971 3 746 0989
Dubai: +971 4 295 6667
Jebel Ali: +971 4 881 1445
Sharjah: +971 6 533 7777
Ras Al Khaimah: +971 7 244 6666
Fujairah: +971 9 222 0172
Email: reservations@budget-uae.com
or book on-line at
www.budget-uae.com

Budget®
Car and Van Rental

Budget Rent a Car is an ISO 9001 certified company and member of the UAE-based Liberty Group.

LIVING IN DUBAI
GETTING AROUND

Importing A Car

It is possible to import or export your car, but be prepared for lots of paperwork. If you're keen to hang onto your chosen four wheels, contact Kanoo Shipping (kanooshipping.com) for help.

If you're buying a car within the UAE but from outside of Dubai you will need to complete export and import procedures. Both buyer and seller will need to be present at the traffic licensing department in the seller's emirate. The department will ask for copies of a passport and driving licence, the vehicle registration card, an insurance policy in the new owner's name (three day policies can be available at the site) and a technical inspection certificate. The seller may also need a no objection letter from their bank if there is an outstanding loan amount. In all emirates aside from Dubai you will be issued with export plates to drive the car home on. You will then have to register it in Dubai. Midland Cars in Karama (04 396 7521, midlandcarsdubai.com) can help you import a vehicle to Dubai from another emirate.

Vehicle Finance

Many new and second-hand car dealers will be able to arrange finance for you, often through a deal with a preferred banking partner. Most official dealers and main financial establishments should be able to sort out monthly automatic payments for you too. Alternatively a personal loan can often have lower interest rates and better terms (plus it's difficult to get an auto loan on cars of a certain age) so it's worth checking. If you go with the bank that receives your salary, the application is often easier. Just make sure you can afford the payments as bad debt is not good news.

Second Opinion

When buying a used car it's well worth having it checked over by a garage or mechanic. Eppco Tasjeel, AAA and Max Garage offer a checking service. Alternatively, speak to the service department at the dealership where the car was originally bought. A thorough inspection will cost about Dhs.250.

New Car Dealers

Bentley Al Habtoor Motors, Port Saeed, 04 294 4492, *emirates.bentleymotors.com*
Bugatti Al Habtoor Motors, Port Saeed, 04 294 4492, *bugatti.com*
Cadillac Liberty Automobiles, Al Qouz Ind. 3, 04 341 9341, *cadillacarabia.com*
Chevrolet Al Ghandi Auto, Al Qouz Ind. 3, 04 231 0800, *chevroletarabia.com*
Chrysler Trading Enterprises, Al Qouz Ind. 3, 04 340 2445, *mideast.chrysler.com*

Dodge Trading Enterprises, Al Qouz Ind. 3, 04 340 2445, *tradingenterprises.ae*
Ferrari Al Tayer Motors, Al Qouz Ind. 1, 04 303 7878, *dubai.ferraridealers.com*
Ford Al Tayer Motors, Al Garhoud, 04 201 1002, *me.ford.com*
Honda Al Futtaim Motors, Al Qouz Ind. 1, 04 347 2212, *honda.ae*
Jaguar Al Tayer Motors, Al Garhoud, 800 668 677, *jaguar.com*
Jeep Trading Enterprises, Al Qouz Ind. 3, 04 340 2445, *mideast.jeep.com*
Land Rover Al Tayer Motors, Al Garhoud, 800 668 677, *landrover.com*
Lexus Al Futtaim Motors, Al Qouz Ind. 3, 04 507 6300, *lexus.ae*
Lincoln Al Tayer Motors, Al Qouz Ind. 1, 04 303 7777, *me.lincoln.com*
Maserati Al Tayer Motors, Al Qouz Ind. 1, 04 303 7878, *maserati.com*
McLaren Dubai The Lofts, Downtown Dubai, Burj Khalifa, 04 382 7500, *dubai.mclarenretailers.com*
Mercedes-Benz Gargash Enterprises, Al Khabaisi, 04 209 9777, *gargash.mercedes-benz.com*
Mitsubishi Motors Al Habtoor Motors, Port Saeed, 04 608 4000, *mitsubishi-uae.com*
Opel Liberty Automobiles, Al Qouz Ind. 3, 04 341 9341, *cadillacarabia.com*
Peugeot Swaidan Trading, Al Qouz Ind. 3, 04 347 9000, *swaidanpeugeot.com*
Ram Trading Enterprises, Al Qouz Ind. 3, 04 340 2445, *tradingenterprises.ae*
Saab Gargash Motors, Al Khabaisi, 04 340 3333, *gargashme.com*
Toyota Al Futtaim Motors, Dubai Festival City, Al Kheeran, 04 206 6000, *toyota.ae*
Volkswagen Al Naboodah Automobiles, Al Qouz Ind. 1, 04 705 3333, *volkswagen-dubai.com*
Volvo Trading Enterprises, Dubai Festival City, Al Kheeran, 04 206 6400, *volvocars.com*

Used Car Dealers

4x4 Motors Al Aweer Auto Market Phase 1, Ras Al Khor Ind. 3, 04 333 2757, *4x4motors.com*
Al Futtaim Automall Nr Times Square, Al Qouz Ind. 1, 04 340 8029, *automalluae.com*
Al Naboodah Automobiles Al Wasl, 04 310 5300, *nabooda-auto.com*
Al Tayer Motors Al Ittihad Rd, Al Khabaisi, 04 266 6489, *altayermotors.com*
House Of Cars > *p.103* Nr Mazaya Centre, Al Wasl, 04 343 5060, *houseofcarsgroup.com*
Liberty Automobiles Shk Zayed Rd, Al Qouz Ind. 3, 04 341 9341, *libertyautos.com*
Reem Automobiles Nr Mazaya Centre, Al Wasl, 04 343 6333, *reemauto.ae*

Home of Performance, Elegance & Luxury motoring

The House of Cars Group was founded in 1998 and has built up to be probably one of the most enthusiastic motor business in Dubai. We are proud that our group provides prestige pre-owned car sales and after sales services with our specialized independant Porsche and BMW garages.

The group offers it's customers outstanding value and superb quality across a full range of vehicles, plus full body or accident repair including vehicle enhancement facilities.

We recognise that "you are our customer and have a choice" we invite you to choose wisely.

HOUSE OF CARS SHOWROOM

P.O. Box 26970 Dubai, U.A.E
Tel.: 04 343 5060
Fax: 04 343 5074
email: showroom@houseofcarsgroup.com
www.houseofcarsgroup.com

HOC INDEPENDENT PORSCHE SPECIALISTS

P.O. Box 26970 Dubai, U.A.E
Tel.: 04 339 3466
Fax: 04 339 3470
email: hocg4you@houseofcarsgroup.com
www.houseofcarsgroup.com

The X Service Centre
INDEPENDENT BMW SPECIALISTS

P.O. Box 26970 Dubai, U.A.E
Tel.: 04 339 5033
Fax: 04 339 5044
email: txsc4you@houseofcarsgroup.com
www.houseofcarsgroup.com

BODY FX
SMART REPAIRS DETAILING SERVICE

P.O. Box 26970 Dubai, U.A.E
Tel.: 04 339 5033
Fax: 04 339 5044
email: carsport@houseofcarsgroup.com
www.houseofcarsgroup.com

www.houseofcarsgroup.com
Opening Hrs Sat. to Thu. from 8:00am-8:00pm
Located between interchange 1 & 2, Exit 49 Shk. Zayed Rd
email: reception@houseofcarsgroup.com

LIVING IN DUBAI
GETTING AROUND

Insurance

Before you can register your car you must have car insurance. The insurers will need to know the usual details such as year of manufacture, and value, as well as the chassis number. If you got a real bargain of a car, make sure you instruct the insurance company to cover it at the market value.

Annual insurance policies last for 13 months (allowing a one-month grace period for when registration expires). It's best to get fully comprehensive cover with personal accident cover, and advisable to be covered for 'blood money'. Rates depend on age and model of your car and your previous insurance history, although no-claims bonuses accrued in your home country are rarely recognised. Expect to pay between 4-7% of the vehicle's value, or a flat rate of 5% for cars over five years old. If you feel your car is worth more than you paid for it, make sure the insurance company covers it at the market value. Insurers will need to see copies of your UAE driving licence, passport and vehicle registration form.

Most insurance agencies now let you request a quote online, and there's a multitude of choice out there from local companies such as AWNIC (awnic.com) to international favourites, AXA (axa-gulf.com), RSA (rsadirect.ae) and Zurich (zurich.ae). If you're driving to Oman you will need additional cover, which can be part of your annual insurance or purchased ad hoc. Also see the UAE's online car insurance comparison websites, which will save you time and are a good starting point; try insurancemarket.ae or insureme.ae.

Fully comprehensive cover with personal accident insurance is highly advisable, and you are strongly advised to make sure the policy covers you for 'blood money'. For more adventurous 4WD drivers, insurance for off-roading accidents is also recommended.

To Oman & Back

It is wise to check whether your insurance covers you for Oman as you may find yourself driving through small Oman enclaves when exploring the UAE (especially if you are off road, near Hatta, through Wadi Bih and in Dibba). Insurance for visit to Oman can be arranged in a short-term basis, usually for no extra cost.

Registering A Vehicle

All cars must be registered annually with the Dubai Police department; if you're buying new, then the dealer should do this for you. All cars over three years old must also have an annual vehicle inspection test, which is part of the registration process.

Vehicle registration, vehicle testing and the renewal of annual car insurance generally take place at the same time. To start the process, first check you have no outstanding traffic offence and fines against your car at dubaipolice.gov.ae as registration renewal can't be completed until they are cleared. Then, renew your insurance as you will be asked to show a valid 13 months certificate. With this done, take your vehicle to a Vehicle Licensing Department-approved service centre.

Pay the Dhs.120 test fee, wait for around 20-30 minutes for the test, and hopefully it should pass and you'll receive a test certificate. If your vehicle fails the inspection, have it repaired and retested within 30 days for no additional fee. Some insurance companies offer to collect your vehicle and handle the test and registration for you – often within a couple of hours.

Once passed and with test certificate in hand, go to a registration office and submit your insurance certificate, current registration card (or that of the previous owner if you are transferring ownership), UAE driving licence and Resident ID, plus the Dhs.100 fee. You'll receive a new registration card plus a new sticker for your vehicle's rear plate. Now you're all legal to drive the vehicle for another year.

You have one month's grace for renewal of your car registration, hence the 13 month insurance policy. This keeps you legal if it's inconvenient to get the car registration renewed at the specified time. After that month though, you will incur fines of Dhs.10 for each month you delay. If renewal hasn't happened for over a year, the charge for re-registration is Dhs.325.

Both EPPCO Tasjeel and Emarat Shamil offer VIP pick-up and drop-off registration services for an extra charge, usually around Dhs.200. Call 800 4258 to make an appointment with Tasjeel or 800 4559 for Shamil. The RTA also recently launched a service enabling owners to carry out vehicle registration online; to sign up to the service, visit rta.ae. Usually a dealer will take care of registering a new car for you.

Vehicle Repairs

By law, no vehicle can be accepted for major 'collision' repairs without an accident report from the Traffic Police, although very minor dents can be repaired without one. Your insurance company will usually have an agreement with a particular garage to which they will refer you. The garage will carry out the repair work and the insurance company will settle the claim. Generally, there is Dhs.500 deductible for all claims, but check your policy details.

If you purchase a new vehicle your insurance should cover you for 'agency repairs', that is, repairs at the workshop of the dealer selling the car, although this is not a guarantee and you may have to pay a

You wouldn't buy a car that doesn't suit you,

so why do it with your car insurance?

With AXA, choose your covers and pay less.

Call 800 4845 or visit www.axa-gulf.com

2013 MENA INSURANCE AWARDS WINNER
Personal Line Insurer & Insurer of the Year

#1 GLOBAL INSURANCE BRAND 2013

AXA / رؤية جديدة / للتأمين
redefining / insurance

AXA Insurance (Gulf) B.S.C (c). Registered in the Insurance Companies Register - Certificate No. (69) dated 22/01/ 2002. Subject to the provisions of Federal Law No. (6) of 2007 concerning the establishment of Insurance Authority and Organization of its work. Agents: The Kanoo Group. Terms and conditions apply.

LIVING IN DUBAI
GETTING AROUND

premium. It's worth it though as your car's warranty (two to three years) may become invalid if you have non-agency repairs done on it. Even if you buy a fairly new second-hand car (less than three years old) it may be beneficial to opt for agency repairs in order to protect the value of the car.

Besides accidents and bumps, you may also have to deal with the usual running repairs associated with any car. Common problems in this part of the world can include the air-conditioning malfunctioning, batteries suddenly giving up and tyres blowing out. With the air-con it may just be a case of having the system topped up, which is a fairly straightforward procedure. Car batteries don't tend to last too long in the hot conditions, and you may not get much warning (one day your car just won't start), so it's always handy to keep a set of jump leads in the boot.

If you do manage to get your car started then it's worth taking a trip to Satwa; before you know it, your car will be surrounded by people offering to fix anything. Haggle hard and you can get a bargain for simple repairs and spares – including a new battery.

When buying a used vehicle, many shoppers like to see a history of agency maintenance, especially for relatively new cars. It may seem ridiculous to have your oil changed at the dealership every 5,000km, but it often pays in the long run when selling your car.

4x4 Garage Nr Oasis Centre, Al Qouz 3, 04 323 2100, *4x4motors.com*
Al Saeedi Automotive Trading Nr Civil Defence, Dubai Investment Park 1, 04 889 5355, *alsaeedi.com*
Al Wataniya Workshop Third Interchange, Al Qouz Ind. 1, 04 340 8546, *aww.ae*
Bosch Service Centre Nr RAK Bank, Al Qouz 3, 04 338 6000, *cmeuae.ae*
Central Motors & Equipment Shk Zayed Rd, Al Qouz 3, 04 338 6000, *cmeuae.ae*
House Of Cars *> p.103* Shk Zayed Rd, Al Qouz Ind 1, 04 339 3466, *houseofcarsgroup.com*
Icon Auto Garage 8th Street, Al Qouz 3, 04 338 2744, *icon-auto.com*
Max Garage Umm Suqeim Rd, Al Qouz Ind. 3, 04 340 8200, *maxgaragedubai.com*
Octane Al Qouz Ind. 1, 04 341 4511

Cycling

The RTA has often talked about the benefits of cycling in the city's most congested districts, and it is working to promote this form of transportation with its 850km Dubai Bicycle Master Plan. You cannot cycle on Dubai's highways and even riding within city neighbourhoods can be dangerous. Also, summer temperatures can reach 45°C, which makes riding to work a very sweaty option. There are, however, a number of places where you can cycle safely for pleasure (See Activities and below). If you do decide to take to two wheels, you are required to wear a helmet and a high visibility jacket, or you could face a fine of Dhs.500.

The RTA has completed various cycling tracks in neighbourhoods across the emirate. There is a 23km-long track along Jumeirah Street, 1.4km track along Street No 7 which links Jumeirah Street with Al Mankhool Street, and a 1.6km track at the Mall of the Emirates station. Also included in the project is the 67km track spanning Seih Assalam Road and Al Qudra Road as well as the 11km track at the centre of Bur Dubai covering Al Fuhaidi, Al Falah, Al Ghubaiba and Al Hisn Roads.

Future plans include tracks in Al Barsha, Al Khawaneej, Al Warqa, Al Qouz 3, Al Sufouh Street, Al Mamzar Park, Mushrif Park, and Hor Al Anz East.

Jumeirah Corniche

Joggers and cyclists will have a new outdoor area to enjoy once the Jumeirah Corniche is built at the end of 2014. Linking six residential areas, the 14km long zone will incorporate jogging and cycling tracks all the way from Dubai Marine Beach Resort down to the Burj Al Arab hotel.

Bike-sharing

For the cooler months, there are now public bike-sharing schemes available. In Downtown Dubai, the Emaar-sponsored bikes are available at docking stations in Mohammed Bin Rashid Boulevard, The Dubai Mall/Burj Khalifa metro station, Emaar Square, Burj Park, Burj Plaza, and next to The Dubai Mall. On the Palm Jumeirah, three are six locations: the Park, the Fairmont, the Shoreline side and three on the outer crescent at Atlantis, Zabeel Saray and Anantara.

You first need to register online at bykystations. com and then you can use your mobile phone to retrieve your registration details once you arrive at a bike station. Bikes can be rented for any time from 30 minutes to 24 hours. The bikes are also available in Marsa Dubai from Marina Walk, Marina Mall and Dubai Marina Yacht Club.

Walking

Cities in the UAE are generally very car-oriented and not designed to encourage walking. Additionally, searing summer temperatures are not conducive to spending any length of time outdoors – within minutes you'll be sweating buckets.

The winter months, however, make walking a pleasant way to get around and people can be found strolling through the streets, especially in the

GREENSHIELD INSURANCE

GREENSHIELD INSURANCE BROKERS LLC

COMMERCIAL LINES
Business Interruption
Contractor's & Erection All Risk
Employee Fidelity
Engineering
General Accident/Disability
Home Contents
Machinery Breakdown
Marine Hull & Cargo
Motor
Property & Fire
Public Liability
Travel
Workmen's Compensation

MEDICAL INSURANCE
Family Medical Plans
Group Medical Plans
Individual Medical Plans

SPECIALIST LINES
Aviation
Bankers Blanket Bond
Credit Insurance
Directors & Officers Liability
Events & Conferences
Film Production & Media
Fine Art & Antiques
Jewellers Block
Kidnap & Ransom
Medical Malpractice
Pleasure Crafts (Yachts)
Professoinal Indemnity
War, Sabotage & Terrorism

LIFE INSURANCE
Group Life Insurance Plans
Investment Linked Insurance Plans
Keyman Insurance
Term Life Insurance Plans

15th Floor, 1503 Emaar Boulevard Plaza Tower 1, P.O. Box 43656, Dubai, UAE
Tel: +971 4 388 2200 I Fax: +971 4 388 2202 I Toll Free: 800(GIB)442
Email: contact@greenshield.ae (Ref: DXBE) I www.greenshield.ae

LIVING IN DUBAI
GETTING AROUND

evenings. Most streets are lined with pavements and there are pedestrian paths either side of the creek, along the seafront in Deira and Jumeira, at The Walk at JBR, and around Marsa Dubai, as well as in the city's parks.

Despite the pavements, it's pretty common to end up with sandy shoes as many car parking spaces are on dusty vacant lots, so if you're off to an important business meeting, take a cloth to clean your shoes. There are also plans underway to build an extra 17 footbridges by 2016, at key locations including Emirates Towers and Al Khail Road. Police are cracking down on jaywalking, and you can be fined Dhs.200 for crossing the road in an undesignated area, so always use the pedestrian crossings available.

Creek Park
Nr Al Garhoud Bridge Umm Hurair 2 **04 336 7633**
dm.gov.ae
Map **2 L7** Metro **Dubai Healthcare City**
It may be in the heart of the city but Creek Park is a welcome slice of green with expansive gardens, fishing piers, jogging tracks, barbecue sites, children's play areas, restaurants and kiosks. Rest your legs and take the cable car that runs the 2.3km length of the park. Alternatively, four-wheel cycles can be hired from Gate 2 for Dhs.20 per hour. Admission costs Dhs.5.

Down By The Creek
Al Souk Al Kabeer
From the embassy area, stroll along the creek to take photos of the much-loved NBD building opposite. Explore Al Fahidi Historical Neighbourhood, where hidden alleyways, secret shops and tiny cafes abound. From here, walk towards the Majlis Gallery, stopping for a much needed juice at XVA Gallery. Continue past the Dubai Museum, through the textile souk and down towards the creek. Take an abra across the creek and you will find yourself at the entrance to the spice souk. You can then wander through the packed streets of Deira towards the gold souk. Fridays are the quietest, as are the early afternoons when stores often close for a break.

Downtown Dubai
Nr The Dubai Mall Downtown Dubai, Burj Khalifa
mydowntowndubai.com
Map **2 F6** Metro **Burj Khalifa/Dubai Mall**
Wander along wide promenades, linger by the lake or get lost in the narrow passageways of the Old Town. This is one of Dubai's trendiest residential communities and was designed for getting around on foot. With cafes, restaurants and coffee shops at every turn, there are plenty of pit-stop possibilities as well as interesting streets to explore. There's also a public bike-sharing scheme available in the area.

The Els Club
Shk Mohammed Bin Zayed Rd Sports City,
Al Hebiah 4 **04 425 1010**
elsclubdubai.com
Map **1 L11**
Inspired by links golf, the beautiful Ernie Els Club golf course has an excellent 10km pedestrian path around its exterior. The Els Club golf course stretches almost 7,000 metres and incorporates natural dunes and plants native to the UAE.

Jumeira Open Beach Running Track
Jumeira 1
Map **2 H4**
An early morning walk on the beach got easier (and less sandy) when the 1.5km track on Jumeira Open Beach opened. With running and cycling lanes, distance markers and regular maintenance, it offers a fun and free way to get active while enjoying some people watching and sunshine. The track starts near Dubai Marine Resort and is open 24 hours.

Jumeirah Beach Residence
Marsa Dubai **04 390 0094**
jumeirahbeachresidences.com
Map **1 K4** Metro **Dubai Marina**
An evening stroll could quickly turn into a shopping spree here along the shorefront development which stretches for 1.7km but there are fountains, grassy areas and benches, plus many eateries. Come evening, this is where people bring their expensive, diamond-encrusted (we're not kidding) cars, to sit in a slow-moving traffic jam and rev their engines in the hope of impressing those strolling by.

Mirdif
Tripoli St Mirdif
Map **2 Q13** Metro **Rashidiya**
Mirdif residential area has two community parks with sprung walking tracks and swings for the kids. Uptown Mirdiff shopping centre also makes for a nice outdoor stroll.

Safa Park
Off Shk Zayed Rd Al Wasl **04 349 2111**
dm.gov.ae
Map **2 D5** Metro **Business Bay**
This huge park is a great place to exercise and escape the hustle and bustle of the city, or simply to enjoy the boating lake, a multitude of play areas, the maze or The Archive library and cafe. Entry costs Dhs.3 (free for children under three years old). There's a great 3km spongy running track around the park's perimeter, not to mention the countless paths that criss-cross the grassy space. On Friday mornings, check out the Ripe Foodie Market. Tuesday is ladies' day, and there is also a permanent ladies' garden within the park.

LIVING IN DUBAI
GETTING AROUND

Mall Walkers
If outdoor activities aren't your thing, or if it's so hot you could fry an egg on the pavement, then combine window shopping at Mall of the Emirates with a brisk walk. To make sure you don't get distracted, the Mall Walkers group will guide you along. Register at the customer service desk on the ground floor near parking area A and turn up at Gate 1 on the ground floor at 8am daily (in suitable shoes).

Public Transport
In an effort to ease the city's congestion problems, the government's Roads & Transport Authority (rta.ae) has made a serious commitment to improving public transport. The Metro is the centrepiece of its efforts and, since its opening in September 2009, has helped to reduce the overall number of daily drivers. Dubai's bus system has also seen major improvements over the past few years with the introduction of air-conditioned bus stops, new buses and an increase in routes. The RTA's fleet of water buses offers commuters and travellers an expanding network of routes along Dubai's waterways; alternatively, there is a more costly water taxi service – operating from Deira across to Jabal Ali.

Nol Card
Nol cards are used to pay for public transport and street car parking. They are rechargeable and can be used on the metro, bus, and water buses, with fares calculated depending on how many zones your journey takes you through. Single journeys start at Dhs.1.80 for up to 3km, rising to Dhs.5.80 for travel across two or more zones. The red Nol card is a paper ticket aimed at tourists. It can be charged for up to 10 journeys, but is only valid on one type of transport – bus, metro or water bus. The silver Nol card costs Dhs.20, including Dhs.14 credit. It can be recharged up to Dhs.500 and can be used across all forms of transport and for street parking. The gold Nol card is identical to the silver, except that holders are charged first-class prices (usually double the standard fare) and can travel in the Gold Class cabins on the metro. There are daily and monthly Nol passes available. A daily unlimited travel pass costs Dhs.14, while the monthly passes range from Dhs.100 to Dhs.270. Student and senior discounts are available on most ticket types. Nol cards can be purchased and topped up at metro and bus stations and at selected supermarkets including Carrefour and Spinneys. Information on the Nol fare structure and a map of the different zones can be found at nol.ae.

As from September 2013, smartphone users can swipe in and out at metro stations, public bus and water bus stations if they have a NFC (Near Field Communication) enabled phone. You can buy NFC SIM cards from Etisalat and du business centres. Transport is free for disabled people on Dubai's metro and buses.

Boat
Crossing Dubai Creek by abra is a common mode of transport for many people. The fare for a single journey across the creek is Dhs.1, and the abras run from 5am to midnight. There are four abra stations, two on the Deira side near the souks and two on the Bur Dubai side near the Ruler's Court. The RTA manages a fleet of air-conditioned water buses costing Dhs.4 per round trip. There are two routes across the creek and four stations. Route 2 between Al Sabkha Station and Dubai Old Souk Station operates 24 hours a day. A route opened in February 2013 between the Festival City Station and Ras Al Khor Wildlife Sanctuary.

Abra Ka Dabra
An abra is a wooden, single engine boat used to carry passengers across the creek. Abras have long been the primary method of crossing the creek. Each one can carry around 20 seated passengers. They tend to depart as soon as all of their seats have been filled.

There is also the Dubai ferry service – two excellent value sightseeing trips aimed at tourists. The first Dubai ferry makes the round trip from Al Ghubaiba station in Bur Dubai to Burj Al Arab and back and the second goes from Dubai Marina Mall and turns around

askexplorer.com 109

LIVING IN DUBAI
GETTING AROUND

near Atlantis The Palm. Each journey lasts around an hour and cost Dhs.50 for silver class and Dhs.75 for gold class, with four trips per day.

The RTA launched the first phase of a new water taxi project in mid-2010. An initial five luxury 10-seater boats shuttle passengers between 26 stops, stretching from JA Jebel Ali Golf Resort to Festival City. Fares range from Dhs.50 to travel one stop, up to a hefty Dhs.570 to travel the whole route. Water taxis are available between 10am and 10pm and some routes are available for families to book at a reduced price.

Tourists can also book a water taxi for an hour for Dhs.400; the number to call is 800 9090. For information about the stops that are open see rta.ae. The RTA has also announced future marine transport stations for the Palm Jumeirah and Dubai Marina – check the RTA website for up-to-date information.

Bus
There are currently around 88 bus routes servicing the main residential and commercial areas of Dubai. While all of the buses and most of the bus shelters are air conditioned and modern, they can be rather crowded during rush hour. Many of the buses from Dubai to Abu Dhabi, Sharjah and Fujairah also have free wi-fi – although there is talk of charging for the wi-fi in the future. There are also on-board catering services on the Bur Dubai to Abu Dhabi bus.

The main bus stations are near the Gold Souk in Deira and on Al Ghubaiba Road in Bur Dubai. Buses run at regular intervals, starting between 5am and 6am and running until midnight or so, and a handful of Nightliner buses operate from 11.30pm till 6am. The front three rows of seats are reserved for women and children only. Cash is not accepted so you need to purchase a Nol card before boarding. For a complete list of the RTA's inter-emirate routes, see rta.ae.

Metro
Dubai's driverless metro currently has two lines. The Red Line, which runs from Rashidiyah to Dubai International Airport, and down Sheikh Zayed Road – passing the financial district, Downtown, Al Barsha and Marsa Dubai – before terminating at Jabal Ali. The Green Line runs from Al Qusais on the Sharjah border to Jaddaf. Most of the stations along the existing lines are now open – you can check dubaimetro.eu for updates. Blue, Gold and Purple Lines are planned to be running by 2030 and the current Red and Green Lines will be further expanded.

Trains run from 5.50am to midnight Saturday to Wednesday; 5.50am to 1am on Thursdays; and 1pm to 1am on Fridays. The frequency is every 3.45 minutes during peak times, and every seven minutes during off-peak hours. Each train has a section for women and children only, and a first or Gold Class cabin. The fare structure operates as a pay-as-you-go system, in which you scan your pre-paid Nol card in and out of stations.

Commuters can also take advantage of du wi-fi at stations and on the trains themselves. Access cards are available for Dhs.20 per hour, or you can pay via credit card at a rate of Dhs.10 per hour.

There is a feeder bus system to transport passengers from stations to local destinations. The buses are free if boarded within 30 minutes of exiting the metro. Each station also has a taxi rank outside the exit to help you reach destinations that aren't accessible by bus.

Monorail
A monorail runs the length of Palm Jumeirah from the Gateway Towers station on the mainland to the Atlantis hotel. Trains run daily from 10am to 10pm and cost Dhs.15 for a single fare or Dhs.25 for a return. Work has also begun on the Al Sufouh Tram which is being designed as a key link for the Dubai Metro and the Palm Monorail. The tram will run along Al Sufouh Road, linking Mall of the Emirates, Marsa Dubai, and Jumeirah Lakes Towers. Construction is underway and the tram is due for completion at the end of 2014.

Plan Your Trip
The best way to work out your public transport options is to use the Roads & Transport Authority's (RTA) online journey planner (wojhati.rta.ae). For further assistance, call the RTA on 800 9090.

Dubai Metro

110 | Dubai Explorer

LIVING IN DUBAI
GETTING AROUND

Taxi
If you don't have a car, taxis are still the most common way of getting around. There are nearly 7,000 metered taxis in Dubai with a fixed fare structure. The cars are beige with different coloured roofs. A fleet of 'ladies taxis' with pink roofs have female drivers and are meant for women or family groups only; In-Safe Hands caters to women, children, students, families and people with special needs; and there is a luxury VIP taxi fleet.

Another World Record
In February 2012, Dubai Metro entered the Guinness World Records Book as the longest driverless metro network in the world, spanning 74.69km.

Taxis can be flagged down by the side of the road or you can call 04 208 0808. If you make a booking, you will pay a slightly higher starting fare. The Dubai Taxi automated phone system stores your address after the first time you call. Each subsequent time you ring from that number, listen to the prompts, hit 1, and a taxi will be dispatched automatically, (or hit 2, then enter a later time using the phone's keypad). Unfortunately, the dispatch centre never gives waiting times, so the taxi could arrive in five minutes or 30. Waits are longer at weekends.

The minimum taxi fare is Dhs.10, and the pick-up fare ranges from Dhs.3 to Dhs.7, depending on the time of day, and whether or not you ordered by phone. The starting fare inside the airport area is Dhs.20. Specialist services charge higher rates. Taxis are no longer exempt from Salik tolls, and crossing the border into Sharjah adds another Dhs.20 to the fare. The rate for stoppage or waiting is 50 fils per minute, so don't be surprised when the meter keeps running in standstill traffic. Taxis can be hired for six hours for Dhs.500 or for 12 hours for Dhs.800.

Finding a taxi in congested areas can be difficult, and in their frustration, many people are using illegal cabs. Be warned though that unlicensed taxis haven't had to meet the same vehicle safety standards that legal cabs do. As these cabs are difficult to trace, there have also been cases where drivers have either been the victim of crimes or have perpetrated them.

The Dubai Taxi fleet also now includes several hybrid taxis – Toyota Camrys – that consume a third less fuel and produce a third less carbon. The fleet also has a few a few specially modified taxis for people with wheelchairs travelling from the airport and around town.

The Hala Taxi fleet is the newest fleet in Dubai. You can't flag them down as they only respond to telephone or online bookings. The cars are black or white, and equipped with wi-fi, Nol and NFC payment systems (for smartphones).

Chauffeur Service
A new app called Uber enables you to summon a chauffeur through your smartphone. Download and input your credit card details and a photo. When you call, the driver can see your location, and, you can track his progress through your phone. There's no need to call to give directions. The app shows your driver's name, type of car, estimated time of arrival and a rating. Once in the car, you will be offered water and a choice of music. The service costs almost double that of a taxi, but for pick-ups in remote or difficult to find areas, it makes sense.

Air Travel
Currently, about 107 airlines take advantage of Dubai's open skies policy, operating to and from over 220 destinations. Dubai International Airport's three terminals are a 15 to 30 minute taxi ride apart, depending on the traffic, and there's also a shuttle bus. All terminals offer car rental, hotel reservations and exchange services. Most of the better-known airlines use Terminal 1, while Terminal 2 is used primarily by flydubai and airlines serving former Soviet countries and central Asia. Terminal 3, which opened in 2008, is the newest and most luxurious of the three and exclusively dedicated to Emirates Airlines. By comparison, Terminal 2 has limited facilities and, invariably, extensive queues, while both Terminal 1 and Terminal 3 have a vast selection of drinking and dining venues, plus a large duty free shopping section. For up-to-date flight information from Dubai International Airport, call 04 216 6666. In addition, Dubai International Airport's Concourse D project is due to open in early 2015.

All three terminals have both short and long-term parking facilities, as well as busy taxi ranks. There are metro stations at both Terminal 1 and Terminal 3 that any traveller can access. The stations are part of the Red Line, which runs throughout Deira, under the creek and along Sheikh Zayed Road all the way to Jabal Ali. Keep in mind that luggage larger than a large holdall or standard case is not permitted on the metro. Airport buses operate to and from the airport. Call 800 9090 or visit rta.ae.

Dubai World Central
A second airport, Dubai World Central – Al Maktoum International opened in 2011 for cargo flights. The airport, which is located at the Jabal Ali end of town, will eventually be the world's largest, with five runways handling passenger flights too. Phase 2 of the airport opened for passenger traffic in October 2013, prior to hosting the Dubai Air Show in December 2013. Budget airline Wizz Air was the first to take off from the airport, flying to various European

askexplorer.com

LIVING IN DUBAI
GETTING AROUND

destinations, with new carriers due to be added throughout 2014.

Airlines

There's an ever-increasing choice of budget airlines based in the UAE including Rotana Jet, flydubai and Air Arabia, each offering no-frills, cheap flights to a wide variety of international destinations. flydubai now offers business class seats that won't break the bank.

Other airlines include Etihad operating out of Abu Dhabi, low-cost carriers Air Arabia in Sharjah and flydubai in Dubai, and RAK Airways. Air Arabia offers a city terminal check-in at Lamcy Plaza. Rotana Jet, the UAE's first domestic airline, connects Abu Dhabi with Al Ain, Fujairah and Sir Bani Yas Island for a reasonable fee.

Abu Dhabi airport is a 90 minute drive from Dubai, and Sharjah airport is 45 minutes away. Etihad also runs its own private bus service, which is free for those with a boarding pass and makes the journey between Abu Dhabi International Airport and Dubai.

Air Arabia 06 558 0000, *airarabia.com*
Air France 800 23 823, *airfrance.ae*
Air India 04 227 6787, *airindia.com*
Air Mauritius 04 221 4455, *airmauritius.com*
Air Seychelles 04 286 8008, *airseychelles.com*
American Airlines 04 316 6116, *aa.com*
Austrian Airlines 04 211 2538, *austrian.com*
Bahrain Air 04 239 9921, *enbahrainair.net*
British Airways 800 0441 3322, *britishairways.com*
Cathay Pacific 04 204 2888, *cathaypacific.com*
China Airlines 04 286 8008, *china-airlines.com*
Cyprus Airways 04 221 4455, *cyprusair.com*
Delta Air Lines 04 397 0118, *delta.com*
Emirates 600 55 5555, *emirates.com*
Etihad Airways 04 407 2200, *etihad.com*
flydubai 04 231 1000, *flydubai.com*
Gulf Air 04 271 6207, *gulfair.com*
IranAir 04 224 0200, *iranair.com*
Japan Airlines 04 217 7501, *jal.com*
Jazeera Airways 04 224 4464, *jazeeraairways.com*
KLM Royal Dutch Airlines 800 556, *klm.com*
Kuwait Airways 04 228 5896
Lufthansa 04 373 9100, *lufthansa.com*
Malaysia Airlines 04 325 4411, *malaysiaairlines.com*
Middle East Airlines 04 223 7080, *mea.com.lb*
Oman Air 04 351 8080, *omanair.com*
Qantas 04 316 6652, *qantas.com*
Qatar Airways 04 231 9921, *qatarairways.com*
RAK Airways 04 294 5666 *rakairways.com*
Rotana Jet 02 444 3366, *rotanajet.com*
Royal Air Maroc 04 286 9499, *royalairmaroc.com*
Royal Brunei Airlines 04 334 4884, *flyroyalrunei.com*
Royal Jet 02 505 5177, *royaljetgroup.com*
Royal Jordanian 04 294 4288, *rj.com*
Saudi Arabian Airlines 04 229 6227, *saudiairlines.com*
Singapore Airlines 04 316 6888, *singaporeair.com*
South African Airways 04 397 0766, *flysaa.com*
SpiceJet 04 396 5186, *spicejet.com*
SriLankan Airlines 04 316 6711, *srilankan.aero*
Swiss International Air Lines 04 381 6100, *swiss.com*
Thai Airways 04 268 1701, *thaiair.com*
Tunisair 04 221 1176, *tunisair.com*
Turkish Airlines 04 444 0999, *turkishairlines.com*
United Airlines 800 0441 5492, *united.com*
Virgin Atlantic 04 406 0600, *virgin-atlantic.com*

e-Gate

Once you have your residence visa you can apply for a smart card to use at the airport e-Gates. Simply swipe the smart card and pass through the gates. Applications for a card are processed within minutes at Dubai International Airport, in the dnata buildings (one on Sheikh Zayed Road and one in Deira near Deira City Centre), or the GDRFA office on Sheikh Khalifa bin Zayed Road. You'll need your passport, with residence visa, and you will be fingerprinted and photographed. The e-Gate card costs Dhs.200 and is valid for two years; however, you can now activate the e-Gate service on your Resident ID and pay just Dhs.150 for two years. Payment can be made by cash or credit card.

For further information, contact 04 316 6966 or see dubai.ae. Better still, you can now check in and out through passport control without having to apply for an e-Gate card. All holders of modern passports with barcodes, including children above the age of seven, can use the new e-Gate service, which has been rolled out across Dubai International Airport.

The Future

The UAE has big expansion plans for its public transport network. Etihad Rail is working on installing a rail network linking the Emirates, and sections of the track are already in place and being utilised by freight trains. The overall plan will see a high-speed passenger rail connection linking Dubai and Abu Dhabi by 2017. Initially this will be aimed at freight transport, but a passenger service between Abu Dhabi and Dubai is likely by 2018. Etihad Rail also plans to extend train lines into other GCC countries and is even looking at expanding its reach as far as Turkey. Once the planned Blue, Gold and Purple metro lines are added to the network by 2030, it could eventually cover 421km with 197 stations – though the size of the expansion will be linked to the official population size. The plan will also see the metro connecting to the Etihad rail network across the Gulf countries. The Al Sufouh Dubai Tram System is another RTA public transport initiative; it will run between Mall of the Emirates and Dubai Marina Mall and is due to open in November 2014.

explorer

there's more to life...

THE REGION'S BEST-SELLING MAPS

askexplorer.com/shop

askexplorer

DIFC – The Gate

FINANCE

Money is a big reason for expats to be in Dubai, so it makes sense to be smart with it when those first tax-free pay cheques come in. From setting up a bank account to credit cards and debt, this chapter will give you the information you need to know in order to watch those dirhams grow.

Main Banks

To open an account in most banks, you will need a residence visa or to have your residence visa application underway. To apply, you will need to submit your original passport, copies of your passport (personal details and visa pages) and an NOC from your sponsor. Some banks set a minimum account limit – this can be anything from Dhs.2,000 for a deposit account and as much as Dhs.10,000 for a current account.

This means at some point during each month your account balance must be over the minimum limit; but if your wages are paid into this account then for most expats that shouldn't be a problem.

There are plenty of ATMs (cash points) available in Dubai, and most cards are compatible with the Central Bank network, though you may pay a small fee if you have to use another bank's ATM. Even if you use your bank card from your home country, you shouldn't have too many issues using an ATM, although the exchange rate given may not always be favourable.

Banks are open from 8am to 1.30pm, Saturday to Wednesday, and 8am to noon on Thursday. Some branches, especially in the malls, stay open until later, even as late as 10pm. All banks are closed on Fridays.

There are also numerous money exchanges; try Al Fardan Exchange (600 522 265, alfardanexchange.com) if you want to buy or sell currency.

LIVING IN DUBAI
FINANCE

Banks that operate internationally rarely have connections with their counterparts in other parts of the world, so you won't be able to manage accounts held in other countries through your Dubai account.

ABN AMRO Bank DIFC, Zaa'beel 2, 04 440 9400, *abnamroprivatebanking.com*
Barclays Nr Dubai Mall, Downtown Dubai, Burj Khalifa, 04 438 1038, *barclays.ae*
Citibank Nr BurJuman Centre, Al Mankhool, 04 507 4104, *citi.com*
Commercial Bank Of Dubai Al Ittihad Rd, Port Saeed, 04 211 2700, *cbd.ae*
Dubai Bank Sunshine Bldg, Al Garhoud, 04 282 9778, *dubaibank.ae*
Dubai Islamic Bank MoE, Al Barsha 1, 04 340 1823, *dib.ae*
Emirates NBD Jabal Ali 1, 04 60054 0000, *emiratesnbd.com*
First Gulf Bank Al Yamamah Tower, Al Khabaisi, 04 294 1234, *fgb.ae*
HSBC Bank Middle East Al Wasl Rd, Al Souk Al Kabeer, 600 554 722, *hsbc.ae*
Mashreq Bank MoE, Al Barsha 1, 04 511 8601, *mashreqbank.com*
RAK Bank Nr Lamcy Plaza, Al Qouz 3, 04 213 0000, *rakbank.ae*
Standard Chartered Bank – Middle East Al Fardan Bldg, Al Mankhool, 600 522 288, *standardchartered.ae*
Union National Bank Omeir Bin Katab Rd, Al Mankhool, 600 566 665, *unb.co.ae*

Mobile Banking

Most banks now offer banking by SMS. You can access your account balance, see your last five transactions, or request a chequebook, simply by sending a text. You'll also get SMS messages to your phone whenever money is paid in or leaves your account.

Online Banking

Banks in the UAE offer online facilities where you can send a transfer, set daily withdrawal limits, check your balance and apply for a loan. It's easy to set up and usually works in conjunction with your mobile phone, in that any security codes required for online transactions will be sent to your mobile for you to then input online.

Credit Cards

It's quite easy to get a credit card and if you're eligible your bank will probably call you to offer you a Visa or MasterCard. For American Express visit americanexpress.ae or call 800 4013. Eligibility usually depends on a minimum salary, a salary certificate detailing your earnings (provided by your employer) and a copy of your passport with your residence visa and work permit. Once you have your card you'll find it's accepted at most shops, hotels and restaurants – though smaller retailers may not always have the facility for credit card payments, or they may charge 5% for processing, even though that is a contravention of the card company rules. However, if you are paying cash you may get a discount! Dubai is relatively safe but the same security measures apply regarding credit cards as anywhere: report lost or stolen cards to your bank immediately, and change your PIN frequently. There will be a limit to the amount of cash that you can withdraw in one day, but you should be able to change this either in your online settings or by contacting your bank.

Pre-paid Cards

Pre-paid cards are available from a number of national banks. These are great for under 18s, as they can shop safely online, can stop the card if it's lost which means they don't lose the money, and parents can track online what they've been spending money on. Using pre-paid cards can mean two for one deals in some eateries can be taken advantage of too.

Cheques

Previously post-dated cheques have mainly been used to secure finances and pay rent, with a year's rent being 'paid' up front in several cheques. The country's first direct debit system came into force in October 2013, with the aim of reducing the need for post-dated cheques in order to guarantee loans.

Bear in mind that if you do write a post-dated cheque, it is a criminal offence if the cheque bounces. More than four bounced cheques in one year will get you blacklisted by the UAE Central Bank, and your account may be closed. Remember too that a cheque cannot be cancelled unless it is lost or stolen, and so think ahead when writing post-dated cheques. In some cases you can be prosecuted, lose your visa or even face a few years in jail.

Financial Planning

Many expats are attracted to Dubai for the tax-free salary and the opportunity to put a something away for the future. However, Dubai's alluring lifestyle can quickly steer you away from your goal. It is often necessary for residents to get credit cards and bank loans to finance their life in Dubai and it is easy to

LIVING IN DUBAI
FINANCE

slip further into debt – you'll find there is little or no support if you do. It is important to plan your finances and arrange a safeguard in case your finances take a turn for the worse.

When choosing a financial planner in Dubai, you should ensure that they are licensed by the Central Bank of the UAE (centralbank.ae), so that you have some recourse in the event of a dispute. You should also consider the company's international presence – you'll still want the same access to advice and your investments if you return home. It may be better to use an independent company or advisor who is not tied to a specific bank, and will objectively offer you the full range of savings products on the market.

Before leaving your home country you should contact the tax authorities to ensure that you are complying with the financial laws there. Most countries will consider you not liable for income tax once you prove you're a UAE resident (a contract of employment is normally a good starting point). However, you may still have to fulfil certain criteria, so do some research before you come (if you are already here, check with your embassy). You may be liable for tax on any income you receive from back home (for example if you are renting out your property).

If you have a pension scheme in your home country, it may not be worth continuing your contributions once you come to Dubai, but rather to set up a tax-free, offshore savings plan. It is always advisable to speak to your financial adviser about such matters before you make any big move.

Financial Advice
There seems to be an overabundance of financial advisors in the city who may contact you over the phone and advertise their services. Most advisors won't ask for money initially; however, they may ask you for contact details of your friends and family members so that they can continue to spread the word.

Pensions
The UAE's first pension scheme for expatriates was launched by the NBAD Trust Company (Jersey) Limited – a wholly owned subsidiary of the National Bank of Abu Dhabi (NBAD). The Wealth Builder Plan is a corporate trust solution that allows employers to offer expat staff greater rewards through corporate savings – the first service of its kinds to be offered by a UAE bank.

The Wealth Builder Plan is underpinned by a range of investment fund options that employees can choose based on their risk appetite. The schemes are tailored for each client, and regular investments can be made solely by the company or by both employer and employee.

Dubai has several international banks

Financial Advisors
These companies are experienced in providing financial advice to expats.

6 Sigma Financial Consultancy Liberty House, DIFC, DIFC, Zaa'beel 2, 04 325 9159, *6sigmagrp.com*
Acuma Wealth Management 703 API World Tower, Al Souk Al Kabeer, 04 332 8582, *acuma.ae*
Ernst & Young Al Attar Business Tower, Trade Center 2, 04 332 4000, *ey.com*
Globaleye VIlla 801, Al Thanya St, Umm Suqeim 3, 04 404 3700, *globaleye.com*
Guardian Life Management Saba Tower 1, JLT, Al Thanyah 5, 04 436 2322, *guardianwealthmanagement.com*
Holborn Assets Al Shafar Tower, Al Thanyah 1, 04 457 3800, *holbornassets.com*
KPMG Emirates Towers, Trade Center 2, 04 403 0300, *kpmg.com*
Mondial (Dubai) Pinnacle Bldg, Al Barsha 1, 04 399 6601, *mondialdubai.com*
Nexus Insurance Emaar Square, Burj Khalifa, 04 323 1111, *nexusadvice.com*
PIC Middle East 414 Emarat Atrium Bldg, Al Wasl, 04 343 3470, *pic-uae.com*

Insurance Companies
Contact one of these companies for insurance advice.

Abu Dhabi National Takaful Company 04 210 8700, *takaful.ae*
Aetna Global Benefits (Middle East) 04 438 7500, *aetnainternational.com*

FIVE DECADES OF TRUST AND EXPERTISE

Worldwide Money Transfer

Foreign Currency Exchange

My Pay-Value Added Services

Travel EZ Visa Prepaid Cards

e-Money Payroll Services

travel ez
beyond the borders

WESTERN UNION
moving money for better

e money
life needs more...

AL FARDAN EXCHANGE
It's about service

alfardanuae   alfardanuae   Call US 600 522265   www.alfardanexchange.com

LIVING IN DUBAI
FINANCE

AFIA Insurance Brokerage Services 04 337 9987, *afia.ae*
Al Ain Ahlia Insurance Company 04 272 5500, *alaininsurance.com*
Al Khazna Insurance Company 04 217 3333, *alkhazna.com*
Alfred's Insurance Market 04 337 9987, *insurancemarket.ae*
Alliance Insurance 04 605 1111, *alliance-uae.com*
Allianz SE 04 702 6666, *allianz.com*
Arab Orient Insurance Company 04 253 1300, *insuranceuae.com*
AXA Insurance (Gulf) > *p.105* 04 324 3434, *axa-gulf.com*
Daman National Health Insurance Company 04 436 0222, *damanhealth.ae*
Emirates Insurance Company 04 294 2949, *eminsco.com*
Gargash Insurance 04 337 9800, *gargashinsurance.com*
Greenshield Insurance Broker > *p.107, 119* 04 388 2200, *greenshield.ae*
Lifecare International 04 331 8688, *lifecareinternational.com*
MedNet UAE 800 4882, *mednet-uae.com*
MetLife Alico 04 360 0555, *metlifealico.ae*
Nasco Karaoglan 04 352 3133, *nascodubai.com*
National General Insurance Co (NGI) 04 211 5800, *ngi.ae*
Neuron 04 399 6779, *neuron.ae*
Nexus 04 323 1111, *nexusadvice.com*
Oman Insurance Company 04 233 7777, *tameen.ae*
Qatar General Insurance & Reinsurance Co 04 268 8688, *qgirco.com*
Qatar Insurance Company 04 222 4045, *qatarinsurance.com*
RSA 800 772, *rsagroup.ae*
Zurich International Life 04 425 2300, *zurich.com*

Debt

Despite the city's reliance on credit, harsh penalties are dealt for late or missed payments. It can be expensive to initially set up here and you may need sizeable loans to purchase a car or cover rent – but if you suddenly lose your job there's no safety net to cover your expenses. However, banks do generally require that you have received six salary payments into your account before they will grant you a loan.

Unlike some countries, where you will receive several reminders for missed payments, if you are late paying for basic household bills such as electricity or water, your services may be disconnected without much warning. Missed payments on credit cards bills will often incur fines or restrictions to services. There are no bankruptcy laws in the UAE and so if you fall into difficulties you are fully liable for your debt. If your bank files a complaint, you could face a visa ban or jail.

Tax

The UAE levies no personal income taxes or withholding taxes. The only noticeable taxes you pay as an expat are a 5% municipality tax on rental accommodation, a 30% tax on alcohol bought at Dubai liquor stores and 50% tax on tobacco (although cigarettes are still comparatively cheap). A municipality tax is included in your DEWA bill, and if you don't pay this your utilities will be cut off. This has resulted in some complaints – the tax is meant to cover refuse collection, street lighting and community road networks, but people renting freehold properties also pay maintenance to cover these things. There is also a 10% municipality tax and a 10% service charge in hotel food and beverage outlets, but you'll find that these are usually incorporated into the displayed price.

Taxing Issues
You may need to register your residency in the UAE with the government in your home country to avoid paying income tax or capital gains tax. It's best to check with your consulate for exact details. British expats can visit the Inland Revenue's website at hmrc.gov.uk/international/abroad.htm for comprehensive advice on tax and National Insurance payments. If you still spend time working in your home country, check with an accountant to see if you are still liable to pay tax at home.

Offshore Accounts

An offshore account works in the same way as a conventional account, but with additional flexibility. Money can be moved where it will produce the best rewards, and cash accessed whenever you need it, in your desired currency. Offshore accounts allow for management through the internet and over the phone, in a range of currencies (commonly in US dollars, euros or pounds sterling). If you are travelling outside the UAE, make sure your account comes with 24 hour banking, internationally recognised debit cards, and the ability to write cheques in your preferred currency.

To open an account, there is usually a minimum balance of around $10,000. Do some thorough research before opening an account, and check the potential tax implications in your home country. It is important to seek independent financial advice, and not just the opinion of the bank offering you an account. To open your account, you may have to produce certain reports or documents from your chosen country. However, for those willing to do the research and undertake the admin, offshore banking can prove to be a lucrative investment.

Medical and Life Insurance from Greenshield

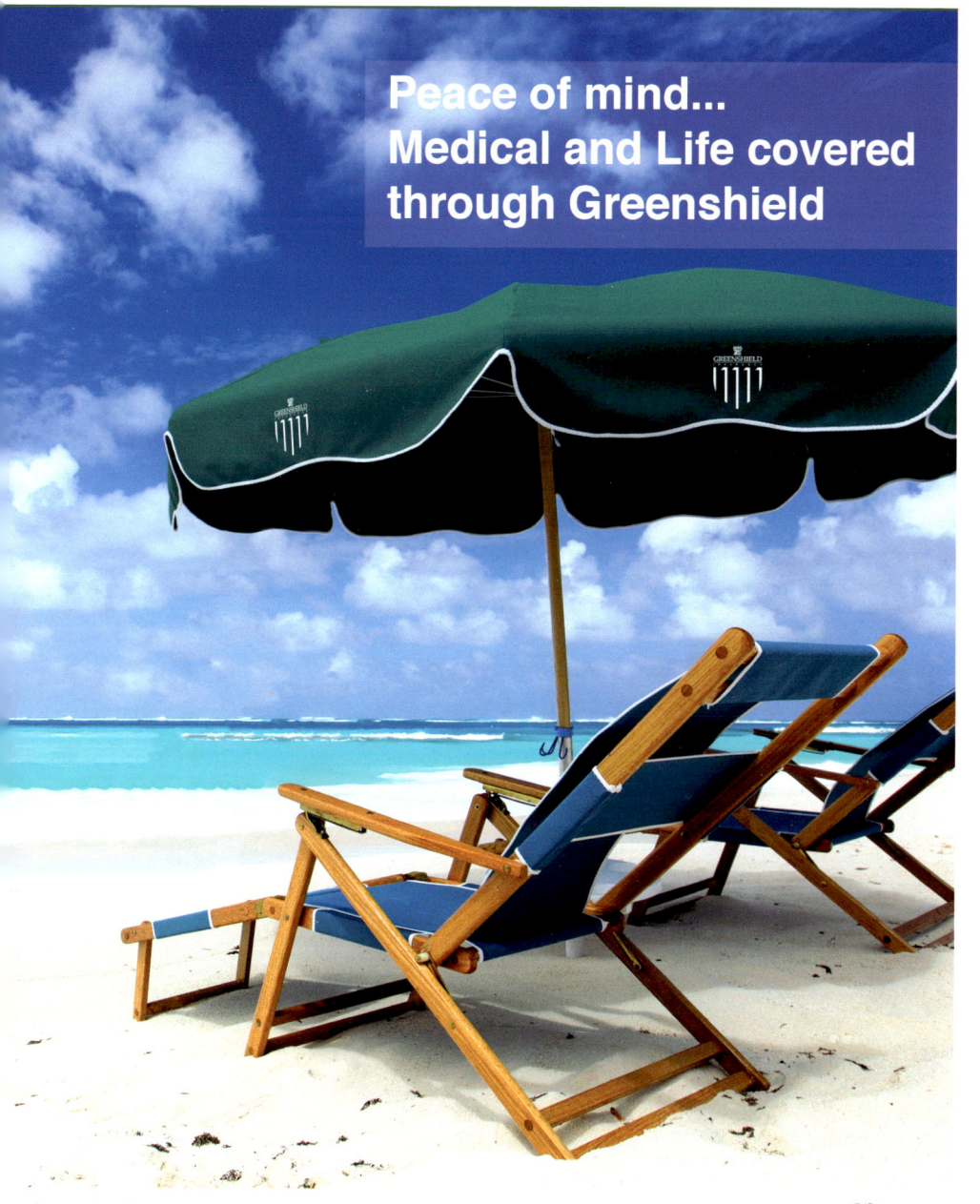

Peace of mind... Medical and Life covered through Greenshield

...ce in a while, life throws us a curve ball. While there's no way of protecting ourselves from the ...oreseen, we can plan ahead. With medical coverage options including local & international ...ns, inpatient & outpatient care, emergency evacuation/repatriation and optional dental & ...ternity benefits, your insurance can cover you when and under which circumstances you desire. ...eenshield Insurance removes the financial burden, so you can focus on life.

...a free consultation, contact Toll Free on 800 GIB (442) or +971 4 388 2200.
...ail: contact@greenshield.ae (Ref: DXBE) I www.greenshield.ae

GREENSHIELD

Life · Medical · Education · Travel · Motor · Savings · Property & Fire · Bankers Blanket Bond · Product Liability

Dubai Healthcare City

HEALTH

Both private and public healthcare services are available in the UAE. General standards are high, with English speaking staff and internationally trained medical staff in most facilities, the main difference being personal service and dorm style rooms rather than private hotel-style rooms (and food!).

Historically, an employer in Dubai can choose to provide access to healthcare for its employees: either the employer pays for a private medical insurance policy, or it pays the cost of obtaining a health card for each employee, which can be used to receive healthcare at any government hospital.

Under a new law introduced in January 2014 (Insurance System for Advancing Healthcare in Dubai – ISAHD), Dubai companies with 1,000 or more employees must cover their staff with private health insurance before the end of October 2014; smaller companies with 100-999 employees will have until the end of July 2015, and companies below 100 employees have until end of June 2016 to cover their employees. Health insurance packages, which must come from a government approved provider, cover all essential health services including emergency care, access to GPs, referral to specialists, tests and investigations, surgical procedures and maternity care.

The new legislation also states that employee's spouses and children must also have health cover – but this may be at the employee's own expense. It is also mandatory for sponsors to provide domestic workers – nannies and maids – with health insurance.

Healthcare in Dubai is managed by the Dubai Health Authority (DHA). As well as introducing compulsory health insurance in 2014, there are plans underway to expand the Rashid Hospital trauma centre, and introduce electronic medical records; all patients will be assigned a password and any doctor in Dubai – whether at a private or public hospital – will be able to access your medical records.

LIVING IN DUBAI
HEALTH

Government Healthcare

In Dubai, the Department of Health & Medical Services (dohms.gov.ae) runs Dubai, Rashid and Latifa hospitals. Dubai Hospital is renowned as one of the best medical centres in the Middle East, while Latifa is a specialised maternity and paediatric hospital. DOHMS also operates a number of outpatient clinics. Al Baraha Hospital is run by the Ministry of Health. The Iranian Hospital, while not a government hospital, provides healthcare subsidised by the Iranian Red Crescent Society. With the exception of emergency care, you will need a health card to access government health services.

Health Card

The Dubai Health Authority issues a health card, which entitles any UAE resident to receive healthcare at a government hospital or clinic. The card costs Dhs.500 and can be applied for at Rashid, Latifa or Dubai hospitals; you will need your residence visa, Resident ID, two passport photos and an application form typed in Arabic. You can also apply online at dha.gov.ae. Even if you already have access to private health insurance, it is perhaps sensible to have a health card as well, as not all policies will cover you for certain treatments and it may be cheaper to go to a government hospital or clinic.

Private Healthcare

If you have private health insurance, you will have access to a network of private hospitals and clinics. Levels of cover vary depending on the policy, so check what you're entitled to. Dental care, maternity and screening tests aren't usually covered as standard, and you may need to have been on the policy for a year before you can receive maternity cover.

Before making an appointment to see a healthcare professional, always check whether the clinic or hospital is part of your insurer's network to avoid being landed with the full costs yourself. Your insurer will also provide details about its payment policy; some companies offer direct billing, which means the insurer pays the hospital or clinic directly and you only pay a nominal fee each time you access medical services, while others require you to pay the cost of the consultation, treatment and medication up front and then file a claim to the insurer.

If your employer is paying for your medical insurance, your employment contract will state whether your spouse and dependants are included in the policy. If you plan to cover the cost of insuring your family yourself, you may need to purchase a separate policy for them as it's not always possible to extend existing policies.

Private hospitals, medical centres and specialist clinics are located across Dubai, and there are over 120 medical facilities in Healthcare City alone, including two hospitals.

Accidents & Emergencies

If you witness an accident or need an ambulance in an emergency situation, the number to call is 999. Anyone can receive emergency treatment in government hospitals but charges apply to anyone without a health card. Some private hospitals have accident and emergency (A&E) departments but unless you have private medical insurance, you'll be landed with a large bill. Your best bet is to check with your insurer that you are covered for treatment in a particular hospital before heading there.

Of the government hospitals, Rashid Hospital (04 219 1000) deals with most emergency cases as it has a well-equipped A&E department. Dubai Hospital also has an emergency unit. Latifa Hospital offers emergency services to children under the age of 12 and women with maternity or gynaecological emergencies; it does not deal with trauma cases. The Iranian Hospital has a busy A&E.

Who You Gonna Call?
Need a doctor urgently? du customers have access to Mobile Doctors, a round-the-clock medical helpline. Licensed and experienced physicians from Dubai Healthcare City are standing by day and night to advise you over the phone and help you make an appointment with leading hospitals, clinics, pharmacies and other health services across the UAE. To subscribe, SMS 'MD' to 2470. For more information and to subscribe online, visit mobiledoctors24-7.com or call 800 63247; there is a daily fee of Dhs.29, and monthly subscriptions are also available.

While finding a place to get emergency treatment is easy, Dubai's paramedic services are somewhat under-developed. Ambulance response times are below those in most western cities but in recent years, a large number of well-equipped response vehicles have been added and times have come down.

When you call 999 (which goes through to Dubai Police) an ambulance will be dispatched to take the patient to the relevant hospital depending on the type of medical treatment needed. Rashid Hospital receives all trauma patients; all other medical emergencies are transported to Dubai Hospital with the exception of cardiac, neurological and gastrointestinal patients, who are taken to Rashid or a speciality hospital.

LIVING IN DUBAI
HEALTH

General Medical Care

There are a few different options available for general, non-emergency medical care. Most hospitals have a walk-in clinic where you can simply turn up, present your health or insurance card, register and queue to see a general practitioner. It's commonplace to be seen by a triage nurse who will take down the details of your medical history and ailment before you see a doctor. These departments usually operate on a first-come, first-served basis. It's advisable to call the hospital prior to visiting to make sure that they have a walk-in service and when it's open. If you are on a private healthcare plan, check in advance that the hospital is on your insurer's network.

Doctor On Call

800 Doctor (800doctor.com, 800 362867) offers a 24/7 doctor on call service. Its team of certified doctors can visit your home, work or business, normally within an hour of your call. They can help with eye infections, sore throat, common viral infections, tonsillitis, asthma, bronchitis, vaccinations and more. A house call will cost Dhs.500 plus medications.

Many hospitals and smaller clinics offer family medicine as part of their outpatient services. You can usually call to make an appointment but there are no guarantees you'll get an appointment on the same day. If your usual family medicine department has no appointments available but you need immediate non-emergency medical care, they may admit you through the A&E department, but they will advise you of this when you call. American Hospital offers a fast-track service through its A&E department for people needing immediate medical attention.

While some people like the convenience of walk-in clinics, others prefer to register with a practice where they are familiar with the administrative procedures and can see the same doctor on return visits. There are countless clinics in Dubai which offer general practice and family medicine. Standards are generally high but it's worth asking friends, neighbours and colleagues for recommendations. Most parts of the city have a local medical centre, so if proximity to your home or office is important, you should be able to find something nearby.

A number of clinics and hospitals offer Well Man, Well Woman and Well Child packages. These care packages involve medical examinations, screenings for common diseases, and routine tests, and offer well-being advice. You can even get your holiday vaccinations topped up as part of some packages. The package that you opt for will depend on factors such as age, gender and medical history.

Al Diyafa Modern Medical Centre 2nd December St, Al Bada', 04 345 4945
Al Mousa Medical Centre Al Wasl Rd, Jumeira 1, 04 345 2999
Al Noor Polyclinic Saif Center, Naif, 04 223 3324, *alnoorpolyclinic.ae*
Amber Clinics Rigga Business Centre, Al Muraqqabat, 04 230 9100, *amber-clinics.com*
Aster Medical Centre Icon Towers, TECOM, Al Thanyah 1, 04 453 4830, *astermedicalcentre.com*
Belgium Medical Services Ibn Sina Bldg, Healthcare City, Umm Hurair 2, 04 362 4711
Belhoul European Hospital Al Satwa, 04 345 4000, *belhouleuropean.com*
Canadian Specialist Hospital Nr Abjar Grand Hotel, Hor Al Anz East, 04 707 2222, *csh.ae*
Crescent Cosmetic Medical Center Villa 39, Nr Mercato, Jumeira 1, 04 342 2288, *crescentmc.ae*
Drs Nicolas & Asp Villa 446, Nr Jumeira Beach Park, Jumeira 3, 04 394 7777, *nicolasandasp.com*
Dubai London Specialty Hospital Jumeira Rd, Umm Suqeim 2, 04 800 352, *dubailondonclinic.com*
Family First Medical Center Al Wasl Rd, Umm Al Sheif, 04 380 5430, *familyfirst.ae*
General Medical Centre > *p.123* Nr Market Shopping Mall, Dubai Investment Park 1, 04 885 3225, *gmcclinics.com*
General Medical Centre > *p.123* Trade Centre Apartments, Trade Center 2, 04 331 3544, *gmcclinics.com*
Health Call Ibn Sina Bldg, Healthcare City, Umm Hurair 2, 04 363 5343, *health-call.com*
Infinity Health Clinic Nr Park n Shop, Jumeira 3, 04 394 8994, *ihcdubai.com*
JTS Medical Centre Jumeirah Terrace, Jumeira 1, 04 379 9954, *jtsmedicalcentre.com*
kidsFIRST Medical Center Villa 1171A, Al Wasl Rd, Umm Al Sheif, 04 348 5437, *kidsfirstmc.com*
Lifeline Medical Centre Dubai Marina Al Fattan Marine Tower 2, Marsa Dubai, 04 399 1119, *lifeline.ae*
Manchester Clinic Jumeira Rd, Jumeira 1, 04 344 0300, *manchester-clinic.com*
Medcare Medical Centre Al Barajeel Oasis Complex Bldg, Mirdif, 04 284 7199, *medcarehospital.com*
Mediclinic Dubai Mall > *p.iv-v* Dubai Mall, Downtown Dubai, Burj Khalifa, 04 449 5111, *mediclinic.ae*
Mercato Family Clinic Nr Mercato Shopping Centre, Jumeira 1, 04 344 8244

Medical History

Be sure to give a copy of your medical history to your new clinic. Most insurance policies don't cover holiday vaccinations; you can save yourself a lot of money if you have a record of which jabs you've already had.

MOH License No: 306/2/1/30/1/2015

GMC JUMEIRAH - MEDICAL
04 349 4880

GMC JUMEIRAH - DENTAL
04 344 9150

GMC GREEN COMMUNITY
MEDICAL | DENTAL - 04 885 3225

GMC TRADE CENTRE APTS.
MEDICAL | DENTAL - 04 331 3544

GMC TECOM
MEDICAL I DENTAL - 04 567 6888

GMC TECOM - LABORATORY
04 567 6800

All major insurances accepted

GMCClinics has been recognized as one of the leading healthcare providers in Dubai for nearly a quarter of a century. We have a team of over 40 internationally experienced medical practitioners who meet the stringent licensing requirements of Dubai and our own rigorous medical standards to ensure you are given the best possible professional care.

Our mission is to care for our patients as we would wish to be cared for ourselves.

Clinical Services

- Cardiology
- Dental Hygienist
- Dentistry
- Ears, Nose and Throat
- Endodontics
- Family Medicine
- Gastroenterology
- General Practice
- Gynaecology
- Implantology and Dental Surgery

- Internal Medicine
- Obstetrics
- Ophthalmology
- Orthodontics
- Osteopathy
- Paediatric Dentistry
- Paediatrics
- Pathologist
- Periodontics
- Physiotherapy
- Prosthodontics

We also offer:

- Corporate Medicals
- Insurance Medicals
- School Medicine
- Sports Medicine
- Travel Medicine
- Vaccinations

gmcclinics.com

GMCClinics
Caring About Health

LIVING IN DUBAI
HEALTH

Government Hospitals

There are four main government hospitals in Dubai that you may need to visit.

Al Baraha Hospital
Nr Dubai Hospital Al Baraha **04 271 0000**
Map **2 P4** Metro **Palm Deira**
This government hospital is commonly referred to as the Kuwaiti Hospital and is one of Dubai's older medical centres. It is on the Deira side of the Shindagha Tunnel. You're unlikely to use this hospital for treatment, but you might need to come here for your blood test when processing your residence visa or for a birth or death certificate.

Dubai Hospital
Nr Baraha Hospital Al Baraha **04 219 5000**
dohms.gov.ae
Map **2 P5** Metro **Palm Deira**
Dubai Hospital is one of the best government hospitals in the UAE. Having opened in 1983, it is one of the oldest, but it's clean and well maintained. The hospital offers a full range of medical, dentistry and general surgical services. It is large and usually busy but has a very efficient emergency department.

Latifa Hospital
Oud Metha Rd Sama Al Jadaf, Al Jadaf **04 219 3000**
dha.gov.ae
Map **2 K7** Metro **Dubai Healthcare City**
The Latifa Hospital specialises in obstetrics, gynaecology and paediatric. Its emergency department provides 24 hour care seven days a week. It cares for children up to the age of 12 with medical, surgical and non-trauma cases, and women with serious problems relating to pregnancy and gynaecology. It's the only hospital to deal with emergency pregnancies and has a special unit for premature and sick neonates. Expat residents admitted in an emergency without a health card are charged Dhs.250 a day plus any medication costs.

Rashid Hospital
Nr Maktoum Bridge Umm Hurair 2 **04 219 1000**
dha.gov.ae
Map **2 L6** Metro **Oud Metha**
Rashid is the main government hospital for A&E, trauma, intensive care and paramedic services. It's likely that you'll be brought here if you have a road accident. It also offers diagnostics, surgery, maternity, paediatrics, physiotherapy and a social affairs unit. The standard of care is good, but it is busy, so seek non-emergency treatment in another government hospital. The hospital is currently undergoing a Dhs.3bn redevelopment; there will be state-of-the-art medical facilities, along with two hotels, residences and a lake.

Private Hospitals

In general private hospitals deliver high standards of care in Dubai. Most hospitals offer a comprehensive range of inpatient and outpatient facilities, so if you like a particular hospital but need to see a specific specialist, the chances are the hospital will be able to cater to your needs. Once you have registered with your chosen hospital it is easier and faster to return for further treatment.

For very specialist treatment you'll be referred to somewhere else in the city. Many of the services offered in hospitals are also offered in clinics and small practices, so if you have a hospital phobia, these might be a better option for non-emergency treatment. See Specialist Clinics & Practitioners. It is worth having a look around the main hospitals to see which one suits you – especially if you are intending to have a baby in Dubai. For more information on Having a Baby in Dubai see Family & Parenting.

Al Garhoud Private Hospital
Nr Millennium Hotel Al Garhoud **04 454 5000**
gph.ae
Map **2 N7** Metro **GGICO**
Almost all areas of medical care are offered at this 52 bed multi-specialty private hospital which offers emergency care, plus general surgery, and obstetrics and gynaecology. There is also an ENT department, plastic aesthetic surgery and physiotherapy.

Private Medical Insurance

Private medical cover in Dubai is available from several providers. Greenshield Insurance (greenshield.ae, 04 388 2200) offers comprehensive medical cover for expats. Their website contains a well-explained guide as to how their policies work. You'll need insurance cover when using private hospitals and clinics; otherwise you'll be landed with the entire bill for your treatment. Using an insurance provider such as Greenshield gives you peace of mind because medical treatment in Dubai can be expensive.

American Hospital Dubai > p.125
Nr Movenpick Hotel Oud Metha **04 336 7777**
ahdubai.com
Map **2 K6** Metro **Oud Metha**
American Hospital is usually pretty busy with its excellent in and outpatient facilities and a fast-track A&E unit. The hospital has top-of-the-range diagnostic equipment and a number of dedicated units including a heart centre and cancer care centre. Its maternity unit is a popular choice, with packages for prenatal care and delivery and private rooms on the labour ward. You can book appointments online.

124   Dubai Explorer

Helping you get back on your feet!

Dr. Ghazwan Maki
Specialist Orthopedic

Dr. Tarek Abuzakuk
Specialist Orthopedic

Ihab Ali
Physiotherapist

The Orthopedic and Total Joint Reconstruction Service at the American Hospital Dubai.

Our commitment to excellence in orthopedic care starts with making sure we deliver outstanding results through innovation and experience.

Under the guidance and support of Dr. Tarek Abuzakuk – Acting Chief of Orthopedics and Joints Replacement Department, the American Hospital Dubai is able to treat a wide range of joint related conditions, guaranteeing higher success rates with shorter recovery time for our patients.

The department has a team of Orthopedic Surgeons trained in Europe and they collectively have decades of surgical experience in total joint replacement procedures, sports medicine and hand surgery, helping you get back on your feet faster.

For more information, please call +971 4 377 6922

Clinical Offerings • Orthopedic Trauma Management • Joint Replacement Surgery of the Shoulder, Hip and Knee Joints • Acute and Reparative Management of Joint Dislocations • Arthroscopic Diagnostic and Therapeutic Surgery of Knees, Ankle, Shoulders Elbow • Sports Medicine, Rehabilitation and Physiotherapy Fractures of Tendons Repair of Hand Injuries.

MOH 3353/2/1/31/1/2014

AMERICAN HOSPITAL DUBAI
المستشفى الأمريكي دبي

Delivering better health in the Middle East

Organization Accredited by Joint Commission International

www.ahdubai.com

The first hospital in the Middle East to be awarded Joint Commission International Accreditation (JCIA)

The first private laboratory to be certified by the College of American Pathologists (CAP)

LIVING IN DUBAI
HEALTH

Belhoul Speciality Hospital
Al Khaleej Rd Al Baraha **04 273 3333**
belhoulspeciality.com
Map **2 N4**
Belhoul Speciality Hospital's nephrology department offers state-of-the-art dialysis machines for kidney disorders. It also has advanced diagnostic technology and health check packages. It has an emergency room and a range of in and outpatient services. The service is efficient as is its customer service.

Cedars Jebel Ali International Hospital
Off Exit 22, Shk Zayed Rd Jabal Ali Port, Mena Jabal Ali **04 881 4000**
cedars-jaih.com
Map **1 D5** Metro **Danube**
Cedars Jebel Ali International Hospital is a private healthcare centre near Jebel Ali Free Zone. Services include a 24 hour emergency clinic and dedicated ambulance (04 881 4000 and 04 881 8816). It specialises in trauma and occupational medicine. A hospital extension is currently under construction.

Healthcare City
Dubai Healthcare City is a centre of excellence dedicated to hospitals and healthcare facilities. There are more than 120 medical facilities and 4,000 doctors spanning all specialities. It's a hub for pioneering research and cutting edge technology. You can find everything from eye doctors to Ayurveda treatments. For more information see dhcc.ae.

Dubai London Specialty Hospital
Jumeira Rd Umm Suqeim 2 **04 80 0352**
dubailondonclinic.com
Map **1 T4** Metro **Noor Bank**
The Dubai London Specialty Hospital is a part of Dubai London Clinic, a well-established clinic with fairly new medical and surgical premises in Umm Suqeim. Another branch is at Festival City (04 232 5751). The Dubai London Dental Centre is on Al Wasl Road. The hospital offers round-the-clock emergency services, inpatient surgery, cosmetic surgery and comprehensive outpatient care.

Emirates Hospital
Nr Jumeirah Beach Park Jumeira 2 **04 349 6666**
emirateshospital.ae
Map **2 D4** Metro **Business Bay**
This small private hospital on Jumeira Road may not be the newest of Dubai's private medical facilities but it delivers a high standard of care. It is primarily a surgical hospital but it also runs outpatient services including a 24 hour walk-in clinic, though the number of doctors available at weekends is limited.

Iranian Hospital
Al Wasl Rd Al Bada' **04 344 0250**
ihd.ae
Map **2 H4** Metro **World Trade Centre**
This mosaic-fronted hospital is affiliated with the Red Crescent Society of Iran, so it isn't strictly a UAE government hospital. It offers its own health card and the fee is reasonable. The card, which costs Dhs.300, offers 20% discount on in and outpatient services, but even without a card, the prices are still affordable. In addition, some of the medicines which they prescribe are free. On the downside the hospital is rather busy, particularly at the walk-in clinic during peak hours.

Medcare Hospital
Nr Safa Park Al Safa 1 **04 407 9100**
medcarehospital.com
Map **2 D5** Metro **Business Bay**
Medcare Hospital is a modern 60 bed private hospital. It offers emergency services and advanced medical care with a particularly strong maternity department. A satellite clinic, Medcare Medical Centre, recently opened in Uptown Mirdiff and takes walk-ins. There is also a multi-speciality clinic on The Walk at JBR.

Medcare Medical Centre
Nr Umm Suqeim Municipality Umm Suqeim 1 **04 395 3115**
medcarehospital.com
Map **2 A5** Metro **Noor Bank**
Offering primary, secondary and tertiary medical services including surgery, dentistry, family medicine, rheumatology, diagnostics, psychiatry, endocrinology, urology and paediatrics. There are also branches at Mirdif, Mirdif City Centre and The Walk at JBR.

Medcare Orthopaedics & Spine Hospital
Off Shk Zayed Rd Al Safa 1 **04 376 8400**
medcareorthopaedics.com
Map **2 C6** Metro **Business Bay**
Medcare Orthopaedics & Spine Hospital, or MOSH, exclusively caters to orthopaedic and spine patients. It specialises in joint replacement, paediatric orthopaedic cases, foot and ankle ailments, sports-related injuries, and hand and spine ailments. It boasts one of the largest and most comprehensive associations of private orthopaedic surgeons in the emirate.

Mediclinic Al Sufouh > *p.iv-v*
Knowledge Village, Al Sufouh 2 **04 366 1030**
mediclinic.ae
Map **1 N5** Metro **Dubai Internet City**
Has everything from its own ambulance services to an operating theatre and 25 outpatient and speciality clinics including day-care surgery, gastroenterology, paediatrics and urgent care. Open 8am to 10.30pm, Saturday to Thursday, 11.30am to 8.30pm on Friday.

LIVING IN DUBAI
HEALTH

Mediclinic City Hospital > p.iv-v
Building 37 Healthcare City, Umm Hurair 2
04 435 9999
mediclinic.ae
Map **2 L7** Metro **Dubai Healthcare City**
Mediclinic City Hospital is a modern, multi-disciplinary hospital delivering world-class healthcare services with the most advanced equipment available. The 229 bed premium facility offers specialised treatment in areas such as cardiology, neurology and neurosurgery, obstetrics and gynaecology, paediatrics, general surgery and radiology. Patient care units provide sophisticated diagnosis and treatments in hand surgery, eye care, kidney stones and breast care. The maternity unit has a dedicated operating theatre for caesarean sections and a neonatal intensive care unit, which is one of the largest in the UAE.

Mediclinic Welcare Hospital > p.iv-v
Nr Dubai Aviation Club Al Garhoud **04 282 7788**
mediclinic.ae
Map **2 N7** Metro **GGICO**
Welcare Hospital's special services include a contact lens clinic, diabetic clinic, holiday dialysis and home call consultations (specialist and GP). Its prenatal and delivery care is considered to be among the best in Dubai. Welcare offers postnatal packages for parents and newborns, which is a nice way for mums to meet. Welcare also operates primary healthcare clinics in Mirdif (04 288 1302) and Al Qusais (04 258 6466) and an ambulatory care unit in Knowledge Village (04 366 1030) that comes highly recommended. Appointments can be booked online.

Neuro Spinal Hospital
Nr Jumeira Beach Park Jumeira 2 **04 342 0000**
nshdubai.com
Map **2 D4** Metro **Business Bay**
The Neuro Spinal Hospital's emergency room is open around the clock and treats all kinds of spinal, neurosurgical and neurological emergencies. The hospital has 40 beds and a multinational team of specialists, doctors and nurses. As well as spinal treatment facilities, the hospital has a stroke centre for treatment of acute cerebro-vascular accidents and its own ambulance, which can be dispatched by calling 04 315 7777.

NMC Hospital
Salahuddin Rd Hor Al Anz **04 268 9800**
nmc.ae
Map **2 Q6** Metro **Abu Hail**
NMC Private Hospital in Deira has a 24 hour walk-in general practice clinic so advance appointments are not necessary. The levels of service are high and the staff are generally efficient. The hospital has an emergency room and its own ambulance with attendant doctors. There is an NMC Specialty Hospital in Al Nahda (04 267 9999), with specialist clinics for allergies, reconstructive surgery, paediatrics and more. Other branches are located in Abu Dhabi and Sharjah.

Saudi German Hospital
Al Hessa Rd Al Barsha 3 **04 389 0000**
sghgroup.ae
Map **1 P6** Metro **Dubai Internet City**
SGH has numerous healthcare establishments located across the MENA region. The Dubai facility is an impressively state-of-the-art 300 bed speciality tertiary care hospital that is extremely convenient for many residents in new Dubai. It offers medical and surgical specialities and subspecialities including cardiac surgery, neurosurgery, oncology, maxillofacial surgery, orthopaedics, and vascular surgery.

Zulekha Hospital
Nr HCT-Dubai Women's College Al Nahda 2
04 267 8866
zulekhahospitals.com
Map **2 T8** Metro **Stadium**
Zulekha is a multi-speciality hospital offering care in fields from cardiology to urology, as well as 24 hour emergency services. The Zulekha Hospital also has a branch in Sharjah and a medical centre in Dubai. In 2012 it was awarded the coveted Dubai Quality Award. It offers health packages to assess your current well-being. Choose from Basic, Executive, Cardiac or Well Woman packages. An initial consultation, followed by blood and urine analysis, analysis of organ functionality and other tests are typically included in the various packages.

Emirates Hospital

askexplorer.com

LIVING IN DUBAI
HEALTH

Specialist Hospitals & Clinics

Whatever your ailment, the chances are you'll find at least one relevant specialist in Dubai. You don't need a referral to be seen by a specialist so you are free to seek whatever medical advice is relevant to your condition. If you are not sure what is wrong with you, or which kind of specialist you should consult, ask your doctor or seek advice from a hospital. Most places will advise you over the phone to save you the hassle of trying to make an appointment. The majority of hospitals also offer a range of outpatient medical specialities, although many people prefer the more personalised environment of smaller practices for long-term medical care. In addition, many general practice clinics offer a range of medical services so it's worth checking at your local clinic before going elsewhere.

Al Borj Medical Center
Al Wasl **04 321 2220**
alborjclinicdubai.com
Map **2 F6** Metro **Business Bay**
Specialises in endocrinology, dermatology, plastic surgery, gynaecology, paediatrics and general surgery.

Al Shifa Al Khaleeji Medical Centre
Abu Baker Al Siddique Rd Al Rigga **04 294 0786**
alshifaalkhaleeji.com
Map **2 N6** Metro **Al Rigga**
This clinic offers paediatrics, gynaecology, dentistry, internal medicine and orthopaedic medical services.

Allied Diagnostics
2nd December St Al Satwa **04 332 8111**
allieddiagnostics.net
Map **2 J5** Metro **World Trade Centre**
Provides diagnostic services for clinics that do not have on-site facilities. You may be referred here for investigative procedures.

Amber Clinics
Rigga Business Centre Al Muraqqabat **04 230 9100**
amber-clinics.com
Map **2 N5** Metro **Al Rigga**
One of a number of Amber establishments in Dubai, the Al Rigga clinic is a large, one-stop 'polyclinic' with numerous specialty departments and laboratories under one roof.

Atlas Star Medical Center
Khalid Bin Al Waleed Rd Al Raffa **04 359 6662**
atlasstar.co
Map **2 L4** Metro **Al Fahidi**
Offers general practice, general surgery, ENT, gynaecology and dental services.

British Medical Consulting Centre
Nr Mercato Jumeira 1 **04 344 2633**
bmccdubai.com
Map **2 F4** Metro **Financial Centre**
Western-trained medical staff specialising in cosmetic surgery, psychotherapy, psychology, dentistry, hair transplantation and marriage counselling. The initial consultation is usually free. Plus they offer psychological support for people with a fear of dentists and dental treatment.

The Diabetes & Endocrine Center
Building 64 Healthcare City, Umm Hurair 2 **04 375 2345**
Map **2 L7** Metro **Dubai Healthcare City**
Screening and treatment clinic for diabetes and thyroid problems.

Dr Al Rustom's Medical & Day Care Surgery Centre
Villa 41, Nr Jumeira Plaza Jumeira 1 **04 349 8800**
skin-and-laser.com
Map **2 H4** Metro **Al Jafiliya**
A specialist dermatology clinic offering cancer services, laser surgery and cosmetic procedures.

Dr Mahaveer Mehta Skin Medical
Al Muraqqabat **04 221 9300**
skinlaserdubai.com
Map **2 N5** Metro **Baniyas Square**
A laser surgery clinic offering treatment for dermatological conditions and cosmetic procedures.

Dr Mohamed Al Zubaidy Clinic
Burger King Bldg, Al Rigga St Al Rigga **04 227 7533**
Map **2 N6** Metro **Union**
Dr Al Zubaidy offers dermatology and venereology investigations and treatments.

Dr Taher H Khalil Clinic
A 22 St, Al Safa 1 **04 268 7655**
Map **2 C6** Metro **Business Bay**
A general medical clinic specialising in hormone therapy including treatment for low fertility, diabetes and thyroid irregularities.

Dubai London Specialty Hospital
Jumeira Rd Umm Suqeim 2 **800 352**
dubailondonclinic.com
Map **1 T4** Metro **Noor Bank**
This is a long-established clinic with brand new medical and surgical premises in Umm Suqeim. Another branch is located at Festival City (04 232 5751) and Dubai London Dental Centre is on Al Wasl Road (see Dentists). The Umm Suqeim branch offers round-the-clock emergency services, inpatient surgery, cosmetic surgery and comprehensive outpatient care.

LIVING IN DUBAI
HEALTH

German Heart Centre Bremen
Building 39 Healthcare City, Umm Hurair 2
04 362 4797
german-heart-centre.com
Map **2 L7** Metro **Dubai Healthcare City**
Cardiac treatment, investigation and intervention services, and after treatment care from Germany's most renowned cardiology clinic.

German Medical Center
Ibn Sina Bldg Healthcare City, Umm Hurair 2
04 362 2929
gmcdhcc.com
Map **2 L7** Metro **Dubai Healthcare City**
Offering medical specialities including urology, andrology, infertility, gynaecology, obstetrics, internal medicine, general and orthopaedic surgeries and ENT.

Health Care Medical Centre
Jumeirah Centre Jumeira 1 **04 344 5550**
Map **2 H4** Metro **Emirates Towers**
A small practice offering ENT, dentistry and ophthalmology.

iCARE Clinics
Oasis Centre Al Qouz 1 **04 384 7272**
icare-clinics.com
Map **2 C6**
The first of 20 proposed iCARE Clinics is now open at the Oasis Centre on Sheikh Zayed Road. The clinics offer a wide range of medical services, including paediatrics, gynaecology, dental, radiology, pathology, family medicine, as well as general practitioner services.

Lifeline Hospital
Nr Jebel Ali Primary School Al Muntazah Complex, Jabal Ali 1 **04 884 5666**
lifeline.ae
Map **1 F6** Metro **Ibn Battuta**
A boutique hospital offering luxury healthcare with chauffeur-driven transfers and private suites. It also has an excellent maternity wing.

Medic Polyclinic
Khalid Bin Al Waleed Rd Al Mankhool **04 355 4111**
Map **2 L5** Metro **BurJuman**
A medical clinic and a diagnostics centre.

Mediclinic Al Qusais > p.iv-v
Dubai Residential Oasis Al Qusais Ind. 2 **04 258 6466**
mediclinic.ae
Map **2 T8** Metro **Dubai Airport Freezone**
This Al Qusais clinic offers patients a wide range of services, from a team of highly experienced staff, including inpatient treatment at the renowned Mediclinic Welcare hospital.

Mediclinic Al Sufouh > p.iv-v
Knowledge Village, Al Sufouh 2 **04 366 1030**
mediclinic.ae
Map **1 N5** Metro **Dubai Internet City**
Has everything from onsite ambulance services to an operation theatre and 25 outpatient and specialty clinics that include day-care surgery, gastroenterology, paediatrics and urgent care.

Mediclinic Arabian Ranches > p.iv-v
Nr Arabian Ranches Community Centre
Arabian Ranches, Wadi Al Safa 6 **04 453 4020**
mediclinic.ae
Map **1 Q13**
An 'ambulatory care centre' with excellent facilities and services. General medicine and day surgery are provided along with specialities such as dentistry, gynaecology, ophthalmology and dermatology.

Mediclinic Beach Road > p.iv-v
Shk Hamdan Awards Complex Madinat Dubai Al Melaheyah **04 379 7711**
mediclinic.ae
Map **2 J4** Metro **Al Jafiliya**
Located in Sheikh Hamdan Complex in Jumeira, this newly-opened medical centre offers a range of specialist services, with facilities including an observation unit and its own in-house laboratory.

Mediclinic Dubai Mall > p.iv-v
Dubai Mall Downtown Dubai, Burj Khalifa
04 449 5111
mediclinic.ae
Map **2 F6** Metro **Burj Khalifa/Dubai Mall**
Offering the full range of general and specialty medicine, from cardiology to urology, this is the region's largest outpatient facility and has the latest facilities to boot.

Mediclinic Ibn Battuta > p.iv-v
Ibn Battuta Jabal Ali 1 **04 440 9000**
mediclinic.ae
Map **1 G5** Metro **Ibn Battuta**
An ultra-modern, fully equipped multi-specialty clinic with its location in Ibn Battuta Mall, making it ideal for residents in the surrounding communities. Has support services like labs and x-rays.

Mediclinic Meadows > p.iv-v
Nr Emirates International School Emirates Living, Al Thanyah 4 **04 453 4040**
mediclinic.ae
Map **1 K6** Metro **Jumeirah Lakes Towers**
Combines advanced medical equipment, an onsite laboratory and diagnostic imaging centre, and a vast range of specialist medical services, including paediatrics, obstetrics and gynaecology.

askexplorer.com

LIVING IN DUBAI
HEALTH

Mediclinic Mirdif > p.iv-v
Uptown Mirdiff Mirdif **04 288 1302**
mediclinicl.ae
Map **2 Q13** Metro **Rashidiya**
Family healthcare clinic specialising in primary medical care, and a wide range of specialised services. Has a direct link to the Welcare Hospital and The Mediclinic City Hospital.

Men's Health Clinic
Al Muhaisnah Medical Fitness Centre Muhaisanah 2 **04 502 3939**
dha.gov.ae
Map **2 R11** Metro **Etisalat**
The region's first men-only clinic specialises in male-related diseases and health concerns such as heart disease, infertility and prostate cancer. The Ministry of Health is due to open more such clinics at its medical centres across the emirate.

Neuro Spinal Centre
Jumeira Rd Jumeira 2 **04 342 0000**
nshdubai.com
Map **2 D4** Metro **Business Bay**
A 40 bed neurosurgical, neurological, spinal and orthopaedic specialist facility offering superior diagnostic, rehabilitative and curative services. Located opposite Jumeirah Beach Park, the centre's facilities include emergency room, operating suite and radiology department.

Panacea Medical & Wellness Centre
Easa Saleh Al Gurg Bldg Al Karama **04 358 2020**
panacea.ae
Map **2 L6** Metro **BurJuman**
A modern clinic that offers everything from the more traditional internal medicine, paediatrics, obstetrics, gynaecology, diagnostics and chiropractics to dietetics and homeopathy. Even has a dentistry department and an emergency department.

Prime Medical Center > p.131
Nr Jumeirah Plaza Al Qouz Ind. 1 **04 349 4545**
pmcdubai.com
Map **2 A6** Metro **Noor Bank**
The Prime Healthcare Group runs six clinics throughout Dubai, offering a wide range of outpatient services, as well as a diagnostics centre in Deira (04 272 0720).

Wooridul Spine Centre
Shk Zayed Rd Al Safa 2 **04 304 6767**
wsc.ae
Map **2 A6** Metro **Noor Bank**
Provides patients with full spinal treatment programmes, from radiological and lab investigations to pain management, physiotherapy and complete surgical plans.

Maternity

The standard of maternity care in Dubai is excellent. Among expats, the most popular maternity hospitals are Welcare, American and Latifa Hospitals (see Hospitals). Latifa Hospital may lack some of the private hospital frills but it has an excellent reputation for maternity care and paediatrics.

Before you decide on a government hospital, check its policy regarding husbands and family members in the labour ward. Some hospitals may not allow husbands in the labour ward (although they can be present at delivery and often, if you are persuasive and there are no local ladies admitted, they will allow access).

All government hospitals now charge expats for maternity services and delivery, and costs vary depending on the package you choose. Private hospitals will be more expensive, but if you shop around you may be surprised to find that sometimes the difference between government and private is not as great as you expected. No matter which you choose, if you have medical insurance check it covers maternity costs. Some have a limitation clause which means you need to have been with the insurer for at least 12 months before conception, and some may not cover any costs at all.

Private hospitals offer maternity packages that include prenatal care, delivery and postnatal care for you and the baby. But remember, the price you are quoted by the hospital is usually for the most basic 'best case scenario' delivery. Should you have additional requirements, such as an epidural (when the anaesthetist must be present) or an assisted delivery (when the paediatrician must be present), you will be charged extra.

If you give birth by caesarean section, for example, the cost is usually significantly higher and the hospital stay is notably longer (five days, compared to just two days for a standard delivery). If you go to an independent gynaecologist for your prenatal care, you will usually be offered a choice of hospitals and delivery packages, where your doctor can attend for the birth. For more information on the practicalities of having a baby in Dubai, see Family & Parenting.

Below is a list of hospitals offering maternity care. For more information on each hospital see the main Hospitals section of this chapter.

Al Zahra Private Medical Centre
Al Safa Tower, Shk Zayed Rd Trade Center 1 **04 331 5000**
alzahra.com
Map **2 H5** Metro **Financial Centre**
A large medical facility offering wellness packages, maternity care and diagnostics in addition to a full range of outpatient services.

130 Dubai Explorer

There's always a **PRIME** nearby!

PRIME
MEDICAL CENTER

Call Centre 04 2720720

Dubai: Deira | Jumeirah | Bur Dubai | Mizhar | Sh. Zayed Road
Sharjah: Al Qasimia 06 5752200 | Al Nahda 06 5251800 Abu Dhabi: Al Falah Street 02 6229993

Prime HealthCare Group LLC: Prime Medical Centers • Premier Diagnostic & Medical Center • Prime Medical Store • MediPrime Pharmacies • Prime Econocare • Prime Hospital

www.primehealth.ae

LIVING IN DUBAI
HEALTH

American Hospital Dubai > p.125
Nr Movenpick Hotel Oud Metha **04 336 7777**
ahdubai.com
Map **2 K6** Metro **Oud Metha**
This hospital's maternity unit is a popular choice, with packages for prenatal care and delivery and private rooms on the labour ward.

Fetal Medicine & Genetic Center
Building 39 Healthcare City, Umm Hurair 2 **04 360 4040**
my-baby.net
Map **2 L7** Metro **Dubai Healthcare City**
The Fetal Medicine & Genetic Center specialises in foetal care, offering first trimester screening tests, prenatal diagnostics, pregnancy assessment and patient care.

Health Bay Clinic
Villa 977, Al Wasl Rd Al Manara **04 348 7140**
healthbayclinic.com
Map **1 U5** Metro **Noor Bank**
This family clinic is known for its high standards of care in several fields including gynaecology and midwifery. Its western-trained physicians also specialise in internal medicine, gastroenterology, dermatology, podiatry and allergies.

Latifa Hospital
Oud Metha Rd Sama Al Jadaf, Al Jadaf **04 219 3000**
dha.gov.ae
Map **2 K7** Metro **Dubai Healthcare City**
Latifa Hospital is a government facility specialising in obstetrics, gynaecology, paediatrics and paediatric surgery. It cares for women with serious problems relating to pregnancy and gynaecology. It is the only hospital in Dubai that deals with emergency pregnancies and has a special baby care unit for premature and sick neonates.

Medcare Hospital
Nr Safa Park Al Safa 1 **04 407 9100**
medcarehospital.com
Map **2 D5** Metro **Business Bay**
Medcare Hospital has a particularly strong maternity department, and staff are qualified to international standards.

Mediclinic City Hospital > p.iv-v
Building 37 Healthcare City, Umm Hurair 2 **04 435 9999**
mediclinic.ae
Map **2 L7** Metro **Dubai Healthcare City**
Mediclinic City Hospital is a modern, multi-disciplinary hospital. Its maternity unit has a dedicated operating theatre for caesarean sections and a neonatal intensive care unit, which is one of the largest in the UAE.

Mediclinic Welcare Hospital > p.iv-v
Nr Dubai Aviation Club Al Garhoud **04 282 7788**
mediclinic.ae
Map **2 N7** Metro **GGICO**
Welcare Hospital's prenatal and delivery care is considered to be among the best in Dubai. Welcare offers postnatal packages for parents and newborns. Welcare also operates primary healthcare clinics in Mirdif (04 288 1302) and Al Qusais (04 258 6466) and an ambulatory care unit in Knowledge Village (04 366 1030) that comes highly recommended.

NMC Speciality Hospital
Nr HCT-Dubai Women's College Al Nahda 2
04 267 9999
nmc.ae
Map **2 S7** Metro **Stadium**
The NMC Specialty Hospital has a maternity ward, as well as other departments.

Rashid Hospital
Nr Maktoum Bridge Umm Hurair 2 **04 219 1000**
dha.gov.ae
Map **2 L6** Metro **Oud Metha**
Amongst other things, the government-run Rashid Hospital offers maternity care.

Obstetrics & Gynaecology

Most hospitals and general practice clinics in Dubai offer gynaecological and obstetrics medical services. In your home country you may be used to receiving reminders when you are due for a smear test or mammogram; in the UAE, you'll need to be more proactive, and while a gynaecologist can advise you on how frequently you should have check-ups, it will be up to you to remember when the time comes. If you are looking for a long-term gynaecologist, try Health Bay Clinic (04 348 7140), which has a gynaecology department. Many clinics offer well woman check-ups that can be done regularly (usually annually) and offer the chance to get all your checks done in one go, at the same time as a general health review. Latifa Hospital (04 219 3000) and Mediclinic City Hospital (04 435 9999) also have gynaecology departments.

Most contraceptives are available in Dubai (the morning after pill is not) and a gynaecologist can advise you on the most suitable form of contraception for you. If you take oral contraceptives, a variety of brands are available over the counter without prescription. Because of the risk of thrombosis, you should make a point of going to your doctor to have your blood pressure checked every six months, just to make sure everything is okay. Note that, while rarely enforced, the law is that you should be married in order to be prescribed or purchase contraceptives.

MEDECINS SANS FRONTIERES
أطبّـاء بــلا حــدود

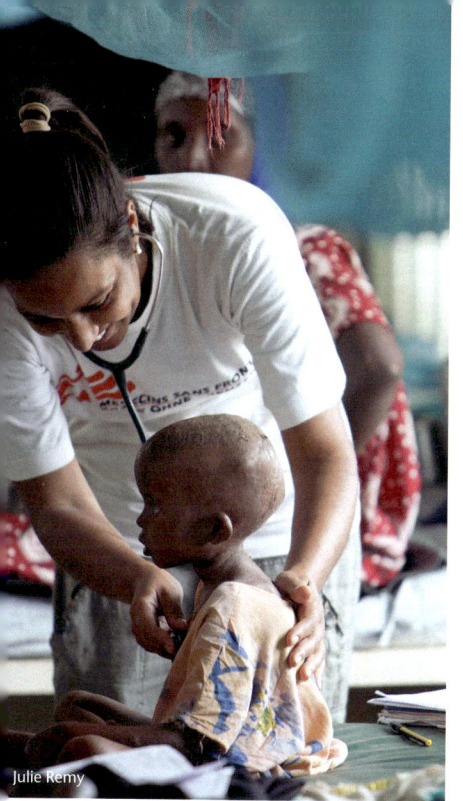

**unconditional
medical care where needed,
when needed**

Médecins Sans Frontières (MSF, or Doctors Without Borders) is an international, independent, medical humanitarian organization that delivers emergency aid in more than 70 countries to people affected by armed conflict, epidemics, natural or man-made disasters or exclusion from healthcare.

www.msf-me.org

Abu Dhabi: P.O. Box 47226, T: +971 2 631 7645, E: office-abudhabi@msf.org
Dubai: P.O. Box 65650, T: +971 4 457 9255, E: office-dubai@msf.org

LIVING IN DUBAI
HEALTH

Bourn Hall Clinic
Shk Hamdan Award Complex Madinat Dubai
Al Melaheyah **04 705 5055**
bournhall-clinic.ae
Map **2 J4** Metro **Al Jafiliya**
A state-of-the-art IVF clinic equipped with the latest technology and staffed by expert physicians, nurses and scientists working in the field of Assisted Reproductive Technology.

Dr Leila Soudah Clinic
Villa 467B, Jumeira Rd Jumeira 3 **04 395 5591**
Map **2 C4** Metro **Business Bay**
An independent gynaecology clinic offering pre and post-natal care. Dr Leila is affiliated with American Hospital, so most of her patients deliver there.

Dubai Gynaecology & Fertility Centre
Building 64 Umm Hurair 2 **04 439 3800**
dgfc.ae
Map **2 L6** Metro **Oud Metha**
This clinic specialises in assisted reproductive technology. It is one of the few facilities in Dubai that offers IVF treatment. A range of gynaecological services are also available.

Fakih IVF
Villa 37, Al Wasl Rd Jumeira 1 **04 349 7600**
fakihivf.com
Map **2 F5** Metro **Burj Khalifa/Dubai Mall**
One of the leading fertility centres in the region, it specialises in IVF and assisted reproductive technology. Dr. Michael Fakih is a recognised leader in the field of assisted reproduction and is responsible for over 10,000 IVF deliveries. His clinic provides infertility treatments as well as PGD for gender selection, PGD for single gene disorders, preserving fertility in cancer patients, and more.

German Clinic
Al Razi Bldg Healthcare City, Umm Hurair 2
04 429 8346
germanclinic-dubai.com
Map **2 K7** Metro **Dubai Healthcare City**
A specialist gynaecology, obstetrics and paediatrics clinic designed to meet German standards of healthcare, based in Dubai Healthcare City. Wellness, fertility and antenatal packages are also available.

Mitera Clinic
Al Razi Bldg Healthcare City, Umm Hurair 2
04 363 5464
miteraclinic.com
Map **2 L7** Metro **Dubai Healthcare City**
Dr Rihab Awad has a number of long term patients who have followed her from American Hospital to her new clinic. She is progressive in terms of stem cell technology and also teaches breast examinations when you have a check-up. If you're looking for a long-term gynaecologist and obstetrician then it's worth getting on her patient list.

Primavera Medical Centre
Al Razi Bldg Healthcare City, Umm Hurair 2
04 375 4669
primaveraclinic.com
Map **2 L7** Metro **Dubai Healthcare City**
This clinic is run by highly recommended obstetrician, gynaecologist and fertility specialist Dr Rosalie Sant.

Orthopaedics

For orthopaedic treatment there are several places to choose from, including Medcare Orthopaedics & Spine Hospital (04 376 8400) in Al Safa, off Sheikh Zayed Road; and the Prime Healthcare Group (042 720 720) hospital in Deira has an orthopaedic unit.

Paediatrics

Most public and private hospitals and medical centres in Dubai have full-time paediatricians on staff, and a growing number have devoted paediatric departments. American Hospital and Mediclinic Welcare Hospital (both private) have teams of specialist paediatric doctors, while Latifa Hospital (government) has dedicated paediatric surgeons and neurodevelopment therapists who care for children with special needs and learning difficulties. Dr Anil Gupta at American Hospital, Dr Zuhair Mahmandar at Emirates Hospital and Dr Loubser at Infinity Clinic (04 394 8994) are popular paediatricians among expat parents. The GMC Clinic in Jumeira has friendly paediatricians who will take the trauma out of doctor's appointments for your child, and who specialise in allergies (04 3494 880). Health Call sends doctors for home visits 24 hours a day, seven days a week and is a handy service if your child is too sick to take to a surgery or hospital (04 363 5343, health-call.com).

Cooper Health Clinic
Nr Choithrams, Al Wasl Rd Umm Suqeim 2
04 348 6344
cooperhealthclinic.com
Map **1 T5** Metro **Noor Bank**
This family medicine clinic offers paediatric, obstetric and gynaecology specialities including pioneering procedures in laser vaginal rejuvenation – popular with women who have given birth. There are also antenatal classes, infant massage and a hypnobirthing course to help pregnant women relax. Dr Khan at the clinic is a popular paediatrician.

LIVING IN DUBAI
HEALTH

Isis The French Clinic
Al Razi Bldg Healthcare City, Umm Hurair 2
04 429 8450
isisclinicdubai.com
Map **2 L7** Metro **Oud Metha**
Located close to the Alliance Francaise and the Ecole George Pompidou (04 337 4101) this practice offers specialist paediatric pulmonary care in addition to asthma, allergies, paediatric general practice and neonatal clinics. Standards are monitored by Dubai Healthcare City and the Harvard Medical School.

Keith Nicholl Medical Centre
Villa 610B, Jumeira Rd Umm Suqeim 1 **04 394 1000**
keithnicholl.com
Map **2 A4** Metro **Noor Bank**
A child-friendly practice in Jumeira staffed by a paediatrician, paediatric nurses and a parent counsellor and educator. In addition to standard paediatric services, there's also a Well Baby Clinic that offers well baby check-ups, immunisations, development checks, as well as first aid courses for parents, nannies and other caregivers.

kidsFIRST Medical Center
Villa 1171A, Al Wasl Rd Umm Al Sheif **04 348 5437**
kidsfirstmc.com
Map **1 S5** Metro **Mall of the Emirates**
In addition to paediatric medicine, kidsFIRST offers occupational therapy, speech therapy and physiotherapy for kids. The kidsFIRST team serves children across a full range of special needs, such as autism, ADHD, cerebral palsy and dyslexia.

Physiotherapy

Many Dubai residents lead an active lifestyle, working hard and then playing harder. But accidents and injuries do happen, so whether you get roughed up playing rugby, pull something in the gym or put your back out moving a wardrobe you'll be pleased to hear that the city has some excellent facilities with specialists from all around the world to help you on the road to recovery.

Popular with expats, Drs Nicolas & Asp offer sports medicine and physiotherapy, as well as a range of other exercises that can help prevent further injury.

Pilates is said to be the safest form of neuromuscular reconditioning and back strengthening available and is often provided by qualified physiotherapists. Classes are offered by a number of gyms as part of their group exercise schedules.

California Chiropractic & Sports Medicine Center
Al Razi Bldg Healthcare City, Umm Hurair 2
04 429 8292
californiachiropracticcenter.com
Map **2 L7** Metro **Dubai Healthcare City**
Partnering a number of the UAE's major sports teams, groups and events, this clinic is a real sports specialist with experts who know their golf, running and cycling every bit as well as they know their bones, tendons and muscles.

Canadian Chiropractic & Natural Health Centre
Al Wasl Rd Jumeira 2 **04 342 0900**
Map **2 E5**
This clinic offers chiropractic treatments and acupuncture as well as reflexology. They also treat sports injuries and give advice for people with long term back problems.

Chiropractic Health & Physio Polyclinic
Villa 967, Al Wasl Rd Al Manara **04 348 8262**
dubaichiropractor.net
Map **1 U5** Metro **Burj Khalifa/Dubai Mall**
This health clinic treats a range of health problems and sports injuries including ADHD, headaches, stress, scoliosis, neck pain, asthma and pain following accidents. A number of physiotherapists and a nutritionist are also based at the clinic.

Dubai Bone & Joint Center
Al Razi Bldg Healthcare City, Umm Hurair 2
04 423 1400
dbaj.ae
Map **2 L7** Metro **Oud Metha**
Focuses on research into and treatment of musculo-skeletal problems. Well-equipped with diagnostic

technologies, the centre offers rehabilitative services including physiotherapy and sports medicine, and has a very high standard of facilities for joint replacements, orthopaedic, and back and neck surgeries.

Dubai Physiotherapy & Family Medicine Clinic
Town Centre Jumeirah Jumeira 1 **04 349 6333**
dubaiphysio.com
Map **2 F4** Metro **Burj Khalifa/Dubai Mall**
Open since 1992, this is one of Dubai's most established clinics. Specialising in physiotherapy for musculoskeletal disorders and sports injuries, it also offers family medicine, sports therapy, osteopathy, acupuncture, nutrition, speech therapy, orthotics, podiatry and psychology.

Emirates European Medical Centre
Villa 119, Al Thanya Rd Umm Suqeim 2 **04 348 1166**
chiropracticdubai.com
Map **1 T5** Metro **First Gulf Bank**
Located in the Emirates European Medical Centre is Chiropractic Dubai, which has a team of experienced chiropractors and physiotherapists who can diagnose all manner of injuries and create a treatment plan to fit the individual's needs. Chiropractor Dr. Samuel Saukkonen is especially skilled in the treatment of lumbar disc herniation.

Orthosports Medical Center
Jumeira Rd Jumeira 1 **04 345 0601**
orthosp.com
Map **2 H4** Metro **Al Jafiliya**
Specialises in orthopaedics and sports medicine, offering physiotherapy, hydrotherapy and orthopaedic surgery to international standards. Sports therapy for fitness and injury rehabilitation and hydrotherapy for a range of conditions including obesity, arthritis, back pain and joint replacements are also available.

Osteopathic Health Centre > *p.137*
Al Wasl Rd Umm Suqeim 2 **04 348 7366**
osteopathydubai.com
Map **1 T5** Metro **Noor Bank**
The serene Osteopathic Health Centre has a number of therapists practising osteopathy in addition to physiotherapy, exercise, sports and massage therapy, chiropractic treatments, homeopathy and counselling.
Specialists at the centre have years' of experience helping clients develop a system of self-help, and giving support to people in pain. The effective, holistic approach of therapists can help reduce muscle tension and relieve pain rapidly and the therapists' bedside manner is sympathetic, friendly and understanding. Centres are also at: Uptown Mirdiff (04 288 8525) and Dubai Healthcare City (04 423 2096).

Up & Running Integrated Sports Medical Center
Al Wasl Rd Al Manara **04 328 4600**
upandrunningdubai.com
Map **1 U5** Metro **Noor Bank**
Another sports medicine and rehabilitation centre that you'll find teaming up with major events and local teams, staff here are mainly UK and Australia-trained with extensive backgrounds in treating sports and occupational injuries. Also offers VO2 max testing, sports massage and sessions such as clinical pilates.

Pharmacies

The UAE has a more relaxed policy on prescription drugs than many other countries and most can be bought over the counter, such as antibiotics (though it is best to seek a doctor's advice before taking antibiotics as over-use can result in a reduction in their ability to cure symptoms).
If you know what you need, it cuts out the hassle of having to see a doctor just to get a prescription. Pharmacists are willing to offer advice, but bear in mind that they don't know your medical history. Always tell the pharmacist if you have any pre-existing conditions and allergies or are taking other medication, and make sure that you understand the administration instructions in case these aren't available in English. You might find it frustrating that certain common medications from your home country are not available here (such as Gaviscon for infants and Pepto Bismol). But there are similar products (such as Infacol instead of infant Gaviscon). There are pharmacies all over the city with some open 24 hours a day, such as Life Pharmacy on Al Wasl Road in Jumeira (04 344 1122). Supermarkets and petrol station convenience stores sell basic medications and first aid equipment.

Medication

Certain medications do require a prescription, and there are some medications (such as codeine, diazepam and temazepam) that are actually banned here in the UAE, even though they are widely available on prescription in other countries. It is a crime to have these medicines in your possession or to take them, unless you can produce an official prescription from your doctor in your home country. The complete list of banned drugs can change regularly, so it is best to check with the Registration & Drug Control Department at the Ministry of Health (moh.gov.ae) before travelling with any medication.
If you have private cover, you'll find that most prescriptions are covered by your insurance, so always be sure to have your card with you as proof.

OSTEOPATHIC HEALTH CENTRE

Uptown Mirdif 04 288 8525
Dubai Healthcare City 04 423 20 96
Umm Suqeim 04 348 7366
www.osteopathydubai.com

Treatment for :

- Back pain
- Neck pain
- Headaches
- Sports Injuries
- Physiotherapy
- Postural Correction
- Ante-natal and Post-natal exercise
- Rehabilitation
- Stress Management

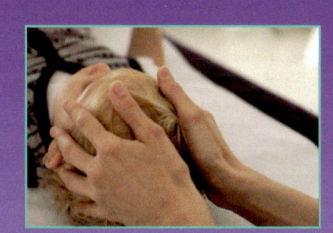

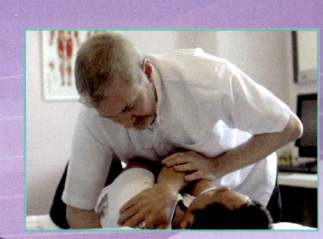

Restoring balance and healing to the body

**LIVING IN DUBAI
HEALTH**

Dentists

Dentistry in Dubai is, like most other medical services, of a high standard with prices to match. Standard health insurance packages don't generally cover dentistry, unless it's for emergency treatment brought about by an accident. You may be able to pay an additional premium to cover dentistry, but the insurer may first want proof that you've had regular, six-monthly check-ups for the previous two or three years.

If you have insurance, you're entitled to basic dentistry at your assigned hospital, and if your hospital doesn't have a dental section, they'll refer you to a public hospital that does, such as Rashid Hospital. You will be charged Dhs.100 for the visit, as well as for any other services that are performed, such as cleaning and filling. Service is generally good, but the rates may not be any lower than at a private dental clinic.

For a standard filling you could be looking at paying anywhere between Dhs.100 and Dhs.1,000. If it is root canal treatment that you need, expect to part with anything from Dhs.600 to Dhs.3,000.

As well as routine and surgical dental treatment, cosmetic dentistry is also big business in Dubai, so if you're looking for a smile make-over, there is plenty of choice.

The clinics listed below are specialist dental clinics. Many primary healthcare clinics and hospitals also offer dental services. For a full listing of dental practices and surgeons in Dubai, visit askexplorer.com.

American Dental Clinic
Villa 54 JMR, Nr Dubai Zoo Jumeira 1 **04 344 0668**
americandentalclinic.com
Map **2 G4** Metro **Financial Centre**
The surgery has a wide range of cutting edge dental services available, and even offers virtual reality movie glasses so patients can watch a film during treatment – while seated in a massage chair!

British Dental Clinic
Nr Emirates NBD Jumeira 1 **04 342 1318**
britishdentalclinic.com
Map **2 F5** Metro **Financial Centre**
The clinic specialises in the most modern dental treatments, cosmetic dentistry, orthodontics, periodontics and implantology. Dentists are from Europe and Canada.

Charly Polyclinic
Sana Fashions Bldg Al Karama **04 337 9191**
charlypolyclinic.com
Map **2 K5** Metro **Al Jafiliya**
This practice offers a range in dental services including cosmetic, laser, implant and general dentistry, orthodontics and oral surgery. They also have an ophthalmologist, gynaecologist and two homeopaths.

The Dental Center
Al Razi Bldg Healthcare City, Umm Hurair 2
04 375 2175
dentalhealthdubai.com
Map **2 L7** Metro **Dubai Healthcare City**
This bright and modern clinic in Healthcare City offers cutting edge dentistry. Routine dentistry and cosmetic procedures, including dental make-overs, are available.

The Dental SPA
Jumeira Rd Jumeira 3 **04 395 2005**
thedentalspa.org
Map **2 B4** Metro **Business Bay**
This clinic offers spa-like surroundings with calming mood music and aromatherapy pillows for your general or cosmetic dental treatment. You can also opt for foot and hand massages during your check-up.

The Dental Studio
Villa 61, Umm Al Sheif Rd Jumeira 3 **04 395 5095**
thedentalstudio.ae
Map **2 B5** Metro **Noor Bank**
This sleek, modern clinic is great to go to if you suffer from fear of the dentist as they are 'dental phobia certified' and will put you at ease. They offer a wide range of treatments, including child dentistry, bridal make-overs and speciality services.

Dr Michael's Dental Clinic
Villa 418 Jumeira 2 **04 349 5900**
drmichaels.com
Map **2 F5** Metro **Burj Khalifa/Dubai Mall**
This clinic prides itself on its personalised service, high safety standards, state-of-the-art dental equipment and an international team of dentists at its two branches in Jumeira and Umm Suqeim (04 394 9433).

Drs Nicolas & Asp
Villa 446, Nr Jumeirah Beach Park Jumeira 3
04 394 7777
nicolasandasp.com
Map **2 D4** Metro **Business Bay**
In addition to regular services, Drs Nicolas & Asp offers a state-of-the-art dental lab for creating implants, veneers and crowns on site. Additionally, cosmetic dentistry, advanced brace fitting and oral maxillofacial surgery are available at its various dental clinics.

Dubai London Clinic Dental Centre
Al Wasl Rd Jumeira 2 **04 378 2921**
dubailondonclinic.com
Map **2 E5** Metro **Burj Khalifa/Dubai Mall**
In addition to routine dental care and cosmetic treatment, the clinic has a periodontics specialist. One treatment available is 'clear braces' – a method of straightening teeth using clear aligner trays.

LIVING IN DUBAI
HEALTH

Dubai School Of Dental Medicine
Building 34 Healthcare City, Umm Hurair 2
04 424 8777
dsdm.ac.ae
Map **2 L7** Metro **Dubai Healthcare City**
A specialist clinic offering a complete range of dental services including fillings, crowns and bridges, cosmetic dentistry, orthodontics, root canal treatment, oral surgery and periodontal treatment. There is also a paediatric dentistry department.

Dubai Sky Clinic
BurJuman Business Tower Al Mankhool **04 355 8808**
dubaiskyclinic.com
Map **2 L5** Metro **Al Fahidi**
Dubai Sky Clinic offers a full range of dental services from its high-tech clinic on the 21st floor of BurJuman Business Tower. Treatment rooms have floor-to-ceiling windows, and patients can watch DVDs or plug in their MP3 players.

GMC Clinics
Magrudy's Mall, Jumeira Rd Jumeira 1 **04 344 9150**
gmcclinics.com
Map **2 B5** Metro **Al Jafiliya**
There are several clinics around Dubai, and each houses a variety of specialists doctors as well as dentists. The clinics' philosophy is to care for the whole family, and they make an extra special effort to make children feel comfortable.

Park Dental Centre
Al Mardoof Bldg, Shk Zayed Rd Al Safa 1
04 346 6111
parkdentalcenter.ae
Map **2 C6** Metro **Business Bay**
Offers a comprehensive list of treatments including orthodontics, implantology, teeth whitening and oral surgery. The practice also offers the latest in root canal therapies and bridge and denture technology, as well as general and cosmetic dentistry.

Sansaya Clinic
Villa 795, Al Wasl Rd Al Safa 2 **04 394 0044**
sansayaclinic.com
Map **2 A5** Metro **Noor Bank**
Services include general, cosmetic and periodontal dentistry, as well as orthodontics and paediatric dental care. The practice also offers specialist restorative procedures, and anxiety-free dentistry.

Seven Dental Centre
Nr HSBC, Jumeira Rd Jumeira 3 **04 395 2177**
sevendentalcentre.com
Map **2 C4** Metro **Business Bay**
Dentists at this practice speak French, English and Arabic and offer a 'no pain' policy. Cosmetic reconstruction, prosthetic and orthodontic procedures available plus routine and children's dentistry.

Swedish Dental Clinic
Nasa Travel Bldg, Al Maktoum St Al Muraqqabat
04 223 1297
Map **2 N5** Metro **Baniyas Square**
This experienced practice, established in Deira back in 1985, offers dental and orthodontic care for patients of all ages. Dr. Nabil Mockbil qualified in Sweden.

Swiss Dental Clinic
Crowne Plaza Trade Center 1 **04 332 1444**
swissdentalclinic.com
Map **2 H5** Metro **Emirates Towers**
Dr Marco Fedele seeks to soothe a patient's anxieties by thoroughly explaining the procedure. General and aesthetic dentistry is available, as well as orthodontic treatments. He speaks English, French, German, Italian and Spanish.

Talass Orthodontic & Dental Center
Villa 114, Nr Dubai Zoo Jumeira 1 **04 349 2220**
talass.com
Map **2 G4** Metro **Financial Centre**
Dr. M. F. Talass and his team of Western-educated, multilingual dental specialists offer family and general dentistry as well as cosmetic dentistry, orthodontics, root canal therapy and TMJ (jaw joint) treatments.

Tower Clinic
Ibn Sina Bldg Healthcare City, Umm Hurair 2
04 362 2939
towerclinic.com
Map **2 L7** Metro **Dubai Healthcare City**
Tower Clinic is one of the UAE's largest private dental clinics. It offers general dentistry and orthodontics plus oral surgery and Zoom!, a one-hour, in-office tooth whitening treatment.

Opticians

You're never far from an optician in Dubai, with most malls and shopping centres having at least one outlet.
The dry, dusty environment in Dubai can cause problems for eyes, even if you've had no trouble in the past. Natural tear or refresher eye drops can increase eye comfort and are available in most opticians and pharmacies. Spending lengthy periods in air-conditioned environments can cause problems for contact lens wearers. Opticians can advise on the most suitable lenses. Sunglasses are an essential accessory in Dubai and prescription lenses are widely available.
For eye problems requiring specialist treatment, many hospitals and clinics, including Moorfields Eye Hospital (moorfields.ae) and The American

LIVING IN DUBAI
HEALTH

Hospital Dubai (ahdubai.com), have well-equipped ophthalmology departments. If you want to ditch the glasses, a number of clinics and medical centres offer laser eye surgery. Prices start from around Dhs.4,000 per eye. All good laser surgery packages should include a complete year's follow-up care.

Even if you've never had an eye test in your life, you will need to undergo one in order to get a driving licence. This test can be carried out at most opticians for a minimal fee, sometimes free of charge.

Al Jaber Optical MoE, Al Barsha 1, 04 341 1322, *aljaberoptical.com*
Anna by Top Vision Optics Nr Dune Centre, Al Satwa, 04 398 4888, *annabytopvisionoptics.com*
Atlanta Vision Clinic Nr Jumeirah Beach Hotel, Umm Suqeim 3, 04 348 6233, *dubailasik.com*
Barakat Optical The Walk at JBR, Marsa Dubai, 04 427 0565, *barakatoptical.com*
Grand Optics MoE, Al Barsha 1, 04 341 0350, *grandoptics.com*
Gulf Eye Center Fairmont, Trade Center 1, 04 329 1977, *gulfeyecenter.com*
Lunettes House of Quality Optics Jumeira 1, 04 349 2270
Lutfi Optical Centre Umm Hurair 2, 04 324 1865, *lutfioptical.com*
Magrabi Optical MoE, Al Barsha 1, 04 341 0445, *magrabioptical.com*
Moorfields Eye Hospital > *p.141* Al Razi Bldg, Healthcare City, Umm Hurair 2, 04 429 7888, *moorfields.ae*
Optic Center Al Mizhar 1, 04 284 5550, *opticcentre.com*
Optivision Ibn Battuta, Jabal Ali 1, 04 368 5540, *dubaioptical.com*
Sharif Eye Center Ibn Sina Bldg, Healthcare City, Umm Hurair 2, 04 423 3664, *sharifeyecenter.com*
Vasan Eye Care Zabeel Plaza, Zabeel Rd, Dubai International Airport, 04 357 9444, *vasaneye.com*
Vision Express Ibn Battuta, 04 368 5926, *alshaya.com*
Yateem Optician Al Mizhar 1, 04 284 5505, *yateemgroup.com*

Alternative Therapies

The Ministry of Health grants licences to and administrates qualified practitioners of alternative medicine through its dedicated department for Traditional, Complementary & Alternative Medicine. Natural medicine can be very specialised, so when consulting with someone, do make sure that you ask questions and explain your needs and expectations. This will ensure that practitioners can indeed help with your situation. Prices vary greatly but are generally comparable to western medicine, however most insurance companies will not cover the costs of alternative therapies. As always, word of mouth is the best way of establishing who might offer the most appropriate treatment.

Yoga and pilates are available at a number of studios and health clubs. Fitness-focused, clinical and classic, meditative forms of yoga are available. There is also a range of clinics that provide 'well-being' services, such as U Concept, which combines personal fitness, a balanced nutrition plan and numerous relaxation techniques, in order to help you achieve the healthy lifestyle you're looking for.

Dubai Herbal & Treatment Centre (04 335 1200) in Oud Metha offers a range of treatments and diagnostic procedures from conventional and alternative medical schools of thought. You can get everything from a tailor-made detox plan, to ozone therapy and allergy testing, as well as massage and a myriad of other complimentary medicines. See dubaihtc.com for more information.

Talise Spa & Wellness Polyclinic at Madinat Jumeirah (jumeirah.com/mjtalise) is a haven of tranquillity that houses a bona fide medical centre, directed by the multilingual Dr Elizabeth Makk. Dr Makk is also qualified in homeopathy and nutrition and offers holistic treatments as well as focusing on disease prevention. Call 04 366 6810 for an appointment.

Cosmetic Treatment & Surgery

Dubai is becoming established as a luxury healthcare destination. Cosmetic surgery is at the heart of this growing industry and the city now boasts a mass of clinics that specialise in reducing, reshaping, removing and enlarging various parts of your anatomy. The clinics listed below are exclusively cosmetic practices, but many of the private hospitals and independent clinics offer cosmetic services including aesthetic and reconstructive surgery. As with all medical facilities, standards are generally high, but it's worth checking out a few different clinics before you go under the knife. If you want a bit of sprucing and don't fancy being sliced into, a lot of the cosmetic clinics will do Botox and other non-surgical treatments.

Aesthetica Clinic Building 39, Healthcare City, Umm Hurair 2, 04 429 8533, *aestheticaclinic.com*
American Academy Of Cosmetic Surgery Hospital Building 73, Healthcare City, Umm Hurair 2, 04 423 7600, *aacsh.com*
Biolite Aesthetic Clinic Villa 57, Al Thanya Rd, Healthcare City, Umm Hurair 2, 04 346 6641, *biolitedubai.com*
CosmeSurge Nr Emirates Hospital, Jumeira 2, 04 344 5915, *cosmesurge.com*

www.moorfields.ae

Bringing over 200 years of UK specialist eye care to the UAE.

Long recognised as one of the leading eye hospitals in the world we have replicated the exceptional standards of our London hospital here in the UAE. Our state-of-the-art facility in Dubai Healthcare City is fully equipped and staffed by highly qualified consultants. If you have any concerns about your vision please contact us.

Call 04 429 7888 or visit www.moorfields.ae today.

Moorfields
Eye Hospital Dubai
A BRANCH OF MOORFIELDS LONDON

LASIK | CATARACT | COSMETIC | PAEDIATRIC | RETINA | CORNEA | GLAUCOMA | STRABISMUS

LIVING IN DUBAI
HEALTH

Dermalase Clinic Nr Jumeirah Beach Park, Jumeira 2, 04 349 7880, *dermalaseclinic.com*
Dubai Cosmetic Surgery Nr Choithrams, Al Wasl Rd, Al Manara, 04 348 5575, *dubaicosmeticsurgery.com*
Dubai Medical Village Nr Sunset Mall, Jumeira 3, 04 346 9999, *medicalvillage.ae*
EuroMed Clinic Villa 611, Jumeirah Rd, Umm Suqeim 04 394 5422, *euromedclinicdubai.com*
General Medical Centre *> p.123* Trade Centre Apartments, Trade Center 2, 04 331 3544, *gmcclinics.com*
Gulf Speciality Hospital Hamarain Centre, Al Muraqqabat, 04 269 9717, *gshdubai.net*
Imperial Healthcare Institute Healthcare City, Umm Hurair 2, 04 439 3737, *imperialhealth.org*
Kaya Skin Clinic Mirdif, 04 283 9200, *kayaskinclinic.me*
London Centre For Aesthetic Surgery Healthcare City, Umm Hurair 2, 04 375 2393, *lcas.com*
Rebecca Treston Aesthetics At EuroMed Jumeira 3, 04 394 5422, *euromedclinicdubai.com*

Nutritionists & Slimming

Slimming clubs offer nutritional advice and hospitals can perform weight loss surgery. Dietary advice for diabetes, allergies, menopause, pregnancy and digestive disorders such as coeliac disease is on hand.

   Mediclinic Welcare Hospital provides a dietary counselling service and unique diet plan. The American Hospital offers a food and nutrition service managed and provided by ADNH Compass. The hospital also runs a Diabetic Centre of Excellence. Emirates Hospital has a weight reduction programme that uses liquid supplements and a very low calorie diet. The hospital also has experts who specialise in medically supervised weight reduction, obesity in children, obesity in diabetic patients and patients with high blood pressure or cholesterol. It also offers gastric band fitting.

   For a more holistic approach to nutrition, the Osteopathic Health Centre offers a complete nutritionist service. You'll find dieticians at Cooper Health Clinic, Dubai London Clinic Medical & Surgical Centre and Drs Nicolas & Asp. The Organic Foods and Cafe sells fresh organic and biodynamic food and supplements, and a nutritionist is on hand at all its stores to give tailor-made advice on supplements and vitamins, detox, weight loss and aromatherapy.

BiteRite
Lotus Apartments Marsa Dubai **04 292 8888**
biterite.ae
Map **1 J5** Metro **Nakheel**
Eat a nutritionally balanced meal in the cafe or use its tailor-made healthy eating service. Healthy meals are delivered to your door. The BiteRite Plan offers an online menu with over 100 varieties of meals.

BodySmart
Meadows Town Centre Al Thanyah 3 **04 363 8318**
bodysmart.ae
Map **1 K13** Metro **Nakheel**
Hypoxi combines cardiovascular exercise with applied pressure to increase blood flow to fatty problem areas. Improvements are within four weeks and goals achieved by week 12. You wear what feels like a wet suit and speed walk on a treadmill or cycle inside a vacuum pod. Results are felt in reduced inches (and each session the trainer will measure your chest, waist and hips). Weight loss can also occur. There's also a Hypoxi studio at the Aviation Club (04 282 4122, *aviationclub.ae*).

Eternal MedSpa
Villa 397, Jumeira Rd Jumeira 2 **04 344 0008**
eternelmedspa.com
Map **2 D4** Metro **Business Bay**
Offers mesotherapy for cellulite treatment, Botox, laser hair removal, slimming treatments as well as general wellness coaching. Mesotherapy involves administering microinjections of conventional or homeopathic medicines, vitamins, minerals or amino acids into the middle layer of skin.

Good Habits
04 344 9692
goodhabitsuae.com
Meetings focused on healthy eating are held every week across Dubai, and often include food tasting and cookery demos. Exercise classes are also organised and individual programmes are offered.

Health Factory
Warehouse 26 Al Qouz Ind. 3 **04 347 3808**
healthfactory.com
Map **1 T7** Metro **First Gulf Bank**
After a consultation you'll be sent three meals a day to help you lose weight or get healthy according to your needs. There's also a diet plan for mothers-to-be, a diabetic meal plan, and healthy eating for kids.

Live'ly
Nr Dubai Cosmetic Surgery Al Manara **04 348 1008**
lively.ae
Map **1 U5** Metro **Noor Bank**
This new centre specialises in nutritional, educational and catering services to help people to manage their weight and live healthier lives.

Perfect Figure
Aviation Club Al Garhoud **050 255 9402**
allbodysolutions.com
Map **2 M8** Metro **GGICO**
This studio creates personal weight loss and toning programmes, which combine exercise using Hypoxi and Vacunaut machines with nutritional advice.

LIVING IN DUBAI
HEALTH

Right Bite
Shk Hamdan Award Complex Madinat Dubai Al Melaheyah **04 338 8763**
right-bite.com
Map **2 J4** Metro **Al Jafiliya**
Right Bite offers a tailor-made healthy eating service. Tasty, low calorie, low fat and low cholesterol meals, devised by their own dieticians, are freshly prepared and delivered to your door.

Slim Spa
Al Attar Tower, Shk Zayed Rd Trade Center 2 **04 343 7987**
slimspa.ae
Map **2 G6** Metro **Financial Centre**
There's a wide range of non-invasive treatments for weight and inch-loss, cellulite reduction, body sculpting, anti-ageing and rejuvenation. Slim Spa also offers personalised programmes, four and eight-week packages, massages and facial treatments.

VLCC
Indigo Central 2 Al Safa 2 **04 338 7897**
vlccwellness.com
Map **1 V6** Metro **Noor Bank**
VLCC offers hair removal, beauty services and customised weight loss programmes which combine dietary advice, exercise and toning and detox therapies. There are women-only centres at Marsa Dubai (04 447 1488) and Uptown Mirdiff (04 288 4880).

Counselling & Therapy

Starting a new life in a different country can be a stressful process, and sometimes it can help just to talk through the emotional aspects. Mental health services in the UAE are not as developed as in some other countries; Al Amal is Dubai's only psychiatric hospital, and Rashid Hospital has a dedicated psychiatric ward.

There are however a number of well-regarded therapy centres offering services including counselling, psychodynamic therapy, family and couples' therapy, paediatric psychiatry, treatment of mental health disorders and learning difficulties support. Dubai Community Health Centre offers a range of counselling and psychiatric services and provides space for support group meetings; it comes highly recommended, as does the Counselling & Development Clinic. In addition to the clinics and centres listed, the British Medical Consulting Centre and Drs Nicolas & Asp have counsellors, family therapists and psychiatrists on staff. Dubai Herbal & Treatment Centre has a psychodynamic counsellor, a psychologist and a learning specialist, and is recommended for child counselling services.

In the neighbouring emirate of Sharjah, Al Tamimi Stables offers Animal Assisted Therapy to help provide people with a positive outlook (tamimistables.com).

Counselling & Development Clinic
Nr Jumeirah Beach Park Jumeira 3 **04 394 6122**
drmccarthypsychologyclinic.com
Map **2 D4** Metro **Business Bay**
This centre caters to adults and children. As well as assessing and treating psychological disorders, the clinic offers counselling, family therapy and couples' clinics. It is well regarded for the treatment and management of bipolar disorder (manic depression), obsessive-compulsive disorder and panic attacks.

Dubai Community Health Centre
Nr Al Nasr Leisureland Oud Metha **04 507 8000**
dubaicommunityhealthcentre.org
Map **2 C4** Metro **Oud Metha**
A private, non-profit facility with counselling, family and marriage therapy, psychology, speech therapy and parenting courses. It also offers occupational therapy, dietetics and special needs education.

Health Psychology UAE
Well Woman Clinic Al Satwa **04 332 7117**
healthpsychuae.com
Map **2 J5** Metro **World Trade Centre**
Dr Melanie C Schlatter is a health psychologist helping people to learn to manage the psychological impact of illnesses and medical conditions that they have. She also offers preventative health psychology in the form of stress management and coping with anxiety, phobias, depression, grief and anger. Her website covers some of the main questions people have about receiving psychological help.

Human Relations Institute & Clinics
Jumeirah Business Center 3 Al Thanyah 5 **04 365 8498**
hridubai.com
Map **1 L5** Metro **Dubai Marina**
The HRI's services include clinical, forensic, organisational, educational and domestic psychology. It offers counselling, life coaching, psychotherapy and workshops for conditions including anxiety, phobias, addiction, behavioural and eating disorders, stress, low self-confidence and depression.

LifeWorks Counselling & Development
996 Al Wasl Rd Umm Suqeim 1 **04 394 2464**
counsellingdubai.com
Map **1 V5** Metro **Noor Bank**
Whether you need self-confidence, personal insight, Cognitive Behavioural Therapy, marriage counselling, help with phobias or would like to join a workshop, this centre can help. Therapists are experienced in treating people from diverse backgrounds.

FAMILY & PARENTING

Al Barsha Pond Park

Bringing your family out to Dubai, or starting one while you're here, can be a fantastic experience. There's plenty of help, great education facilities and a whole range of activities for the kids. This section covers much of that, but also takes a look at some of the more sobering topics like bereavement and divorce; issues that you may be faced with during your time here.

Marriage

When living in the UAE under Shariah law, marriage is the only legal bond for a man and a woman to establish a relationship and have children. It is illegal to live together as a couple if you are unmarried and you cannot have children out of wedlock.

If you're Christian or Catholic, you can marry in a church; if you'd prefer a non-religious marriage, you may be able to tie the knot at your embassy. Muslim weddings take place before a Shariah court; the man must be a Muslim while the woman can be non-Muslim, and a Muslim woman cannot marry a non-Muslim man in the UAE. Whatever your nationality, you should contact your embassy to notify them of your intent to get married and find out the exact process and paperwork necessary. Once wed, you will need to register the marriage with your embassy to get it validated internationally.

The Big Day

This chapter outlines the basics to get you started organising your wedding and reception. For step-by-step procedures, including specifics on which documents to take where, see Explorer's *Dubai How-To* guide, which covers Christian, Catholic, Muslim and Hindu weddings.

LIVING IN DUBAI
FAMILY & PARENTING

The Ceremony
While the wedding must be conducted in either a church, court or at your embassy, you have a large choice of where to have a wedding blessing and the reception. Many couples choose to have a small church ceremony and then celebrate at one of the luxury hotels, on the beach or even aboard a yacht.

Anglican wedding ceremonies can take place at the Holy Trinity Church, Dubai at Christ Church in Jabal Ali, Dubai, St Andrew's Church in Abu Dhabi or St Martin's Church in Sharjah, all of which are recognised by the UAE government. Ministers from the Anglican Church can also marry people at other approved locations.

Roman Catholic marriages can take place at St Mary's Catholic Church in Dubai (saintmarysdubai.com). To marry in a Roman Catholic church, at least one of the partners must be Roman Catholic, and both of them must be resident in Dubai. Women must be at least 18, men must be over 21.

Hindu marriages are conducted by the maharaj at Dubai's Hindu Temple in Bur Dubai. The Hindu Temple is run in conjunction with the Indian consulate who solemnise the marriage. Both parties must be Hindu and at least one of the couple should be an Indian citizen with a Dubai residence visa; there should also be three witnesses who have a UAE residence visa.

People of other religions (Buddhist, Sikh or Bahai) may be able to get married at their embassies or consulates. A Muslim marrying another Muslim can apply at the marriage section of the Dubai Courts, next to Maktoum Bridge.

Fees for a church wedding are around Dhs.2,000 and you can get married on any day of the week if a minister/vicar is available. You will typically need two or three witnesses who are UAE residents.

There are certain conditions for a church wedding:
- At least one member of the couple has to have been baptised (or equivalent)
- At least one of the couple must have a UAE residence visa; expats on a visit visa cannot get married in the UAE
- Both people must be aged 18 or over

Depending on your faith and denomination, you may have to go for counselling sessions and regular church services. You will also need to register certain documents including birth and christening certificates, and written evidence that each is single and free to marry (divorce papers or a letter from your embassy). You will need a Banns certificate or certificate of no impediment, which takes up to three weeks to process and needs to be applied for at your home embassy. For example, the British embassy will display a notice of marriage for 21 days and, assuming no one objects, you are then free to tie the knot.

The Paperwork
In order to register the marriage, your wedding certificate has to be translated into Arabic by a court-approved legal translator. Take this, and the original, along with your essential documents to the Notary Public Office at the Dubai Courts. They will certify the documents for a fee of about Dhs.80. Next you will need to go to the Ministry of Justice (ejustice.gov.ae) to authenticate the signature and the Notary Public seal. Just when you think it's all over, you still have to go to the Ministry of Foreign Affairs (behind the distinctive Etisalat building in Deira) to authenticate the seal of the Ministry of Justice. Now you just need to pop back to your embassy for final legal verification.

In Preparation
Get organised! Visit the Dubai Bride Show (thebrideshow.com/dubai), held every April at the Dubai International Exhibition Centre; it covers everything you'll need for your big day.

The Reception
When it comes to your reception, any one of Dubai's stunning hotels would make the perfect venue and they will assist you with everything from the music and menus to floorplans and florists.

Arabian Ranches Golf Club
Shk Mohd Bin Zayed Rd Arabian Ranches, Wadi Al Safa 6 **04 366 3000**
arabianranchesgolfdubai.com
Map **1 Q13**
Choose between the spacious Baker-Finch indoor venue or one of the magnificent terraces featuring stunning views of the golf course. Packages start from Dhs.270 per person.

Atlantis The Palm > p.275
Crescent Rd Nakhlat Jumeira **04 426 0376**
atlantisthepalm.com
Map **1 N1** Metro **Nakheel**
Choose from various unique venues, from the private tent at Asateer, or the grand luxurious Atlantis Ballroom, or a personalised venue such as the idyllic Dolphin Bay Beach for a more unique touch, The Lost Chambers Aquarium, or even the picture perfect Palm Grove for an intimate setting.

Bateaux Dubai
Nr British Embassy Al Hamriya **04 814 5553**
bateauxdubai.com
Map **2 M5** Metro **Baniyas Square**
Opt for a unique and tasteful reception on the water, where the wedding planner will take care of every last detail from floral arrangements to signature menus.

LIVING IN DUBAI
FAMILY & PARENTING

Park Hyatt

Park Hyatt Dubai
Nr Dubai Creek Golf & Yacht Club Port Saeed
04 602 1234
dubai.park.hyatt.com
Map **2 M7** Metro **GGICO**
Packages including catering, floral arrangements and special guest room rates are available in the ballroom and garden, for an indoor or outdoor day to remember.

The Westin Dubai Mina Seyahi Beach Resort & Marina
Al Sufouh Rd Marsa Dubai **04 399 4141**
westinminaseyahi.com
Map **1 M5** Metro **Nakheel**
The Serdaal Ballroom can accommodate up to 450 guests in gala dinner set-up style, while the outdoor Arabian Terrace offers breathtaking views of the Gulf and the Palm Jumeirah.

XVA Art Hotel
Al Fahidi Historical Neighbourhood Al Souk Al Kabeer **04 353 5383**
xvahotel.com
Map **2 M4** Metro **Al Fahidi**
This boutique hotel in the heart of the historical Al Fahidi neighbourhood makes for a stylish setting for a reception – the alfresco courtyard is relaxed, casual and stunning when candlelit at night.

All the Frills
One of the challenges of getting married outside your country of origin is being far away from your support network; if this is the case, a wedding planner can provide invaluable assistance and ensure that the big day runs smoothly.

Try C'est La Vie (clvweddings.com), wedding.ae or Fonoon (fonoon-uae.com) or check out Couture Events who will help you every step of the way – from the paperwork to the seating plan (coutureevents.ae). Upscale & Posh offers a tailored service for flowers and wedding reception decorations (upscaleandposh.com). Brides needn't worry about missing out on the princess treatment since most spas offer tailor-made services for them.

Try the following photographers for your big day: Sue Johnston (imageoasisdubai.com) or Charlotte Simpson (hotshotsdubai.com).

Wedding Ideas
There are numerous resources available in Dubai to help you plan your wedding and provide inspirational ideas. Bride Club ME (brideclubme.com) is an online portal with a comprehensive list of vendors (offering everything from dresses, to food, to venues), as well as features, forums and photos of weddings they've helped organise. If you want to wow your guests with a stunning, otherworldly theatrical wedding venue design, check out Ali Bakhtiar Designs LLC (alibakhtiardesigns.com).

Family Law
All matters of family law, from divorce and child custody cases through to wills and inheritance, are generally dealt with under Shariah (Islamic) law or by the laws of your home country. In any instance it is best to contact your embassy for an approved list of law firms to assist you, and then deal with a company that is familiar with both the law in your home country and here in Dubai.

Afridi & Angell Emirates Towers, Trade Center 2, 04 330 3900, *afridi-angell.com*
Al Tamimi & Company DIFC, Zaa'beel 2, 04 364 1641, *tamimi.com*
Bayat Legal Services Canadian Consulate Bldg, Al Souk Al Kabeer, 04 355 4646, *ilsgroup.com*
The Rights Lawyers Building 8, Media City, Al Sufouh 2, 04 390 3646, *therightslawyers.com*
Trench & Associates Albwardy Bldg, Al Mankhool, 04 355 3146, *trenchlaw.com*

Wills
It is essential that you have a will in place, and it's especially important to seek legal advice if you become a property owner in Dubai. That's because,

LIVING IN DUBAI
FAMILY & PARENTING

under Shariah law, the rules for who inherits property after someone's death differ from those in other countries. For example, in the event of your death, it may be that your sons (or brother, if you don't have any sons) are first in line for inheritance and your wife could end up with nothing.

The UAE does claim to guarantee a woman's right to inherit property, but it's worth making your will watertight to this. Also, if a family member dies, the government can freeze his/her accounts until all liabilities of your husband are cleared such as loans, credit cards and business debts; this can happen very quickly but can easily be overturned if a UAE will is in place. Providing each other with a 'Power of Attorney' document in addition to a will is also recommended to prevent this.

A Dubai-based lawyer can assist you with a locally viable will (do check that they are authorised by the government to write wills), or contact The Wills Specialists (willsuae.com), or Just Wills (just-wills.net), part of a UK-based estate planning organisation with a UAE presence.

Making A Will
Firstly, make an appointment with a licensed estate planner, preferably one with knowledge of the law of your home country; you'll need passport copies, contact details of executors and proof of assets. A will can be drawn up, and needs to be attested at your embassy or consulate. Have this attested document translated at an authorised typing centre, and then attested by a notary public in the emirate you live in.

Divorce
Divorce, like other matters of family law, is either governed by UAE law, Shariah law, or by the laws of the individuals' originating country. If the parties are from different countries, the applicable law is that from where the marriage was solemnised.

The first step in any divorce hearing is to look at reconciliation with the aid of the Family Guidance and Reformation Centre, which functions under the Department of Justice at Dubai Courts (04 334 7777). Anyone experiencing marital problems or family disputes can use this service, and you can file a complaint against your spouse by simply providing the centre with copies of your ID (passport or Resident Identity Card) and your marriage certificate.

If counsellors at the centre are unable to help a couple to reach an amicable settlement then the case may get referred to the Court of First Instance, Dubai Courts for legal proceedings to take place. This is when you need to seek legal advice. At this stage you will need the services of an expat law firm, who can advise you which 'jurisdiction' (either UAE or your home country) is the most appropriate for you in terms of cost, timescale and outcome.

If the case is straightforward and uncontested you may not even need to attend court, and you can expect to pay around Dhs.10,000, inclusive of all court fees and other expenses. The procedure is fairly standard for Christian, Roman Catholic and Hindu religions: the couple apply to the court for a decree nisi, stating their reasons for divorce, and if the judge finds the reasons to be convincing, the divorce will be granted.

In cases of child custody, the paramount concern of the court is the child's welfare. In Shariah law, the custody of a child classed as a minor, will be the mother's unless there are compelling reasons to decide otherwise.

Death
There's never a more tragic time than when a friend or relative dies. While there is a lot of bureaucracy surrounding a death here, there are companies who can take care of the practical matters and advise you on all aspects of the mourning process.

In the event of a death outside a hospital, notify the police by dialling 999. The police will then file a report and the body will be taken to Rashid Hospital where a doctor will determine the cause of death and produce a report; this usually takes three to seven days.

If the death occurs in a hospital, that hospital will be responsible for completing the initial death report and transferring the deceased to the mortuary.

The first administrative step is to get a death certificate, which is needed before you can arrange a local burial or cremation, or send the body home. Thereafter, the process for registering a death will vary depending on the deceased's religion and whether he or she was an expat or not.

It's best to get in touch with the relevant embassy for guidelines on what the next steps are. To help guide you through the process, contact the private company, Middle East Funeral Services (mefs.ae).

Helping Hand
Middle East Funeral Services (mefs.ae) has partnered up with a network of Worldwide Repatriation Specialists, and are able to manage the entire process, from the initial stages (including obtaining death certificates and registrations) until the deceased is at the funeral home of choice.

Death Certificate
On receipt of the doctor's report, the hospital will issue a death certificate declaration (not to be confused with the actual death certificate). Take this, along with the deceased's passport, to the nearest police department, which will issue a No Objection

LIVING IN DUBAI
FAMILY & PARENTING

Certificate (NOC) addressed to Al Baraha Hospital. You should also request NOCs addressed to the mortuary for embalming, the airport for transportation and the hospital for the release of the body. This letter, plus the death declaration certificate, original passport and copies should be taken to the Department of Preventative Medicine at Al Baraha Hospital, where the death certificate will be issued in Arabic. This must be translated into the appropriate language if the body is being sent home.

The certificate must then be attested for by the Ministry of Health, the Ministry of Foreign Affairs and registered at the General Directorate of Residency and Foreign Affairs (GDRFA). You will also need to cancel the deceased's visa at the GDRFA. Since Islam requires that the body be buried immediately, the death certificate and registration procedures for deceased Muslims can be performed after the burial.

You will also need to inform the embassy of the deceased's home country – the embassy will register the death, issue an embassy death certificate and cancel the passport. This can cost up to Dhs.1,000 depending on which country's embassy you are dealing with.

Local Burial Or Cremation

Before the deceased can be buried or cremated locally, you will need the following documentation: cancelled passport, death certificate, proof that the visa was cancelled and an NOC from the sponsor stating that all debts have been settled.

For a Hindu cremation, you must also provide written permission from the next of kin, as well as that person's passport. The procedure for local cremation and burial can be complicated and changes often, so you will need to contact the Dubai Municipality (04 221 5555, dm.gov.ae), the Christian Cemetery (04 337 0247), or the Hindu Temple in Bur Dubai (04 353 5334) for the latest information.

If you want to arrange a local burial it can be done at the Muslim or Christian cemeteries in Dubai. The cost of a burial is Dhs.1,100 for an adult and Dhs.350 for a child. You will need to get a coffin made, as well as organise transport to the burial site. Cremation is also possible, but the deceased must have had a valid Dubai residence visa, and a cremation permit must be obtained from the municipality, which costs Dhs.1,100. It's also a Dhs.2,500 fee for the cremation

Transporting Ashes Back Home

If the deceased has been cremated in Dubai, you might want to send their ashes back to their home country. The best people to contact are at the dnata Export Office, Cargo Village. Call them on 04 211 1111. They can provide further assistance and information.

Returning The Deceased Home

To return the deceased to his or her country of origin, you will need to book your own ticket with the airline of your choosing (if you want to travel with the body) as well as make shipping arrangements through dnata (04 211 1111), which will handle the body at Cargo Village and process any required documentation.

The deceased will need to be embalmed before reaching Cargo Village, and you will need the original death certificates (both the local certificate and the embassy certificate), the NOC from Dubai Police, an NOC from the embassy of the deceased (which must be the same as the destination to which they are being sent), the cancelled passport and visa and a copy of the air tickets specifying flight details.

You will also need to purchase a coffin. Embalming can be arranged through the Dubai Health Authority and will cost around Dhs.1,000, which includes the embalming certificate. The body must be identified before and after embalming, after which it should be transferred to Cargo Village for shipping.

Cargo fees are calculated by the kilo and distance travelled. The total charge can be anywhere between Dhs.1,500 to Dhs.30,000. A coffin costs upwards of Dhs.1,200. When preparing the documentation, remember that dnata will require seven copies of each document and the translation.

You'll also need to arrange for a funeral company to receive the body when it reaches its destination. It is not obligatory for anyone to accompany the body during the flight home.

Having A Baby

The standard of maternity healthcare in Dubai, either private or government, is excellent. As long as you have insurance or the means to pay, there is no reason to return to your home country to give birth. It's also easier to get by with one income in Dubai, meaning that many mothers get to stay at home with their new babies rather than having to return to work. And, you will have access to cheap childcare and babysitting services here.

However, there are a few disadvantages to be aware of. Maternity leave is paltry: just 45 days paid leave, and no paternity leave. You can take another month unpaid, provided your employer agrees. If you need extra time for medical reasons, you can take up to 100 days, although this is only granted upon production of a medical certificate from your doctor. Plus, there's also the absence of the family support network you may have had back home. Fortunately, there are strong networks of other parents who meet up regularly and offer plenty of support to each other; for example, see dubaimums.com and expatwoman.com.

Registering Your New Baby

If you're planning to have a baby in Dubai, the following is an essential checklist to ensure your child is properly registered once born.

Get a UAE birth certificate
You have 30 days after the birth to get your newborn's UAE birth certificate, which is needed to apply for a passport and residence visa.

After the baby is born, the hospital will issue a notification of birth upon receipt of copies of both parents' passports, the attested marriage certificate, and a fee of Dhs.50.

To get the actual UAE birth certificate, take the birth notification and the above documents to the Mediexpress office (04 272 7190) at Al Baraha Hospital. For a fee of Dhs.490, they will issue the English birth certificate and the Arabic birth certificate, and have both attested by the Ministry of Health and the Ministry of Foreign Affairs.

Register the birth with your embassy
Once you have the UAE birth certificate, you can register the birth with your embassy. They will issue you with a registration of birth certificate that can be used to apply for the passport. (Note that this is not the birth certificate from your home country; that will need to be applied for separately). The fees and process will vary depending on nationality. Visit your embassy's website to download the application form and find out more about the procedure.

Apply for your baby's passport
Once the birth is registered with your embassy, you can apply for the passport. You'll need to provide the birth certificate (UAE or home nationality), the registration of birth certificate (issued by your embassy), one parent's birth certificate and two passport-sized photos of your child. The fees for the passport and courier service will vary depending on nationality. The procedure should take four to six weeks.

Apply for a birth certificate from your home country
Depending on your nationality, you may have to wait up to six months from registering the birth with your embassy to request a birth certificate, either at your embassy or in some cases, online. The certificate will then be couriered to you.

Get a residence visa for your baby
You have 120 days from the birth to get a UAE residence visa for your newborn or risk being fined Dhs.100 a day. To qualify, the parent (sponsor) must earn at least Dhs.4,000 (or Dhs.3,000 plus accommodation) per month. You'll need the following documents (originals and copies unless otherwise specified):

- Typed application form
- Baby's passport
- Baby's attested birth certificates (both in English and Arabic)
- Three passport-sized photos of the baby
- Attested marriage certificate
- Sponsor (parent)'s passport (copy)
- Mother's passport and visa page (copy)
- Sponsor's attested salary certificate (copy)
- Ejari tenancy contract
- Resident ID of the sponsor
- Last three months' bank statements (not printed online statements)
- Dhs.310 application fee and typing fee

Pick up an application form from a typing office and have them complete it for you. Then, visit the residency section of the General Directorate of Residency & Foreigners Affairs. Hand in the completed form and supporting documents at the Family Entry Permit counter. The residence visa will be sent to you through a courier service or can be collected.

Born Back Home
Babies born abroad to expat mums with UAE residency are required to have a residence visa or visit visa of their own to enter the UAE. The application should be filed by the father or family provider, along with the essential documents, a salary certificate and a copy of the newly born child's birth certificate.

LIVING IN DUBAI
FAMILY & PARENTING

Let's just clear up some of the misunderstandings and urban myths about having a baby in Dubai.
Here we go:
- Your baby will have an Arabic birth certificate
- He/she will not have UAE citizenship or a passport
- Breastfeeding is allowed in the UAE, just be discreet
- Home births are not permitted in the UAE
- You must be married before giving birth
- The husband is allowed to be present at the birth at most private hospitals

Overseas Births
If you have your baby back in your home country, you will need to organise their residence or visit visa before entering the UAE. The application should be filed by the father along with his passport and residence visa, salary certificate, and a copy of the birth certificate.

Pregnant Out Of Wedlock
If you fall pregnant but are not married then there is no reason to panic, but there are several decisions that you will need to make fairly quickly. It is illegal to have a baby out of wedlock while you are a resident in the UAE and if you deliver your baby at any hospital here, private or public, and can't produce a marriage certificate, you will most likely face a prison sentence. Therefore, as soon as you see the blue lines on the pregnancy test, you need to sort a few things out.

The easiest solution is to have a quick wedding, after which you can go on to have antenatal care in a government or private hospital without any fear of punishment. If this is not an option, you can stay in Dubai until a reasonable time before you are due to give birth, and even have your antenatal check-ups in a private hospital. But you will need to ensure that you return to your home country to actually deliver the baby. Once you have delivered you can return to Dubai with the baby: there are no rules against being a single mother here.

From Bump To Birth
As soon as you find out that you're going to have a baby, you need to choose where to go for your maternity care. Most expecting expat mothers opt for a private hospital rather than a government hospital, and as long as you have private health insurance this should be affordable, if not free. Bear in mind that some hospitals may charge extra for certain procedures, such as caesarean sections, costing around Dhs.20,000, and epidurals, which normally cost about Dhs.2,000. Having twins, triplets or more will cost you more, too. There are also additional costs for resuscitation after the birth, Neonatal Intensive Care Unit (NICU), your husband staying overnight in the room with you, and, in some hospitals, baby's nappies and wet wipes.

Unlike some other countries, in the UAE the delivery will be performed by the doctor who treats you throughout your pregnancy, rather than a midwife. Therefore, it's important to find a doctor that you are comfortable with from the beginning, as he or she will be with you from bump to birth'. You can choose to have all your antenatal care at a local clinic, as many obstetricians are then authorised to deliver at a certain hospital. It's also more than likely that you will be able to receive more frequent check-ups and scans in the run up to the birth as part of your care, including a 4D scan.

See the Health section for listings of maternity clinics; Mediclinic City Hospital, which has one of the largest Neonatal Intensive Care Units (NICU) in the UAE, and American Hospital are by far the most popular. There is also an NICU at the government-run Latifa Hospital; this is the largest NICU facility in the Middle East and provides treatment for babies from 24 weeks onwards.

Water Births
While water births are not available in Dubai, you can go to the Al Ain Cromwell Women and Children's Hospital (alaincromwell.com). However, you'll need to sign up to their whole delivery package which will cost you between Dhs.12,000 and Dhs.14,000 if you don't have insurance, or if your insurance won't cover it.

Healthy Pregnancy
To prepare you for parenthood why not sign up to an antenatal class. Health Bay Polyclinic in Umm Suqeim (healthbayclinic.com) runs classes costing Dhs.1,500 for four hour-long sessions; Mediclinic City Hospital has an antenatal programme (Dhs.1,725 for eight classes or Dhs.250 per class); and Cooper Clinic (cooperhealthclinic.com) offers one-day courses including an introduction to baby massage.

Compulsory Vaccinations
By law, parents are required to ensure that their baby's immunisation shots are up to date. While the first vaccines are given as soon as your baby is born, you will be required to return to your hospital or clinic every two months until the baby is one year old. At 18 months, babies receive three booster shots and then do not have any more until they are aged five.

The UAE's national immunisation programme includes Hepatitis A + B, polio, MMR (measles, mumps and German measles), chicken pox, Hib and whooping cough. Do bring copies of your child's vaccination records from your home country with you when moving to Dubai.

LIVING IN DUBAI
FAMILY & PARENTING

Adoption

While you can't adopt a UAE National baby, many couples in Dubai adopt children from Africa, Asia and Far Eastern countries. Adoption regulations vary according to which country the child comes from, but once you clear the requirements of that country, and complete the adoption process, you will have no problems bringing your new child into the UAE on your sponsorship. Check with your embassy about the procedure for applying for citizenship of your home country for your new child.

You are advised to go through the Hague Adoption Convention, an internationally recognised process. You'll be required to provide a file of essential documents, undergo a police check, and complete a 12 hour home-study programme – which involves psychological analysis and parental preparation. After a home visit and final interview, you will receive 'approval', and your home study file can be handed over to any international adoption agency recognised by the UAE, and your name added to their adoption list. It is then a matter of waiting for the phone to ring. If you are considering adopting a child, a good place to start is the Adoption Support Group Dubai. Join the Yahoo group (groups.yahoo.com/group/asgdubai), or email asgdubai@yahoogroups.com.

Single Parents

It is possible to live in Dubai and sponsor your children as a single parent, even if you are a woman. There will, however, be a number of extra requirements that you need to meet, including a minimum salary level and a letter of no objection from the other parent (or a death certificate, in the case of a deceased spouse). You may also need to show your divorce certificate but it is best to visit the Immigration Department to find out the exact requirements, as these may change.

Being a working single parent in Dubai may seem daunting for a number of reasons. Firstly, as an expat, your support system may not be as great as back home, where friends and family can help out, and, secondly, in a country where marriage and family are so important you may feel a little like the 'odd one out'. However, once you get used to people enquiring where your husband is (if you have a child with you, people assume you're married), there are actually lots of advantages of living in Dubai as a working single parent. For one thing, there's the standard of childcare: the nurseries in Dubai are very good and a few offer full day-care; they are also generally much more affordable than in your home country. There is also the option of having a live-in nanny, which means that you cannot only work as a single parent but can enjoy an active social life too.

Mother & Baby Groups

Dubai is a great place for young families because it is safe, has great weather and close-knit expat communities. While you may not have the helpful hand of family close by, there are lots of mother and baby groups to keep you and your baby happy. The city's parks make great spots for mothers to meet, and many of them have walking tracks which are excellent for a bit of pram pushing exercise. As pavements are rare in Dubai, going for a stroll with your pushchair may be a challenge – malls are of course an option, The Walk at Jumeirah Beach Residence has nice wide walkways and Uptown Mirdiff's pedestrianised area provides traffic-free space, as does much of the Downtown Dubai area.

Dubai Mums Club
dubaimumsclub.com
This group operates via its online site and through meet-ups. Registered members have access to the club forum, as well as special discounts. Members can also consult an online paediatrician and fitness instructor.

Mirdif Mums Dubai
Mirdif **055 735 4759**
mirdifmums.webs.com
Metro **Rashidiya**
As Mirdif has a strong family population it is only fitting that the mums get together to share coffee mornings, afternoons in the park and various activity days. The group also has some social outings without the kids, which is a great way to make new friends.

Mumcierge
050 640 8322
mumcierge.com
An online concierge club for busy parents wanting to set up activities for their children. The group has weekly coffee meetings at Lime Tree Cafe & Kitchen in Al Qouz.

Hiring A Nanny

Many families choose to hire live-in, full-time maids (nannies) to assist them with childcare and babysitting. It is a relatively simple process, detailed in Explorer's *Dubai How-To* guide, which explains all the documents you will need and procedures to follow to organise a domestic worker visa.

If both you and your spouse work full time then a live-in maid is really your best option as there is no official network of childminders. Your maid can also help with cleaning, washing, cooking and other household jobs.

LIVING IN DUBAI
FAMILY & PARENTING

Finding the right live-in person can certainly be a challenge. There are a number of registered agencies in Dubai, which organise everything from interviews through to airfares and the visa; they will charge an agency fee of around Dhs.3,500. It is preferable to recruit someone who is already in Dubai, and therefore your best bet would be to find an expat who is leaving the country and no longer needs their maid. Speak to other parents and check/put up notices on Spinneys and community noticeboards, as check the ads on expatwoman.com and dubizzle.com.

Residence Visa

If you employ a full-time live-in maid you will need to sponsor her for a residence visa. You can only sponsor a maid from the following countries: India, Sri Lanka, Philippines, Ethiopia, Bangladesh, and Indonesia. You must have a salary above Dhs.6,000 per month and be able to provide her with housing (many apartments and villas have a maid's room inside or outside), medical insurance and benefits, which include an airfare back to her home country at least once every two years, food, clothing and toiletries. Depending upon the nationality of your live-in maid (and whether or not you need to organise her entry permit into the UAE) you may have to visit their local embassy to get a contract drawn up before beginning the sponsorship process (see When You Arrive).

Can You Afford It?

Once you've made the decision to employ a nanny, you'll need to work out if you can actually afford to do so. The average monthly wage is around Dhs.2,000 although you should allow an extra Dhs.400 for things like phone credit, food, clothes and toiletries. One of the prerequisites is an airfare to her home country, which is likely to cost about Dhs.3,500. The residence visa is Dhs.5,080 a year and her annual medical will cost Dhs.325. You'll also need to make a few one-off payments: Dhs.600 for health insurance, Dhs.140 for a Resident ID card and a refundable residence visa deposit of Dhs.2,030.

First Aid Courses

Make sure that you and your maid are able to cope with minor medical emergencies and take a first aid course. The Perfect Help (theperfecthelp.com) run a number of training courses for maids, including first aid. Back To Basics also run courses in several languages (backtobasicsme.com).

Pros & Cons

There are plenty of advantages to having a live-in nanny. Not only is it relatively inexpensive, but having someone to look after your child means that you have reliable childcare support as and when you need it, and can enjoy the odd night out!

On the other hand, you should keep in mind that first aid and childcare qualifications are not legally required for your babysitters or childcare workers in the UAE, so it's worth doing your research to find someone with experience. Networking and word of mouth can pay dividends as many parents with young children will be in the same boat as you.

Babysitting

Domestic help agencies can provide part-time babysitters, although there is no guarantee that you will get the same babysitter every time.

Ask around your neighbourhood to see if any of the local maids or teenagers are available for ad hoc evening babysitting, or try your child's nursery, as classroom assistants are often up for a bit of extra work and they will already have a rapport with your children. If you do manage to find someone for part-time babysitting, the rate ranges from Dhs.30 to Dhs.40 per hour. Western childminders are most likely to charge more than this.

Activities For Kids

During the cooler months (October to May), kids can enjoy the parks and beaches around Dubai, which house playgrounds for varying ages, as well as tennis and basketball courts. Try the boating lake in Safa Park, the petting zoo in Mushrif Park, and the camel and pony rides in Creek Park. There are also water parks in and around the city; however, while swimming is obviously popular, there are few public pools. Mushrif Park has separate women's and men's pools but, outside the hotels and health clubs, the only other options are villa compound pools or the beach. See Things to See & Do for more information.

During the warmer months (June to September) the many amusement centres and kids' play areas keep your brood from getting bored. Fun Corner is a soft play centre with a few arcade games and small rides located in Bin Sougat Centre, Al Ghurair City, and the Spinneys Centre on Al Wasl Road. Fun City (funcity.ae) offers similar facilities, plus scheduled classes, and can be found in the Arabian Center, Oasis Centre, Reef Mall, Ibn Battuta, Mercato, Lamcy Plaza and Century Mall. Located near Dubai Garden Centre along Sheikh Zayed Road, Mini Monsters (minimonsters.ae) is the UAE's largest indoor soft play venue.

There are various sports and activity clubs that run after-school activities and summer camps, plus some great kids' attractions such as KidZania. The Activities chapter covers a range of hobbies for children. Visit uae4kidz.biz for up-to-date information on family events and activities.

LIVING IN DUBAI
FAMILY & PARENTING

Keep an eye on the local press too as, most months, there's something going on for families whether that's shows on the ice, exhibitions or one-off entertainment. Many malls have specific kiddie entertainment during Eid, DSF and other popular calendar events.

After-School Activities

Many schools will run ECAs (Extra Curricular Activities) from kindergarten upwards. Generally, the younger years only have one ECA a week for around 30-60 minutes directly after school, while the older years may have multiple classes at various times. School-run ECAs are often included in the school fees, however, independent companies also hold classes at schools during the afternoons and evenings and charge term fees (which are far from cheap), as well as at weekends and holidays.

Turning Pointe runs ballet classes for all ages in various schools around Dubai, as does Kids' Theatre Works, and Active Sports Academy has a range of sports classes. If your kids are sports players (or you want them to be) there are a number of academies that can develop their talents – would-be Federers should sign up with the Clark Francis Tennis Academy, budding Beckhams can hone their skills with the International Football Academy or UAE English Soccer School of Excellence, wanna-be Olympic gold medallists should dive in with Australian International Swim Schools and potential Bruce Lees can kick it with various clubs around Dubai (see Martial Arts). Many parents get together in the parks (in the winter) and play centres (in the summer) around Dubai for their own impromptu after-school activities, so new families shouldn't worry about long afternoons and bored kids.

Keep The Kids Happy

For a taste of the past, and guaranteed to get the little ones excited, flag down the Desert Chill ice cream van. Complete with melodic tinkling tunes, this classic van travels around several communities in Dubai all week long. See desertchill.ae for the schedule or call 050 612 2108.

Indoor

From around May to September, having fun in air-conditioned venues like these is often the best option.

Aquaplay
Mirdif **04 231 6307**
theplaymania.com
Map **2 P12** Metro **Rashidiya**
An indoor play centre dedicated to water fun, this gem in Mirdif City Centre boasts a swinging pirate ship, log flume ride, water guns and bumper boats.

It's a child-friendly change from the usual outdoor water parks and available at a fraction of the cost. Plus, the fact that it's indoors makes it perfect for the summer months.

Cheeky Monkeys Playland
Al Barsha Mall Al Barsha 2 **04 385 0875**
cheekymonkeys.ae
Map **1 Q7** Metro **Sharaf DG**
This hugely popular play centre is well suited to little ones, thanks to its toddler-friendly soft play areas as well as Art Garden, Sports Room and Princess Room. It's a great spot for hosting birthday parties, and there's a cafe selling snacks and freshly squeezed juices where mums and dads can relax while the kids play.

Children's City
Gate 1, Creek Park Umm Hurair 2 **04 334 0808**
childrencity.ae
Map **2 L7** Metro **Dubai Healthcare City**
An edutainment venue in Creek Park with hands-on interactive displays and learning zones where kids have fun and can swot up on subjects like science, geography and even astronomy at the planetarium. In addition to the permanent displays, there are regular events such as drum shows and light displays.

Favourite Things
Marsa Dubai **04 434 1984**
favouritethings.com
Map **1 K5** Metro **Jumeirah Lakes Towers**
The perfect place to leave your kids happily playing for an hour or two, Favourite Things, in Dubai Marina Mall,

Kids Connection

LIVING IN DUBAI
FAMILY & PARENTING

has more than enough activities to keep the rug rats happy. There's everything from toddlers' soft play area to a mini race track, jungle gym and dressing up area. Parents can join in, watch from the comfort of the cafe, or even leave the tots in the centre's capable hands while they go shopping.

Kids Connection
Wafi Umm Hurair 2 **04 327 9011**
Map **2 L7** Metro **Dubai Health Care City**
Located on the first floor of Wafi Mall, this bright, colourful attraction brings the outside in with a variety of wooden park attractions in a very green, woodland inspired setting. Kids can climb, swing, seesaw and slide while mum and dad enjoy a coffee in the Cafe Court – or burn off some energy on the trampolines, bouncy castle and climbing wall. The soft play area with a ball pool is great for toddlers too. Prices range from Dhs.3 to Dhs.27.

Kidz Venture
Ibn Battuta Jabal Ali 1 **04 368 4130**
kidzventure.ae
Map **1 G5** Metro **Ibn Battuta**
Open seven days a week, from 7am to 10pm, Kidz Venture offers a variety of childcare options as and when you need them. From nursery and after-school programmes, to drop 'n' shop babysitting, birthday parties, and arts and crafts activities, there is always something to keep your little one amused.

Le Petit Palais
Downtown Dubai, Burj Khalifa **04 382 7333**
Map **2 F7** Metro **Burj Khalifa/Dubai Mall**
Located in the ever-sophisticated Galeries Lafayette in The Dubai Mall, the French-themed play centre is the perfect place for kids to have fun while parents shop. It's like a miniature city where children can play at being grown-ups, with a mini supermarket, salon and even a karaoke room, as well as other games and soft play areas to keep them entertained.

Little Explorers
Mirdiff City Center Mirdif
Map **2 P12** Metro **Rashidiya**
Little Explorers at Playnation Mirdif City Centre is an edutainment centre for children from two to seven years old. Focused on acquiring skills in a fun and safe environment, this venue is set out in five distinctly themed zones offering plenty of variety to keep kids interested; there's everything from seeing how fast you can run, to scientific experiments that investigate the natural environment. With games and activities spanning over 97 different exhibits that get the brain ticking and stimulate the senses, children can discover hidden talents and new skills. There are also a variety of birthday party packages available.

Magic Planet
Mall of the Emirates Al Barsha 1 **04 341 4444**
magicplanet.ae
Map **1 R6** Metro **Mall of the Emirates**
A blaring and boisterous play centre that's a huge hit with families, Magic Planet's many attractions include bowling lanes, bumper cars and video games. Play the arcade games and collect tickets to exchange for prizes or, for a more exhilarating game experience, check out the XD Theatre with its interactive 3D and 4D cinema effects.

Peekaboo Creative Play Centre
The Village Jumeira 1 **04 344 7122**
peekaboo.ae
Map **2 H4** Metro **Emirates Towers**
Here there's a packed schedule of organised activities, which aim to be fun while developing the children's creativity and providing an educational experience. Children aged zero to seven can join in with cooking, nursery rhymes, yoga, arts, crafts and more. Kids under three-and-a-half must be accompanied by an adult. The centre operates an hourly fee structure with memberships also available. Also at Mall of the Emirates and Ibn Battuta.

Play A Round @ Some Place Nice
Jewels Tower Marsa Dubai **04 457 0455**
playaround.ae
Map **1 J5** Metro **Jumeirah Lakes Towers**
Play A Round @ Some Place Nice provides fun for all the family, with its neon, nine-hole mini golf course, soft play areas and party room. Once you're done competing on the glow-in-the-dark course, grab a bite to eat at the on-site cafe or try some arts and crafts. There's a special area for tots aged one to three.

Quay Skillz Youth Facility
Madinat Jumeirah Al Sufouh 1 **050 480 7670**
skillz.ae
Map **1 R5** Metro **Mall of the Emirates**
Dedicated children's gym with secure entry and specialised trainers who provide an environment for kids aged seven to 16 to exercise, while adults can use the extensive club facilities. Includes running machines, spinning bikes, cross trainers, fitness trampolines and rowing machines all tailored to the needs and interests of the younger gym-goer.

Zebra Crossing
Nr Noor Islamic Bank MS Al Qouz Ind. 1 **050 559 4903**
zebra-crossing.com
Map **2 A6** Metro **Noor Bank**
Join Ziggi the Zebra at this play centre, which boasts a host of soft play areas and bouncy castles. It's the perfect spot for a party, with activities ranging from arts and crafts and face painting to magic shows and

NEW
Delivery
ON DEMAND
Desert
Chill
ICE CREAM
www.desertchill.ae
You choose
HOME DELIVERY OFFICE VISITS
BIRTHDAY PARTIES & EVENTS
050 6122108 BBpin: 2B4E0B23
www.desertchill.ae

LIVING IN DUBAI
FAMILY & PARENTING

puppet shows. There's even the option to host a spa party at the Zebra Lounge, where little princesses can enjoy mini mani-pedis.

Classes
Keep the grey matter working and learn something new or perfect an existing skill with classes and courses from these clubs and service providers.

Apple Seeds
Al Quoz Ind. 3 **04 380 6064**
appleseedsdubai.com
Map **1 S6** Metro **Mall of the Emirates**
This New-York themed indoor playground has some innovative ideas and features an NYC taxi cab and apartment, yoga block skyscraper, shape sorter garden, deli with play foods, Lego table, magnet wall and even more. There are also classes covering everything from science to ballet, cooking to art – so lots to keep the little ones amused. They also have character and confidence building programmes for four to 13 year olds.

Desert Sport Services
Palace Tower 2 Nadd Hessa **056 644 1742**
desertsportservices.com
Desert Sport Services runs swimming programmes for all ages, from parent & baby/toddler through to learn to swim and stroke development; sessions are held at various sites including Emirates International School, English College Primary, Jebel Ali Club and Horizon School. The club also organises pool parties for children, staffed by fully qualified lifeguards.

DuGym Gymnastics Club
050 553 6283
dugym.com
DuGym offers gymnastics and trampoline coaching to children of all ages and abilities. Established in 2000, the club now operates at 15 locations including Wellington International School, Jumeirah English Speaking School and Emirates International School. Classes are held from Sunday to Thursday. Contact Suzanne on the above number for more details.

Kids' Theatre Works
DUCTAC Al Barsha 1 **050 158 5653**
kidstheatreworks.com
Map **1 R6** Metro **Mall of the Emirates**
This club holds classes in creative drama, musical theatre, acting, dance, youth theatre, music and scene work for children aged three and over; if your kids are budding superstars, Kids' Theatre Works is a good start. It runs classes at DUCTAC (the theatre inside Mall of the Emirates), Uptown Mirdiff Primary, Jabal Ali, Gems Academies and the American School of Dubai.

Kidville
The Walk at JBR Marsa Dubai **04 440 1220**
mykidville.ae
Map **1 K4** Metro **Jumeirah Lakes Towers**
Based on an innovative concept pioneered in New York, Kidville offers newborns to six year olds a unique range of classes that include musical journeys on the Rockin' Railroad, building 3D art projects in Construction Junction, and exploring a variety of paints, dough, crayons, chalk and collage in My Big Messy Art Class. There's also the Kidville University, an alternative programme for pre-schoolers. Other branches include MotorCity (04 454 2760) and Uptown Mirdiff (04 236 3648).

My Gym UAE
Villa 520, Jumeira Rd Jumeira 3 **04 394 3962**
mygymuae.com
Map **2 B4** Metro **Noor Bank**
Offering a wide range of programmes for kids up to 13 years old, the expert staff lead classes that combine increases in strength, agility, coordination and flexibility with the development of social skills and self-esteem.

Tickles & Giggles
The Walk at JBR Marsa Dubai **04 432 8681**
ticklesandgiggles.com
Map **1 K4** Metro **Jumeirah Lakes Towers**
Tickles & Giggles has a kids' salon and spa, and offers unique classes such as baby yoga, etiquette classes, arts and crafts and nursery rhymes. It also hosts ultra-trendy parties for kids (no bears or tank engines in sight), and will match decorations and the menu to your chosen theme. You can become a member on the website, where you can order party supplies as well as make online bookings.

Scouts & Guides
Girls can join the Girl Guides, Brownies or Rainbows clubs in Dubai. Email girlguidingdubai@gmail.com for more information about meeting times and places. Scout groups operate too. Contact gasplampke@msn.com for information on Cub Scouts and hoytjk2@aol.com for information on Boy Scouts of America.

The majority of Scout and Guide groups in Dubai are held at schools, so check with your child's school. With each new group comes a need for adult volunteers. If you have experience with Scout or Guide groups, or your child was once a member, contact Mary Dunn (alistair@emirates.net.ae) to get involved.

British Guides In Foreign Countries
girlguidingdubai.wordpress.com
Groups for girls of various ages include Rainbows (five to seven years), Brownies (seven to 10), Guides (10 to 14), and Senior Section (14 to 25) with groups in Al

LIVING IN DUBAI
FAMILY & PARENTING

Safa, Jabal Ali, Dubai Investment Park, Mirdif, Silicon Oasis, Emirates Living and Arabian Ranches.

The Scouts Association (British Scouting Overseas)
britishscoutingoverseas.org.uk
The Scouts Association encourages the development of youngsters through weekly activities and outings for ages six to 18 and 18-25. Contact Steve Sutton (dc_middle-east@bsomail.org.uk) for more information.

Scouts Abroad
From April 2012, the existing Scout Areas of British Scouts in Western Europe (BSWE) and British Groups Abroad (BGA) were merged into a new Scout Area referred to as 'British Scouting Overseas' (BSO), which functions to support UK Scouting based outside the UK. The area is classed as an independent educational UK charity.

Summer Camps
Soaring temperatures that have everyone cooped up indoors can make summer a challenging time to entertain the kids. To help keep boredom at bay, various organisations throughout Dubai run summer camps during the hottest months, while several nurseries also offer summer day-care for young children.

While many activities will be inside air-conditioned buildings there are plenty that will have your little ones getting a good dose of fresh air. Most language schools run summer courses for kids (see Language Courses), or if you'd rather see them having fun over the holidays, many leisure clubs offer summer camps that focus on sports, arts and crafts. Alternatively, contact Active Sports Academy, which arranges sporty summer camps at various venues around the city.

Another option is to sign them up for sailing lessons – if there's a breeze, then being out on the water can be significantly cooler than on land, and that way, they're still getting some fresh air. Clubs such as Dubai Offshore Sailing Club (DOSC – dosc.ae) run dinghy sailing courses for kids.

Active Sports Academy
106 Corner City Al Kheeran 050 559 7055
activeuae.com
Map **2 M9** Metro **Emirates**
In operation for 14 years, Active Sports Academy organises various coaching classes in multiple venues around Dubai, including at campuses after school. It teaches tennis, soccer, cricket, basketball, swimming and gymnastics and runs various tournaments, as well as holiday camps through all school break periods, including spring, Eid, Christmas and summer.

Blossom Village Nursery
Villa 43, Street 21C Umm Suqeim 1 04 394 8837
theblossomnursery.com
Map **2 A5** Metro **Noor Bank**
This vibrant nursery will give your child plenty of stimulation as it emphasises creativity, play and personal development – and its summer camp, Passports, is no different. Based on the British Early Years Foundation Stage and aimed at children aged two and older, it's an imaginative summer adventure that includes arts and crafts, mini Olympics, swimming, baking and more. Flexible enrolment and pick up at 1pm, 3pm, 5pm or 6pm are available, making it a good choice if both parents work full time.

Dubai Holiday Camps
Grosvenor House Business Tower Al Thanyah 1 04 420 3732
dubaiholidaycamps.com
Map **1 P6** Metro **Dubai Internet City**
One of the longest established camps in the UAE, Dubai Holiday Camps has been provides a range of holiday activities for children aged three to 14 since its inception in 1998. Juniors take part in classroom-based fun like arts and crafts, storytelling, movie time and face painting, while older kids (those aged five to 14) can try their hands at a range of sports as well as talent shows, dance, drama and cooking classes. The experienced staff are English speakers with additional languages and trained to handle large groups of kids.

E-Sports
Al Garhoud 04 282 4540
esportsuae.com
Map **2 M8** Metro **GGICO**
Each day follows a set structure at E-Sports Holiday Camps – there are around 20 activities to choose from that are rotated throughout the week with kids taking part in five activities a day. (Guaranteed to tire them out!) These range from sports like football, tennis and swimming to arts and crafts, and dodgeball. Led by professional, enthusiastic teachers and assistants, E-Sports camps are a firm favourite with youngsters and a popular choice for busy parents.

Gulf Star Sports
050 429 4860
gulfstarsports.com
These action-packed, multi-activity camps are targeted at children aged from two to 17. There's a strong focus on sports and children and teens can try their hands (and feet) at everything from football, cricket and basketball to martial arts, dance, and water polo, as well as drama and crafts. Professional, enthusiastic staff and top notch facilities make for an unforgettable experience. Staff are happy to meet with parents to discuss their children's needs.

PETS

Having a pet is always a comfort, and Dubai has no shortage of abandoned animals in need of homes. If you're not sure you can commit for the long term, there are also options to foster animals as cat and dog homes especially are overcrowded.

You should check with your landlord what the pet policy is before you move in. In many cases it is not permitted to keep a pet, particularly in apartments. Some landlords will be amenable if you negotiate, but it is advisable to get any permission in writing to avoid difficult situations further down the line.

Pets are banned from parks and beaches, and popular walkways such as The Walk at JBR are also off limits, so finding a place for a good long walk can be a challenge. Paws Pet Planet (pawspetplanet.com) has a 20,000 square feet outdoor and indoor dog park, where you can let your pooch run off the leash.

When walking your dog, keep it on a short leash. Remember that dogs are considered by many conservative Muslims as unclean and are traditionally only kept for guarding property, so just be mindful of these attitudes when you are out in public. Be sure to keep your pet indoors or within your garden to avoid contact with strays and to prevent any problems with frightened neighbours. Dubai has a significant problem with strays, although both Feline Friends (050 451 0058) and K9 Friends (04 887 8739) are hard-working animal charities that take in as many as they can. The Dubai Municipality is also helping to fix the stray problem.

In addition to having dogs kept on leads at all times when walking, certain dogs have to be muzzled in Dubai when walked in public (see dkc.ae for details). All cats and dogs must be registered, microchipped and vaccinated, or you could face fines and confiscation.

Hot Dogs

The summer heat in Dubai is a serious health risk for cats, dogs and other pets. They cannot sweat to regulate body temperature as humans can, and so are at risk from heat-related issues, which can be fatal. Never walk your dog in the summer sun – be prepared to get up at dawn to ensure your dog gets the exercise it needs in a bearable temperature. Remember too that hot pavements will burn your pooch's paws. If your dog is bred for colder climes, think very carefully before you subject your pet to desert heat. Keeping the animal penned up inside with the air conditioning on is not a healthy option either; a dog needs regular exercise.

While rare, there have been reports of dogs being stolen, either to be sold to unscrupulous pet shops or for dog fighting. Ensure your garden is secure and don't let your dog roam around on the street. If you witness animal abuse see dm.gov.ae for advice or call 04 289 1114.

Sleek Salukis

The saluki is the breed of dog most commonly associated with the region; they are used in traditional forms of hunting and resemble a greyhound in many ways. The Arabian Saluki Centre (02 575 5330) offers a wealth of information and care for these thoroughbred dogs and even welcomes visitors to learn about them.

Moving Your Pet

Pets may be brought into the UAE without quarantine as long as they are microchipped and vaccinated with verifying documentation, including a government health certificate from the country of origin; however, you'll also need an import permit. You cannot import cats and dogs under four months old and all pets must arrive as manifest cargo with a valid rabies vaccination more than 21 days before their arrival. Imports from some countries will also be subjected to a rabies test. For more information visit petimport.moew.gov.ae and create an account.

There are certain breeds of dog that are banned from being imported into the UAE: pit bull terriers, Argentinean and Brazilian mastiffs, Japanese tosa inu, American Staffordshire terriers, Rottweilers and any wolf hybrids; the UAE also bans any dogs crossed with any of the banned breeds listed. There are other breeds which, while not banned outright, have restrictions on them too. Make sure you check with the municipality before you embark on the process. Dubai Kennels & Cattery provides a detailed guide to importing and exporting pets.

The international removal company Crown Relocations (crownrelo.com/uae, 04 230 5300) offers a pet relocation service and can provide useful information on how best to transport your pet.

Buying a Pet

If you want to buy a pet it makes sense to start by visiting some of the rescue centres in Dubai – there are many abandoned animals in need of a home. K9 Friends (04 887 8739) helps to rehome stray and injured dogs, many of which are abandoned family pets looking for a second chance. See k9friends.com for more information. Another useful website for

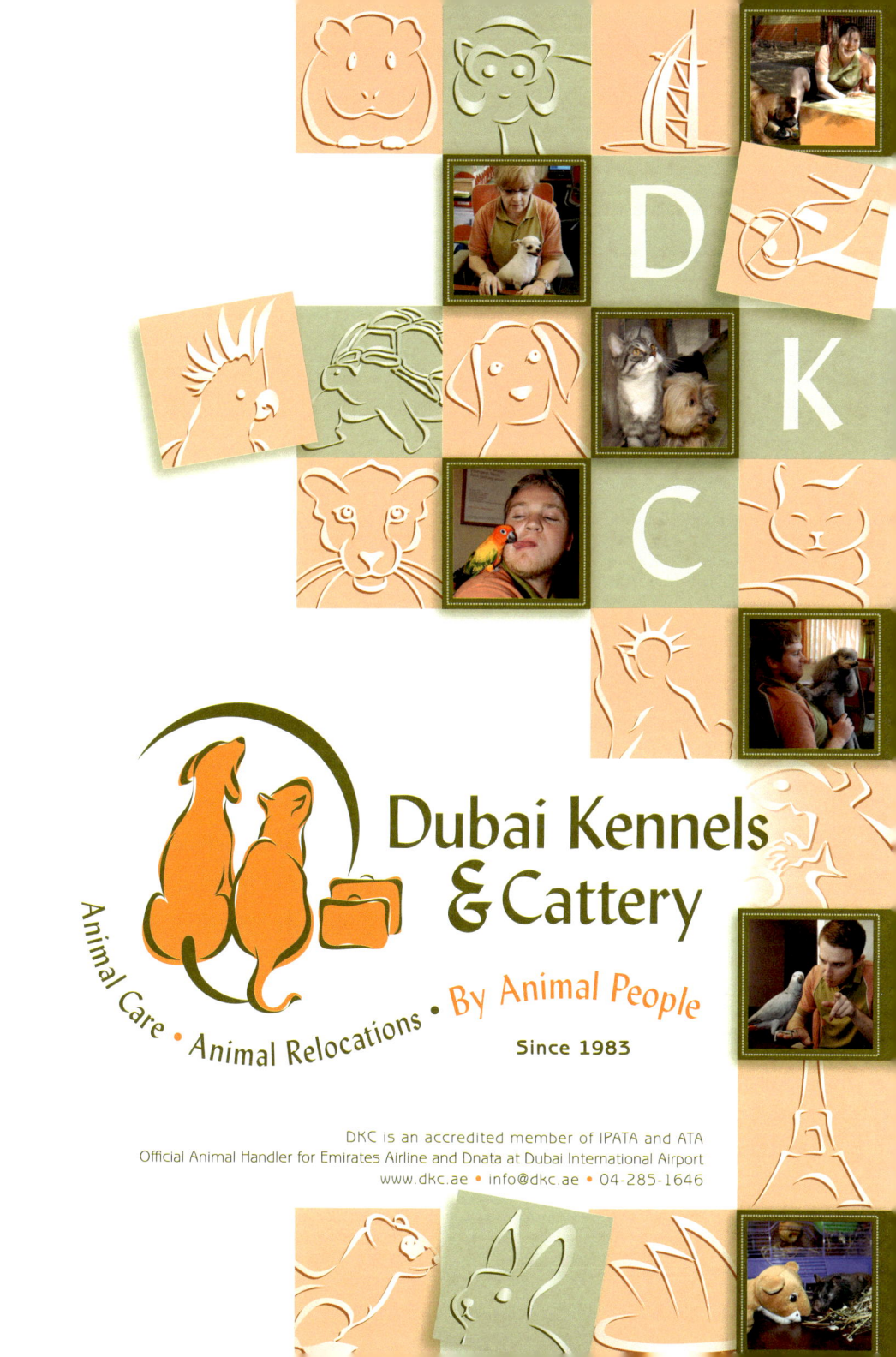

Dubai Kennels & Cattery

Animal Care • Animal Relocations • By Animal People

Since 1983

DKC is an accredited member of IPATA and ATA
Official Animal Handler for Emirates Airline and Dnata at Dubai International Airport
www.dkc.ae • info@dkc.ae • 04-285-1646

LIVING IN DUBAI
PETS

pet owners in the Emirates is petdubai.com. Feline Friends (050 451 0058) is a non-profit organisation, aiming to improve the lives of cats by rescuing and rehoming stray cats and kittens. It has a 24 hour telephone answering service as well as a useful website, felinefriendsdubai.com. The saluki is a breed of dog most commonly associated with the region; they are used in traditional forms of hunting. The Arabian Saluki Center (02 575 5330) can provide information on all aspects of the care of these animals. Many 'desert dogs' descend from the saluki. If you'd like to adopt your own desert dog, contact K9 Friends (k9friends.com).

Vaccinations & Registration

You should inoculate dogs annually against rabies, distemper, canine hepatitis, leptospirosis, parainfluenza virus and parvovirus. There is an optional vaccination against kennel cough which is recommended for all dogs going to kennels, doggy day-care or dog-training in mixed classes. Cats have to be vaccinated against rabies, feline rhinotracheitis, calicivirus and panleukopnia. You must also register your pet with the Dubai Municipality (04 289 1114); this is an annual registration which requires all cats and dogs to have the above vaccinations. They are then microchipped and given a plastic neck tag (there's a different colour for each year), as well as normal ID tags. If the municipality picks up an animal without a tag and chip, it is treated as a stray and there is a strong chance it will be put down. Registration can all be done at any vets or at Dubai Municipality Veterinary Services, and costs approximately Dhs.1,000.

Taking Care Of Turtles
Turtles are native to the waters off Dubai, but with more construction, boats and pollution, they are having a tough time. Luckily, there are organisations doing their bit to help save the turtles. One such rehabilitation project is a collaboration between the Jumeirah Group and the Wildlife Protection Office, with veterinary support provided by Dubai Falcon Clinic & Central Veterinary Research Laboratory. To see how you can help, go to facebook.com/turtle.rehabilitation.

Taking Your Pet Home

To take your pet home contact the airline you will be using – the animal may be able to travel with you or as unaccompanied cargo. Many boarding kennels and vets offer an export service, including Dubai Kennels & Cattery and The Doghouse (dubaidoghouse.com).

Vets, Kennels & Boarding

Standards of care at Dubai's veterinary clinics are reasonably high. Prices do not vary dramatically, but the Deira Veterinary Clinic (04 258 1881) and Al Barsha Veterinary Clinic (04 340 8601) are a little cheaper than the rest. Dubai Municipality has a veterinary services department (04 289 1114) next to Mushrif Park that only vaccinates animals.

There are also several new seven-star pet resorts such as Urban Tails, with luxury suites, landscaped gardens, a pet gym with treadmills, a doggie bootcamp, an outdoor swimming pool and fountains. Paws Pet Planet is another posh pad for pooches (see Where To Walk Your Dog). The Nad Al Shiba Veterinary Hospital (04 323 4412) also treats more exotic animals and birds. Kennels are generally of a good standard, although spaces are limited during peak times (summer and Christmas) – try Dubai Kennels & Cattery (see below).

An alternative is to use an at-home pet-sitting service – someone will come into your house at least once a day to feed and exercise your pet for a reasonable fee (for a bit extra they might even water your plants). For further information on pet shops see Shopping. There are a number of firms that offer a variety of grooming treatments from the basic (shampooing, medicated baths and nail clipping) to the more indulgent, like fashion advice.

Below is our pick of just some of the many vets and boarding and training schools

For more listings see askexplorer.com

Al Barsha Veterinary Clinic Nr Centro Rotana, Al Barsha 1, 04 340 8601, *abvc.ae*
Doggies Palace Nr Al Quoz Cemetery, Al Qouz 1, 04 339 3737, *doggiespalace.com*
Dubai Kennels & Cattery > *p.159* 34th Street, Umm Ramoul, 04 285 1646, *dkc.ae*
Energetic Panacea Al Wasl Rd, Jumeira 2, 04 344 7812, *pets-uae.com*
European Veterinary Centre Villa 63, Umm Al Sheif St, Al Rigga, 04 380 4415, *evc.ae*
Jumeirah Veterinary Clinic 35A Street, Jumeira 3, 04 394 2276
Modern Veterinary Clinic Al Wasl Rd, Al Rigga, 04 395 3131, *vetdubai.com*
Pampered Pets Dreams Tower 2, Marsa Dubai, 04 447 5330, *pamperedpets.ae*
Poshpaws Kennels & Cattery The Animal Care House, Sharjah, 050 273 0973, *poshpawsdubai.com*
Positive Paws Umm Suqeim Rd, Al Qouz Ind. 4, 04 379 0996, *positivepaws.ae*
Urban Tails Pet Resort > *p.163* Nr Green Community, Dubai Investments Park 2, 04 884 8847, *urbantailsdubai.com*
World of Pets Jumeira Rd, Jumeira 3, 04 395 5701, *worldofpetsme.com*

homes
for life

k9 friends
homes for life

We are a voluntary organisation that rescues and rehomes stray & abandoned dogs in the UAE. Our finances are solely dependent on fundraising and donations.

This is how you can help:
- Give a dog a home
- Foster a dog
- Volunteer at the kennel
- Sponsor a kennel or a dog on an annual basis
- Help with fundraising, marketing or organising events

T. 04 887 8739
E. info@k9friends.com
www.k9friends.com

Proud sponsor of
K9 Friends dog food
Eukanuba

Where To Walk Your Dog

Dogs are not as widely accepted in Dubai as they are back home, and there are far more restrictions on dog-walking here. But we've sniffed out some places where your pet can stretch his paws.

Dogs are banned from many areas including Jumeirah Beach Residence (JBR) waterfront, and are frowned upon along Marina Walk and some areas on Palm Jumeirah. Walking a dog off-leash is not permitted and many beaches and parks have large signs up clearly stating these rules. Dubai Municipality will slap you with a Dhs.200 on-the-spot fine (per dog) if you flout the law. Fortunately, you do have a few options when it comes to pooch-friendly spots.

Doggy day-care

This safe, sociable dog park in Dubai, Paws Pet Planet (pawspetplanet.com) is ideal for letting your dog play with other dogs. A first of its kind in the Middle East, the park welcomes all sizes, ages and breeds of dogs and puppies; there are individual dog areas depending on size and the dog's nature. The 2,000 sq m indoor arena is climate-controlled with splash pools, bridges, tunnels and obstacles. All dogs are supervised and if you are unable to be there, the park also runs a doggy day-care centre. To attend, all dogs must have a prior assessment and have up-to-date vaccinations (including kennel cough). Dogs must also pass a mandatory temperament assessment. See website for timetable and prices.

Desert and beach walks

As long as you're vigilant that a snake or scorpion doesn't bite your dog, you can walk your pet in the desert. For a long off-the-lead run, dog-owners get together to organise doggy play dates at various locations. Head out to the open desert behind Arabian Ranches, in Mirdif and Al Barsha 1 (behind the Mall of the Emirates).

In Nadd Al Shiba, there is also a popular area behind the camel market, which is safe, and far away from main roads. Meanwhile, in Al Warqa there is a large area for long walks, only a seven-minute drive from Mirdif.

In Jabal Ali, many people walk dogs on the beach next to the JA Jebel Ali Golf Resort & Spa, while other dog owners drive to Abu Dhabi where dogs are permitted in 'open water' beaches, away from the public and any shops. Also try Shahama Harbour and the beach club and bungalows at the Al Jazira Hotel near Ghantoot.

Dog-walking groups

Find fellow dog owners on the following websites: dubaidogclub.com, k9friends.com and petwatchdubai.com. Expatwoman.com is also a great forum for sharing local dog knowledge and news.

Dog-Friendly Cafes

Some cafes do welcome well-behaved dogs. The Lime Tree Café, on Jumeira Road and the new Tim Horton's and Coffeol cafes at Al Wasl Square don't seem to mind dogs passing through with their owners. There are even some trees close by for some much-needed shade in the summer months.

URBAN tail
PET RESORT

7 star vacations for your furry friends

Luxury Pet Destination
Short & Long Term Boarding For Cats & Dogs
Doggie Daycare
Pet Relocations – Import & Export
Pet Boutique
Live Webcam Access
Qualified Pet Carers
24/7 Supervision
Modern Air-Conditioned Custom Built Facility
Large Shaded Garden & Pool

Located in DIP only 5 minutes from the Green Community

For info and reservations please **call +971 4 884 8847** or drop us an email at **info@urbantailsdubai.com**
w w w . u r b a n t a i l s d u b a i . c o m

Gyms are of a high standard in Dubai

FITNESS

Gyms & Fitness Clubs

While the Dubai lifestyle can be conducive to inactivity and overindulgence, the good weather throughout most of the year means that it's a pretty good place to be active too. So, whether you need to shift that 'Dubai stone' or want to hit the beach bootcamp-style to ramp up your endurance, you'll find plenty of ways to get off your sofa and on your feet.

If it's a new sport you're after there's a wide variety of team sports to choose from (see also Activities & Hobbies). If you prefer to hit the treadmill or cross-trainer, you may be lucky to find accommodation with its own gym, particularly in apartment blocks and new housing complexes.

There are also plenty of gyms to join, and hotels offer health club memberships if your complex doesn't have facilities. Independent gyms usually offer day passes for Dhs.100, or monthly membership from Dhs.350-1,000. With 27 branches across the UAE, Fitness First is one of the leading gym brands in the region; standard membership costs Dhs.4,199 per year including all exercise classes and two free personal training sessions, after which you will receive a personalised programme.

Fitness 360 offers unusual fitness classes such as dancing in heels and partner yoga; U Concept is a boutique gym with DJ decks, art on the walls and a UFC cage in the basement; Engine offers a class-only package at Dhs.450 per month (including suspended yoga using a padded hammock); and Symmetry Gym offers personalised workouts in a small gym environment. The Circuit Factory (circuitfactory.ae) sets the four-week challenge of circuit sessions and a diet. So, there is plenty of choice and no excuse to fester on the sofa or in the bar!

LIVING IN DUBAI
FITNESS

American Fitness Umm Suqeim 1, 056 103 5581, *americanfitness.me*
The Aviation Club Jumeirah Creekside, Al Garhoud, 04 230 8560, *jumeirah.com*
Bodylines Health & Fitness Centre Trade Center 1, 04 312 2556
Cleopatra's Spa & Wellness Umm Hurair 2, 04 324 7700, *cleopatrasspaandwellness.com*
Core Fit Dreams Tower 2, Marsa Dubai, 050 922 6247, *coredirection.com*
Crowne Fitness Crowne Plaza, Trade Center 1, 04 3311111, *crowneplaza.com*
Dubai Ladies Club Jumeira Rd, Jumeira 2, 04 349 9922, *dubailadiesclub.com*
Exhale Marsa Dubai, 04 424 3777, *exhaledubai.com*
Fidelity Fitness Club Almas Tower, Al Thanyah 5, 04 451 1133, *fidelityfitnessclub.com*
Fitness First DIFC, DIFC, Zaa'beel 2, 04 363 7444, *fitnessfirstme.com*
Fitness O2 Nr Mall of the Emirates, Al Barsha 1, 04 379 2757, *fitness02.com*
Goal Attained 056 693 9258, *goalattained.com*
The Health Club Emirates Towers, Trade Center 2, 04 319 8888, *jumeirahemiratestowers.com*
In Shape Ladies Fitness Club Al Joud Bldg, Al Qouz Ind 1, 04 395 5718, *inshapeme.com*
India Club Nr Indian High School, Oud Metha, 04 337 1112, *indiaclubdubai.com*
Insportz Club Nr Dubai Garden Centre, Al Qouz Ind. 3, 04 347 5833, *insportzclub.com*
Motion Fitness Center Villa 24, Street 25, Umm Suqeim 3, 04 328 2538, *motionfitnesscenter.com*
Original Fitness Fairmont, Trade Center 1, 04 311 6571, *originalfitnessco.com*
The Pavilion Marina & Sports Club Jumeira Beach, Umm Suqeim 3, 04 406 8800, *jumeirahbeachhotel.com*
The Quay Health club Madinat Jumeirah, Al Sufouh 1, 04 366 6821
Sharjah Wanderers Sports Club Nr Sharjah English School, Sharjah, 06 566 2105, *sharjahwanderers.com*
ShuiQi Spa & Fitness Atlantis, Nakhlat Jumeira, 04 426 1020
Sports Fit Al Mizhar 1, 04 236 2111
Spring Dubai 050 378 7367, *springdubai.com*
Symmetry Gym Gold & Diamond Park, Al Quoz Industrial 3, 050 887 4707, *symmetrygymdubai.com*
Synergy Fitness Al Samrey Bldg, Al Barsha 1, 04 454 1471
Talise Fitness Trade Center 2, 04 319 8660, *jumeirah.com*
U Energy Gate Village, DIFC, Zaa'beel 2, 04 422 8721, *uenergy.me*

Mother & Child

If you want to give your kid a mind, body and soul workout, then My Gym (mygym.com/dubai) is the place to go for gymnastics and Mommy & Me sessions. The Little Gym (thelittlegym.com) runs gym classes from four months to 12 years. Urban Energy runs prenatal fitness classes in the park using weights and gentle exercises. And for mums looking to get back into shape, Pure Fitness (purefitnessuae.com) offers BuggEfit Bootcamp and a baby-friendly, four-week Results programme.

Ladies Only

There are several ladies-only gyms and fitness clubs in Dubai including Fitness 360 at J3 Mall, the Dubai Ladies Club, and Curves, which is based around a circuit of machines, both cardio and toning, which, along with stretching, is completed twice in 30 minutes. Dance Fit is a ladies-only centre running classes in Zumba, hip-hop, tap-dancing and Bootylicious, as well as a six-week course in the flirty Burlesque.

Yoga & Pilates

If pumping iron or running a marathon isn't for you, the ancient art of yoga and the ever more popular pilates method are gentle yet effective alternatives to help you get and stay in shape. Pilates is said to be the safest form of neuromuscular reconditioning and back strengthening available and is often delivered by trained physiotherapists. The method can help you become stronger, fitter, more toned and more flexible – either as a means to treat a problem, or as an exercise regime in small groups or one-on-one sessions. Classes are offered by a number of gyms as part of their group exercise schedules.

Yoga is a low-impact (but deceptively challenging) form of holistic exercise which has been practised for thousands of years. It involves holding sequences of poses or 'asanas' that, combined with breathing exercises, gently but powerfully help your body become stronger and more flexible. Many health and fitness clubs and dance schools offer yoga as part of their weekly schedule, as do some alternative therapy centres.

Club Stretch
Nr Mercure Hotel, Al Mina Rd Al Hudaiba **04 345 2131**
clubstretch.ae
Map **2 J4** Metro **Al Jafiliya**
Club Stretch offers reformer pilates classes taught by highly qualified instructors who also teach Bikram yoga at the studio.

Exhale
Marsa Dubai **04 424 3777**
exhaledubai.com
Map **1 K4** Metro **Dubai Marina**
This ladies-only centre specialises in pilates and yoga. Prices start at Dhs.80 for a single pilates reformer class.

LIVING IN DUBAI
FITNESS

A set of 10 Exhale classes costs Dhs.750 and is valid for two months. Exhale has another studio in Dubai MotorCity (04 447 4220).

The Hundred Pilates Studio
Healthcare City, Umm Hurair 2 **04 429 8433**
thehundred.ae
Map **2 L7** Metro **Dubai Healthcare City**
Personalised pilates sessions are available, as well as small group classes with a maximum four participants. Prices start at Dhs.90 for a single class.

Real Pilates
Palm Strip Mall, Jumeira Rd, Jumeira 1 **04 345 3228**
real-pilates.com
Map **2 H4** Metro **Emirates Towers**
At its bright studio, Real Pilates focuses on STOTT pilates and has high-quality equipment and well qualified instructors. Single sessions start at Dhs.65 with block booking offers available; mat and reformer pilates are on offer. There's also a studio at JLT (nearest metro: Dubai Marina).

Zen Yoga
BBC Bldg Emirates Living, Al Thanyah 4 **04 367 0435**
yoga.ae
Map **1 K8** Metro **Dubai Marina**
Mat and reformer pilates (using a machine to increase intensity) are available, with yogilates also offered. Expectant mums can join prenatal pilates classes. A trial lesson costs Dhs.90, with five classes for Dhs.450. Emirates Living (04 422 4643), Dubai Media City (04 367 0435), Town Centre Jumeirah (04 349 2933).

Personal Training

Whether your goal is a rippling six pack, to run a marathon, or just to feel fitter, the support, encouragement and expertise of a good personal trainer might be just the shot.

A personal trainer will assess your fitness, design the perfect regime for you – and motivate you to show up. There are a number of indoor and outdoor personal trainers in Dubai, some attached to gyms or health and fitness centres, others employed by fitness companies, and some working for themselves. Make sure your trainer is properly qualified with an internationally recognised certificate and registered with the International Register of Exercise Professionals.

Quick Fix
Exercise will relax you, provide you with that vital mental break from stress, and give you the physical strength to power on when you don't feel like it. Research shows that even if you only have time for 10-15 minutes activity at a time, the benefits can still be significant. So even a 10 minute run on the beach after work is worth the effort.

Original Fitness
Fairmont Trade Center 1 **04 311 6571**
originalfitnessco.com
Map **2 J5** Metro **World Trade Centre**
All ages and fitness levels are catered for by the trainers at Original Fitness. They also run bootcamps on the beach for those who like to push themselves.

Regime Fitness
Marina Yacht Club Marsa Dubai **04 366 3234**
regime.ae
Map **1 K5** Metro **Jumeirah Lakes Towers**
Regime Fitness offer a free initial personal training consultation, and also provide wellness programmes for companies.

UAE Active
Abu Dhabi **055 348 6377**
uaeactive.com
With the philosophy that 'your body is your gym', UAE Active trainers are a dab hand at helping you figure out how to train in almost any environment – so even if you can't get to the gym, or have no equipment at home, they'll design a programme to suit you.

WPT Dubai Women Personal Training
04 452 0194
wptfitness.com
Personal trainers just for women, who are specialised in women's needs. Several training programmes are available including pre-natal and post-natal.

Exercise Your Options

Getting fit in Dubai is easy. There are several types of exercise classes available.

Military style
If you like a really good, hard workout in a gym or outdoors, then try bootcamp, a demanding regime of sprints, boxing, pushups, squats and bicep curls designed for military recruits. It will dramatically and quickly increase your strength and fitness levels but be warned. You're going to be shouted at. A lot. Down a megaphone. At dawn. Original Fitness runs camps on the beach at JBR, in Safa Park and in Downtown Dubai – both early mornings and evenings.

Martial arts
Martial arts have been a form of self defence for thousands of years. The idea was to use physical and mental discipline to take control of your attacker without doing harm. Try Muay Thai boxing (dubaikarate.com), jiu jitsu and kickboxing (mmafitcenter.com), or capoeira (capoeiradubai.com), a Brazilian blend of martial arts, dance and acrobatics set to music.

Gym classes
A well air-conditioned gym is a lifesaver during the Dubai summer. Good gyms offer an array of classes with almost countless combinations of aerobics and floor exercises, weights, circuit training, and cycling, all set to a great sound track. They're a fun and effective way to burn fat, build muscle, lose weight, and improve heart health. Ask about joining discounts. In addition, many hotels offer memberships to their in-house gyms. They're often more expensive but can be quieter and include access to the hotel spa. Some of the more popular ones are Le Meridien Mina Seyahi, the Grand Hyatt and JA Jebel Ali Golf Resort.

Dance
So you think you can't dance? Try Irish, tango, salsa, ballet, African or flamenco at a Dubai dance school (jamesandalex.com), gym, or even a meetup group. Other classes blend dance and aerobics such as Zumba, or Fitness First's Dance Mania. Xtend Barre borrows elements from ballet training (real-pilates.com).

Yoga & pilates
For a subtle yet powerful exercise try yoga, a holistic form of exercise in which holding a series of asanas, or poses, will make you stronger and more supple, as well as helping to balance emotions. Pilates classes are designed to build core strength, or try water aerobics. Bikram yoga takes yoga and adds a heated room to make things even tougher, which you can take part in at Raw Yoga (rawryoga.com). Real Pilates runs Xtend Barre classes, combining pilates with ballet.

Cross Fit
This is a really demanding workout that pushes the super fit to their physical limit and it's booming in Dubai. Check out Fitness First at Knowledge Village and Reebok CrossFit LifeSpark at Jumeirah Lakes Towers, if you think you're up to the challenge.

SensAsia Urban Spa

WELL-BEING

Beauty Salons & Nail Bars

Beauty is big business in Dubai, and you're never far from a salon where you can pop in for a quick mani-pedi, massage or facial. You can expect to pay around Dhs.60 for a manicure and Dhs.80 for a pedicure. Fridays tend to be the busiest day for salons, with customers prepping for the weekend ahead, so book in advance. Keep an eye out for discounts for spas on websites such as groupon.ae, which can offer surprisingly big savings on a variety of treatments.

Branches of Mary Foot Spa, a pleasant, no-frills spa, are located throughout the city, where you can expect to be pampered by therapists who really know their stuff, within a calm, candlelit, soothing atmosphere.

Branches of N.Bar and Nail Lounges can be found pretty much all over Dubai and they're a popular spot for waxing, threading, massages and mani-pedis, and the chain of Tips & Toes offers everything from gelish mani-pedis to Turkish and Moroccan hammams. Most nail salons now offer in the chair head, neck and shoulder massages too.

Unbelievably, there are also a number of spas specifically aimed at children, such as Hello Kitty Spa and Tickles & Giggles (800 82634). Increasingly, men's spas such as Urban Male Lounge are popping up in the city to provide metrosexual gents with some pampering too.

Many beauty salons and spas offer the traditional art of henna or mendhi, for special occasions or a fun experience for visitors. A design is drawn on your skin with henna paste that dries, flakes off, and leaves a stain that darkens, then fades after two or three weeks. Prices vary depending on the complexity of the design you choose. Try Rachna on Jumeira Rd (04 394 4489) that has designs from Dhs.100, or Aroushi on Oud Metha Rd (04 336 2794), with prices from Dhs.40.

LIVING IN DUBAI
WELL-BEING

Aroushi Beauty Salon Nr Lamcy Plaza, Oud Metha, 04 336 2794, *aroushibeautysalon.com*
Chez Toi 04 369 5338, *cheztoibeauty.com*
Clarins Boutique Dubai Mall, Downtown Dubai, Burj Khalifa, 04 434 0522, *clarins.com*
Color Nail Beauty Lounge Al Qouz Ind. 1, 04 341 8848
Dermalogica Dubai Mall, Downtown Dubai, Burj Khalifa, 04 339 8250, *dermalogica.com*
Elyazia Beauty Center Nr Uptown Mirdiff, Mirdif, 04 288 8300, *elyaziabeautycenter.com*
Essentials Hair & Beauty Salon Nr Al Safa Centre, Jumeira 3, 04 395 5909, *essentialsdubai.com*
Hello Kitty Beauty Spa Jumeira 1, 04 344 9598, *hellokittybeautyspa.com*
Mary Foot Spa The Walk at JBR, Marsa Dubai, 04 440 4888, *maryfootspa.com*
N Bar Jumeira 1, 04 346 1100, *thegroomingcompany.com*
Nail Moda Umm Hurair 2, 04 327 9088, *nailmoda.com*
The Nail Spa Dubai Mall, Downtown Dubai, Burj Khalifa, 04 339 9078, *thenailspa.com*
Nail Station Jumeira 1, 04 349 0123
Nail Zone Nr Jumeirah Beach Park, Jumeira 2, 04 344 6969
Nails At Home 04 298 0707, *nailsathome.ae*
Natalie Beauty Saloon JLT Gold Crest Views -1, JLT, Al Thanyah 5, 04 435 8066, *nataliebeautysalon.com*
NStyle Nail Lounge MoE, Al Barsha 1, 04 341 3300, *nstyleintl.com*
The Organic Glow Beauty Lounge Nr Safa Park, Al Wasl Rd, Jumeira 3, 04 380 4666
Pastels Nr Choithrams, Al Wasl Rd, Umm Suqeim 2, 04 388 3534, *pastels-salon.com*
Sisters Beauty Lounge Jumeira 1, 04 342 0787, *sistersbeautylounge.com*
Tilia & Finn The Walk at JBR, Marsa Dubai, 04 438 0636, *tiliaandfinn.ae*
Tips & Toes JBR, Marsa Dubai, 04 429 3477, *tipsandtoes.com*
Version Francaise Marina Heights Tower, Marsa Dubai, 04 360 5260, *version-francaise.com*

Organic
These salons use natural toxin-free ingredients.

Nails Trident Tower, Marsa Dubai, 04 447 3688, *nailsorganicspa.com*
The Organic Glow Beauty Lounge Nr Safa Park, Al Wasl Rd, Jumeira 3, 04 380 4666

Kids
Spas for children are growing ever-popular, particularly for birthday parties. Here tots to tweens can enjoy a manicure, pedicure, nail design, hair style, temporary hair colour, braiding, body sprays, body glitter, body tattoos, make-up and more.

Hairdressers

In Dubai, you'll find ladies and gents hairdressers to suit every budget, from small salons where fellas could pay as little as Dhs.30 for a simple wet cut to larger, branded salons where prices start at around Dhs.165 (with a junior stylist). For higher quality styling and colouring prices start at Dhs.350. Straightening treatments can cost upwards of Dhs.1,000) and extensions will set you back from Dhs.500. Recommendations from friends and colleagues are a good way to find a stylist that you like; Salon Ink, Ted Morgan and Pastels are all popular spots with the city's expats. Men in search of something more than a simple barbershop should try male spas Man/Age or Urban Male Lounge.

Alain & Milad CNBC Bldg, Media City, Al Sufouh 2, 04 390 2815
Amaya Salon & Spa Oud Metha, 04 335 1101, *idm.ae*
Baré Gents Salon Ibn Battuta, Jabal Ali 1, 04 368 5111, *baresalongroup.com*
Bilal Le Salon Dubai Marine Beach Resort, Jumeira 1, 04 346 1111
Camille Albane Al Badia, Al Kheeran, 04 232 8550, *camillealbane.com*
Carla K Styling Nr Mazaya Centre, Al Wasl, 04 343 8544, *carla-k.com*
Code Men's Salon Shk Hamdan Award Complex, Madinat Dubai Al Melaheyah, 04 386 9909
De La Mer Day Spa Al Wasl Rd, Al Manara, 04 328 2775, *delamerspa.com*
The Edge Hair & Beauty Salon Wafi Residence, Umm Hurair 2, 04 324 0024
Elyazia Beauty Center Nr Uptown Mirdiff, Mirdif, 04 288 8300, *elyaziabeautycenter.com*
Essentials Hair & Beauty Salon Nr Al Safa Centre, Jumeira 3, 04 395 5909, *essentialsdubai.com*
Franck Provost MoE, Al Barsha 1, 04 341 3245, *franckprovostdubai.com*
The Gold Salon Al Attar Tower, Shk Zayed Rd, Trade Center 2, 04 321 1423, *goldsalondubai.com*
The Hair Corridor Al Safa Centre, Al Wasl Rd, Al Safa 1, 04 394 5622, *thehaircorridor.com*
The Hair Shop Capitol, Madinat Dubai Al Melaheyah, 04 345 8566, *hairshop-uae.com*
Hair Station Mirdif, 04 288 6483, *hairstationladiessalon.com*
Hair@Pyramids Umm Hurair 2, 04 324 0000, *pyramidsrestaurantsatwafi.com*
Jen's Hair Studio White Crown Bldg, Trade Center 1, 04 800 5367, *jenshairstudio.com*
JetSet Grosvenor, Marsa Dubai, 04 399 5005
Juan Hair Salon Indigo Tower, JLT, Al Thanyah 5, 04 438 9570, *juansalon.com*
Maison de Joelle Kempinski Mall of the Emirates, Al Barsha 1, 04 323 6011, *maisondejoelle.com*

LIVING IN DUBAI
WELL-BEING

Maria Dowling Nr Capitol Hotel, Al Hudaiba, 04 345 4225, *mariadowling.com*
Pace e Luce Al Manzil Mall, Burj Khalifa, 04 420 1165, *paceeluce.com*
Pastels Nr Choithrams, Al Wasl Rd, Umm Suqeim 2, 04 388 3534, *pastels-salon.com*
Patsi Collins Hair Beauty Nails Nr RTA, Al Garhoud, 04 286 9923, *dubaibeautysalon.com*
Reflection Hair & Beauty Centre Umm Suqeim 1, 04 394 4595, *reflectionhairandbeautycentre.com*
Roots Salon Nr Jumeirah Beach Park, Jumeira 2, 04 344 4040, *rootssalons.com*
Saks Hair Salon Downtown Dubai, Burj Khalifa, 04 430 8572, *saks.co.uk*
Salon Ink Jumeira 2, 04 385 4402, *saloninkdubai.com*
ShuiQi Salon Atlantis, Nakhlat Jumeira, 04 426 1020, *atlantisthepalm.com*
Sisters Beauty Lounge Jumeira 1, 04 342 0787, *sistersbeautylounge.com*
SOS Beauty Salon Jumeira 1, 04 349 1144
Ted Morgan Hair Shoreline Apartments, Nakhlat Jumeira, 04 430 8190, *tedmorganhair.com*
Toni & Guy The Gate, Marble Walk, DIFC, Zaa'beel 2, 04 330 3345, *toniandguy.com*
Top Style Hair Salon Aviation Club, Al Garhoud, 04 282 9663, *topstylesalon.com*
Top Style Salon Nr Grand Millennium Hotel, Al Thanyah 1, 04 422 5633, *topstylesalon.com*
VOG Color Your Life Jumeira 3, 04 380 8960, *vog.ae*
Youngsters Hair & Spa Cluster T 1 Lake Plaza, JLT, Al Thanyah 5, 04 434 3911
Zouari Hair Salon Palace At One&Only Royal Mirage, Al Sufouh 2, 04 399 9999, *oneandonlyresorts.com*

Barbers & Male Salons

Caractere Gents Saloon Jumeira 3, 04 380 4188, *caracteresalongroup.com*
Chill Salon Loft Office 1, Media City, Al Sufouh 2, 04 446 2991, *chill-salon.com*
Julian Hairdressing Jumeira 1, 04 344 9006
Man/Age Al Barsha 2, 04 385 0350, *managespa.com*
Urban Male Lounge (UML) MoE, Al Barsha 1, 04 395 1103, *nstyleintl.com/uml*
Y12 Ritz-Carlton DIFC, DIFC, Zaa'beel 2, 04 372 2712, *y12salons.com*

Kids

Caboodle Pamper & Play Dubai Mall, Downtown Dubai, Burj Khalifa, 04 325 3367, *caboodle.ae*
Fun City Jumeira 1, 04 349 9976, *funcity.ae*
Hello Kitty Beauty Spa Jumeira 1, 04 344 9598, *hellokittybeautyspa.com*
Kiddo Cuts Al Manara, 052 909 9164, *kiddocuts.ae*
Kids Cuts Marsa Dubai, 04 434 1984, *favouritethings.com*
Tickles & Giggles The Walk at JBR, Marsa Dubai, 04 432 8681, *ticklesandgiggles.com*

Spas

Whatever your pampering budget, you'll find a spa to suit you in Dubai. The city is blessed with world-class luxury spas within five-star hotels as well as small, independent establishments that offer fewer bells and whistles but better value for money. As well as the usual massages, body scrubs and wraps, you'll also find more unusual treatments such as the ancient practice of Ayurvedic massage, reflexology and traditional hammams. Budget and mid-range spas are perfect for regular indulgence, but if you want to splash your cash for a special occasion, there are some amazing treatments – think royal hammams and 24 carat gold facials – to leave you feeling like a million bucks. Expect to pay around Dhs.700 for a 90 minute treatment at a hotel spa or around Dhs.300 at smaller spas.

Relaxing Prices

Certain spas will offer special treatments at certain times of year such as Ramadan, as well as reductions on packages. If you're thinking about indulging yourself check out sites like groupon.com, which often has discounts on spa treatments. Also, get the Entertainer Body book or app and enjoy BOGOF deals year-round.

Budget

There are spas of all sizes and styles ready to rub, scrub and knead you into relaxation. And here are handful of the more independent places that offer better value for money, but you may have to forego some of the most luxurious facilities.

Kalm Beauty
Riva Beach Club Nakhlat Jumeira **04 451 9988**
kalmbeauty.com
Map **1 N3** Metro **Nakheel**
Located on the Shoreline of Palm Jumeirah, Kalm is a firm favourite among local residents wanting a soothing aromatherapy massage, relaxing mani-pedi or reviving facial, all of which are reasonably priced. Kalm also has monthly specials on discounted packages such as Keratin hair treatments and full body massages.

Lotus Salon
Lotus Apartments Marsa Dubai **04 440 2805**
lotus-hospitality.com
Map **1 J5** Metro **Jumeirah Lakes Towers**
This no-frills spa in the lobby of Lotus Hotel Apartments has a more casual, relaxed mood and a relatively minimalist menu. Its massages include hot stone, Thai, deep tissue, anti-cellulite and chakra balance. There are also reasonably priced grooming treatments including threading, waxing and mani-pedis.

LIVING IN DUBAI
WELL-BEING

B/Attitude Spa

ShuiQi Spa & Fitness

Talise Ottoman Spa

LIVING IN DUBAI
WELL-BEING

The Nail Spa
Dubai Mall Downtown Dubai, Burj Khalifa
04 339 9078
thenailspa.com
Map **2 F7** Metro **Burj Khalifa/Dubai Mall**
With branches located throughout the UAE, the Nail Spa is the perfect spot for some reasonably priced pampering. Try the Minty Chocolate Sole Scrub or the Lavender Heel Peel as add-ons to your pedicure. For the ultimate pick-me-up, opt for a blissful shoulder massage along with your mani-pedi.

SpaDunya Club
The Walk at JBR Marsa Dubai **04 439 3669**
spadunyaclub.com
Map **1 K4** Metro **Jumeirah Lakes Towers**
This wallet-friendly spa specialises in colour therapies that harmonise the body's energy levels. You'll find an range of treatments including face reflexology and a Body Harmonising Colour Treatment that includes a colour consultation, scrub, wrap and massage. There's also a hammam, steam room, sauna and beauty rooms.

Tips & Toes
209 Pinnacle Bldg Al Barsha 1 **04 399 0550**
tipsntoeshaven.com
Map **1 Q6** Metro **Sharaf DG**
This popular pampering chain has branches all over Dubai and has a menu of manicures, pedicures, waxing, threading and massages. Visit the larger Al Barsha branch and try the Turkish hammam, a combination of being scrubbed, steamed and massaged that will leave you squeaky clean and relaxed.

Mid-range
Plenty of hotels and boutique spas dotted around Dubai have pitched mind and body treatments somewhere in the middle – affordable but with extra personal touches.

Amara Spa
Park Hyatt Port Saeed **04**
Map **2 M7** Metro **GGICO**
Amara boasts amazing private treatment rooms with all the facilities of a changing room, as well as a relaxation corner. After your scrub or wrap, you can rinse off in the lovely private outdoor shower, then dry off and soak up some rays in the secluded relaxation area.

Cleopatra's Spa & Wellness
Pyramids at Wafi Umm Hurair 2 **04 324 7700**
cleopatrasspaandwellness.com
Map **2 K7** Metro **Dubai Healthcare City**
While the entrance and changing facilities may lack the opulence of some hotel spas, Cleopatra's plush relaxation area is a lovely ancient Egypt-themed affair with drapes, silk cushions and majlis-style seats. There is also a small plunge pool with a Jacuzzi and sauna. Enjoy facials, body wraps and anti-ageing miracles.

The Cure
Building 10 Media City, Al Sufouh 2 **04 391 6485**
thecure.ae
Map **1 M5** Metro **Nakheel**
A friendly haven in the heart of Media City, the Cure is the answer to whatever ails you, whether you're in need of a rejuvenating facial or a relaxing massage. The menu is extensive, the therapists are highly knowledgable and well trained, and the quality of the treatments is exceptional given the reasonable prices.

Dreamworks Spa & Massage
Shoreline Apartments Nakhlat Jumeira **04 447 5511**
dreamworks.ae
Map **1 N3** Metro **Nakheel**
If it's a massage you're after, then you can't go wrong with a trip to Dreamworks Spa, which specialises in kneading out your knots. Let go of your daily stresses by treating yourself to some foot reflexology, a Balinese head massage or even an exquisite four hands massage. There's also a home service option, so you can get pampered in the comfort of your own place.

Perfect Shape Up Beauty Centre
Villa 160A, Off Al Wasl Rd Jumeira 3 **04 342 7722**
perfectshapeup.com
Map **2 F5** Metro **Noor Bank**
This spa bridges the gap between five-star luxury and a neighbourhood salon – the quality is just that little bit higher, the ambiance just that little bit more

LIVING IN DUBAI
WELL-BEING

relaxing. Behind the doors of this unassuming villa you'll find a world of beauty services delivered by friendly and knowledgeable staff, including tanning, waxing, nails and hair care.

Hammam
The Oriental hammam is a traditional pampering experience in the Middle East, which shares similarities with Turkish baths. It involves being bathed, steamed, washed with black soap, scrubbed with a loofa and massaged on a hot marble table – an intense treatment that leaves your skin squeaky clean and glowing. Try the hammam at the One&Only Royal Mirage (04 315 2130, royalmirage.oneandonlyresorts.com) for a real treat.

Spaces Spa & Salon
Oasis Centre Al Qouz 1 **04 515 4400**
spacessalon.com
Map **2 C6** Metro **Noor Bank**

This small salon is split into gents' and ladies' quarters and offers massages that are just as good as a premium spa's, but without the exorbitant five-star hotel prices. Service is polite and exceptionally friendly. Offering a range of services from a deep tissue massage and facials to hair and nail treatments, Spaces is a nice, affordable option. And not breaking the bank makes it all the more relaxing.

Thai Elite Spa
Mercure Gold Madinat Dubai Al Melaheyah
04 345 9992 thaielitespa.com
Map **2 J4** Metro **Al Jafiliya**

This quaint spa on the upper level of the Gold Swiss-Belhotel may lack the facilities you'll find in some of the city's other spas, but its laid-back approach is refreshing. All the usual therapies are on offer, with the full-body scrub followed by a Thai oil massage a particularly relaxing and yet invigorating choice. Long opening hours and reasonable prices also make it attractive.

Luxury
These spas will customise every detail of your treatment for a blissful experience – and a massage or facial at one of these havens usually means you can wallow in Jacuzzis, saunas and steam rooms before and after your treatment – but you'll often pay top dollar.

Angsana Spa Arabian Ranches
Arabian Ranches, Al Hebiah 2 **04 361 8251**
angsanaspa.com
Map **1 N13**

Minimalist decor, exotic oils and soft music set the tone for relaxation at Angsana Spa. The impeccably trained staff work wonders, turning tight muscles to putty and sending overworked minds to cloud nine.

The massage menu includes Balinese, Hawaiian and Thai, and you get a heated massage table.

Armani/Spa
Armani Downtown Dubai, Burj Khalifa **04 8883888**
dubai.armanihotels.com
Map **2 F6** Metro **Burj Khalifa/Dubai Mall**

Armani/Spa is modern, elegant and sleek. There are three categories of treatment – Stillness (relaxing), Freedom (rejuvenating) and Fluidity (detoxifying), encompassing massages, facials and body wraps. The pod-like treatment rooms create a feeling of being truly cocooned from the stress of the outside world.

Assawan Spa & Health Club
Burj Al Arab Umm Suqeim 3 **04 301 7338**
jumeirah.com
Map **1 S4** Metro **First Gulf Bank**

Assawan is an elaborate affair. There are saunas, steam rooms, plunge pools and two relaxing infinity pools decorated in mosaic and gold leaf tiles – swim to the edge, put your nose to the window, and enjoy the amazing views of Dubai. For pure unadulterated indulgence, try the caviar body treatment.

B/Attitude Spa
Grosvenor House Dubai Marsa Dubai
04 399 8888 battitudespa-dubai.com
Map **1 L5** Metro **Dubai Marina**

An Asian-inspired spa with treatments ranging from Eastern massages to Ayurvedic facials, exotic body wraps and Swiss Bellefontaine treatments. The overall vibe is Oriental chic – think Tibetan relaxation techniques, sacred stones and Ayurveda, all delivered in treatment rooms that are named after the chakras.

Residence&Spa At One&Only Royal Mirage
Al Sufouh Rd Al Sufouh 2 **04 399 9999**
oneandonlyroyalmirage.com
Map **1 M4** Metro **Nakheel**

Understated decor, natural light and soft music create a serene effect in the treatment rooms of this spa. There are a variety of treatments including Swedish lymphatic drainage, slimming and sports massages, as well as an energy-balancing massage using warm and cool stones 'charged' in the moonlight and cleansed with salt. The hammam is not to be missed. Alternatively, opt for a peel, wrap or oil bath, exclusively with Espa products.

Rixos Royal Spa
Rixos The Palm Nakhlat Jumeira **04 4575 555**
rixos.com
Map **1 P3** Metro **Nakheel**

Treatments at this white and ice-blue spa vary from facials to traditional massages, and the signature packages offer a complete head-to-toe experience for extravagant pampering. The spa promises a relaxing

LIVING IN DUBAI
WELL-BEING

experience from start to finish, with well-trained therapists who are friendly and attentive, and an indulgent fruit platter to give you an energy boost after your treatment.

Saray Spa
Marriott Harbour Marsa Dubai **04 319 4630**
marriott.com
Map **1 L5** Metro **Dubai Marina**
The treatments at the stunning Saray Spa are inspired by the ancient healing and beautifying rituals of the Arabic world, with the highlight of the menu undoubtedly being the Signature Dead Sea Journey. This treatment is over two hours long and incorporates a salt scrub, mud mask wrap and a soothing soak in a heated flotation tank, salinated to imitate the Dead Sea itself.

Satori Spa
Bab Al Shams Mugatrah **04 809 6232**
meydanhotels.com
This spa makes the most of its desert location – the treatment rooms feature a window with a blind; unusual for spas in Dubai, which are usually cosseted away in the heart of a hotel. The sense of being close to the desert wilderness seeps into the gently lit room, and the quiet music empties your mind of everything but the rhythmic strokes of the therapist. Aromatherapy Associates is the oil of choice here, and a beguiling scent surrounds you as you are kneaded and massaged into a state of semi-conscious bliss.

ShuiQi Spa & Fitness
Atlantis Nakhlat Jumeira **04 426 1020**
Map **1 N1** Metro **Nakheel**
This spectacular spa has around 27 treatment rooms set over two floors, and offers a personal touch. Whether you choose a simple massage and facial to the intricate Japanese ritual Shiseido spa journey, you can expect the undivided attention of expertly trained therapists. Be sure to stock up on spa goodies in the boutique area at the entrance.

Softouch Spa
Kempinski Mall of the Emirates Al Barsha 1
04 409 5909
softouchspa.com
Map **1 R6** Metro **Mall of the Emirates**
You wouldn't expect to find such a sanctuary of calm in the midst of a mall, but the Softouch Spa is a true haven. Specialising in treatments based on Ayurveda, it's one of the few spas in the UAE with therapists that are fully trained in this tradition. It's also open 24 hours. Try the detoxifying warm Aromatic Moor Mud Wrap followed by a bliss-inducing massage with lavender essential oils.

The Spa At The Palace Downtown Dubai
The Palace Downtown Downtown Dubai, Burj Khalifa
04 428 7805
theaddress.com
Map **2 F6** Metro **Burj Khalifa/Dubai Mall**
This spa truly makes the most of its enviable location with its lakeside spa cabanas. These luxurious treatment beds directly overlook Burj Khalifa lake, providing gorgeous views of the world's tallest building and the Dubai Fountain, while ensuring the utmost privacy despite the glamorous outdoor setting. Attentive therapists ensure that your treatment is personalised to meet your needs.

Talise Ottoman Spa
Jumeirah Zabeel Saray Nakhlat Jumeira **04 453 0456**
jumeirah.com
Map **1 L3** Metro **Nakheel**
With 50 treatment rooms, mineral pools, majlis areas, saunas, ice chambers, couples' suites, gyms and stunning hammams, Talise Ottoman Spa is one of the biggest in the Middle East and amongst the largest in the world. Relax with an indulgent massage in a private outdoor cabana, or splash out on the authentic Turkish hammam for true top to toe pampering.

Talise Spa At Jumeirah Emirates Towers
Hotel Tower Trade Center 2 **04 319 8181**
jumeirah.com
Map **2 H6** Metro **Financial Centre**
This compact spa is a suitably suave affair for the prestigious address in one of Dubai's most established five-star hotels. The menu features a handful of facials, but the real emphasis is on the body treatments. Massages range from Swedish to Hawaiian Lomi Lomi and reflexology; however, the real stars of the show are the signature spa rituals, many of which include flotation in the spa's fantastic salt water pool.

Day Spas
If you fancy more than a quick treatment, these places can help you make a day of it. Most spas will actually offer some kind of day-long service which generally involves use of pool areas, saunas and steam rooms.

De La Mer Day Spa
Al Wasl Rd Al Manara **04 328 2775**
delamerspa.com
Map **1 U5** Metro **Noor Bank**
This spa is perfect for a day-long girly gathering with body wraps, facials, massages, manicures and pedicures. Soak up some sun in the secluded garden, which has a swimming pool and Jacuzzi. The spa is great for occasions such as hen parties, birthdays and baby showers – you can book the VIP suite and bring your own food, drink and decorations.

One&Only
Royal Mirage, Dubai

Oriental Hammam

The traditional Hammam, has long played a part in the cultural and social life of eastern cities. An 'oasis of retreat' from daily stresses entering the Hammam is akin to a journey.

Located at Residence & Spa, One&Only Royal Mirage

Open daily 9.30am - 10pm
Ladies only 9.30am - 2pm, Gentlemen only 8pm - 10pm

Telephone +971 4 399 99 99   oneandonlyroyalmirage.com

LIVING IN DUBAI
WELL-BEING

Lime Spa
Desert Palm Warsan 2 **04 323 8888**
desertpalm.ae
More of a retreat than a spa; with any treatment you get use of the facilities for the day. Six stunning treatment rooms are all naturally lit by large windows overlooking the polo fields. The couples' room has its own plunge pool and private relaxation area.

Raffles Spa
Raffles Umm Hurair 2 **04 314 9870**
raffles.com
Map **2 K7** Metro **Dubai Healthcare City**
Raffles Spa is pure lavish indulgence. Try the Dubai Decadence treatment – a full six hours of head-to-toe pampering including a steam bath, body scrub, hot stone massage, facial, manicure and pedicure. There's also a gym, pool, sauna and steam room if you wish to delay your departure even further.

Talise Spa Madinat Jumeirah
Madinat Jumeirah Al Sufouh 1 **04 366 6818**
madinatjumeirah.com
Map **1 R5** Metro **Mall of the Emirates**
This is a true destination spa, with a wonderful steam room, sauna and plunge pools. Indoor sunbeds provide lazing-around space, and there's even a lounge with sofas to chill on. There's an extensive range of therapies, with a strong focus on using natural oils, and the expertly trained staff ensure that your treatment is meticulously tailored to your needs. Yoga, including the popular classes held under the stars, is also available.

Kids' Spas
It's not just grown-ups that can be pampered. Other spas may accommodate kids too, if asked nicely.

Caboodle Pamper & Play
Dubai Mall Downtown Dubai, Burj Khalifa
04 325 3367
caboodle.ae
Map **2 F7** Metro **Burj Khalifa/Dubai Mall**
A lovely spot for some mother-daughter pampering, Caboodle Pamper & Play uses organic, chemical free products. It's also a great place for kids' haircuts, as little ones get DVDs, games and toys while they sit in the styling chair.

Hello Kitty Beauty Spa
Town Centre Jumeira 1 **04 344 9598**
hellokittybeautyspa.com
Map **2 F4** Metro **Burj Khalifa/Dubai Mall**
Girls can get a 'kitty-cure' to match their mum's manicure and have their nails painted with stars and flowers. Facials use organic ingredients such as oatmeal, honey and chocolate.

Tickles & Giggles
The Walk at JBR Marsa Dubai **04 432 8681**
ticklesandgiggles.com
Map **1 K4** Metro **Jumeirah Lakes Towers**
A salon and spa aimed at little ones, offering child-friendly face masks using natural ingredients and non-toxic, water-based polishes for mini mani-pedis. There's more to this venue than pint-sized pampering – it also hosts fun classes such as arts and craft as well as ultra-trendy parties for mini stylistas.

Male Spas
Damaging sun, skin-drying air conditioning and usual daily stresses can make the world of massages, facials and spas start looking like a good idea, even for men.

1847
Grosvenor Marsa Dubai **04 399 8989**
thegroomingcompany.com
Map **1 L5** Metro **Dubai Marina**
Men are the centre of attention at 1847, which was the first dedicated 'grooming lounge' for men in the Middle East. Skilled therapists offer traditional shaves, beard styling, facials, massages, manicures and pedicures, and simple haircuts.

Kalm Grooming Lounge
Riva Beach Club Nakhlat Jumeira **04 451 9888**
kalmgrooming.com
Map **1 N3** Metro **Nakheel**
Located on Shoreline of Palm Jumeirah, above Riva Beach Club, Kalm Grooming Lounge has a good range of treatments on offer, from express manicures to haircuts, waxing and massages. Try the unusual Hot Lava Shell Massage, which uses warmed shells to melt the tension from your muscles.

Man/Age
Media City Arjaan Media City, Al Sufouh 2
04 437 0868
managespa.com
Map **1 M5** Metro **Nakheel**
This luxury men's spa offers male grooming including haircuts and shaving, manicures, massages and facials. It also has a Moroccan bath. All the treatments on offer are very reasonably priced and there are annual and six month memberships.

Urban Male Lounge (UML)
Precinct Building 2 DIFC, Zaa'beel 2 **04 425 0350**
nstyleintl.com/uml
Map **2 G6** Metro **Financial Centre**
This award-winning male-centric spa offers a chic, relaxed setting. With locations in the DIFC and the Mall of the Emirates, Urban Male Lounge is the perfect spot for gents to indulge in a massage or sharpen up their look with a hip new cut.

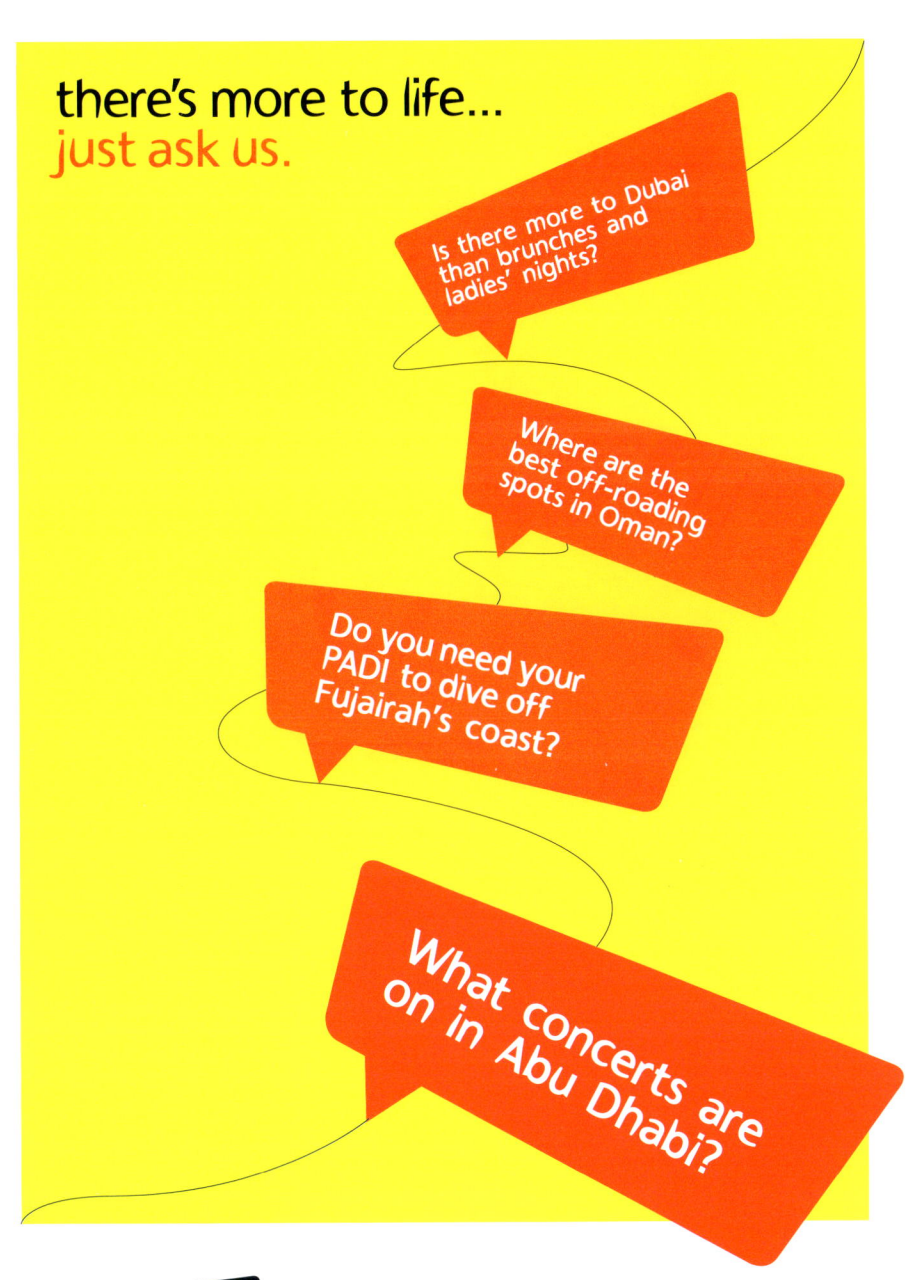

Bikers join the National Day parade

CLUBS & GROUPS

All the different cultures converging in Dubai bring a diverse range of activities with them. Everything from jumping out of an airplane to scrapbooking is covered in this section and, for every traditional pursuit such as tennis, running or football, there is the opportunity to try something you never even dreamed of doing back home, such as kitesurfing, sandboarding, yogilates or even caving. For the adventurous, the UAE's topography lends itself to outdoor pursuits including rock climbing, mountain biking, dune bashing, wadi driving and skydiving. Thanks to the miles of coastline, watersports are popular, with scuba diving, snorkelling, sailing, surfing and water-skiing all firm favourites. You need not leave behind those hobbies you enjoyed back home either. From dance classes to photography, there are like-minded people in the city who will be more than happy to hear from you. How these activities are organised varies from regular meetings and paid-for classes to forum or social media based groups. If one of your interests isn't catered for, there's nothing to stop you from starting your own group or club – and you're likely to find plenty of takers in this active city. Alternatively, a trip to Abu Dhabi can often help you find clubs and groups that aren't available in Dubai.

Team Spirit

More than 10,000 members are signed up for Duplays recreational sports leagues in the UAE – a phenomenal number given that the organisation was set up by expats in 2009. What better way to keep fit, meet new people and settle in to a new city. Players of all skill levels are welcome. Get stuck into five- or seven-a-side football, beach volleyball, kickball or badminton, to name a few. Individuals joining can be assigned a team. For details visit duplays.com.

LIVING IN DUBAI
CLUBS & GROUPS

Sport

American Football
The Emirates American Football League offers full-contact American football in the UAE for players of all skill levels, from beginner to experienced. There are adult and youth teams, as well as recreational flag league teams. Contact info@eafl.ae for info. To find out how to join the Duplays Mighty Eagle I flag football league, as an individual or a team, visit duplays.com.

Active Sports
A fun sports club for kids offering everything from swimming, football and tennis, to cheerleading, basketball and gymnastics. There are several venues across the city, which are detailed on the website (activeuae.com). Co-founder, Cees Valk has previously coached tennis stars, Stefan Edberg and Emile Sanchez.

Badminton

Badeemonz Badminton Club Dubai
facebook.com/BadeemonzBadmintonClubUaeDubai
Founded in 2008, the club also organises tournaments. Check their Facebook page for more information.

Badmintown
Al Safa Sports Centre Al Wasl **050 770 6711**
Map **2 E5** Metro **Business Bay**
A group of badminton players who meet to play and take part in tournaments. They also offer coaching and discounted Yonex items.

Emirates Badminton Club
Muhaisanah 2 **04 204 3491**
emiratesbadminton.com
Map **2 S10** Metro **Etisalat**
The club was formed in 1986 and practises every day at the Etisalat Academy in Muhaisanah. Members take part in international tournaments (representing the UAE) in countries including Saudi Arabia, Iran and Malaysia.

India Club
Nr Indian High School Oud Metha **04 337 1112**
indiaclubdubai.com
Map **2 L6** Metro **Oud Metha**
This members club has been in existence since 1964 and offers a range of sports and entertainment activities including badminton (four courts), basketball, squash, bowling, tennis, a gym and table tennis. Experienced coaches are on hand and the club hosts numerous tournaments throughout the year.

Baseball

Dubai Little League
Nr Al Qouz Pond Park, Off Al Khail Rd Al Qouz 2 **050 293 3855**
eteamz.com/DubaiLittleLeague
Map **2 D7** Metro **Business Bay**
Parent volunteers field more than 20 baseball teams for boys and girls aged five to 16. Beginners welcome. Dhs.1,200 registration includes season fees, team picture, uniform and year-end trophy.

Basketball
Dubai has a number of public basketball courts but getting a game on them in the evenings can be tricky because they're so popular. There are courts near the Canadian University of Dubai, at Hamriya Park in Abu Hail and on 2nd December St in Satwa, next to Chelsea Plaza Hotel. You can also go to Safa Park and Al Barsha Pond Park and get regular pick-up games on Wednesday, Thursday and Sunday evenings. Air-conditioned indoor courts can be hired for Dhs.35 per person per hour at Chevrolet Insportz (insportzclub.com), behind Dubai Garden Centre in Al Qouz 3. Duplays organises men's and women's recreational and competitive leagues (duplays.com).

Basketball Academy Of Dubai
Umm Suqeim 3 **050 731 6745**
badubai.com
Map **1 S5** Metro **First Gulf Bank**
Children can learn everything there is to know about basketball at this academy, from slam dunking for beginners to clinics, camps, leagues and pick-up sessions. Highly qualified staff are properly trained to teach children. Call Academy Director, Marc Roberts, on 056 683 0665 for more info.

Boxing

Al Nasr Leisureland
Nr American Hospital Oud Metha **04 337 1234**
alnasrll.com
Map **2 L6** Metro **Oud Metha**
Boxing classes are Saturdays, Mondays and Wednesdays from 8.30pm to 10.30pm. A 12 lesson package costs Dhs.550. For more information on the different weight classes, contact the coach, Iraj Dortolouee, on the above number.

Colosseum Muay Thai Health & Fitness Club
Zaabeel Rd Al Karama **04 337 2755**
colosseumuae.com
Map **2 L6** Metro **BurJuman**
Gym specialising in boxing, Muay Thai (Thai boxing), kickboxing and street fighting. Group classes meet daily between 8.30pm to 10pm. Costs Dhs.75 per session.

LIVING IN DUBAI
CLUBS & GROUPS

Dubai Fight Academy
Nr ACE Hardware Al Qouz Ind. 1 **050 712 9333**
fightacademy.ae
Map **1 U6** Metro **Noor Bank**
The academy offers Thai boxing lessons and holds tournaments. Membership is Dhs.1,500 for six months including use of gym and pool. Another branch is in Jumeira (050 650 1184).

Climbing
See Activities, Things To See & Do.

Cricket
On weekends you'll see informal cricket games springing up on scratchy patches of open space on the outskirts of the city. Zabeel and Safa parks are favourite spots if you prefer a little more green for your stumps. There are also several small-scale training centres, such as the Emirates Cricket Training Centre (050 497 3461). International matches are regularly hosted in the United Arab Emirates, particularly at the state-of-the-art cricket ground in Dubai Sports City (dubaisportscity.ae) where it's possible to see some of the world's best teams in action.

ICC Global Cricket Academy
Nr Autodrome Sports City, Al Hebiah 4 **04 448 1355**
iccglobalcricketacademy.com
Map **1 M11**
The ICC cricket Dubai Sports City offers cricket coaching for all ages with ICC-affiliated coaches and some of the most advanced facilities in the cricketing world.

Insportz Club
Nr Dubai Garden Centre Al Qouz Ind. 3 **04 347 5833**
insportzclub.com
Map **1 S6** Metro **First Gulf Bank**
Insportz has three main net courts with a scoreboard and one side court, available for social games as part of a league, or just for practice.

Last Man Stands
Al Kifaf
lastmanstands.com
Map **2 K6** Metro **Al Jafiliya**
Amateur T20 cricket league with several Dubai teams taking part. Registration fees are Dhs.640 per year. Matches are played at Zabeel Park.

Cycling & Mountain Biking
Dubai is not a particularly bicycle-friendly city, but there are pleasant areas where you can ride such as along both sides of the creek and Jumeira Road, and on the cycle tracks at Mamzar Park and Jumeirah Open Beach. Also, try out the Meydan Cycle Park, a converted camel racing track with varying distances (4km, 6km and 8km), and the Dubai Autodrome. Dubai Autodrome and Yas Marina Circuit in Abu Dhabi host weekly track cycling sessions. Check the CycleSafeDubai Facebook page discussion threads for the next event.

Wolfi's Bike Shop and Probike offer equipment, advice on technique and recommend weekly riding groups. For cycling as a mode of transport in Dubai, see Getting Around.

Away from the cities, the UAE has a lot to offer outdoor enthusiasts, especially mountain bikers. On a mountain bike it's possible to see the most remote and untouched places that are not even accessible in 4WDs. For hardcore, experienced bikers there is some good terrain, from super-technical rocky trails in areas like Fili and Siji, to mountain routes like Wadi Bih, which climb to over 1,000m and can be descended in minutes. The riding is mainly rocky, technical and challenging.

Even if you are experienced, always be sensible and go prepared – the sun is strong, you will need far more water than you think, and it's easy to get lost. Wide, knobbly tires work much better on the loose, sharp rocks. For further information on mountain biking in the UAE, including details of possible routes, refer to the *UAE Off-Road Explorer*.

The Cycle Hub
Dubai MotorCity Grandstand MotorCity, Al Hebiah 1 **04 425 6555**
thecyclehub.com
Map **1 N12**
Organises numerous trails and weekly group rides for mountain bikers and also offers a rider development programme for beginners to elite. You can also get your bike serviced here and buy new bikes and spare parts.

The mountains offer many biking routes

LIVING IN DUBAI
CLUBS & GROUPS

Cycle Safe Dubai
050 680 4528
cyclesafedubai.com
A road biking club that organises races including the Spinneys Dubai 92 Cycle Challenge, Friday morning rides between 35km and 100km and the Saturday morning Bab Al Shams coffee ride. It is also the brains behind the Wednesday cycle nights at the Dubai Autodrome, where expert cyclists are on hand to teach beginners the basics. For Dhs.500 a year, you can join Team CSD and get a range of services and discounts (as well as a team jersey) but membership is not mandatory to join in the rides.

Dubai Mountain Bikers UAE
facebook.com/pages/Dubai-Mountain-Bikers-UAE-Dubikers
Also known as Dubikers, this mountain-biking club aims to encourage more people to the sport and is best for those who don't yet have elite technical riding experience. They regularly organise rides – see their facebook page for more information.

Dubai Roadsters
04 339 4453
dubairoadsters.com
Possibly the more serious of the organised road-biking groups and rides, the Friday ride offers options of 80km, 120km and, occasionally, 140km. Weekday rides range from 30km to 50km. There are also special events, from the epic twice-yearly 240km coast-to-coast ride to group training rides in the Hatta hills. The group's socials are a great place to meet like-minded people.

Hot-Cog Mountain Bike Club
056 170 8087
hot-cog.com
An active group of enthusiasts who organise weekend trips all over the country and midweek off-road mountain-biking night rides. They also camp, hike and barbecue, and new riders are always welcome.

Dragon Boat Racing
Training sessions in the ancient eastern sport of dragon boat racing are held most mornings and evenings at either Dubai Festival City or Le Meridien Mina Seyahi. There are several teams in Dubai which compete against each other and teams from Abu Dhabi. Most are more than happy to accept new members with little or no experience.
Dragon boats are low-lying vessels that are paddled along by hardworking teams (hence why the sport is also referred to as 'paddling').
　　The UAE Dragon Boat Association lists all of the country's teams. For details and a history of the sport visit dubaidragonboat.com.

Dubai Dawn Patrol
The Westin Marsa Dubai 050 879 5845
dubaidawnpatrol.org
Map 1 M5
Dawn Patrol members make up a diverse group which started in 2008. They combine serious sporting dedication with a fun environment and general love of the water and the outdoors. Training takes place on Tuesday and Thursday mornings (5.45pm to 7pm) and Saturday evenings (4.30pm to 6pm) in the Dubai marina area. The first three sessions are free and then there's an annual membership fee of Dhs.1,000.

Dubai Diggers
Jumeirah Beach Hotel Umm Suqeim 3 050 718 5104
dubai-diggers.com
Map 1 S4 Metro First Gulf Bank
Dubai Diggers are coached by Nick Hando, who founded Australia's Bondi Diggers team. The Dubai Diggers train three times a week. Beginners can attend any session, although the sessions held from 7.30am to 9.30am on Friday mornings at Jumeirah Beach Hotel (which include circuit training) are recommended for a first taste of the sport. Other sessions are Mondays and Wednesdays between 6am and 7am.

Dubai Flying Dragons
Le Meridien Mina Seyahi Marsa Dubai 050 640 9017
dubaidragonboat.com
Map 1 M4 Metro Nakheel
Holds training sessions at Le Meridien Mina Seyahi. Beginners' sessions are on Saturdays at 4pm – email info@dubaidragons.com for more information. The first Saturday of every month is 'social Saturday' where members can get to know each other better.

Dragon Warriors Dubai
056 174 0305
dragonwarriorsdubai.com
Dubai's first all-Filipino dragon-boat race team trains on weekday evenings and weekend mornings and are aiming to join the 2014 Club Crew World Championship in Italy. New paddlers of any age or ability are welcome.

Dubai Sea Dragons
Le Meridien Mina Seyahi Marsa Dubai 050 354 9193
dubaiseadragons.net
Map 1 M4 Metro Nakheel
An independent dragon boating club, affiliated with the International Dragon Boat Federation and DBA Federation. The Sea Dragons participate in local and international competitions. Newcomers are welcome. The one-hour training sessions take place Mondays and Wednesdays (8am and 5pm), and Saturday mornings at 8am. All are on the beach at Mina Seyahi and cost Dhs.50 per session.

LIVING IN DUBAI
CLUBS & GROUPS

Fencing

MK Fencing Academy
Umm Suqeim 3 **050 794 4190**
mkfencingacademy.com
Map **1 S5** Metro **First Gulf Bank**
Offers individual (Dhs.200) and group (Dhs.55) training in épée (épée is French for sword) and foil for all levels. Fencers receive masks, gloves and weapons, with three fencing paths. Electrical scoring and weapons are available for advanced levels.

UAE Fencing Federation
Nr Ramada Hotel Al Mankhool **04 269 9866**
dubaifencingclub.com
Map **1 D5** Metro **Al Fahidi**
This body organises and supervises fencing in the UAE and has affiliations with local competition organisers and the UAE national team.

Fishing

The Dubai government has introduced regulations to protect fish stocks but you can still fish as long as you have the right permit or you charter a licensed tour guide. The best fishing is from September to April, although it is still possible to catch sailfish and queen fish in the summer.

Fish commonly caught in the region include king mackerel, tuna, trevally, bonito, kingfish, cobia and dorado. Beach or surf fishing is popular along the coast and, in season, you can even catch barracuda from the shore. The local hammour, however, is being over-fished, and so anglers are advised not to pluck this species from the sea.

The creek front in Creekside Park is a popular spot. On a Friday, you can hire an abra for the morning at the Bur Dubai or Deira landing steps and ask your driver to take you to the mouth of the creek. You could also consider a deep-sea fishing trip with one of the charter companies listed under Tours.

For more competitive anglers, the UAQ Marine Club (uaqmarineclub.com) sponsors a fishing competition twice a year, in April and October. Call 06 766 6644 for more details. A good selection of fishing rods, tackle and equipment is available at Barracuda Dubai (barracudadubai.com). You can even post your catch of the day on their website.

Licence To Krill

To throw a fishing line into the water you'll first need a fishing licence from Dubai government. Either that or go with a registered fishing charter. There are different permits for leisure boats and offshore fishing. Both are free and can be applied for through the government portal, dm.gov.ae.

Club Joumana
JA Jebel Ali Golf Resort Mena Jabal Ali **04 8836000**
jaresortshotels.com
Metro **Jebel Ali**
Budding fishermen will soon be reeling them in by chartering one of these fully-equipped fishing boats complete with experienced crew and refreshments. Serious contenders can fish under IGFA rules.

Dubai Creek Golf & Yacht Club
Nr Deira City Centre Port Saeed **04 295 6000**
dubaigolf.com
Map **2 M7** Metro **Deira City Centre**
Charter the club's yacht, Sneak Away, and head out into the Arabian Gulf for big game sport fishing. The 32 foot Hatteras carries up to six passengers and the Dhs.3,500 hire fee includes four hours at sea (or Dhs.4,500 for eight hours) plus tackle, bait, ice, fuel and a friendly crew.

Ocean Active
Al Qouz Ind. 3 **050 502 2924**
oceanactive.com
Map **1 S6** Metro **First Gulf Bank**
This experienced boat charter company offers live-aboard and day fishing trips to locations in the UAE and Oman. Fishing charters across the Middle East are also available.

Soolyman Sport Fishing
Jumeirah Beach Umm Suqeim 2 **050 886 6227**
soolymansportfishing.com
Map **1 T4** Metro **First Gulf Bank**
Operates a fleet of fishing boats captained by an experienced South African crew. Costs Dhs.2,300 for four hours, Dhs.2,800 for six hours or Dhs.3,300 for eight hours.

Xclusive Yachts Sport Fishing & Yacht Charter
Marina Yacht Club Marsa Dubai **04 432 7233**
xclusiveyachts.com
Map **1 K5** Metro **Jumeirah Lakes Towers**
Two-hour cruises and four-hour fishing trips are available. An impressive 37 foot sport fishing boat operates from the Dubai Marina Yacht Club.

Football

Football (or soccer) is much loved here in the UAE. Teams train and compete on a regular basis and you'll see plenty of impromptu kickabouts in parks. Insportz (insportzclub.com) in Al Qouz has five indoor five-a-side pitches, and some universities and schools rent out their outdoor and five-a-side pitches. If you'd rather watch than play, the UAE league has regular fixtures in Dubai. Gaelic Football fans should contact Dubai Celts GAA.

LIVING IN DUBAI
CLUBS & GROUPS

Dubai Amateur Football League
dubaifootball.leaguerepublic.com
The 'Expat League' hosts two divisions of 12 teams. It runs an 11-a-side league and cup games between September and April at various locations, and seven-a-side games during the summer.

Dubai Football Academy
04 282 4540
esportsdubai.com
Provides comprehensive training for youngsters at various locations. Players are encouraged to join one of the teams competing in the Dubai Junior Football League. A 15-week course costs Dhs.1,400 for one session a week or Dhs.2,500 for two sessions a week.

Dubai Schools Football League
04 296 6804
dsfl.leaguerepublic.com
This is the umbrella organisation that oversees league football for girls and boys in Dubai. Children wishing to participate in school league football should do so through their schools, but questions about league set-up, results and fixtures can usually be answered here.

Dubai Women's Football Association
Hessyan 1 **050 659 8767**
dubaiwfa.com
Features 15 women's teams that compete across two divisions. Players train once a week, and play weekly matches. Matches take place at the Jebel Ali Centre of Excellence, in the Jebel Ali Shooting Club.

Duplays
Indigo Icon Tower JLT, Al Thanyah 5 **04 447 2394**
duplays.com
Map **1 K5** Metro **Jumeirah Lakes Towers**
Duplays runs competitive and recreational five-a-side indoor and seven-a-side outdoor leagues, and has recently added a women's five-a-side league as well as the Mighty Eagles, an outdoor flag football league.

International Football Academy
04 454 1683
ifasport.com
Offers training for four- to 16-year-olds from internationally qualified coaches. Provides tailored coaching to schools, as well as existing teams. Teams play in several leagues. Pitch hire also available and the academy can organise birthday parties packed full of events.

It's Just Football
JA Centre of Excellence Hessyan 2 **055 296 2963**
itsjustfootball.com
Metro **Jebel Ali**
The club welcome beginners through to elite players with sessions running throughout the week. The dedicated UEFA, A & B licensed coaches have all played and coached at the highest levels and bring years' of experience to their training. The club also hosts tournaments, social events and fitness training and runs English Football Association Coach Education courses for men and women over the age of 16 looking to become coaches.

Dubai has many football camps for kids

LIVING IN DUBAI
CLUBS & GROUPS

McGettigan Irish Football Club
dubaiirish.leaguerepublic.com
Dubai Irish consists of players of all nationalities and participates in the Dubai Amateur Football League. Despite competing in the more competitive division one, the team welcomes players of all skill levels.

Socatots
Sports City, Al Hebiah 4 **04 425 1111**
footballacademydubai.com
Map **1 M12**
This is a fun, musical, soccer play programme for toddlers from walking age to five years. It covers aspects of physical, mental and social development and involves parent participation. Sessions, held from Thursdays to Saturdays, also take place at Emirates International School.

Soccer Circus Dubai
Mirdif City Centre Mirdif **800 586**
soccercircusme.com
Map **2 P12** Metro **Rashidiya**
Playnation is where you'll find this fun football activity which is a big hit with families and groups of youths. It's also a fantastic place for boys' birthday parties. Participants undergo a series of challenges to improve skills. If the Training Academy and Powerplay simulated stadium experience whet the appetite, there's a huge indoor multisports pitch that can be hired for matches.

UAE English Soccer School Of Excellence
050 476 4877
soccerkidsdubai.com
Soccer Kids Dubai offers soccer training in locations across Dubai for ages three to 16 years. Soccer camps during the school holidays are also available. The school also offers children's parties.

Gaelic Games

Dubai Celts GAA
055 660 8357
dubaicelts.com
Dubai Celts GAA holds games and organises training in men's and ladies' Gaelic football, hurling and camogie. Monthly matches are played within the UAE, and international tournaments are held in Bahrain (November) and Dubai (March) each year. Training sessions are held every Monday and Wednesday at 7pm. To join, call the above number.

Gymnastics

Whether you're looking for professional coaching, something to keep the kids active or to just try out a new activity, there are gymnastics classes for every skill level.

Dubai Olympic Gymnastics Club
Nr Jumeira Post Office, Off Al Wasl Rd Al Wasl
050 765 1515
dubai-gymnastics.com
Map **2 F5** Metro **Burj Khalifa/Dubai Mall**
UK gymnastics champion Dean Johnstone runs this club which offers courses for gymnasts of all levels. Classes correspond with school terms as they are geared towards children.

DuGym Gymnastics Club
050 553 6283
dugym.com
Gymnastics and trampoline coaching for children of all abilities is offered during classes from Sunday to Thursday. DuGym runs gym tots lessons as well as club competitions throughout the year at locations including the GEMS World Academy, the Jumeirah English Speaking School and Emirates International School. Contact Suzanne for more info.

GymnastEx
Prism Tower Business Bay **04 445 8244**
gymnast-ex.com
Map **2 E6** Metro **Business Bay**
GymnastEx combo classes blend three disciplines – rhythmic, arobatics and sports aerobics – in one session. Martial arts instruction for boys and yoga for parents is also available, as well as classes for babies and educational gymnastics.

Hashing

Billed as 'drinking clubs with a running problem', Hash House Harriers is a global network of clubs with an emphasis on taking part and socialising afterwards, rather than serious running. A fun way to get fit and meet people.

Creek Hash House Harriers
Al Qouz 2 **050 451 5847**
creekhash.net
Map **2 B8** Metro **Noor Bank**
This men-only group meets every Tuesday, and runs take pace in the desert around sunset for around 45 minutes. They then gather around a camp fire to socialise. They also hold regular curry nights and spit-roast dinners.

Desert Hash House Harriers
050 614 6621
deserthash.org
This group runs every Sunday, an hour before sunset. Prior to the run, one or more members, the Hares, set a trail using straws, paint, chalk or flour. This trail is then followed by the remainder of the group The fee is Dhs.50 including refreshments. There's no need to worry if you're not an athlete – everyone is welcome.

LIVING IN DUBAI
CLUBS & GROUPS

Hockey

Dubai Hockey Club
Nr Cricket Stadium Sports City, Al Hebiah 4
055 917 0622
dubaihockeyclub.com
Map **1 L11**

The club plays in local tournaments on grass and takes part in friendly games. Club training sessions are every Sunday and Wednesday evening. All abilities are welcome. Men and women can join. International tours to locations such as Singapore, Hong Kong and the UK are organised fairly regularly.

Horse Riding

There are a number of excellent stables and equestrian clubs in Dubai. While keeping your own horse can be very expensive, you may find that riding lessons cost less here than in your home country. Though there may be a waiting lists for lessons. There are a few places, such as The Desert Palm Riding School, where you can take your kids for a 10 minute horse ride around the track. If you are a dressage rider and would like to get involved in shows in the UAE contact stables such as Godolphin (godolphin.com), the Abu Dhabi Equestrian Club (emiratesracing.com), or Al Zobair Stud Farm in Sharjah (alzobairstud.com). Horse racing in Dubai is extremely popular. Most races, including the Dubai World Cup – the richest horse race in the world – take place at the Meydan racetrack.

Al Ahli Horse Riding Club
Nr LuLu Hypermarket Al Nahda 1 04 298 8408
alahliclub.info
Map **2 R7** Metro **Stadium**

A well-established club offering a wide range of activities including bare back lessons, dressage and jumping. There's also pony clubs and horsemanship clubs for riders aged four and up.

Al Jiyad Stables
Nr Dubai International Endurance City Al Yalayis 2
050 599 5866
aljiyad.com

Offers lessons for riders of all levels of experience. It also runs individual or group desert hacks. The excellent stables are home to more than 60 horses.

Al Sahra Desert Resort Equestrian Centre
Al Sahra Desert Resort Heritage Vision, Al Yufrah 1
04 427 4055
jaresortshotels.com

Horse riding for individuals and groups is available at this eco-tourism resort in the Dubai desert. Private livery is also offered for a limited number of horses, and corporate team-building exercises are available.

The Desert Equestrian Club
Wadi Al Amardi Wadi Al Amardi 050 309 9770

If you have your own horse, the Desert Equestrian Club offers livery services for Dhs.1,500 a month. Accomplished riders can pay Dhs.100 to use one of the stable's horses. Private lessons are Dhs.80 for adults and Dhs.50 for children under 16.

The Desert Palm Riding School
Desert Palm Warsan 2 050 451 7773
desertpalm.ae

This state-of-the-art riding school offers group or semi-private classes for all ages, and one-to-one sessions. Prices are Dhs.95 per 30 minutes for child beginners and Dhs.175 per hour for adults, including all equipment. Relax after riding in the club's Lime Spa, or enjoy dinner at the Arabian-influenced restaurant.

Dubai Polo & Equestrian Club
Al Qudra Rd Arabian Ranches, Al Hebiah 2
04 361 8111
poloclubdubai.com
Map **1 N13**

This top-notch centre features a sandplast arena (one of the best surfaces to ride on), a riding school and a polo club. Horseriding lessons are available for all abilities. Beginners' courses start at Dhs.1,400 for 10 lessons. Enjoy a picnic pitchside during chukkas, held every weekend during the winter. Bring your own sandwiches or order bespoke picnics through the website. The club also houses several top-quality restaurants and a branch of Angsana Spa, and the venue is available for weddings and conferences.

Emirates Equestrian Centre
Nr Bab Al Shams Desert Resort & Spa Al Yalayis 2
050 553 7986
emiratesequestriancentre.com

This centre is home to more than 80 horses. Facilities include an international size floodlit arena, a riding school, and dressage and lunging rings. It can cater to very small children and hosts regular competitions, gymkhanas and shows. The centre also has regular clinics and stable management courses.

Hoofbeatz
Arabian Ranches, Al Hebiah 2 050 181 0401
hoofbeatz.com
Map **1 N13**

The Hoofbeatz Horsemanship Club runs every Friday and Saturday, from 4pm until 6pm, for beginner and novice horse lovers aged eight to 18 years. The centre also runs an all-round horsemanship course covering stable management and caring for horses. If you're unfamiliar with horses, then try the two-hour 'Meet the Horse' experience. Also on offer are birthday parties, educational visits for schools, and holiday camps.

LIVING IN DUBAI
CLUBS & GROUPS

JA Jebel Ali Golf Resort
Nr Palm Jebel Ali Mena Jabal Ali **04 814 5555**
jaresortshotels.com
Metro **Jebel Ali**
The riding centre has nine horses and air-conditioned stables. Instructors give private lessons from Tuesday to Sunday, while experienced riders can tackle one-hour desert rides. Half-hour lessons cost Dhs.200 (private) and Dhs.150 (semi-private).

Jebel Ali Equestrian Club
Nr Jebel Ali Hospital Al Thanyah 2 **04 884 5101**
Map **1 N7** Metro **Dubai Internet City**
Qualified instructors teach all levels of dressage, jumping, gymkhana games and hacking. Newcomers can try one lesson, after which a 10-lesson package costs Dhs.800 for children and Dhs.1,000 for adults, plus a Dhs.120 annual registration fee.

Riding For The Disabled Association Of Dubai
Desert Palm Warsan 2 rdad.ae
A charity that uses horseriding and hippotherapy (physical and speech therapy using the movement of a horse) to achieve therapeutic goals for those suffering from autism, cerebral palsy, Down Syndrome, spina bifida and learning disabilities. The aim is to improve poise, posture, strength and flexibility while boosting confidence. Classes last around 45 minutes.

Ice Hockey
Ice hockey has been a fixture on the local sports scene ever since Al Nasr Leisureland opened in 1979. With the opening of Dubai Ice Rink, teams now have two Dubai venues. The Skate Shop next to the ice rink at The Dubai Mall stocks hockey kit including skates, sticks, body armour, jerseys and helmets for children and adults. Call Dubai Ice Rink for stock details (04 448 5111).

Dubai Mighty Camels Ice Hockey Club
Al Nasr Leisureland Oud Metha
dubaimightycamels.com
Map **2 L6** Metro **Oud Metha**
This amateur ice hockey league has more than 120 members and competes in the Emirates Hockey League (EHL). The club also hosts an annual tournament in April, which attracts up to 20 teams from the Gulf, Europe and the Far East.

Dubai Sandstorms Ice Hockey Club
Oud Metha **050 775 8713**
eteamz.com/dubaisandstorm
Map **2 L6** Metro **Oud Metha**
Practice sessions are held twice a week for youngsters aged four to 18. The emphasis is on teamwork and sportsmanship. Matches are played against teams from Dubai, Abu Dhabi, Al Ain Oman and Qatar. The Sandstorms website has a noticeboard for buying and selling ice hockey equipment.

Kayaking
See Activities, Things To See & Do.

Kitesurfing
See Activities, Things To See & Do.

Martial Arts
Aspiring Bruce Lees are well catered for with many centres offering courses in judo, aikido, karate, kickboxing and other martial arts. In addition, many fitness clubs and gyms offer Thai boxing, kung fu, self-defence alongside their group exercise programmes. For kids, the Active Sports Academy has an excellent range of disciplines for all ages and runs after-school classes as well as holiday camps.

Colosseum Muay Thai Health & Fitness Club
Zaabeel Rd Al Karama **04 337 2755**
colosseumuae.com
Map **2 L6** Metro **BurJuman**
Classes are daily from 8.30pm to 10pm, except Fridays (Dhs.50). Personal training is available for those over eight years old. Colosseum organises competitions with area clubs.

Dubai Karate Centre
Nr Safa Park Al Safa 1 **04 344 7797**
dubaikarate.com
Map **2 C5**
This club is a member of the Japanese Karate Association (JKA) and has a team of black belt, JKA qualified instructors who teach a range of martial arts that include shotokan karate, taekwondo, aikido, Muay Thai, judo, kudo, iado, laido and wingtzun. This centre also runs regular self-defence courses. Registration Dhs.100. Monthly memberships from Dhs.380.

Dubai Kendo Club
050 900 2661
The focus here is on a martial art based on the ancient Japanese swordsmanship traditions. The club meets Wednesdays at 7.45pm and Saturdays at 4pm at Emirates International School Jumeirah. The two-hour classes cost Dhs.50 for adults, Dhs.30 for children.

EBMAS School Of Self Defense
DUCTAC Al Barsha 1 **055 605 8128**
ebmas-selfdefense.com
Map **1 R6** Metro **Mall of the Emirates**
Emin Boztepe Martial Arts System (EBMAS) is a popular form of self-defence that has become so popular it is now taught in more than 40 countries. This school teaches armed and unarmed forms of

LIVING IN DUBAI
CLUBS & GROUPS

EBMAS. Classes are held on Sundays and Wednesdays from 8.30pm to 9.45pm.

Golden Falcon Karate Centre
Nr Choithrams Al Karama 04 336 0243
goldenfalconkarate.com
Map **2 L5** Metro **Al Karama**
Established in 1990, the centre is affiliated with the International Karate Budokan and the UAE Judo, Taekwondo & Karate Federation. The centre is open throughout the week. Training costs Dhs.150 for two classes per week. Classes are also taught at Jabal Ali, Meadows, Oud Metha and JLT.

Golden Fist Karate Club
Al Riffa Plaza Al Raffa 04 452 5599
goldenfistkarate.net
Map **2 L4** Metro **Al Raffa**
This club is popular for the flexible times it provides for training in martial arts including karate and kung fu. A nine-month black belt crash course is available too. Two and six classes a week, from Dhs.150 to Dhs.320 per month (plus a Dhs.50 admission fee). For those of a more gentle disposition, yoga, swimming and aerobics classes are also offered.

Raifet N Shawe
Trade Center 2 050 495 4446
Map **2 H6** Metro **Financial Centre**
A black belt teacher in karate, kickboxing, judo and Muay Thai holds classes at Emirates Towers (04 319 8660) on Mondays, Wednesdays and Saturdays from 5.30pm to 6.30pm.

Zanshinkan Aikido Club Dubai
Al Raizi Boys School Al Safa 1 050 795 2716
aikido.ae
Map **2 C5** Metro **Business Bay**
Classes for children and adults are held throughout the week at the Dubai Karate Centre. Once-only registration Dhs.100. Kids' classes are Dhs.350 for eight classes a month and adult training costs Dhs.500 for 12 sessions a month.

Motorsports

Automobile & Touring Club Of The UAE
Nr Century Mall Al Mamzar 04 296 1122
atcuae.ae
Map **2 R6** Metro **Al Qiyadah**
The club is the UAE's FIM (Fédération Internationale de Motocyclisme) representative. Regular motocross and off-road enduros are held between September and April, and activity centres at the DMX Club and in Umm Al Quwain host quad and drag races. It organises the Abu Dhabi Desert Challenge, and the opening round of the FIA Cross Country Rally.

Dubai Autodrome
Shk Mohammed Bin Zayed Rd MotorCity,
Al Hebiah 1 04 367 8700
dubaiautodrome.com
Map **1 N12**
Dubai's motorsport home has six track configurations, including a 5.39km FIA-sanctioned GP circuit, state-of-the-art pit facilities and a 7,000 seat grandstand. Events hosted include rounds of the FIA GT Championship.

Dubai Motocross Club (DMX)
Nr Jebel Ali Go Kart Track Hessyan 1 050 452 6489
dubaimotocross.com
Metro **Jebel Ali**
Dubai Motocross (DMX) runs classes for cadets, juniors, 65cc, 85cc, 125cc and adults. The facility features two tracks, one for juniors and one for seniors, and organises eight championship events per year. The entry fee is Dhs.150 for members and starts at Dhs.250 for non-members. Practice fees for members are Dhs.50 during the week and Dhs.75 at weekends. Non-members pay Dhs.100 or Dhs.150.

Emirates Motor Sports Federation
Villa 1, Casablanca Rd Al Garhoud 04 282 7111
emsf.ae
Map **2 M8** Metro **GGICO**
Emirates Motor Sports Federation organises events throughout the year, such as the 4WD 1000 Dunes Rally, the Champions Rally for saloon cars, road safety campaigns and classic car exhibitions. Membership including competition licence is Dhs.500 per year; non-members can race for a fee.

The Chase street-racing festival at Dubai Autodrome

LIVING IN DUBAI
CLUBS & GROUPS

Harley Owners Group Dubai Chapter
04 339 1909
hoguae.com
The group meets at various locations for rides across the region, including the Middle East HOG Rally in Fujairah. See its website for a full events calendar and map links to meet locations.

Royal Enfield Dubai
Nr Times Square Al Qouz Ind. 1 04 340 1855
royalenfielduae.com
Map **1 U6** Metro **Noor Bank**
The social club organises city rides, long-distance trips and informal gatherings, as well as an annual gala. Although the club is named Royal Enfield Dubai, riders of any bikes are welcome.

Netball
Netball is not just for school girls – here in Dubai it's alive and kicking for all age groups, and is a well-established sport. Even if you've no prior experience, you'll be welcomed by Dubai's teams if you want to give it a try.

Dubai Netball League
The Sevens Al Marmoom 055 817 6624
dubainetballleague.com
Four divisions compete between September and May. Training is on Sundays or Mondays. League nights are on Wednesdays. Players also have the chance to be selected for the annual inter-Gulf championship. New players of all levels are welcome.

Duplays
Indigo Icon Tower JLT, Al Thanyah 5 04 447 2394
duplays.com
Map **1 K5** Metro **Jumeirah Lakes Towers**
Duplays' competitive women's league plays Sunday evenings, and games in the recreational league take place on Monday evenings. Players can sign up as individuals and be allocated to a team for Dhs.450. Enter a full team for Dhs.3,900 per season.

Polo

Dubai Polo & Equestrian Club
Al Qudra Rd Arabian Ranches, Al Hebiah 2
04 361 8111
poloclubdubai.com
Map **1 N13**
The very best players in the world are attracted to this venue's regular local and international polo competitions held on its two full-sized pitches. Coaching is offered for all levels, from 40 minute lessons to six-day courses. An introductory 1.5 hour lesson is Dhs.800.

Polo
For a fun twist on the game, head to the Dubai polo and Equestrian Club for a spot of camel polo. It's not as fast-paced as the real thing but you'll come away with plenty of good stories. Any group of eight or more is welcome to book a session. Call 04 404 5880 for reservations or for more details email camelpolo@gulfventures.com.

Netball

Rugby

Dubai Exiles Rugby Football Club
dubaiexiles.com
The Exiles is Dubai's most serious rugby club and has a 1st and 2nd XV that competes in the AGRFU leagues. It also has a veterans, U19s, ladies', girls' U17s and a minis and youth section. The Exiles club also hosts a tournament alongside the annual Dubai IRB Sevens Tournament.

Dubai Hurricanes Rugby Football Club
The Sevens Al Marmoom 050 288 1491
dubaihurricanes.com
Having started as a social outfit, the Hurricanes now compete in the Dubai Sevens. The club also has a ladies' team and players aged from four to over 50 and abilities are welcome. Training is on Mondays and Wednesdays at 6.30pm. Touring is a key activity of the club and is used to develop the Midi and Youth sections – tours to date include Australia, Japan, Spain and more.

LIVING IN DUBAI
CLUBS & GROUPS

Running

For more than half the year, Dubai's weather is perfect for running. There are lots of groups to try and a number of events to train for, such as the excellent Creek Striders Half Marathon (dubaicreekstriders@gmail.com), the Dubai Marathon (dubaimarathon.org), and the Wadi Bih Race (wadibih.com). For suggestions of places to run, see askexplorer.com.

Dubai Creek Striders
dubaicreekstriders.org
The Striders meet Friday mornings (on the road opposite the Novotel next to the Trade Centre) for a long-distance run. This club started in 1995 and training is designed for members to take part in the 42.2km Dubai Marathon in January. For more info email them on dubai.creek.striders@gmail.com.

Dubai Road Runners
Safa Park Al Wasl **050 624 3213**
dubai-road-runners.com
Map **2 D5** Metro **Business Bay**
Meet up with the Road Runners on Saturdays at 6.30pm by gate 4 of Safa Park to run between 3.4km and 7km (the park charges Dhs.5 entrance fee). For fun, runners predict their times, with a prize for the winner.

Nike+ Run Club
werundubai.com
Beginners or intermediates are best suited to these sessions at Festival City (Tuesday evenings) and Downtown (Friday mornings) and are expertly coached, not to mention free.

Reebok Running Club
Marsa Dubai **055 369 5664**
urbanenergyfitness.com
Map **1 K5** Metro **Jumeirah Lakes Towers**
Ignite your passion for running with this club for all abilities and fitness levels. Members meet twice a week at Dubai Marina Mall to run in a fun, motivating atmosphere and share advice on training, nutrition and health tips. Organised in partnership with fitness experts Urban Energy.

Stride For Life
050 657 7057
strideforlife.com
Stride for Life offers aerobic walking and running for people of all ages and abilities. Anyone interested in joining should first undergo a fitness assessment. Following this, a thrice-weekly programme is recommended. Stride for Life also does Nordic and mall walking, and 'training journeys' for novices preparing for long distance events. Fees are Dhs.1,600 for a one-year membership.

Sailing
See Activities, Things To See & Do.

Skating & Rollerblading
See Activities, Things To See & Do.

Skiing

Dubai Ski Club
Al Barsha 1
dubaiskiclub.com
Map **1 R6** Metro **Mall of the Emirates**
The club has over 1,400 members and meets at 6pm on the last Saturday of every month, next to Ski Dubai's ticket counter, for social skiing or snowboarding, race training and races, followed by apres ski. Membership benefits include a reduced fee for the slope pass and use of the 'advance booking' lane when purchasing tickets, plus special offers on equipment, clothing, accessories and holidays. Membership is Dhs.300.

Softball

Dubai Softball League
Shk Zayed Rd Business Bay **050 651 4970**
dubaisoftball.com
Map **2 D6** Metro **Business Bay**
Over 16s can join one of more than 20 teams in three leagues (two for men, one mixed) and take part in the Middle East Softball Championships in April. The season runs from September to December and from January to May.

LIVING IN DUBAI
CLUBS & GROUPS

Duplays
Indigo Icon Tower JLT, Al Thanyah 5 **04 447 2394**
duplays.com
Map **1 K5** Metro **Jumeirah Lakes Towers**
Duplays runs a mixed recreational softball league on Wednesdays. Matches are held at the sports field near Business Bay on Sheikh Zayed Road.

Squash

Dubai Squash
The Greens, Al Thanyah 3
dubaisquash.com
Map **1 M6** Metro **Nakheel**
The league has been active in Dubai and Sharjah since the 1970s and is run by the UAE Squash Association. Around 250 competitors in 25 teams play three 10 week seasons. Teams meet on Mondays at 7.30pm and each team fields four players.

Surfing
See Activities, Things To See & Do.

Swimming
Dubai has some great swimming spots at various public beaches, private pools, at beach clubs or one of the beach parks. The water temperature rarely dips below 20°C in winter, although during the summer it can feel like stepping into a bath. Be aware that rip tides and undertows in the sea can catch out even the strongest swimmer, so never ignore flags or signs ordering you not to swim.

You might also run into quite a lot of jellyfish towards the end of the summer. Around the UAE there are occasional outbreaks of red tide, a naturally occurring algal bloom which turns the water red and gives it an unpleasant smell. These generally affect the east coast and are relatively uncommon in Dubai.

Many hotels, beach clubs and health clubs have swimming pools open to the public for a day entrance fee. Swimming lessons are available from health and beach clubs too. For children's lessons, check with your school. Keen swimmers can sign up for the Wild Wadi Swim Around the Burj annual challenge, held each February in aid of Medecins Sans Frontieres (swim.msf-me.org). There are two distances to choose from – an 800m swim and a 1,600m swim – and swimmers are given plenty of encouragement from spectators watching from the beach.

Active Sports Academy
106 Corner City Al Kheeran **050 559 7055**
activeuae.com
Map **2 M9** Metro **Emirates**
Classes, held in various locations, include water babies, parent and toddlers, and lessons for beginners to advanced swimmers.

Aqua Sports Academy
King's Dubai Umm Suqeim 3 **050 574 7942**
aquaswim.ae
Map **1 S5** Metro **First Gulf Bank**
Aqua Sports runs mainly from the 25m pool at Kings' School in Umm Suqeim. Sessions include everything from parent-and-baby sessions, kids' swim lessons and one-to-one clinics, competitive squads and holiday camps. It also runs the city's most popular masters' swim programme for swimmers aged 16 and up. Casual, keep-fit swimmers and competitive age-group swimmers and triathletes all welcome. See the website for session times and special events.

Australian International Swim Schools (AISS) > p.191
Al Shafar Tower 1 Trade Center 1 **04 368 9226**
aiss.ae
Map **2 J5** Metro **World Trade Centre**
AUSTSWIM-certified instructors provide swimming lessons at pools throughout Dubai. This company also runs many of the schools' swimming programmes. Swimming training is provided at all levels, from classes for parents and babies, to adult triathlon swimming squads. Lessons are available in Al Qouz, Jumeira, The Lakes, Emirate Hills, Springs, Victory Heights, Sharjah, Mirdif and Al Twar.

Desert Sport Services
Palace Tower 2 Nadd Hessa **056 644 1742**
desertsportservices.com
The swimming programme offers classes for parents and babies, learn-to-swim, stroke development, and competitive training sessions. There is also a full adult swimming programme. Instructors are all Swimming Teacher Association (STA) qualified, and conduct classes based on the Total Immersion philosophy.

Excel Sports
050 223 9235
excelsportsuae.com
Excel Sports offers coaching in swimming, cricket, soccer and gymnastics. The emphasis is firmly on having fun and being confident in the water. The company also runs holiday camps that include swimming in the programme, as well as other activities such as tennis, soccer and softball.

Hamdan bin Mohammed Sports Complex
Nr Emirates Rd Umm Nahad 2 **04 306 2666**
hamdansc.com
The HSC is the largest sports Aquatic Sports Centre in the world. It houses three swimming pools and specialises in swimming, diving, water polo and synchronised swimming. It also offers track and field sports and hosts events. A monthly swimming pass is Dhs.200 – see the website for further prices.

AISS

Australian International Swim Schools

SWIM TIME
LEARN TO SWIM CENTRE

Dubai's First dedicated specialised Learn to Swim Centre Programs for Babies to Adults and has Full Disabled Access.

AREAS COVERED INCLUDE
Al Quoz, Jumeirah, Al Sufouh, Umm Suqeim and Al Barsha.

Located between Times Square and Limetree Cafe Street 4b Al Quoz 1 Phone: 043233388 Email: swim@aiss.ae

AISS

CLASSES AT VARIOUS VENUES INCLUDE
Learn to Swim Classes, Parent and Child Classes, Infants Swimming Stroke Development, Stroke Correction, Mini Swim Squads, Junior Squads, Adult Learn to Swim, Adult Fitness Squads.

PROGRAMS COVERING
Al Barsha, JBR, The Lakes, Emirate Hills, Al Twar, Sharjah, Mirdif, Al Quoz, Al Sufouh, Jumeirah, Umm Suqeim, Tecom, The Greens, Motor City, Sports City, Victory Heights, Media City and The Springs.

A Devision of
AISS
Australian International Sports Services

Office: +971 43689226 Mobile: +971 556014549 Email: swim@aiss.ae

LIVING IN DUBAI
CLUBS & GROUPS

Hamilton Aquatics
04 450 8832
hamiltonaquaticsdubai.com
Hamilton Aquatics is currently one of the largest swimming academies in the Middle East. Hamilton's Learn to Swim Academy develops children and adults from non-swimmers to advanced swimmers with over 210 classes and 1,200 spaces a week for every level of swimmer. Operating across numerous locations in Dubai, it runs a swim development programme to enhance swimming skills and a dedicated Squad Academy for elite swim training.

Speedo Swim Squads
Arabian Ranches, Wadi Al Safa 6 **04 354 9525**
speedodubai.net
Map **1 Q13**
This private club offers tuition for all ages and abilities, from 'duckling' to squad training. It also offers ASA teacher training and water polo classes. Lessons take place at a number of locations including Horizon School, Uptown High School, Dubai International Academy and Emirates International School.

Synquatics
Raffles International School
Umm Suqeim 3 **055 448 5381**
synquatics.com
Map **1 S5** Metro **First Gulf Bank**
Opened in 2012 by former Olympian sisters, Sarah and Hebel Abdel Gawad, this club teaches synchronised swimming; a hybrid of swimming, dance and gymnastics. Locations include Safa School, Raffles and Fitness First (Meadows). Swimmers can choose to train either once, twice or three times a week in 60 minute sessions, though during term time only block bookings are accepted.

Table Tennis
Table tennis can be played for Dhs.40 per hour, including equipment, at Insportz just behind Dubai Garden Centre on Sheikh Zayed Road. Booking is required. Several of the older leisure clubs provide table tennis, although the equipment is usually a bit rusty. The UAE Table Tennis Association is in Dubai (04 254 7111), and can provide information on how to get into leagues and high level competitions, but unfortunately most of the local clubs only accept UAE Nationals.

Tennis
Dubai is firmly established on the international tennis circuit, with the annual Dubai Duty Free Tennis Championships attracting the best players in the world. There are plenty of venues to enjoy a game. Outdoor courts are available at most health and beach clubs, many of which are floodlit. There are indoor courts for hire at InSports (04 347 5833).

Ace Sports Academy
Emirates Grand Trade Center 2 **04 55452 2066**
acesportsacademy.com
Map **2 G6** Metro **Burj Khalifa/Dubai Mall**
This tennis school offers everything from tots' tennis and junior development to ladies' mornings, adult

Emirates Golf Club

Dubai Explorer

LIVING IN DUBAI
CLUBS & GROUPS

lessons and tournaments. Private, semi-private and family lessons are available, and ball machines can be hired. Membership and lesson costs vary. Check the website for details. Also at Mirdif Tennis Courts, near Mirdif City Centre.

The Atlantis Tennis Academy
Atlantis Nakhlat Jumeira 04 426 1433
Map **1 N1** Metro **Nakheel**
Provides world-class coaching for players of all ages and levels. The state-of-the-art facilities include the latest court surfaces plus video technology for technique analysis. The academy also organises social events and tournament afternoons for members.

Clark Francis Tennis Academy
04 282 4540
clarkfrancistennis.com
This tennis school offers group and individual tennis coaching for children and adults. A ladies' morning is held at the Grand Hyatt on Mondays from 8.15am. Cardio Tennis classes (a cross between tennis and circuit training) are every Tuesday from 6.45pm at the Aviation Club. It also organises competitive leagues in a variety of categories including juniors. Ball kid training (for the Dubai Tennis Championships) is available, and the service centre can have your racket restrung and returned to you within 12 hours.

Dubai Tennis Academy
American University Al Sufouh 2 04 399 1125
dubaitennisacademy.com
Map **1 M5** Metro **Nakheel**
Provides training for all levels, with internationally qualified coaches, at American University Dubai, and the five-star Grand Hyatt hotel Dubai (which has four courts). Programmes include private lessons, group clinics, competitions, ladies' tennis mornings and school holiday camps. Check the website for prices for members and non-members. The academy sometimes offers discounts and promotions on its website.

DUET Sports Club
Dubai Men's College Academic City, Al Rowaiyah 2
055 881 1974
This club has thousands of members and so you are sure to find your hitting partner, tennis coach or tennis buddy among DUET's more than 1,200 registered members. This active social tennis group has a good website about the sport in the region, and can provide players with partners, organise tennis events, and offer professional coaching to all ages and levels. The club has branched out to offer other sports including football leagues, and basketball and swimming lessons.

Emirates Golf Club
Shk Zayed Rd The Greens, Al Thanyah 3 **04 417 9999**
dubaigolf.com
Map **1 M6** Metro **Nakheel**
Open to non-members of all levels for coaching by qualified USPTR professionals. The centre has four courts. Two teams play in the ladies' Spinneys League and one in the men's Prince League.

Triathlon

SuperTRI
050 873 1989
supertridubai.com
If you fancy getting really fit this year then train with certified triathlon coach, Trace Rogers, who can help you gain the skills and techniques you need to perform in a triathlon and reach your best ever time. Training focuses on all areas of swimming, running and biking and programmes are offered to suit your lifestyle and budget.

TriDubai
tridubai.org
Support for everyone from complete beginners to world-class athletes; for those training for sprint distance to Ironman races (or just training for the love of it); for those starting out, starting again or wanting to break records. The club welcomes new members and training sessions are free of charge.

Ultimate Frisbee

Duplays
Indigo Icon Tower JLT, Al Thanyah 5 **04 447 2394**
duplays.com
Map **1 K5** Metro **Jumeirah Lakes Towers**
Duplays (duplays.com) organises a friendly league which you can enter as a team or individual and be placed in a team. Games are on Monday nights on the field near Business Bay. Pickup games are held in Safa Park on Saturday afternoons.

Volleyball

EK Volleyball Club
050 358 1603
ekvolleyballclub.com
Organises various events around Dubai including pickup nights, indoor and beach volleyball. Prices vary but a two-hour community game starts from Dhs.25. Many players play at Kite Beach/Beach Volleyball Park on Fridays and Saturdays after 10am.

Watersports
For information on diving, kayaking, kitesurfing and other watersports, see Activities, Things To See & Do.

LIVING IN DUBAI
CLUBS & GROUPS

Hobbies

Arts & Crafts

There's a thriving arts and crafts scene in Dubai with classes available for beginners and children. During the hot summer months, an arty activity could be just what you need to keep occupied. And, if you need to buy supplies, see our Shopping section for listings.

Art Labs
04 374 6208
artlabs.me
Courses are held at Dubai Ladies Club and The Pavillion Downtown on everything from *sospeso trasparente* and sugar wires to jewellery making and decorating techniques. There's also an online store to buy supplies. The group creates beautiful, glitzy accessories for weddings and corporate events, as well as invites – some of which are decorated with Swarovski crystals.

Cafe Ceramique
Dubai Festival City Mall Al Badia, Al Kheeran
04 232 8616
cafe-ceramique.com
Map **2 L9** Metro **Emirates**
Paint your own teapot or a whole dinner set. Choose your piece of blank pottery, which the cafe will glaze and fire for you after you decorate it. Events include Art4fun Workshops and the Kidz4art Summer Camp. The cafe also serves a great selection of healthy breakfasts, lunches and snacks to keep you energised while you get creative.

Cafe Ceramique

Craft Land
Town Centre Jumeirah Jumeira 1 **04 342 2237**
mycraftland.com
Map **2 F4** Metro **Burj Khalifa/Dubai Mall**
Everything you'd like to learn about machine sewing, quilting, hand embroidery, knitting and crocheting is taught here. There are needlecraft workshops, courses, clubs and clinics. Classes are for beginners and the more experienced. Most sessions last around 90 minutes. Some are charged per class (roughly Dhs.40) while for others you pay for a full course (prices vary). Club meetings are Tuesday mornings and Saturday afternoons and membership is Dhs.50.

Creative Hands
Mayfair Bldg Dubai Investment Park 1 **04 884 9343**
creativehandsdubai.com
Map **1 G10** Metro **Ibn Battuta**
Creative Hands has a store in The Green Community and another online. The company also offers workshops and sessions in crafts such as scrapbooking and card making.

Dubai Community Theatre & Arts Centre > p.437
Mall of the Emirates Al Barsha 1 **04 341 4777**
ductac.org
Map **1 R6** Metro **Mall of the Emirates**
Decorative arts, drawing, painting, photography, sculpture, paper craft and the performing arts are just some of classes DUCTAC runs for adults and children. Details are listed online and updated regularly. DUCTAC also has a theatre, art galleries and studios for exhibitions and performances. There's a cafe, art supplies shop and The Old Library, an English language lending library run by volunteers. DUCTAC is open daily 9am to 10pm and 2pm to 10pm on Fridays.

Dubai International Art Centre
Villa 27, Street 75B Jumeira 1 **04 344 4398**
artdubai.com
Map **2 F4** Metro **Financial Centre**
Villa-based art centre offering six- to eight-week courses in more than 70 subjects, including painting, drawing, dressmaking, etching, pottery and photography. Annual membership starts from Dhs.350 for adults, Dhs.450 for families and Dhs.120 for under 18s.

Ikebana Sogetsu Group
Villa 13, 132 Street 15 Al Wuheida **04 262 0282**
Map **2 Q5** Metro **Al Qiyadah**
Ikebana is the intricate and beautiful Japanese art of flower arranging. This Dubai group attempts to deepen cultural understanding among the city's multinational society with exhibitions, demonstrations and workshops. Classes are taught by a qualified teacher from Japan.

LIVING IN DUBAI
CLUBS & GROUPS

the jamjar
Nr Dubai Garden Centre Al Qouz Ind. 3 **04 341 7303**
thejamjardubai.com
Map **1 S6** Metro **First Gulf Bank**
A canvas, paints and the obligatory jam jar are yours starting at Dhs.195 for four hours of self-inspired creativity. All you need to bring is your inspiration. The 'Jam-To-Go' service brings the experience to you – a novel idea for a party or corporate event. Open weekdays from 10am to 8pm; Fridays 2pm to 8pm; closed on Sundays.

Objects & Elements
Street 8 Al Qouz Ind. 1 **04 323 6182**
objectsandelementsgroup.com
Map **1 U6** Metro **Noor Bank**
A sewing group where you can get your 'sewing machine driving licence' and learn how to make everything from ironing board covers to retro soft toy owls. They also teach embroidery.

Paper At Artisans of the Emirates
Time Square Center Al Qouz Ind. 1 arte.ae
Map **1 T6** Metro **Noor Bank**
Paper@ARTE is part of ARTE Souk, held at the Times Square Center or Festival Centre most Fridays. All scrapbookers can join the workshops.

Paper Lane
Town Centre Jumeirah Jumeira 1 **04 344 3633**
mypaperlane.com
Map **2 F4** **Metro** Burj Khalifa/Dubai Mall
One of the city's biggest scrapbooking shops, Paper Lane carries all the materials you'll need to create a memorable album. It also runs classes for all ages and levels. Families welcome.

Birdwatching

Emirates Bird Records Committee
uaebirding.com
Local and visiting birders are invited to submit details of sightings to this committee which collates information on birds in the UAE and on request. A weekly roundup of bird sightings and a monthly report are available via email from Tommy Pedersen at 777sandman@gmail.com.

Bridge

Dubai Ladies Bridge Club
Jumeira 1 **050 659 1300**
Map **2 F4** Metro **Business Bay**
The sociable females of Dubai meet for ladies-only bridge mornings at 9am on Sundays and Wednesdays. Contact Marzie Polad on the number above or Jan Irvine on 050 645 4395.

Chess

Dubai Chess & Culture Club
Nr Century Mall Al Mamzar **04 296 6664**
dubaichess.ae
Map **2 R6** Metro **Al Qiyadah**
The home of the UAE's national chess team. Members can play at the club seven nights a week, and competitions are organised on a regular basis. The club also promotes international competitions, including the Dubai International Open, Emirates Open and Dubai Junior Open. Membership costs Dhs.100 a year.

Cooking Classes
Many hotels run cookery classes by special request if you particularly like one of their dishes, or as an organised series of classes. There are also wine tasting classes and courses for budding oenophiles or those just wanting to up their dinner party game.

Armani Hotel Dubai
Downtown Dubai, Burj Khalifa **04 888 3888**
dubai.armanihotels.com
Map **2 F6** Metro **Burj Khalifa/Dubai Mall**
The teams of chefs at several of the Armani Hotel's most popular restaurants teach willing students how to make some of their specialities at home. Between Saturdays and Wednesdays, 4.30pm to 6pm, you can learn to prepare a classic three-course Italian meal, master Indian cuisine or perfect the intricacies of Japanese fare. Classes range in price from Dhs.1,100 to Dhs.1,300.

The Balance Cafe Cookery School
Al Qouz 1 **04 384 7010**
balance-wellness-centre.com
Map **2 C6**
Award-winning chefs from restaurants across Dubai, including Carluccio's, Ushna and Mango Tree offer hands-on training in a variety of cuisines such as Thai, Italian, sushi and Indian, all with a focus on healthy eating. The Balance Cafe cookery courses are designed for everyone from amateurs to professionals, with prices starting at Dhs.250 per class and Dhs.800 for any four classes.

Blue Flame
Jumeirah Creekside Al Garhoud **04 230 8459**
jumeirah.com
Map **2 M8** Metro **GGICO**
Learn the secrets of preparing gourmet dishes such as brick baby chicken and seafood papillote at the Blue Flame cookery school. Classes are held every day at 7pm in a state-of-the-art cooking pod. Prices start at Dhs.300, which includes a signed copy of the menu and Blue Flame apron.

LIVING IN DUBAI
CLUBS & GROUPS

Cooking At Home
056 244 5082
Learn how to prepare traditional Italian family recipes, with two-hour weekly classes for Dhs.150 or weekend courses for Dhs.180. Private classes are also available.

Children's Classes
Kids can learn to cook at several places including Sway 2the Heart (sway2the heart.net, Dhs.80 per class) or Le Meridien Dubai's Little Pastry Chef sessions at L'atelier des Chefs (atelierdeschefsdubai.com, Dhs.150. They also teach adults).

De Dietrich Cuisine Academy
Dubai Ladies Club Jumeira 2 **050 550 1612**
de-dietrich-academy.ae
Map **2 D4** Metro **Business Bay**
Brush up on your culinary skills with courses in French, Italian, Asian, sushi and special pastries. Learn how to make the perfect seasonal menu, prepare mocktails, cook fresh and healthy cuisine, or make special meals for kids. Classes cost from Dhs.130 to Dhs.350, and special packages for birthdays, baby showers and bridal parties are also available.

International Centre For Culinary Arts Dubai
Al Jafiliya **04 398 9745**
iccadubai.ae
Map **2 J5** Metro **Al Jafiliya**
There's a wide range of cookery classes available, from industry training for professionals to cooking for fun courses for amateurs. This culinary training centre is accredited by City & Guilds London.

Jones The Grocer
Indigo Central 8 Al Manara **04 346 6886**
jonesthegrocer.com
Map **1 T6** Metro **First Gulf Bank**
Australia's gourmet deli and cafe hosts weekly cooking classes where you can master the art of pastries and breads, learn how to make pasta, or create your own soups – and then enjoy what you've cooked with selected beverages and desserts. A chocolate masterclass is also held once a month. Classes start at 6pm and cost Dhs.375, and prior booking is necessary.

L'atelier des Chefs
Le Meridien Al Garhoud **056 690 0480**
atelierdeschefsdubai.com
Map **2 N8** Metro **Airport Terminal 1**
This French cooking school offers a wide range of classes including Arabic, Indian and French cuisine, plus sushi, seafood and pastry making. Classes cost from Dhs.120 for half an hour to Dhs.350 for two hours, depending on the type of class.

Nobu
Atlantis Nakhlat Jumeira **04 426 2626**
atlantisthepalm.com
Map **1 N1** Metro **Nakheel**
Learn how to cook like the master chef Nobu Matsuhisa at Nobu's three-hour class on the first Saturday of every month. Costs Dhs.1,250 per person with lunch.

Prego's
TECOM, Al Thanyah 1 **04 435 0201**
rotana.com
Map **1 P6** Metro **Dubai Internet City**
Cooking has been in Chef Mauro's family for generations, and he makes for a charismatic and easy guide through some of his kitchen's most famous Italian dishes.

Rococo
Sofitel Jumeirah JBR, Marsa Dubai **04 448 4848**
Map **1 K5** Metro **Jumeirah Lakes Towers**
These two-and-a-half hour Italian cookery classes can be privately organised for groups of eight or more and offer great value at Dhs.250 per person, including dinner.

Spice & Aroma
Al Wasl Plaza Al Wasl **04 349 2577**
spiceandaroma.com
Map **2 E5** Metro **Burj Khalifa/Dubai Mall**
Learn the art of spice-friendly cooking at this master class in Indian and oriental cuisine. Costs Dhs.150-Dhs.200 (inclusive of meal).

Tavola
Jumeira 1 **04 344 5624**
tavolashop.com
Map **2 H4** Metro **Al Jafiliya**
Cake decoration, with an authorised Wilton method instructor. A course consists of four three-hour sessions and costs Dhs.750.

Thai at the Blue Elephant
Al Bustan Rotana Al Garhoud **04 282 0000**
blueelephant.com
Map **2 N8** Metro **Airport Terminal 1**
Al Bustan Rotana offers Thai cookery classes at the Blue Elephant on the first Saturday of the month. Cost is Dhs.199.

Thiptara
The Palace Downtown Downtown Dubai, Burj Khalifa **04 888 3444**
Map **2 F6** Metro **Burj Khalifa/Dubai Mall**
Culinary classes with Chef Mac cost Dhs.295, including the two-hour demonstration, some hands-on practice, lunch and a diploma in Thai cuisine.

LIVING IN DUBAI
CLUBS & GROUPS

Zuma
Gate Village DIFC, Zaa'beel 2 **04 425 5660**
zumarestaurant.com
Map **2 G6** Metro **Financial Centre**
As the man behind arguably the city's best sushi counter, Zuma's Masaharu Kondo is the perfect host for these two-hour sushi masterclasses which cost Dhs.500 and allow for plenty of delicious sampling.

Dance
Whether you prefer to tap your feet to classical or contemporary rhythms, all dancing tastes are catered for in Dubai. Dancing schools, health clubs, restaurants and even bars hold weekly sessions in flamenco, salsa, samba, jazz dance, ballroom and so much more.

Belly Dancing
The ancient art of belly dancing is a great way to keep fit. The Ballet Centre (04 344 9776) holds lessons for Dhs.40 on Tuesdays and Saturdays. Milla Tenorio teaches at the Rotana Towers on Sundays and Tuesdays at 6pm; classes cost from Dhs.50 (050 395 5983). Nora Dance Group also offers belly dancing classes and Exhale Fitness offers belly dance fitness classes (exhaledubai.com).

The Address Dubai Marina
Nr Dubai Marina Mall Marsa Dubai **04 436 7777**
theaddress.com
Map **1 K5** Metro **Jumeirah Lakes Towers**
Every Wednesday is Havana Night at Blends with instructor Aloy Junco, Cuban-Latino sounds and complimentary Cuban salsa classes and beverages for the ladies, from 7pm till midnight.

Arthur Murray Dance Centre
201 Reef Tower JLT, Al Thanyah 5 **04 448 6458**
arthurmurraydubai.com
Map **1 K5** Metro **Jumeirah Lakes Towers**
Teaches rhythm and Latin, smooth and standard, country western and speciality dances in line with the Arthur Murray method. There's a second branch at Souk Al Bahar (04 450 8648).

The Ballet Centre
Nr Jumeira Plaza Jumeira 1 **04 344 9776**
balletcentre.com
Map **2 H4** Metro **World Trade Centre**
Study ballet, tap, modern, salsa, Irish, jazz and belly dancing. Classes are for adults, and children three years and over. Training for the Imperial Society for Teachers of Dancing (ISTD) and the Royal Academy of Dance examinations is encouraged. There are seven dance studios situated inside two villas and also a cafe and clothing shop.

Cello Music & Ballet Centre
Oasis Centre Al Qouz 1 **04 380 8282**
cellodubai.com
Map **2 C6** Metro **Noor Bank**
Offering dance and music classes to children and adults of all ages at eight locations across Dubai: Springs, Lakes, Arabian Ranches, JBR, Umm Suqeim, Marsa Dubai, Palm Jumeirah, Al Qouz and Sheikh Zayed. There are also classes in belly dance, jazz, modern, tap dance, Irish dance, hip-hop and martial arts.

Ceroc Arabia
Trade Center 1 **050 514 4603**
Map **2 G5** Metro **Financial Centre**
This modern jive is easy to learn and similar to salsa but without the fancy footwork. It can be danced to all kinds of different music, including club and chart hits, classics, swing, Latin and rock 'n' roll. Classes, socials and private tuition are available.

Dance Horizons 1
Al Wasl **04 360 7691**
dancehorizons.ae
Map **2 D5** Metro **Business Bay**
A specialist ballet school that offers the Royal Academy of Dance Examination syllabus for beginners and advanced dancers, and a specialised music and movement programme for age three and older. Classes are at Horizon School near Safa Park and Safa School on Meydan Road in fully equipped ballet studios with sprung floors, barres and mirrors, and are led by highly qualified, RAD-registered teaching staff.

Disco Dance Dubai
Umm Suqeim 3 **050 289 6735**
Map **1 S5** Metro **Financial Centre**
Dance routines to Hannah Montana, Mamma Mia and songs from High School Musical are taught by RAD and IDTA trained director, Becky Kerrigan. Contact Becky for times and prices.

Dubai Liners
Al Satwa **050 654 5960**
Map **2 G5** Metro **Financial Centre**
It's not all country and western. Line dance to disco, rock 'n' roll, salsa, jazz, R&B and waltzes. Beginners' classes are held on Saturdays from 9.30am to 11.30am, and intermediates dance from 11am to 1pm, with another class on Wednesdays from 7pm to 8.30pm.

El Firulete BNF Dance Company Dubai
Al Sufouh 2 **04 364 4882**
elfiruletebnf.com
Map **1 N5** Metro **Dubai Internet City**
The BNF is a celebrated Columbian dance school and the Dubai branch offers private and group instruction in tango, salsa and belly dancing, among other styles.

LIVING IN DUBAI
CLUBS & GROUPS

El Malecon
Dubai Marine Beach Resort Jumeira 1 **04 346 1111**
dxbmarine.com
Map **2 H4** Metro **Emirates Towers**
Salsa dancing every Saturday night from 10pm onwards for Dhs.40. Dancing is free if you order food.

Familia De La Salsa
050 277 7475
familiadelasalsa.com
Salsa dancing lessons for beginners and enthusiastic salseros/salseras in a friendly and relaxed atmosphere at locations across Dubai. There are also children's dancing classes at the Dubai Ballet Centre every Saturday. Classes start from Dhs.40.

First International Dance Studio
One Lake Plaza Al Thanyah 5 **04 252 5080**
firstids.com
Map **1 L5** Metro **Jumeirah Lakes Towers**
Hip-hop and breakdance are the main disciplines offered at this school, but other modern and classical styles are also available. Dhs.800 per month for three group classes a week; get a taster with a free introductory lesson. Classes are for kids, teenagers and adults.

Highland Dance Dubai
Dubai Lagoon, Dubai Investments Park 1
050 765 8007
highlanddancedubai.com
Map **1 F12**
Certified instructor, Clarissa Crowley, teaches traditional Scottish dancing to male and female students of all ages and abilities. The first class is free, so you can try before you buy. Further classes cost Dhs.35-50 per hour, depending on your level. Visit the website for timings and more information.

James & Alex Dance Studios
Media City, Al Sufouh 2 **04 447 0773**
jamesandalex.com
Map **1 M5** Metro **Nakheel**
Salsa-dancing partners James and Alex offer a variety of classes for adults and children from ballet and jazz to belly dance and salsa. There's also pole fitness classes for beginners and intermediates, as well as private classes for one-on-one tuition.

Nora Dance Group
050 875 0111
noradancegroup.com
Learn hip-hop, ballet, jazz, tango and modern freestyle, as well as belly dancing and Bollywood. Classes are held at Knowledge Village, DUCTAC and Dubai Marina Mall. Available for adults and children, group lessons or private instruction.

Prima Performing Arts
Dubai Investments Park 1 **055 771 4526**
primauae.com
Map **1 F9**
Prima Performing Arts offers a fun way for children to learn to dance and get fit. There's classes for all ages, with Dinky Dances for babies aged 18 months, fun movement classes for mums and toddlers, and ballet classes for three to 18 year-olds. The dance academy also holds annual exams and performances in hip-hop, contemporary, dance/gymnastics, musical theatre, jazz and tap.

Ritmo De Havana
DUCTAC Al Barsha 1 **050 696 3520**
ritmo-de-havana.com
Map **1 R6** Metro **Mall of the Emirates**
Del Piero is a certified instructor. His courses start from Dhs.600 per person and run in batches so check the website for the most up-to-date timings.

Salsa Dubai
Umm Hurair 2 **050 565 6420**
Map **2 L7** Metro **Dubai Healthcare City**
Instructor Phil has 13 years' experience in Cuban, New York and Spanish dance styles. Classes are tailored to the individual, and members can learn the famous La Rueda Cuban dance. Find schedules on 'The Original Salsa Dubai' Facebook page.

Savage Garden
Capitol Madinat Dubai Al Melaheyah **04 346 0111**
Map **2 J4** Metro **Al Jafiliya**
On Monday, Tuesday, Thursday and Friday nights, this Latin American restaurant and nightclub serves up Latino food with a side order of salsa and merengue classes. Beginners' lessons are from 8pm to 9pm and intermediate and advanced dancers take to the floor from 9pm to 10pm. Classes cost Dhs.40 a pop. Contact George or Tatiana on 050 597 5058 for more details.

Solid Rock
Pinnacle Bldg Al Barsha 1 **04 395 7808**
solidrockdubai.com
Map **1 Q6** Metro **Sharaf DG**
A complete performing arts studio offers music and dance, with hip-hop, salsa and jazz on the menu. The first group lesson is free, so you can try before you buy. Classes are available from beginners through to advanced dancers.

Tango Dubai
DUCTAC Al Barsha 1 **050 451 6281**
tangodubai.com
Map **1 R6** Metro **Mall of the Emirates**
Tuesday classes are held for beginners and advanced dancers at Evory Bar, Kempinski Hotel and at DUCTAC,

LIVING IN DUBAI
CLUBS & GROUPS

Mall of the Emirates. Call Eleanor on the number listed, or Maya on 050 622 3679. Lessons cost Dhs.200 for four beginners' classes and Dhs.240 for advanced. Tango Dubai also runs dance nights at Sezzam and Pachanga restaurants.

Turning Pointe Music
Russia Cluster Warsan 1 **04 422 1592**
turningpointe.ae
Metro **Rashidiya**
Turning Pointe has over 35 studios throughout the UAE, offering everything from ballet for children aged three and over (with Royal Academy of Dance Syllabus and Examinations). There's also hip-hop, street jazz and Jazz2Pop, plus the popular TP Glee Club! All teachers fully qualified and recruited from the UK.

Salsa
If you fancy a bit of salsa there are a number of places you can learn seriously, or just have a bit of fun. Check out dubaisalsa.com for more information.

Drama

Drama Dubai
DUCTAC Al Barsha 1 **050 986 1761**
dramaworkshopsdubai.com
Map **1 R6** Metro **Mall of the Emirates**
This very active drama school runs classes for children and adults on the elements and techniques of acting. School workshops include circus fighting, comedy and Shakespeare. Private tuition and corporate training can be arranged.

Dubai Drama Group
DUCTAC Al Barsha 1
dubaidramagroup.com
Map **1 R6** Metro **Mall of the Emirates**
Members of this group include actors, directors, singers, dancers and backstage crew. Dubai Drama Group stages four productions a year, and there are workshops, socials and an internet forum. Annual membership is Dhs.100.

Manhattan Film Academy
Al Sufouh 2
mfacademy.com
Map **1 N5** Metro **Dubai Internet City**
The Dubai branch of this world-famous New York film school offers workshops in screenwriting, directing and acting.

Flying

Al Jazirah Aviation Club
Jazirah Airport Ras Al Khaimah **07 244 6416**
jac-uae.net
Dedicated solely to microlight/ultralight flying. The club also offers training and pleasure flights. A Microlight Pilot's Licence course, with around 25 hours flying time, costs Dhs.500 per hour.

Emirates Flying School
Dubai International Airport **04 299 5155**
emiratesaviationservices.com
Map **2 N8** Metro **Airport Terminal 1**
The only approved flight training institution in Dubai offers private and commercial licences, and will convert international licences to the UAE equivalent. A Private Pilot's Licence course costs upwards of Dhs.48,720.

Environment
In recent years, the determined clamour of environmentally conscious campaigners and groups has begun to make an impact in a country where concepts like carbon-offsetting, recycling and re-using are still nascent. In 1998, HH Sheikh Mohammed bin Rashid Al Maktoum, then Crown Prince of Dubai, established an environmental award which recognises an individual or organisation for work carried out on behalf of the environment. At an everyday level, there are increasing numbers of glass, plastic and paper recycling points around the city, mainly around shopping centres. However, overall, little seems to be done to persuade the average citizen to be more environmentally active, for instance by encouraging the reduction of littering. If you want to take action, there are a couple of groups, including Emirates Environmental Group, who always need volunteers and funds.

LIVING IN DUBAI
CLUBS & GROUPS

Dubai Natural History Group
Umm Suqeim 3 **04 282 3952**
dnhg.org
Map **1 S5** Metro **First Gulf Bank**
Learn more about the UAE's fascinating natural history at monthly meetings where experts lecture about flora, fauna, geology, and archaeology. Members go on regular field trips and can borrow from a library of natural history publications. Annual membership is Dhs.100 for a family and Dhs.50 for individuals. Contact chairman Gary Feulner (04 306 5570; grfeulner@gmail.com).

Emirates Environmental Group
Villa JMR 68-117A Jumeira 1 **04 344 8622**
eeg-uae.org
Map **2 G4** Metro **Emirates Towers**
A voluntary organisation devoted to helping protect the environment through education, action programmes and community involvement. Activities include evening lectures and special events such as recycling collections and clean-up campaigns. Annual membership costs Dhs.300 for adults and Dhs.100 for college students.

Music
There are a number of specialist music schools in Dubai where you and your kids can have lessons. In addition, you may find that some schools offer extra-curricular music programmes (for a fee) for students.

Centre For Musical Arts
Al Qouz Ind. 3 **04 341 8872**
cmadubai.com
Map **1 S6** Metro **Mall of the Emirates**
Budding musicians can get instruction in string, woodwind and brass instruments, as well as piano. Group lessons start at Dhs.975 and individual lessons from Dhs.1,625 per term. Visit the website for details of their popular Saturday Sessions.

Dubai Music School
Stalco Bldg, Zabeel Rd Al Karama **04 396 4834**
dubaimusicschool.com
Map **2 L6** Metro **Al Karama**
This school offers one-hour lessons in guitar, piano, organ, violin, brass, drums, singing and composing, leading to Trinity College of Music examinations.

Juli Music Center
Nr Mazaya Shopping Centre Al Wasl **04 321 2588**
imi-jmc.net
Map **2 F6** Metro **Burj Khalifa/Dubai Mall**
Juli Music Center offers lessons in various instruments from Dhs.180 per hour. They also sell a variety of musical instruments including new and used pianos, brass, woodwind, strings, and percussion.

Jumeirah Music Centre
Jumeirah Plaza Jumeira 1 **04 349 2662**
jumeirah-music.com
Map **2 H4** Metro **Emirates Towers**
Lessons in piano, guitar, flute, violin, drums and voice for all ages at Dhs.90 per half hour. All children are welcome to audition for the choir, which puts on a concert every year.

Little Musicians
055 364 9421
littlemusiciansdubai.com
Holds classes all over Dubai (Arabian Ranches, Jumeirah Ballet Centre, Dubai Marina Yacht Club, Dubai Marina Mall and Indigo Icon Office Tower JLT) with all manner of fun and brightly coloured instruments. The emphasis is very much on making music enjoyable and achievable.

The Music Chamber
Time Square Center Al Qouz Ind. 1 **04 346 8056**
musicchamber.net
Map **1 T6** Metro **Noor Bank**
The Music Chamber gives lessons in all instruments, from electric and classical guitar to cello, piano and percussion. The school is recognised by the Associated Board of Royal Schools of Music in London. It boasts a large variety of instruments, accessories and books. It also offers vocal training and theory lessons.

The Music Institute
The Walk at JBR Marsa Dubai **04 424 3818**
tmi.ae
Map **1 K4** Metro **Jumeirah Lakes Towers**
Piano, violin, guitar and drum lessons with musical theory for all ages, plus group guitar and violin lessons. Practice rooms available to hire. Recitals are also held.

Popular Music Institute
Umm Hurair 2 **04 324 2626**
thomsunpuremusic.com
Map **2 L7** Metro **Dubai Healthcare City**
Thomsun Pure Music is in Wafi and runs the Popular Music Institute and the Sing & Swing Training Centre. Students learn instruments, musicianship, theory and performance, and prepare for music exams.

Solid Rock
Pinnacle Bldg Al Barsha 1 **04 395 7808**
solidrockdubai.com
Map **1 Q6** Metro **Sharaf DG**
Teaches modern music and dance at its Al Barsha studios. There is a particular focus on piano, guitar and drums – the staples of rock music. Private and group classes are available, and the school offers the first group session for free, so you can check it out before you sign up.

LIVING IN DUBAI
CLUBS & GROUPS

Orchestras & Bands

Centre For Musical Arts
Al Qouz Ind. 3 **04 341 8772**
cmadubai.com
Map **1 S6** Metro **First Gulf Bank**
The centre is home to a number of adult and children's musical groups, including ensembles for string, flute, saxophone and guitar players. It also offers instrumental and choral tuition and has an instrument hire and repair service.

Dubai Chamber Orchestra
04 349 0423
The chamber orchestra practises every Wednesday evening and gives three public performances a year. It was founded by an international group of musicians now residing in the UAE. There are currently more than 40 members hailing from more than 15 countries and more are always welcome. Its varied programme includes chamber and modern orchestral pieces.

Dubai Classical Guitar Orchestra
DUCTAC Al Barsha 1 **04 341 4666**
dcgo.ae
Map **1 R6** Metro **Mall of the Emirates**
This classical guitar ensemble rehearses at DUCTAC every Tuesday from 6pm to 8pm. People of all ages and levels of skill are welcome to join or learn. Regular performances are also staged.

Dubai Drums
Building 8 Media City, Al Sufouh 2 **04 347 4790**
dubaidrums.com
Map **1 M5** Metro **Nakheel**
Dubai Drums runs African Djembe drumming circles every Monday. A leader guides the group from simple rhythms right through to more complex performances. Classes cost Dhs.50 with drums provided. On Saturdays, Kidz Drum Club is held at DUCTAC, from 10.15am to 11.15am. Cost Dhs.50. Dubai Drums organises other events throughout the year, such as Full Moon and Desert Drumming.

Gardening

Dubai Gardening Group
Villa 97, Street 16D Jumeira 1 **04 344 5999**
Map **2 G4** Metro **Emirates Towers**
This group shares its communal gardening know-how in a friendly and informal atmosphere, with seminars and practical demonstrations from experts, trips to garden nurseries and members' gardens also arranged. If you want advice on how to improve your gardening skills, or just want to mingle with other green-fingered Dubaians and chat plants, then this group is for you.

Photography & Film
Photography and film are increasingly popular in the region. Although three film festivals, DIFF, ADFF and Gulf Film Festival shine an encouraging spotlight on the region's film-making, there is still a dearth of serious funding. For amateur film fans, there are groups that bring the filmmaking community together for screenings, workshops and presentations.

Photography
For photographers, Emirates Photography Club (meetup.com/emiratesphotoclub) is a web-based community where local photography enthusiasts can exchange tips and ideas. The group meets twice a month on alternating Tuesdays.

Gulf Photo Plus
Alserkal Avenue Al Qouz Ind. 1 **04 380 8545**
gulfphotoplus.com
Map **1 U6** Metro **Noor Bank**
Digital photography classes for beginner to intermediate photographers, and workshops and events with master photographers. Introductory classes to Photoshop are also available. Check out their store selling lenses, lights and literature.

the jamjar
Nr Dubai Garden Centre Al Qouz Ind. 3 **04 341 7303**
thejamjardubai.com
Map **1 S6** Metro **First Gulf Bank**
The award-winning filmmaker, Mahmood Kabour, holds a film series called Mahmovies! at the jamjar (an art studio space). He screens art house offerings for the general public in an informal atmosphere; totally free of charge and encourages discussion amongst viewers. Mahmood is the director of the documentary Champ of the Camp – a film about life in the UAE's labour camps. Further details are available on the Mahmovies! group Facebook page (facebook.com/mahmovies).

Lightform
lightform.ae
An International Filipino Photographer's Guild photographic society, it organises regular workshops, field trips and events for members. Members must complete a basic class to join.

The Picturehouse
Dubai Mall Downtown Dubai, Burj Khalifa
reelcinemas.ae
Map **2 F7** Metro **Burj Khalifa/Dubai Mall**
The Picturehouse at Reel Cinemas in Dubai Mall screens arthouse films and documentaries that don't make it onto the main screens.

LIVING IN DUBAI
CLUBS & GROUPS

SAE Institute Dubai
Knowledge Village, Al Sufouh 2 **04 361 6173**
sae.edu
Map **1 N5** Metro **Dubai Internet City**
The world's largest private college for film and audio production, animation and multimedia offers a degree in filmmaking, as well as photography bootcamps.

The Scene Club
Building 2 Media City, Al Sufouh 2 **04 391 0051**
thesceneclub.com
Map **1 M5** Metro **Nakheel**
Dubai's first film club for true movie buffs offers workshops as well as screenings of films and documentaries that may not make box office history but are felt to be culturally significant. Screenings generally take place once a month.

Shelter Dubai
Alserkal Ave Al Qouz Ind. 4 **04 380 9040**
shelter.ae
Map **1 S7** Metro First Gulf Bank
Shelter (shelter.ae) has a small screening room and holds regular film nights which are open to non-members. Visit their website for schedules.

Scrabble

Dubai Scrabble League
050 653 7992
Meets once a month for friendly games between players of all levels. Regular competitions are held, and players also attend competitions overseas. The UAE Open is the qualifier for the Gulf Open in Bahrain. For more information, contact Selwyn Lobo.

Singing

Dubai Chamber Choir
dubaichamberchoir.com
Established in 2003, the choir provides choral education and training, and performs concerts throughout the year. The seasonal Christmas series is a highlight. Contact the choir if you're interested in joining up. There are a limited number of members, therefore, auditions are held for all new members, and re-auditions for the full choir take place on a biennial basis.

Dubai Harmony
Al Safa 1 **056 690 7052**
dubai-harmony.com
Map **2 C5** Metro **Noor Bank**
A barbershop quartet-style group with an all-female ensemble. New members are always welcome and previous musical training is not required – just the desire to sing with enthusiasm.

Dubai Singers
Kindermusik, 15B Street Umm Suqeim 3 **04 344 8883**
dubaisingers.info
Map **1 S5** Metro **First Gulf Bank**
This is a group of amateur singers who meet regularly to create music in a variety of styles. Repertoire includes requiems, choral works, Christmas carols, musicals and variety shows. Membership is open to everyone; sheet music is provided.

Snooker

Dubai Snooker Club
Nr Karama Post Office Al Karama **04 337 5338**
dubaisnooker.com
Map **2 L6** Metro **Oud Metha**
The club's facilities include 12 tournament-class snooker tables, 13 pool tables, two private snooker rooms and a private pool room. Table charges are Dhs.30 per hour, and food is available. You don't have to be a member to play.

Take A Shot
Knight Shot (04 343 5678), near the Mazaya Centre, sells all manner of pool and billiards equipment and, as one of the main sponsors of the games in the region, it's a good place to chat to staff and find out about local tournaments.

Yoga
A low-impact (but deceptively challenging) form of holistic exercise, yoga involves holding sequences of poses or 'asanas' that, combined with breathing exercises, gently but powerfully help your body become stronger and more flexible. Many health and fitness clubs offer yoga as part of their weekly schedule, as do some alternative therapy centres.

Bharat Thakur's Artistic Yoga
800 9642
artisticyoga.com
The latest twist in this flexible form of inner and outer exercise combines ancient yogic techniques with modern cardio training. Morning and evening classes, from Dhs.65, are held at Angsana Spa, Body & Soul Spa Al Ghusais and Al Hana Centre.

Club Stretch
Nr Mercure Hotel, Al Mina Rd Al Hudaiba **04 345 2131**
clubstretch.ae
Map **2 J4** Metro **Al Jafiliya**
A popular studio offering Bikram yoga, which is practised in a hot room to aid muscle warming and stretching. Pilates is also offered. An unlimited 10 day introduction pass costs Dhs.120.

LIVING IN DUBAI
CLUBS & GROUPS

Advanced yoga

Exhale
Marsa Dubai **04 424 3777**
exhaledubai.com
Map **1 K4** Metro **Dubai Marina**
This ladies-only fitness offering vinyasa, ashtanga and power yoga, as well as yoga for pregnant women. The cost per session is Dhs.75, with packages of 10 costing Dhs.650 and valid for two months.

Fitness First
DIFC DIFC, Zaa'beel 2 **04 363 7444**
fitnessfirstme.com
Map **2 G6** Metro **Financial Centre**
Great for yoga newbies, hatha classes are held most days of the week, with power yoga also available. Prices start at Dhs.100 for non members. Other studios at The Meadows and Lakes.

Gems Of Yoga
White Crown Bldg, Shk Zayed Rd Trade Center 1
04 331 5161
gemsofyogadubai.com
Map **2 H5** Metro **Emirates Towers**
Hatha, ashtanga and power yoga as well as classes for ladies, children and the elderly. Dhs.650 for 10 classes.

Rawr Yoga
Concord Tower Media City, Al Sufouh 2 **04 423 2808**
rawryoga.com
Map **1 N5** Metro **Nakheel**
A stylish, state-of-the-art Bikram yoga studio in the heart of Media City. Offers 90 minute Bikram yoga classes, as well as hour-long express classes and a few other types of yoga. Open to all ages and levels of fitness, with a range of membership packages from its Dhs.125 introductory offer to Dhs.700 for unlimited monthly membership.

Yoga Room
Swiss Tower JLT, Al Thanyah 5 **050 518 9966**
yogaroom.ae
Map **1 L6** Metro **Dubai Marina**
Ashtanga and vinyasa yoga for all levels and workshops hosted by visiting yoga experts. Packages start from Dhs.80 for a single class.

Yogalates Bliss
Fraser Suites Al Sufouh 2 **050 328 9642**
yogalatesblissindubai.com
Map **1 P5** Metro **Dubai Internet City**
Yogalates is a fusion of yoga and pilates to relieve muscular tension, improve core and pelvic floor strength and inspire balance. Classes are on an outdoor terrace. There's also Funky Fireflies kids yoga, as well as yoga teacher training workshops.

Zen Yoga
BBC Bldg Dubai Media City, Al Sufouh 2 **04 367 0435**
yoga.ae
Map **1 P5** Metro **Dubai Internet City**
Zen Yoga is a yoga and pilates specialist. Its three modern centres have mirrored walls to help you check your posture. A one-month unlimited yoga trial costs Dhs.750 and regular classes are Dhs.80. The studios are in Emirates Hills (04 422 4643), Dubai Media City (04 367 0435), and Town Centre Jumeirah (04 349 2933).

Take the knowledge with you

Relocating is a big opportunity, we'll help make sure you're ready for it.

Tel: +971 4 230 5300
dubai@crownrelo.com

Go knowing
www.crownrelo.com/uae

CROWN RELOCATIONS

WORKING IN DUBAI

Employment **207**
Free Zones **212**
Business **214**
Starting A Business **216**
Voluntary & Charity Work **218**

WORKING IN DUBAI

Dubai is a land of opportunity for skilled professionals with plenty of rewards on offer.

The Gate building with Emirates Towers in the background

Expat workers come to Dubai for a number of reasons: to advance their career, enjoy a higher standard of living, or to take advantage of new opportunities. Whatever the reason, there are various advantages to making the move.

While the biggest bonus of working in Dubai may seem to be tax-free salaries, the cost of living (or your newly acquired lifestyle) can somewhat balance out this benefit. All-inclusive packages with accommodation and education allowances are not as common as they once were, although basic benefits still apply (such as annual flights home, health insurance and around 22 calendar days of annual leave). That said, Dubai is still very much is a a land of opportunities for skilled professionals. It is comparatively easier to change industries, as skill sets are less 'pigeon-holed' than in other countries, and jobs in certain industries (such as construction and property) are more readily available.

Expats can work in either the public (government) or private sectors; many companies in the private sector operate within Free Trade Zones (FTZs), where foreigners can work, trade or establish their business under more relaxed laws.

To work anywhere in Dubai you need to be aged 18 to 65 years, be sponsored by an employer, and have a residence visa. The visa permits you to live and work anywhere in the UAE; it is valid for two years (or three years for those working in some free zones or in government jobs). All companies are governed by UAE Labour Law, although there is a noticeable difference in salaries, benefits, holidays, annual leave, and end of service payments between the public (government) and private sectors.

WORKING IN DUBAI
EMPLOYMENT

EMPLOYMENT

Getting Started

If you're looking to live and work in Dubai you have three options. You can search for jobs while in your home country; you'll often be interviewed by phone or Skype, rather than here in the UAE. Once you have a job offer, your employer will start to process your residence visa. Depending on your contract, your employer may pay for your flight to Dubai (and often tickets for any family members), one month's temporary accommodation, shipping costs, vehicle hire, and the services of a relocation company to help you find a new home. Alternatively, you can arrive in Dubai on a visit visa, which means that you have 30 days (or up to 60 days if you renew it) to legally look for work and live in the country. Or, you may already be living and working in the UAE and looking to transfer jobs. In this instance, you will need to cancel your existing residence visa; your new employer will then sponsor you on a new residence visa.

Job Hunting

Start by registering with a recruitment agency in Dubai. The agency will then set up an interview where you are usually required to fill out a form summarising your CV; you will also need a few passport photos. The agency takes its fee from the registered company once the position has been filled. It is illegal for a recruitment company to levy fees on candidates for this service, although be warned that some might try.

Boutique Recruitment Services

If your field is office support, but you are looking for an executive position, then Miller Hay (millerhay.com) could be the best recruitment company for you to contact. They specialise in finding high-calibre secretarial and office support staff.

Employers also use local newspapers and headhunters (also known as executive search companies) to advertise job opportunities, as well as their own websites. It is easier to look for a job once you are in Dubai. Get your hands on the Gulf News appointments supplement (gnads4u.com), published every day except Fridays and Saturdays, or the Khaleej Times Appointments (khaleejtimes.com) every day except Friday. The National has a careers section that is available to those who subscribe online.

Also, check listings on online versions of international newspapers as companies within the UAE often post jobs on these sites. Websites for The Guardian (guardian.co.uk) and The Times (timesonline.co.uk) newspapers in the UK and The Washington Post (washingtonpost.com) in the US are often a good resource. You can also upload your CV to sites like monstergulf.com, naukrigulf.com, bayt.com and gulftalent.com. Job advertisements are posted on dubizzle.com and expatwoman.com. Also try contacting companies directly and start networking, using sites such as linkedin.com.

What To Expect

According to the Bayt.com Job Index Survey (August 2013), the time is ripe for many jobseekers. There is a demand for qualified professionals in the UAE, as engineering (27%), business management (24%) and commerce (23%) top the list of most desirable qualifications among UAE employers. The most attractive industries in the UAE for jobs are perceived to be banking and finance (34%), construction (33%) and oil, gas and petrochemicals (33%). Recruitment agency Charterhouse lists the following average monthly salaries for key sectors:

HR Manager: Dhs.25,000
Head Of Corporate Bank: Dhs.60,000
Senior Civil/Structural Engineer: Dhs.35,000
Financial Accountant: Dhs.20,000
Chief Financial Officer: Dhs.60,000
Finance Director: Dhs.50,000
Senior Project Engineer: Dhs.55,000
Senior Architect: Dhs.30,000
Legal Secretary: Dhs.20,000
General Manager (Construction): Dhs.75,000
Designer: Dhs.18,000
Key Account Manager: Dhs.20,000
Head of IT: Dhs.20,000-30,000
Communications Manager: Dhs.22,000-35,000
Marketing Manager: Dhs.25,000
Partner (Law Firm): Dhs.60,000-70,000 plus

Recruitment Agencies

BAC Middle East Liberty House, Zaa'beel 2, 04 439 8500, *bacme.com*
Bayt.com Grosvenor Business Tower, Al Thanyah 1, 04 449 3100, *bayt.com*
Charterhouse Middle East Maze Tower, Shk Zayed Rd, Trade Center 1, 04 372 3500, *charterhouseme.ae*
Hays Middle East Dubai Knowledge Village, Al Sufouh 2, 04 361 2882, *hays.ae*
Manpower Middle East Dubai Internet City Bldg 1, Al Sufouh 2, 04 391 0460, *manpower-me.com*
Parsons Brinckerhoff The H Dubai Office Tower, Trade Center 1, 04 376 7222, *pbworld.com*

WORKING IN DUBAI
EMPLOYMENT

Permit To Work

Once you receive a job offer, your employer, and sponsor, will start to process your residence visa with the General Directorate of Residency and Foreigners Affairs (GDRFA). All the paperwork should be taken care of by your PRO (see Getting Started); you will need to take a medical test and hand over your passport and attested education certificates. Your labour card or free zone ID – your permit to work – will be processed at the same time. Your PRO should also help with your application for your Resident ID.

Labour Card

Employees working outside a free zone will receive a labour card, processed by the Ministry of Labour. If you work in a free zone, however, you will receive a free zone ID, which is processed by the free zone authority and can be ready in as little as 24 hours. Both cards feature your photo and details of your employer. The labour card costs Dhs.1,000 (paid for by your company) and is valid for as long as your residence visa is. A free zone ID is valid for either one, two or three years.

You will need to sign your labour contract before the labour card/free zone ID is issued. This contract is printed in both Arabic and English. The plan is for labour cards to be phased out in favour of the Resident ID, but, for now, the labour card is still required. The Ministry of Labour has also voiced plans to replace the labour card with an electronic work permit; this could be issued within 48 hours, compared to the current waiting time of up to 14 days.

Family Sponsored

If you are sponsored by your husband or wife on a family visa, you can still legally work. Your employer will simply need to apply for your labour card; you will need an NOC from your sponsor as well as your passport with residence visa, your sponsor's passport and your attested education certificates.

Temporary Work Permits

Non-GCC nationals who are above 18 years of age can now enter the UAE on a short-term work permit which is valid for 60 days; these can be extended/renewed up to six times (subject to a fee and bank guarantee).

Employment Contracts

Once you have accepted a job offer you will be asked to sign an employment contract; this should list the starting date, type of employment, location, terms and conditions, duration and the salary. This is a legally binding agreement that should be written in both Arabic and English. You can check or print your labour contract and card online at mol.gov.ae. There is often confusion over the offer letter and the contract. An offer letter should give details of the terms of the job you are being offered, such as salary, leave, hours and other benefits; if you accept the terms of this offer, it becomes a legally binding contract.

An employment contract can be terminated if both parties agree, provided that the employee's written consent is given; the employer will then need to cancel your residence visa. See Changing Jobs.

Probation

Probation periods can be set for a maximum of six months. Some companies delay the residency process until the probation period is up, which can make settling in difficult – no residency means you can't sponsor family members, buy a car or get a bank loan.

By law, employees are not entitled to paid sick leave during probation and most firms do not grant paid annual leave to be taken during this time – you will continue to accrue annual leave though that you can take over the course of the year.

Leave

While on sick leave, the first 15 days are with full pay, the next 30 days are with half pay, and any subsequent days are unpaid. Annual holiday starts at one calendar month per year, roughly 22 working days.

Working Hours

Working hours differ dramatically between companies; straight shifts vary from 7am to 2.30pm for government organisations to the common 9am to 6pm for private companies. Most retail outlets tend to be open from 10am to 10pm but often operate shifts. Teachers start early at around 7.30am and classes finish around 2.30pm, although their hours aren't as predetermined as other roles. Although less common nowadays, some offices and shops operate split shifts, which allow for a longer break in the afternoon (hours are usually 8am to 1pm and 4pm to 7pm).

The maximum number of hours permitted per week according to UAE Labour Law is 48, although some industries, such as hospitality and retail, have longer stipulated hours. Annual holiday allowance starts at one calendar month per year, or roughly 22 working days. Some employees, especially those in management, have more than this and long service usually adds to holiday allowance.

Friday is the Islamic holy day and therefore a universal day off for offices and schools. Consumer demand means that the hospitality and retail industries are open seven days a week. Saturday is the second day of the weekend; some companies work five and a half days a week and some operate a six-day week, taking only Friday as a rest day. Public holidays are set by the government, while the timing of religious holidays depends on the sighting of

We design and build – feasible, functional and dynamic workplace. From a simple home office to corporate headquarters.

Great offices, *delivered.*

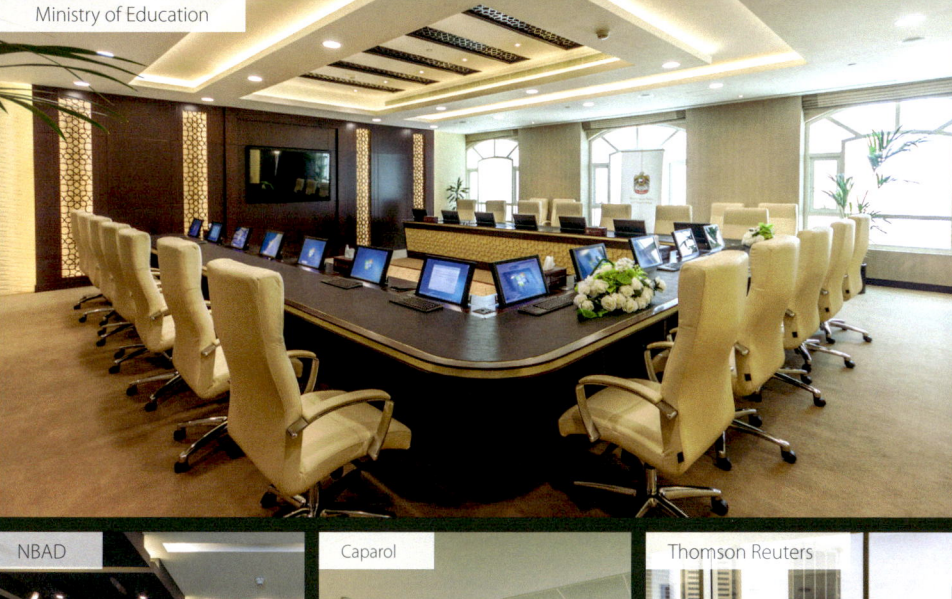

Ministry of Education

NBAD

Caparol

Thomson Reuters

300 BAFCO ▪ bafco.com

بافكو
BAFCO

WORKING IN DUBAI
EMPLOYMENT

the moon. This can mean that it is difficult to plan holidays, as confirmation of public holidays can come just days before the event. All employees (even non-Muslims) are entitled to a shorter working day during Ramadan, although lawyers would advise you not to insist on this if you are not fasting.

Health Insurance
A new health insurance law (Insurance System for Advancing Healthcare in Dubai – ISAHD) will be rolled out from 2014-16 in Dubai, which makes it compulsory for employers to provide all workers, and their spouses and dependants, with basic health insurance; this covers all businesses in the emirate including those in free zones. Under the law, employers must pay for private health cover with any insurance company holding a health insurance permit from the DHA. This replaces the previous system whereby employers could choose to enrol their staff into a private healthcare scheme. This mandatory health cover also applies to domestic workers such as maids and nannies.

Gratuity Payments
An employee on a fixed-term contract, who has completed one or more years of continuous service, will be entitled to 21 days pay for each of the first five years of service, and 30 days pay for each additional year as an end-of-service gratuity payment; this compensates for the lack of a pension system. This is based on your basic salary (not including basic housing, transport and utilities). The total end-of-service gratuity should not exceed the salary of two years. Leaving before the end of your fixed-term contract or being fired for breaking UAE Labour Law could result in the loss of your gratuity payment.

Maternity Leave
Under UAE Labour Law, women are entitled to 45 days maternity leave, on full pay, once they've completed one year of continuous service. Fathers are not entitled to paternity leave. If you've been with your employer for less than a year you can claim 45 days on half pay.

UAE Labour Law

The UAE Labour Law outlines information on employee entitlements, employment contracts and disciplinary rules. The law is employer friendly, but it also clearly outlines employee rights. You can download a copy of the document from the Ministry of Labour website (mol.gov.ae); the document has not been fully updated for some time but amendments and additions are often posted on the site.

If you find yourself in the situation where you have not been paid (including women on maternity leave), you can file a case with the UAE Labour Department which will take the necessary action. You could also get a lawyer to deal with the claim on your behalf. Although lawyers are expensive in Dubai, the employer will have to bear the cost if the case is settled in your favour.

Changing Jobs
If you decide to leave a company before the end of your contract you will require permission from your existing employer in the form of an NOC. Your employer will also need to cancel your residence visa. You will then be able to switch to a new job and your new employer will process a new residence visa and labour card.

Officially, anyone working in the private sector who breaks their contract could face a six month ban from working for any other company in the UAE (if you are working in a free zone, this ban may be restricted to jobs within that free zone only). However, banning rules are increasingly relaxed and job transfers have become much more flexible. Stay on good terms with your employer, and you shouldn't face a problem. If you complete your contract period, either two or three years, you can legally move jobs without an NOC.

Always check if there is a non-compete clause in your contract, particularly if your new role is with a direct competitor to your current employer.

There are some exceptions where you can transfer your sponsorship without the approval of your current sponsor; such as death of your sponsor, change of company ownership, company closure and cancellation of your company's trade licence.

Transferring A Visa
If you are planning to transfer your visa, your new employer will first need to gain permission from your previous employer, after getting approval from the Ministry of Labour. Free zone visas can usually be transferred from one employer to the next. However, the previous employer needs to agree to the transfer and may need to provide a no objection certificate (NOC). Keep in mind that this NOC may also need to be translated into Arabic, on headed notepaper, and signed by the local sponsor.

Non-free zone visas need to be cancelled before you can apply for a new one. You should also sign a document instructive of a six-month work ban. This ban can be lifted with an NOC from a previous employer. When a non-free zone visa is cancelled, the new employer may have to pay a fine for the duration of the remainder of the visa, if the employee has not completed a specified period of work.

Absconding
Anyone leaving the country or their job permanently without informing their employer and cancelling the residence visa with their sponsor will be classed as 'absconding' and may receive a ban; employers have

MILLER HAY

www.millerhay.com

Gateway to opportunity

Miller Hay specialises in recruitment solutions for high calibre secretarial and office support staff

With a passion for uncompromising quality, Miller Hay has a market-leading reputation for providing an honest, transparent and personal service where the long term needs of clients and candidates take priority over all else.

- Executive Assistants
- Personal Assistants
- Team Assistants
- Office Administrators
- Legal Secretaries and Paralegals
- Office Managers
- Receptionists

Al Fattan Currency House, Tower 1, Office 114, DIFC, PO Box 506761, Dubai
T: +971 4 388 7367 | F: +971 4 388 7463 | www.millerhay.com

WORKING IN DUBAI
FREE ZONES

to wait six months to report absconders who have left the country. If you remain in the country, that period is reduced to seven days.

Absconders are reported to the Ministry of Labour, who then pass information on to the GDRFA and the Dubai police. If a ban is on your computer file, any applications from a new employer for a residence visa and labour card will be refused. Also, if you leave the country or are unaccountable for seven days in a row or 20 days in total, your company can terminate your employment contract without awarding you gratuity pay or any outstanding benefits.

Company Closure
If the company you work for closes, you are still entitled to outstanding holiday pay and gratuity. The Ministry of Labour would need to be involved though. You are allowed to transfer sponsorship to a new employer; but if you can't find a new job your visa will be cancelled and you will have to leave the country. To transfer the visa you'll need an attested certificate of closure, issued by the court and submitted to the Ministry of Labour. If your company were to close without cancelling their trade licence, you could receive a short-term ban from taking a new role with a new employer. Consult the appropriate government offices to get your paperwork right, or consider investing in the services of a specialist labour lawyer.

Redundancy
If you are made redundant, the first thing to discuss with your employer is whether they are prepared to be flexible with your visa status. If you have a good relationship with your company, you should have room to negotiate the terms under which you are leaving, and it's a good idea to request a few months leeway so that you have the opportunity to find a new employer and sponsor. If this is not possible and your company wishes to cancel your visa immediately, you have a standard 30 day grace period within which to leave the country before incurring any fines for overstaying your visa. Similarly, if you are in company accommodation, try to negotiate the date on which you need to move out. If your company has paid for your villa or apartment up front, they may let you stay for a fixed period.

It is always a good idea to plan for every eventuality by putting money aside to act as a buffer should you lose your job; rather than incur large debts, this money can help pay for key bills like rent and car loans.

FREE ZONES

Dubai is home to more than 20 free zones, which service a wide range of industries, including healthcare, education, commodities and technology companies. Unique laws regarding taxation, recruitment of labour, and income apply to these areas. Various benefits make free zones an ideal

Dubai Media City

WORKING IN DUBAI
FREE ZONES

option for companies wishing to establish a distribution, manufacturing and service base for trade outside of the UAE.

Free zones in the UAE work on a 'one-stop shop' principle – so, as an employer or company owner, you'll only have one authority to deal with. This should simplify the process of running your business considerably. If you want to work as a consultant or you wish to set up a small business, free zones are your best bet. The process and fees for getting a visa varies between each free zone. Note that the cost of commercial property can be quite high in popular free zones, such as Dubai Media City and the Jebel Ali Free Zone.

Employees of companies in free zones have different sponsorship options to choose from, depending on which free zone they inhabit. For example, in the Jebel Ali Free Zone you can either be sponsored by an individual company or by the free zone authority itself.

Whether you are in the Jebel Ali Free Zone, Dubai Internet City, Dubai Media City, Knowledge Village, Healthcare City or any other free zone, the respective authority will process your residence visa directly through the General Directorate of Residency and Foreigners Affairs (GDRFA), without having to get employment approval from the Ministry of Labour. This speeds up the process significantly, and residence visas can sometimes be granted in a matter of hours.

Once the GDRFA has stamped your residence visa in your passport, the free zone will issue your free zone ID – this also acts as your security pass for entry to the free zone. A big advantage of working in a free zone is the lack of red tape encountered if you move jobs to another free zone company. This is because the free zone itself is actually your sponsor, so when you switch jobs to another employer you won't be switching sponsors.

The validity of a free zone residence visa permit will depend on how long the labour card is valid for (either one, two or three years, depending on the zone).

Designed to encourage investment from overseas, free zones allow 100% foreign ownership and offer exemption from taxes and customs duties. There are plenty to choose from across the emirate: the most well-known being Dubai Media City and Jebel Ali Free Zone.

Choosing A Free Zone

If the idea of working for yourself in a free zone appeals to you, then begin by checking out the Dubai free zones' individual websites or see freezonesuae.com, which provides a fact sheet on each zone. This will give you a good idea of which zone is best suited to your business plan, as well as the conditions to fulfil to obtain a licence. Licences for businesses vary from Dhs.5,500 in the Jebel Ali Free Zone to Dhs.20,000 in JLT.

Freelance Work

Freelancers can apply for a work permit and residence visa from a select number of free zones in Dubai, including International Media Production Zone, Dubai Technology and Media Free Zone, Dubai Media City and Knowledge Village. Your profession needs to be related to these free zones' activities, which are predominantly media-related: artists, editors, directors, writers, engineers, producers, photographers, camera operators and technicians in the fields of film, TV, music, radio and print media.

Freelancers are granted a freelance permit, which identifies you as a sole practitioner and enables you to conduct your business in your birth name as opposed to a brand name. You will also be given a UAE residence visa, and have access to a 'hot desk' and business facilities (including a PO Box address) within the free zone that sponsored you. Both the permit and visa are valid for one year. This costs between Dhs.20,000-30,000. The process varies between free zones, and check individual websites for specific requirements and to download forms.

An alternative option, depending on your line of work, may be to set up or register your own Dubai-based company. This has become a little easier to do than it used to be (check out Explorer's *Dubai How-To* guide for step-by-step information on setting up a company). Or, contact the Department of Economic Development (dubaided.gov.ae) to get started. See also Part-time work in this chapter for other options.

Virtuzone

Virtuzone is officially part of Fujairah Creative City free zone, and was set up with the express aim of helping those who want to either set up a small company or relocate it to the UAE while keeping costs as low as possible. Start-up costs begin at around Dhs.10,000 and Virtuzone looks after the whole process; significantly, there's no need for a UAE sponsor, companies can be 100% foreign owned and there are no corporate or income taxes. Also, there's no requirement to take commercial premises – something that really drives up the price of setting up in other free zones.

If you're looking to move your small business from your home country or are thinking about taking a skill and going solo, it's probably the easiest and cheapest way to set up. Visit vz.ae or the physical office on The Walk at JBR.

Dubai Media City

Media professionals in the following categories are eligible to apply for a freelance permit and visa in Dubai Media City: artists, editors, directors, writers, engineers, producers, photographers, camera operators and technicians in the fields of film, TV,

WORKING IN DUBAI
BUSINESS

music, radio or print media. They will be subject to the conditions listed below:
- The freelance permit includes a residence visa, access to 10 shared work stations, and a shared PO Box address and fax line
- A minimum of three hours per week and no more than three hours per day must be spent at the hot desk
- A business plan, CV, bank reference letter and portfolio must be submitted along with your application

Costs at DMC include:
- Dhs.5,000 security deposit (refundable)
- Dhs.5,000 joining fee (one-off payment)
- Dhs.8,000 annual freelance permit fee
- Dhs.4,000 annual membership fee

Working On The Move
MAKE Business Hub (makebusinesshub.com) near JBR at The Walk offers freelancers a workspace and a cafe rolled into one; there are work stations, work pods for private meetings and a tasty menu serving breakfast through to dinner.

Part-time Work
In the past, it has been extremely difficult to organise part-time work. What little there is has been offered 'off the books' to those already in Dubai under their partner's sponsorship. But new legislation now allows residents to take on work part-time in Dubai, which is good news for everyone from mothers returning to work to teenagers wanting to earn some spending money in their spare time.

Since January 2011, teenagers from 15 to 18 years of age can find jobs in the UAE upon obtaining a teenage work permit from the Ministry of Labour. Part-time work permits can be also be issued for any of the following: workers below the age of 65 with valid residence visas who are registered with the Ministry of Labour; government workers; or women living with their parents, husbands, sons or daughters with valid residence visas.

However, part-time work is still a relatively new concept in Dubai and it may be a while until there's the wide variety of casual work available that you'll find in most other countries, but there are an increasing number of opportunities. For more information, contact the General Directorate of Residency and Foreigners (dnrd.ae).

It is up to the employer to pay for the part-time work permit (which costs Dhs.500) rather than the employee. It's also essential that both sign a contract which explicitly states the wage before the permit can be issued. To request a part-time work permit, visit the Ministry of Labour website (mol.gov.ae). You will need to provide a number of documents including copies of the company's trade licence, a photo of the employee as well as a copy of his passport and his education certificates attested by the Ministry of Foreign Affairs.

BUSINESS

Business Culture
Like anywhere in the world, doing business in the UAE has its own unique idiosyncrasies. Even if you work for a western company, the chances are that some of your business transactions will be with Emiratis, whether on a customer or client basis.

One of the key aspects to realise is that family ties, friendship, honour and trust are crucial. So much so that those who have built good relationships can often see rules bent; the system of favours being given and not forgotten is an integral, if unspoken, part of things. Age, money and social connections are also significant in establishing your status, and older people are treated with respect. Often elders in a room are greeted first and served first at meals.

All of this can mean that things can take longer to get done than expats are used to; which can, in turn, lead to frustrations and difficulties meeting expected deadlines if you work for a western company.

Networking is important

Entrepreneurs' Guide

Dubai is one of the most exciting cities in the world for entrepreneurs and start-up companies. The fast-changing nature of the region means that opportunities abound for small business ventures here. It is advisable to do your market research before you arrive and then come along with endless endurance to tackle the bureaucratic procedures that will need to be followed.

Getting started
All companies setting up outside a free zone in Dubai must have a trade licence, which determines which business activities you are permitted to practise. One of your first points of call should be the Department of Economic Development (DED) which issues trade licences and is the integral authority for business in the UAE.

You will need sponsorship from a UAE national (who will have a 51% stake in your business) if setting up a Limited Liability Company (LLC) or public/private shareholding company. Alternatively, you will need sponsorship from a local service agent if setting up a branch company, sole proprietorship or civil business.

Applying for a trade licence
This is a multi-step process that requires you to register your trade name, apply for an Initial Approval Certificate, rent/buy commercial premises, and obtain special licensing approvals (if required). These procedures are dealt with by the DED and Ministry of Economy. Only then will you receive a full trade licence. This is usually valid for one year.

Getting a PO Box
You will need to organise a company PO Box as part of the set-up procedure. All mail is then sent to a PO Box address, registered at your company premises. See emiratespost.ae for details.

DCCI
All commercial and industrial businesses in Dubai must be registered with the Dubai Chamber of Commerce & Industry (DCCI), responsible for registering and attesting members, and recording information on companies.

Setting up in a free zone
Free zones offer business licences to companies 100% owned by foreign nationals. This negates the need for a UAE national sponsor or local service agent; you simply apply to the relevant Free Zone Authority (FZA) – there are more than 20 to choose from in Dubai, each designed around one or more industries. While the initial minimum capital requirement to set up in a free zone can be substantial, there are plenty of benefits.

Get, set, go!
The following companies can assist you in setting up a business, dealing with licensing, start-up and free zone applications, as well as offering ongoing services such as audits and accounting, HR and recruitment:

Commit *commitbiz.com*
Healy Consultants *healyconsultants.com*
HLB Hamt Chartered Accountants *hlbhamt.com*
Middle East and Africa Monitor *meamonitor.com*

For the full procedure of how to set up your business, see Explorer's *Dubai How-To* guide.

WORKING IN DUBAI
STARTING A BUSINESS

Warm greetings are commonplace, with long handshakes, effusive compliments and enquiries about the health of families. Avoid enquiring after female family members though, as this is kept extremely private. Similarly, when meeting someone of the opposite sex it's likely that a handshake will not be given and is best to refrain unless they extend their hand to you. Always use your right hand to meet, eat or hand over items as Muslims reserve the left hand for bodily hygiene and consider it unclean. Avoid showing the bottom of your shoes in meetings too as this is considered an insult.

If you're attending a business meeting at an Arab-owned company, it's likely that you'll be served traditional Arabic coffee, or *kahwa*. Sharing coffee is an important social ritual in the Middle East so you should drink some when offered. Cups should be taken in the right hand and if there is a waiter standing by, replenishing your cup, there are two ways to signal that you have had enough: either leave a small amount of coffee in the bottom of your cup or gently tip the cup from side to side.

Networking & Events

With Dubai still being a relatively small city, made up of communities that are smaller still, networking is critical, even across industries. Everyone seems to know everyone else and getting in with the corporate 'in-crowd' definitely has its plus points.

Business acumen here can, at times, be more important than specific industry knowledge so it pays to attend business events and trade shows. Make friends in government departments and this will often land you in the front line for opportunities.

Likewise, bad news is rarely made public here, so staying in tune with the grapevine can help prevent wrong decisions. Social networking sites like LinkedIn (linkedin.com) are a great resource when looking for new jobs or contacts, while groups like Heels & Deals (heelsanddeals.org) arrange regular meet-ups. Eleqt.com is an exclusive social networking site for high-level executives and entrepreneurs willing to pay the Dhs.18,000 joining fee.

Business Councils

American Business Council Of Dubai & The Northern Emirates 04 379 1414, *abcdubai.com*
Arab Business Club 04 358 3000, *arabbusinessclub.org*
Australian Business Council Dubai 04 367 2437, *abc-dxb.com*
British Business Group 04 397 0303, *britbiz-uae.com*
Canadian Business Council 04 359 2625, *cbc-dubai.com*

Danish Business Council Dubai 050 625 0092, *danishbusinessdubai.com*
French Business Council Dubai & The Northern Emirates 04 312 6700, *fbcdubai.com*
German Emirati Joint Council For Industry & Commerce 04 447 0100, *vae.ahk.de*
Indian Business & Professional Council 04 332 4300, *ibpcdubai.com*
Iranian Business Council 04 335 9220, *ibc.ae*
Italian Business Council 04 321 3082, *italianbusinesscouncil.com*
Malaysia Business Council 04 335 5528, *mbc-uae.com*
Netherlands Business Council 050 559 2272, *nbcdubai.com*
Pakistan Business Council Dubai 04 335 9991, *pbcdubai.com*
Singapore Business Council 04 393 7758, *sbcuae.com*
South African Business Council 04 390 0433, *sabco-uae.org*
Spanish Business Council 04 427 0379, *spanishbusinesscouncil.ae*
Swedish Business Council 04 429 8600, *sbcuae.se*
Swiss Business Council 04 368 7702, *swissbcuae.com*

STARTING A BUSINESS

Starting a business requires meticulous market research, a strict and realistic business plan and responsive action to take advantage of fleeting openings in the market. Bankruptcy laws are not as defined as in other countries and mismanagement of funds could result in harsh repercussions, including deportation or even jail time.

These days there is legislation which aids the start-up process – for example, there is no minimum capital requirement to start a business, unless you opt for a Limited Liability Company, in which case the capital requirement is Dhs.300,000.

One of the main hesitations that entrepreneurs have about starting a business here is the traditional requirement of having a local sponsor control a majority stake of the company. An eagerly awaited revamp of the commercial companies' law is in the drafting, although clauses removing the requirement for a local sponsor or a local service agent have already been rejected by the Federal National Council.

The exception to the above are free zones, where full private foreign ownership is already permitted. The licensing process for opening a business in a free zone is also more streamlined and helped by the free zone organisation.

explorer

there's more to life...

THE ULTIMATE CAREER GUIDE

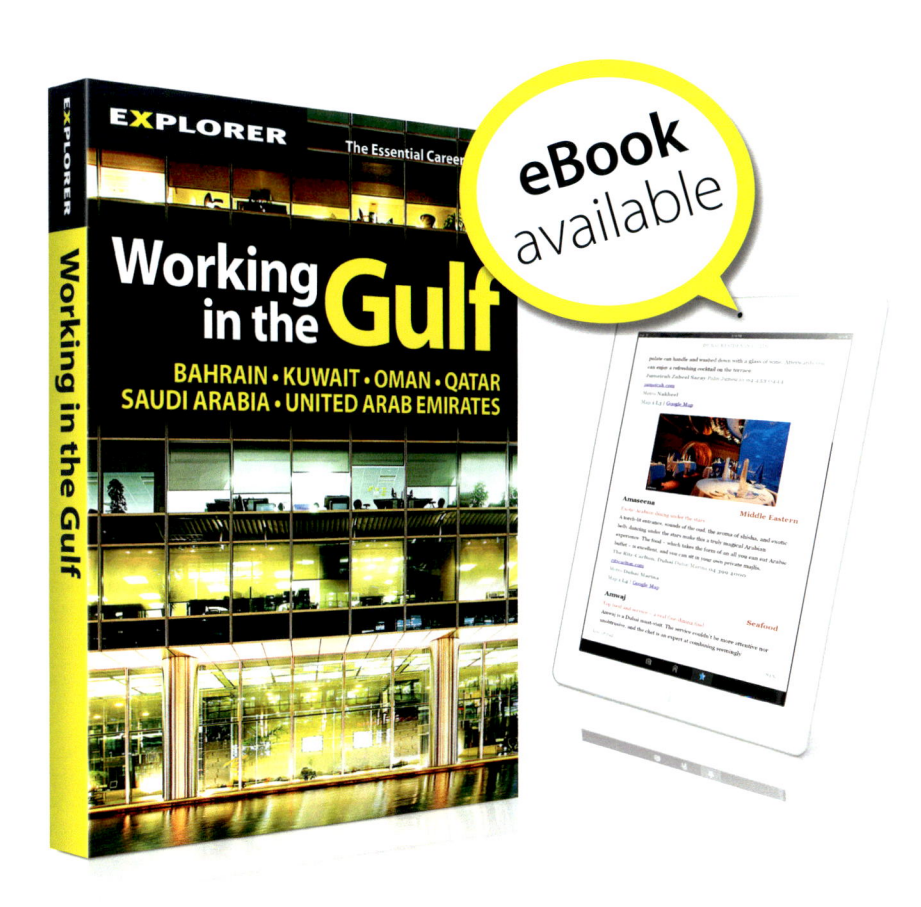

Working in the Gulf

BAHRAIN • KUWAIT • OMAN • QATAR
SAUDI ARABIA • UNITED ARAB EMIRATES

eBook available

askexplorer.com/shop

askexplorer

WORKING IN DUBAI
VOLUNTARY & CHARITY WORK

Government and privately sponsored initiatives are also helping to spur growth and educate potential business owners. The Mohammed Bin Rashid Establishment for SME Development (sme.ae) was set up to help entrepreneurs understand the procedures and potential costs of setting up in Dubai. The organisation provides guidance and information to Emiratis and expats hoping to start their own business. Among its varied schedule of events, arts community hub Shelter (shelter.ae) also hosts a programme of workshops for entrepreneurs, as well as providing hot desk facilities for creatives. If you want someone to handle all of the red tape for you, companies like Sentinel Business Centres (sentinelbusinesscentres.com) and Creative Zone (creativezone.ae) can help you set up in a free zone or even help find a local sponsor for your business.

There are various business groups in Dubai that help facilitate investments and provide opportunities for networking. Some provide information on trade with their respective countries, as well as business opportunities in Dubai and internationally. Most arrange social and networking events. Before you set up, contact the Dubai Chamber of Commerce & Industry (dubaichamber.com) and the Ministry of Economy (economy.gov.ae). Both can offer excellent advice. Embassies or consulates can also be a good business resource and may be able to offer contact lists for the UAE and the country of representation. For further information, refer to Explorer's *Working In The Gulf*, the Dubai Commercial Directory or the Hawk Business Pages.

Business Domain Name
You can register your domain name through Etisalat (etisalat.ae) which handles domain name registration through UAEnic (United Arab Emirates Network Information Center), or through du (du.ae) which is an accredited registrar of the .ae Domain Administration (.aeDA). It can also register other top-level domains such as those ending with .com and .net.

Consultants & Chartered Accountants
It pays in the long run to get professional advice if you want to set up your own business or become a freelancer. Listed below are just some of the consultants who can help and advise. For more, see askexplorer.com.

Commit Dubai World Trade Centre, Trade Center 2, 04 386 7444, *commitbiz.com*
Healy Consultants Khalid bin Al Waleed Bldg, Al Souk Al Kabeer, *healyconsultants.com*
HLB Hamt Chartered Accountants City Tower 2, Trade Center 1, 04 327 7775, *hlbhamt.com*
Middle East & Africa Monitor *meamonitor.com*

VOLUNTARY & CHARITY WORK

There are a number of opportunities to do voluntary or charity work in Dubai and the organisations listed below are always looking for committed volunteers. The Dubai Volunteering Centre, run by the Community Development Authority (CDA), regulates, promotes and encourages people to get involved in voluntary work. To register as a volunteer, call the CDA on 800 2121 or visit the website at cda.gov.ae.

If you're not entirely sure which charity you'd like to help, or want to volunteer for more than one charity, check out volunteerindubai.com – the website matches volunteers with the needs of specific drives or events.

All As One
Fairmont Dubai Trade Center 1 **04 311 6707**
allasone.org
Map **2 H5** Metro **World Trade Centre**
A non-profit organisation that cares for abandoned, disabled, abused and destitute children of Sierra Leone at the All As One Children's Centre. Operating costs are funded through donations, child sponsorship and charity events.

Breast Cancer Arabia
055 147 6435
breastcancerarabia.com
A charity that raises money to pay for breast cancer treatment for women who cannot afford it. Monies are raised at events such as golf days organised by the Breast Cancer Arabia Foundation, as well as through donations. Email foundation@breastcancerarabia.com for further information.

Feline Friends Dubai
050 451 0058
felinefriendsdubai.com
This non-profit organisation, with volunteers who rescue and re-home stray cats and kittens, promotes the control of street cats by sterilisation and provides care and relief to sick and injured cats. Rescue volunteers and foster homes are always needed.

Gulf For Good
International Humanitarian City
Dubai Industrial City **04 368 0222**
gulf4good.org
Metro **Jebel Ali**
This organisation raises funds for selected worthy causes around the world by organising sponsored

WORKING IN DUBAI
VOLUNTARY & CHARITY WORK

expeditions and treks to locations across the globe. Challenges include hikes in the Himalayan foothills and a trek through Palestine's remote highlands, wadis and deserts.

K9 Friends > p.161
04 887 8739
k9friends.com
A group of volunteers who rescue, care for and re-home unwanted dogs from all over the UAE. Running costs are met entirely through public donations and corporate sponsors. Assistance is always welcome.

Medecins Sans Frontieres (MSF) > p.133
Al Shafar Bldg, Shk Zayed Rd Al Thanyah 1
04 457 9255
msf-me.org
Map 1 N6 Metro Dubai Internet City
An international, non-profit emergency medical relief organisation. Volunteers can become involved locally with fundraising and awareness campaigns. Annual events include the Dubai Vertical Marathon, where participants climb the Emirates Towers' 1,334 steps, and Wild Wadi's Swim Burj Al Arab.

Riding For The Disabled Association Of Dubai
Desert Palm Retreat Warsan 2
rdad.ae
Launched by HH Sheikha Hassa bint Mohammed bin Rashid Al Maktoum, the association provides therapeutic benefits for children with special needs through gentle horse riding. Reliable volunteers are always needed to lead the horses and assist riders.

Women For Women International
050 342 4949
womenforwomen.org
Informal charity events organised by a group of ladies to help Women for Women International, a charity giving aid to war survivors. Contact Julie Wilkinson for details on 050 342 4949 or at jwilkinson@valleyforge.com.

Environmental Groups

The UAE government and local municipalities have started making efforts towards reducing waste and consumption and raising environmental awareness. Masdar City in Abu Dhabi is being hailed as a groundbreaking green project and will be one of the world's most sustainable places to live, powered by renewable energy sources (masdarcity.ae).

In Dubai, The Change Initiative is a flagship store in Al Barsha for environmentally friendly services and products. The first company of its type in the region, it specialises in eco-friendly goods including sustainable cleaning products, solar panels, household appliances and building solutions.

Dubai's Emirates Environment Group (eeg-uae.org) is devoted to environmental protection through education, action and community involvement. It also has a recycling centre. Call 04 344 8622.

Dubai Desert Conservation Reserve (ddcr.org) allows visits and sometimes accepts volunteer workers to help with the monitoring of endangered species.

In neighbouring Abu Dhabi the government effort is being accelerated by various environmental organisations who aim to protect the environment, as well as to educate the population about environmental issues. The Environment Agency Abu Dhabi (ead.ae) assists the Abu Dhabi government in the conservation and management of the emirate's natural environment, resources, wildlife and biological diversity.

Sir Bani Yas Island, which is part of the Abu Dhabi emirate, is home to an internationally acclaimed breeding programme for endangered wildlife. Created as a private wildlife sanctuary by the late Sheikh Zayed, it is now an exclusive eco-resort (call 02 801 5400 or visit anantara.com).

Emirates Wildlife Society is a national environmental NGO that operates in association with the WWF (panda.org). In addition, The Breeding Centre for Endangered Arabian Wildlife (06 531 1212) at Sharjah Desert Park has a successful breeding programme for wildlife under threat, particularly the Arabian leopard. The breeding centre is off-limits to visitors but the Arabian Wildlife Centre (06 531 1999), also at the Desert Park, is open to the public.

Several environmental groups help native wildlife

Shows & Exhibitions

The MICE industry in Dubai is growing rapidly, as both local and international companies choose to host events in the emirate.

With its vast transport hub, Dubai is an increasingly popular location for international trade fairs and conferences. The emirate's central location and abundance of five-star accommodation options means worldwide organisations are likely to choose Dubai as their meeting point.

There are a growing number of industry and trade events in Dubai that are lucrative for companies – or a fantastic day of entertainment for local families.

The Dubai World Trade Centre hosts more than 500 events every year, receiving more than 1.4 million visitors and about 6,000 exhibitors.

Each year the Abu Dhabi National Exhibition Centre (ADNEC) also stages more than 100 events, which bring millions of dollars to the UAE capital.

The Big Three

Gitex Shopper
Residents wait for Gitex Shopper so they can purchase electronics or IT goods. This is where manufacturers release their latest products and retailers offer them at discounted prices. In 2013, there were two events, one in April and another in October. Gitex Shopper retailers reported sales in excess of Dhs.245 million at the October event alone, which was an increase on figures from 2012.

Big Boys Toys
If it's fast, powerful or expensive, you'll find it at Big Boys Toys – the showcase of sleek and luxurious products. Check out the latest Lamborghini or the biggest from Bang and Olufsen. Other interesting products previously showcased include the smallest folding electric bike in the world.

Arabian Travel Market (ATM)
The leading international travel and tourism event in the Middle East for inbound and outbound tourism professionals from across the globe. Residents also flock to see what travel promotions are running in tandem with the exhibition. With Dubai winning the right to host the World Expo 2020, this event is even more important as a way for the city to market itself to visiting tourism authorities.

2014 Highlights

March
Dubai International Boat Show 4-8 March
boatshowdubai.com
Cabsat Mena 11-13 March 2014
cabsat.com
Dubai International Horse Fair 20-22 March
dihf.ae
25 Years of Arab Creativity 27 January-20 April
abudhabifestival.ae

April
The Bride Show Dubai 2-5 April
thebrideshow.com
Gulf Education & Training Exhibition 9-11 April
mygetex.com
CItyscape Abu Dhabi 22-24 April
cityscapeabudhabi.com
GITEX Shopper 23-26 April
gitexshopperdubai.com

May
Arabian Travel Market (ATM) 5-8 May
arabiantravelmarket.com
Beauty World Middle East 27-29 May
gulfbeautyexpo.com

June
Dubai Summer Surprises June and July
mydsf.ae

October
Big Boys Toys 3-5 October *bigboystoysuae.com*
GITEX Technology Week 12-16 October *gitex.com*
Green Middle East at Sharjah Expo Centre
20-22 October *green-middleeast.com*

November
Big Five Exhibition 17-20 November
thebig5.ae

December
Abu Dhabi International Motor Show
17-21 December *reedexpo.com*

MICE Venues

Aside from the Dubai World Trade Centre, Dubai has many hotels that offer conference and event facilities, which are suitable for events ranging from 20 people in a boardroom meeting, to 500-plus at a company conference.

The Fairmont (fairmont.com) in Dubai offers 'sustainable meetings' packages for socially and environmentally conscious delegates, or you could arrange a seminar in JA Jebel Ali Golf Resort's (jaresortshotels.com) bio garden.

Sheikh Zayed Rd skyline

fashion, graphic,
& interior design.
painting &
printmaking.
art history.

www.qatar.vcu.edu

vcuqatar | virginia commonwealth university in qatar
جامعة فرجينيا كومنولث في قطر

by imen ibala, interior design, 2013

EDUCATION

Nurseries & Pre-Schools **225**
Selecting A School **230**
Primary & Secondary Schools **232**
Universities & Colleges **247**

EDUCATION

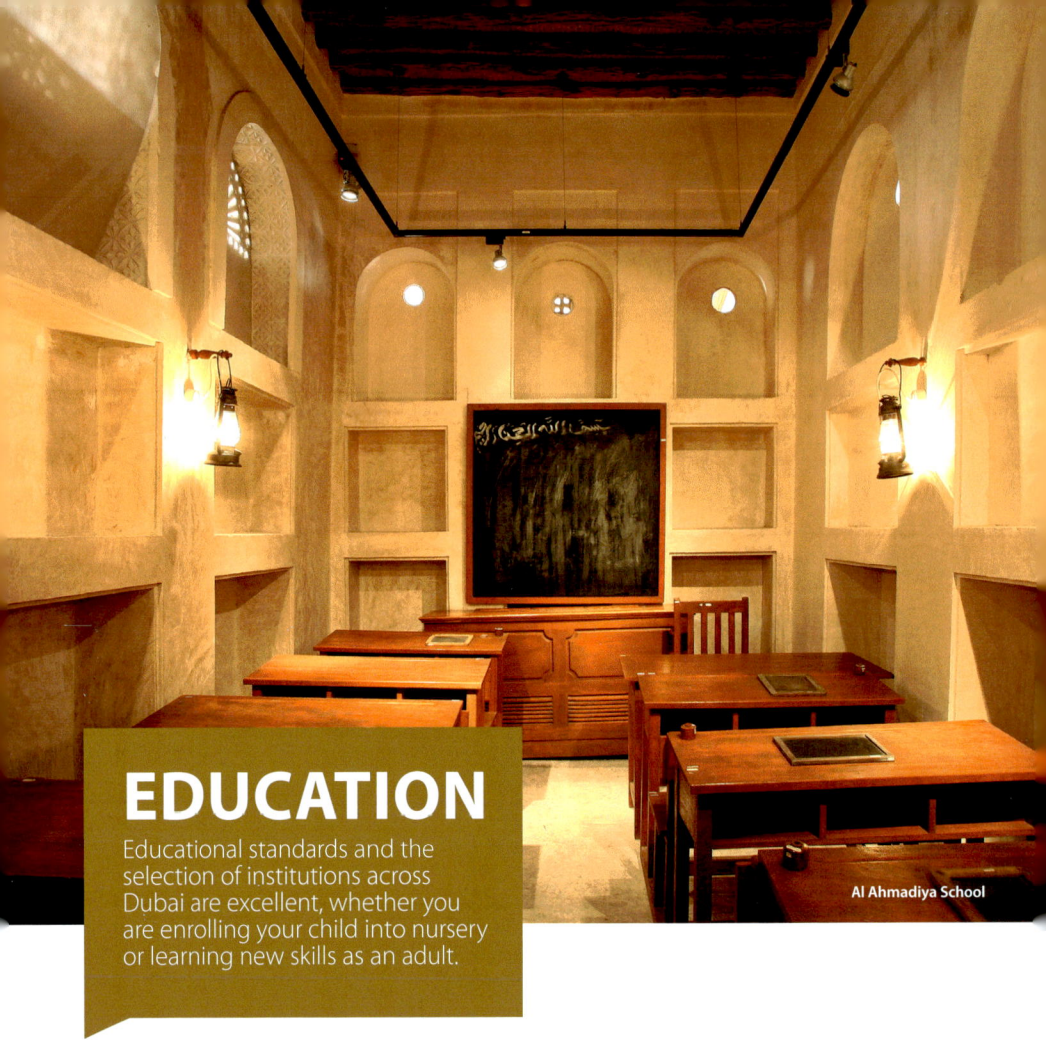

Educational standards and the selection of institutions across Dubai are excellent, whether you are enrolling your child into nursery or learning new skills as an adult.

Al Ahmadiya School

Dubai is home to various international and government nurseries, schools and universities offering top quality education. There has been a high level of investment and rapid expansion within a relatively short time frame in the emirate – and the educational landscape continues to change and improve. School inspections are now compulsory, and teachers will be soon have to be 'licensed' (as in western countries).

Local schools are restricted primarily to Arabic speaking Emiratis, so you will need to enrol your child in a private school. Although prices can be high, your child will learn Arabic and other languages from a young age, the facilities are world-class, and schools are a melting pot of nationalities. There are currently 225,000 students enrolled in private schools across the emirate – and plans to build more new schools by 2020. There is also a growing number of internationally accredited colleges and universities offering courses in the arts, sciences, business and engineering sectors. Although the majority of university places in Dubai are filled by locals, there are both expat and mature students studying here too.

The first thing anyone will tell you about education in the UAE is to get your child's name on several schools' waiting lists as soon as possible. The demand for spaces at the more popular schools is high, and you can never apply too early. Secondly, try to negotiate school fees in your employment package with your employer. Also, check to see if your company has a corporate debenture with a particular place, as that will move you up the waiting list.

Whether you are a parent or a mature student, this chapter will guide you on the path to education...

EDUCATION
NURSERIES & PRE-SCHOOLS

NURSERIES & PRE-SCHOOLS

Some nurseries, or kindergartens, accept babies from as young as three months, although most prefer to take on children who have started walking (around 12 months). Fees and timings vary dramatically, so it's best to call around and visit a few nurseries to get an idea of what's available. As a general rule of thumb, most nurseries are open for four or five hours in the morning and charge anything from Dhs.3,000 to Dhs.12,000 per term. You can pay extra in many nurseries if you need to drop your child off earlier (for a 7am breakfast club) or collect them later, often until 6pm. In general, classes of between 10 and 20 children are staffed by a nursery teacher and as many as three teaching assistants.

The more popular nurseries have unbelievably long waiting lists, so, if you're after a particular establishment, it may be necessary to enrol your child before he or she is even born just to make sure you get a spot. Some of the bigger primary schools also have nursery sections or an affiliated nursery – if you've got a primary school in mind for your child, it is worth checking to see if they have a nursery, as this may help you secure a place in the school itself a few years down the line.

Selecting A Nursery

The Ministry of Social Affairs is currently developing a nursery rating system to help you choose a school but, for the time being, parents will have to make this decision based on their own research. This chapter should serve as a useful guide.

Some nurseries in Dubai only operate morning hours which may rule them out if you are working full time. However, many will also run late classes until 6pm for an extra fee and a number of them have early-bird drop-offs. They may also organise summer camps and other sessions during the holiday periods.

Also, don't be surprised if your child starts learning Arabic or even French from as young as one. Another factor worth thinking about when selecting your child's nursery is whether or not they provide meals – having to make a packed lunch every morning when you're trying to get ready for work may not be suitable for you.

The location of your nursery will also be a key factor in your decision making progress. You may prefer a nursery that is within walking distance of your home or en route to the office. Bear in mind that traffic can often get very congested at pick-up and drop-off time during term time.

International

Most nurseries will follow one particular curriculum – mainly International, English (Early Years Foundation Stage) or Montessori – so bear that in mind. Quite often there will be an amalgamation of approaches with more of a focus on children's social and personal development than on any one particular country's curriculum. Kidville Nursery (kidville.com) in Marsa Dubai, for example, runs its Kidville University programme with a focus on preparing toddlers for the transition to school through creativity and play.

Early Years Foundation Stage

In line with the National Curriculum for England, children between the ages of three and five follow the EYFS (Early Years Foundation Stage) curriculum which is specifically designed to prepare them for entry to Key Stage 1 (Years 1 & 2) at school. EYFS focuses on: communication and language, and physical, personal, social and emotional development. Assessments are made throughout a child's time at the nursery, creating a profile to help teachers understand the child and tailor a curriculum to suit their development. Children typically attend nursery until Foundation Stage 1. Once they are aged four, they start Foundation Stage 2 at a primary school. It's a good option to prepare children for a British school education.

Blossom Children's Nursery
Villa 37, 10A St Umm Al Sheif
04 348 6275
theblossomnursery.com
Map **2 B5** Metro **First Gulf Bank**
Structured play programmes include dance, drama, music, water play, and foreign languages. A smartbook keeps parents informed of their child's development and there's a big focus on sensory learning. There are also branches in Downtown and Umm Suqeim; its Early Learning Centre at Academic City teaches up to FS2 level. **Age:** 6 months to 4 years. **Fees:** Available on request.

British Orchard Nursery
Nr Al Karama Metro Station Al Mankhool
04 398 3536
britishorchardnursery.com
Map **2 K5** Metro **Al Karama**
Timings are from 8am to 12.30pm and there are two out-of-school daycare clubs, Little Apples and Breakfast Club, which run from 7.30am to 5pm. Parents can log on to a secure website to see their children through the in-class CCTV. There are also branches in Jumeira, Silicon Oasis and Media City. **Age:** 6 months to 4 years. **Fees:** Available on request.

askexplorer.com

225

EDUCATION
NURSERIES & PRE-SCHOOLS

Building Blocks Nursery & Child Enrichment Centre
Apex Atrium MotorCity, Al Hebiah 1 **04 453 4363**
building-blocks.ae
Map **1 N11**
Building Blocks follows the UK's Early Years Foundation Stage curriculum framework, which concentrates on helping babies and toddlers to learn and grow through play. The nursery has an 'enrichment centre' where children can learn the basics of dance, music, sport, language and cooking. **Age:** 4 months to 5 years. **Fees:** Dhs.10,100-13,700/term.

Burj Daycare Nursery
Downtown Dubai, Burj Khalifa **04 431 8320**
burjdaycarenursery.com
Map **2 F6** Metro **Burj Khalifa/Dubai Mall**
Open 8am until 2pm, this one-classroom nursery follows the UK's Early Years Foundation Stage programme, including classes in music and movement, Kidzart and French. There's a dedicated outdoor space, which includes a wave pool and 'splash maze', as well as an area for bikes and push-along toys. **Age:** 18 months to 4 years. **Fees:** Dhs.18,000-21,000/term.

The Children's Garden
Green Community, Dubai Investment Park 1
04 885 3484
childrensgarden.ae
Map **1 F10**
The Children's Garden was Dubai's first multi-lingual preschool and has three branches: Green Community, Barsha (tcgbarsha.ae, 04 399 0160), and Jumeira (tcgjumeira.ae, 04 349 2985). The syllabus officially offers children exposure to multiple languages: English, Arabic, French and German. In total, the staff speak 19 languages. The school implemented the preschool ICLA in 2005 – the International Curriculum for Languages and Creative Arts – under the auspices of Taaleem, a UAE school management organisation. It requires teaching resources to come from a variety of international sources. The goal is for children to be at least bilingual when they graduate. **Age:** 2 to 5 years. **Fees:** Dhs.28,500-50,000.

Emirates British Nursery
Al Wasl Rd Umm Al Sheif **04 348 9996**
emiratesbritishnursery.com
Map **1 R6** Metro **Mall of the Emirates**
This nursery regards playtime as an important factor in a child's early development. Its three locations (including Mirdif and MotorCity) are spacious, with multilingual staff and an in-house nurse. A summer school is available during July and August and late classes are available until 3pm. **Age:** 3 months (Mirdif only) to 4 years. **Fees:** Available on request.

Golden Beach Nursery
Street 17A Umm Suqeim 3 **04 380 9336**
goldenbeachnursery.com
Map **1 S5** Metro **First Gulf Bank**
Follows the British Early Years Foundation Stage curriculum, with a focus on qualified staff and healthy meals. Facilities include two indoor play areas and a large outdoor shaded play area, and the curriculum includes water play, music, French and art classes. Open 50 weeks a year from Sunday to Thursday (7am to 6pm). **Age:** 14 months to 5 years. **Fees:** Dhs.10,833-11,666/term.

Home Grown Children's Eco Nursery
Villa 33, Street 9 Umm Suqeim 2 **04 330 7008**
homegrownnursery.ae
Map **1 U5** Metro **Noor Bank**
Billed as Dubai's first 'eco-nursery', Home Grown follows the British Early Years Foundation Stage curriculum, uses eco-friendly resources and equipment, and many of the activities are focused on nature and the outdoors. **Age:** 12 months to 4 years. **Fees:** Dhs.10,800-15,900/term.

Hopscotch Nursery
Villa 48, 15th Street Al Manara **04 328 2226**
hopscotchnursery.net
Map **1 U6** Metro **Noor Bank**
Using the British Early Years Foundation Stage curriculum, this nursery aims to care for, develop, motivate and educate children in equal measures, with the help of some excellent facilities and a broad range of sporting activities. **Age:** 4 months to 4 years. **Fees:** Dhs.7,000-9,000/term approx.

Horizon Kids Nursery
29B Street Al Safa 2 **04 380 9077**
horizonkidsnursery.com
Map **2 A6** Metro **Noor Bank**
Linked to Horizon School, this is a wonderful bright and spacious nursery with a sensory room, library, art studio, gym and outdoor play area. There are optional afternoon football, dance and yoga classes. Timings are 7.30am to 12.30pm, with later pick-ups available at 3pm and 5pm. **Age:** 3 months to 5 years. **Fees:** Dhs.10,000/term (5 days a week).

Jumeirah International Nursery School
Villa 8, Street 13 Al Wasl **04 349 9065**
jinschools.com
Map **2 F5** Metro **Burj Khalifa/Dubai Mall**
One of the oldest in Dubai, this nursery follows the UK's Ofsted standards; individual attention is given in a safe and balanced environment. Classes run from 8am to 12.30pm. There are also branches near Safa Park (04 394 5567) and in Downtown (04 456 4955). **Age:** 18 months to 4 years. **Fees:** Available on request.

OPEN DOORS. OPEN MINDS.

- Private Tours
- Arabic Classes
- Cultural Events
- Cultural Workshops
- Cultural Meals

ABOUT US

The Sheikh Mohammed Centre for Cultural Understanding (SMCCU) was established under the patronage of His Highness Sheikh Mohammed bin Rashid Al Maktoum in 1998. Operating under the philosophy and banner of "Open doors. Open minds." the SMCCU strives to remove barriers between people of different nationalities and raise awareness of the UAE's local culture, customs and religion. Located in a traditional wind tower house in the heart of Al Fahidi Historic District, the SMCCU regularly conducts various activities that aim to improve cross-cultural understanding and communication between locals and foreigners across the UAE.

CULTURAL MEALS

The most popular offering of the SMCCU is its Cultural Breakfasts & Lunches. Introduced for 2013 is our new Brunch & Dinner events where guests can also indulge in traditional Emirati meals in a relaxed and friendly ambience while a knowledgeable Emirati host chats to them about the local customs and traditions.

Breakfast: Every Mon & Wed at 10am, AED 70 pp.
Lunch: Every Sunday & Tuesday at 1pm, AED 80 pp.
Brunch: Every Saturday at 10:30am, AED 85 pp.
Dinner: Every Tuesday at 7pm, AED 95 pp.
Duration 90 minutes, (Reservations are essential).

JUMEIRAH MOSQUE VISIT

The Jumeirah Mosque has become renowned as the focal point of SMCCU's "Open doors. Open minds." programme. Till recently, it was the only mosque in Dubai open to the public and dedicated to receiving non-Muslim guests.
Every Saturday through Thursday at 10am. (closed Friday). Please arrive at 9:45am for registration.
Guests are requested to dress modestly; traditional attire can also be borrowed from the mosque. AED 10 pp.
Duration 75 mins (*No* reservations required).

HERITAGE TOUR

Enjoy a guided walk through the Al Fahidi Historic District and visit and talk inside the Diwan Masjid (Mosque), followed by a Question & Answer session at the SMCCU house with freshly brewed Arabic coffee and dates.
Every Saturday at 9am & every Sunday, Tuesday and Thursday at 10:30am, AED 65 pp.
Duration 90 minutes, (Reservations are essential).

WALKING TOUR

This tour includes a walk through the Al Fahidi Historic District and a Question & Answer session at the SMCCU house. Guests will be treated to Arabic coffee and dates.
Daily Sunday to Thursday at 9am, Duration 60 minutes, AED 50 pp.
Duration 60 minutes, (Reservations are essential).

Located in House 26, Al Musallah Road,
Al Fahidi Historic District, Bur Dubai
Tel: +971 4 353 6666, Fax: +971 4 353 6661
smccu@cultures.ae
www.cultures.ae

Follow us
SMCCUDubai

EDUCATION
NURSERIES & PRE-SCHOOLS

Kensington Nursery
Umm Al Sheif Rd Umm Suqeim 1 **04 394 4473**
thekensingtonnursery.com
Map **2 B5** Metro **Noor Bank**
With locations in Umm Suqeim and Dubai Silicon Oasis, this nursery follows the British Early Years Foundation Stage curriculum. It is open 7.30am to 6pm with full and half-day options, operates a transport service, and runs holiday camps. **Age:** 4 months to 5 years. **Fees:** Dhs.40,950/year approx.

Kids Island Nursery
Al Hamra St Jumeira 3 **04 394 2578**
kidsislandnursery.com
Map **2 B5** Metro **Noor Bank**
This nursery school follows a British curriculum and is open all year round, with late classes running until 1pm. There are large, shaded outdoor play areas, an activity room and a playroom. It is partnered with Cocoon Nursery in Jumeira 3 (04 394 9394). **Age:** 12 months to 5 years. **Fees:** Available on request.

Kids Zone Nursery
The Villa Community Al Barari, Wadi Al Safa 3 **04 452 6474**
kidszonenursery.com
Map **2 A13**
Kids Zone Nursery uses the British Early Years Foundation Stage curriculum and also adopts the Reggio approach to teaching. The school runs holiday programmes outside of term time. Timings are from 8am to 1pm with early drop off times from 7.30am and extended pick-up options until 6pm. **Age:** 6 months to 4 years. **Fees:** Available on request.

Little Discoverers Nursery
Villa 38, 35th Street Al Safa 1 **04 394 6066**
littlediscoverers.com
Map **2 B6** Metro **Noor Bank**
Open between 7am and 6pm, this nursery follows the British curriculum and kids can enjoy a wide range of facilities including a jungle gym, herb garden and bike tracks. There's also an indoor play area, themed classrooms and a cosy library. **Age:** 3 months to 4 years. **Fees:** Available on request.

Little Wonders Nursery
Villa 5, 3rd St Al Manara **04 348 7195**
littlewonders.ae
Map **1 U6** Metro **Noor Bank**
This nursery in Al Manara uses the British curriculum with a range of activities and subjects including music, science and outdoor play. Facilities include an indoor play area and covered swimming pools. Breakfast and lunch are provided at extra cost. **Age:** 2 months to 4 years. **Fees:** Available on request.

My Nursery
Nr Dubai Zoo, Street 2B Al Bada' **04 344 1120**
mynursery.ae
Map **2 H4** Metro **Emirates Towers**
This nursery delivers a bilingual English-Arabic curriculum aimed at educating children to the same level of proficiency in both languages. After-school care and school transport are available, and the nursery will soon be opening a class for children aged one year and eight months, and upwards. **Age:** 2 to 4 years. **Fees:** Available on request.

Raffles International School
Nr Burj Al Arab, Street 20 Umm Suqeim 3
04 427 1228
rafflesis.com
Map **1 S5** Metro **First Gulf Bank**
Raffles operates nine nurseries at various locations throughout Dubai including Arabian Ranches, Marsa Dubai, Springs, Lakes, Emirates Hills and Umm Suqeim. Nursery timing are 8am to 2pm, and there is a choice of two curriculums: the British Early Years Foundation Stage and Montessori. A healthy lunch is served every day. **Age:** 18 months to 4 years. **Fees:** Dhs.11,000/term approx.

Safa Kindergarten Nursery
Nr Shangri-La Al Satwa **04 344 3878**
safanurseriesdubai.ae
Map **2 G5** Metro **Burj Khalifa/Dubai Mall**
This British curriculum nursery uses the popular Montessori learning principles. Activities include educational play, water play and singing. Arabic or French as a second language is introduced to children when they turn three. **Age:** 12 months to 4.5 years. **Fees:** Available on request.

Seashells Nursery
Nr Mall of the Emirates Al Barsha 2 **04 341 3404**
seashellsnursery.com
Map **1 R7** Metro **Mall of the Emirates**
Seashells follows the British curriculum, has two indoor playrooms, an indoor gym, a project room for cooking and experiments, and shaded outdoor play areas. There are organised field trips too. After-school activities include football, gym and languages, and a school holiday programme is also available. **Age:** 18 months to 4 years. **Fees:** Available on request.

Small World Nursery
Nr Archaeological Site Jumeira 2 **04 349 0770**
smallworldnurserydubai.com
Map **2 D4** Metro **Business Bay**
Small World combines academic learning with physical education. Facilities include a discovery garden, swimming pool and outside play area. There is a late class until 1.30pm. Another branch in Umm

EDUCATION
NURSERIES & PRE-SCHOOLS

Suqeim (04 348 0788) offers the UK curriculum with the Waldorf-Steiner philosophy, a swimming pool, and a late class until 3pm. **Age:** 1 to 4 years. **Fees:** Dhs.8,100-9,775/term approx.

Willow Children's Nursery
Villa 75, Off Al Wasl Rd Umm Suqeim 2
04 346 5078
willownurserydubai.com
Map **1 U5** Metro **Noor Bank**
This bright and pleasant nursery, with large gardens and play areas, is run by British staff teaching the Early Years Foundation Stage curriculum. Flexible hours are offered and a home-cooked lunch can be provided. There is a dedicated baby area, Little Willows. **Age:** 3 months to 4.5 years. **Fees:** Available on request.

Yellow Brick Road Nursery
Nr Irish Village Al Garhoud 04 282 8290
yellowbrickroad.ws
Map **2 N8** Metro **Airport Terminal 1**
This huge and very popular British curriculum nursery (with a long waiting list) accommodates 180 children in nine classes and a dedicated baby room. A cooked breakfast and lunch are provided. Late classes run until 6pm. Another branch, Emerald City Nursery (04 349 0848), is in Jumeira 2. **Age:** 4 months to 4.5 years. **Fees:** Dhs.9,500/term.

Montessori

Montessori is a popular teaching method that encourages a more flexible approach to learning than a strict academic curriculum. Children are encouraged to discover new things through imaginative play, social interaction and physical activity. The method is also used to help children to develop their own instinct to learn and is a good foundation for the International Baccalaureate curriculum.

Alphabet Street Nursery
Villa 11, Al Manara Rd Al Manara 04 348 5991
alphabetstreetnursery.com
Map **1 U5** Metro **Noor Bank**
Alphabet Street employs a mix of the Montessori teaching method and the UK's Early Years Foundation Stage Programme to develop each child's communication, control and coordination. Facilities include a library, computer room and paddling pool. The school offers the possibility of a 7.30am start, and also provides holiday care outside of term time. A late class is available until 5.30pm. Staff are highly trained and certified St John Ambulance lifesavers for babies and children. **Age:** 14 months to 4+ years. **Fees:** Available on request.

Baby Land Nursery
Al Wasl Rd Al Manara 04 348 6874
babylandnursery.com
Map **1 T5** Metro **Noor Bank**
Children participate in a series of practical activities specially designed to improve their independence, concentration, hand-eye coordination, fine motor skills, patience and judgement. Baby Land offers late classes until 4pm and a summer school, and there's a large, supervised outdoor play area. **Age:** 12 months to 4.5 years. **Fees:** Available on request.

First Steps Nursery Dubai
Villa 10, Nr Burj Al Arab Umm Suqeim 3 04 348 6301
Map **1 S5** Metro **Mall of the Emirates**
This Montessori nursery opens from 7.30am to 6pm. It encourages child development through arts and crafts, reading, educational videos and indoor and outdoor play areas. It's open on Saturdays too, when it also accepts children up to the age of 10. In addition, it runs summer camps during the holidays. **Age:** 18 months to 5 years. **Fees:** Available on request.

GEMS Modern Nursery
Nadd Al Shiba 3 04 326 3339
Map **2 H13**
Dubai Modern High School in Nadd Al Shiba offers a one year pre-kindergarten programme to help prepare children for kindergarten by having them spend some time away from home. It follows the self-directed learning principles of both the Reggio and Montessori methods. **Age:** 2 to 4 years old. **Fees:** Available on request.

Gulf Montessori Nursery
Nr Choithrams Al Garhoud 04 282 7046
gulfmontessori.com
Map **2 N8** Metro **Airport Terminal 1**
This Gulf Montessori Nursery has fully equipped classrooms and its facilities include a dedicated art room, a swimming pool and a large outdoor play area. The curriculum takes a child-centred approach to academic and social development. Children are required to wear a uniform. **Age:** 2 to 5 years. **Fees:** Available on request.

Hope Montessori Nursery
Nr Children's Library Al Mankhool 04 398 2494
hopemontessorinursery.ae
Map **2 K5** Metro **Al Karama**
This private multi-cultural, multi-lingual nursery located in Bur Dubai follows an English-speaking, Montessori curriculum. There's a wide variety of activities on offer, including water play, arts and crafts, aerobics and even yoga. In addition, the school organises a number of extracurricular activities. **Age:** 2 to 4 years. **Fees:** Available on request.

EDUCATION
SELECTING A SCHOOL

Kidz Venture
Ibn Battuta Jabal Ali 1 **04 368 4130**
kidzventure.ae
Map **1 G5** Metro **Ibn Battuta**
Children are free to experiment through multiple activities like gardening, music, drama, cooking and games at this nursery for infants through to pre-schoolers. It offers a Montessori programme as well as the British Early Years Foundation Stage curriculum. Open 7am to 7pm Sunday to Thursday. **Age:** 6 months to 4 years. **Fees:** Dhs.10,200-17,700/term.

Ladybird Nursery
Villa 8, Street 25A Al Wasl **04 344 1011**
ladybirdnursery.ae
Map **2 E5** Metro **Business Bay**
Ladybird strikes an interesting balance between a traditional nursery and a Montessori school by providing a bright and cheerful environment, toys, dressing-up clothes and soft play. Late classes are available until 1.30pm. **Age:** 1 to 4 years. **Fees:** Available on request.

Little Land Nursery & Montessori Centre
Nr Saga World Umm Suqeim 1 **04 394 4471**
littlelandnursery.com
Map **1 U4** Metro **Noor Bank**
At Little Land Nursery there are six classrooms, three of which are traditional nurseries for toddlers aged from 14 months old, and three Montessori classrooms for kids aged from 2.5 years old. All of the teachers have pre-school teaching qualifications. **Age:** 14 months to 4 years. **Fees:** Available on request.

Mulberry Tree Nursery
Villa 5, Al Safeena St Jumeira 3 **04 394 9909**
Map **2 B4** Metro **Noor Bank**
This nursery offers both the Montessori and British curriculum, with a range of activities and subjects including music, science, cooking and outdoor play. The nursery welcomes children with special educational needs and its facilities include an indoor gym and puppet theatre. **Age:** 12 months to 4 years old. **Fees:** Available on request.

Tiny Home Nursery
Villa No.9, Street 29 Al Manara **04 346 5240**
tiny-home.com
Map **1 T6** Metro **First Gulf Bank**
Tiny Home Nursery has been running in Dubai since 1989 and was founded under supervision of the London Montessori Centre. Times are from 8am to 12.30pm, with enrollment for two, three and five days per week available. It also offers a Busy Bees after school club that runs until 2pm. Yoga classes are now incorporated into the curriculum. **Age:** 18 months to 4 years. **Fees:** Dhs.5,000-8,950/term.

SELECTING A SCHOOL

Things to consider when selecting a school:
Curriculum Pick the best curriculum for your child based on your nationality and future plans; there are as many as 15 curriculae on offer.
KHDA rankings The government inspected all schools in 2012-13 and rated them accordingly.
School fees These can vary considerably between schools, and primary and secondary.
School transport Dubai's rush-hour traffic can turn a short journey into a tedious trek every day – check for the availability of school transport.

Curriculum

There is a wide choice of international curriculums at Dubai's primary and secondary schools, but you will find that many schools follow either the English (UK) National Curriculum, American Curriculum or International Baccalaureate Programme (IB). International schools are typically open to all nationalities, and so the choice is yours. To help you get started, this chapter features an overview of schools teaching the English, American and IB curriculums; see also askexplorer.com for a more comprehensive list covering other curriculums.

Other curriculums include the Indian CBSE/ICSE, which is taught at Apple International School (apple.sch.ae) amongst others; the German International School Dubai (germanschool.ae) is based on the curriculum of the German federal state of Thuringia, and the Lycee Francais International de Dubai (aflec-fr.org/lfidubai) teaches the French syllabus. There is also the Japanese School Dubai (japanese.sch.ae), the Russian International School Dubai (dubairuschool.com) and the Swedish School in Dubai (svenskaskolandubai.com). For full details on these and other schools, visit askexplorer.com.

Indian Curriculum
The CBSE/ICSE is an ideal option for Indian nationals who want to continue their children's education internationally, but expect to settle back in India. It educates students to CBSE and ICSE level to the end of Year 12. There are many choices for Indian schools in the emirate, including The Indian High School – Dubai, Our Own Indian High School – Dubai, and Global Indian International School – Dubai.

EDUCATION
SELECTING A SCHOOL

KHDA Rankings

The Knowledge and Human Development Authority (KHDA) is Dubai's regulatory body for private education at all levels, from early childhood to adult learning. Since inspections began in 2008, KHDA reports have ranked every school in Dubai from Outstanding and Good to Acceptable and Unacceptable; schools that perform well can increase their fees at a steeper percentage than poorer schools. School inspections are carried out annually by the Dubai Schools Inspection Bureau (DSIB). Assessments are based on a wide range of criteria, from academic achievements in core subjects to the attitude of students; higher rankings often come hand in hand with the quality of teaching of Islamic and Arabic subjects. See khda.gov.ae for more information and for a breakdown of each school's result.

British schools can now apply for inspection and British School Overseas certification by the British government; the KHDA plans to make this compulsory and also to introduce a similar quality assurance scheme for US curriculum schools. According to the KHDA rankings for 2012/13, nine out of the 12 Outstanding schools in Dubai follow a UK curriculum.

Top Scores

In the latest 2012/13 report, two new schools were ranked Outstanding – namely Dubai English Speaking College and Horizon School. One school – Jebel Ali Primary School – reverted to its Good ranking of 2010/11, although it is still rated Outstanding in many elements of the KHDA report. The percentage of students attending Good and Outstanding schools in Dubai has risen by 19% since 2008. According to the KHDA, 49% of all private school students are now studying at either Good or Outstanding schools.

School Fees

School fees are a contentious issue for many. For a good school, you can expect to pay Dhs.25,000 plus per year during the primary years, Dhs.30,000 and up for the middle primary years, and as much as Dhs.60,000 per year for secondary school. Ouch! If you're lucky, your company may include an education allowance for school fees as part of your employment package, so it's worth trying to negotiate for this when accepting a job offer. However, you should note that this is no longer very common. Additionally, you will usually pay around Dhs.500 to put your child's name on a waiting list, and a registration fee (around Dhs.2,000), which is deducted from your annual costs. Crucially, you must sign your child up for your chosen school as soon as you can (sign-up is usually in February) as competition for places is extremely fierce.

Financial Headache

They say what goes up must come down, but not when it comes to UAE school fees, it seems. A recent survey found that fees are causing parents a great deal of financial worry. WhichSchoolAdvisor.com surveyed 1,072 UAE parents. Results revealed that 90% said school fees were a source of financial stress, one in three said they paid fees late, and two out of 10 have taken personal loans to pay them. A total of 77% said they never sent their kids on a school trip and 19% never sent them to extracurricular activities, due to the cost. UAE schools don't usually offer grants, bursaries and scholarships.

Parents struggling with fees are advised to notify the school, which may agree to a payment plan. Banks can advise on a savings scheme or loans; Barclays, for example, offers an Education Loan.

OUTSTANDING SCHOOLS

The Knowledge and Human Development Authority (KHDA) ranks every school as Outstanding, Good, Acceptable or Unacceptable. The schools below were ranked Outstanding, and are shown with highlights from the report. See whichschooladvisor.com for the latest rankings.

Dubai College	Large proportion of leavers enrol in high ranking 'red brick' UK universities
GEMS Jumeirah Primary School	A unique parental engagement programme to boost achievement
GEMS Wellington Int'l School	State-of-the-art facilities and a reputation for academic excellence
Jumeirah College	Consistently high grades with a strong emphasis on personal development
JESS Jumeirah	Ranked Outstanding three years in a row. Hugely popular with parents
Kings' Dubai	Renowned for engaging curriculum and positive attitudes of students
Dubai English Speaking College	Exceptional achievement in core subjects, teaching standards and parent support
Horizon School	High quality student-staff relationships promote personal development
JESS Arabian Ranches	Over 99% of students achieved 5 grades A* to C at GCSE in 2013
Dubai American Academy	Renowned for high IB diploma pass rate and modern facilities
Dubai Modern High School	Praised for outstanding leadership of staff and high attainment
The Indian High School	Exceptional attainment in core subjects and notable students' work ethic

EDUCATION
PRIMARY & SECONDARY SCHOOLS

School Transport

If you are not able to do the school run every day, you can make use of the bus services offered by most schools. The advantages are that you avoid having to deal with heavy traffic, and strict regulations mean that bus safety standards are high.

The disadvantages are that it can be very expensive – you pay the same fees regardless of how close you live to the school – and if your child is one of the first to be picked up, it will mean an early start and a long journey while the bus collects the other kids.

The very identifiable bright yellow school buses are heavily regulated: bus drivers must have valid school bus driver permits, a supervisor must accompany pupils below the age of 11, and drivers are not permitted to exceed a speed of 80km/h.

Drive Safe
School Transport Services LLC (STS) is used by over 40 schools in the UAE. You can visit schooltransportservices.com to register your child and make online payments; you can also see the existing routes and pick-up times.

PRIMARY & SECONDARY SCHOOLS

Having selected a school, you will need to register your child on the waiting list (there's usually a Dhs.500 non-refundable fee). If places are available, your child will be assessed and then either offered a place or placed on a waiting list. Assessments are usually held at the child's nursery or at the school, and tend to just 'observe' the child at play. It's a stressful time for parents, especially as schools' registration procedures happen at different times of the year; apply to three or four schools and you are more than likely to get a place. Your chances increase with siblings, who get priority, or if your child is in an affiliated nursery.

School Regulator

Education standards in private schools are high. The Knowledge and Human Development Authority (KHDA) has been set up to ensure that education in Dubai is delivered consistently and to an acceptable standard. All schools have to apply to the KHDA if they want to increase their fees; these can be upped annually based on each school's ranking. Outstanding schools are allowed an increase of up to 6%, schools assessed as good get up to 4.5%, and those in the acceptable and unsatisfactory category can ask for a 3% increase.

School Uniforms

Most private schools here in Dubai will insist on students wearing the official school uniform. Each school will use a particular uniform supply shop, and this will be the only place where you can buy official school items. Before heading out and spending a fortune on uniforms, check with the school and with other parents which items are compulsory and which are not: a sturdy pair of black school shoes and a pair of non-marking trainers are usually essential items, whereas a branded school bag is often not.

Uniforms bought from the official suppliers are usually priced very highly, and can often be of poor quality, so if your school offers any flexibility on the uniform issue (such as your child wearing a plain white collared shirt as opposed to a white shirt with the school badge on the pocket), you may want to take it. A final word on uniforms: if you leave your uniform shopping until the last few days before the beginning of term, chances are you'll get to the uniform shop to find several items have sold out. This is definitely one task where it pays to shop in advance. Find out from your school who its uniform supplier is, and stock up on as early as possible.

School Lunches

Many private schools in Dubai do not offer school meals, so children have to bring a packed lunch. This is worth bearing in mind if you know you won't have time to prepare packed lunches every morning when you're busy getting your children ready for school and yourself ready for work.

Holiday Calendar

Be prepared to accept that there are a lot of school holidays here in Dubai. The summer holidays stretch for 10 long weeks over the hottest months of July and August, when many kids return to their home countries for extended holidays, or attend summer camps. There are also holidays in April and December.

Schools close for at least a week twice a year for Eid Al Fitr and Eid Al Adha, and will most likely also open for reduced hours during the month of Ramadan. If one of you is a stay-at-home parent, then this poses few problems in terms of childcare; however, if both of you work, you will need to make sure that you have alternative arrangements for childcare during school holidays and random days off.

Schools which follow an Indian or Pakistani curriculum follow a different academic calendar, with the term starting in April and ending in March the following year. As a result, they follow different schedules for school exams and holidays too.

EDUCATION
PRIMARY & SECONDARY SCHOOLS

School Transfers

If you are transferring within Dubai, you will need a transfer certificate. If you are leaving Dubai, you may need a 'student leaving certificate' to prove the years of study in school in Dubai. In both cases, the school supply these and verify them through the KHDA.

Other Options

Boarding Schools

Repton School Dubai was the first boarding school to open in Dubai, and has boarding facilities for up to 100 boys and 20 girls. Abu Dhabi is set to have its first boarding school when Cranleigh Abu Dhabi opens on Saadiyat Island in 2014. Cranleigh Abu Dhabi will cater for over 1,600 boys and girls aged three to 18, on what will be the UAE's largest school campus. Most will be day students. Boarding fees for Cranleigh Abu Dhabi have not been released but Repton Dubai charges up to Dhs.161,000 per year.

Some parents opt to send their children abroad – usually back to their home country – for a boarding school education. There are various boarding school agents in the UAE who provide impartial advice and guidance on selecting a school, such as Sue Anderson Consultants (andersoneducation.co.uk). For the past nine years the UK Boarding School Exhibition Dubai has also been held in the city, with over 30 UK schools represented at the last event. Entrance is free, yet it can be an invaluable resource in getting a feel for the school you're interested in sending your child to.

Home Schooling

One of the main reasons for home schooling in the UAE is to avoid the hefty private school fees. There are very few private schools in Dubai that offer home schooling curriculums. K12 in Knowledge Village offers some online courses (visit k12.com/int/arabian_gulf//index.html). The Ministry of Education offers home schooling for all nationalities but the curriculum is only available in Arabic.

Schools in your home country will be able to provide you with the curriculum, materials and online testing, for a fee. Many expats with multiple children find that whilst nurseries tend to be more affordable than in their home countries, when it comes to schooling it makes more financial sense to return home, where free public education is often available.

American Curriculum

A popular curriculum, the American curriculum is an option that is well-suited to parents who are thinking of moving Stateside before their children graduate.

Students aged four start in KG1 and progress through to Grade 12 when, aged 17, they take their High School Diploma exams. There is some variation in US curriculums and students might be tested in a range of methods from IQ assessments to exams based on understanding and recollection. Usually private schools in Dubai will choose the curriculum of one of the larger accreditation bodies in the US, such as the New England Association of Schools and Colleges or the Middle States Association of Colleges and Schools. For younger children, there is a greater emphasis on learning through play, with a gradual move to more formal education as they get older.

As well as developing students' core and essential skills, the American system has a well-regarded holistic approach to learning, cultivating a capacity for critical thinking and creativity as well as promoting students' characters, their skills as young leaders, and their sense of civic responsibility.

Al Mizhar American Academy
Nr Arabian Centre Al Mizhar 1 **04 288 7250**
americanacademy.ae
Map **2 R12**

Located in Mizhar and offering an American curriculum, Al Mizhar American Academy has a co-educational early years programme for dual language learners leading to an all-girls school. It is well equipped for sporting activities including swimming and basketball. There are also computer labs, interactive whiteboards, art and music studios, science labs, and a mini auditorium. **Age:** 3 to 18 years (Pre-KG to Year 12). **Fees:** Dhs.35,530- 55,385. **Transport:** Bus. **KHDA ranking:** Good.

Raffles International School

EDUCATION
PRIMARY & SECONDARY SCHOOLS

American International School
Nr Lulu Hypermarket Al Qusais 1 **04 298 8666**
aisch.net
Map **2 R7** Metro **Stadium**
Established almost a decade ago, AISCH follows a curriculum that leads to both US and UAE High School Diplomas, making this school popular with Americans, Canadians and Emiratis. **Age:** 3 to 18 (KG1 to Grade 12). **Fees:** Available on request. **Transport:** Bus. **KHDA ranking:** Acceptable.

American School Of Dubai
Nr Saudi German Hospital Al Barsha 1 **04 395 0005**
asdubai.org
Map **1 P6** Metro **Dubai Internet City**
The school's 23-acre site includes two multipurpose gyms, a 700-seat performing arts theatre, an indoor climbing wall and two 25m swimming pools. After Grade 6 there is a 1:1 laptop programme. **Age:** 4 to 18 years (K1 to Grade 12). **Fees:** Dhs.52,730-82,070. **Transport:** Bus **KHDA ranking:** Good.

Bradenton Preparatory Academy
Sports City, Al Hebiah 4 **04 449 3600**
bradentonprepdubai.com
Map **1 M12**
The curriculum is based on the American Common Core standards, with venues for art, music, drama, laboratory sciences, as well as a library and full-sized gym. The academy has small class sizes. On graduating students receive the American High School Diploma. **Age:** 3 to 18 (KG to Grade 12). **Fees:** Dhs.30,000-70,790. **Transport:** NA. **KHDA ranking:** Acceptable.

Collegiate American School
34th Street Umm Suqeim 2 **04 427 1400**
casdubai.com
Map **1 U5** Metro **Noor Bank**
This American school centres on a technology-enabled learning environment that focuses on digital learning. Facilities include a library, art rooms, dance studio, music rooms, swimming pools and sports hall. **Age:** 3 to 15 years (Pre-KG to Grade 9). **Fees:** Dhs.36,000-65,000. **Transport:** Bus. **KHDA ranking:** Acceptable.

Dubai American Academy
Nr Lulu Hypermarket Al Barsha 1 **04 347 9222**
gemsaa-dubai.com
Map **1 R7** Metro **Mall of the Emirates**
DAA offers the International Baccalaureate Diploma and an enriched American curriculum; there is also an extensive after-school programme. Facilities include computer and science labs, a gymnasium, library, pool, athletics track and an auditorium. **Age:** 4 to 18 years (KG1 to Grade 12). **Fees:** Dhs.18,688-69,186. **Transport:** Bus. **KHDA ranking:** Outstanding.

DWC High School > *p.235*
Al Nahda 2 **04 208 9700**
dwchighschool.hct.ac.ae
Map **2 S7** Metro **Al Nahda**
Located on the campus of the HCT Dubai Women's College, one of the major education institutions for young UAE women. The school shares facilities with the college, which includes a well-stocked library, cutting-edge technology, state-of-the-art fitness centre, swimming pool and a cafeteria – all in a landscaped setting. Uniquely, the school offers a dual curriculum, which allows its students to follow the UAE Ministry of Education syllabus in parallel with a US syllabus through a hybrid learning model. **Age:** 14 to 17 years (Grade 9 to 12). **Fees:** Dhs.50,000 approx. **Transport:** Bus. **KHDA ranking:** Not available.

International School Of Arts & Sciences
Al Warqa'a 1 **04 280 0185**
isas.sch.ae
Map **2 M13** Metro **Rashidiya**
ISAS follows an American, English-speaking curriculum with additional subjects such as Arabic and Islamic Studies set according to UAE Ministry of Education guidelines. It boasts outstanding facilities including four modern science laboratories, two computer labs, a visual arts centre, a library and a medical clinic staffed by a full-time doctor and nurse. There's also an indoor swimming pool and three indoor playgrounds. **Age:** 3 to 18 years. **Fees:** Dhs.26,000-48,900. **Transport:** Bus. **KHDA ranking:** Acceptable.

Universal American School Dubai
Nr Al Badia Residence Al Badia, Al Kheeran **04 232 5222**
uasdubai.ae
Map **2 M10** Metro **Emirates**
UASD follows an American curriculum culminating with the American High School Diploma. The campus has a gymnasium, Olympic-size track and football field, as well as computer and science labs, libraries and a swimming pool. **Age:** 4 to 18 years old (Pre-KG to Grade 12). **Fees:** Dhs.28,650-64,740. **Transport:** Bus. **KHDA ranking:** Good.

English National Curriculum

Taught by many private schools in Dubai and in British schools around the world, the English National Curriculum or British Curriculum is popular with many nationalities. It encourages children to reach educational milestones each year and standardised tests assess students, who are assigned targets suited to their academic performance.

The Early Years Foundation Stage (EYFS, Foundation Stages 1 and 2) for children aged three to five, is

DWC HIGH SCHOOL
كلية دبي الثانوية للطالبات
The Knowledge to Compete

Empower yourself.
Empower your community.

DWC High School is an innovative new private high school located on the campus of Dubai Women's College. Combining onsite instruction with online learning from K12, America's leader in online learning, DWC High School will provide its students with the high quality education and independent organization skills needed to succeed in a modern and changing global society.

On the attractive campus of the Dubai Women's College which has established itself over the past 20+ years as one of the major education institutions for young UAE women, the school shares facilities which are second to none. These include a world class library, cutting edge technology and a state-of-the-art fitness centre and swimming pool all in an inspiring landscaped setting.

For information about enrollment in our international school for girls, grades 9-12, please call 042089700.

EDUCATION
PRIMARY & SECONDARY SCHOOLS

focused on developing the social and academic skills of young children through the use of milestones and communication with parents, with an emphasis on play as well. Students then move on to the Key Stages 1 to 4, until they complete their GCSEs, aged 16 and A-Levels, aged 18.

Cambridge International School Dubai
Nr American College Of Dubai Al Garhoud
04 282 4646
gemscis-dubai.com
Map **2 M8** Metro **GGICO**
This school follows the English National Curriculum and aims to encourage creativity and critical thinking alongside academic rigour. Set in a spacious campus, the school is divided into two sections: Primary and Secondary. There's a variety of activities and good facilities. **Age:** 4 to 18 (FS1 to Year 13).
Fees: Dhs.16,000-25,000 approx. **Transport:** Bus.
KHDA ranking: Good.

City School International
Nadd Al Hamar **04 289 9722**
tcs-uae.com
Map **2 L12** Metro **Rashidiya**
A Pakistan-based organisation with sister schools in Pakistan, Saudi Arabia, Malaysia, Bangladesh and the Philippines, the school follows a UK-based curriculum leading to IGCSE exams in Grade 11. A fairly limited range of subjects is offered – in addition to compulsory ones like English, Maths and ICT, students also have to choose one of three pairs: chemistry/accounting, physics/economics and biology/business. **Age:** 4 to 17 years. **Fees:** Dhs.12,349-21,892.
Transport: Bus. **KHDA ranking:** Acceptable.

Deira Private School
Nr Terminal 2 Al Twar 3 **04 264 1595**
deps-sch.ae
Map **2 Q11** Metro **Rashidiya**
Deira Private School is a combined first and middle school that follows a British curriculum, the Cambridge International Primary Programme. It produces strong results in science with solid attainment in English and maths, and offers a good range of educational trips and extra-curricular activities including football, cricket and even yoga. There is good support for students with special educational needs. **Age:** 3 to 11 years. **Fees:** Dhs.19,500-30,475. **Transport:** Bus. **KHDA ranking:** Acceptable.

Dubai British School
Springs 3 Emirates Living, Al Thanyah 4 **04 361 9361**
dubaibritishschool.ae
Map **1 K8** Metro **Jumeirah Lakes Towers**
Offering high quality facilities and set in a convenient location for residents in the Emirates Living area, DBS follows the English National Curriculum. Modern facilities include a swimming pool, gymnasium and library. **Age:** 3 to 18 years old (FS1 to Year 13). **Fees:** Dhs.38,843-58,265. **Transport:** Bus.
KHDA ranking: Good.

Dubai College
Off Al Sufouh Rd Al Sufouh 2 **04 399 9111**
dubaicollege.org
Map **1 P5** Metro **Dubai Internet City**
Following the English National Curriculum, the facilities at Dubai College include a science block with 13 laboratories, and a music centre with a recording studio. Sporting activities range from athletics, rugby, and football to netball, tennis and swimming. **Age:** 11 to 18 (Year 7 to 13). **Fees:** Dhs.67,773. **Transport:** Bus.
KHDA ranking: Outstanding.

Dubai English Speaking College
Nr Al Ghurair University Academic City,
Al Rowaiyah 2 **04 360 4866**
descdubai.com
This English curriculum secondary school opened in 2005. It has been praised for the quality of teaching, student behaviour and partnerships with parents. There's a dedication to sport with top notch facilities (a 25m pool, several pitches and double sports hall). The school also offers rugby, football, netball, basketball, badminton and volleyball. **Age:** 11 to 18 (Year 7 to 13). **Fees:** Dhs.66,061-71,003. **Transport:** Bus. **KHDA ranking:** Outstanding.

Dubai English Speaking School
Nr St Mary's Catholic Church Umm Hurair 2
04 337 1457
dessdubai.com
Map **2 L7** Metro **Oud Metha**
DESS is a highly respected school offering the English National Curriculum. It's renowned for the positive attitudes of students and consistently high attainment in core subjects. Facilities and activities include IT labs, music, swimming, dance and a library, and the school is successful at sport. **Age:** 3 to 11 (FS1 to Year 6). **Fees:** Dhs.37,452. **Transport:** Bus. **KHDA ranking:** Good.

Dubai GEMS Private School
Nr Iranian Club Oud Metha **04 337 6661**
dubaigem.org
Map **2 L7** Metro **Oud Metha**
This established school has a reputation for strong attainment in English, maths and science. It follows the British curriculum, leading to IGCSE exams in Grade 11, AS Levels in Grade 12 and A-Levels in Grade 13. There's a range of facilities, including computer rooms, art rooms, and a sports centre. **Age:** 3 to 18 years. **Fees:** Dhs.10,000-20,366. **Transport:** Bus.
KHDA ranking: Good.

Little people, big responsibility

Leaving home is difficult for everyone, but we give extra help to the youngest relocators.

Crown service offerings include:
- International & Domestic Shipments
- Storage, Airfreight
- Transit Insurance
- Immigration & Legalization
- Home Search
- School Search

Tel: +971 4 230 5300
dubai@crownrelo.com

Go knowing
www.crownrelo.com/uae

CROWN RELOCATIONS

EDUCATION
PRIMARY & SECONDARY SCHOOLS

Foremarke
Dubiotech Al Barsha South 3 **04 818 8600**
foremarkedubai.org
Map **1 R10**
Foremarke is a co-educational junior school which opened in September 2013. It is partnered with Foremarke Hall in the UK and follows the English National Curriculum. Years 3 to 5 start September 2014. **Age:** FS1 to Year 5. **Fees:** Dhs.65,000-85,000. **Transport:** NA. **KHDA ranking:** NA.

GEMS Jumeirah Primary School
Nr Park N Shop Al Safa 1 **04 394 3500**
jumeirahprimaryschool.com
Map **2 C5** Metro **Noor Bank**
GEMS Jumeirah Primary School teaches the National Curriculum for England. The school has excellent facilities, including a library and Discovery Centre and 25m swimming pool. The whole campus is bright, spacious and comfortable. **Age:** 3 to 11 (FS1 to Year 6). **Fees:** Dhs.32,775-41,315. **Transport:** Bus. **KHDA ranking:** Outstanding.

GEMS Royal Dubai School
Nr Arabian Centre Al Mizhar 1 **04 288 6499**
royaldubaischool.com
Map **2 S13**
GEMS Royal Dubai School offers high quality education in line with the English National Curriculum. The school employs British-trained, experienced teachers and the spacious building provides cutting-edge facilities. **Age:** 3 to 11 (FS1 to Year 6). **Fees:** Dhs.31,438-39,639. **Transport:** Bus. **KHDA ranking:** Good.

GEMS Wellington Academy
Silicon Oasis Nadd Hessa **04 342 4040**
gemswellingtonacademy-dso.com
Metro **Rashidiya**
GEMS Wellington Academy – Silicon Oasis is based on the English National Curriculum, and educates children from Foundation Stage to Sixth Form. Students benefit from excellent, purpose-built facilities at this well-designed campus, including a swimming pool and visual arts suite. **Age:** 3 to 18 (FS1 to Year 13). **Fees:** Dhs.31,000-70,000. **Transport:** Bus. **KHDA ranking:** Good.

GEMS New Millennium School Al Khail
Hadaeq Sheikh Mohammed Bin Rashid **04 339 6533**
gemsnewmillenniumschool-alkhail.com
Map **1 U9** Metro **Noor Bank**
This school takes on students from kindergarten to Year 7, and there are plans to expand to Year 12 in the future. The English National Curriculum is followed, and there are state-of-the-art facilities including music rooms, sports fields, libraries and a pool. **Age:** 3-12. **Fees:** 20,000-27,000. **Transport:** Bus. **KHDA ranking**: NA.

GEMS Wellington International School
Shk Zayed Rd Al Sufouh 1 **04 348 4999**
wellingtoninternationalschool.com
Map **1 Q5** Metro **Sharaf DG**
Following the English National Curriculum, and the International Baccalaureate programme in Years 12 and 13, students benefit from access to digital editing suites, and a television studio and radio station – a first for UAE schools. Other premium facilities include an indoor swimming pool, state-of-the-art gym and three science laboratories. **Age:** 3 to 18 (FS1 to Year 13). **Fees:** Dhs.35,244-76,675. **Transport:** Bus. **KHDA ranking:** Outstanding.

GEMS Wellington Primary School
Nr Shangri-la Al Satwa **04 343 3266**
gemswps.com
Map **2 G5** Metro **Financial Centre**
The curriculum at GEMS WPS complies with the National Curriculum in England. It has well-equipped music, art and IT departments, as well as a library, gymnasium, shaded play areas and two swimming pools. **Age:** 3 to 11 (FS1 to Year 6). **Fees:** Dhs.36,063-45,458. **Transport:** Bus. **KHDA ranking:** Good.

GEMS Winchester School Dubai
Nr American Hospital Oud Metha **04 337 4112**
gemswinchesterschool-dubai.com
Map **2 L7** Metro **Oud Metha**
One of the most recent additions to the GEMS network of international schools. The school follows the Early Years Foundation Stage set by the English National Curriculum. Years 10-13 are set to open in 2014. **Age:** 3 to 14 (FS1 to Year 9). **Fees:** Dhs.9,377-14,846. **Transport:** Bus. **KHDA ranking:** Acceptable.

Horizon School
Nr Safa Park Al Wasl **04 342 2891**
horizonschooldubai.com
Map **2 D5** Metro **Business Bay**
Horizon is based in a large complex complete with top-class facilities, offering the British curriculum to primary students. Facilities include a fantastic music room, library and outdoor swimming pool. **Age:** 3 to 11 (FS1 to Year 6). **Fees:** Available on request. **Transport:** Bus. **KHDA ranking:** Outstanding.

Jebel Ali Primary School
Jabal Ali Village, Jabal Ali 1 **04 884 6485**
jebelalischool.org
Map **1 F6** Metro **Ibn Battuta**
JAPS teaches the English National Curriculum as well as offering an excellent range of after-school activities, including football, netball, golf, gymnastics, swimming, squash, drama, dance, cooking, and music. **Age:** 4 to 11 (Reception to Year 6). **Fees:** Dhs.36,297. **Transport:** Bus. **KHDA ranking:** Good.

Mackenzie Art

ART · MURALS · TROMPE L'OEIL · DECORATION

ENHANCE YOUR ENVIRONMENT

Manhattan Mural – Ramada Hotel, Doha

Dome Mural in Spa, Dubai

Exterior Wall garden mural

Abstract Painting

Trompe L'Oeil Mural Design

Mural Design

Gold Mural – Prayer Room

Gold Leaf Panel

Trompe L'Oeil Arches – Palace, Abu Dhabi

Trompe L'Oeil Fountain

"From small to tall – we paint it all!"
Interior, exterior, walls and canvases – we provide personalised paintings for your homes, offices and projects

www.mackenzieart.com

EDUCATION
PRIMARY & SECONDARY SCHOOLS

Jumeirah College
Nr Park N Shop Al Safa 1 **04 395 5524**
gemsjc.com
Map **2 C5** Metro **Noor Bank**
Jumeirah College uses the English National Curriculum. The student body is multicultural with members from more than 59 countries represented, and the school has a reputation for high academic standards. **Age:** 11 to 18 (Year 7 to 13). **Fees:** Dhs.58,542-73,177. **Transport:** Bus. **KHDA ranking:** Outstanding.

Jumeirah English Speaking School
16th Street Al Safa 1 **04 394 5515**
jess.sch.ae
Map **2 C5** Metro **Noor Bank**
JESS is one of the most in-demand British schools in Dubai, with a long waiting list. The campus has a gymnasium, music rooms, playing areas, a football pitch and a swimming pool. **Age:** 3 to 11 (FS1 to Year 6). **Fees:** Dhs.32,043-40,164. **KHDA ranking:** Outstanding.

Jumeirah English Speaking School
Arabian Ranches, Wadi Al Safa 6 **04 361 9019**
jess.sch.ae
Map **1 Q13**
This second JESS school offers the English National Curriculum, with facilities including a swimming pool, tennis and netball courts. The majority of the pupils live within the Arabian Ranches complex, making it a close-knit community. **Age:** 3 to 11 (FS1 to Year 6). **Fees:** Dhs.32,043-40,164. **Transport:** Bus. **KHDA ranking:** Outstanding.

Kings' School Dubai
Umm Suqeim 3 **04 348 3939**
kingsdubai.com
Map **1 S5** Metro **First Gulf Bank**
Also known simply as Kings' Dubai, this popular school teaches the English National Curriculum through an innovative, creative approach. It is the only school to achieve the Outstanding ranking five years in a row. Facilities include a swimming pool and sports fields. **Age:** 3 to 11 years (FS1 to Year 6). **Fees:** Dhs.33,441-50,892. **Transport:** NA. **KHDA ranking:** Outstanding.

Kings' School Nad Al Sheba
Nr Repton School Nadd Al Shiba 3 **04 348 3939**
kingsdubai.com
Map **2 H13**
This new project from the renowned Kings' School is set to open in September 2014, along with another school, Kings' School Al Barsha. Both will offer classes from Foundation stage to Year 9. Parents are advised to apply early, as waiting lists for the original Kings' School in Umm Suqeim are long. **KHDA ranking:** NA.

Nord Anglia International School Dubai > p.241
Off Hessa St Al Barsha South 2 **04 361 4330**
nainternationalschool.ae
Map **1 P10** Metro **Dubai Internet City**
Founded in 1972, Nord Anglia Education is a family of 27 international schools providing a premium education to more than 16,000 students around the world. The new Dubai school will open in September 2014 offering both British and IB curriculum. **Age:** 3 to 13 years (up to Year 8). **Fees:** Dhs.49,400-75,000. **Transport:** Bus. **KHDA ranking:** NA.

Oasis School
Street 8B Al Safa 1 **04 388 1388**
oasisschool.ae
Map **2 C5** Metro **Noor Bank**
The Oasis School offers the English National Curriculum with a full inclusion approach for special needs students. Students can obtain either their AS and A-Levels or vocational qualifications such as Edexcel and BTEC. **Age:** 3 to 16 years. **Fees:** Dhs.35,244--65,874. **Transport:** Not in 2014. **KHDA ranking:** NA.

Pristine Private School
Nr Emarat Petrol Station Al Nahda 2 **04 267 4299**
pristineschool.com
Map **2 S7** Metro **Stadium**
One of the most affordable Dubai schools with the 'Good' KHDA ranking. It follows the National Curriculum for England and Wales, as well as the Ministry of Education Framework for Islamic Education and Arabic. Support for students with special educational needs is good, and facilities include art studios, computer labs, a swimming pool and a grand auditorium. **Age:** 3 to 18 years. **Fees:** Dhs.8,500-16,000. **Transport:** Bus. **KHDA ranking:** Good.

Raffles International School
21st Street Umm Suqeim 3 **04 427 1200**
rafflesis.com
Map **1 S5** Metro **First Gulf Bank**
The South Campus follows the Cambridge Curriculum at primary and secondary level, and offers the Montessori programme at preschool. There is a theatre, art rooms, dance studio, swimming pools, tennis courts and sports hall. **Age:** 4 to 12 years (KG1 to Grade 5). **Fees:** Dhs.26,125-61,446. **Transport:** Bus. **KHDA ranking:** Outstanding.

Regent International School
The Greens The Views, Al Thanyah 3 **04 360 8830**
risdubai.com
Map **1 N6** Metro **Dubai Internet City**
Regent International School offers the English National Curriculum. Facilities include state-of-the-

NORD ANGLIA INTERNATIONAL SCHOOL DUBAI
A NORD ANGLIA EDUCATION SCHOOL

OPENING SEPTEMBER 2014

THE FINEST BRITISH EDUCATION
British Curriculum and IB Diploma, Ages 3+

+971 (0)4 361 4330
sally.embley@nordanglia.com
nainternationalschool.ae

School opening and operations are subject to the completion of the building and final approval from KHDA.

EDUCATION
PRIMARY & SECONDARY SCHOOLS

art technology, multimedia zones, library, computer, science and language labs, as well as a football pitch, playing fields, gymnasium and a swimming pool. **Age:** 3 to 18 years (FS to Year 13). **Fees:** Dhs.34,172-78,375. **Transport:** Bus. **KHDA ranking:** Good.

Repton School
Nr ENOC Petrol Station Nadd Al Shiba 3 **04 426 9393**
reptondubai.org
Map **2 H3**
This prestigious school offers the English National Curriculum and has premium educational and sporting facilities on its vast campus, including sports fields, a performing arts centre, music room and library. Repton is also the first school in Dubai to offer boarding for students from 11. **Age:** 3 to 18 years (Nursery to Year 13). **Fees:** Dhs.47,599-95,199. **Transport:** Bus. **KHDA ranking:** Good.

Safa School
Meydan Rd Al Qouz 1 **04 388 4300**
safaschooldubai.com
Map **2 D7** Metro **Business Bay**
Also known as Al Safa Private School, this Al Qouz establishment follows a British curriculum and its largest demographic comes from the UK. It has been recognised for the quality of its teaching and student support, as well as consistent attainment in core subjects. The school also boasts a wide range of modern facilities and extra-curricular activities including badminton, checkers and music composition. **Age:** 3 to 11 years. **Fees:** Dhs.20,942-45,847. **Transport:** Bus **KHDA ranking:** Good.

Sheffield Private School
Doha Rd Al Nahda 2 **04 267 8444**
sheffield-school.com
Map **2 T8** Metro **Dubai Airport Freezone**
Sheffield Private School follows the English National Curriculum. Its campus facilities include music and art studios, an ICT lab, covered play areas and swimming pools. **Age:** 3 to 18 years (FS1 to Year 13). **Fees:** Dhs.19,117-36,050. **Transport:** Bus. **KHDA ranking:** Acceptable.

St Mary's Catholic High School
Nr Rashid Hospital Umm Hurair 2 **04 337 0252**
stmarysdubai.com
Map **2 L6** Metro **Oud Metha**
St. Mary's retains the discipline of a convent education but welcomes all students of all religions. The school teaches the English National Curriculum and offers sports activities alongside drama, music, debating class, cookery and chess. **Age:** 5 to 19 (KG to Grade 12). **Fees:** Dhs.6,460-14,920. **Transport:** Bus. **KHDA ranking:** Good.

Star International School
Nr New Airport Terminal, Street 7B Al Twar 2 **04 263 8999**
starschoolaltwar.com
Map **2 R9** Metro **Al Qusais**
This popular school follows the English National Curriculum. With a 700-seat auditorium, the school aims to be an important location for the promotion and teaching of arts and culture in the community. **Age:** 4 to 15 years (FS1 to Year 9). **Fees:** Dhs.17,510-34,640. **Transport:** Bus. **KHDA ranking:** Acceptable.

Star International School Mirdif
Nr Uptown Mirdiff Mirdif **04 288 4644**
starschoolmirdif.com
Map **2 Q13** Metro **Rashidiya**
This school offers the English National Curriculum at primary level and will phase in secondary school levels over the next few years. Focussed on promoting arts and culture in the community. **Age:** 3 to 11 years (FS1 to Year 6). **Fees:** Dhs.29,940-45,250. **Transport:** Bus. **KHDA ranking:** Acceptable.

Star International School Umm Sheif
9A Street Umm Al Sheif **04 348 3314**
starschoolummsheif.com
Map **1 S6** Metro **First Gulf Bank**
One of three Star International schools in Dubai teaching the Early Years Foundation Stage and the National Curriculum of England, with great facilities including splash pools, a large indoor play area, an ICT suite with programmable robots, and sports hall. **Age:** 3 to 15 years (F1 to Year 9). **Fees:** Dhs.29,600-51,300. **Transport:** Bus. **KHDA ranking:** Good.

Dubai International Academic City

EDUCATION
PRIMARY & SECONDARY SCHOOLS

Victory Heights Primary School
Victory Heights Sports City, Al Hebiah 4 **04 423 1100**
vhprimary.com
Map **1 M11**
At this relatively new primary school, the curriculum is based on the English National Curriculum, but expands upon it to recognise Dubai's diverse population. There's a strong emphasis on personal and social, as well as academic, development. Modern facilities including a library, art studio, music room and science lab. **Age:** 3 to 11. **Fees:** 13,200-18,000. **Transport:** Bus. **KHDA ranking:** NA.

Westminster School
Al Ghusais School Zone Al Qusais 1 **04 298 8333**
gemsws-ghusais.com
Map **2 R7** Metro **Al Nahda**
The spacious premises provide separate facilities for boys and girls from Year 5 onwards and, with students from over 72 nationalities, the school has a rich, multicultural environment. **Age:** 3 to 18 (FS1 to Year 13). **Fees:** Dhs.5,557-10,484. **Transport:** Bus. **KHDA ranking:** Acceptable.

Winchester School
The Gardens, Jabal Ali 1 **04 882 0444**
thewinchesterschool.com
Map **1 G6** Metro **Ibn Battuta**
Winchester School provides a high quality, relatively affordable education to students of all nationalities, following the English National Curriculum. It has a multipurpose auditorium for indoor games, when students aren't developing their musical and theatrical talents, as well as science laboratories, arts and crafts rooms and multiple sports fields. **Age:** 3 to 18 years (FS1 to Year 13). **Fees:** Dhs.10,816-24,127. **Transport:** Bus. **KHDA ranking:** Good.

International Baccalaureate Programme

A third option is the International Baccalaureate, also known as the IB curriculum, which is the best choice for parents who don't know where they will be in the next few years. It is compatible internationally, so your child should be able to fit into any school around the world. The programmes, aimed at students aged three to 19, aim to develop the intellectual, personal, emotional and social skills of children. They focus on a range of subjects including literature, arts, humanities, sciences and mathematics, with the choice to take certain subjects as specialist options. The IB Primary Years Programme is designed for students aged three to 12, and the IB Middle Years Programme, aimed at students aged 11 to 16, then prepares these final year students for the IB Diploma.

Dar Al Marefa Private School
58C Street Mirdif **04 288 5782**
daralmarefa.ae
Map **2 R13** Metro **Rashidiya**
Dar Al Marefa Private School offers a bilingual education in Arabic and English, with a strong emphasis on respecting local culture and values. The curriculum includes all major areas of study such as languages, maths, science, technology and the arts. There's a range of facilities including sports fields, outdoor playgrounds, a library and clinic. **Age:** Grade KG to 10. **Fees:** 25,750.00-50,000.00. **Transport:** Bus. **KHDA ranking:** Acceptable.

Deira International School
Nr Al Badia Residence Al Badia, Al Kheeran **04 232 5552**
disdubai.ae
Map **2 M11** Metro **Rashidiya**
DIS offers GCSE/IGCSE, A-Levels and the International Baccalaureate programme. Facilities within the school include a gymnasium, a full-sized track and football field, music rooms, computer and science labs, libraries, a large auditorium and a swimming pool. **Age:** 3 to 18 (EY1 to Year 13/IB2). **Fees:** Dhs.34,765-70,050. **Transport:** Bus. **KHDA ranking:** Good.

IGCSE

The International General Certificate of Secondary Education (IGCSE), which is recognised as being equivalent to the English system of GCSEs. It prepares students for further academic study, including progression to AS Level and A Level, and the IB Diploma Programme, and is taught at both several schools in Dubai.

Delhi Private School Academy
Dubai Intl Academic City Al Rowaiyah 2 **04 326 5556**
dpsacademy.ae
This school follows the Indian Curriculum laid down by the Central Board of Secondary Education (CBSE), with the aim being to create a lifelong love of learning. Plenty of modern facilities include a well-equipped sports field, vibrant learning rooms, computer labs and science labs. **Age:** 3-18. **Fees:** Dhs.8,460-11,850. **Transport:** Bus. **KHDA ranking:** Good

Dubai International Academy
Nr Jebel Ali Racecourse Emirates Living, Al Thanyah 4 **04 368 4111**
diadubai.com
Map **1 M7** Metro **Dubai Marina**
DIA delivers the full IB curriculum, from primary to secondary. The school has more than 80 classrooms, as well as music, art, and drama rooms, science and

EDUCATION
PRIMARY & SECONDARY SCHOOLS

computer labs, libraries, swimming pools, playing fields, basketball and tennis courts. **Age:** 3 to 18 years (KG1 to Year 13). **Fees:** Dhs.33,618-59,565. **Transport:** Bus. **KHDA ranking:** Good.

Dubai Modern High School
Nr ENOC Petrol Station Nadd Al Shiba 3 **04 326 3339**
gemsmhs.com
Map **2 H3**
Dubai Modern High School teaches the Indian School Certificate Examinations and the IB syllabus. The school teaches academics in the morning, then Activities for Curriculum Enrichment (ACE), which includes a supervised study session with clubs and games. **Age:** 2 to 18 years (Pre-KG to Grade 12). **Fees:** Dhs.26,780-42,050. **Transport:** Bus. **KHDA ranking:** Outstanding.

Emirates International School – Jumeirah
Al Thanya Rd Umm Al Sheif **04 348 9804**
eischools.ae
Map **1 T6** Metro **First Gulf Bank**
EIS-Jumeirah was the first school in Dubai to be authorised to offer the International Baccalaureate Diploma Programme. It accepts children at primary, middle school and senior school levels and runs an alumni programme for graduates. **Age:** 4 to 18 years (KG2 to Grade 13). **Fees:** Dhs.30,140-63,870. **Transport:** Bus. **KHDA ranking:** Good.

Emirates International School – Meadows
Meadows Drive Emirates Living, Al Thanyah 4 **04 362 9009**
eischools.ae
Map **1 K6** Metro **Jumeirah Lakes Towers**
The Meadows campus of EIS offers the International Baccalaureate curriculum. The school facilities include large classrooms, computer and science labs, a library and a theatre, alongside a free after-school activity programme offering sporting, artistic, cultural and social activities. **Age:** 3 to 18 years (KG1 to Grade 13). **Fees:** Dhs.23,045-68,345. **Transport:** Bus. **KHDA ranking:** Good.

GEMS International School Al Khail
Al Khail Rd Mohammed Bin Rashid Garden, Hadaeq Sheikh Mohammed Bin Rashid **04 60056 7771**
gemsinternationalschool-alkhail.com
Map **1 U9** Metro **Noor Bank**
This establishment's curriculum is currently under development with the intention to follow the International Baccalaureate programmes, making it a good choice for expats who are not sure which country they may move to next. The core subjects are language arts (English and Arabic), maths, science and social studies. **Age:** 4-18 years. **Fees:** Dhs.46,000-6000. **Transport:** Bus. **KHDA ranking:** NA.

GEMS World Academy Dubai
Al Khail Rd Al Barsha South 1 **04 373 6373**
gemsworldacademy-dubai.com
Map **1 Q9** Metro **Sharaf DG**
The GWA Discovery World is at the heart of this IB school, with computer rooms, a robotics lab, and design and technology studios. There's also a planetarium, rooftop peace garden and music centre. **Age:** 3 to 18 years (Pre-KG to Grade 12). **Fees:** Dhs.55,386-96,140. **Transport:** Bus. **KHDA ranking:** Good.

Greenfield Community School
Green Community Dubai Lagoon, Dubai Investment Park 1 **04 885 6600**
gcschool.ae
Map **1 F12**
Located in Dubai Investments Park just beyond the Green Community, Greenfield Community School teaches the IB curriculum. GCS has excellent facilities and a progressive special needs policy. **Age:** 4 to 18 years (KG1 to Grade 12). **Fees:** Dhs.36,915-67,980. **Transport:** Bus. **KHDA ranking:** Acceptable.

The Indian Academy
Nr Madina Mall Muhaisanah 4 **04 264 6746**
indianacademydubai.com
Map **2 T9** Metro **Al Qusais 1**
Offers the Indian Certificate of Secondary Education. Its focus in on holistic learning, with an emphasis on social, emotional and physical development as well as academic. Facilities include a music room, library and an after school kinder club for foundation stage children. **Age:** 3 to 11 years (KG1-Grade 6). **Fees:** Dhs.10,000-16,000 **Transport:** Bus. **KHDA ranking:** NA.

JSS International School
Al Barsha South 1 **04 325 6886**
jssisdubai.com
Map **1 P9** Metro **Sharaf DG**
This private school in Barsha follows the Indian Central Board of Secondary Education Curriculum. English is the primary language – secondary languages include Arabic, Hindi, French and (from Grade 6) Sanskrit. There's a good selection of extra-curricular activities. **Age:** 4 to 14 years. **Fees:** Dhs. 13,133-24,720. **Transport:** Bus. **KHDA ranking:** Acceptable.

Jumeira Baccalaureate School
53B Street Jumeira 1 **04 344 6931**
jbschool.ae
Map **2 G4** Metro **Financial Centre**
This co-educational school offers the English Early Learning Goals at kindergarten level, the International Primary Curriculum, and the International Baccalaureate Middle Years and Diploma Programmes. **Age:** 3 to 18 years (KG1 to Grade 12). **Fees:** Dhs.50,000-75,000. **Transport:** Bus. **KHDA ranking:** Good.

EDUCATION
PRIMARY & SECONDARY SCHOOLS

Raffles World Academy
7th Street Umm Suqeim 2 **04 427 1300**
rafflesis.com
Map **1 U5** Metro **Noor Bank**
This is an authorised World School for the International Baccalaureate Diploma Programme (IBDP), offering the Primary Years Programme (PYP), the Cambridge Secondary 1(CS1) and the International General Certificate of Secondary Education (IGCSE). **Age:** 4 to 18 (KG1/IB PYP to Grade 12/IB2). **Fees:** Dhs.26,125-73,150. **Transport:** Bus. **KHDA ranking:** Good.

Uptown Primary School
Algeria St Mirdif **04 251 5001**
uptownprimary.ae
Map **2 Q13** Metro **Rashidiya**
Uptown Primary follows the International Baccalaureate programme. Its facilities include a swimming pool, computer labs, art studios, music rooms, play areas and science labs. Students can remain here into the IB's Middle Years Programme. Grade 11-12 are set to open in 2014. **Age:** 3 to 16 (Pre-K to Grade 10). **Fees:** Dhs.34,950-59,950. **Transport:** Bus. **KHDA ranking:** Good.

Special Needs Education

The UAE boasts an excellent private school system for expats; however, it is sometimes more difficult to find quality education for children with special needs. There is increasing awareness, and so the situation does seem to be slowly improving.

If your child has physical or learning difficulties, there are several organisations that can help; the Dubai Dyslexia Support Group, for example, holds regular meetings for families affected by dyslexia. There are also schools that seem to be leading the way in terms of opening doors to children with special needs, while certain other private schools in Dubai will offer places to children with mild dyslexia or Down's syndrome.

Unfortunately, the picture is not so bright for children with more severe learning difficulties or special needs. While in an ideal world it may be desirable for these children to attend 'normal' schools, the truth is that the majority of private schools in the UAE do not have sufficient facilities or support to cope with severe disabilities or to meet the special needs of some children. While this may result in, for example, a child with a physical disability not being able to attend a mainstream school despite not having any cognitive impairment, some parents feel that there is little point pushing the issue.

Organisations such as the British Institute for Learning Development aim to bridge a gap between private schools that may lack adequate facilities and more extreme solutions in the form of centres for children with severe disabilities. Although it focuses more on learning support and sensory therapy than on helping children with physical disabilities, the institute seeks to address children's learning and behavioural problems through occupational therapy and neuro-developmental therapy (Sensory Integration). Students are supported through work with speech therapists, psychologists and specially qualified teachers.

Special needs education is available

Al Noor Training Center For Children With Special Needs
Nr Emirates NBD Al Barsha 1 **04 340 4844**
alnoorspneeds.ae
Map **1 R6** Metro **Mall of the Emirates**
This centre provides therapeutic support, and educational and vocational training to special needs children from three to 18 years of age. The centre is also active in the community with fundraisers, various events such as swimming galas, programmes to help parents learn how best to support their children, and a summer camp.

All 4 Down Syndrome Dubai
050 880 9228
downsyndromedubai.com
This support group is open to families whose lives have been affected by Down's syndrome. The group is part of an awareness-raising campaign, and offers advice on health, education and care for people with Down's. Social mornings are held every Sunday. See their website for more information.

EDUCATION
PRIMARY & SECONDARY SCHOOLS

Dubai Autism Center
6B Street Hudaiba 04 398 6862
dubaiautismcenter.ae
Map **2 J4** Metro **Al Karama**
This non-profit organisation provides a variety of services for children with autism including diagnosis, family support, training and school services.

Dubai Centre For Special Needs
Nr Gulf News Al Wasl 04 344 0966
dcsneeds.ae
Map **2 D5** Metro **Business Bay**
A learning institution offering individualised therapeutic and educational programmes to its 130 students. A pre-vocational programme is offered for older students, including arranging work placements.

Rashid Paediatric Therapy Centre
Nr Mall Of The Emirates Al Barsha 1 04 340 0005
rashidc.ae
Map **1 R6** Metro **Mall of the Emirates**
An educational centre that runs classes for students with learning difficulties aged between three and 15, and a senior school offering functional academic and practical life skills education for 13 to 17 year olds. Classes are taught in both Arabic and English.

Riding For The Disabled Association Of Dubai
Desert Palm Warsan 2rdad.ae
Metro **Rashidiya**
A unique and therapeutic riding programme designed to help children with disabilities and special needs, such as autism, cerebral palsy and spina bifida to develop their abilities through interaction with horses. Sessions usually take place at Desert Palm Dubai. For more information, please contact the instructors at lessons@rdad.ae.

Special Needs Future Development Centre
Karama Centre Al Karama 04 337 6759
snfgroup.com
Map **2 L5** Metro **Al Karama**
An educational and vocational training centre for children and young adults with special needs. The centre also aims to help the families and communities of children with special needs.

After-School Activities

Most schools pride themselves on offering a broad spectrum of after-school extracurricular activities and often see these as important parts of a child's overall development. Activities include anything from sports teams, drama and computer clubs to dance lessons, singing or even gardening classes. According to the whichschooladvisor.com Fees and Financing Survey 2013, 70% of UAE parents pay less than Dhs.1,000 per month for extra-curricular activities, with others paying far more. One in 10 respondents claims to be spending more than Dhs.30,000 annually. If your school doesn't offer anything suitable, there are plenty of independent options, such as sports academies like the Clark Francis Tennis Academy. Budding Beckhams can hone their skills with the International Football Academy or the UAE English Soccer School of Excellence, and Turning Pointe run ballet classes in several Dubai schools.

Many schools have also embraced the UK's Duke of Edinburgh Award youth achievement programme. Established in 1956 by Queen Elizabeth's husband, the scheme encourages youngsters to learn skills, build confidence and engage in voluntary work.

Scouts & Guides
The majority of Scout and Guide groups in Dubai are held at schools, so check with your kids' school to find out if they run a programme. Alternatively, you can contact the British Guides in Foreign Countries (bgifc.org.uk) and the Scouts Association (scouts.org.uk).

Summer Camps
Due to the sweltering hot weather, children can find themselves cooped-up indoors for much of the long summer holidays – but fortunately many of Dubai's nurseries and schools offer camps and activities during this and all other holidays to keep them entertained. See Family & Parenting for more information on independent summer camps.

Activities for children

EDUCATION
UNIVERSITIES & COLLEGES

UNIVERSITIES & COLLEGES

In the past, the vast majority of expat teenagers returned to their home countries when moving from secondary to tertiary education. Now, a growing number of institutions within Dubai and the other emirates entice more people into studying in the UAE, with degrees and diplomas offered in the arts, sciences, business, and engineering and technology. There are also a number of opportunities for post-graduate study here in the UAE. Many institutions are based at Knowledge Village near Media and Internet Cities, and Dubai International Academic City, on the outskirts of Dubai.

Public institutions are free for UAE citizens, but the amount of international universities is increasing in Dubai as the interest in higher education grows. In particular, many UK institutions are looking to tap into the growing number of business schools in Dubai; the London Business School (london.edu) is based in DIFC, as is Cass (cass.city.ac.uk, formerly City University Business School). The latter specialises in energy and Islamic finance. Warwick Business School (wbs.ac.uk) has been offering MBAs in Dubai since 2003. In addition, there are also plenty of college options available.

Some of the universities, including several of the ones above, offer students the opportunity to study part-time, or in a structured e-learning environment through the use of a range of learning strategies. International correspondence courses and distance learning schemes, are other available options for learning skills and gaining new qualifications.

The UK-based Open University (open.ac.uk) is a popular choice, as is the South African-based UNISA (University of South Africa). UNISA recently opened an office in Dubai (unisa.ac.za). *Gulf News'* classifieds section carries adverts for the numerous other study options for short courses.

Education UK Exhibition
Organised annually by the British Council, Education UK Exhibition (EDUKEX) is part of an initiative to enhance educational relations between the UK and the Middle East. Students from across the region can attend the event to gather information on UK universities, whether they have campuses in the UAE or in the UK. The event usually takes place in January at the Dubai International Convention and Exhibition Centre. See britishcouncil.org.

Getting A Place
Typically, in Years 11 and 12 students take an interests test and psychometric evaluation to help them select their A-Levels or equivalent. In Year 13, many schools invite universities to come for an open day, after which students can draw up a shortlist of the five that they will apply for; the universities will tell the student what grades they are expected to achieve. The majority of students opt for the UK, as well as universities in the US, Australia, Canada, New Zealand and Hong Kong – but some do stay here in the UAE.

Fashion: An Opportunity
If you're interested in studying fashion, keep an eye out for the latest short courses offered by the London School Of Fashion in Dubai. Programmes last between one and five days, and cover a whole range of subjects including: fashion journalism, fashion communication and PR, luxury brand management, fashion marketing, design and styling, and starting your own fashion label. The courses are all led by tutors who have extensive experience in the fashion world, including designers, journalists and image consultants. The programmes are held throughout the year, so check the website (fashion.arts.ac.uk) for up to date news and how to register.

Academic City
Dubai International Academic City (diacedu.ae) hosts international universities including: American University in the Emirates, Cambridge College International Dubai, Dubai English Speaking College, EHSAL, French fashion university Esmod Dubai, Hamdan Bin Mohamed e-University (HBMeU), Heriot-Watt University, Hult International Business School, the Institute of Management Technology, Islamic Azad University, JSS Education Foundation, Mahatma Gandhi University, MAHE, Manipal-Dubai Campus, Manchester Business School Worldwide, Michigan State University Dubai, Middlesex University, Murdoch University International Study Centre Dubai, PIM International Center, S P Jain Center of Management, SAE Institute, Saint-Petersburg State University of Engineering and Economics, Shaheed Zulfikar Ali Bhutto Institute of Science and Technology (SZABIST), Syrian Virtual University, the British University in Dubai, the University of Exeter, the University of Wollongong in Dubai (UOWD), Universitas 21 Global Pte Ltd, University of Bradford and University of Phoenix.

Knowledge Village
Knowledge Village prides itself on creating an environment conducive to education, the business of education and networking. The operating rules and regulations are relatively straightforward

EDUCATION
UNIVERSITIES & COLLEGES

and they simplify the application process for a one-year student's resident visa, too. Some of the tertiary institutions to be found here are: European University College Brussels, Institute of Management Technology, Islamic Azad University, Mahatma Ghandhi University, UAE University, Royal College of Surgeons and the University of New Brunswick in Dubai. Find out more at kv.ae.

Transform Your Life
If you want to enhance personal and professional skills, increase your capabilities, fulfil your highest potential and promote creativity, innovation and transformational change, then sign up for a course at the Transformations Institute (04 344 0115). As well as counselling and therapy, they offer career and life make-overs and professional development courses. See transforminst.com for more information.

International Universities
A number of leading international universities have an established presence in the emirate, and are open to students of all nationalities.

American University In Dubai
Shk Zayed Rd Al Sufouh 2 **04 399 9000**
aud.edu
Map **1 M5** Metro **Nakheel**
With its impressive main building that has become something of a landmark along Sheikh Zayed Road, the American University in Dubai is a well-established institution with over 2,000 students of various nationalities. The campus boasts excellent sporting facilities and the university offers a number of courses including business, engineering, information technology, visual communication, interior design and liberal arts. **Best for:** Engineering

Overseas Study
For students looking to travel further afield within the Middle East, there are several higher education institutions in Qatar. Virginia Commonwealth University (qatar.vcu.edu) specialises in research and education in art and design; UCL Qatar (ucl.ac.uk), the first British university to open a campus in Qatar, offers postgraduate degree programmes in archaeology, conservation, cultural heritage and museum studies; and Carnegie Mellon University (qatar.cmu.edu) offers full-time, coeducational, English-language undergraduate degree programmes in business administration and computer science in Doha.

American University Of Ras Al Khaimah
Shk Saqr Bin Khalid Rd, Seih Al Hudaibah
Ras Al Khaimah **07 2210 900**
aurak.ae
Set up in 2009, the American University of Ras Al Khaimah offers a wide variety of degree courses including BScs in Biotechnology, Business Administration, Computer Engineering, and Electronics and Communications Engineering. There are also BAs in English Language and Communication.
Best for: Sciences.

American University Of Sharjah
Sharjah **06 515 5555**
aus.edu
This university offers a wide range of undergraduate programmes in areas such as language, literature, communications, business, finance and engineering. Postgraduate courses are also offered from the schools of Arts and Sciences, Architecture and Design, Business and Management, and Engineering.
Best for: Commerce, and Art and Culture.

Amity University
Block 10 Academic City, Al Rowaiyah 1 **04 455 4900**
amityuniversity.ae
With campuses in Dubai and India, Amity University offers a wide range of MBA, BBA and B Tech courses in subjects as wide-ranging as hospitality, tourism, real estate, civil engineering and aerospace. Open evenings are held every Thursday.
Best for: Technology.

The British University In Dubai
Block 11 Knowledge Village, Al Sufouh 2 **04 391 3626**
buid.ac.ae
Map **1 N5** Metro **Dubai Internet City**
The British University In Dubai, established in 2004, is the region's first postgraduate research-based university. BUID offers postgraduate degrees including an MSc in Environmental Design of Buildings, MSc in Information Technology and various PhD programmes, and welcomes international students from outside the UAE. **Best for:** Postgrad research.

Canadian University Of Dubai
Nr Shangri-La Hotel Al Satwa **04 321 9090**
cud.ac.ae
Map **2 G5** Metro **Burj Khalifa/Dubai Mall**
CUD is one of the few Canadian universities within the UAE and strives to create an international academic experience for its students, with credit transfer if you wish to continue your studies in Canada. It offers various accredited degrees including business and marketing, human resource management, interior design and architecture, telecommunication engineering and health management. As well as

EDUCATION
UNIVERSITIES & COLLEGES

academic achievement, the importance of extra-curricular activities such as sport, music and drama is also emphasised. **Best for:** Business and marketing.

Cass Business School City University London
DIFC DIFC, Zaa'beel 2 **04 401 9316**
cass.city.ac.uk
Map **2 G6** Metro **Financial Centre**
Part of City University London, the Cass Executive MBA is targeted towards Middle East business executives, with a focus on Islamic Finance or Energy. It's a two-year course and the lectures are delivered over the weekends to avoid disruption to the working week. Students have direct access to City of London contacts, and students can take electives at the London campus. Degrees include accounting, business studies, and actuarial science.
Best for: Middle East-focused business.

Libraries
There are a number of libraries in Dubai. Several come under the jurisdiction of Dubai Culture & Arts Authority and can be found at dubaipubliclibrary.ae. For French books go to the Alliance Francaise Dubai (afdubai.org), and find English books at The Old Library (theoldlibrary.ae) in Mall of the Emirates. For a full list of libraries in Dubai see askexplorer.com.

Esmod Dubai
Academic City, Al Rowaiyah 1 **04 429 1228**
esmod-dubai.com
The French Fashion University is the only university in the Middle East that is dedicated to fashion. Accredited by the French Ministry of Education, it offers three-year BA courses, fashion workshops, trend forecasting master classes, merchandising training sessions, and an MBA in Fashion Management. Three and six-month courses are also available, plus classes on everything from make-up to marketing. One-month summer workshops can provide a foundation for the three-year course. **Best for:** Fashion.

European University College
Ibn Sina Bldg Umm Hurair 2 **04 362 4787**
dubaipostgraduate.com
Map **2 L7** Metro **Dubai Healthcare City**
Formerly Nicholas & Asp University College, this is the first postgraduate dental institution to offer international training programmes in the UAE, including masters degrees, speciality training, certificates, diplomas, and CPD courses. Other areas covered include oral implantology, paediatric dentistry, and orthodontics. There is also an associate degree in dental assisting. **Best for:** Dentistry.

Heriot Watt University Dubai Campus
Academic City, Al Rowaiyah 1 **04 435 8700**
hw.ac.uk
One of the UK's oldest universities, Heriot-Watt offers undergraduate and postgraduate courses in business, management, finance, accounting, and IT at its purpose-built campus in the heart of Dubai International Academic City. Comprehensive English language programmes are also available.
Best for: Business.

Hult International Business School
Dubai Internet City Al Sufouh 2
04 427 5800
hult.edu
Map **1 N5** Metro **Dubai Internet City**
This highly-ranked global business school offers US accredited further education. Courses offered at the Dubai campus include a one-year, full time MBA programme, a part-time Executive MBA programme, and a Master's degree in International Marketing and International Business. Students can choose to take electives at the school's campuses in London, Boston, San Francisco and Shanghai. **Best for:** Business.

Manchester Business School
Knowledge Village, Al Sufouh 2 **04 446 8664**
mbs.ac.uk
Map **1 N5** Metro **Dubai Internet City**
Affiliated to the UK's University of Manchester, this business school was established in Knowledge Village in 2006, and offers a range of MBAs in subjects including engineering, construction, sports and finance, plus doctoral programmes and executive education courses. **Best for:** Business.

Manipal University Dubai Campus
Academic City, Al Rowaiyah 1 **04 429 0777**
manipaldubai.com
A branch of India's Manipal University, this campus offers certificate programmes and bachelor's and master's degree programmes in a range of subjects including information systems, engineering, bio-technology, media and communications, as well as fashion and interior design. **Best for:** Technology

Michigan State University Dubai
Knowledge Village, Al Sufouh 2 **04 446 5147**
dubai.msu.edu
Map **1 N5** Metro **Dubai Internet City**
This non-profit institution offers UAE and international students bachelor's and master's degree programmes in line with those at MSU in the US. Programmes covered include business administration, computer engineering, construction management, media management, human resources and family community services. The university encourages a

EDUCATION
UNIVERSITIES & COLLEGES

combination of teaching methods including lectures and seminars, online classes, and internship/study abroad options.
Best for: Engineering and construction.

Middlesex University Dubai
Knowledge Village, Al Sufouh 2 **04 367 8100**
mdx.ac
Map **1 N5** Metro **Dubai Internet City**
The UK's Middlesex University recently opened a campus at Knowledge Village. Students have the option of studying for single or joint honours degrees in various subjects including accountancy, business studies, tourism, human resource management, journalism, advertising, public relations and media, marketing and computing science. Student accommodation is available at The Halls, on the outskirts of the city.
Best for: Public relations and media.

Murdoch University International Study Centre Dubai
Block 10 Academic City, Al Rowaiyah 1 **04 435 5700**
murdoch.edu.au
Murdoch University offers undergraduate degrees in business, environmental management, information technology and media, and postgraduate degrees in business and media. Their impressive campus houses a fully professional HD TV studio, an advanced editing suite and three radio studios. Students can transfer all credits to Murdoch in Australia if they wish to continue their studies there. **Best for:** Business and media.

New York University Abu Dhabi
Nr ADIA Tower, Al Nasr St Abu Dhabi
02 628 4000
nyuad.nyu.edu
This research university's arts and science undergraduate programmes are affiliated with the US campus. The university aims to give students the full, traditional college experience and its approach is firmly set on creating a campus where students will learn and develop in residences, clubs and campus events, as well as in lectures. Although it does not currently offer a graduate programme, most of NYU's selective graduate and professional schools will offer special consideration to applications from NYU Abu Dhabi graduates.
Best for: Arts and sciences.

Paris Sorbonne University Abu Dhabi
Abu Dhabi **02 656 9555**
sorbonne.ae
The legendary Sorbonne arrived in Abu Dhabi in 2006. This French-speaking university focuses on a wide range of majors in humanities and law, with undergraduate and master's degrees in subjects such as archaeology and history of arts, economics and management, French and comparative literature, international business and languages. Classes are either in French (with translation) or in English.
Best for: Arts and social sciences.

University Of Wollongong In Dubai > p.251
Knowledge Village, Al Sufouh 2 **04 367 2400**
uowdubai.ac.ae
Map **1 N5** Metro **Dubai Internet City**
The University of Wollongong offers undergraduate and postgraduate programmes in business and IT, in addition to certificates and awards in accounting, banking and management. This Australian university was on Jumeira Road, but moved its campus in 2005, making it one of the more established universities in the city. **Best for:** Business and IT.

Public Universities

The Higher Colleges of Technology (HCT) and Zayed University are the two most prominent local universities in Dubai. The HCT is the largest, with around 16,000 students (all UAE nationals) studying at 16 campuses; it offers higher diplomas, bachelor's and master's degrees across over 80 different programmes. Prior to 2009, Zayed University only offered its degree programmes to UAE nationals; however, it now invites all UAE residents and international students to apply.

Higher Colleges Of Technology
Baghdad St Al Nahda 2 **04 267 2929**
dwc.hct.ac.ae
Map **2 S7** Metro **Al Nahda**
With more than 20,000 students studying at 16 campuses across the UAE, HCT is the largest higher education institution in the UAE. English-taught programmes include Applied Communication, Business, Computer & Information Science, Engineering Technology, Health Sciences and Education at various levels. **Best for:** Technology.

Zayed University
Knowledge Village Knowledge Village, Al Sufouh 2 **04 402 1111**
zu.ac.ae
Map **1 P5** Metro **Dubai Internet City**
This university was established in 1998 and has a solid reputation. Zayed University's campuses in Academic City and Abu Dhabi Khalifa City now accept female and male students of all nationalities, whether international or UAE residents. It offers bachelor's and master's programmes in the arts, sciences, business, communication and media, sustainabilty, education and IT.
Best for: Media and communications.

WHATEVER YOUR ACADEMIC REQUIREMENT, UOWD HAS A PROGRAM FOR YOU
CONNECT: UOWD

Undergraduate programs
BBA/Accountancy/Finance/HR/International Business/Management/Marketing/Computer Science/Information Technology/Engineering (Computer/Electrical/Telecommunications)

Postgraduate programs
MBA/International Business/Strategic Marketing/Strategic HR/Logistics/Quality Management/Finance/IT Management/Engineering Management/Media & Communication/International Studies

Language programs
Language Training/Corporate Language Training/Teacher Training/IELTS Preparation/IELTS Testing

Call 04-3672400, visit Block 15, Dubai Knowledge Village
www.uowdubai.ac.ae

UOWD - Your Australian University in Dubai

UNIVERSITY OF WOLLONGONG IN DUBAI

20 YEARS IN THE UAE

EDUCATION
UNIVERSITIES & COLLEGES

Institutes & Colleges

Recently, more and more expat students have been considering staying in Dubai to continue their education once they have left school. Traditionally many ventured further afield, or travelled back to their home countries, but as the choice of further education institutes in Dubai grows, so does the appeal of staying.

American College Of Dubai
Nr Emarat Petrol Station Al Garhoud **04 282 9992**
acd.ac.ae
Map **2 M8** Metro **Airport Terminal 1**
The American College of Dubai offers courses that will provide students with university-level credits, allowing them to transfer to institutions in the US, UK, UAE, Canada, Europe, India, or elsewhere in the world. Additionally, associate degrees in the liberal arts, business and information technology are also available.

Dubai School Of Dental Medicine
Building 34 Healthcare City, Umm Hurair 2
04 424 8777
dsdm.ac.ae
Map **2 L7** Metro **Dubai Healthcare City**
This home-grown dental institution was launched in 2013. The postgraduate school offers students a three-year MSc degree in a range of specialisations such as oral surgery, orthodontics, paediatric dentistry, and fixed and removable prosthodontics. Students will have the opportunity to sit a membership examination in their dental speciality from The Royal College of Surgeons of Edinburgh.

EMDI Institute Of Media & Communication
Knowledge Village, Al Sufouh 2 **04 433 2833**
emdiworld.com
Map **1 N5** Metro **Dubai Internet City**
EMDI specialises in providing education and qualifications in media and communications. Full-time and part-time courses are available in everything from journalism, advertising and PR, through to graphic design, DJing, events and wedding planning. There's also a range of journalism courses to arm students with the fundamental skills of print, broadcasting and new media.

Emirates Academy Of Hospitality Management > p.253
Nr Burj Al Arab Umm Suqeim 3 **04 315 5555**
emiratesacademy.edu
Map **1 S5** Metro **Mall of the Emirates**
EAHM, one of the world's leading hospitality business management schools and a part of the global luxury hotel company, Jumeirah Group, specialises in providing business management degrees with a hospitality focus. The school offers an MBA, a BBA and an ABA in International Hospitality Management. EAHM provides students with job opportunities to gain valuable work experience within the hospitality industry in Jumeirah Group, Dubai or worldwide.

European University College
Ibn Sina Bldg Umm Hurair 2 **04 362 4787**
dubaipostgraduate.com
Map **2 L7** Metro **Dubai Healthcare City**
This pioneering college offers master's degrees, speciality training, certificates, diplomas, and CPD courses, and is a reputable college to attend in order to train for a career in dentistry. Students also study oral implantology, paediatric dentistry, endodontics, and orthodontics or dental assisting. For additional information refer to the listing under International Universities previously in this chapter.
Best for: Dentistry.

Lotus Educational Institute
Knowledge Village, Al Sufouh 2 **04 391 1718**
lotus.ae
Map **1 N5** Metro **Dubai Internet City**
Located in Knowledge Village, Lotus Education Institute provides professional training in arts and design subjects, development programmes in business studies and holistic self development, as well as preparatory classes in English and IT. There's a strong focus on painting, with courses in classical, abstract and cubist art as well as workshops to introduce students to various techniques.
Best for: Art and design.

The Emirates Academy Of Hospitality Management

THE EMIRATES ACADEMY
OF HOSPITALITY MANAGEMENT
In academic association with Ecole hôtelière de Lausanne

Study Hospitality Business Management in Dubai
Scholarships available — Ask us how!

"I am excited about the many job opportunities awaiting me!"

Andreas Wicksell
BBA student, Swedish

Earn your degree and start your career in the world's fastest growing industry!

Internationally Accredited and Recognised Programmes:

- Master of Business Administration in International Hospitality Management [MBA] (1 year)
- Bachelor of Business Administration (Hons.) in International Hospitality Management [BBA] (3 years)
- Associate of Business Administration in International Hospitality Management [ABA] (18 months)
- English as a Foreign Language Programme (Basic / Intermediate) (3 months per level)
- Study Abroad Programme (3-6 months + optional internship component)

EXPO 2020 DUBAI UAE

JUMEIRAH GROUP

+971 4 315 5555 www.emiratesacademy.edu info@emiratesacademy.edu
The Emirates Academy of Hospitality Management @EmiratesAcademy

EDUCATION
UNIVERSITIES & COLLEGES

Mohammad Bin Rashid School Of Government
Trade Centre Trade Center 2 **04 329 3290**
dsg.ae
Map **2 J6** Metro **World Trade Centre**
Mohammad Bin Rashid School Of Government (formerly known as the Dubai School Of Government) is a research and teaching institution that focuses on Arab world politics, public policy and administration, and economics. It offers two graduate programmes, the Master of Public Administration, in cooperation with Harvard Kennedy School, and the Executive Diploma in Public Administration. Its executive education programmes provide courses in public policy, leadership and management for government and non-government leaders.

Rochester Institute Of Technology
Techno Point Bldg Silicon Oasis, Nadd Hessa **04 371 2000**
dubai.rit.edu
Currently RIT Dubai mirrors the degree programmes of RIT in the United States, offering master's degrees in Business Administration (MBA), engineering (electrical and mechanical), fine arts, architecture, science, service leadership and innovation and networking and systems administrations. An undergraduate programme is also offered in subjects as diverse as accounting, ceramics, 3D digital graphics, woodworking, and furniture design.

SAE Institute Dubai
Knowledge Village, Al Sufouh 2 **04 361 6173**
sae.edu
Map **1 N5** Metro **Dubai Internet City**
This large and respected Australian film institute, which has branches on every continent, has an impressive multimedia training facility in Dubai's Knowledge Village. The perfect choice for budding movie makers, SAE offers degree courses in audio engineering, digital animation, film making and web development, with short courses available too. Online courses in music, film, 3D animation, games and business are also on offer.

Language Courses

As you would expect from a city with such a diverse range of nationalities, there are plenty of options if you would like to learn a different language. While English is widely spoken by many in the workplace, some people may need to hone their English-speaking skills at a language centre. Living in Dubai can also be a great reason to give Arabic lessons a go, or to learn the mother tongue spoken in your next port of call. Most institutes cater for adults as well as children with a range of classroom times, making morning, afternoon or evening lessons possible.

Generally speaking, a course will cover between 28-36 hours with varying levels of intensity. Some will last just seven weeks while others will run over 12 weeks. Expect to pay between Dhs.1,800 and Dhs.2,000 for your chosen course.

You can also opt for private one-to-one lessons, but these will cost more.

International House Dubai > p.255
Addiyar Bldg Al Wasl **04 321 3121**
ihdubai.com
Map **2 D6** Metro **Business Bay**
With a team of teachers speaking 16 different languages, including Arabic, English, Spanish, Hindi, Farsi and Japanese, IH Dubai specialises in teaching languages, teacher training and industry-specific professional qualifications. It also delivers the National Development Programme, with tailormade induction courses to help Emirati nationals to enter the workforce.

Teaching English
If you're interested in a career move or would like to expand your skill set, consider a TEFL (Teaching English as a Foreign Language) or TESOL (Teaching English to Speakers of Other Languages) course offered at plenty of institutions within Dubai's Knowledge Village (kv.ae). The four-week courses cost around Dhs.9,000. If you can't find anything to suit in Dubai, Abu Dhabi Men's College (hct.ac.ae) offers courses, as do the British Council (britishcouncil.org) and Abu Dhabi Higher Colleges of Technology (hct.ac.ae).

Alliance Francaise Dubai Nr Dunes Hotel Apartments, Oud Metha, 04 335 8712, *afdubai.org*
Arabic Language Centre Trade Centre, Trade Center 2, 04 331 5600, *arabiclanguagecentre.com*
Berlitz Language Center Nr Dubai Zoo, Jumeira 1, 04 344 0034, *berlitz-uae.com*
British Council Nr Rashid Hospital, Umm Hurair 2, 04 8002 2 5522, *britishcouncil.org/uae*
Confucius Institute University of Dubai, Riggat Al, Buteen, 04 207 2678
Dar El Ilm School Of Languages Trade Centre, Trade Center 2, 04 331 0221, *dar-el-ilm.com*
Eton Institute Knowledge Village, Al Sufouh 2, 04 438 6800, *eton.ac*
Goethe-Institut German Language Center Dubai Al Raffa, 04 325 9865, *goethe.de*
Inlingua Nr Lamcy Plaza, Oud Metha, 04 334 0004, *inlingua.com*
Lotus Educational Institute Knowledge Village, Al Sufouh 2, 04 391 1718, *lotus.ae*

IH Dubai celebrating 10 years of Professional Training and Development

The corner stone of any successful career is a solid grounding in skills and practical knowledge. We equip you and your team with the tools needed to succeed in your professional careers by molding our training and development programmes to fit your career path.

Essential training courses include:
- English Language Courses
- Professional Qualifications
  (Marketing, Accounting, Leadership, HR & Personnel Development programs)
- Teacher Training
- Exams for University entrance and/or immigration purposes

We have trained some of the biggest names in the UAE including Al Futtaim, Emirates Airlines, LUKOIL and National Bank of Abu Dhabi, to name a few. Our reputation is built on trust, high level expertise and our training heritage dating back to 1953.

If you feel you need training and development support, don't hesitate to call on the professionals. IH Dubai, 10 years of training excellence... and counting.

04 321 3121 or 800 LEARN

International House Dubai

.hdubai.com

DUBAI SPORTS CITY

Bringing together a city of SPORTS, LIFESTYLE AND LIVING

18 hole Championship Golf Course and Club House

THE ELS CLUB
DUBAI SPORTS CITY

Academies Campus

ICC Academy

Butch Harmon School of Golf

Spanish Soccer Schools

ALREADY IN OPERATION

- Dubai International Stadium
- ICC Academy
- The ELS Club
- Butch Harmon School of Golf
- Football Academy
- Rugby Park
- Spanish Soccer Schools
- Events

CONTACT US
Tel : +971 4 4251111 | email : marketing@dxbsport.com | www.dubaisportscity.ae

THINGS TO SEE & DO

Places Of Interest **259**
Art & Culture **266**
Attractions **273**
Parks & Beaches **278**
Sports & Leisure **283**
Activities **294**
Tours **307**
Hotels **313**

THINGS TO SEE & DO

From world-class sports to desert tours – there's no time to be bored when you live in Dubai.

Abras on Dubai Creek

Dubai has put itself well and truly on the global map over the past decade as one of the top places to visit. Its desire to build the biggest and best of everything has, as planned, caught much of the world's attention. The city's ever-growing skyline, audacious manmade islands, mega malls, seven-star service and permanently sunny weather have combined with its position as a major airline hub to transform Dubai into an international holiday destination, a regional shopping magnet, and the Middle East's most ostentatious, glamorous party capital.

Expats can also enjoy the emirate's culture and traditions as well as a host of leisure activities. The city's art scene is growing too, with more modern galleries popping up in the industrial area of Al Qouz, and there's a full calendar of international events to keep sports fans happy. During the cooler months, there are some excellent outdoor options for get-togethers with family and friends; Dubai's green parks are superbly maintained, while the beaches draw crowds of sunbathers and swimmers at the weekends. There's family fun to be had at the various water parks, aquariums and amusement centres. The larger attractions (and many hotels) often offer discounted residents' rates. You're not likely to tire of enjoying the urban attractions anytime soon, but even if you do, there's a huge adventure playground just beyond the city limits that's waiting to be explored. Head off-road to make the most of the awe-inspiring desert sands and wadi beds, hike in the mountain peaks, go camping or take to the sea for some excellent diving, snorkelling and sailing. And that's just Dubai – there are six other emirates to get to know too – see the Out Of The City section to find out more.

THINGS TO SEE & DO
PLACES OF INTEREST

PLACES OF INTEREST

To get a sense of the city, simply exploring is a good place to start. There's a definite divide between the old and the new parts of town. Head to the creek and its surrounding areas of Deira and Bur Dubai for a flavour of what Dubai used to be like. Souks, narrow side streets, heritage sites, local restaurants and a bustling waterway make this a great part of town to investigate. In contrast, the mind-boggling modern developments that make up new Dubai – Downtown Dubai, Palm Jumeirah and Marsa Dubai accommodate spectacular buildings, first-class hotels, shopping delights, and more besides.

Deira & The Creek

Once the central residential hub of Dubai, Deira remains an incredibly atmospheric area. Narrow convoluted streets bustle with activity while gold, spices, perfumes and general goods are touted in its numerous souks. Likewise, Dubai Creek, beside which Deira sits, was the original centre of Dubai commerce, and it still buzzes today with boats plying their transport and cargo trades. Both sides of the creek are lined by corniches that come alive in the evenings as residents head out for a stroll and traders take stock. Take the time to meander along the Deira side, where men in traditional south Asian garb unload wooden dhows docked by the water's edge, tightly packed with everything from fruit and vegetables to televisions and maybe even a car or two, often traded with Iran, the UAE's neighbour across the Gulf.

Creek Tours

A cruise on Dubai Creek is a wonderful way to enjoy views of new and old parts of the city side by side. Many of the tours are in traditional wooden dhows, but even these often have air conditioning inside to avoid the summer heat and humidity. Prices per adult range from about Dhs.45 for a daytime trip to Dhs.325 for a top-class evening cruise with fine food. For more information see Boat Tours.

Across the creek in Bur Dubai you'll find a multitude of nationalities squeezed together alongside busy shopping streets, seedy bars in older hotels, and some of the best historical and cultural attractions in Dubai. A walk along the Corniche between Al Fahidi and Shindagha will take you through crowds of people buying and selling fabrics from the Textile Souk, jostling to board an abra, or heading for prayers at one of the mosques or the atmospheric Hindu temple.

Dubai's Oldest History

For a full creek experience, start at Al Fahidi Historical Neighbourhood (formerly Bastakiya), where you'll step out of the modern world and into a pocket of the city that harks back to a bygone era. Situated in Bur Dubai by the creek, it is one of the oldest heritage sites in Dubai and certainly the most atmospheric. The area dates from the early 1900s when traders from the Bastak region of southern Iran were encouraged to settle there by tax concessions granted by Sheikh Maktoum bin Hashar, the ruler of Dubai at the time.

The area is characterised by traditional windtower houses, built around courtyards and clustered together along a winding maze of alleyways. The distinctive four-sided windtowers (*barjeel*), seen on top of the traditional flat-roofed buildings, were an early form of air conditioning. There are some excellent cultural establishments in and around the area, including Dubai Museum and XVA Gallery.

Water Taxis

A fleet of James Bond-style water taxis serve waterfront destinations from Al Mamzar and the creek all the way to Jabal Ali. The smart-looking taxis are available for private hire with fares starting from Dhs.50 and rising to Dhs.570 for the longest distance. They can also be hired on an hourly basis, starting at Dhs.400 per hour. Passengers can call the RTA on 800 9090 to be picked up from one of 23 taxi stops.

Souk Up The Atmosphere

From Al Fahidi, wander through the Textile Souk and then on to Shindagha, another interesting old area where you'll find Sheikh Saeed Al Maktoum's House and the Heritage & Diving Villages. Then take an abra towards Deira; a must for Dubai residents, you can make a single crossing on a communal abra for Dhs.1, or take a private tour between Maktoum Bridge and Shindagha (the official RTA rate is Dhs.100 for an hour).

Once on the Deira side, cross the corniche and head towards the souk district. First stop is the Spice Souk, where the aroma of saffron and cumin fills the air. Nearby, the streets in and around the Gold Souk are crammed with shops shimmering with jewellery.

Take a wander around the area behind the souks to discover alleyways with shops that deal in almost any kind of goods imaginable. Tiny cafeterias, old barbershops and odd knick-knack stores appear around almost every corner, and life in general seems to move at its own energetic pace.

askexplorer.com 259

THINGS TO SEE & DO
PLACES OF INTEREST

Deira Tower on Al Nasr Square is worth a visit if you're after rugs. Around 40 shops offer a colourful profusion of carpets from Iran, Pakistan, Turkey and Afghanistan. For dinner with a view, head to the top of the Hyatt Regency where Al Dawaar hosts an incredible buffet within its rotating dining room. Afterwards, you can burn off the buffet belly by strolling along the Gulf-side Deira corniche, where you'll find the atmospheric Fish Market and Mamzar Beach Park, a great spot for a day out by the sea.

Good As Gold
The Gold Souk is an Aladdin's cave of gold shopping. Bargaining is expected, and discounts depend on the season and the international gold rate. Dubai Shopping Festival and Dubai Summer Surprises are the main periods for low prices, when huge discounts attract gold lovers from around the world. Individual pieces can be made, or copies done to your own specifications, within a few days. Even if you aren't buying, an evening stroll through the Gold Souk, when it's glistening, is worth the experience.

Architectural Delights
Further up the creek, on the other side of the souks, are some fascinating buildings that seemed years ahead of their time when they were built. The large golf ball that sits atop the Etisalat building is testimony to the unique imagination of Dubai's modern architecture. The sparkling glass building housing the National Bank of Dubai (known fondly as the 'pregnant lady') is a sculptural vision, standing tall like a magnificent convex mirror that reflects the bustling activity of the creek.

It is also in this area that you can find three of Dubai's original five-star hotels: Hilton Dubai Creek, Sheraton Dubai Creek, and the Radisson Blu, Dubai Deira Creek. Nearby is the dhow wharfage area where more of the large wooden trading boats dock.

Inland is Deira City Centre, one of Dubai's first mega malls, while bordering the creek for about 1.5km between Maktoum and Garhoud bridges is an enticing stretch of carefully manicured greenery, home to the Dubai Creek Golf & Yacht Club. The impressive golf clubhouse is based on the shape of a dhow sail (the image of this famous building is found on the Dhs.20 note), while the yacht club is aptly in the shape of a yacht. This is also the site of one of the city's top five-star hotels, the Park Hyatt Dubai, which features Mediterranean-style low buildings offering creek views and some great restaurants.

To the south-west of Bur Dubai is Port Rashid, where you'll find the Dubai Ports Authority building, a large glass and chrome construction imaginatively designed like a paddle steamer.

Downtown Dubai
This spectacular mix of shops, restaurants, entertainment and architecture is a showstopper destination that attracts hordes of tourists and residents every day.

At the heart of Downtown is the world's tallest tower, the shimmering Burj Khalifa, which points like a needle more than 800m skywards and contains exclusive apartments, the At The Top observatory, and the Armani Hotel Dubai. By its base are The Dubai Mall and Old Town, while the centrepiece is the spectacular Dubai Fountain, which draws crowds to witness the regular evening shows where jets of water shoot 150m into the air along the length of Burj Lake to modern and Arabic music. Take a seat at any of the restaurant terraces that line the lake for a perfect view; Mango Tree at Souk Al Bahar is particularly well placed.

Inside The Burj Khalifa
After growing like a beanstalk before the eyes of residents over the years, the Burj Khalifa reached its zenith in 2010, and at over 828m in height, is officially the world's tallest building. Visitors can ride high-speed lifts all the way to the 124th floor to take in the staggering 360° views from the observation deck, At The Top (burjkhalifa.ae). Fine dining restaurant At.mosphere, found on the 122nd floor, is officially the world's highest restaurant from ground level, too.

The Dubai Mall, one of the largest malls in the world, is full of top-end retail brands, an array of excellent eateries and some fantastic entertainment options such as Dubai Aquarium & Underwater Zoo, Dubai Ice Rink, Reel Cinemas and SEGA Republic.

The Dubai Fountain
The world's largest dancing fountain is located in Burj Lake. The very best views are from either the restaurants on the waterfront promenade of The Dubai Mall, or those that line Souk Al Bahar. You can get an entirely different view if you head for drinks at Neos, The Cigar Lounge or At.mosphere, or time your ascent of the Burj Khalifa. Set to modern, Arabic and classical music, the fountain sends spray up to 150m, with 22,000 gallons of water airborne at some points, all lit up by 1.5 million lumens of projected light. Performances are daily at 1pm and 1:30pm, and then every 30 minutes from 6pm.

There are two Address hotels in the area, and the views from the 63rd floor Neos bar at The Address Downtown are well worth taking in. Old Town, which is home to the atmospheric Souk Al Bahar,

THINGS TO SEE & DO
PLACES OF INTEREST

takes strong influences from traditional Arabia, with windtowers, mosaics, courtyards, passageways and fortress-like finishes, all of which are beautifully lit at night. Other hotels in the area include The Palace and Al Manzil, which are home to Asado steakhouse and upmarket sports bar Nezesaussi Grill respectively. Circling the Downtown complex is Sheikh Mohammed bin Rashid Boulevard, which has a growing number of alfresco eateries and hangouts, including the ever-popular Reem Al Bawadi. It's a wide and pleasant place to stroll, and popular with joggers.

Just behind Downtown, the buzzing strip over on Sheikh Zayed Rd is known for the striking architecture of its high-rise residential buildings, office towers and top-class hotels including Jumeirah Emirates Towers and the Shangri-La. From Dubai World Trade Centre to Interchange One (known as Defence Roundabout), the wide, skyscraping 3.5km stretch is the subject of many a photo, as well as after-hours hook ups in the various happening hotspots.

With so many residents, tourists and business people around, this area really comes to life at night, as the crowds flit from restaurants to bars to clubs.

Marsa Dubai

Known by most as Dubai Marina, this area has been renamed under the new addressing system as 'Marsa Dubai'. The epitome of new Dubai's rise to modern prominence, apartment buildings line every inch of the man-made waterway, while between the marina and the shore is the massive Jumeirah Beach Residence (JBR) development, which dwarfs nearby beach resorts, such as the Hilton and the Ritz-Carlton.

The pedestrianised walkways that run around the marina and parallel to the coast have evolved into lively strips of cafes and restaurants, which throng with people in the evenings when the lit-up skyscrapers are at their most impressive.

Marina Walk boulevard provides continuous pedestrian access around the 11km perimeter of the water and is a popular circuit for morning joggers, skaters and cyclists. It is a great place for a stroll any time but it really comes to life in the evenings and cooler months when you can sit and gaze out across the rows of gleaming yachts and flashing lights of high-rise hotels and apartments. Dubai Marina Mall sits along the walkway with a number of alfresco cafes connecting the mall with the boulevard bustle. Nearby, The Walk at JBR is an outdoor parade of shops, restaurants and hotels parallel to the beach that has become a huge leisure-time draw for Dubai visitors and residents. Walking from one end to the other of this 1.7km promenade will take you past a whole host of retail and eating options, with the scores of alfresco diners and Saturday strollers creating a lively atmosphere and providing some excellent people-watching opportunities.

There's a good beach here, which is massively popular during the cooler months. The spaces in front of the hotels are reserved for guests, but there are areas in between that fill with crowds of families and groups of friends at weekends. The waters are fairly

Marsa Dubai

THINGS TO SEE & DO
PLACES OF INTEREST

calm here and the shallow areas are scattered with bathers, while the hotels offer a variety of watersports such as parasailing and boat rides that anyone can sign up for.

There is some construction going on in this area as a new shopping mall is being built, and the Dubai Eye project will see the building of Bluewaters Island off the southern canal entrance to hold the world's tallest observation wheel, along with leisure amenities and residential developments.

Jumeira

Jumeira might not have the exotic atmosphere or history of Deira, but its beaches, shopping centres and pleasant, wide streets make up for it. The area is traditionally one of the most desirable addresses for well-off expats, and the origin of the infamous 'Jumeira Jane' caricature – well-to-do expat women who fill their days shopping, spa-ing or lunching with fellow Janes in the establishments along Jumeira Road. The area is home to a range of stylish boutiques and shopping centres, Mercato Shopping Mall, and excellent cafes such as The Lime Tree Cafe & Kitchen and THE One restaurant.

It's a great part of town for hitting the beach too. The popular Jumeirah Open Beach has showers and lifeguards, but it unfortunately attracts a few voyeurs, so you may prefer to try the more private Jumeirah Beach Park opposite Chili's, where you can hire sun loungers and parasols.

That's not to say Jumeira is all sun, sea and shopping – there are some interesting cultural spots here too. Jumeirah Mosque is one of the most recognisable places of worship in the city and welcomes visitors with tours and educational programmes, while a couple of galleries will keep art enthusiasts happy.

Jumeirah Corniche
The new corniche will run from Dubai Marine Beach Resort down to the Burj Al Arab hotel and will be the longest beachfront in Dubai. The new walkway with jogging and cycle tracks is due to open late 2014.

Just outside Jumeira, on the border with Satwa, lies 2nd December Street. It offers a completely different vibe to the sedate Jumeira suburbs; it's a hectic thoroughfare lined with shops and restaurants, and is the main destination for anyone needing to feed their post-club hunger, show off their expensive customised car, or watch the city pass by as they enjoy some street-side Lebanese fare. If you're out past midnight, don't miss having a bite at either Al Mallah

Burj Khalifa from the beach

or the Dubai institution that is Ravi's.

At the other end of Jumeira is Umm Suqeim, where the ultimate attraction has to be the iconic Burj Al Arab – be sure to visit its restaurants or spa at least once while you live here.

Souk Madinat Jumeirah is a picture perfect leisure destination in itself, brimming with popular bars and restaurants amongst its waterways and Arabesque architecture, and packed with shops and stalls.

The wave-shaped Jumeirah Beach Hotel is another popular spot for dining and nightlife and is home to 360 Bar & Lounge, which sits at the end of its own pier and has fabulous views of the city's shoreline.

Sun and water lovers are well catered for in this area too, with a great public beach that has views of the Burj Al Arab, and the excellent water park, Wild Wadi.

Streetlife: Karama and Satwa
They may not offer too much in the way of spectacular modern developments or five-star luxury, but for a dose of interesting street life, plus a real flavour of the Indian subcontinent and the Philippines, Karama and Satwa are well worth a visit.

Karama mainly consists of low-rise apartment buildings, but is also home to a range of shops selling all kinds of cheap clothing and goods – not always the genuine article. Karama's merchants are a far cry from their mall counterparts, and you can expect to have to haggle to get your bargain. The other big draw for Karama is the range of excellent, low-budget south Asian restaurants, serving fiery Indian, Sri Lankan and Pakistani fare. Highlights include Saravana Bhavan and Karachi Darbar.

Dubai Explorer

THINGS TO SEE & DO
PLACES OF INTEREST

Satwa's character shines through on its busy main thoroughfares, 2nd December Street, Plant Street and Satwa Road. 2nd December Street is the heartbeat of the area, where people go to eat, socialise and be seen. Satwa Road branches off this road, and Plant Street runs parallel; here you'll find pots and plants, pet shops, fabric shops and hardware outlets, and a small area full of car repair shops. It's also a great spot to find a bargain tailor. Head here on a Saturday evening to soak up the atmosphere, but women are advised to cover up to avoid being stared at.

Dubai Canal

Dubai Creek is being extended from Business Bay to Jumeira beach. The 3km stretch of water will cut through Sheikh Zayed Road, Safa Park, Al Wasl Road and Jumeira Road and will be peppered with pedestrian bridges and waterside walkways leading to new hotels, malls and restaurants. The whole project is due for completion by 2017 and will be known as Dubai Canal.

Palm Jumeirah

Stretching several kilometres out to sea between Marsa Dubai and Al Sufouh is the Palm Jumeirah, Dubai's original, mind-boggling man-made island built in the shape of a palm tree. Stretching out along the exclusive 'fronds' are countless luxury villas, while the 'trunk' is lined with desirable apartments along the Golden Mile (accessed by the left fork onto the Palm) and the Shoreline.

Standing boldly at the seaward-most point of the island is the Disney-esque Atlantis hotel, which has become an icon in itself. Dotted along the east and west 'crescents', are a raft of deluxe hotels including One&Only The Palm, Jumeirah Zabeel Saray, the Kempinski, and gorgeous new offerings from Sofitel and Anantara.

Aquaventure is Atlantis' thrilling water park, and you can get up close to the marine life at Dolphin Bay and The Lost Chambers aquarium.

The Palm is also home to several top restaurants, including Nobu at Atlantis and West 14th at Oceana, as well as more relaxed hangouts such as Aussie surf shack-inspired BidiBondi and Riva Beach Club along the same strip as the Shoreline Apartments.

You can drive the length of the Palm and around its perimeter for great views back to the shore, and the sea wall here has a pleasant sidewalk for a stroll. Plans are afoot to widen this into a boardwalk that will be dotted with kiosks, and for two piers to be built out into the water.

If you want to avoid having to drive, you can take a ride on the monorail for a more interesting trip up the Palm, and for an elevated view of the luxury-villa-lined fronds. The picturesque Al Ittihad Park, which stretches beneath the monorail, may not have the open lawns and acres of space found elsewhere, but it bustles with dog walkers, joggers making use of the springy, 2.9km running track and kids enjoying the play areas dotted throughout.

Atlantis The Palm

Al Qouz – The Unlikely Art District

Some of Dubai's most significant culture is hidden away among the sand-covered warehouses and factories of Al Qouz.

Tucked away in massive warehouses – often out of sight – are a collection of galleries and impressive interior design shops that are some of Dubai's best bets for truly joining the global arts landscape. Add to that an endless selection of cheap south Asian cafeterias, several trendy cafes, the Gold & Diamond Park, Times Square Center, the treasure trove of goods at Dubai Antique Museum and community arts hub The Courtyard, Al Qouz quickly becomes a destination worth exploring.

Although less-publicised than massive state-sponsored cultural projects in Abu Dhabi or Doha, the Al Qouz art scene, and Alserkal Avenue in particular, are the heart of the Arab art world. It is here that lesser-known artists can find exhibition space, and the galleries are working to promote Arab art on an international scale.

At one end of the spectrum sit smaller galleries such as **4 Walls Art Gallery** (4walls-dubai.com) and, at the other end, are the well-known, relatively long-established galleries that have experienced art collectors as their main clients. One of the best recognised is **The Third Line**. The gallery itself is impressive and contains some of the most innovative art in the city. In addition to monthly exhibitions, the gallery hosts alternative programmes which include film screenings, debates and international multimedia forums, all promoting interaction between regional artists and the public.

Along with the promotion and exhibition of regional art, Al Qouz has also become a centre for the creative process. **The jamjar** offers an extensive schedule of workshops and open studio sessions geared towards amateur artists looking for a welcoming outlet. Workshops range from advanced painting skills to the basics of lomography. The jamjar also hosts several exhibitions each year in its gallery space.

Shelter (shelter.ae) promotes regional creatives with a host of entrepreneurial services including office space, business setup assistance and an environment to nurture contacts. Along with its office spaces and meeting rooms, Shelter includes a brasserie run by MORE Cafe and a boutique shop selling design-centric gifts and clothing produced by its members. Elsewhere in Al Qouz, you'll find great galleries like **Artsawa**.

Alserkal Avenue

This arts district is home to around 20 creative spaces, and it's a great place to spot new talent from the UAE and abroad. The easiest way to explore it is with the aid of ArtMap (visit artinthecity.com).

There's **Salsali Private Museum**, a non-profit museum, and hip gallery **Mojo**, both of which are known for championing local artists.

Gulf Photo Plus is a photography studio and gallery that runs courses as well as exhibitions, and **The Fridge** has become something of a hidden gem for performance art and music events.

Ayyam Art Center runs the Shabab Ayyam Project, a programme that encourages the development of new talent in the region, while **Carbon 12 Dubai** states its mission as bringing together a colourful variety of international movements with one common point: contemporary at its best.

Gallery Etemad Dubai's large open space showcases works by established and emerging international artists, and **Gallery Isabelle Van Den Eynde** has become a significant player, credited with discovering and nurturing the talent of some of the most promising figures in the Middle East's contemporary art scene – including Rokni and Ramin Haerizadeh, Reza Aramesh and Lara Baladiwell.

Green Art Gallery exhibits international fine art, and **Lawrie Shabibi** focuses on modern art from the Middle East, North Africa, South and Central Asia with regular artist talks and screenings.

The Courtyard

A stone's throw from Alserkal is The Courtyard, home to the Total Arts Gallery, which has long showcased Middle Eastern art with an emphasis on Iranian artists, and the venue frequently exhibits traditional handicrafts and antique furniture. There's also an innovative performing arts theatre here, The Courtyard Playhouse, and on Saturday mornings Ripe hosts a farmer's market.

Trendy tastes

Popular cafes in the area include the buzzing MORE Cafe at the Gold & Diamond Park, hip newcomer Tom & Serg (behind ACE Hardware) and Lime Tree Cafe. All are worth the trip into dusty Al Qouz.

Highlights of Al Qouz

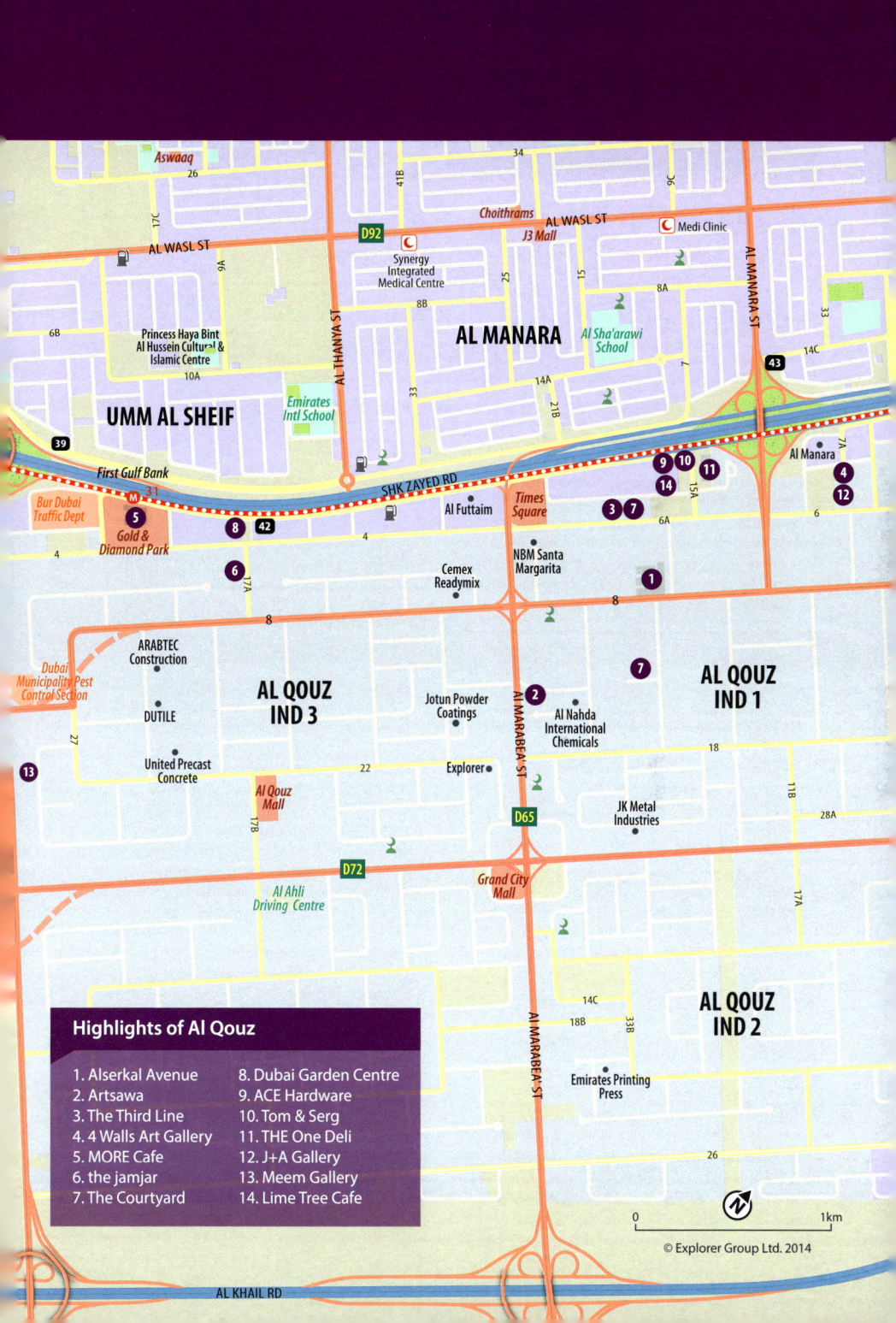

1. Alserkal Avenue
2. Artsawa
3. The Third Line
4. 4 Walls Art Gallery
5. MORE Cafe
6. the jamjar
7. The Courtyard
8. Dubai Garden Centre
9. ACE Hardware
10. Tom & Serg
11. THE One Deli
12. J+A Gallery
13. Meem Gallery
14. Lime Tree Cafe

© Explorer Group Ltd. 2014

THINGS TO SEE & DO
ART & CULTURE

ART & CULTURE

Along with well-curated heritage sites and some fascinating museums, there's a thriving art scene in the city that's well worth exploring.

Art Galleries

While there's nothing like the Tate or the Louvre in Dubai yet, there are a number of galleries that have interesting exhibitions of art and traditional Arabic artefacts, and more are springing up, particularly in the Al Qouz area. Most operate as a shop and a gallery, but some also provide studios for artists and are involved in the promotion of art within the emirates. The Majlis Gallery, The Courtyard and the XVA Gallery are all worth visiting for their architecture alone; they provide striking locations in which you can enjoy a wide range of art, both local and international, while at Opera Gallery you'll find the odd Renoir and Picasso. Many art shops also have galleries as well.

Modern Art

Dubai is following in Abu Dhabi's footsteps with plans for a new cultural district in the emirate. The Opera House District, which is under construction in Downtown Dubai, will include a 2,000 seat opera house (due to open in 2015), a modern art museum, two 'art hotels' and several new galleries.

Alserkal Avenue
8th Street Al Qouz Ind. 1 **04 416 1900**
alserkalavenue.ae
Map **1 U6** Metro **Noor Bank**
This cool complex off Manara Road is home to several galleries and event spaces. See the feature on the previous page for more information about this thriving arts centre.

Art Couture
Al Badia Golf Club Al Badia, Al Kheeran **04 601 0101**
artcoutureuae.com
Map **2 M10** Metro **Emirates**
With a number of regional and international solo and group exhibitions each year, this gallery also hosts the interesting Art & Coffee mornings that offer art fans a chance to chat to artists, watch live demonstrations and participate in discussions around a set theme.

Artsawa
Al Marabea Rd Al Qouz Ind. 1 **04 340 8660**
artsawa.com
Map **1 T7** Metro **Noor Bank**
Artsawa focuses on the promotion of contemporary Arab art in a variety of mediums including collage, etching, installation, painting, photography, sculpture and video. It also hosts performing arts performances, music recitals and educational workshops aimed at engaging the local and international communities.

Abu Dhabi Art
Establishing itself as a major artistic centre is high on the agenda for Abu Dhabi. Exciting attractions to come are branches of the Louvre and the Guggenheim at Saadiyat Cultural District on Saadiyat Island, which are due in 2015 and 2017 respectively. Emirates Palace already regularly plays host to some excellent international exhibitions in association with some of the world's leading institutions, while Manarat Al Saadiyat is already making waves (saadiyatculturaldistrict.ae). There's also an increasingly important annual event on the calendar, Abu Dhabi Art (abudhabiartfair.ae), which is held in November.

DIFC Gate Village
DIFC Zaa'beel 2
difc.ae
Map **2 G6** Metro **Emirates Towers**
An arts hub to service the trendy DIFC area, Gate Village is home to several impressive spaces and hosts regular events. Artspace is one of Dubai's most sophisticated galleries, specialising in showcasing contemporary art from Middle Eastern artists. Cuadro Fine Art Gallery has a space every bit as beautiful as the art it displays. Exhibitions concentrate on contemporary pieces focusing on painting, paper, photography and sculpture. These are enhanced by the Cuadro Education Program, which organises lectures, workshops and panel discussions.

The Empty Quarter deals exclusively in fine art photography, staging exhibitions from both emerging and established artists from across the globe and works from abstract art to photo journalism. The Farjam Collection features rotating exhibitions from the private collection of a local arts patron, including Quranic scripts, regional art and international masterpieces. The gallery hosts guided tours and an art camp for kids in the summer.

Opera Gallery is part of an international chain, and has a permanent collection of art on display and for sale, mainly European and Chinese, with visiting exhibitions changing throughout the year. The permanent collection also includes several masterpieces, so look out for the odd Dali or Picasso.

THINGS TO SEE & DO
ART & CULTURE

Rira Gallery hosts solo and group exhibitions featuring a strong selection of emerging and well-known artists from the Arab world. Its monthly exhibitions and programme of alternative events are making it a notable player in the Dubai art scene.

Dubai International Art Centre
Nr Mercato Shopping Mall Jumeira 1 **04 344 4398**
artdubai.com
Map **2 F4** Metro **Burj Khalifa/Dubai Mall**
This large gallery and shop has eight showrooms with a wide range of original art, framed maps, and Arabian antiques and gifts. The gallery specialises in the restoration of antiques and furniture, and also offers picture framing.

The Flying House
House 18, 25 Street Al Qouz 1 **04 265 3365**
flyinghouse.net
Map **2 C6** Metro **Business Bay**
A non-profit organisation dedicated to contemporary Emirati artists, with a collection of important Emirati works that have been assembled over a period of 30 years. This includes early works by some of the pioneers of contemporary art in the UAE, and recent works by both established and young artists.

The ArtBus
The ArtBus runs regular art gallery tours and offers transport to the major exhibitions during the annual art fairs including Art Dubai and Abu Dhabi Art Fair. For more information, visit artinthecity.com.

Hunar Gallery
Villa 6, Street 49A Al Rashidiya **04 286 2224**
hunargallery.com
Map **2 P10** Metro **Etisalat**
Open since 1998, this gallery features international portraits, landscapes, calligraphy and abstract art, as well as promoting up and coming local artists and works by women. There have been exhibitions from artists from many continents. Open Saturday to Thursday from 9am to 8pm, and Friday by appointment.

J+A Gallery
Warehouse 15, Street 4A Al Qouz Ind. 1
055 395 0495
ja-gallery.com
Map **2 A6** Metro **Noor Bank**
With a focus on rare industrial antiques and vintage items from the early 20th century, this gallery highlights the transition from traditional craft to industrial mass production after the First World War. There's also an impressive collection of contemporary German art.

the jamjar
Nr Dubai Garden Centre Al Qouz Ind. 3 **04 341 7303**
thejamjardubai.com
Map **1 S6** Metro **First Gulf Bank**
A studio and workshop space for creatives, the jamjar also hosts several exhibitions each year in its gallery, as well as hosting other arts events such as film screenings. Team-building days can be organised, and it's also a great place to introduce kids to the joys of art, with painting sessions and parties available.

The Majlis Gallery
Al Fahidi Neighbourhood Al Souk Al Kabeer
04 353 6223
themajlisgallery.com
Map **2 M4** Metro **Al Fahidi**
A converted traditional house with windtowers, the building also has small whitewashed rooms leading off the central courtyard where exhibitions by contemporary artists are held. You can also see hand-made glass, pottery, fabrics and unusual furniture.

Meem Gallery
Umm Suqeim Rd Al Qouz Ind. 3 **04 347 7883**
meemartgallery.com
Map **1 S7** Metro **First Gulf Bank**
Features work from modern and contemporary Middle Eastern artists. It's also home to The Noor Library of Islamic Art, which houses a comprehensive collection of books, journals and catalogues on regional and Islamic art. Open Saturday to Thursday.

Miraj Islamic Art Centre
Jumeira Rd Umm Suqeim 1 **04 394 1084**
mirajislamicartcentre.com
Map **2 B4** Metro **Noor Bank**
A fantastic collection of Islamic art objects from silver, metalware and marble, to intricate astrolabes (ancient astronomical 'computers'), painstakingly crafted carpets and textiles, and displays of calligraphy and engraving. At nearby Saga World you can buy a range of Middle Eastern and Indian handicraft products similar to those on display here.

New Masters Art Gallery
Majestic Al Mankhool **04 359 8888**
Map **2 L5** Metro **Al Fahidi**
An offering of collectible European, Asian and American art within a reasonable price range, and also provides art advice and education.

The Pavilion Downtown Dubai
Nr Burj Khalifa Burj Khalifa **04 447 7025**
pavilion.ae
Map **2 F6** Metro **Burj Khalifa/Dubai Mall**
A non-profit contemporary art space that not only showcases new regional artists but provides a space

THINGS TO SEE & DO
ART & CULTURE

for artists and aficionados to meet, with its restaurant, cinema, library, espresso cafe and lounge.

Pro Art
Palm Strip Mall Jumeira 1 **04 345 0912**
proartuae.com
Map **2 H4** Metro **World Trade Centre**
This fine art gallery is a lovely space where you can browse and buy artworks by international artists, including several masters. It also has a framing service.

Read All About It
The Archive (thearchive.ae.) is a new library dedicated to Middle Eastern and North African art literature. Located near Gate 5 in Safa Park, it hosts various activities and events including public art initiatives as well as live music jams, magazine fairs and food markets. There is also a modern cafe and espresso bar.

Tashkeel
Nr Nad Al Sheba Health Center Nadd Al Shiba 1 **04 336 3313**
tashkeel.org
Map **2 F11**
A creative hub for artistic activity, members have access to fantastic studio facilities and resources, including a dark room. Public creative workshops are also hosted by practising artists, and there are regular exhibitions. There's a great skatepark onsite that's free to use all day, every day, and the peaceful location complements the relaxed, creative atmosphere.

The Third Line
Nr Times Square Al Qouz Ind. 1 **04 341 1367**
thethirdline.com
Map **1 U6** Metro **Noor Bank**
One of the leading lights of the Dubai art scene, this gallery in Al Qouz hosts exhibitions by artists originating from or working in the Middle East. There are indoor and outdoor spaces for shows. Open Saturday to Thursday 10am to 7pm.

Total Arts
The Courtyard Al Qouz Ind. 1 **04 347 5050**
Map **1 U6** Metro **Noor Bank**
Occupying two floors of The Courtyard in Al Qouz. This large gallery exhibits works from a variety of cultures and continents, although there is a leaning towards regional talent (particularly Iranian). There are over 300 paintings on permanent display, and regular shows of traditional handicrafts and antique furniture. One of the main attractions is the beautiful cobbled courtyard itself, surrounded by different facades showcasing building styles from around the world.

Art Dubai
This annual get-together of industry people from across the Middle East and Asian art world is held in March at Madinat Jumeirah. Several exhibitions and events also run alongside the forum, drawing thousands of visitors.

XVA Gallery
Al Fahidi Neighbourhood Al Souk Al Kabeer **04 353 5383**
xvagallery.com
Map **2 M4** Metro **Al Fahidi**
Located in the centre of Al Fahidi Historical Neighbourhood (formerly Bastakiya) this is one of Dubai's most interesting galleries. A restored windtower house, it is worth a visit for its architecture and displays of local and international art. The gallery hosts many exhibitions throughout the year, as well as free film screenings. It is also home to Dubai's hippest hotel and a great cafe. Another branch is open at DIFC.

Heritage Sites
Old Dubai features many fascinating places to visit, offering glimpses into a time when the city was nothing more than a small fishing and trading port. Many of the pre-oil heritage sites have been carefully restored, paying close attention to traditional design and using original building materials. You'll marvel at how people coped in Dubai before air conditioning. Most of these attractions are closed on Friday mornings, and they charge a nominal entrance fee.

The Third Line

THINGS TO SEE & DO
ART & CULTURE

Al Ahmadiya School & Heritage House
Nr Dubai Public Libraries Al Ras 04 226 0286
definitelydubai.com
Map **2 M4** Metro **Al Ghubaiba**

This was the earliest regular school in the city, established in 1912 for Dubai's elite. Situated in what is becoming a small centre for heritage in Deira (Al Souk Al Kabeer), it sits just behind the Heritage House, an interesting example of a traditional Emirati family house and the former home of the school's founder, Mr Ahmadiya, dating back to 1890. Both buildings have been renovated and are great places for a glimpse of how life used to be. Admission to both is free. Open Saturday to Thursday 8.30am to 8.30pm and 2pm to 8.30pm on Friday.

Al Fahidi Historical Neighbourhood
Nr Al Seef Rd Al Souk Al Kabeer 04 353 9090
dubaiculture.ae
Map **2 M4** Metro **Al Fahidi**

Escape the skyscraper valleys of the city centre and travel back in time with a trip to Al Fahidi, previously known as Bastakiya. This atmospheric area in Bur Dubai is one of the oldest heritage sites in the city, with a neighbourhood that dates back to the early 1900s. A wander around offers a beguiling glimpse into the Dubai of a bygone era, with its traditional windtowers, bustling courtyards and maze of winding and beautiful alleyways.

There are some great cultural attractions to visit in the area, including the Dubai Museum. Located in Al Fahidi Fort, this family friendly attraction showcases all aspects of traditional Emirati life, from souks and oases to archaeological finds and local wildlife. After a wander around the museum, head for the art galleries. The Majlis Gallery and XVA Gallery are in restored traditional houses and both host a variety of contemporary art. There are also several shops in selling good quality handicrafts and souvenirs.

Heritage & Diving Villages
Nr Shk Saeed Al Maktoum House Al Shindagha
04 393 7139
definitelydubai.com
Map **2 M4** Metro **Al Ghubaiba**

For a fascinating glimpse into Dubai's history, the Heritage & Diving Villages are an excellent spot to spend the day. Located near the mouth of Dubai Creek, this cultural attraction focuses on Dubai's maritime past, pearl diving trade, arts, customs and architecture. Here you can observe potters and weavers practising their craft the way it has been done for centuries, get close to local wildlife or sample genuine Emirati cuisine served by local women in traditional dress.

The best and liveliest time to visit is during the Dubai Shopping Festival or Eid celebrations, when it comes alive with a variety of performances including traditional sword dancing. Open daily 8am to 10pm (Fridays 3.30pm to 10pm).

Jumeirah Mosque
Nr Palm Strip, Jumeirah Rd Jumeira 1 04 353 6666
cultures.ae
Map **2 H4** Metro **World Trade Centre**

The much-photographed Jumeirah Mosque is one of Dubai's most famous landmarks and features on the Dhs.500 note. The Sheikh Mohammed Centre for Cultural Understanding organises tours for non-Muslims everyday at 10am except for Fridays, during which you'll be guided around the impressive building and given a talk on Islam and prayer rituals.

Pre-booking is recommended and there is a registration fee of Dhs.10. It is essential that you dress conservatively and remove your shoes before entering. Do not wear shorts or sleeveless tops, and women must cover their heads with a scarf or shawl.

Majlis Ghorfat Um Al Sheif
Off Jumeira Rd Jumeira 3 04 852 1374
definitelydubai.com
Map **2 C4** Metro **Business Bay**

Constructed in 1955 from coral stone and gypsum, this simple building was used by the late Sheikh Rashid bin Saeed Al Maktoum as a summer residence. The ground floor is an open veranda (known as a *leewan* or *rewaaq*), while upstairs the majlis is decorated with carpets, cushions, lanterns and rifles. The roof terrace was used for drying dates and even sleeping on and the site has a garden with a pond and traditional *falaj* irrigation system.

The Majlis is located just inland from Jumeira Road on Street 17, beside Reem Al Bawardi Restaurant – look for the brown municipality signs. Entry is Dhs.1 for adults and free for children under six years old.

Sheikh Mohammed Centre For Cultural Understanding > *p.227*
Al Fahidi Neighbourhood Al Souk Al Kabeer
04 353 6666
cultures.ae
Map **2 M4** Metro **Al Fahidi**

Located close to Dubai Museum, the SMCCU was established to help visitors and residents understand the Emirati culture, as well as the customs and religion of the UAE, by involving expats in various activities. These include cultural meals, fascinating and informative tours of Dubai's historic district, and a Jumeirah Mosque visit programme. The building that houses the centre is also worth a look for the majlis-style rooms located around the courtyard and great views through the palm trees and windtowers. Open Sunday to Thursday 9am to 5pm and Saturday 9am to 1pm.

Don't Leave Dubai Without…

There are some attractions that you simply must see during your time in Dubai to get the whole experience.

At The Top, Burj Khalifa
You'll spend a lot of time gazing at the heights of the tallest tower in the world, if only to get your bearings from practically any point in the city. But you can't leave Dubai without visiting the 124th floor and turning the perspective around.

Desert safari
Dubai's biggest playground is waiting to be explored, whether you go bashing through the dunes in a 4WD or rampaging through the sands on a dune buggy. End the day with shisha and Arabic entertainment as the sun sets and the rolling dunes take on a lustrous orange hue.

Ski Dubai > p.293
To try an experience that is beyond comprehension, skiing in the desert tops the lot. Leave the bikini at home, don some thermal gear and take to the snowy slopes of Ski Dubai, where the temperature hovers around a chilly -3 degrees.

Dubai Museum/Al Fahidi/Creek
Get to the heart of Dubai with a wander around the creek area. This ancient trading hub oozes character, from the old traditional windtowers of Al Fahidi Historical Neighbourhood to the abras that continue to transport people across the water.

Downtown Dubai
After a day spent navigating Dubai Mall, marvelling at the enormous window of Dubai Aquarium and having fun at SEGA Republic, watching the Dubai Fountain is a must. Join the crowds lining Burj Lake, waiting for the nightly spectacular to begin, or settle on the candlelit terrace at Souk Al Bahar's Mango Tree or Rivington Grill for a romantic evening.

Skydive Dubai
For the ultimate in adrenaline experiences, it doesn't get more exciting – or maybe just plain scary – than a UAE skydive and nothing says you've 'done Dubai' like plummeting towards it from 12,000 feet. Take in the stupendous views of the desert, the city and the sea, while the perfectly formed Palm Jumeirah is laid out beneath you.

High tea at the Burj Al Arab
This Dubai icon is as extravagant inside as its spectacular architecture suggests. Head to Sahn Eddar for a champagne afternoon tea, followed by a cocktail at the Skyview Bar to enjoy the stunning vistas. It's the pinnacle of the Dubai high life.

Aquaventure
This sprawling water park at the famous Atlantis, The Palm is worth visiting for its multitude of adrenaline-fuelled rides. Take the monorail for a great view of the Palm Jumeirah's exclusive fronds and then head to the top of the Tower of Neptune for panoramic views of the Dubai skyline – before whizzing down the Leap of Faith through tunnels surrounded by shark-infested waters.

Souks
You may have shopped till you drop in one of the city's gigantic malls, but you haven't had the true Middle East experience until you'd haggled in one of the souks – head to the Gold and Spice souks in Deira, or the Textile Souk across the creek.

Dhow cruise
Step aboard an atmospheric wooden dhow and cruise the calm waters of the creek amid the twinkling evening lights. Dhow dinner tours also take place along Dubai Creek and from Marsa Dubai at the other end of town. Traditionally trading crafts that ship cargo between the Gulf and Iran, these dhows have been converted to become floating restaurants; the two to three hour tours typically see diners sit on the top deck, beneath the stars, while an Arabian buffet is served up.

Friday polo
The Dubai Polo & Equestrian Club stages Friday and Saturday chukka events during the polo season (the cooler winter months) and rather spiffing events they are too. Don't worry if you don't know the first thing about polo – you'll be in good company, plus polo events are all about the social aspect anyway. For Dhs.50, you can drive pitchside and set up your picnic chairs and blanket, bringing along a cool box full of the finest fare you could find.

Burj Khalifa and Downtown

THINGS TO SEE & DO
ART & CULTURE

Sheikh Saeed Al Maktoum House
Nr Heritage & Diving Villages Al Shindagha
04 393 7139
definitelydubai.com
Map **2 M4** Metro **Al Ghubaiba**
This 19th century restored house-turned-museum was constructed in a way typical of the time and era, using coral covered in lime and sand-coloured plaster. Located in Shindagha, one of the oldest neighbourhoods in Dubai, the house was once home to the visionary leader Sheikh Saeed Al Maktoum and centuries ago it provided the ruling family with unparalleled views of the shipbuilding district and Arabian Gulf.

Today, it is home to an impressive collection of Emirati artefacts including historic documents and maps, and wonderful rare photographs that capture the Dubai of a bygone era. Entry is Dhs.2 for adults.

Ramadan Timings
During Ramadan, timings for many companies change significantly. Museums and heritage sites usually open slightly later in the morning than usual, and close earlier in the afternoon.

Museums

Dubai Moving Image Museum
MCN Hive Bldg TECOM, Al Thanyah 1 **04 421 6679**
dubaimovingimagemuseum.com
Map **1 P6** Metro **Dubai Internet City**
This rich museum in TECOM charts the history of the moving image prior to the advent of cinema. There's an incredible array of lovingly preserved antiques, some from as early as 1730, and the museum explores how light and shadow have been played around with to create moving images for millennia. There are some cool reproductions to play with, optical illusions and videos to watch. Entry costs Dhs.50 (Dhs.25 for students and children under 18) and it's worth paying the extra Dhs.10 for the guided tour.

Dubai Museum
Al Fahidi St Al Souk Al Kabeer **04 353 1862**
definitelydubai.com
Map **2 M4** Metro **Al Fahidi**
Housed in Al Fahidi Fort, a traditional Arabic fort that dates back to 1787, this family friendly museum was once the home of the ruler of Dubai and also functioned as a sea defence. Today, the impressive building presents all manner of interesting artefacts and relics from Dubai's past. Galleries and dioramas have been used to depict life from a bygone era; you'll find souks from the 1950s, stroll through an oasis, step into a traditional house and even get up close to local wildlife. Tickets cost just Dhs.3 for adults and Dhs.1 for children under six.

Falcon Museum & Heritage Sports Centre
Nr Nad Al Sheba Market Nadd Al Shiba 1
04 338 0201
Map **2 D9**
A hub for breeders and owners, this heritage landmark of Dubai offers a truly Arabian falconry experience. The centre has a souk for falcon traders and falcon breeders, as well as a small mosque, (a replica of the old Masjid Bin Suroor in Shindagha), a cafe and gift shop. Be dazzled by falconry displays in the outdoor courtyard and learn all about these fascinating birds at the museum, which showcases the history of falcons in three halls and a 3D light and sound show. The souk is open from 9am to 10pm every day, except Friday, with some shops closing between 12pm and 2pm.

Naif Museum
Naif Fort Naif **04 226 0286**
definitelydubai.com
Map **2 N4** Metro **Baniyas Square**
Situated in the heart of Deira, Naif Fort gives a fascinating insight into the history and development of Dubai's police force, as well as the city's justice system. Built in 1939, almost entirely of clay, the fort is home to life-size models, interactive exhibits and museum displays. The fort, which has been extensively restored, was the former police headquarters and has also served as a prison. Open Saturday to Thursday 8am to 7.30pm, and Friday 2.30pm to 7.30pm.

Dubai Museum

THINGS TO SEE & DO
ATTRACTIONS

ATTRACTIONS

There's no shortage of fun to be had in Dubai, whatever your age and interests. The whole family will find more than enough thrills and spills at the water parks such as like Wild Wadi, and theme parks like SEGA Republic.

Several family attractions get you pretty close to some wildlife too, from swimming with dolphins at Dubai Dolphinarium to feeding rays at The Lost Chambers aquarium.

Amusement Centres

There are plenty of children's play zones around the city, from parks to soft play areas, and you can find more information on these in Family and Parenting, as well as outdoor activities and summer camps. The following amusement centres offer fun for the whole family.

Aquaplay
Mirdif City Centre Mirdif **04 231 6307**
theplaymania.com
Map **2 P12** Metro **Rashidiya**
An indoor play centre that's dedicated to water fun; kids will love it here. Perfect for two to eight year olds, Aquaplay features a variety of interactive and educational games and water rides. There are arcade-style amusement games with an aqua twist, as well as an experimentation 'lab' with water guns, a swinging pirate ship, a seahorse carousel, and a more boisterous bumper boat ride that's fun for mums and dads too. Rides cost between Dhs.10 and Dhs.35.

Children's City
Gate 1, Creek Park Umm Hurair 2 **04 334 0808**
childrencity.ae
Map **2 L7** Metro **Dubai Healthcare City**
This themed activity centre in Creek Park is the first of its kind and offers kids their own learning zone and amusement facilities. It's designed to complement what they've been learning at school, with interactive, hands-on displays to keep things interesting. A planetarium focuses on the solar system and space exploration, a nature centre provides information on the world around them, and the Discovery Space explores the miracles and mysteries of the human body. There's something to suit everyone; while the exhibition space is aimed at visitors aged five to 15, toddlers and older teens are also well catered for.

Extreme Fun
Nr Spinneys MotorCity, Al Hebiah 1 **04 452 5525**
extremefunuae.com
Map **1 N12**
Big, bright and noisy, Extreme Fun is every child's dream. There are play areas, a birthday party room and kiddie rides, as well as arcade games and a Kidz Kutz salon. There's also plenty for youngsters to do with soft play and toddler areas, while parents can enjoy a relaxing coffee or snack in the cosy cafe.

Fantasy Kingdom
Al Qusais 1 **04 263 0000**
al-bustan.com
Map **2 R7** Metro **Al Nahda**
Themed as a medieval castle, Fantasy Kingdom offers adventure and excitement for the little ones. The centre has a 2,200 sq m indoor play area which is divided into sections for different age groups. Younger children can enjoy the merry-go-round, cars to ride and the soft-play area, while older kids can play interactive games, video games, bumper cars, pool and air hockey. There is also a children's cafe.

Fun City
Mercato Shopping Mall Jumeira 1 **04 349 9976**
funcity.ae
Map **2 F4** Metro **Al Jafiliya**
A combination of rides, games, sports and an indoor playground, Fun City caters to all younger family members and is especially popular for kids' parties, with a range of packages available from Dhs.55 per child. The daily (Sunday to Thursday) Mother's Club coffee mornings are also popular. There are branches at malls across the city, including Ibn Battuta Mall, Arabian Center, Reef Mall, Lamcy Plaza and BurJuman.

KidZania
Dubai Mall Downtown Dubai, Burj Khalifa **04 448 5222**
kidzania.ae
Map **2 F7** Metro **Burj Khalifa/Dubai Mall**
A truly unique attraction that will keep the kids entertained for hours, this fantastic edutainment zone gives kids the chance to become adults for the day. Billed as a 'real-life city' for children, youngsters can dress up and act out more than 80 different roles, including everything from a policeman or fireman in an emergency response team – compete with a fire truck and fake fire – to being a pilot, doctor or a designer.

Little Explorers
Mirdif City Centre Mirdif **800 386**
theplaymania.com
Map **2 P12** Metro **Rashidiya**
Not your average play centre, Little Explorers offers an exciting mix of education and entertainment for children from two to seven, this bright and spacious

THINGS TO SEE & DO
ATTRACTIONS

attraction is divided into five zones: I Discover Myself, I Can Do, I Locate Myself, All Together and I Experiment. And each one is jam-packed with fun learning experiences, such as the building site with foam bricks, chutes and miniature wheelbarrows, where little construction workers can dress up in hard hats and tabards for role play fun. There are more than 80 different activities in all, and you can leave the kids under supervised care while you shop.

Magic Planet
Deira City Centre Port Saeed **04 295 4333**
magicplanet.ae
Map **2 M7** Metro **Deira City Centre**
There are branches of this entertainment hub in various malls throughout the UAE, including Mirdif City Centre, Deira City Centre and Mall of the Emirates. It's a blaring, boisterous play area that's hugely popular with kids accompanying their mums and dads on long shopping trips.

There are various rides, bowling lanes and the latest video games, as well as amusement games that give out tickets to collect and exchange for prizes. Entry is free, and you can use the facilities on a 'pay as you play' basis, or buy a Dhs.85 special pass for unlimited fun and entertainment.

Playnation
Mirdif City Centre Mirdif **04 800 0386**
theplaymania.com
Map **2 P12** Metro **Rashidiya**
A dedicated leisure and entertainment destination at Mirdif City Centre, Playnation offers a range of exciting activities (and not just for younger family members). There are five 'experiences': indoor skydiving at iFLY Dubai (see Sports & Leisure), Soccer Circus Dubai, Little Explorers edutainment centre, Yalla! Bowling and Magic Planet, which includes the nerve-wracking Sky Trail attraction. Parents can even drop their children off at Playnation while they enjoy a movie at VOX Cinemas – see the website for more information.

Theme Parks
SEGA Republic
Dubai Mall Downtown Dubai, Burj Khalifa
04 448 8484
segarepublic.com
Map **2 F7** Metro **Burj Khalifa/Dubai Mall**
Don't be fooled by the somewhat dated, amusement arcade feel to this indoor theme park located in The Dubai Mall – SEGA Republic is really, really fun and, unlike many other shopping mall amusement centres, is for all ages.

Big kids as well as little ones will find enough thrills to satisfy, with some familiar characters for company.

There are some genuinely unique rides at SEGA Republic, including the dizzying Halfpipe Canyon, which sees you working your 'snowboard' to spin higher and faster in order to beat your opponent. SpinGear goes beyond the usual arcade racing game, flipping you 360 degrees as you race your opponents on a virtual bobsled run. There's also a soft play area and more than 170 amusement games that allow you to win tickets to exchange for prizes.

Water Parks
Aquaventure
Atlantis Nakhlat Jumeira **04 426 0000**
atlantisthepalm.com
Map **1 N1** Metro **Nakheel**
The ultimate destination for thrill-seekers. To get the adrenaline pumping, there's the Leap Of Faith, a near-vertical drop that shoots you through a series of tunnels surrounded by shark-infested waters, or try the largest waterslide in the world. There's rapids and a lazy river, and a waterslide system that takes you up on a travelator, so you don't even have to get off your rubber tube.

Out of the water, there's the longest zip line in the Middle East, or you can make use of a sun lounger on the park's private beach. Splashers is a giant water playground specifically for little ones with slides and a giant tipping bucket.

Splash Land
WonderLand Umm Hurair 2 **04 324 3222**
wonderlanduae.com
Map **2 L8** Metro **Dubai Healthcare City**
It may feel at times like a bit of a ghost town, but the water park within WonderLand offers fun for kids and adults with nine rides, including slides and twisters, a lazy river, an adults' pool and a children's activity pool with slides, bridges and water cannons. Alternatively, you can just relax by the pool and sunbathe. Lockers and changing rooms are available.

Water, Water Everywhere
Ridden the Tantrum Alley so many times you've screamed yourself hoarse? Taken the Leap Of Faith so often you're on first-name terms with the sharks? It's time for a new water challenge. Umm Al Quwain is home to Dreamland Aqua Park, with over 30 rides and attractions, plus camping facilities. Also, Ice Land Water Park in Ras Al Khaimah is just 80km from Dubai and features more than 30 slides, plus water football and a rain dance pool. Or, you can pop down to Yas Waterworld Abu Dhabi and brave the Liwa Loop – a full 360 degree looping waterslide.

Come Play for The Day at Atlantis, The Palm

*Special rates for UAE Residents**

NEW!

Make a new friend at **Dolphin Bay** and **Sea Lion Point**. Experience a close encounter that you'll treasure for a lifetime.

Release the thrill-seeker in you with **NEW** record breaking rides at **Aquaventure Waterpark,** the No.1 waterpark in the Middle East and Europe.

Rediscover the explorer in you at **The Lost Chambers Aquarium**, home to a mythical lost city and 65,000 amazing marine animals

Book today on atlantisthepalm.com for the best available rates

*Proof of UAE residency required. Resident rate not applicable for Dolphin Bay.

ATLANTIS
THE PALM, DUBAI

THINGS TO SEE & DO
ATTRACTIONS

Wild Wadi > *p.x, 277*
Nr Burj Al Arab Umm Suqeim 3 **04 348 4444**
wildwadi.com
Map **1 S4** Metro **First Gulf Bank**

There's fun for all ages at this perennially popular water park beside Jumeirah Beach Hotel. The highlight is the Jumeirah Sceirah, the tallest and fastest freefall slide outside of the United States. A trapdoor floor opens to shoot you down a 120m long slide at speeds of up to 80kph. For something more sedate, float round the lazy river or simply bob about in the wave pool. There's also a great water play area for younger kids, and life jackets are available.

Wildlife & Sealife

While Dubai Zoo may not be the best facility in the world, there are several places beyond the city limits that are worth a visit for animal lovers. Al Ain Zoo contains excellent facilities for an impressive range of animals from around the globe, including rare breeds like the white lion, or there's Emirates Park Zoo in Abu Dhabi, which lets you get pretty close to a lot of the animals. Sharjah also has several places to get up close to birds, beasts and fish: it has its own aquarium; plus Arabia's Wildlife Centre and Children's Farm; and Al Tamimi Stables, with pony rides, nature trails, a petting farm, equestrian and falconry shows. See Out of the City for more information on these.

Closer to Dubai is Ras Al Khor Wildlife Sanctuary, a stopping off point for thousands of migrating birds each year, including about 1,500 flamingos. There are a number of hides from where to view the action: one beside Ras Al Khor Road, and two off Oud Metha Road (wildlife.ae, 04 606 6822/26).

Al Hurr Falconry Services
Falcon & Heritage Sports Centre Nadd Al Shiba 1 **04 323 4829**
alhurrfalconry.com
Map **2 D9**

Located in Nadd Al Shiba, Al Hurr is where you can discover all you've ever wanted to know about falcons and falconry – one of the traditional symbols of Arabia. The trained handlers educate visitors about the majestic falcons and it's well worth visiting to see the amazing shows these graceful creations put on.

Desert Ranch
Al Sahra Heritage Vision, Al Yufrah 2 **04 427 4055**
alsahra.com

This eco-tourism concept is part of Jebel Ali International Hotels. The 2.4 sq km Desert Ranch runs a wide variety of fun, desert-themed nature activities ranging from campfire Fridays, family picnics and educational field trips, to horse riding, children's clubs, ranch tours, Bedouin farm tours and camel cuddling.

Dolphin Bay
Atlantis Nakhlat Jumeira **04 426 1030**
atlantisthepalm.com
Map **1 N1** Metro **Nakheel**

Playing with a bottlenose dolphin at Dolphin Bay is an unforgettable experience. Touching, hugging, holding 'hands', playing ball and feeding are all encouraged, under the supervision of the marine specialists. A 90 minute session will set you back Dhs.790 per person (with discounts for hotel guests) and is open to all ages. Your family and friends can watch and take photos from the beach for Dhs.300, but this also grants them access to Aquaventure and the private beach. There's a deep water experience too, where visitors can swim and snorkel alongside the mammals with the aid of an underwater scooter.

Dubai Aquarium & Underwater Zoo
Dubai Mall Downtown Dubai, Burj Khalifa
04 448 5200
thedubaiaquarium.com
Map **2 F6** Meto **Burj Khalifa/Dubai Mall**

Located, somewhat bizarrely, in the middle of The Dubai Mall, this aquarium displays over 33,000 tropical fish to passing shoppers free of charge. For a closer view of the main tank's inhabitants, which include fearsome looking sand tiger sharks, you can pay to walk through the 270° viewing tunnel and see them swimming overhead. Also well worth a look is the Underwater Zoo, which is home to residents such as penguins, turtles and alligators.

Dubai Aquarium

TIME TO REFRESH YOUR WORLD.

Get a fresh take on life and discover a different Dubai with Wild Wadi's splashy attractions and sunny surprises. Exciting rides and even more exciting adventures await you at the wildest park in town!

www.wildwadi.com | Call: +971 4 348 4444

Wild Wadi
WATERPARK

LIFE. REFRESHED.

JUMEIRAH GROUP

Jumeirah Hotel guests can access the park with compliments of the Jumeirah Group

Jumeirah Sceirah · Master Blaster · Tunnel of Doom · Flowriders · Lazy River · Wave Pool · Flood River · Children's Play Structure · Family Rides

THINGS TO SEE & DO
PARKS & BEACHES

You can also scuba dive in the tank (call ahead to book), and even take a PADI diving course. For those who don't fancy being eyed up as a shark's potential dinner, you can cage snorkel or take a ride in a glass-bottomed boat.

Dubai Dolphinarium > p.279
Gate 1, Creek Park Umm Hurair 2 **04 336 9773**
dubaidolphinarium.ae
Map **2 L7** Metro **Dubai Healthcare City**
Splashing about with Flipper is surely every child's fantasy, and the Dolphinarium is absolutely guaranteed to delight the kids. The main attraction is the seal and dolphin show, during which you will meet the resident Black Sea bottlenose dolphins and northern fur seals. Afterwards, you can have your picture taken with them, or even jump in for playtime, and grab onto a firm fin to be whizzed across the pool.

The Dolphinarium has some additional fun attractions to while away the hours, including a Mirror Maze in which to lose the kids, a 5D cinema, and there's an onsite restaurant and gift shop too. The Dolphinarium also runs an exotic bird show in Creek Park, where you can watch a cockatoo paint.

Dubai Zoo
Jumeira Rd Jumeira 1 **04 349 6444**
dm.gov.ae
Map **2 G4** Metro **Financial Centre**
This is an old-fashioned zoo, with lions, tigers, giraffes, monkeys, deer, snakes, bears, flamingos, giant tortoises and other animals housed in small cages. The curator and his staff do their best, with the woefully inadequate space and resources, to look after the animals, but it's not a place that animal lovers will enjoy. There are plans to replace this ageing zoo with a safari-style park in Al Warqa. Entry costs Dhs.2 per person, under twos go free. Closed on Tuesdays. Female visitors must cover shoulders and knees.

The Lost Chambers Aquarium
Atlantis Nakhlat Jumeira **04 426 1040**
atlantisthepalm.com
Map **1 N1** Metro **Nakheel**
The ruins of the mysterious lost city provide the theme for this enormous aquarium at Atlantis, The Palm. Guests can see quite a lot from the hotel windows, but it's worth splashing out for the views inside. A maze of underwater halls and tunnels provide ample opportunity to get up close to the aquarium's 65,000 inhabitants, ranging from sharks and eels to rays and piranhas, as well as multitudes of exotic fish. For an insight into the aquarium's residents, join one of the hourly guided tours, and there's also a twice-daily show at the Seven Sage Chamber. Other activities are available at extra cost, including a behind-the-scenes tour with the animal experts.

PARKS & BEACHES

Blessed with warm weather, calm ocean waters and long stretches of sand, Dubai offers its residents the choice of several beautiful beaches. There are three types of beach to choose from: public beaches (limited facilities but no entry fee), beach parks (good facilities and a nominal entrance fee), and private beaches (normally part of a hotel or resort).

Beaches
Several beaches in Dubai have been awarded the internationally recognised Blue Flag award for cleanliness and safety: JA Jebel Ali Golf Resort, Jumeirah Open Beach, Al Mamzar Beach Park, Le Meridien Mina Seyahi, Jumeirah Beach Hotel, Le Royal Meridien and the Sheraton Jumeirah Beach Resort.

Regulations for public beaches are quite strict. Dogs are banned and so is driving on the sand. Officially, other off-limit activities include barbecues, camping without a permit and holding large parties. Contact the Public Parks & Recreation Section (04 221 5555) for clarification. It is fine to wear swimming costumes and bikinis on the beach, as long as you keep both parts on.

Swim Safely
Although the waters off the coast generally look calm and unchallenging, very strong rip tides can carry the most confident swimmer away from the shore very quickly and drownings have occurred in the past. Take extra care when swimming off the public beaches where there are no lifeguards.

Black Palace Beach
Al Sufouh Rd Al Sufouh 1
Map **1 P4** Metro **Dubai Internet City**
This section of public beach, known unofficially as Black Palace Beach or 'secret beach', is on Al Sufouh Road, in a gap amid the grand palaces between Madinat and the Palm. There are no facilities whatsoever, but the beach gets nice waves and has a great view of the Palm and the Burj Al Arab.

JBR Beach
Nr The Walk at JBR Marsa Dubai
Map **1 K4** Metro **Dubai Marina**
The waters are fairly calm here and the shallow areas are scattered with bathers, while the hotels

DUBAI DOLPHINARIUM

DAILY DOLPHIN & SEAL SHOW
(EXCEPT SUNDAY)

A 45-minute interactive extravaganza showcases these amazing animals astounding skills. Watch in wonder as the dolphins and seals dance, sing juggle, play ball, jump through hoops and even paint.

For Details & Tickets Visit

www.dubaidolphinarium.ae

Dubai Dolphinarium Presents

UAE'S ONLY EXOTIC BIRD SHOW

Bird Show Timings
Mon to Thu: 12.30pm, 2pm, 4.30pm
Fri & Sat: 10am, 12.30pm, 2pm & 4.30pm

Location: Creek Park, Gate 1, Dubai, Call: +971 4 336 9773; Toll Free: 800-DOLPHIN (800-3657446)

Our Vision: To create an excellent city that provides the essence of success and comfort of living.

THINGS TO SEE & DO
PARKS & BEACHES

offer a variety of watersports such as parasailing, wakeboarding and banana boating that anyone can sign up for, as well as camel rides. It is by far one of the most fun, family friendly beaches in Dubai, and the skyscrapers of Marsa Dubai provide a spectacular backdrop to your activities, all just a quick stroll away from the cafe culture of The Walk at JBR.

Jumeirah Beach Park
Jumeira Rd Jumeira 2 **04 349 2555**
dm.gov.ae
Map **2 D4** Metro **Business Bay**
You get the best of both worlds here with plenty of grassy areas and vast expanses of pristine, palm-lined beach with clear blue waters that are perfectly safe for swimming. Facilities include sunbed and parasol hire – these cost Dhs.20 but get there early to ensure they haven't run out. There are also lifeguards on lookout, toilets, showers, and a budget-friendly beachfront snack bar serving chips, burgers and all things fried. Away from the beach, the grassy areas and landscaped gardens are great for setting up picnics or a game of cricket, football or frisbee. There are children's play areas and barbecue pits available for public use.

Kite Beach
Nr Dubai Offshore Sailing Club Umm Suqeim 1
kitesurf.ae
Map **2 A4** Metro **Noor Bank**
Dubai's sportiest beach – also known as Woollongong Beach – is by far its coolest, and a favourite with local kitesurfers. The long sweeping stretch of uninterrupted sand makes it the perfect playground, or if you prefer to stay on dry land it's also a great spot for flying a kite. Family events are held here throughout the year. There are kayaks for hire, a small kids' play area, volleyball and a Dutch waffle kiosk, as well as showers and toilets. Be careful not to get in the way of the kitesurfers, though!

Mamzar Beach Park
Al Khaleej Rd Al Mamzar **04 296 6201**
dm.gov.ae
Map **2 T4** Metro **Al Qiyadah**
With four clean beaches, green open spaces, private chalets for hire and imaginative play areas, this is a park and a half, and can be pleasantly empty during the week. The well-maintained beaches have sheltered, safe areas for swimming and there are also two swimming pools with changing rooms with showers, plus parasols and lifeguards. There are barbecue areas, a restaurant and several snack bars scattered around the park. You can also hire bikes, jet skis and other watersports equipment. Further along from the beach park are beaches on the lagoon that are free to use.

Umm Suqeim Beach
Nr Jumeirah Beach Hotel Umm Suqeim 3
Map **1 T4** Metro **First Gulf Bank**
This popular stretch of sand, also known as Sunset Beach or Surfers' Beach, is one of the busiest public beaches at weekends. Extending from Jumeirah Beach Hotel to Dubai Offshore Sailing Club, its spot next to the Burj Al Arab allows for some stunning photos. There aren't any cafes or toilet facilities, but there are plenty of options on Jumeirah Beach Road for picking up a picnic. You will also find surfers out whenever there's a swell, though the surf club is currently closed until they can get new permissions to re open. The beach is also popular with stand up paddleboarders.

Blue Flag Status
Al Mamzar Beach Park and Jumeirah Open Beach, as well as three Dubai hotel beaches – Jumeirah Beach Hotel, Le Royal Meridien and the Sheraton Jumeirah Beach Resort – have been awarded an internationally recognised Blue Flag. The flag highlights cleanliness, safety and environmental management.

Beach Clubs

For those looking for that holiday beach experience, the many beachfront hotels in Dubai offer annual membership and day passes. From Dhs.13,000 (single) for Dubai Marine Beach Resort to Dhs.22,000 for the Ritz-Carlton Beach Club, you can use the hotels and the facilities. Day passes start at around Dhs.100, but average at around Dhs.300.

Barasti
Le Meridien Mina Seyahi Marsa Dubai **04 318 1313**
barastibeach.com
Map **1 M5** Metro **Nakheel**
The best value beach 'club' by far as it's free. This small beach by the hugely popular bar is scattered with sun loungers and square sunbeds large enough for two. It gets really busy from 2pm onwards on weekends when the beach starts to fill, the music starts playing, and there's a lively atmosphere. People come here to relax rather than swim, and under 21s are not allowed entry.

Dubai Marine Beach Resort & Spa
Nr Jumeirah Mosque Jumeira 1 **04 346 1111**
dxbmarine.com
Map **2 H4** Metro **World Trade Centre**
Pay for a day pass here (from Dhs.100 on weekdays) and you get the run of three great swimming pools, a private beach, a pool bar, and loads of restaurants and bars. Highly recommended is Flooka for

THINGS TO SEE & DO
PARKS & BEACHES

some delicious, fresh Arabic cuisine. There's also a supervised playroom where you can leave kids in air-conditioned comfort. The resort is also home to several popular nightspots.

Meydan Beach
The Walk at JBR Marsa Dubai 04 433 3777
meydanbeach.com
Map **1 K4** Metro **Dubai Marina**
Arriving at this beach club feels as if you've been superimposed onto an art deco painting. The please-dive-in infinity pool complete with floating sun loungers and delightfully manicured green lawns create a picture postcard setting for the ultimate beach club experience. It's Monaco in the heart of JBR, and this celeb-style living will set you back Dhs.495 for a day pass, but this includes Dhs.250 credit on food and drink.

Nasimi Beach
Atlantis Nakhlat Jumeira 04 426 2626
atlantisthepalm.com
Map **1 N1** Metro **Nakheel**
The beach of the 'it' crowd – complete with white four-poster beds to lounge on. A DJ spins chilled tracks all day, cocktails are sipped by elegant clientele in floaty dresses and the Mediterranean kitchen turns out fancy food for diners on the beach terrace. The calm waters of the Palm are easy to swim in, and mainland Dubai's city skyline makes a great backdrop for your photos. Access is free with an obligatory minimum spend of Dhs.150 during the week and Dhs.200 on Fridays and Saturdays.

Riva Beach Club
Shoreline Apartments Nakhlat Jumeira 04 430 9466
riva-beach.com
Map **1 N3** Metro **Nakheel**
This standalone beach club on the Palm Jumeirah has a laid back feel, and manages to accommodate both families and the fashionable crowd. For Dhs.150 (Dhs.100 on weekdays) you can make use of the chilled swimming pool, sun lounger bar service and private beach. Go for a yummy Pina Colada served in a pineapple. Also in the building are a couple of spas, a gym, a restaurant and a great cafe called Sophie's.

Rixos The Palm Dubai
East Crescent Nakhlat Jumeira 04 457 5555
rixos.com
Map **1 P3** Metro **Nakheel**
With a great location at the end of Palm Jumeirah, this beach club is well worth the drive. Members get access to the gym, the longest private beach on the Palm, a lap pool, the spa, tennis courts, beach volleyball and beach football areas. You also get 20% discount on dining at Rixos' restaurants and bars. Annual membership starts from Dhs.20,000, or day passes are available from Dhs.175.

Parks

Dubai has a number of excellent parks, with lush green lawns and a variety of trees and shrubs creating the perfect escape from the concrete jungle of the

Meydan Beach

THINGS TO SEE & DO
PARKS & BEACHES

city. Children's play areas and even fitness equipment are often provided. In the winter months, the popular parks are very busy, especially at weekends. Most have a kiosk or cafe selling snacks and drinks, and some have barbecue pits (take your own wood or charcoal, and remember that it is forbidden to cook pork at public barbecue areas).

Regulations at the parks vary, with some banning bikes and rollerblades, or limiting ball games to specific areas. Pets are not permitted and you should not take plant cuttings. Some parks have a ladies' day when entry is restricted to women, girls and young boys, and certain smaller ones actually ban anyone other than ladies through the week, while allowing families only at the weekends. Entrance to the smaller parks is generally free, while the larger ones charge up to Dhs.5 per person. Opening hours of most parks change during Ramadan.

Al Barsha Pond Park
23rd Street Al Barsha 3
Map **1 Q7** Metro **Sharaf DG**
A welcome focal point for the Al Barsha community, this compact but incredibly well-equipped park has tennis and basketball courts and football pitches (book at the onsite office) as well as a cushioned 1.5km running track and additional cycling path. Scattered around a large central lake are lots of green spaces to enjoy picnics on (as hundreds of families do at the weekend), kiosks and play areas to keep children amused.

Al Ittihad Park
Nr Shoreline Apartments Nakhlat Jumeira
nakheel.com
Map **1 N4** Metro **Nakheel**
This serene park on the Palm Jumeirah boasts more than 60 species of indigenous trees and plants. Located between the Golden Mile and Shoreline residential developments, and running under the track for the Palm Jumeirah Monorail, the park covers around 10 hectares and has a cushioned 3.2km jogging track. It's free, open 24 hours a day and features various play areas for children, and fitness equipment is scattered throughout.

Al Qouz Pond Park
Al Khail Rd Al Qouz 2 **050 852 8513**
Map **2 C7** Metro **Business Bay**
In an unlikely semi-industrial location in Al Qouz 2, at the intersection of Al Khail Road and Al Meydan Street, is this peaceful and little-known park. It's free to enter and there's a large fenced-off pond, which is encircled by a cushioned running track. You'll also find green lawns, flowers and a scattering of trees, as well as a toilet and drinking water fountain. A handy lunchtime escape if you're working in Al Qouz.

Creek Park
Nr Al Garhoud Bridge Umm Hurair 2 **04 336 7633**
dm.gov.ae
Map **2 L7** Metro **Dubai Healthcare City**
Situated in the heart of the city but blessed with acres of gardens, fishing piers, jogging tracks, barbecue sites, children's play areas, mini golf, restaurants and kiosks. Get a bird's eye view of the park, the creek and Old Dubai in a scenic half-hour cable car ride, and check out some more traditional attractions: a mini falaj system of canals, a desert garden and camel and pony rides near Gate 1. Four-wheel cycles can be hired, and the park is also home to Dubai Dolphinarium and Children's City.

Jumeirah Lakes Towers Park
Al Thanyah 5
Map **1 K5** Metro **Jumeirah Lakes Towers**
Where 'Lake C' once commanded attention at the centre of the JLT development, a new JLT park now stands in its place and, in the process, has become the longest public park in the vicinity and is a popular place for dog-walkers.

Miracle Garden
Arjan Al Barsha South 3 **04 422 8902**
dubaimiraclegarden.com
Map **1 P11**
This explosion of colour has been developed with the vision of becoming the world's biggest flower garden – no mean feat in the arid climate of Dubai. The sheer volume of blooms is astonishing, and you can walk under beautifully designed flower-covered arches and blooms fashioned into the shapes of hearts and stars.

Mushrif Park
Al Khawaneej Rd Mushrif **04 288 3624**
dm.gov.ae
Spread over 526 hectares, this desert park near Mirdif is full of surprises, including play areas, a 5km walking, cycling and jogging track, two 25-metre swimming pools (Dhs.10 for adults and Dhs.5 for children), Mushrif Equestrian and Polo Club, and even a miniature village. The park is so vast you can drive through it, and there's a petting zoo and aviary.

Safa Park
Off Shk Zayed Rd Al Wasl **04 349 2111**
dm.gov.ae
Map **2 D5** Metro **Business Bay**
This huge artistically landscaped park is a great place to escape the commotion of nearby Sheikh Zayed Road. Its sports fields, barbecue areas and play areas make it one of the best parks in the city. There's lots to entertain the kids, including a boating lake in the centre and a small maze. The Archive arts library and

THINGS TO SEE & DO
SPORTS & LEISURE

cafe (thearchive.ae) makes for a welcome pit stop, especially for breakfast, and regular markets run throughout the winter months. Bikes are available for hire, and there's a great running track around the park's perimeter. Entrance is Dhs.3.

Umm Suqeim Park
Nr Jumeirah Beach Hotel Umm Suqeim 2
04 348 4554
dm.gov.ae
Map **1 T4** Metro **First Gulf Bank**

This ladies' park is closed to men except for at weekends. It is fairly large and has three big, well-equipped sandy playgrounds. There are also plenty of shady, grassy areas so that mums can sit and rest while the kids let off steam. The park has become a popular venue to hold children's parties. Entrance is free.

Zabeel Park
Nr Trade Centre R/A Al Kifaf **04 398 6888**
dm.gov.ae
Map **2 K6** Metro **Al Jafiliya**

This green oasis straddles Sheikh Zayed Road in the shadow of Trade Centre roundabout – but you wouldn't even know it from the inside. The northern half of the park is home to a wonderful and well-shaded children's adventure play area, with all kinds of obstacles and some funky slides. There's also a large amphitheatre and a football pitch. Cross the pedestrian bridge over the highway (or catch the mini train) and explore the southern half, which has a serene lake with motorised boats available for hire and a great view of the SZR skyline.

Al Barsha Pond Park

SPORTS & LEISURE

There is one dedicated sports hub in the emirate, Dubai Sports City, which will feature four stadia: a 60,000 seat multi-purpose outdoor stadium for rugby, soccer and track and field events, a swimming pool, a 25,000 seat capacity dedicated cricket stadium, a 10,000 seat multi-purpose indoor arena for hard court games, ice hockey, concerts and other events, and a rugby stadium. So far the Dubai International Cricket Stadium, and the 18 hole championship golf course, The Els Club, are both open.

Elsewhere in the emirate there is the Etisalat Academy Sports & Leisure Club (eacademy.ae), The Aviation Club (aviationclub.ae) and the Dubai Ladies Club (dubailadiesclub.com). There's also a multitude of sports and leisure facilities within Dubai's malls, hotels and park areas. With everything from bowling and paintballing to skiing and skydiving, there's no time to get bored.

Archery

Dubai Archers
Nr Sharjah National Park Sharjah **050 454 3099**
dubaiarchers.com

Dubai Archers meet at Sharjah Wanderers Golf Club, just inside the E611 on the Sharjah-Al Dhaid Road, every Friday. Timings change according to the season, but are usually around 9am to noon and cost Dhs.70 for two hours including equipment and instruction for those who require it.

Sharjah Golf & Shooting Club > p.vi-vii
Shk Mohammed Bin Zayed Rd Sharjah **06 548 7777**
golfandshootingshj.com

The shooting club's indoor range offers target practice at Dhs.60 for 20 arrows for members and Dhs.70 for non-members. You can try your hand at pistol and rifle shooting, and there's also several superb arenas for paintballing.

Bowling

There are a number of places that you can go bowling. At independent centres the lanes are cheap and you can have an alcoholic drink while you play. If you want to join a bowling league, contact Dubai International Bowling Centre and they will put you in touch with Dubai's leagues.

askexplorer.com   283

THINGS TO SEE & DO
SPORTS & LEISURE

Al Nasr Leisureland
Nr American Hospital Oud Metha **04 337 1234**
alnasrll.com
Map **2 L6** Metro **Oud Metha**
This large leisure complex has eight lanes and the bonus of a licensed bar. Booking is recommended, and the first game costs Dhs.15, including shoe rental. The complex also houses an outdoor swimming pool with a wave machine, slides and a baby pool, plus an Olympic-size ice skating rink, squash and tennis courts, arcade games and restaurants.

Bowling City
Dubai Festival City Mall Al Kheeran **04 232 8600**
bowling-city.com
Map **2 L9** Metro **Emirates**
Located on the balcony level, this centre has 12 hi-tech bowling lanes with various special effects to jazz up the experience, including synchronised coloured lighting and fog and mist effects. Bumpers and ramps are available for beginners and little ones, and there are billiard tables, PlayStation booths, a 24 station PC gaming network and karaoke cabins.

Dubai Bowling Centre
Meydan Rd Al Qouz 1 **04 339 1010**
bowlingdubai.com
Map **2 D6** Metro **Business Bay**
With 24 professional-series lanes you can either bowl for fun or compete in a league. The centre caters for professional tournaments, corporate events and kids' parties – there's also a gaming area. Prices are from Dhs.15 per game or Dhs.130 per hour for a lane.

Dubai International Bowling Centre
Nr Century Mall Al Mamzar **04 296 9222**
Map **2 R6** Metro **Al Qiyadah**
Dubai's biggest bowling centre boasts 36 state-of-the-art computerised lanes as well as amusement games, snooker, billiards and food outlets. Several of Dubai's clubs and leagues are based here and the centre hosts regular competitions.

Funky Lanes Bowling Centre
Arabian Center Al Mizhar 1 **04 239 3636**
Map **2 R13** Metro **Rashidiya**
This 10 lane bowling centre also has a billiards lounge, arcade games zone and a private party room. It runs a daily Ladies' Happy Hour offering free bowling for women between 10am and 2pm.

Magic Planet
Mall of the Emirates Al Barsha 1 **04 341 4444**
magicplanet.ae
Map **1 R6** Metro **Mall of the Emirates**
Magic Planet has bowling lanes in its games arcade. Prices per player per game start at Dhs.20 on weekdays and Dhs.25 on weekends.

Switch Bowling Dubai
Ibn Battuta Jabal Ali 1 **04 440 5961**
switchbowlingdubai.com
Map **1 G5** Metro **Ibn Battuta**
Set within the Indian Court, Switch Bowling has state-of-the-art lighting and sound effects, and 12 glow-in-the-dark lanes that are served by waiters who bring food and refreshments. The decor is pretty funky too, and there are professional billiard tables, network gaming facilities, private karaoke and PlayStation rooms, and a cafe and lounge area. From Dhs.25 per game.

Yalla! Bowling Lanes & Lounge
Mirdif City Centre Mirdif **04 80 0386**
theplaymania.com
Map **2 P12** Metro **Rashidiya**
Yalla! is within Mirdif City Centre's Playnation. It features 12 illuminated lanes of dayglo bowling, along with video simulators, video games and pool tables. Open daily 10am to midnight.

Golf

Design collaborations with stars such as Colin Montgomerie, Ernie Els and Ian Baker-Finch have helped cement Dubai as a world-class golf destination. Several of the game's biggest events are hosted here, including the annual Dubai Desert Classic at Emirates Golf Club, and the DP World Tour Championship at Jumeirah Golf Estates. For amateur enthusiasts

THINGS TO SEE & DO
SPORTS & LEISURE

there are local monthly tournaments and annual competitions open to all such as the Emirates Mixed Amateur Open, the Emirates Ladies' Amateur Open (handicap of 21 or less), and the Emirates Men's Amateur Open (handicap of five or less).

To get your official handicap in the UAE, register with Emirates Golf Federation and submit three score cards. You will then be issued with a member card and handicap card enabling you to enter competitions.

If you don't want to join a golf club – the fees are pretty steep – you can join an amateur golf society such as the Kegs or Dubai Divots, or start one yourself as large groups can often get concessionary rates.

The Address Montgomerie Dubai
Emirates Hills Emirates Living, Al Thanyah 4 **04 390 5600**
theaddress.com
Map **1 L7** Metro **Dubai Marina**
Set on 265 acres of land, the 18-hole, par 72 course has some unique characteristics, including the mammoth 656 yard 18th hole. Facilities include putting greens and a swing analysis studio. The clubhouse is managed by The Address and boasts an Angsana spa and a number of places to dine, including Nineteen.

Al Badia Golf Club By InterContinental Dubai Festival City
Dubai Festival City Al Badia, Al Kheeran **04 601 0101**
albadiagolfclub.ae
Map **2 M10** Metro **Emirates**
This Robert Trent Jones-designed course features a plush clubhouse, 11 lakes and eco-friendly salt-tolerant grass, meaning the 7,303 yard, par 72 championship course can be irrigated with sea water.

Arabian Ranches Golf Club
Arabian Ranches Wadi Al Safa 6 **04 366 3000**
arabianranchesgolfdubai.com
Map **1 Q13**
Designed by Ian Baker-Finch and Nicklaus Design, this par 72 grass course incorporates natural desert terrain and indigenous plants. Facilities include an academy, an extensive short-game practice area, GPS-enabled golf carts and a pleasant clubhouse.

Dubai Creek Golf & Yacht Club
Nr Deira City Centre Port Saeed **04 295 6000**
dubaigolf.com
Map **2 M7** Metro **Deira City Centre**
Offers one of the most scenic 18-hole championship courses in Dubai, and it's in the heart of the city. Peak winter rates are Dhs.795 for an 18-hole round, but nine-hole rounds and off-peak rates are also available. There's also a par 3 (Adults: Dhs.80; members and juniors: Dhs.60). For bookings, call 04 380 1234 or email golfbooking@dubaigolf.com.

The Els Club
Dubai Sports City Al Hebiah 4 **04 425 1010**
elsclubdubai.com
Map **1 L11**
This 7,538 yard, par 72 signature course in Sports City was designed by Ernie Els and includes a Butch Harmon School of Golf for players of all ages and skills. It also includes a Mediterranean-style clubhouse managed by Troon Golf.

Emirates Golf Club
Shk Zayed Rd The Greens, Al Thanyah 3 **04 417 9999**
dubaigolf.com
Map **1 M6** Metro **Nakheel**
Home of the European Tour Omega Dubai Desert Classic, this club has two of the city's best courses. Peak winter rates including green fees, cart hire and range balls are Dhs.995 for a round on the Majlis course and Dhs.695 on the Faldo course. Look out for off-peak or night golf reductions. For bookings, call 04 380 1234 or email golfbooking@dubaigolf.com.

Emirates Golf Federation
Creek Golf Club Port Saeed **04 295 2277**
ugagolf.com
Map **2 M7** Metro **Deira City Centre**
Affiliated to R&A (golf's rulemaking body) and the International Golf Federation, this non-profit organisation is the governing body for amateur golf in the UAE. It supports junior players, develops the national team and issues official handicap cards. It also has a hole-in-one club for golfers to record their glorious moments. The affiliate membership rate is Dhs.200 for a quarter.

JA Jebel Ali Golf Resort
Nr Palm Jebel Ali Mena Jabal Ali **04 814 5555**
jaresortshotels.com
Metro **Jebel Ali**
Peacocks and Gulf views may be a little distracting at this nine-hole, par 36 course which hosts the Jebel Ali Golf Resort & Spa Challenge, Omega Dubai Desert Classic Challenge Match, the curtain raiser to the main event. For family members who take their golf a little less seriously, there's a mini golf course too.

Jumeirah Golf Estates
Nr Dubai Sports City Al Hebiah 4 **04 375 9999**
jumeirahgolfestates.com
Map **1 H9**
The home of the DP World Tour Championship offers themed courses designed by Greg Norman. The Fire course features desert terrain and greens, with red sand bunkers; Earth is reminiscent of European parklands. The Wind and Water courses are under construction. Annual membership packages include access to both courses.

Spectator Sports

From local competitions to world-class headliners, Dubai's sports calendar draws crowds from across the globe.

The UAE's sunny winter climate, central location, excellent sporting facilities and ability to stump up monstrous sums as prize money mean the country is growing ever more attractive as a venue for international sporting events. From headliners like the Dubai Desert Classic to tennis tournaments and international cricket, and even local horse and camel racing meets, there's an awful lot going on.

Camel racing
This local sport is serious business, with racing camels changing hands for as much as Dhs.10 million each, while up to Dhs.25 million in prizes is won each year. Races take place during the winter months, usually early on Thursday and Friday mornings, and admission is free. Dubai's camel racetrack is on the Al Ain Road, just past the Sevens (take the Al Lisali exit).

Cricket
Dubai Sports City is home to the world-class, 25,000 seat Dubai International Cricket Stadium (dubaisportscity.ae), and well as the headquarters of the International Cricket Council, which runs a cricket academy at the stadium, creating a global hub for the sport. The stadium hosts its fair share of major international matches; the likes of India, Pakistan, England, Australia, South Africa and Sri Lanka have played here.

Football
Football is as popular in the UAE as it is the world over. There's a strong domestic competition – the UAE Football League – and attending one of these games makes for a really colourful experience.

Golf
Each February, the Dubai Desert Classic is staged at Emirates Golf Club (dubaidesertclassic.com). Part of the European PGA Tour, previous winners include Tiger Woods and Rory McIlroy. The DP World Tour Championship, staged annually at the Jumeirah Golf Estates, is the culmination of the European Tour's Race To Dubai. Golf fans also have another major international tournament to look forward to: the Abu Dhabi HSBC Golf Championship, staged at Abu Dhabi Golf Course each January.

Horse racing
The richest horse race in the world, the glitzy Dubai World Cup, is held at the Meydan Racecourse in March, and there are also race nights throughout the season. Futuristic trackside The Meydan Hotel offers special racing packages; gambling is not allowed in the UAE, but there are raffles and cash prizes.

For horse excitement of a different kind, Dubai Polo & Equestrian Club stages Friday chukka events during the polo season. For Dhs.50 you can drive pitchside and set up your picnic chairs and blanket.

Motorsports
Dubai's own Autodrome hosts events such as the Dunlop 24H endurance series, for which admission is free, but the real action is down on Abu Dhabi's Yas Island, where the Formula 1 Grand Prix takes place at Yas Marina Circuit each November.

Rugby
The Sevens stadium on the Al Ain Road is host to the Emirates Airline Dubai Rugby Sevens (dubairugby7s.com) – three days of rugby and revelry. This 'light' version of the sport is fast paced and competitive, with young, up-and-coming international stars taking centre stage. As much about the atmosphere as the sport, it's a great day out for groups of friends.

Tennis
Dubai Duty Free Tennis Championships, which is held at The Aviation Club every February, is a great opportunity to catch some of the top players in the game at close quarters, and features both men's and ladies' tournaments. Tickets for the later stages sell out in advance so keep an eye out for sale details, although entrance to some of the earlier rounds can be bought on the day. See dubaidutyfreetennischampionships.com.

Watersports
An important part of Dubai's heritage, many sailing and dhow racing events take place off Dubai's shoreline, including the 10 day Maktoum Sailing Trophy, which takes place every February (dimc.ae).

The emirate's waters are also a venue for the Class 1 World Powerboat Championship (class-1.com).

UIM Class 1 World Powerboat Championship

THINGS TO SEE & DO
SPORTS & LEISURE

The Track Meydan Golf
Meydan Racecourse Nadd Al Shiba 1 **04 381 3733**
meydangolf.com
Map **2 E10**
This 'pay-and-play' golf course designed by Peter Harradine can be played as nine or 18 holes. Located at the famous Dubai racecourse, it challenges golfers of all skill levels as it works its way between a series of natural lakes. There's no membership fee, so casual golfers can simply book a tee time to play. Tuition packages and one-off lessons are also available.

Ice Skating

Al Nasr Leisureland
Nr American Hospital Oud Metha **04 337 1234**
alnasrll.com
Map **2 L6** Metro **Oud Metha**
This Olympic-size rink is part of a large leisure complex that includes a bowling alley. Entry is Dhs.10 for adults and Dhs.5 for children under 10, with skate hire at Dhs.20 for two hours. There is a skating school and regular ice shows. Call ahead as the rink is sometimes closed for practice sessions.

Dubai Ice Rink
Dubai Mall Downtown Dubai, Burj Khalifa **04 448 5111**
dubaiicerink.com
Map **2 F7** Metro **Burj Khalifa/Dubai Mall**
An Olympic-sized arena on the ground floor of The Dubai Mall. Skating aids are available to help little ones feel safe on the ice and there are also Mom and Tots sessions. Regular public sessions are held at various times during the day, and on certain days the rink is transformed into an ice disco with a DJ. Lessons are available for skaters of all different abilities.

The Galleria Ice Rink
Hyatt Regency Al Corniche **04 209 6550**
Map **2 N4** Metro **Palm Deira**
Public skating costs Dhs.35 per person (including skate hire). Membership rates start at Dhs.400 per month, or Dhs.2,075 per year, with unlimited skating. Lessons are available and start at Dhs.200 for members and Dhs.300 for non-members for five 15 minute classes. Other packages include figure skating coaching, birthday celebrations, and disco nights.

Queen Of Ice World
Al Nasr Leisureland Oud Metha **050 200 1095**
queenoficeworld.org
Map **2 K6** Metro **Oud Metha**
Everyone from toddlers to experienced skaters looking to jump, spiral and dance are catered for in classes run by the Queen of Ice World school at Al Nasr Leisureland. The school is also the biggest supplier of skating equipment and clothing in the Middle East, and organises a popular summer skate programme.

Karting

Emirates Kart Zone
Al Wasl Sports Club Sama Al Jadaf, Al Jadaf
050 426 3424
emirateskartzone.net
Map **2 J7** Metro **Dubai Healthcare City**
Operating under the Emirates Motor Sports Federation, this is a huge, state-of-the-art floodlit outdoor track and visitors of all ages can take on a Formula 1-style circuit complete with hairpin turns and chicanes. Professional and junior karts are available, and at the end of each session, computerised race results reveal the fastest lap times on a big screen.

Blokarting
Get involved with the latest extreme sports craze in Dubai. Blokarting, or landsailing, takes the principles of windsurfing and applies them on land – or to a buggy on land, to be specific. A Blokarting experience for two costs Dhs.550 through Dreamdays (dreamdays.ae) and once you've got the bug, join Duplays' blokart racing league at Jumeirah Beach Park. Find out more at duplays.com

Kartdrome
MotorCity Al Hebiah 1 **04 367 8744**
Map **1 N12**
The Autodrome in MotorCity has a 500 metre indoor circuit as well as a 1.2km outdoor track with a challenging 17 corners. After a safety briefing you take to your 390cc kart (there are 120cc karts for kids over seven years) and hit the tarmac. There are timed races for the International Leisure Ranking, plus the Dubai Autodrome Championship for more serious racers. Races are Dhs.100 (indoor track) or Dhs.110 (outdoor track), including kart and clothing, and they last 15 minutes. Those with their own karts can use the track at certain times.

Mini Golf

Hyatt Regency Dubai Golf Park
Hyatt Regency Al Corniche **04 209 6817**
Map **2 N4** Metro **Palm Deira**
Bring your own clubs and golf balls for the nine-hole pitch-and-putt grass course (Dhs.30 for one round) or rent it all at the 18-hole crazy golf course (Dhs.15 per person). No membership required.

THINGS TO SEE & DO
SPORTS & LEISURE

Dubai Ice Rink at The Dubai Mall

Mini Golf

Emirates Kart Zone

askexplorer.com 289

THINGS TO SEE & DO
SPORTS & LEISURE

JA Jebel Ali Golf Resort
Nr Palm Jebel Ali Mena Jabal Ali **04 814 5555**
jaresortshotels.com
Metro **Jebel Ali**
Right on the beach in the serene gardens of the resort, this course features a range of obstacles, from awkward bends and jumps to tricky loops and putts. Prices start at Dhs.20, although you will have to pay for a day pass at Jebel Ali Golf Resort on top, with rates starting at Dhs.180 (weekdays) for non-members (Dhs.90 for children).

Play A Round @ Some Place Nice
Jewels Tower Marsa Dubai **04 457 0455**
playaround.ae
Map **1 J5** Metro **Jumeirah Lakes Towers**
Intended as a space for parents and kids to play together, Play A Round is an indoor, neon nine-hole mini golf course with an underwater theme. There are also arts and crafts activities, a soft play area and a cafe.

Tee & Putt Mini Golf
Umm Hurair 2 **04 357 3290**
teeandputt.com
Map **2 N7** Metro **Airport Terminal 1**
A glow-in-the-dark world of UV lights and surreal outer space designs, all set to a lively pop soundtrack. There are 18 holes, all with different obstacles that follow the space theme. There's also the opportunity for kids to paint their own designs onto glow-in-the-dark t-shirts or get their faces painted, and the venue has a space for hosting parties.

Motorsports

Dubai Autodrome
MotorCity Al Hebiah 1 **04 367 8700**
dubaiautodrome.com
Map **1 N12**
Dubai's motorsport home has six track configurations, including a 5.39km FIA-sanctioned GP circuit, state-of-the-art pit facilities and a 7,000 seat grandstand. The venue hosts events including rounds of the FIA GT Championship. A number of experiences are available from getting behind the wheel of an Audi R8 V10 to trying out an F1-style single seater.

Multi-sports

The Aviation Club
Jumeirah Creekside Al Garhoud **04 230 8560**
jumeirah.com
Map **2 M8** Metro **GGICO**
This leisure facility offers more activities than your average gym – beach volleyball, bocce, badminton, croquet, along with tennis and some great swimming pools – even a glass-bottomed rooftop one.

Dubai Ladies Club
Jumeira Rd Jumeira 2 **04 349 9822**
dubailadiesclub.com
Map **2 D4** Metro **Business Bay**
There's lots going on at this club exclusive to the fairer sex, including facilities for squash, tennis and volleyball, with tournaments organised regularly for members. There's also a 1km running track, swimming pool and wellness centre with a group fitness studio.

Etisalat Academy Recreation & Sports Complex
Off Shk Mohd Bin Zayed Rd Muhaisanah 2
04 204 3491
eacademy.ae
Map **2 S10** Metro **Etisalat**
This large sports and recreation facility close the Dubai International Airport is open to visitors, with football, volleyball, basketball and squash courts, as well as a running track and swimming pool.

Shooting, Paintballing & Laser Games

JA Shooting Club
Nr Jebel Ali Golf Resort Hessyan 1 **04 883 6555**
jaresortshotels.com
Metro **Jebel Ali**
If you are ready to feel like a champ, and would like to feel the cold steel of a firearm in your hands, the JA Shooting Club is one of the most popular destinations in Dubai. Five floodlit clay shooting ranges consisting of skeet, trap and sporting clays. Instructors give detailed lessons. Both members and non-members are welcome.

Laserdrome Dubai
MotorCity, Al Hebiah 1 **04 436 1422**
Map **1 N12**
Players wear special vests that detect their enemies' lasers. At the end of each round, contestants can see how many times they got shot and who shot them. The charges are Dhs.80 per person for 15 minutes.

Pursuit Games
WonderLand Umm Hurair 2 **04 324 4755**
paintballdubai.com
Map **2 L8** Metro **Dubai Healthcare City**
The Pursuit Games version of paintball is a combination of speedball and paintball and this arena capitalises on the desert terrain. Sessions start at Dhs.90 for two hours, including 100 paintballs and all the necessary gear.

DUBAI AUTODROME
YOUR TURN
EXPERIENCE IT
ADRENALINE EXPERIENCES
AUDI R8 V10 THRILL EXPERIENCE
AUDI TT EXPERIENCE
FIRST DRIVE EXPERIENCE
KARTDROME EXPERIENCE
KIDS KARTING EXPERIENCE
SINGLE SEATER - STAGE 1 EXPERIENCE
CLIO CUP RACE CAR EXPERIENCE
AVAILABLE NOW!
WWW.DUBAIAUTODROME.COM

THINGS TO SEE & DO
SPORTS & LEISURE

Thrill Zone
Oasis Centre Al Qouz 1 **04 388 3551**
thrillzoneuae.com
Map **2 C6** Metro **Noor Bank**
A dinosaur-themed laser tag centre that's suitable for the whole family – and great for competitive groups of friends looking for a fun afternoon. There's also a 6D cinema, a party area and a cafe. Prices for laser tag start at Dhs.55 per person.

Sharjah Golf & Shooting Club > *p.vi-vii*
Shk Mohammed Bin Zayed Rd Sharjah **06 548 7777**
golfandshootingshj.com
Trigger-happy activities are well served with superb shooting facilities and three fantastic paintball parks. The shooting range boasts indoor pistols, rifles and revolvers, and 25m and 50m ranges. Thirty minute beginner lessons with .22 calibre weapons cost Dhs.170 for non-members and Dhs.130 for members. Twenty-five shots with standard weapons are charged at Dhs.90 for non-members and Dhs.70 for members. For paintball, there are two innovative outdoor parks to choose from: a World War I battlefield and a giant outdoor jungle. Indoors, there's a London-themed battlefield complete with black taxis, red telephone booths and even a Harrods to hide in.

Skateparks

Dubai's many parks provide some excellent locations for skating. The likes of Creek Park and Safa Park have plenty of wide pathways, relatively few people and enough slopes and turns to make it interesting. Alternatively, check out both sides of Dubai Creek, the seafront near the Hyatt Regency Hotel or the promenades at the Jumeira Beach corniche and in Deira along towards Al Mamzar Beach Park, where the views are an added bonus. Sheikh Mohammed bin Rashid Boulevard, running through the Downtown area, The Walk at Jumeirah Beach Residence, and the promenade running around Marsa Dubai also have wide promenades that are great for skating. Dubai also has a women's roller derby team. Not sure what that is? Check out dubairollerderby.com for more.

Rage Bowl
Dubai Mall Downtown Dubai, Burj Khalifa **04 434 1549**
rage-shop.com
Map **2 F7** Metro **Burj Khalifa/Dubai Mall**
This indoor skateboarding bowl is open Sunday to Wednesday, 10am to 10pm, and until midnight at weekends. Two-hour sessions cost Dhs.25; helmets can also be hired for Dhs.10. Lessons are available at Dhs.85 per hour on weekdays and Dhs.125 on weekends, and no previous experience is required. Check the website for happy hour timings.

Tashkeel
Nr Nad Al Sheba Health Center Nadd Al Shiba 1 **04 336 3313**
tashkeel.org
Map **2 F11**
Art meets skateboarding at this gallery in peaceful Nadd Al Shiba. The creative hub has a fantastic, free-to-use skate ramp and bowl that's open every day. Skate lessons are available, and so is equipment.

Skiing

Ski Dubai > *p.293*
Mall of the Emirates Al Barsha 1 **04 409 4090**
skidxb.com
Map **1 R6** Metro **Mall of the Emirates**
Leave the sun and sand outside and head to this winter wonderland, complete with 22,500 sq m of real snow, where the temperature hovers around -2°C. Competent skiers and boarders can choose between five runs of different difficulty (there's even a black run) and a freestyle area, but lessons are available for beginners. There's also a huge Snow Park, where you can take little ones tobogganing and get up close with penguins. If you don't ski, you can even roll down the slope inside a giant inflatable ball or zip line from the top of the slope on the brand new Snow Bullet. Slope pass and lesson prices include the hire of jackets, trousers, boots, socks, helmets and equipment, but it's worth bringing your own gloves as you'll be charged extra for these.

Skydiving

iFLY Dubai
Mirdif City Centre Mirdif **04 231 6292**
theplaymania.com
Map **2 P12** Metro **Rashidiya**
Like the idea of a skydive but don't have the budget or the head for heights? Visit iFLY at Playnation. Giant vertical wind tunnels simulate the sensation of jumping from a plane – you hover over powerful fans while being blasted up to 10 metres in the air by winds of up to 200kph. It's a remarkable sensation and it may sound scary, but instructors are on hand to help. You can even take kids as young as three.

SkyDive Dubai
Off Al Sufouh Rd Marsa Dubai **04 377 8888**
skydivedubai.ae
Map **1 L4** Metro **Dubai Marina**
Stunning skydives over The Palm Jumeirah and Marsa Dubai. A first-time tandem jump costs Dhs.1,999 (with photos and DVD). You can also sign up for skydive school, and licensed jumpers can rent gear.

CHAIRLIFT

TUBING RUN

SKI SCHOOL

DO SOMETHING DIFFERENT

SKIING

SNOW PENGUINS

THE GIANT SNOW BALL

SNOWBOARDING

ooking for an action-packed day out?
lit the slopes with your skis and snowboards or take on the exciting rides
ke The Giant Ball or tubing runs. Or if you're just looking for a place to chill,
ome hang out with our adorable Snow Penguins or have a blast at the Snow Park.
here is something for everyone at the coolest destination in town.

Ski Dubai. Do something different.

SKI DUBAI
سكي دبي

or more information visit www.skidxb.com and /SKIDXB   /SKIDXB   /SKIDUBAI   /SKIDXB

THINGS TO SEE & DO
ACTIVITIES

ACTIVITIES

Speedboats in Dubai's marina

The UAE's diverse topography lends itself perfectly to a wide range of outdoor pursuits, including mountain biking, dune bashing, wadi driving and camping. Thanks to the endless kilometres of coastline, watersports are particularly popular as well, with scuba diving, sailing, wakeboarding and kayaking all firmly within the realms of possibility. With so many different cultures converging in Dubai, it's little surprise that there is such a diverse range of activities available to fill your free time with.

Biking

Away from the cities, the UAE has a lot to offer outdoor enthusiasts, especially mountain bikers. On a mountain bike it's possible to see untouched places that are not even accessible in 4WDs.

Beginner bikers: head to the Hatta Fort Hotel, a secluded mountain retreat which has an off-road bike track on its grounds.

Advanced bikers: from super-technical rocky trails in areas like Fili and Siji, to mountain routes like Wadi Bih, which climb to over 1,000m and can be descended in minutes, there really are plenty of fantastic routes for experienced riders to try where riding is mainly rocky and quite challenging. Even if you are experienced, always be sensible and go prepared – the sun is strong, you will need far more water than you think, and it's easy to get lost. Wide, knobbly tyres work much better on the loose, sharp rocks. For further information on mountain biking in Dubai, including details of possible routes, refer to the *UAE Off-Road Explorer*. See also the Clubs & Groups section in this book for more details of other biking groups.

Boating

With calm waters and year-round sunshine, the UAE offers ideal conditions for those wishing to sample life on the ocean waves. An evening aboard a dhow, either on Dubai Creek or sailing along the coast is a wonderfully memorable experience. A number of companies in Dubai provide boat charters, offering everything from sundowner cruises of a couple of hours and overnight trips with snorkelling stopovers, to scuba diving excursions to remote destinations such as Musandam. Large sailing yachts, catamarans, speedboats and other motorboats can be hired for private charter and corporate events; other companies offer outings on dhows and also cater to weddings and birthday parties. Fishing trips and watersports packages are also available. If you're on the east coast and fancy a traditional boating experience, large independent groups can charter a dhow from the fishermen at Dibba. If you're a boating enthusiast, make sure you pick up Explorer's *UAE Boating & Yachting* book.

Membership at one of Dubai's sailing clubs allows you to participate in club activities and to rent sailing and watersports equipment. You can also use leisure facilities and the club's beach, and moor your boat at an additional cost. If you've not found your sea legs but would like to, there are a few places that will teach you.

Exclusion zones
There are many exclusion zones set around the offshore sites such as the Palms, The World and other in-water development sites around Dubai's coast. These exclusion zones not only detract sightseers, but are also in place for the safety of the boat owner, so it is advisable to stay well clear. Approaching any oil installations areas is strictly prohibited.

Dubai International Marine Club
Al Sufouh Rd Marsa Dubai **04 399 5777**
dimc.ae
Map **1 M5** Metro **Nakheel**
Offers sailing lessons for children. A 12 hour course sets members back Dhs.1,500. See the website for more details on lessons and membership.

THINGS TO SEE & DO
ACTIVITIES

Dubai Offshore Sailing Club
Jumeira Rd Umm Suqeim 1 **04 394 1669**
dosc.ae
Map **2 B4** Metro **Noor Bank**
This Royal Yachting Association Training Centre offers dinghy and keelboat courses throughout the year. Members enjoy weekly regattas and a busy social calendar. The restaurant is very reasonably priced and has a large terrace with views over the quaint marina. There's also a small private beach and private function area. To gain membership, you have to prove that you're an active sailor and gain points in your sailing logbook in order to be considered.

Sailing Events
Sailing is an important part of Dubai's heritage and this is reflected in the number of sailing events that take place each year. The traditional dhow races are an exciting spectacle, while the long distance races such as the annual Dubai to Muscat race attracts many sailors. The emirate's waters are a major venue for the popular Class 1 World Power Boating Championship (class-1.com). These stylish heavyweights of the powerboating world race around a grand prix circuit through Mina Seyahi lagoon at speeds of up to 257kph, just metres from the beach. Held at the end of November, the twin Dubai competitions represent the finale of the European circuit, which has seen Dubai's Victory Team win the series eight times.

In Sharjah, the UIM F1 H2O World Championship takes place every December as part of Sharjah Water Festival. For a quieter but still vigorous display of boating prowess, look out for the various dragon boat events held throughout the year (dubaidragonboat.com), and keep an eye open for the many sailing and dhow racing events that take place off Dubai's shoreline, including the 10-day Maktoum Sailing Trophy, which takes place every February (dimc.ae).

Ports Of Call
If you've already established that sailing is your pastime, and you either have a boat or are currently looking to buy one, you're going to need to store it somewhere. There are still waiting lists at a few of the UAE's most established marinas but, by and large, there is availability. Rates start from Dhs.245 per month.

Buying A Boat
Whether you're purchasing your first vessel, or you're a serious skipper, there are a few rules and regulations you need to be aware of. You will need the following:
- Marine craft registration and licence
- Marine craft inspection report
- Coastguard approved transponder
- Boat insurance
- Permit to sail
- Marine driver's licence

Both private vessels – also known as 'pleasure', leisure or marine craft – and commercial vessels, must be registered annually with the Dubai Maritime City Authority (DMCA) before they can be used. As part of this process, you will need to insure your vessel (Dubai Insurance and AXA Gulf both offer boat insurance), take it to the DMCA at the dry docks for a marine inspection report, and get a transponder fitted.

Before you reach the water, you will need to obtain a permit to sail, which is authorised by the Dubai Coastguard; its patrol boats are often on the look out to make sure boat owners have complied with all these regulations. You will also need to apply to the DMCA for a marine driver's licence, a relatively new rule to ensure that all boat owners have the theoretical and practical knowledge and expertise to drive light marine vessels and leisure crafts.

Explorer's *Dubai How-To* guide gives full information on all procedures required in buying and registering a boat and a jet ski.

Camping
To really appreciate the surroundings that Dubai has to offer, you need to venture out and experience the natural wonders of the Arabian countryside for at least a night or two. There are an awe-inspiring array of safe and secluded locations to make camping a much-loved activity in Dubai and the UAE. While the weather is rarely bad – there's hardly ever any rain – the ideal time for a camping trip is between October and April. Such warm temperatures mean you can camp with much less equipment and preparation than in other countries, and many first-timers or families with children find that camping becomes their favourite weekend break.

Choose between the peace and tranquillity of the desert, or camp among the wadis and mountains next to trickling streams in picturesque oases. Generally speaking, there are no restrictions on where you can camp, with the exception of some beaches, but obviously people's privacy and property need to be respected at all times.

About 140km west of Abu Dhabi, Mirfa is a small, quiet town located on the coast. While there are not a lot of attractions, the long stretch of beach is a kitesurfer's paradise and many choose to pitch tents here, especially during the popular Al Gharbia Watersports Festival which takes place in March each year. Or head to Ras Khumais. Turning off the main road 15km after Sila (6km before the Saudi Arabia boarder), this small road takes you up to the headland of Ras Khumais. Before you hit the military post, there are a few areas where you can drive onto the beach

THINGS TO SEE & DO
ACTIVITIES

and camp right beside the sea while watching pink flamingos as they bob around in the turquoise sea.

Luckily, in the UAE there's a great selection of stores that offer a huge variety of camping equipment whatever your budget. Head to the Shopping section for listings.

Child's Play
The long stretch of beach in Fujairah is ideal for those travelling with kids. Hotels line some of these beaches and, so, if your attempt at a beach BBQ goes awry, you can always head to a restaurant to fill empty bellies. Toilets in the hotels can also be a sight for sore eyes for those with kids too. Other good locations include Jabal Ali and Hatta as they all have hotels nearby.

Glamping
Love camping but hate pitching? In these parts, you can always take to the great outdoors with a few extra luxuries. There are several tour companies that organise desert camping trips which make for a completely hassle-free experience all round. These firms usually offer a full desert safari, complete with dune bashing, camel riding, belly dancers and a BBQ dinner, as well as an overnight stay, but usually tourists choose to skip the staying over part. Check the list of tour companies for more. For those who want to try the very best in glamping experiences try Banyan Tree Al Wadi, where tented luxury awaits. Expect four-poster beds, tent-service and unrivalled extravagance.

Places To Pitch Up
You can camp just about anywhere but there are some stand-out spots that are super places to pitch up. Many good camping spots are easily accessible from tarmac roads too, so a 4WD is not always required. Jebel Yibir is the UAE's highest peak and, as such, camping out on the mountain (there's a road up to the summit) is a good option for the warmer months as the temperatures up there are much cooler than down below. The Wadi Sidr off-road route leads to a plateau that offers some good places to camp, with great views, while both Fossil Rock and the drive from Madam to Madah provide terrific, accessible dune driving and camping spots.

The ultimate camping experience, however, is to be had in the sea of dunes at Liwa, where you can go to sleep beneath a starry sky and wake up completely surrounded by one of the world's most mesmerising dunescapes (see Out Of The City). For more information on off-road adventuring and camping, refer to the *UAE Off-Road Explorer*.

Don't forget that while the UAE has comparably low rainfall, care should always be taken in and near wadis as flash floods, although rare, can occur; remember, it may be raining in the mountains miles from where you are.

Caving

The cave network in the Hajar Mountains is extensive and much of it has yet to be explored. Some of the best caves are near Al Ain, the Jebel Hafeet area and just past Buraimi near the Oman border. Many of the underground passages and caves have spectacular displays of curtains, stalagmites and stalactites, as well as gypsum flowers.

In Oman, the range includes what is still believed to be the second-largest cave system in the world, as well as the Majlis Al Jinn Cave – the second-largest chamber in the world.

Within the region, caving ranges from fairly safe to extremely dangerous and, as no mountain rescue services exist, anyone venturing out into the mountains should always be well-equipped and accompanied by an experienced leader.

Mountain High Middle East
050 659 5536
mountainhighme.com
A company providing exciting adventure experiences and motivational and teambuilding activities. Mountain-climbing and trekking are just some of the trips they can organise.

UAE & Oman Rock Climbing & Outdoor Adventures
Abu Dhabi **055 770 8629**
Providing rock climbing adventures around the UAE, Oman and further afield, UAE & Oman Rock Climbing & Outdoor Adventures welcomes everyone from beginners to experienced climbers. The type of climbing includes traditional, bouldering, DWSing, sport climbing, spelunking, and aid climbing, and the company aims to build a large community of keen climbers in the region.

Climbing

Excellent climbing can be found in various locations around the UAE, including Ras Al Khaimah, Hatta and the Al Ain/Buraimi region. More than 600 routes have been recorded since the 1970s. These vary from short outcrop routes to difficult mountain routes of alpine proportions. Most range from very severe up to extreme. There are several easier routes for beginner climbers, especially around Wadi Bih and Wadi Khab Al Shamis.

To meet like-minded people, head to Wadi Bih where you'll find climbers nearly every weekend, or go to one of the climbing walls listed below. For more information, contact John Gregory on 050 647 7120. Other excellent resources are uaeclimbing.com and the book *UAE Rock Climbing* by Toby Foord-Kelcey.

WHAT TO CARRY WHEN CAMPING

- ☐ Tent (to avoid creepy crawlies, heavy dew, wind and goats)
- ☐ Lightweight sleeping bag
- ☐ Air bed
- ☐ Torches and spare batteries
- ☐ Maps or a GPS system
- ☐ Cool box (fully stocked)
- ☐ Water
- ☐ Food and drink
- ☐ Camping stove, firewood or BBQ and charcoal
- ☐ Newspaper to light the fire
- ☐ Matches or lighters
- ☐ Insect repellent and antihistamine cream
- ☐ First aid kit (including any personal medications)
- ☐ Sun protection (hats, sunglasses, sun cream)
- ☐ Warm clothing for cooler evenings
- ☐ Toilet roll
- ☐ Rubbish bags
- ☐ Mobile phone (fully charged)
- ☐ Explorer's Camping Shower

THINGS TO SEE & DO
ACTIVITIES

Climbing wall at Playnation

Adventure HQ
Al Quoz Ind. 1 **04 346 6824**
adventurehq.ae
Map **1 T6** Metro **Noor Bank**
As well as being arguably the best place in the UAE to pick up climbing gear, Adventure HQ has a state-of-the-art climbing wall and cable obstacle course. Climbing rates starting from Dhs.50 per person. Test your climbing gear for cold conditions in the Chill Chamber.

Cleopatra's Spa & Wellness
Umm Hurair 2 **04 324 7700**
cleopatrasspaandwellness.com
Map **2 K7** Metro **Dubai Healthcare City**
The indoor climbing wall at Cleopatra's Spa and Wellness in Wafi offers courses for all abilities, including beginners' classes as well as sessions for experienced climbers. The wall has routes of varying difficulty and crash mats are provided for bouldering. Lessons cost Dhs.62 per hour and are limited to six people per instructor.

Climbing Dubai
Trade Centre Apartments Trade Center 2 **04 306 5061**
dorellsports.com
Map **2 H6** Metro **World Trade Centre**
The Middle East's tallest outdoor climbing wall can be found at Dubai World Trade Centre Hotel Apartments. Learn to scale the impressive 16 metre wall with an introductory lesson for Dhs.85. Courses for adults are Dhs.350 for five classes and for kids are Dhs.250 for five classes. A day pass costs Dhs.60. Climbing Dubai also has an eight-metre climbing tower at Horizon School Dubai, next to Safa Park Gate 4 (050 659 8500).

E-Sports
Al Garhoud **04 282 4540**
esportsuae.com
Map **2 M8** Metro **GGICO**
E-Sports offers climbing lessons for children and adults at GEMS World Academy, Jumeirah Primary School and GEMS Wellington International School. Advanced outdoor classes teach how to classify a climb, examine ropes and equipment for faults, evaluate the safety of a climb and know exactly what to do in an emergency situation. E-Sports also organises climbing and hiking holidays to destinations such as the French Alps.

Desert Activities

When it comes to the UAE, there's one place that demands our attention more than any other: the desert. It makes up more than 90% of the country and it's the biggest outdoor adventure playground you could imagine. In all directions the desert offers a varied and fascinating landscape that has great potential for exploring and leisure-time activities. In Dubai, there are a number of organisations who offer professional desert driving and off-road courses (see opposite for details). A number of tour companies provide desert safari trips, or lease out dune buggies and quad bikes; these companies are listed under Desert & Mountain Tours.

Dubai Explorer

THINGS TO SEE & DO
ACTIVITIES

Al Futtaim Training Centre
Nr Dubai Duty Free Umm Ramoul **04 292 0555**
traininguae.com
Map **2 N9** Metro **Emirates**
Classroom and practical tuition for off-road driving enthusiasts to learn how to venture safely out and into the desert.

Desert Rangers
Nr American Hospital Oud Metha **04 357 2200**
desertrangers.com
Map **2 K6** Metro **Oud Metha**
Experience a four-hour desert driving safari with the chance to spend an hour behind the wheel. The costs are Dhs.1,000 with own vehicle, or Dhs.1,800 without.

Emirates Driving Institute
Nr Galadari Engineering Al Qouz Ind. 3 **04 340 0449**
edi-uae.com
Map **1 T7** Metro **First Gulf Bank**
Offers an eight-hour desert driving course from Dhs.500 or Dhs.550 on Fridays.

OffRoad-Zone
8th Street Al Qouz Ind. 1 **04 339 2449**
offroad-zone.com
Map **2 A6** Metro **Noor Bank**
Drivers are taught how to handle a 4WD on a training course in Jabal Ali which covers all terrains from deep water crossings to sandy descents. Bring your own 4WD or rent one from OffRoad-Zone. Dhs.850 per person for three hours.

Drive With Care
To protect the environment from damage, you should try to stick to existing tracks rather than create new tracks across virgin countryside. While it may be hard to deviate from the track, dunes are ever changing so obvious paths are less common. Although the sandy dunes may look devoid of life, there is a surprising variety of flora and fauna that exists. Check out Explorer's *UAE Off-Road* series for more information.

Desert Driving
Dune bashing, desert driving or off-roading is one of the toughest challenges for both car and driver, but once mastered, it's great fun if you do it safely. Taking special off-road driving lessons enables you to make the most of your 4WD and learn how to tackle driving in the desert without getting stuck in the sand. Learn what to do if you do get bogged in, or learn more about driving your own vehicle safely in the sand – a good idea if you plan to go camping. See Off-roading for some of the best and most peaceful places in the region to visit away from the city.

Dune Buggying
Unless you've got Dhs.60,000 to spare for a neat motorised vehicle used solely for the pleasure of revving up and down dunes, chances are you've not got a dune buggy, but ask almost every adventure junkie in the UAE and they'll tell you that getting out to the dunes to shred some sand is top on their list on fun. Dune buggying is a full-on adrenaline bender spent rocketing across the desert plains in custom-made two-seater buggies that resemble something you might see on a lunar landing. See Desert & Mountain Tours.

Quad Biking
More adrenaline-fuelled than a desert hack and closer to the action than a 4WD tour, on a quad you're down at sand level feeling every dune contour. It is especially exciting as the routes get more challenging. Just remember to listen to the instructions of the professionals accompanying you.

Sandboarding
Sandboarding is a sport of its own and requires balance, strength and no small amount of tenacity. Once you climb your way to the top of the dune, it's best to wax the bottom of the board to reduce friction between the board and the sand. Strap your feet onto the board, bending your back knee slightly and slide on down, using your heels and toes to turn. All major tour operators in Dubai (see Desert & Mountain Tours) offer sandboarding experiences with instruction.

Mountain Biking
Away from the city, Dubai also has a lot to offer mountain bikers. On a mountain bike, it's possible to see the most remote and untouched places that are not even accessible in 4WDs. For hardcore, experienced bikers there is some good terrain from super-technical rocky trails to mountain routes above the desert. See Biking for further details.

Diving
The UAE offers diving that's really very special; the warm seas and clear, calm waters of the lower Arabian Gulf and the Gulf of Oman will satisfy all tastes and levels of experience for divers and snorkellers alike and are perfect places for exploring the region's varied underwater life. The UAE's coastal waters are home to a variety of marine species, coral life and shipwrecks. You'll see some exotic fish, like clownfish and seahorses, and possibly even spotted eagle rays, moray eels, small sharks, turtles, dolphins, barracuda, jellyfish, sea snakes and stingrays.

Most of the wrecks are on the west coast, while the beautiful flora and fauna of coral reefs can be seen

THINGS TO SEE & DO
ACTIVITIES

on the east coast. Cement Barge, Mariam Express and the MV Dara wreck are some of the more popular dive sites. Off the east coast, one well-known dive site is Martini Rock, a small, underwater mountain covered with colourful soft coral, with a depth range of three to 19 metres. North of Khor Fakkan is the Car Cemetery, a reef that has thrived around a number of cars placed 16 metres below water. Visibility off both coasts ranges from five to 20 metres.

Another option for diving enthusiasts is to take a trip to Musandam. This area, which is part of the Sultanate of Oman, is often described as the 'Norway of the Middle East' due to the fjord-like inlets and the way the sheer cliffs plunge directly into the sea. It offers some spectacular dive sites. Straight-down wall dives with strong currents and clear waters are more suitable for advanced divers, while the huge bays, with their calm waters and shallow reefs, are ideal for the less experienced. Visibility here is between 10 and 35 metres.

If you plan to travel to Khasab, the capital of the Musandam region, you may not be able to take your own air tanks across the border and will have to rent from one the dive centres there. You may also require an Omani visa. Alternatively, from Dibba on the east coast, you can hire a fast dive boat to take you anywhere from five to 75km up the coast. The cost ranges from Dhs.150 to Dhs.500, for what is usually a two-dive trip.

There are plenty of dive companies in the UAE that can help you should you want to try diving for the first time, or improve on your existing diving skills (see below). PADI training is available from beginner level through to instructor qualifications. Most companies offer both tuition and straightforward dive outings, with equipment. Online PADI e-learning courses are also available via Al Boom Diving (alboomdiving.com).

Underwater Explorer
Check out the *UAE Underwater Explorer* for further information on the best diving and snorkelling sites in the area as well as detailed info on diving companies and clubs. Go to askexplorer.com to purchase a copy.

7 Seas Divers
Nr Safeer Centre, Al Hayawa Khor Fakkan
09 238 2971
7seasdivers.com
This PADI dive centre offers day and night diving trips to sites around Khor Fakkan, Musandam and Lima Rock. Training is provided from beginner to instructor level, in a variety of languages.

Al Boom Diving
Nr Iranian Hospital Jumeira 1 04 342 2993
alboomdiving.com
Map **2 H4** Metro **World Trade Centre**
Al Boom's Aqua Centre on Al Wasl Road (there are centres in Fujairah, Dibba and Jabal Ali too) is a purpose-built school with a diving shop. There are diving trips daily. PADI certification starts from Dhs.1,750 for Scuba Diver; novices can try a disco very dive experience for Dhs.150. Al Boom also runs the Diving With Sharks experience in Dubai Aquarium at The Dubai Mall where you can experience a 40 minute dive in a tank filled with these sharp toothed creatures. For more, see thedubaiaquarium.com.

Arabian Divers & Sportfishing Charters
Marina Al Bateen Abu Dhabi 050 614 6931
This dive centre has a complete range of diving courses and adventure packages, all based in the waters surrounding the Musandam Peninsula. Guests can enjoy a fusion of Caribbean and Arabian seafood onboard, as well as activities such as environmental education classes.

Atlantis Dive Centre
Atlantis Nakhlat Jumeira 04 426 3000
atlantisthepalm.com
Map **1 N1** Metro **Nakheel**
This top level, accredited PADI facility is one of the best equipped in the country with indoor saltwater pools, classrooms, good quality equipment and boat rental. All major courses are available from discovery to advanced, as well as a variety of trips and tours. Its Family Fun Days provide a free introduction to diving for the whole family.

Diving

THINGS TO SEE & DO
ACTIVITIES

BSAC 406 Wanderers Dive Club
Shj Wanderers Sharjah **06 566 2105**
bsac406.com
This club is a member of the British Sub Aqua Club and follows its training, certification and diving practices. Clubhouse facilities include a training room, social area, equipment room, compressors, dive gear and two dive boats. The club dives mainly shipwrecks in the Arabian Gulf, and launches boats from both Sharjah and Dubai, depending on which dive site they are visiting.

Desert Sport Diving Club
Street 40A Al Qouz 1 desertsportsdivingclub.net
Map **2 C7** Metro **Noor Bank**
Dubai's only independent diving group meets on Mondays and Wednesdays at the clubhouse near Sheikh Zayed Road to plan dives. The group has two boats in Dubai and one on the east coast. A Dhs.1,000 fee entitles members to unlimited free dives on club boats. Guests pay Dhs.200 per dive.

Divers Down UAE
Iberotel Miramar Al Aqah Fujairah **09 237 0299**
diversdown-uae.com
Offers PADI courses for all abilities, and organises a variety of diving adventures including wreck dives, wall dives, deep dives and night dives, as well as dives in the Gulf of Oman. It runs two boats, operates three dives per day, and is open seven days a week; transport can be provided. In 2013, a centre also opened at RIVA Beach Club on the Palm Jumeirah. As well as regular dives, this centre offers: a Travel Club, which organises international diving excursions; diving for youngsters; and an extensive schools programme incorporating the Duke of Edinburgh Award, International Baccalaureate (IB CAS Projects), holiday camps, specialised 'Week Without Walls' programme and GAP year courses with training for future dive instructors.

Emirates Diving Association
Al Shindagha **04 393 9390**
emiratesdiving.com
Map **2 M4** Metro **Al Ghubaiba**
A non-profit organisation that seeks to protect the UAE's marine resources. It runs a coral monitoring project and annual Clean-Up Arabia campaigns. Divers are encouraged to join for Dhs.100 per year.

Freediving UAE
Abu Dhabi **050613 0486**
freedivinguae.com
This Abu Dhabi-based company teaches you how to dive deep without the aid of scuba equipment. Allowing divers to enjoy a whole new sense of freedom, freediving is rapidly gaining in popularity. Freediving UAE offers all levels of training courses.

Freestyle Divers
Royal Beach Fujairah **09 244 5756**
freestyledivers.com
A quality dive centre with learning premises on Al Wasl Road as well as a dive centre at the Royal Beach Hotel in Dibba. Offers courses and certification from beginner to advanced divers and organises regular trips. The full PADI Open Water Diver course costs Dhs.2,100.

Nomad Ocean Adventures
Nr The Harbour, Al Biah Dibba **+968 26 836 069**
discovernomad.com
This very friendly dive centre offers dive, dhow and overnight camping trips which can be tailored for individual parties. A two-dive trip with equipment starts at Dhs.450, a beginner's trial dive costs Dhs.500. You can also spend the weekend at its wonderfully charismatic eco-lodge and complete your open water course (including nine dives and certification). Rates for this start at Dhs.1,800. Call Christophe on the number above or +968 98 155 906.

The Pavilion Dive Centre
Jumeirah Beach Hotel Umm Suqeim 3 **04 406 8828**
jumeirah.com
Map **1 S4** Metro **First Gulf Bank**
This PADI Gold Palm IDC Centre is run by PADI course directors. Daily dive charters for certified divers are available in Dubai; charters to Musandam can be organised upon request from Dhs.650 with equipment. Open Water certification is Dhs.1,850.

Sandy Beach Diving Centre
Sandy Beach Fujairah **09 244 5555**
sandybm.com
Located in a chalet beach resort, the centre, which sells dive equipment, is open year-round. Nearby Snoopy Island, alive with hard coral and interesting marine life, is an excellent spot for snorkelling and diving.

Scuba 2000
Al Bidiya Beach, Al Bidiyah Fujairah **09 238 8477**
scuba-2000.com
This east coast dive centre provides daily trips to Dibba and Khor Fakkan, as well as a range of courses starting at Dhs.400 for Discover Scuba and rising to Dhs.2,200 for Open Water certification.

Scubatec Diving Center
Nr LuLu Hypermarket Al Karama **04 334 8988**
scubatecdiving.greensmedia.com
Map **2 K5** Metro **Al Jafiliya**
A five-star IDC operator, licensed by PADI and TDI, offering courses from beginner to instructor level. Dives are available in Dubai and on the east coast.

THINGS TO SEE & DO
ACTIVITIES

Sheesa Beach Dive Centre
Musandam Dibba 968 26836551
sheesabeach.com
The perfect dive centre for those wanting to explore the amazing dive sites of Musandam – said to be amongst the world's very best. As well as its resort in Dibba, Sheesa offers all manner of diving, from kids' courses and speciality diving to PADI certification. It also offers more private trips on speedboats as well as social dhow trips, from a few hours' duration to a full weekend or several days.

Decompression Sickness
While diving is generally a safe sport, there is always a risk of decompression sickness if a diver stays too deep for too long or ascends too rapidly. One of the first symptoms is aches and pains in the joints, and following that there may be a skin rash or dizziness and other neurological symptoms.

If you notice any of these symptoms after diving, consult a doctor as soon as possible – it is likely that you will need oxygen and possibly hyperbaric re-compression. Before you can receive treatment in a re-compression chamber, a qualified diving doctor must sign a consent form – there's no point just turning up at the chamber.

In Dubai you can contact Dr Barbara Karin Vela for diving-related questions at Dubai London Clinic and Speciality Hospital on Jumeirah Beach Road in Umm Suqeim (800-DLC/800-352). In an emergency, call 050 885 8172. The UAE only has two hyperbaric re-compression chambers – one at Zayed Military Hospital in Abu Dhabi (02 444 8100) and another at Aqua Marine Diving Services in Al Qouz industrial area (aqua-diving-services.com).

Snorkelling
If you'd like a glimpse of underwater life without making the investment to become a certified diver, snorkelling is the way to go. It's a great hobby regardless of your age or fitness level and you can pretty much snorkel anywhere off a boat – all you need is a mask and fins. The dive sites listed before are perfect for snorkellers and divers alike. Snorkelling offers a different experience to diving, with many interesting creatures such as turtles, rays and even sharks seen near the surface. It's also a great way for the family to enjoy an activity together, and all you need is some basic equipment. You can snorkel anywhere off a boat or off any beach.

The east coast is a great area for snorkelling and has the most diverse marine life compared the Dubai's coast. Most dive centres take snorkellers out on their boats (along with divers) and the trip last for about two hours. Some centres can make arrangements to take you to Shark Island (also called Khor Fakkan Island) where you can spend the day.

You can also go to Sandy Beach Hotel in Fujairah and spend the day on the beach and swim out to Snoopy Island, just a short distance from shore. In winter time, the water recedes a long way and the distance you have to swim is even less – but the water temperature will be considerably cooler too. Musandam offers good snorkelling too, but the waters can have strong currents so it's a good idea to go with a tour company and have a guide to point out the best sites. The best fish life is to be found between the surface and 10 metres below, so try to snorkel along the side of rocks and islands. There are a number of tour companies that offer dhow trips for dolphin watching and snorkelling, and the boats usually moor in areas that are safe for snorkelling in.

Hiking
If you've always wanted to get into hiking but were daunted by the prospect of setting out into the wild on your own, then going on an organised hike is the best way to step out into the UAE's great outdoors. It's easy in Dubai to get out of the habit of walking, and so even the most gentle of hikes can be good for the heart.

Safety First
As with any trip into the UAE 'outback', take sensible precautions. Tell someone where you are going and when you should be back, and don't forget to take a map, compass, GPS equipment and robust hiking boots. Don't underestimate the strength of the sun – take sunscreen and, most importantly, lots of water. Be particularly careful in wadis (dry riverbeds) during the wet season (November to January) as flash floods can immerse a wadi in seconds. Also note that there are no mountain rescue services in the UAE.

Despite Dubai's flat terrain, spectacular hiking locations can be found just a few hours outside the city limits. In the very north of the UAE, the Ru'us Al Jibal Mountains contain the highest peaks in the area, standing proud at over 2,000m, while the impressive Hajar Mountains stretch from Musandam in the north all the way down to the Empty Quarter desert in the south. Inland, Al Ain provides some excellent hiking routes, with plenty of mountains, including the imposing Jebel Hafeet, teamed with seven lush oases. Routes range from short, easy walks leading to spectacular viewpoints, to all-day treks over difficult terrain, and can include major mountaineering. Some hikes follow centuries-old Bedouin and Shihuh mountain paths, a few of which are still being used.

One of the easiest places to reach is the foothills of the Hajar Mountains on the Hatta Road, near the

THINGS TO SEE & DO
ACTIVITIES

Oman border. After passing through the desert, the flat, stark, rugged outcrops transform the landscape. Explore any turning you like, or take the road to Mahdah, along which you'll find several hiking options. Other great areas for hiking and exploring include the mountains in and around Musandam, and the mountains near the east coast. The mountains in the UAE don't generally disappoint, and the further off the beaten track you get, the more likely you are to find interesting villages where residents live in much the same way as they did centuries ago. You can find details of local hikes in the *UAE Off-Road Explorer*; and for somewhere a bit further afield see *Oman Trekking*, a guide book from Explorer with pull-out maps covering major signed routes in Oman.

Absolute Adventure
Al Diyafah Centre Al Bada' 04 345 9900
adventure.ae
Map **2 J5** Metro **Al Jafiliya**
This adventure tour operator offers a range of treks, varying in difficulty, including extreme trekking at Jebel Qihwi and an eight-hour coastal village trek. The activity centre, right on the beach at Dibba, can accommodate 14 people for group stays – and beach barbecues. The group also organises treks for serious hikers to destinations further afield, such as Nepal. Check the website for details of upcoming trips.

Arabia Outdoors
055 955 6209
arabiaoutdoors.com
Organises individual, group and corporate hikes along routes such as Jebel Qihwi, Jebel Hafeet and Stairway To Heaven. Other activities include camping, climbing and kayaking, and team-building camps and events.

Desert Rangers
Nr American Hospital Oud Metha 04 357 2200
desertrangers.com
Map **2 K6** Metro **Oud Metha**
Offers hikes for individuals and groups of up to 100 people by dividing them into smaller teams to tackle different trails to the summit. A variety of routes are offered according to age and fitness. Locations include Fujairah, Dibba, Masafi, Ras Al Khaimah and Al Ain, with prices starting at Dhs.275 per person.

Off-roading

Getting out into the deserts and wadis by 4WD is a must-do while you're a Dubai resident and, once you're out there, there are some super hiking and camping spots to take advantage of too. If you're desert driving for the first time, go with an experienced person – driving on sand requires very different skills to other surfaces. Tour companies offer a range of desert and mountain safaris (see Tour Operators). 4WDs can be hired from most car hire companies (see Car Hire Companies).

OffRoad-Zone
If you're really keen to learn to off-road in a controlled environment, then OffRoad-Zone (offroad-zone.com) runs a driving centre at the Jebel Ali Shooting Club where you can practise tackling all manner of obstacles that you might find while off-roading, including deep water, loose rocks and steep descents. Tutors are on hand to show you the proper technique too.

Northern Emirates: For a weekend away, with some of the best driving in the UAE, combine the mountains around Wadi Bih, near Ras Al Khaimah, with one of the interesting wadi routes on the east coast.
East Coast: From Dubai, the east coast can be reached in about two hours. The mountains and beaches are fantastic spots for camping, barbecues and weekend breaks, as well as various other activities. There are some great wadi and mountain routes here, and the area is also renowned for its diving and snorkelling opportunities, particularly around Snoopy Island.
Hatta: The Hatta region is home to the popular Big Red sand dune, a huge draw and a must-do challenge for off-roaders and quad bikers, as well as the Hatta Pools, a great swimming spot in the Hajar Mountains.
Al Ain: The oasis town is worthy of a visit in its own right, but nearby the imposing Jebel Hafeet and Hanging Gardens have great trekking spots.
Liwa: A trip to Liwa is one you'll never forget – it's one of the few remaining chances to experience unspoiled dunes. The drive from Dubai is long, more suitable for a two or three day camping trip, but the journey is worth it. Prepare for the most adventurous off-road driving the UAE has to offer. For further information and tips on driving off-road, check out both the *UAE Off-Road Explorer* and the *Oman Off-Road Explorer*. These books feature a multitude of detailed routes and give advice on how to stay safe, where to camp and things to do along the way. If you want a wilderness adventure but don't know where to start, contact any of the major tour companies. All offer a range of desert and mountain safaris.

Top Day Trips
If you want more ideas for the best day trips in Dubai and the region, get a copy of Explorer's *UAE Day Tripper*. The book features detailed reviews of some of the region's top attractions and sightseeing highlights. See askexplorer.com.

THINGS TO SEE & DO
ACTIVITIES

Water Activities

Temperatures throughout the year make Dubai the perfect place for sailing, swimming and watersports generally. The emirate's stunning stretch of beaches offer plenty of opportunities for water-based fun, from the latest craze of flyboarding to the more relaxed thrills of stand up paddleboarding, and the different ocean breaks allow for a wide range of activities to take place within close proximity.

Before grabbing your kayak or board and making a dash for the ocean, make sure that you are allowed to kitesurf or surf there. Some beaches have restrictions in place to protect swimmers, so check the signs before hitting the waves. Also remember that some beaches in the UAE may not be open to the public, or if they are, are not patrolled as diligently as some European beaches (if at all).

Swimming

Dubai has some great swimming spots, whether it's at the public beaches, in the private pools, in a beach club or one of the beach parks. The water temperature rarely dips below 20°C in winter, although during the summer it can feel like stepping into a bath. As with sea swimming elsewhere, rip tides and undertows can catch out even the strongest swimmer, so never ignore flags or signs ordering you not to swim. You might also run into quite a lot of jellyfish towards the end of the summer.

For details on where to swim or where to go to for swimming lessons in Dubai, see Clubs and Groups.

Swim Around The Burj Challenge

Keen swimmers can sign up for the annual Wild Wadi Swim Around The Burj challenge, held each year in aid of Medecins Sans Frontieres (swim.msf-me.org). Over 500 participants tackle the 1km distance and all swimmers are given plenty of encouragement from beach spectators.

Fishing

A boat isn't necessarily required to enjoy a great afternoon or evening of fishing. There are plenty of places along Dubai's coast where fishermen tend to congregate, but be aware that you must first obtain a recreational licence. You can apply and pay online (it costs Dhs.250) for a fishing licence via Dubai Municipality at dm.gov.ae/en. September to April is the peak fishing season here, although it's still possible to catch queenfish and sailfish in the summer months.

For a chance of hooking bigger bites, or to let someone else handle the licence admin, it's best to get out on the water and hire a fishing guide or charter a boat. For more information see Clubs & Groups.

Canoeing and Kayaking

Canoeing and kayaking are great ways to get close to the varied marine and birdlife of the UAE. Khor Kalba on the east coast is a popular canoeing spot, as are the mangrove-covered islands in Umm Al Quwain. Sea canoes can be used in Musandam to visit secluded bays and spectacular rocky coastlines where many species of turtles can often be found soaking up the sun. There are a number of specialist tour companies who offer canoeing and kayaking trips to all of these areas, including Desert Rangers and Noukhada. Alternatively, you can test your skills at the artificial whitewater rafting venue at Wadi Adventure (wadiadventure.ae).

For leisurely paddles along the coastline, many of the beach hotels provide hourly kayak hire (from around Dhs.100 per hour). Kite Beach, for instance charge Dhs.25 per hour and an adult must show ID or a driver's licence before heading out. A particularly pleasant kayaking route starts at the Hilton hotel along JBR and follows around clockwise past the Skydive Dubai centre, into the marina and out the other side back onto JBR. It's a peaceful route that should take a beginner kayaker an hour to complete. Just beware of the water taxis and other large vessels sailing swiftly in the marina.

Kitesurfing

Kitesurfing is an extreme sport that fuses elements of windsurfing, wakeboarding and kite flying. You may see kitesurfers showing off along several of Dubai's beaches, but the Kite Beach in Umm Suqeim (behind Sunset Mall, between the Dubai Offshore Sailing Club and Jumeirah Beach Park) is the only place where kiting is officially permitted. The Dubai Kite Forum (dubaikiteforum.com) is a good place to find out the latest on regulations. Kite People (kitepeople.ae) and Kitesurfing in Dubai (dubaikiters.com) are good online resources for buying equipment and locating IKO instructors.

Stand Up Paddleboarding

For a great workout and a good way to get out on the water when conditions are less than ideal for surfing or kitesurfing, the new craze of stand up paddleboarding or SUP, as it has become known, is a welcome addition to the watersport scene. Since the length and width of the board is a generous size, balancing on top of one is far easier than a surfboard. Get in contact with Surfing Dubai (surfingdubai.com) and Dukite (dukite.com/standup-paddle) for lessons, demos, sales and rentals. If you fancy getting your pulse racing a little harder, head to the Black Palace beach in between the Palm and Madinat Jumeirah with Oceanman UAE (oceanmanuae.com) where the team combine paddleboarding with an on-beach fitness regime comprising burpees, sprints and push

THINGS TO SEE & DO
ACTIVITIES

Watercooled

ups. Oceanman UAE also organises the popular monthly full moon paddleboarding sessions which takes paddlers out to the Burj Al Arab towards Pierchic under the stars and moonlight. Don't forget to bring your glow sticks and a head torch.

Wakeboarding
Wakeboarding is the cool, young upstart that has become the newest, hippest watersport around. If you don't have a boat, you'll find that many of the big hotels' beach clubs offer the sport with a going rate of about Dhs.140 for 15 minutes. Better still, there are now are few excellent wakeboarding-specific companies that offer hourly sessions with equipment hire included. See Watersports Centres and Companies at the end of this section for details.

Cable-Boarding
A popular sport in the US and Europe, cable-boarding allows you to wakeboard while being pulled along by a zip line. The Al Forsan International Sports Resort in Abu Dhabi has two excellent – and world-renowned – cable-boarding lakes.

Jet-skiing
Due to complaints of noise pollution and safety issues concerning swimmers, the Dubai Maritime City Authority has introduced licences and regulations for jet-skiing. You must now obtain a licence through DMCA (dmca.ae) and are only allowed to jet-ski within restricted areas between sunrise and sunset. If you do go jet-skiing, it may be worth checking that your medical insurance covers you. You may also want to consider whether you have any personal liability insurance in case you injure a third party. There are several places that offer jet ski rental, with prices varying significantly.

Flyboarding
Flyboarding is the new craze in watersports, where you'll be strapped onto a miniature wakeboard that's connected to a giant hose, that in turn is connected to a jet ski. As soon as your jet-skier flips the throttle, water is sent through the hose at a very high pressure into the board on your feet giving you powerful propulsion. Your job? Harness that power, balance on a cushion of water pressure – and fly. Check out flyboards-uae.com for information. Sessions start at Dhs.300 per 30 minute experience.

Surfing
Dubai isn't well-known as a surfing destination but if you're looking to catch some waves, you'll find an enthusiastic community of surfers who are out whenever there's a swell. Dubai Municipality has also periodically cracked down on surfing at public beaches in the past – check with Surfing Dubai for the latest before paddling out. Sunset Beach (Umm Suqeim open beach) has smallish but decent waves as does the Sheraton Beach between the Hilton and Sheraton in Marsa Dubai.

Watersports Centres and Companies

Al Forsan International Sports Resort
Khalifa City, Abu Dhabi **02 556 8555**
alforsan.com
If you've tried wakeboarding behind a boat, then you'll already have the general gist of what is required to cable board. The main difference, of course, is that there is no need for a boat and, instead, the strong cable links that are wired around the lakes pull you along.

Bristol Middle East Yacht Solution
Marina Walk Marsa Dubai **04 366 3538**
bristol-middleeast.com
Map **1 L5** Metro **Dubai Marina**
Has a watersports division that covers water skiing, wakeboarding, surf skiing, kneeboarding, banana boating, donut rides and speed boat trips.

Club Joumana
JA Jebel Ali Golf Resort Mena Jabal Ali **04 814 5023**
jaresortshotels.com
Metro **Jebel Ali**
Windsurfing, waterskiing, kayaking, catamaran, Laser sailing and banana boat rides are available at this club at JA Jebel Ali Golf Resort. Non-residents are charged an additional fee for day access to the beach and pools.

askexplorer.com   305

THINGS TO SEE & DO
ACTIVITIES

Dubai International Marine Club
Al Sufouh Rd Marsa Dubai **04 399 5777**
dimc.ae
Map **1 M5** Metro **Nakheel**
DIMC is the home of Mina Seyahi Watersports Club. Kayaks, surfskis, Lasers, catamarans, wakeboards, jet skis and kneeboards are available to hire.

Dubai Offshore Sailing Club
Jumeira Rd Umm Suqeim 1 **04 394 1669**
dosc.ae
Map **2 B4** Metro **Noor Bank**
This Royal Yachting Association Training Centre offers dinghy and keelboat courses throughout the year. See Boating in this chapter for more information.

Dubai Paddling School
Kite Beach Umm Suqeim 1 **050 640 6087**
Map **2 A4** Metro **Noor Bank**
This club organises the annual Shamaal International Surfski Race and a range of leisurely kayaking trips. Prices range from Dhs.1,200 for membership with berth, Dhs.250 without.

Dubai Surfski & Kayak Club
Nr Saga World Umm Suqeim 1 **055 498 6280**
dskc.hu
Map **1 U4** Metro **Noor Bank**
This club has a paddling school offering training for surfski or kayak beginners, and coaching for advanced paddlers. Activities include the 10km DSKC Squall on the last Friday of every month at Mina Seyahi.

Duco Maritime
Jumeira 3 **050 870 3427**
ducomaritime.com
Map **2 B4** Metro **Business Bay**
Classes are available every day by request on beaches in Dubai, RAK and Abu Dhabi. Two-hour lessons by IKO qualified instructors are available for beginners, charged at Dhs.300 per hour including equipment. Stand Up Paddleboarding lessons also available.

Explorer Tours
Nr Nadd Shamma Park Umm Ramool **04 286 1991**
explorertours.ae
Map **2 N10** Metro **Emirates**
Take a canoe or kayak trip in Umm Al Quwain from Dhs.300 per person with transport, or Dhs.200 per person without. Explore the tranquil mangroves of the east coast, famous for its variety of birds and marine life.

Sea Riders
Dubai Marina Mall Dubai Marina **055 510 3739**
searidersuae.com
Sea Riders has been in operation since summer 2013 but its fully-loaded boat complete with enormous speakers and laid back staff will no doubt make it a Dubai favourite. Sessions cost Dhs.500 for one hour (weekdays) and Dhs.550 per hour (weekends). Sea Riders also offer excellent private fishing and boating charters for competitive prices.

Sky & Sea Adventures
Sheraton Jumeirah Marsa Dubai **04 399 9005**
watersportsdubai.com
Map **1 K4** Metro **Jumeirah Lakes Towers**
Offers bodyboarding, kayaking, waterskiing, snorkelling, parasailing, windsurfing and wakeboarding.

Surf Dubai
3A Street Umm Suqeim 3 **050 504 3020**
surfingdubai.com
Map **1 T4** Metro **First Gulf Bank**
There was a great community of surfers linked together by this popular surf school, but sadly, the authorities prohibited the school from operating in 2013. Whilst the previous services of surfboard/SUP rental, surf/SUP lessons and surfboard repair are not currently available, they are still selling equipment, and attempting to gain the necessary permits to re-open, so check with them for the latest.

Surf School UAE
Riva Beach Club Nakhlat Jumeira **055 601 0997**
surfschooluae.com
Map **1 N3** Metro **Nakheel**
Owned and managed by keen and experienced surfers, and certified by the International Surf Association. Surf lessons are currently on hold due to a municipality ruling, but stand up paddleboarding lessons are available at Riva Beach Club. Keep an eye out for the latest on surfing and SUP in Dubai.

Wadi Adventure
Off Al Ain Fayda Rd Al Ain **03 781 8422**
wadiadventure.ae
The waves aren't always reliable in Dubai, unless you head for the hills that is. Located near Jebel Hafeet, entry to Wadi Adventure costs Dhs.50 to Dhs.100, with an hour in the surf pool (where waves reach three metres) costing Dhs.100 further, including equipment.

Watercooled
JA Jebel Ali Golf Resort Mena Jabal Ali **04 887 6771**
watercooleddubai.com
Metro **Jebel Ali**
Offers a wide range of watersports – from dinghy and catamaran sailing to wakeboarding – as well as a variety of RYA courses. Call in advance to reserve the kit you want. There's also a small bar with delicious mocktails, and guests can use the facilities at the adjacent JA Jebel Ali Golf Resort hotel for a limited time if hiring equipment at Watercooled.

THINGS TO SEE & DO
TOURS

TOURS

As befits a leading international tourist destination, Dubai is well geared up for taking people on tours of its attractions and highlights. It's generally a rite of passage for Dubai residents to go on a desert safari, and there are plenty of other popular options for seeing the country via land, sea or air.

Tour Tips
If you are booking a tour, make sure you ring around to get the best price. Dubai is dedicated to discounts and you can often get a better rate as a resident. Just remember it is all about putting on the charm – not being a cheeky customer.

Some tours are offered by most operators, particularly desert experiences and dhow cruises; both of these are great options for when you have guests in town. Other companies run memorable, specialised tours, such as diving trips, aerial sightseeing and trekking, while almost all the firms listed here will tailor programmes to suit individual needs.

Bus
If you've got visitors here on a short visit or on a whirlwind stopover in Dubai before they jet off elsewhere, a bus tour of the city is a great way to take in all the highlights in one go. It's also a good way to get acquainted with what's where when you first move to Dubai.

Shopping Tours
Dubai's reputation as the shopping capital of the Middle East is well deserved. From designer clothes, shoes and jewellery in the malls, to electronics, spices and gold in the souks, everything is available. A half-day shopping tour takes you round some of the best shopping spots.

ArtBus
04 341 7303
artinthecity.com
This service runs from the jamjar to galleries across town and Madinat Jumeirah during major art festivals and exhibitions.

Big Bus Tours
04 340 7709
bigbustours.com
A fleet of double-decker buses that provide a hop-on hop-off service, with audio commentary, to major attractions across town. Tickets are valid for either 24 or 48 hours.

Boulevard Bus Tour
Dubai Mall Downtown Dubai, Burj Khalifa
800 38224 6255
dubaimall.com
Map **2 F7** Metro **Burj Khalifa/Dubai Mall**
Whisks you around Downtown and, with a day ticket, you can hop on and off at any of the seven stops. There are four pick-ups per hour, and the bus runs from 10am to 10pm during the week and until midnight at weekends.

Easy Tour Dubai
04 388 3410
easytour.ae
Offers day and night guided bus tours around Dubai at 10am, 2.30pm, 4pm and 8pm. The four and two-hour round trips include free entrance to Dubai Museum and a walking tour in The Dubai Mall.

Wonder Bus Tours
Al Mankhool **04 359 5656**
wonderbustours.net
Map **2 L5** Metro **Al Fahidi**
Book a two-hour mini tour which travels along, and on, Dubai Creek in an amphibious bus. The tour covers Creek Park and Dubai Creek Golf & Yacht Club, and heads under Maktoum Bridge towards Garhoud Bridge, then returns to BurJuman.

Desert & Mountain
Desert safaris are by far the most popular variety of tours available, perhaps because a good safari offers many activities in one day. Expert drivers blast 4WD vehicles up, down and around massive dunes (dune bashing) while passing old Bedouin villages and pointing out beautiful natural attractions. Mountain safaris lead passengers through the narrow wadis and steep passes of the Hajar Mountains.

Some tours include sand skiing or boarding and end the day at a replica Bedouin camp where you can watch a belly dancer, eat Arabic delicacies, hold a falcon, ride camels and smoke shisha. Many operators even run overnight safaris that combine desert and mountain safaris. Most driving safaris include pick-up from your place of residence and lunch. The approximate cost for a desert safari is Dhs.150 to Dhs.350 (overnight up to Dhs.500).

THINGS TO SEE & DO
TOURS

Most tour operators offer variations on the main types of excursions: city tours, desert safaris and mountain safaris. Some offer more unique activities, such as fishing or diving trips, expeditions to the Empty Quarter, helicopter tours and desert driving courses. The main tour companies, and those that offer something a little bit different, are listed in this section – contact them directly for information on their full programmes and tours and overnight camping options.

Alpha Tours
Al Owais Bldg, Al Ittihad Rd Port Saeed **04 294 9888**
alphatoursdubai.com
Map **2 K7** Metro **Dubai Healthcare City**
Provides a full range of tours including shopping trips, desert safaris, flights and cruises.

Arabian Adventures
Emirates Holiday Bldg Business Bay **04 214 4888**
arabian-adventures.com
Map **2 E6** Metro **Business Bay**
Offers a range of tours and itineraries including desert safaris, city tours, sand skiing, dhow cruises, camel riding, and wadi and dune bashing.

Dadabhai Travel
Sama Bldg, Al Ittihad Rd Al Nahda 1 **04 220 9393**
dadabhaitravel.ae
Map **2 R7** Metro **Stadium**
One of the operators with the most extensive ranges of tours, covering everything from shopping and culture to overnight camps, it has a great Bedouin camp out near Al Aweer.

Desert Adventures
Al Barsha Boutique Bldg Al Barsha 1 **04 450 4450**
desertadventures.com
Map **1 Q6** Metro **Sharaf DG**
Offers a full range of city and desert tours throughout the emirate with interesting and creative city tours.

Desert Rangers
Nr American Hospital Oud Metha **04 357 2200**
desertrangers.com
Map **2 K6** Metro **Oud Metha**
Runs a wide variety of standard and specialist desert and mountain tours, including activities such as rock climbing, helicopter tours and kayaking.

Desert Rose Tourism
Platinum Business Centre Al Nahda 2 **050 778 5707**
desertrose-tourism.com
Map **2 S7** Metro **Al Nahda**
Offers city discovery tours with a guide, plus various trips around the UAE and Oman, including desert, camel safaris and dhow dinner cruises.

Desert Safari Abu Dhabi & Dubai
Lake View 316 Bldg Al Thanyah 5 **04 361 7530**
desertsafariabudhabi.ae
Map **1 M5** Metro **Jumeirah Lakes Towers**
Specialising in desert safaris, dune bashing and dune buggying, this company also offers city tours and water-based excursions.

Dream Explorer
Meena Bazaar Al Souk Al Kabeer **04 354 4481**
dreamexplorerdubai.com
Map **2 H5** Metro **Al Fahidi**
Desert and mountain tours, dune buggying, plus white-knuckle jet boat rides. A luxury option combines dune driving with a visit to the Bab Al Shams Desert Resort.

Dubai Tourism & Travel Services
Al Abbar Bldg Al Karama **04 336 7727**
dubai-travel.ae
Map **2 K6** Metro **Al Karama**
City shopping tours, creek dinner cruises, cultural tours to Sharjah and Ajman, plus desert, mountain and east coast excursions.

Gulf Ventures > p.309
Business Bay **04 404 5880**
gulfventures.com
Map **2 D6** Metro **Business Bay**
There's a wide range of activities including Bedouin camps, creek cruises and east coast tours on land and sea, plus fishing, polo and ballooning. More unusually, camel polo is a fun-packed day out, with the rare opportunity to learn the basics of polo.

Lama Tours
Al Sayegh Bldg Oud Metha **04 334 4330**
lamadubai.com
Map **2 L6** Metro **Oud Metha**
Tours include an excellent desert safari experience, dhow cruises, city excursions and fishing tours.

Net Tours
Al Zarouni Bldg Al Barsha 1 **04 376 2333**
nettoursuae.ae
Map **1 Q6** Metro **Sharaf DG**
Offers mountain tours and treks, theme park excursions, helicopter and balloon flights, dhow dinner cruises and desert safaris, plus of course the usual Bedouin desert campsite experience.

Oasis Palm Tourism
Royal Plaza Bldg, Al Rigga Rd Al Rigga **04 262 8889**
opdubai.com
Map **2 N5** Metro **Al Rigga**
One of the biggest and best known tour operators, Oasis Palm offers desert safaris, dhow dinner cruises

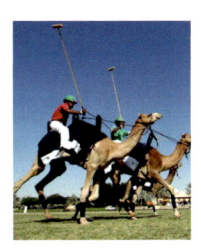

Think you know Dubai? Wait till you experience it with us.

We've been thrilling visitors to the United Arab Emirates and Oman for over two decades. Off-road desert action; polo and golf to camel-trekking and sandboarding; incredible rides by balloon and sea-plane; wedding celebrations and days that end in the romance of our Bedouin desert camp. All of this tailored to groups, families, couples or solo travellers—and wrapped in luxurious hospitality.

Call us today and discover why Gulf Ventures is your natural partner.

T: +971 4 404 5880
E: enquiries@gulfventures.com

gulfventures.com

Leisure Services / Event Services / Tours & Excursions

GULF VENTURES

Destination Management Specialists

THINGS TO SEE & DO
TOURS

and wadi trips, plus east coast tours, diving and deep sea fishing trips.

Orient Tours
Nr Le Meridien Fairway Al Garhoud **04 282 8238**
orient-tours-uae.com
Map **2 N7** Metro **GGICO**
City tours, including trips to the horse and camel races, desert safaris, sea safaris around Musandam, off-road trips to Hatta and day tours of the Empty Quarter in Liwa.

Planet Travel & Tourism
Abulhoul Bldg, Airport Rd Port Saeed **04 282 2199**
planetgrouponline.com
Map **2 N7** Metro **GGICO**
A large travel company with plenty of resources to call on, Planet Travel offers coach, heritage and shopping tours within Dubai, as well as safari and desert tours.

Dune Dinners
Enjoy some thrilling off-road desert driving before settling down to watch the sun set behind the majestic Arabian dunes. Starting around 4pm, tours typically pass camel farms and fascinating scenery that provide great photo opportunities. At a traditional Arabian campsite, enjoy a delicious dinner and the calm of a starlit desert night, before returning around 10pm.

Full-Day Safari
This day-long tour usually passes through traditional Bedouin villages and camel farms in the desert, with a drive through sand dunes of varying colours and heights. Tours often visit either Fossil Rock or the Hajar Mountains. A cold buffet lunch may be provided in the mountains before the drive home.

Hatta Pools Safari
Hatta is a quiet, old-fashioned town nestled in the foothills of the Hajar Mountains, famed for its fresh water rock pools that you can swim in. The full-day trip usually includes a stop at the Hatta Fort Hotel, where you can enjoy the pool, landscaped gardens, archery, and nine-hole golf course. Lunch is served either in the hotel, or alfresco in the mountains. The trip costs Dhs.260-Dhs.350.

Mountain Safari
Normally a full-day tour takes you across to the east coast, heading inland at Dibba and entering the spectacular Hajar Mountain range. You will travel through rugged canyons onto steep winding tracks, past terraced mountainsides and old stone houses. It returns via Dibba, where the journey home to Dubai stops off at the quaint Masafi Market on the way, where you can buy everything from rugs to beach inflatables.

Overnight Safari
This 24 hour tour starts at about 3pm with a drive through the dunes to a Bedouin-style campsite. Dine under the stars, sleep in the fresh air and wake to the smell of freshly brewed coffee, before heading for the mountains. The drive takes you through spectacular rugged scenery, past dunes and along wadis, before stopping for a buffet lunch and returning to Dubai.

Boat

An evening aboard a dhow, either on Dubai Creek or sailing along the coast, is a wonderfully atmospheric experience. Some companies run regular, scheduled trips, while others will charter out boats to private parties. Many boats also offer dinner cruises from the Bur Dubai side of the creek. Charters of luxury yachts, catamarans and fishing boats are available from several operators, and many firms will consider letting out their tour boats for the right price. If you want to go further afield, a dhow cruise in Musandam is a must and some dhow cruise companies offer transfers from Dubai. Alternatively, a number of dive companies, such as Al Boom Diving, offer sightseeing cruises – either as part of a dive trip or as a separate offering.

4Yacht Arabia
JAFZA View 18 Jabal Ali Ind. 2 **04 886 5755**
4yachtarabia.ae
Map **1 B7** Metro **Jebel Ali**
A luxury yacht charter and sales company with five Dubai-based yachts for charter, plus water taxis, and three vessels moored in Greece, if you fancy a cruising holiday.

Al Boom Tourist Village
Nr Al Garhoud Bridge Umm Hurair 2 **04 324 3000**
alboom.ae
Map **2 L8** Metro **Dubai Healthcare City**
Operates several dhows on the creek, with capacities ranging from 20 to 350 passengers. Various packages are available.

Al Marsa Tours & Cargo
University City Rd Sharjah **06 544 1232**
almarsamusandam.com
Runs dhow voyages off Musandam for divers, snorkellers and sightseers, lasting from half a day to a whole week.

Al Wasl Cruising & Fishing
Al Owais Bldg Hor Al Anz **04 239 4760**
cruiseindubai.com
Map **2 P6** Metro **Abu Baker Al Siddique**
Specialises in a variety of deep sea fishing trips and yacht charters with a fleet of modern vessels.

THINGS TO SEE & DO
TOURS

ART Marine
Shk Zayed Rd Al Qouz Ind. 1 04 338 8955
artmarine.net
Map **2 A6** Metro **Noor Bank**
Offers chartered yacht experiences from locations around the region, including Jumeirah Beach Hotel in Dubai, Emirates Palace and Yas Marina in Abu Dhabi, and the stunning Zighy Marina in Oman.

Athena Charter Yacht
Marina Yacht Club Marsa Dubai
Map **1 K5** Metro **Jumeirah Lakes Towers**
A 50 foot yacht available for cruises around Marsa Dubai, the Palm Jumeirah and along the Jumeira coastline, for up to 12 people at a time. On-board dining is also available.

Bateaux Dubai
Nr British Embassy Al Hamriya 04 814 5553
bateauxdubai.com
Map **2 M5** Metro **Baniyas Square**
This sleek sightseeing vessel offers daily tours but it's the dinner cruises that offer the best and most unique experience. The boat can also be privately chartered to cater for parties of up to 300 people.

Bristol Middle East Yacht Solution
Marina Walk Marsa Dubai 04 366 3538
bristol-middleeast.com
Map **1 L5** Metro **Dubai Marina**
Marina-based company that offers charters and packages on boats of all shapes and sizes, from luxury yachts to its old wooden dhow, Captain Jack, which regularly takes one-hour pleasure cruises along the coast from Marsa Dubai. The firm puts together land and air tours too.

Cruise With Nakheel
Nakheel Sales Centre Al Sufouh 2
nakheel.com
Map **1 N5** Metro **Nakheel**
Experience striking views of the Palm Jumeirah from the deck of a double-decker houseboat or smaller vessel. The 'Cruise with Nakheel' service runs trips for groups of up to 12, 15 and 30 people around the landmark island, with prices starting from around Dhs.1,000 per boat.

Divaz
Jebel Ali Golf Resort Mena Jabal Ali 04 814 5604
Metro **Jebel Ali**
More of a floating party than traditional boat trip, Divaz offers chilled dining experiences including a seafood buffet with a selection of fresh fish for only Dhs.250 per person. It also caters for raucous brunches or elegant night-time gatherings... all out on the open waves.

El Mundo
DIMC Marsa Dubai 050 551 7406
elmundodubai.com
Map **1 M5** Metro **Nakheel**
El Mundo is a 60 foot catamaran that offers four-hour cruises on Thursdays and Fridays, and can be privately chartered for all manner of occasions.

JA Jebel Ali Golf Resort
Nr Palm Jebel Ali Mena Jabal Ali 04 814 5555
jaresortshotels.com
Metro **Jebel Ali**
One or two-hour long leisure boat trips for up to seven people on board Club Joumana's 36ft fishing boat.

Khasab Travel & Tours
Al Muraqqabat 04 266 9950
khasabtours.com
Map **2 P6** Metro **Al Rigga**
Runs a dhow cruise from Khasab in Musandam that includes lunch, refreshments, snorkelling gear and a spot of fishing. Khasab Travel & Tours can also organise pick-ups from Dubai.

OCEAN Independence
Wafi Residences Umm Hurair 2 04 324 3327
oceanindependence.com
Map **2 L7** Metro **Dubai Healthcare City**
Provides a range of luxury yacht charters from short trips to overnight stays and holidays on the water. Also sells vessels and runs charters internationally.

Sheesa Beach Dive Center
Musandam Dibba 968 26836551
sheesabeach.com
Exceptionally fun day, overnight and week-long dhow cruises in Musandam, with transfers from Dubai available. Diving trips, PADI training and camping are also offered.

Tour Dubai
Oud Metha 04 336 8407
tour-dubai.com
Map **2 L6** Metro **Oud Metha**
Offers a variety of creek dhow tours and charter packages that range from romantic dinners for two to corporate hospitality for up to 200 guests.

Ultimate Charter
Fairmont Trade Center 1 04 346 4194
dubaiultimatecharter.com
Map **2 H5** Metro **World Trade Centre**
As well as two-hour dhow dinner cruises along Marsa Dubai and the Palm Jumeirah, there are catamaran party cruises, luxury motor yachts, super yachts and mega yachts available for charter, and fishing boats offering a guaranteed catch.

THINGS TO SEE & DO
TOURS

Waterworld Yacht Rental
Marina Yacht Club Marsa Dubai **04 422 8729**
waterworldyachtrental.com
Map **1 K5** Metro **Jumeirah Lakes Towers**
As well as yacht rentals from Dhs.699 per hour, this company offers deep sea fishing trips, BBQ cruises and dhow dinner cruises.

Xclusive Yachts Sport Fishing & Yacht Charter
Marina Yacht Club Marsa Dubai **04 432 7233**
xclusiveyachts.com
Map **1 K5** Metro **Jumeirah Lakes Towers**
Offering everything from 22ft to 90ft boats, Xclusive can organise sightseeing or fishing trips for groups of family or friends, or you can simply charter a boat and follow your own itinerary. Watersports including banana boating and parasailing can be included.

Dhow And Out
An option for large independent groups is to charter a dhow from the fishermen at Dibba on the east coast to travel up the coast to Musandam. If you're prepared to haggle you can usually knock the price down substantially, especially if you know a bit of Arabic. Expect to pay around Dhs.2,500 per day for a dhow large enough to take 20-25 people, or Dhs.100 per hour for a smaller one. You'll need to take your own food and water, as nothing is supplied onboard except ice lockers suitable for storing supplies. Conditions are basic, but you'll have the freedom to plan your own route and to see the beautiful fjord-like scenery of Musandam from a traditional wooden dhow.

The waters in the area are beautifully clear and turtles and dolphins can often be seen from the boat, although sometimes unfavourable weather conditions can seriously reduce visibility for divers. If you leave from Dibba (or Daba), Omani visas are not required, even though you enter Omani waters.

It is also possible to arrange stops along the coast and it's worth taking camping equipment for the night, although you can sleep on board. This kind of trip is ideal for diving but you should hire any equipment you may need before you get to Dibba. If diving is not your thing, you can just spend the day swimming, snorkelling and soaking up the sun.

Aerial Tours
With its soaring skyscrapers, rolling sand dunes and spectacular man-made islands, Dubai from the air is an impressive and truly unique sight. Swoop over the cityscape in a helicopter, fly along the coast in a seaplane, or take in the serenity of the desert from a graceful hot air balloon flight – any one of these experiences will live long in the memory. As with boat tours, most aerial tour companies offer a seat on a set tour as well as charter options.

Aerogulf Services
Dubai International Airport **04 877 6120**
aerogulfservices.com
Map **2 N7** Metro **GGICO**
Provides helicopter tours over the city and its main landmarks. A half-hour tour for four people costs Dhs.3,200 or you can opt to charter a chopper by the hour and choose your route.

Amigos Balloons
04 289 9295
amigos-balloons.com
Take a dawn hot air balloon flight over the desert out near Fossil Rock and watch the changing colour of the sands as the sun rises. Flights operate from September to June and cost Dhs.950 per person.

Balloon Adventures Emirates > p.19
Nr Bin Sougat Centre Al Rashidiya **04 285 4949**
ballooning.ae
Map **2 P11** Metro **Rashidiya**
There's nothing better than taking in the serenity of the desert from a graceful hot air balloon flight. Balloon Adventures Emirates organises tours, with flights departing before sunrise. Flights depart before sunrise between October and May, and are followed by dune driving.

Fujairah Aviation Academy
Fujairah **09 222 4747**
fujaa.ae
An enthralling bird's-eye view of Fujairah's coastline, rugged mountains, villages and date plantations. Flights can accommodate one to three people.

Gulf Ventures > p.309
Business Bay **04 404 5880**
gulfventures.com
Map **2 D6** Metro **Business Bay**
In addition to offering desert and mountain tours, Gulf Ventures also offers several ways for you to view the emirate from great heights. Fly over Fossil Rock in a hot air balloon, take a private helicopter along the coastline and over the Palm and Burj Al Arab, or soar through the sky in a sea plane.

Seawings > p.xxvi
JA Jebel Ali Golf Resort Mena Jabal Ali **04 807 0708**
seawings.ae
Metro **Jebel Ali**
A Seawings flight is often top on most residents' bucket list. Take off from the water in a seaplane from Jabal Ali or Dubai Creek for spectacular flights over the Gulf and city. Various package options are available.

THINGS TO SEE & DO
HOTELS

HOTELS

There are a vast array of hotels in Dubai, ranging from one of the most superlative and opulent in the world, the Burj Al Arab, with a rack rate in the region of Dhs.11,000 for a night in a standard suite, right down to the cheapest digs in areas such as Deira costing under Dhs.200 a night. There is an increasing number of internationally branded budget hotels, plus a handful of B&Bs, and there's even a youth hostel. While the hotels at the higher end of the market offer superb surroundings and facilities, those at the cheaper end vary – you get what you pay for. There are dozens of the world's leading hotel brands to be found here, many of them housed in some of the city's most iconic buildings.

The Dubai Department of Tourism & Commerce Marketing (DTCM) oversees a hotel classification system that gives an internationally recognised star rating to hotels and hotel apartments. This is being updated to include a budget hotel category, and Gold and Platinum Accolades for outstanding hotels and resorts.

Record breakers

Dubai's penchant for showing off has resulted in some stupendously extravagant places to stay. From one of the most expensive hotels in the world, the Burj Al Arab, to the tallest hotel in the world, the JW Marriott Marquis. Then there's The Meydan Hotel, which hosts the richest horse race in the world, the Dubai World Cup, and the Armani Hotel, nestled at the base of the tallest man-made structure in the world, practically every inch of which has been personally designed by Armani himself, one of the most famous designers in the world. And that's before you head out to Atlantis on the Palm Jumeirah – once the world's largest man-made island.

Staycations

Living in Dubai allows you to make the most of a destination that millions of tourists save up their hard earned cash to visit. With a wealth of showstopper hotels and all the amenities they provide – sumptuous spas, gorgeous swimming pools, five-star restaurants and incredible views – it's no bad thing to forgo the hassle of travel and take a staycation. Many hotels also offer seasonal discounts to GCC residents, particularly in the hot summer months when prices can be 50% lower than at peak times, providing a great opportunity for a bargain weekend 'away'. These hotels are the best Dubai has to offer for a luxurious beach break.

Anantara Dubai The Palm
East Crescent Nakhlat Jumeira 04 567 8888
anantara.com
Map **1 Q3** Metro **Nakheel**
This stunning hotel on the eastern crescent of Palm Jumeirah combines the hospitality of Thailand, the luxury of Arabia and the iconic over-water accommodation of the Maldives. Splash out on a villa on stilts hovering above the ocean, or opt for a lagoon villa, where you can step straight into the pool from the balcony of your stylish room. Impeccable service, a stunning infinity pool and beach side dining round off the incredible experience.

Atlantis The Palm > p.275
Crescent Rd Nakhlat Jumeira 04 426 0376
atlantisthepalm.com
Map **1 N1** Metro **Nakheel**
With a staggering 1,539 rooms and suites, all with views of the sea or the Palm Jumeirah, Atlantis is certainly one of Dubai's grandest hotels. It has no less than four fancy restaurants featuring the cuisine of Michelin-starred chefs, including a branch of the world-famous chain Nobu. It is also home to Aquaventure and the Lost Chambers aquarium.

Burj Al Arab
Off Jumeira Rd Umm Suqeim 3 04 301 7777
jumeirah.com
Map **1 S4** Metro **First Gulf Bank**
Standing on its own man-made island, this dramatic Dubai icon's unique architecture is recognised around the world. Suites have two floors and are serviced by a team of butlers. To get into the hotel as a non-guest, you will need a restaurant reservation.

Dubai Marine Beach Resort
Nr Jumeirah Mosque Jumeira 1 04 346 1111
dxbmarine.com
Map **2 H4** Metro **World Trade Centre**
This beachside hotel has 195 villa-style rooms nestled among lush, green landscaped gardens, waterfalls and streams. The grounds offer three swimming pools, a spa, a health club and a small private beach. The restaurants and bars are perennially popular, especially the Ibiza-esque Sho Cho and beautiful hangout, Boudoir.

Fairmont The Palm
The Trunk Nakhlat Jumeira 04 457 3388
fairmont.com
Map **1 N3** Metro **Nakheel**
Located on the trunk of the Palm Jumeirah, this hotel enjoys impressive views of Marsa Dubai. Relax and unwind at the Willow Stream Spa; enjoy the great outdoors at the hotel's private beach club with four swimming pools and outdoor leisure facilities; and

THINGS TO SEE & DO
HOTELS

take your pick from seven restaurants and lounges, serving Brazilian, pan-Chinese, Middle Eastern, Indian, Mediterranean and Asian cuisine. The Cigar Room features a walk-in humidor.

Jumeirah Beach Hotel
Jumeira Rd Umm Suqeim 3 **04 348 0000**
jumeirah.com
Map **1 S4** Metro **First Gulf Bank**
Shaped like an ocean wave, with a fun and colourful interior, the hotel has 598 rooms and suites and 19 private villas, all with a sea view. It is also home to some excellent food and beverage outlets, including Jamie's Italian restaurant, Uptown for happy hour cocktails and a great view of the Burj Al Arab.

Jumeirah Zabeel Saray
West Crescent Nakhlat Jumeira **04 453 0000**
jumeirahzabeelsaray.com
Map **1 L3**
So opulent, it was used for the lavish party scenes in Mission Impossible: Ghost Protocol, Zabeel Saray is an architectural wonder, drawing on Arabic and Turkish influences. It's a huge hotel with a gorgeous outdoor pool overlooking the sea. There are several excellent outlets including the super cool Voda bar, although the real draw is the spa which is one of the world's biggest and best.

Madinat Jumeirah
Nr Burj Al Arab Al Sufouh 1 **04 366 8888**
jumeirah.com
Map **1 R5** Metro **Mall of the Emirates**
This extravagant resort has two hotels, Al Qasr and Mina A'Salam, with no fewer than 940 luxurious rooms and suites, and the exclusive Dar Al Masyaf summer houses, all linked by man-made waterways navigated by wooden abra boats which whisk guests around the resort. Nestled between the two hotels is the Souk Madinat, with a plethora of popular shops, bars and restaurants all located inside a faux Arabian-style market. A third hotel is due to open in 2015.

One&Only Royal Mirage > p.175
Nr Palm Jumeirah Al Sufouh 2 **04 399 9999**
oneandonlyresorts.com
Map **1 M5** Metro **Nakheel**
This stunningly beautiful resort is home to three different properties: The Palace, Arabian Court, and the Residence & Spa. The service and dining (opt for the Beach, Bar & Grill for a romantic evening out; try delectable Moroccan cuisine in the opulent Tagine; or enjoy cocktails with a view in The Rooftop and Sports Lounge) are renowned, and a luxury spa treatment here is the ultimate indulgence. Its equally extravagant sister property sits across the water on the outer reaches of the Palm Jumeirah.

Rixos The Palm
East Crescent Nakhlat Jumeira **04 457 5555**
rixos.com
Map **1 P3** Metro **Nakheel**
Located on the eastern crescent of the Palm Jumeirah, Rixos The Palm boasts incredible views in all directions – the Arabian Gulf, the Palm and the Dubai coastline – with many of the city's landmarks in sight, not least the Burj Al Arab, Burj Khalifa and Marsa Dubai. It is a relaxing resort on a peaceful slice of beach, with a few dining options, great lounging areas and luxurious spa.

Sofitel The Palm
East Crescent Nakhlat Jumeira **04 455 6677**
sofitel.com
Map **1 P1** Metro **Nakheel**
The sunny Polynesian island theme to this hotel, with its fresh flowers on the walls and Maui beach bar, makes this a great escape from the city. Lounge in private cabanas discretely dotted around the large main pool, find yourself one of the secret Jacuzzi pools, or take a pedalo from the beach jetty. By night, you can enjoy sundowners on the rooftop bar before dining at one of Dubai's most fantastic restaurants (you will be wowed), Studio du Chef. The kids' pool with waterslides is more than enough to keep the little ones happy, too.

Visitors In Town?

Dubai's popularity as a tourist destination means that you may soon find a continual stream of friends and family arriving and needing a place to stay. Putting your visitors up in a hotel is something you may need to do. Fortunately, most hotels are excellently geared up for holidaymakers, with many located on the beach or near to some of the main attractions. We recommend a range of hotels that offer something to visitors, be it great spa facilities or popular restaurants, at a variety of budgets.

The Address Downtown Dubai
Shk Mohd Bin Rashid Blvd Downtown Dubai, Burj Khalifa **04 436 8888**
theaddress.com
Map **2 F7** Metro **Burj Khalifa/Dubai Mall**
With three main properties in prime glitzy locations, this group of hotels is sure to please. The Address Downtown has breathtaking views of the Burj Khalifa, beautiful interiors and eight dining outlets (including Neos, the panoramic bar on the 63rd floor), while The Address Dubai Mall and The Address Dubai Marina are handily attached to major shopping and leisure hotspots making them a perfect choice for shopaholics. The marina location has a terrific infinity pool overlooking the stunning Marsa Dubai skyline.

THINGS TO SEE & DO
HOTELS

The Address Downtown Dubai and Dubai Fountain

One&Only Royal Mirage Dubai

Madinat Jumeirah and the Burj Al Arab

THINGS TO SEE & DO
HOTELS

Al Bustan Rotana
Casablanca Rd Al Garhoud **04 282 0000**
rotana.com
Map **2 N8** Metro **Airport Terminal 1**
A central location near the airport, Deira City Centre and the Dubai Creek makes this hotel accessible for tourists and business visitors. Renowned for its good restaurants, with Benihana (Japanese), Blue Elephant (Thai) and Rodeo Grill (steakhouse) standing out.

Al Manzil Downtown Dubai
The Old Town Downtown Dubai, Burj Khalifa **04 428 5888**
almanzilhotel.ae
Map **2 F7** Metro **Burj Khalifa/Dubai Mall**
In the heart of Old Town, this beautiful four-star hotel is conveniently located for business and leisure trips. It also houses Nezesaussi Grill, the popular Antipodean sports bar, and The Courtyard, a beautiful and atmospheric mezze and shisha cafe.

Al Murooj Rotana
Al Saffa St Trade Center 2 **04 321 1111**
rotana.com
Map **2 G6** Metro **Burj Khalifa/Dubai Mall**
A luxurious resort hotel that is popular with both leisure tourists and business travellers, being ideally located right between Downtown and DIFC. It has a number of good bars and restaurants, including the popular and often raucous Double Decker bar.

Amwaj Rotana Jumeirah Beach Residence
JBR Marsa Dubai **04 428 2000**
rotana.com
Map **1 K5** Metro **Jumeirah Lakes Towers**
Located on the bustling strip along new Dubai's seafront, this smart 200 room hotel features an outdoor pool, a fitness centre and great dining venues including Italian bar Rosso and teppanyaki restaurant Benihana.

Armani Hotel Dubai
Downtown Dubai, Burj Khalifa **04 888 3888**
dubai.armanihotels.com
Map **2 F6** Metro **Burj Khalifa/Dubai Mall**
This luxurious (and expensive) hotel, in the world's tallest tower, is remarkably without pretension, but its designer credentials are noticeable down to the nuts and bolts. As well as elegant suites kitted out with Armani/Casa goods, it is home to an Armani spa and a clutch of excellent dining venues.

Asiana Hotel
Salahuddin Rd Al Muraqqabat **04 238 7777**
asianahoteldubai.com
Map **2 N5** Metro **Salah Al Din**
With a choice of four restaurants specialising in Chinese, Filipino, Japanese and Korean, this Deira-based five-star hotel is worth the trip. And if the quality, value and variety of food doesn't lure you in, then the trendy decor with Asian flair will do its very best to.

Bonnington Jumeirah Lakes Towers
Cluster J JLT, Al Thanyah 5 **04 356 0000**
bonningtontower.com
Map **1 K5** Metro **Jumeirah Lakes Towers**
Containing both hotel suites and serviced apartments, as well as six restaurants and bars and a leisure deck with infinity pool, it has great connections to Marsa Dubai via the nearby metro.

Conrad Dubai
Shk Zayed Rd Trade Center 1 **04 444 7444**
hilton.com
Map **2 H5** Metro **Emirates Towers**
For stunning views over the skyline and the Arabian Gulf, head to the luxurious Conrad Dubai. It boasts some of the best nightlife spots in the city, including the Parisian-inspired bar Cave and the Marco Pierre White Grill.

Crowne Plaza Dubai
Shk Zayed Rd Trade Center 1 **04 331 1111**
ihg.com
Map **2 H5** Metro **Emirates Towers**
One of Dubai's older five-star hotels, with an excellent collection of food and beverage outlets including Trader Vic's, Wagamama and Oscar's Vine Society. It's centrally located on Sheikh Zayed Road, so it's only a short drive to the beaches, malls and nightspots.

Al Manzil Downtown Dubai

THINGS TO SEE & DO
HOTELS

Crowne Plaza Dubai Festival City
Nr Dubai Festival City Mall Al Badia, Al Kheeran 04 701 2222
ihg.com
Map **2 L9** Metro **Emirates**
On the banks of the Creek, this Crowne Plaza is excellently positioned within the Festival City complex. One of its highlights is the Belgian Beer Cafe, an atmospheric bar that serves a great selection of European beers and is extremely popular with Dubai residents and visitors alike.

Dubai Marriott Harbour
Al Sufouh Rd Marsa Dubai 04 319 4000
dubaimarriottharbourhotel.com
Map **1 L5** Metro **Dubai Marina**
With 261 spacious suites, each with its own fitted kitchen, staying in The Harbour is like having your very own luxury apartment. The hotel is home to a range of dining options including The Observatory (offering great views from the 52nd floor) and 24 hour deli Counter Culture.

Dusit Thani Dubai
Shk Zayed Rd Trade Center 2 04 343 3333
dusit.com
Map **2 G6** Metro **Burj Khalifa/Dubai Mall**
This member of the upmarket Thai hotel chain is situated in the 'clasped hands' (or 'pair of trousers') building on the main stretch of Sheikh Zayed Road. It features 321 rooms, and several food and beverage outlets including Benjarong, the 'royal Thai' restaurant and the Champagne Lounge.

Emirates Grand Hotel
Shk Zayed Rd Trade Center 2 04 323 0000
emiratesgrandhotel.com
Map **2 G6** Metro **Financial Centre**
Next to the Burj Khalifa and the Dubai Mall, this non-alcoholic hotel boasts serious style. The rooftop terrace is a must-see for its panoramic city and sea views, and you can also relax there with a traditional Arabic shisha. Chill out further at the wellness centre with its sauna, hot tub and steam room, or pump some iron at the gym. The hotel is completed with four restaurants, which serve a variety of food including Lebanese and Turkish.

Fairmont Dubai
Shk Zayed Rd Trade Center 1 04 332 5555
fairmont.com
Map **2 H5** Metro **World Trade Centre**
Home to the legendary Spectrum On One restaurant, a beautiful rooftop pool and the renowned The Spa at Fairmont Dubai, this hotel is as notable for its modern interior as it is for its striking architecture, which is based on traditional Arabian windtowers.

Grand Excelsior
Nr Mall of the Emirates Al Barsha 1 04 444 9999
grandexcelsior.ae
Map **1 R7** Metro **Mall of the Emirates**
With a striking cruise ship-style exterior, this 230 plus room hotel offers luxury amenities including a pretty rooftop swimming pool and well-equipped gym. F&B outlets include an all-day dining restaurant, the Oak 'n' Barrel pub, a new Mediterranean venue, pool bar, and club.

Grand Hyatt
Nr Al Garhoud Bridge Umm Hurair 2 04 317 1234
dubai.grand.hyatt.com
Map **2 L8** Metro **Dubai Healthcare City**
The eye-catching design of this huge hotel near the Garhoud Bridge is not random: from the air the shape of the building spells out the word 'Dubai' in Arabic. It has excellent leisure facilities, a great selection of restaurants, and one of the most impressive lobbies in Dubai.

Grosvenor House
Al Sufouh Rd Marsa Dubai 04 399 8888
grosvenorhouse-dubai.com
Map **1 L5** Metro **Dubai Marina**
This neon-blue skyscraper at the mouth of Marsa Dubai is run by Le Meridien group, and features guest rooms, serviced apartments and some iconic nightlife venues: Buddha Bar, Gary Rhodes' Mezzanine and the crow's nest Bar 44 are all well worth a visit, with a second tower adding the likes of Toro Toro and Embassy. There's also a branch of luxury male-only spa 1847 here.

H Hotel
One Shk Zayed Rd Trade Center 1 04 501 8888
h-hotel.com
Map **2 J5** Metro **World Trade Centre**
Previously The Monarch, this stylish hotel may have changed names but its popular restaurants including Okku and Ruth's Chris, thankfully, stay the same. With 236 rooms and suites, including 53 serviced residential apartments, this hotel has one of the most desirable addresses in Dubai: One Sheikh Zayed Road.

Habtoor Grand Beach
Al Sufouh Rd Marsa Dubai 04 399 5000
habtoorhotels.com
Map **1 L4** Metro **Dubai Marina**
The twin-towered Habtoor Grand, on the beach at the northern end of Marsa Dubai, offers 442 spacious rooms and suites with garden or sea views. Pools, restaurants and bars are set amid the hotel's tropical gardens bordering the Arabian Gulf, while The Underground bar draws in the expat football fan crowd for its multiple screens.

THINGS TO SEE & DO
HOTELS

Hilton Dubai Creek
Nr Dubai Chamber of Commerce Riggat Al Buteen **04 227 1111**
hilton.com
Map **2 M6** Metro **Al Rigga**
With very flash yet understated elegance, this ultra-minimalist hotel features interiors of wood, glass and chrome. Centrally located and overlooking the Dubai Creek, with splendid views of the Arabian dhow trading posts, the hotel has two renowned restaurants: Glasshouse Brasserie and the Dubai gastronomic darling, Table 9 with its recently installed new chef, Darren Velvick, who has spent more than 14 years working with Gordon Ramsey and Marcus Wareing.

Hilton Dubai Jumeirah Resort
The Walk at JBR Marsa Dubai **04 399 1111**
hilton.com
Map **1 K4** Metro **Jumeirah Lakes Towers**
Situated between The Walk and the JBR beach, the Hilton Dubai Jumeirah features excellent restaurants, including the Italian BiCE and the Latin American meat feast venue Pachanga, as well as a sports bar, Studio One. There's a beach bar too – Wavebreaker – which is a great spot for sundowners. Marsa Dubai is within walking distance.

Hyatt Regency
Al Corniche 04 209 1234
dubai.regency.hyatt.com
Map **2 N4** Metro **Palm Deira**
The restaurants alone in this hotel are well worth fighting the Deira traffic for – particularly Al Dawaar, Dubai's only revolving restaurant which boasts amazing views of the creek and coast. All 400 rooms have creek views too.

InterContinental Dubai Festival City
Nr Dubai Festival City Mall Al Badia, Al Kheeran **04 701 1111**
ichotelsgroup.com
Map **2 L9** Metro **Emirates**
Worth a visit if only to taste fine fare served up in Michelin-starred chef Pierre Gagnaire's excellent restaurant, or to enjoy the panoramic views from the Eclipse bar. The hotel also features an excellent spa, 498 rooms and suites, and access to the Festival Waterfront Centre.

JA Ocean View
The Walk at JBR JBR, Marsa Dubai **04 814 5599**
jaresortshotels.com
Map **1 K5** Metro **Jumeirah Lakes Towers**
A great location right on the edge of The Walk at JBR, this hotel boasts to be 'Dubai's only four-star hotel on the beach'. All rooms have sea views, and aqua-lovers can enjoy the swimming pool, the local beach or jump on a complimentary shuttle to the private beach at JA Jebel Ali Golf Resort. Dining highlights include Fogo Vivo, a Brazilian steakhouse with an open kitchen, and The Whistler, a cheese and wine bar. A popular choice for families, the hotel has a shaded children's pool and kids' club for three to 11 year olds.

Jumeirah Creekside
Nr Aviation Club Al Garhoud **04 230 8555**
jumeirah.com
Map **2 M8** Metro **GGICO**
A sleek yet eclectically designed hotel with an abundance of venues. Start your day at the lively Italian cafe, go light and healthy on lunch at Plumeria, choose either steak or seafood at Blue Flame or south Asian flavours at Nomad for dinner, and then finish off the evening with mint and rum infused mojitos at the rooftop lounge Cu-ba. From the statement art, to the personalised service, to the new concept menus, this hotel breathes boutique and is sure to 'wow'.

Jumeirah Emirates Towers
Shk Zayed Rd Trade Center 2 **04 330 0000**
jumeirah.com
Map **2 H6** Metro **Financial Centre**
Sophisticated and elegant, this hotel forms one part of Dubai's iconic twin skyscrapers. It has 400 rooms, some excellent restaurants and bars (including Harry Ghatto's for hilarious karaoke nights), as well as an exclusive shopping mall. Other leisure facilities include the Talise spa and health club offering massage treatments and a sauna.

JW Marriott Marquis
Nr Dubai Airline Centre Business Bay **04 414 0000**
marriott.com
Map **2 D6** Metro **Business Bay**
This long awaited five-star hotel which opened in 2012, rises above Business Bay at a staggering 355m, making it the world's tallest freestanding hotel. Spread across two iconic towers, there are some top-notch restaurants, including the hyped restaurant Rang Mahal by Atul Kochhar, the fine-dining steakhouse Prime 68 and the impressive and elegant Italian restaurant, Positano.

Kempinski
MoE Al Barsha 1 **04 341 0000**
kempinski.com
Map **1 R6** Metro **Mall of the Emirates**
With over 400 deluxe rooms this hotel features a spa, infinity pool, fitness centre, tennis court and the attached Ski Dubai. Check into one of the 15 exclusive and unique ski chalets, remove your snow boots, put your feet up by the (fake) fire and tuck into an après-ski afternoon tea while enjoying the view of the piste from your room.

THINGS TO SEE & DO
HOTELS

JW Marriott Marquis

Le Meridien Dubai
Airport Rd Al Garhoud **04 217 0000**
lemeridien-dubai.com
Map **2 N8** Metro **Airport Terminal 1**
Just a stone's throw from Dubai Airport and the Aviation Club, guests and visitors can enjoy many excellent restaurants inside the hotel, many of which share a large alfresco terrace in the cooler months. With 383 rooms, the hotel is also home to trendy nightspot Warehouse and Antipodean restaurant Yalumba, which offers a famous Friday brunch.

Le Meridien Mina Seyahi
Al Sufouh Rd Marsa Dubai **04 399 3333**
lemeridien-minaseyahi.com
Map **1 M5** Metro **Nakheel**
Home to legendary beach bar and ever-popular expat hangout, Barasti, this hotel has a great stretch of beach overlooking the Palm, with watersports on offer. There's also a rooftop pool and some rooms come with a personalised butler service.

Le Royal Meridien Beach Resort
Nr Jumeirah Beach Residence Marsa Dubai **04 399 5555**
leroyalmeridien-dubai.com
Map **1 L5** Metro **Dubai Marina**
Large-scale beach resort at Marsa Dubai. Good leisure facilities and a big selection of bars and restaurants including Mexican Maya and seafood outlet Me Vida. A shuttle bus transfers guests through the Marina to allow access to the facilities of the Grosvenor House.

Media One
Dubai Media City Al Sufouh 2 **04 427 1000**
mediaonehotel.com
Map **1 M5** Metro **Nakheel**
This fun, funky and functional hotel is great if you need to be in reach of Media City. The rooms are geared towards the business traveller's needs, with workspaces, wi-fi and flat screen TVs, but they certainly don't lack style. Z:ONE and the Dek on 8 are popular post-work haunts, while The Med hosts a fun Friday brunch.

Media Rotana
Nr American School of Dubai TECOM, Al Thanyah 1 **04 435 0000**
rotana.com
Map **1 P6** Metro **Dubai Internet City**
Ideally located close to Dubai Media City and Dubai Internet City, this city hotel boasts an outdoor pool and massage rooms. On the dining front, Prego's restaurant offers a cosy ambience with an open kitchen; Channels features live cooking; or you can try designer beers at Nelson's pub. Hugely popular is the alfresco brunch on The Terrace, held every Friday.

Melia Dubai
23 Kuwait St Al Raffa **04 386 8111**
melia-dubai.com
Map **2 K4** Metro **Al Fahidi**
Contemporary and elegant, the Melia stands out in Bur Dubai for all the right reasons. Featuring two high-profile restaurants – Titanic and Signature – and a

THINGS TO SEE & DO
HOTELS

luxurious spa, this is a hidden gem worth discovering. The rooms are tastefully decorated, and the TVs disguised as mirrors add a stylish touch.

The Meydan
Meydan Racecourse Nadd Al Shiba 1 04 381 3333
meydanhotels.com
Map **2 D10**
There's no better place to watch the racing action at The Meydan horserace track than from the rooftop infinity pool of this decadent, five-star, landmark hotel, but the striking modern design, spa and excellent outlets including Prime and Shiba make this hotel a deluxe destination in itself. Guests can also enjoy The Track; the hotel's stunning pay-to-play golf course for all abilities. Guests can make use of free shuttle buses to destinations around Dubai.

Movenpick Hotel Ibn Battuta Gate
Nr Ibn Battuta Mall Jabal Ali 1 04 444 0000
moevenpick-hotels.com
Map **1 G5** Metro **Ibn Battuta**
Catering for travellers who want easy access to Marsa Dubai and Jabal Ali, this five-star, strikingly designed hotel is themed on the territories to which the 14th century explorer Ibn Battuta travelled. The pool terrace offers stunning views over 'new Dubai' and its food outlets represent the cuisines of the world. Guests can also take the free shuttle to the Palm and use the fabulous facilities at Oceana, which overlooks the marina.

Movenpick Hotel Jumeirah Beach
Nr The Walk JBR, Marsa Dubai 04 449 8888
moevenpick-hotels.com
Map **1 K5** Metro **Jumeirah Lakes Towers**
Situated on The Walk at JBR this five-star, 300 room hotel has much to recommend it, not least its beachfront location and stunning sea-view pool bar, but also a couple of decent restaurants.

The Oberoi
The Oberoi Centre Business Bay 04 444 1444
oberoihotels.com
Map **2 E6** Metro **Business Bay**
The latest hotel to open up in the Business Bay district is The Oberoi Dubai – the first high-end Indian hotelier to hit the UAE's shores. Everything from the beautifully modern decor to the perfectly mannered staff ensures that a stay here is a peaceful and magical one. In addition to the pampering services of an on call butler – yes, each of the hotel's 252 rooms are sated with this gem – there's also in-room check-in, famous nightclubs and a fantastic tapas-style brunch at Nine7One. You'll probably never want to leave the hotel, but if you really must, Dubai Mall is only a 10 minute drive away.

One&Only The Palm
The West Crescent Nakhlat Jumeira 04 440 1010
oneandonlyresorts.com
Map **1 L3** Metro **Nakheel**
A stunning boutique resort and the end of the west crescent on the Palm intended to create an intimate and indulgent setting. Designed in an Andalusian style, the 64 rooms, 26 suites and four beachfront villas feature free-standing bath tubs and rain showers, plus private terraces or balconies that take in the lights of Marsa Dubai. Among the highlights is restaurant STAY by Yannick Alléno and the romantic alfresco 101 Dining Lounge and Bar.

The Palace Downtown Dubai
Nr Dubai Mall Downtown Dubai, Burj Khalifa
04 428 7888
theaddress.com
Map **2 F6** Metro **Burj Khalifa/Dubai Mall**
Palatial indeed, The Palace, and many of its luxurious and beautifully designed suites look out onto the mighty Burj Khalifa and the Dubai Fountain, and boasts a beautiful spa – guests can even have a treatment at a poolside cabana while the Dubai Fountain is in full swing. There are some excellent restaurants, including the renowned Argentinian restaurant Asado and Thiptara.

Park Hyatt Dubai
Nr Dubai Creek Golf & Yacht Club Port Saeed
04 602 1234
dubai.park.hyatt.com
Map **2 M7** Metro **GGICO**
Enjoying a prime waterfront location within the grounds of Dubai Creek Golf & Yacht Club, the Park Hyatt is Mediterranean in style with low-rise buildings, natural colours and stylish decor. The hotel has 225 rooms and suites, all with beautiful views, as well as some great dining outlets and a luxurious spa, which features a luxury couple's massage option. Excellent restaurants inside the hotel include The Thai Kitchen and Traiteur.

Pullman Deira City Centre > p.xvi, IBC
Deira City Centre Port Saeed 04 294 1222
pullmanhotels.com
Map **2 N7** Metro **Deira City Centre**
The Pullman is in a great spot overlooking Dubai Creek and the Golf & Yacht Club. Its vibrant, modern and spacious rooms have fantastic creek views and the 24 hour chic lobby lounge always has a welcoming coffee on hand. The hotel's Medley restaurant offers the added entertainment of live cooking stations and after dinner, guests can enjoy the stunning rooftop bar Azure – a great place to watch the dusk roll in. Relaxation is available at Soma Spa, with its crisp, clean and white decor.

THINGS TO SEE & DO
HOTELS

Radisson Royal
Nr Emirates NBD Trade Center 1 **04 308 0000**
radissonblu.com
Map **2 H5** Metro **Emirates Towers**
Within walking distance of the World Trade Centre Metro Station, this city centre hotel is a popular choice with business travellers. But its appeal is far-reaching, thanks to its spa, Japanese restaurant Icho and, above all, trendy London nightclub Mo*Vida.

Raffles
Nr Wafi Umm Hurair 2 **04 324 8888**
raffles.com
Map **2 K7** Metro **Dubai Healthcare City**
With 248 stunning suites, the renowned Raffles Spa and a unique Botanical Sky Garden, this is one of Dubai's most noteworthy city hotels. Eight food and beverage outlets offer a mix of international and far eastern cuisine.

Ritz-Carlton Dubai
Nr The Walk, Jumeirah Beach Residence Marsa Dubai **04 399 4000**
ritzcarlton.com
Map **1 L4** Metro **Dubai Marina**
Even though it is the only low-rise building amid the sea of marina towers behind it, all 138 rooms have beautiful views of the Gulf – The Ritz-Carlton was, after all, here years before the rest of Marsa Dubai was built. Afternoon tea in the Lobby Lounge is a must, and there are several other excellent restaurants and a very good spa onsite. The Ritz-Carlton has also added another property to its offerings, with a 341 room hotel in the DIFC area.

Shangri-La
Shk Zayed Rd Trade Center 1 **04 343 8888**
shangri-la.com
Map **2 G6** Metro **Burj Khalifa/Dubai Mall**
Featuring great views of the coast and the city from Sheikh Zayed Road, this hotel has 301 guest rooms and suites, 126 serviced apartments, a health club and spa, two swimming pools and a variety of restaurants and bars including majestic Moroccan Marrakech and seafood specialist Amwaj.

Sheraton Jumeirah Beach
Al Sufouh Rd Marsa Dubai **04 399 5333**
sheratonjumeirahbeach.com
Map **1 K4** Metro **Jumeirah Lakes Towers**
An older waterfront resort right at the southern end of JBR beach, this hotel has a secluded stretch of the golden sands to itself, plus green gardens and a couple of decent restaurants, including Peacock Chinese Restaurant and The Grill Room. It hosts a chill-out evening on Fridays, Ocean Club, which is popular with local residents.

Sofitel Jumeirah Beach
JBR Marsa Dubai **04 448 4848**
sofitel-dubai-jumeirahbeach.com
Map **1 K5** Metro **Jumeirah Lakes Towers**
This chic, five-star, seafront property stands tall on Jumeirah Beach Residence's The Walk, and the hotel offers direct access to the beach as well as a host of boutiques and cafes along the promenade. It features a beauty salon, a pool bar, popular Irish sports bar The Hub and signature French restaurant Rococo.

Waldorf Astoria Palm Jumeirah
East Crescent Nakhlat Jumeira **04 818 2222**
waldorfastoria.com
Map **1 P1** Metro **Nakheel**
This iconic brand's first foray in Dubai is an opulent affair that oozes class and benefits from a stunning, peaceful location on the Palm Jumeirah.

Westin Dubai Mina Seyahi
Al Sufouh Rd Marsa Dubai **04 399 4141**
westinminaseyahi.com
Map **1 M5** Metro **Nakheel**
Set on 1,200 metres of private beach, The Westin has 294 spacious rooms and suites with all the luxury amenities you would expect of a five-star hotel, including the aptly named Heavenly Spa. Ample dining venues include perennially popular Italian Bussola and wine and cheese bar Oeno.

Other Options
Bur Dubai and Deira have plenty of notable (and affordable) hotels for guests staying in this buzzing end of town. The Crowne Plaza Dubai Deira is home to legendary buffet restaurant Spice Island, and the JW Marriott Hotel Dubai is known for its theme nights and brunches. The Dhow Palace Hotel and the Park Regis Kris Kin Hotel also offer great facilities with rooms available at competitive prices.

Radisson Blu (radissonblu.com), Novotel, Rotana (rotana.com), Sheraton and Holiday Inn all have various branches around the main areas of the city, each with its own popular brunch options and bars.

Guesthouses are not hugely common in Dubai but are becoming more popular. Smaller in size, B&Bs offer a homely feel and are ideal for guests who want to see more of the 'real Dubai'. Located in residential areas, they won't have access to private beaches, but there is no shortage of good public beaches to enjoy. Some will have their own pool, while owners will be only too happy to give personal recommendations on what to see, and things to do.

Villa 47 (04 286 8239, villa47.com) has only two guest rooms, but is located close to the airport in Garhoud. It's also just a stone's throw from the Irish Village, which has ample dining and drinking venues. You can book through the usual online portals.

HOME OF ELEGANT RETAILERS AND UPSCALE DINING
Shop in the contemporary beauty of Sunset Mall.
Visit our boutiques and you're sure to find a style of shopping that suits your taste
Jumeirah Beach Road, Jumeirah 3
www.sunsetmall.ae

Sunset Mall

SHOPPING

Need To Know **325**
Shopping Districts **328**
Places To Shop **334**
Buyers' Guide **352**

SHOPPING

Spending money is something of a national sport in the UAE; whatever your budget, you'll find no shortage of opportunity when it comes to opening those purse strings.

Souk Madinat Jumeirah

Dubai is well and truly positioning itself as the retail capital of the world – where else would you get a festival dedicated specifically (and reverently) to shopping? The largest shopping mall in the world is here, as well as plenty more leisure and retail havens. Dubai's development is inextricably linked to shopping, and with each new development comes a new mall.

Practicality plays a large part in the mall culture; during the hotter months, malls are oases of cool in the sweltering city – somewhere to walk, shop, eat and be entertained.

But it doesn't end there – the city's shopping highlights include traditional souks and quirky markets, boutiques, a few thrift shops, a plethora of designer names and a growing number of original independent stores. There are new unique shopping hubs cropping up all the time, and several residential areas now have something akin to a high street.

The thing that makes shopping here so appealing is the fantastic range of products; there is very little that is not available and for most items there is enough choice to fit any budget, from the streets of Karama with its fake designer goods, to the shops in the malls that sell the real thing.

With the population being largely transitory, there is no shortage of second-hand goods, and it's worth venturing out of the city for bigger items; Sharjah and Ajman are known for their cheaper prices.

One thing's for sure, there are not many places that can beat Dubai's range of goods and services. You'll be spoilt for choice, and the frequency of sales means that if you look in the right places at the right time, you'll be sure to bag a bargain.

SHOPPING
NEED TO KNOW

NEED TO KNOW

Most shops are open until 10pm every night and even later at the weekends. You can often do your grocery shopping till midnight, and a few of the major supermarkets are open 24 hours a day. The malls are particularly busy at the weekend, especially on Friday evenings. Things change slightly during Ramadan, when some shops close from noon until around 7pm.

You may find that imported items and brands, particularly from the international high-street stores, carry an extra few dirhams to compensate for the cost of importing the goods.

Bizarrely, the fashions here follow the European seasons, so just as the weather cools down from the extreme heat of the summer and you're ready to get kitted out for the beach, you'll find the stores are full of winter boots and heavy coats. You may want to stock up at the beginning of summer.

How To Pay

You'll have few problems parting with your money. Credit cards (American Express, Diners Club, MasterCard and Visa) and debit cards (Visa Electron) are accepted in shopping malls, supermarkets and many independent shops. Cards mainly use the chip-and-pin system. Aramex also offers a Web Surfer card, a pre-paid MasterCard for use online.

It's better to pay with cash for fuel at petrol stations, although some are now offering card payment. You are never too far from an ATM in the city and it is preferable to pay with cash in souks and smaller shops – try to have a variety of denominations, because it is better to hand over close to the exact amount. US dollars and other foreign currencies are accepted in some larger shops (and in airport duty free).

Loyalty Cards

Many stores and malls in the UAE participate in nationwide loyalty card schemes. These allow you to earn points while shopping, which can then be redeemed against purchases, and so can be well worth collecting. Shukran, from the Landmark group, has lots of participating shops from fashion to electronics, including Iconic, New Look, Centrepoint and Emax, as well as restaurants. Alshaya is another popular card with H&M, Debenhams, Boots and many more participating stores. Several brands have their own loyalty schemes, including Virgin Megastore, and Carrefour with its MyClub loyalty card.

Bargaining

Bargaining is common practice in the souks and shopping areas of the UAE; you'll need to give it a go to get the best prices. Before you take the plunge, try to get an idea of prices from a few shops, as there can often be a significant difference. Once you've decided how much to spend, offer an initial bid that is roughly around half that price. Stay laidback and vaguely uninterested. When your initial offer is rejected (and it will be), keep going until you reach an agreement or until you have reached your limit. If the price isn't right, say so and walk out – the vendor will often follow and suggest a compromise price. The more you buy, the better the discount. When the price is agreed, it is considered bad form to back out of the sale.

Bargaining isn't commonly accepted in malls and independent shops. However, some shops such as jewellery stores and smaller electronics stores do operate a set discount system so you never know: ask whether there is a discount on the marked price and you may bag a bargain.

Canny Coupons

It's no secret that there are bargains to be had across the city. As well as the Entertainer books and app, check out groupon.ae and cobone.com for discounts on everything from shopping to dentistry to holidays.

Shopping Events

At certain times of the year, Dubai sees sweeping discounts and promotions. It can be worth holding out for these events to buy certain items, including cars and electronics. While prices are slashed in the shops, many malls hold raffles for big prizes when you spend money – these include cars and large cash prizes. The malls are pretty busy during these periods.

Art Dubai
Madinat Jumeirah Al Sufouh 1 **04 384 2000**
artdubai.ae
Map **1 R5** Metro **Mall of the Emirates**
A commercial art fair that draws together artwork from many of Dubai's galleries. The event will run from 19 to 22 March 2014, and is a great opportunity to check out the variety of art on offer in the city.

Dubai Shopping Festival
04 445 5642
dubaievents.ae
A month dedicated to consumerism that takes place annually between January and February. There are sweeping discounts, entertainment and promotions across the entire city.

askexplorer.com   325

SHOPPING
NEED TO KNOW

Dubai Summer Surprises
600 545 555
dubaievents.ae
Another city-wide event that takes place in the summer months, aimed at attracting visitors despite the sweltering heat. There are vast sales and promotions, as well as all sorts of family entertainment to draw shoppers into the malls.

Online Shopping

Without the local presence of online stores like Amazon and ASOS, knowing where to go online for what is perhaps a little trickier than at home. But there's still plenty of choice locally, and delivery is available to your home or office. More online stores are cropping up all the time, and the range is always improving. Geant is the first hypermarket to offer online grocery shopping, with delivery across Dubai (geantonline.ae).

International websites are a popular option (such as Amazon UK or US), and while not all companies ship to the UAE (or they charge high prices), there are several options for getting round this. Aramex provides a 'Shop & Ship' service which sets up a mailbox in both the UK and US, great for dealing with sites which do not offer international shipping. Borderlinx (borderlinx.com) provides a similar service for stores that will only ship to the USA.

There are sites based in the UAE that will arrange for gifts to be delivered both here and internationally, such as quickdubai.com and papagiftexpress.com, which delivers to India, Sri Lanka, Qatar, Oman and the UAE. International sites such as moonpig.com and Interflora are great for sending cards and gifts within the delivery country, often with same or next day delivery.

Deliveries & Shipping

The high number of international and local shipping and courier agencies means it is possible to transport just about anything. Both air freight and sea freight are available; air freight is faster and you can track the items, but it's more expensive and not really suitable for large or heavy objects. Sea freight takes several weeks to arrive but it is cheaper and you can rent containers for larger items. It is worth getting a few quotes and finding out what will happen when the goods arrive; some offer no services at the destination while others, usually the bigger ones, will clear customs and deliver right to the door. See the Getting Started section for more information. The companies listed above (right) are best to use for sending small packages.

Aramex
Dubai Internet City Al Sufouh 2 600 544 000
aramex.com
Offers a great service called 'Shop & Ship'. For a one-off payment of $45, Aramex will set up a mailbox for you in both the UK and US. Deliveries can be arranged up to three times a week; packages can be tracked. There are branches in Media and Internet Cities, and also in Garhoud.

Empost
Deira Main Post Office Bldg Hor Al Anz 600 565 555
empostuae.com
Offers both local and international courier and air freight services – its prices are competitive and packages can be tracked.

Refunds, Exchanges & Consumer Rights

Policies on refunds and exchanges vary from shop to shop. It is common to be offered an exchange or credit note rather than a refund. Even with tags attached, many stores will not even consider an exchange unless you have the receipt. For some items, such as those in sealed packages, shops insist that the packaging should be intact so that the item can be resold – a fairly illogical stance if the item proves to be faulty.

If you're having no success with customer services, ask to speak to the manager, as the person on the shop floor is often not authorised to deviate from standard policy whereas managers may be more flexible.

The Consumer Protection Department of the UAE Ministry of Economy has been established to safeguard the interests of shoppers. The department tracks and regulates retail prices and has rejected planned price increases for staple goods. It has also mandated that all retail outlets display a notice of their consumer rights policy in the store. Consumers wishing to complain about a retailer can complete a form on the website economy.gov.ae, send an email to consumer@economy.ae, or call the freephone hotline on 600 522 225. In Dubai, the Consumer Rights Unit at the Dubai Economic Department (600 545 555, dubaided.gov.ae) primarily deals with unfit food, but can be contacted to report faulty goods or to complain if a guarantee is not honoured.

Buyer Beware
Traps for the unwary shopper do exist. Some of the international stores sell items that are far more expensive than in their country of origin (you can often even still see the original price tags). Prices can be as much as 30% higher, so beware.

Hallmark
Life IS A SPECIAL OCCASION.

www.hallmarkgcc.com

SHOPPING DISTRICTS

A souk in Old Dubai

If you're moving to a new area in Dubai or just planning a shopping trip, it helps to know what your options are across the city. While there is generally a mall or shopping centre within striking distance of anywhere you end up, different areas can also conjure up some different shopping treats.

If venturing into the gargantuan Dubai Mall exhausts you at the very thought, try Dubai Marina Mall, handy for the Marsa Dubai end of town, or Mercato Shopping Mall towards the northern end of Jumeira Road. Both are a more manageable size and usually pretty calm, but have a good range of shops.

For a breath of fresh air – literally – head to Wasl Square or Citywalk, both in Jumeira. These outdoor complexes have a more interesting range of shops, as well as lovely alfresco cafes and several amenities.

For the true Middle Eastern shopping experience, head for Dubai Creek, where the buzzing souks of Deira and Bur Dubai are and haggle to your heart's content.

Al Barsha

The main draw in this area is the city's second biggest shopping hub, Mall of the Emirates, but the neighbourhood has an urban residential feel with lots of cafes and independent shops. The huge LuLu Hypermarket just off Umm Suqeim Road is worth the journey, and there's a cluster of handy shops accessed from this main artery, including furniture emporium, Pan Emirates.

Al Barsha Mall
24th Street Al Barsha 2 **04 284 3663**
Map **1 Q7** Metro **Mall of the Emirates**
A large Union Co-operative Society supermarket is the main draw for this handy community mall, plus there's a range of services available, a few fashion brands, electronics store Sharaf DG, Japanese value store Daiso and some rides to entertain the kids.

SHOPPING
DISTRICTS

Al Qouz

Head into this industrial wilderness and you'll find some real gems, which make use of the space and versatility of the warehouses. Al Qouz 1 is home to The Courtyard, which has some interesting shops and galleries, and hosts a farmers' market on Saturdays. Nearby Dubai Antique Museum is an enormous wonderland of furniture, souvenirs and much more, and then there's Alserkal Avenue, with a host of edgy art galleries.

Lining Sheikh Zayed Road are a number of retail outlets and car dealerships; dig a little deeper and you'll find stores such as Safita, which sells well-priced wooden Indian furniture. Kidz Inc sells furniture and toys for children, while Just Kidding has all the latest baby equipment. The nearby branch of Lime Tree Cafe has some lovely edible and kitchen goodies that make great gifts. Dubai Garden Centre has everything for the garden, and the Sun & Sand Sports outlet behind the Gold & Diamond Park has lots of bargains.

Gold & Diamond Park   > p.367
Nr First Gulf Bank Metro Station
Al Qouz Ind. 3 **04 362 7777**
goldanddiamondpark.com
Map **1 S6** Metro **First Gulf Bank**
The Gold & Diamond Park (at junction four on Sheikh Zayed Road) has branches of many of the same shops as the Gold Souk but in a calmer, air-conditioned atmosphere. You can still barter, and there is the added bonus of cafes, including the popular MORE Cafe. There are a few other shops, such as Just Kidding.

Oasis Centre
Shk Zayed Rd Al Qouz Ind. 1 **04 515 4000**
oasiscentremall.com
Map **2 C6** Metro **Noor Bank**
A good selection of outlets including Home Centre, New Look, Carrefour Express and Centrepoint. A small food court offers the usual fast food outlets, or head to Balance Cafe for a guilt-free, healthy lunch.

Times Square Center
Shk Zayed Rd Al Qouz Ind. 1 **04 341 8020**
timessquarecenter.ae
Map **1 T6** Metro **Noor Bank**
Outdoor and adventure sports megastore Adventure HQ, which has a climbing wall and aerial obstacle course, is the biggest draw for this small but modern mall. You'll find large branches of Sharaf DG, Intersport, Toys R Us and Yellow Hat (for car accessories), and a good branch of Al Manama Hypermarket. Head to the Chillout ice lounge (unlicensed) for a sub-zero mocktail. The ARTE craft market takes over the ground floor once a month.

Bur Dubai

Al Fahidi Street is perfect for a bit of local colour and some great shopping. It is part of the commercial area that runs from Al Fahidi Historical Neighbourhood (formerly Bastakiya) all the way to Shindagha and takes in Dubai Museum, the Electronics Souk and the Textile Souk. There is a good range of inexpensive places to eat, including some fantastic vegetarian restaurants. This area is always busy but it really comes to life at night – if you're not sure you're in the right place, just head for the neon lights.

Karama is one of the older residential districts in Dubai, and is one of the best places to find a bargain. The best spot is the Karama Complex, a long street running through the middle of the district that is lined by shops on both sides. The area is best known for bargain clothing, sports goods, gifts and souvenirs (from toy camels to mosque alarm clocks and stuffed scorpions to pashminas) and it is notorious for being the hotbed of counterfeit items in Dubai. As you wander round you will be offered 'copy watches, copy bags' with every step, and if you show any interest you will be whisked into a back room to view the goods. If you're not interested, a simple 'no thank you' will suffice, or even just ignore the vendor completely – it may seem rude, but sometimes it's the only way to cope with the incessant hassle. The most popular shops are Blue Marine, Green Eye and Asda. With loads of small, inexpensive restaurants, you won't go hungry while pounding the streets of Karama. Try Chef Lanka, Aryaas or Saravana Bhavan, or head for the large fish, fruit and vegetable market.

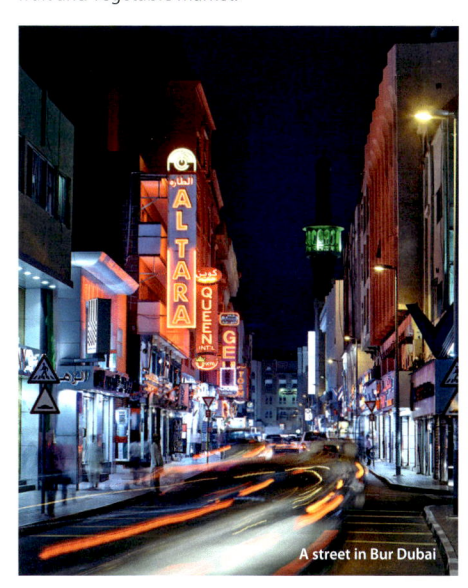

A street in Bur Dubai

askexplorer.com

SHOPPING
DISTRICTS

Lamcy Plaza
Shk Rashid Rd Oud Metha **04 335 9999**
lamcyplaza.com
Map **2 K6** Metro **Oud Metha**

Large and consistently popular, there's a great variety of shops and entertainment. Services include a play area, pharmacy, a money exchange, a florist and a post office counter. There's fashion stores aplenty, including Dorothy Perkins and Guess; baby stores include Mothercare and Pumpkin Patch. Mexx for Less sells discounted clothing, and Peacocks and Matalan sell reasonably priced fashion.

Deira

This chaotic urban jungle is crammed with independent shops that cater to all tastes and budgets, and the area hides some great shopping centres, both large and small. While Deira City Centre has all the modern amenities and attractions, a major draw is the atmospheric district that incorporates the winding Gold Souk, where you can barter for some bargain bling, and the fragrant Spice Souk on the banks of the Creek.

Century Mall
Nr Al Shabab Club, Al Wuheida Rd Al Mamzar **04 296 6337**
mysafeer.com
Map **2 R6** Metro **Al Qiyadah**

Shopping meets entertainment here, with 75 speciality stores selling the latest in electronics, mobiles, fashion, lifestyle, gift ideas, home furnishings, jewellery, and health and beauty products. There's a Carrefour, a foodcourt and an indoor themed amusement centre.

Madina Mall
Beirut St Muhaisnah 4 **04 238 1111**
madinamalldxb.ae
Map **2 T9** Metro **Al Qusais**

This strikingly designed shopping mall is packed with outlets selling everything from homewares to fashion, and is home to the Middle East's first Poundstretcher, a popular UK bargain basement brand. There's also a Carrefour and a family entertainment area.

Reef Mall
Salahuddin Rd Al Muraqqabat **04 224 2240**
reefmall.com
Map **2 N5** Metro **Salah Al Din**

This surprisingly large mall has branches of Emax, Daiso, Babyshop, Home Centre and a range of fashion brands. There's a huge Fun City for kids to burn off a bit of energy, plus a small foodcourt, several cafes and a supermarket.

Souk Al Bahar

Downtown Dubai

This area has grown into a key place to meet, eat and shop. The Dubai Mall won't disappoint with its extensive store listing. For a more laidback atmosphere, Souk Al Bahar's passageways, resembling a traditional souk, cater well to tourists. Some great restaurants are here, with prime position over the nightly Dubai Fountain show. The Boulevard is also lined with cafes, shops and hotels. Further afield, Jumeirah Emirates Towers has a promenade of high-end shops.

Dubailand

This enormous development that stretches down the desert side of the city has a long way to go to completion, but there are some great pockets of leisure and retail. With a slightly out of town location, they are surprisingly easy to get to and for the most part traffic free. Check out Global Village during the winter months, a major attraction with plenty of shopping, plus fairground rides and entertainment.

Dubai Investments Park
Dubai Investments Park 1 **04 885 1188**
dipark.com
Map **1 F10**

Park n Shop fans should head here for the brand's large and blissfully quiet Cash and Carry branch. There's a Carrefour Market here too, and a pleasant local shopping centre at Green Community.

SHOPPING
DISTRICTS

Uptown MotorCity
Al Hebiah 1 **04 932 7520**
Map **1 N12**
This neighbourhood has become desirable thanks to its pleasant high street. With a huge Spinneys at one end, the promenade is lined with cafes, shops and useful services, including a Party World, Pet Corner, Beyond the Beach and more.

Marsa Dubai
This trendy residential district is a hub of retail and leisure. Dubai Marina Mall is a manageable size, and outside and there's plenty more along the waterways.

Marina Walk
Marsa Dubai
Map **1 L5** Metro **Dubai Marina**
By night the promenade that hugs the waters of Marsa Dubai is buzzing with strolling families and friends enjoying the alfresco lifestyle at the many cafes and restaurants that line the Walk. Marina Market takes up the promenade outside Marina Mall with a mix of stalls from Wednesday to Saturday.

The Walk at Jumeirah Beach Residence
Jumeirah Beach Residence Marsa Dubai
04 390 0091
dubaipropertiesgroup.ae
Map **1 K4** Metro **Jumeirah Lakes Towers**
This cobbled strip embraces alfresco cafe culture, with street-side shops, cute stalls and plenty of outdoor restaurant seating, perfect for an evening amble. Outlets are located either on the ground level or on the plaza level of six clusters of towers called Murjan, Sadaf, Bahar, Rimal, Amwaj and Shams.

Jumeira & Umm Suqeim
The community feel of this area is a pleasant contrast to the large malls that shoppers are used to in Dubai. The whole strip is a bit long to walk (Jumeira Road and Al Wasl Road stretch from Souk Madinat Jumeirah up to 2nd December Street), but there are clusters of stores, restaurants and cafes all the way along both streets, several community malls and shopping arcades, and a couple of larger malls. Shops range from high-end boutiques to high-street chains; from furniture to fancy dress. Many businesses in the area are located in villas; these are mostly spas, dentists, hairdressers, and cosmetic surgery clinics.

On Al Wasl Road there are a variety of art galleries, garden stores, hair salons, dentists and vets – all accessed by service roads. The popular Spinneys Centre and Al Safa Centre, a community shopping centre that's home to Park n Shop and Pizza Express, are expat favourites. At the Satwa end of Al Wasl Road is the Al Ghazal Complex, perhaps most well known by partygoers for Mr Ben's Costume Closet. There's also supermarkets including Choithrams, Waitrose and the Union Co-operative Society.

Beach Centre
Nr Dubai Zoo, Jumeira Rd Jumeira 1 **04 344 7077**
Map **2 G4** Metro **Emirates Towers**
This good community mall has a number of interesting independent shops that sell everything from books to furniture and jewellery. Two branches of White Star Bookshop stock craft materials and teachers' supplies respectively. It also houses the Music Room, which has the largest supply of sheet music in Dubai, plus Kuts 4 Kids, a children's hairdressers, an opticians and a pharmacy.

Citywalk
Nr Al Wasl Rd & Al Safa St Al Wasl
meraas.com
Map **2 F5** Metro **Burj Khalifa/Dubai Mall**
This brand new retail space on Al Wasl Road is characterised by pleasant open spaces, water features, play areas, alfresco cafes and boutiques.

J3 Mall
Al Wasl Rd Al Manara **04 388 4433**
j3mall.com
Map **1 U5** Metro **Noor Bank**
This compact shopping centre has a good Choithrams, funky women's sportswear at Lorna Jane, SPERA fashion boutique and an indoor play centre for kids.

The Walk at JBR

SHOPPING
DISTRICTS

Jumeira Plaza
Jumeira Rd Jumeira 1 **04 349 7111**
Map **2 H4** Metro **Emirates Towers**
The 'pink mall' has an interesting range of independent shops selling everything from furniture to greeting cards. Prose is a popular second-hand bookshop; Melange has an interesting selection of clothing, jewellery and soft furnishings from India. There's a play area for kids, a Dome Cafe and a small branch of the Dubai Police – great for paying fines without having to queue.

Jumeirah Centre
Jumeira Rd Jumeira 1 **04 349 9702**
jumeirahcentre.net
Map **2 H4** Metro **Emirates Towers**
Packs a lot into a small space. Chains like Benetton and Nike join a number of independents, including Elves & Fairies for crafts and hobbies, Panache for accessories made only from natural materials, and the Wedding Shop. Kazim has a good range of stationery and art supplies, and there are some interesting clothes shops plus a gallery.

Palm Strip
Jumeira Rd Jumeira 1 **04 346 1462**
dipllc.ae
Map **2 H4** Metro **World Trade Centre**
Across the road from Jumeirah Mosque, this shopping arcade is dominated by upmarket boutiques, plus there are beauty salons and a pharmacy. Often quiet during the day, it gets a little livelier in the evenings with the popular Japengo Cafe. Other outlets include: Beyond the Beach, Elite Fashion, Oceano and Zara Home.

Spinneys Centre
Al Wasl Rd Al Safa 2 **04 394 1657**
spinneys-dubai.com
Map **2 B5** Metro **Noor Bank**
Just off Al Wasl Road, there's a number of shops centred around a large Spinneys supermarket, including Early Learning Centre and Mothercare, Tavola (for kitchenalia), and Disco 2000, one of Dubai's better music and DVD shops. There are branches of both MMI and A&E, a large play area, and services include dry cleaning and a pharmacy.

Sunset Mall
Jumeira Rd Jumeira 3 **04 330 7333**
sunsetmall.ae
Map **2 C4** Metro **Business Bay**
Stretching along Jumeira Road, this boutique mall has a sleek glass and steel exterior, and is home to premium fashion and lifestyle brands as well as unique dining experiences in town. Provedore, a delicatessen with a difference, Taste of Fame, a unique celebrity themed restaurant, and other niche venues such as I Love F Cafe, Gizia, Valleydez, West La and more, are featuring this elegant and stylish shopping destination.

Town Centre Jumeirah
Jumeira Rd Jumeira 1 **04 344 0111**
towncentrejumeirah.com
Map **2 F4** Metro **Burj Khalifa/Dubai Mall**
This community mall has an interesting blend of outlets and several cafes, including Cafe Ceramique where you can customise a piece of pottery while you dine. There are beauty salons, as well as clothing shops including Heat Waves (for beachwear), Anne Klein (fashion accessories), TKD Lingerie for the more well-endowed lady, a large branch of Paris Gallery plus an Empost counter and an Etisalat machine.

Village Mall
Jumeira Rd Jumeira 1 **04 349 4444**
Map **2 H4** Metro **World Trade Centre**
With its Mediterranean theme, this has more of a community feel than many of the malls in Dubai. The niche boutiques are great for something different, whether it's clothing or something for the home, with outlets like S*uce, Ayesha Depala and Shakespeare & Co. There's a bright and fun children's play area for younger children and a number of places to eat.

Wasl Square
Nr Al Wasl Rd & Hadiqa St Al Safa 1 **04 800 9275**
waslproperties.com
Map **2 D5** Metro **Business Bay**
This lovely open-air development next to Safa Park has a number of interesting stores, restaurants and services, including S*uce Gifts, a gourmet butcher,

Shops are open late in Dubai

SHOPPING DISTRICTS

a Japanese bakery and salons for men and women. There are several cafes, including popular gourmet venue The Pantry and Bookmunch, where you can peruse and purchase books while you eat.

Mirdif

The family suburb of Mirdif is mostly collections of small cornershops and supermarkets, usually centred around a mosque, but Uptown Mirdiff is a pleasant open air complex, and the huge Mirdif City Centre mall is a destination worth heading to, especially for the variety of attractions at Playnation.

Arabian Center
Al Khawaneej Rd Al Mizhar 1 **04 284 5555**
arabiancenter.ae
Map **2 R13** Metro **Rashidiya**
This small mall still manages to tick all the boxes. You can pick up home appliances or creature comforts (Homes R Us, Sharaf DG and Eros Digital) as well as high-street fashion including New Look and Mango. A good selection of sports stores includes Adidas. There's also a cinema, hypermarket, a play area for kids and a salon.

Bin Sougat Centre
Airport Rd Al Rashidiya **04 286 3000**
binsougatcenter.com
Map **2 P10** Metro **Rashidiya**
Anchored by a large Spinneys, there is an interesting mix of stores including Emirates Trading which sells professional art supplies and equipment, Dubai Library Distributors, which is excellent for stationery, and Orient Curios Furniture. There is also a Secrets Boutique which sells a limited range of lingerie in larger sizes.

Etihad Mall
Al Khawaneej Rd Muhaisnah 1 **04 284 3663**
etihadmall.ae
Map **2 R12** Metro **Rashidiya**
A community mall with numerous fashion brands – including several aimed squarely at the Arab market – as well as services like opticians, banks and pharmacies. There's an indoor amusement centre for kids, and a good sized foodcourt.

Uptown Mirdiff
Nr Uptown Primary School Mirdif **04 288 9333**
uptownmirdiff.ae
Map **2 Q13** Metro **Rashidiya**
This open air complex has a sense of community about it that attracts plenty of families living in the area. It has all the essentials: a Spinneys, an A&E liquor store, banks, pharmacy, gym, cafes and restaurants.

Satwa

One of Dubai's original retail areas, Satwa has something of a village feel about it. It is best known for its fabric shops and tailors, but holds a real mix of stores. The area tends to cater to the lower end of the market and is great fun to look around. Popular reasons to visit Satwa include buying traditional *majlis* seating and getting your car windows tinted. The pick of the fabric shops is Deepak's, with an amazing range, reasonable prices and helpful staff.

There are a number of shops on 'Plant Street' with good indoor and outdoor plants; this is also the street for upholstery and paint. Animal lovers should probably avoid the pet shops – conditions are awful, despite regulations, and the animals are often in a sorry state. Shop around, because whatever you are looking for there's bound to be more than one outlet selling it and prices vary.

Satwa is renowned for its fast food outlets and reasonably priced restaurants. Ravi's is an institution in Dubai, serving good Pakistani food at incredible prices; Mini Chinese has been going for years and Rydges Plaza Hotel has a number of popular, licensed bars and restaurants. Satwa is also home to some great salons, where you can get various treatments at low prices. They might not be as smooth as the upper-end salons, but they are great for a quick fix.

2nd December Street (still often called by its former name, Al Diyafah Road) is a great place for a lively evening stroll. There's an eclectic mix of shops and fast food outlets; Al Mallah, a popular Lebanese restaurant, is highly recommended (arguably the best falafel and shawarma in Dubai).

Out Of Town

Venture slightly out of the city and you can find some serious bargains. Dubai Outlet Mall is 15 minutes along the Al Ain Road and great for cut-price labels, or head to Sharjah or Ajman for cheap furniture, carpets and electronics.

Dragon Mart
Al Aweer Rd Warsan 1 **04 433 6200**
dragonmart.ae
This huge concentration of Chinese traders (shaped like a dragon and over a kilometre long) is vaguely divided into zones by commodity; from building materials to toys, household items to quad bikes, everything is available – and cheaper than elsewhere in the city. There's an incredible amount of tat, but if you're looking for something cheap and for the short haul, you can't go wrong. Items worth looking out for include garden furniture and fancy dress costumes. See the website for opening hours.

The waterfall at The Dubai Mall

PLACES TO SHOP

Depending on what you need to buy, or how you want to spend your day, Dubai has a place to shop that will match your mood. While the magnificent malls are fantastic places to be entertained, eat and buy from many top international stores, there are also smaller shopping centres, hypermarkets and souks to help you spend your dirhams.

The souks and markets offer a surprisingly authentic Middle Eastern shopping experience – bargaining can be fun and rewarding, and you never know what you might come home with, from fresh fish to Iranian plant pots. The hypermarkets, on the other hand, stock all manner of international brands and you can shop knowing what to expect.

Overall, don't panic that you can't head to your favourite organic grocery store or department store – you're bound to have a new favourite in no time, and many of the chains you are used to are right here.

Department Stores

Department stores are at the heart of some of Dubai's biggest malls and in addition to British stalwarts like Marks & Spencer and Debenhams, South Africa's trusted Woolworths and regional powerhouse Jashanmal provide essentials for the whole family.

Bloomingdale's
The Dubai Mall Burj Khalifa **04 350 5333**
bloomingdales.com
Map **2 F7** Metro **Burj Khalifa/Dubai Mall**
The first Bloomingdale's to open outside the USA brings with it the exclusivity that attracts well-heeled New Yorkers. Three storeys of high-end lines of fashion include jewellery, accessories and homewares. Classic touches include the store's famous 'big brown bags' and a taste of Manhattan at Magnolia's Bakery.

SHOPPING
PLACES TO SHOP

Centrepoint
Oasis Centre Al Qouz 1 **04 809 4000**
Map **2 C6** Metro **Noor Bank**
Shopaholics will love this store, a one-stop shopping destination that houses Babyshop, Splash, Lifestyle, Shoe Mart and Beautybay all under one roof. You can dress your family head to toe in one easy shopping trip – and without breaking the bank. Also at Mall of the Emirates and Mirdif City Centre.

Debenhams
The Dubai Mall Burj Khalifa **04 339 9285**
debenhams.com
Map **2 F7** Metro **Burj Khalifa/Dubai Mall**
A mainstay of the British high street, it's a go-to for perfumes, cosmetics, homewares and clothing for men, women and children. Brands include Evans, for plus-size clothing, Warehouse and Miss Selfridge, as well as John Rocha and Jasper Conran. Also located at Deira City Centre, Ibn Battuta Mall, Mirdif City Centre and Mall of the Emirates.

Galeries Lafayette
The Dubai Mall Burj Khalifa **04 339 9933**
galerieslafayette-dubai.com
Map **2 F7** Metro **Burj Khalifa/Dubai Mall**
This French department store adds more designer brands to The Dubai Mall's extensive store list; from glamorous frocks and stylish shoes to cosmetics, children's wear, lingerie and a homeware section. The Lafayette Gourmet food store stocks a range of original and innovative edible treats, and there's the option to dine in too.

Harvey Nichols
Mall of the Emirates Al Barsha 1 **04 409 8888**
harveynichols.com/stores-abroad
Map **1 R6** Metro **Mall of the Emirates**
The epitome of chic shopping, 'Harvey Nics' offers a large selection of high-rolling fashion (for men, women and kids), beauty and homeware brands. You'll find Jimmy Choo and Diane Von Furstenberg rubbing shoulders with other swish brands. There is a small range of gourmet products in the Foodmarket and restaurant Almaz by Momo.

Jashanmal
Dubai Festival City Mall Al Kheeran **04 232 9023**
jashanmal.ae
Map **2 M9** Metro **Emirates**
The go-to shopping destination for dinnerware, cookware, bed and bath accessories, home appliances as well as luggage. It also sells a small range of clothing and underwear, perfume and books, and its luggage section is particularly good. Also located at Mall of the Emirates, The Dubai Mall, Dubai Marina Mall, Mirdif City Centre and Al Ghurair Centre.

Marks & Spencer
The Dubai Mall Burj Khalifa **04 339 8890**
marksandspencerme.com
Map **2 F7** Metro **Burj Khalifa/Dubai Mall**
A renowned UK brand, 'M&S' sells clothes and shoes for men, women and children, including a revered underwear range, along with a small selection of food and sweets. It's a good bet for seasonal items such as Christmas cards and Easter eggs. Also at Wafi, Mall of the Emirates, Festival City, Mirdif and Deira City Centre.

Mudo City
The Dubai Mall Burj Khalifa **04 325 3246**
mudo.com.tr
Map **2 F7** Metro **Burj Khalifa/Dubai Mall**
One of the most famous brands in Turkey, Mudo City is a lifestyle store with a collection of furniture, home furnishings, kitchen, bathroom and personal accessories, and home textiles. It's an eclectic mix of fashion and home decor, all with a modern-classic style; you can pick up an affordable T-shirt for Dhs.70 or a quirky, designer table for Dhs.10,000.

Redtag
Ibn Battuta Mall Jabal Ali 1 **04 445 6966**
redtag.ae
Map **1 G5** Metro **Ibn Battuta**
A big name in fashion in Saudi Arabia, with more than 40 stores across the Kingdom, this store offers value ranges of men's, women's and children's clothing. It's a popular regional choice, with several locations including Ibn Battuta Mall, Arabian Centre in Mirdif and Lamcy Plaza.

Saks Fifth Avenue
BurJuman Al Mankhool **04 501 2700**
saksincorporated.com
Map **2 L5** Metro **Burjuman**
Even in Dubai's cultured retail sector, this store has an air of sophistication. Along with cosmetics, perfumes, designer sunglasses and the Saks Nail Studio, there are boutiques from Jean Paul Gaultier, Prada and D&G, plus children's designer clothes, a men's store, and a chocolate bar and cafe. There's also an exclusive bridal salon that stocks Vera Wang gowns.

Salam Studio & Stores
Wafi Umm Hurair 2 **04 704 8484**
salaminternational.com
Map **2 K7** Metro **Dubai Healthcare City**
This local department store has a swanky decor and a good mix of brands, including LA brand Gypsy 05 and designer names such as Betsey Johnson, Roberto Cavalli and Missoni. Its spacious store in Wafi stocks a good range of homeware and jewellery, as well as a particularly good selection of photography accessories from well-known brands.

askexplorer.com

335

SHOPPING
PLACES TO SHOP

Hypermarkets

For a one-stop shop for almost anything you can think of, hypermarkets are the place to go. With a range that goes far beyond food, most sell a variety of electronics and home appliances at competitive prices, as well as toys, homewares, luggage, clothes, shoes, music and DVDs and much, much more.

Carrefour
Mall of the Emirates Al Barsha 1 **800 73232**
carrefouruae.com
Map **1 R6** Metro **Mall of the Emirates**
Renowned for its competitive pricing and special offers, branches of this French chain can be found throughout the city. As well as a good range of French food products there's a comprehensive range of electronics and household goods. Camping gear, car accessories, garden furniture and hardware are also on sale. Non-food items can be ordered online. Also located in Mirdif and Deira.

Geant
Ibn Battuta Mall Jabal Ali 1 **04 368 5880**
geant-uae.com
Map **1 G5** Metro **Ibn Battuta**
Stocks a massive selection of products. It is well worth a visit for the cheap fruit and vegetables and the huge selection of nuts (great almonds). You'll also find very reasonably priced towels and bedding, a good selection of electronics, a car accessories section and it's also a good destination for DVD box sets. Comprehensive online grocery shopping is also available – a first for the UAE.

HyperPanda
Dubai Festival City Mall Al Kheeran **04 232 5997**
panda.com.sa/dubai
Map **2 M9** Metro **Emirates**
Enormous but quieter than similar stores, so it's a good choice when you need hypermarket shopping without the hyperactive crowds. The selection of produce isn't as extensive as in some of the other hypermarkets, but it does have a healthcare department, electronics and more than the basic range of goods.

LuLu
Nr Mall of the Emirates Al Barsha 1 **04 341 8888**
luluhypermarket.com
Map **1 R6** Metro **Mall of the Emirates**
Great for those on a budget; LuLu's hot food counters, salad bars and fishmonger are particularly good value, as is the wide-ranging fruit and vegetable section. While you may not find all of your favourite Western brands, it stocks a good range of ethnic food. Most stores have a range of home appliances. Also located in Mirdif, Karama and Al Qusais.

Fruit and veg is imported

Convenience Stores

Aside from the larger supermarkets and hypermarkets, Dubai has a huge number of smaller convenience stores selling many of the basic food and drink needs. If you live close to a convenience store it's quite usual that you can phone them up and have them deliver small amounts of groceries to you too, with the only extra cost being a tip for the delivery guy.
There are also branches of Spinneys Market, Carrefour Market and Carrefour Express around the city offering convenience from a trusted name.

Al Maya
Reef Mall Al Muraqqabat **04 2229898**
almaya.ae Map **2 N5** Metro **Al Rigga**
This city-wide chain can be relied on for a good range of items, a bakery and fresh meat and fish. It also has a pork section selling a wide range of goods. Many of its branches are open 24 hours and offer free home delivery for a minimum order of Dhs.50.

Lifco
Al Nahda 1 **04 2545763**
lifco.com Map **2 S7** Metro **Stadium**
Stocks a great range of items in terms of convenience, and it is a good place to go for fresh olives. The store has regular special offers where you can buy two or three items banded together for a discount.

Blue Mart
bluemartgroup.com
All Day Mini Mart
alldayuae.com

SHOPPING
PLACES TO SHOP

Supermarkets

Unlike hypermarkets, supermarkets concentrate solely on food and domestic necessities such as cleaning products and toiletries. They all tend to have their own kitchens that cook up freshly baked goods, with some larger stores offering quite an impressive range of pies, samosas and pasties. Some even have fish and meat counters for you to peruse. Carrefour Market (with various locations) is a more condensed and less frantic version of the hypermarket.

You may find that the prices between different brands of supermarket can vary quite dramatically, while the quality of some items like fruit and vegetables can be equally varied; this means it can pay to visit a couple of different supermarkets to get the best balance of quality and price when completing the grocery run.

Choithrams
Nr Safa Park, Al Wasl Rd Jumeira **04 394 3852**
choithram.com
Map **2 D5** Metro **Business Bay**
With branches across the city, Choithrams stores are renowned for stocking British, American and Asian products that can't be found elsewhere (such as the Quorn range), but they are also known for being fairly expensive. Stores have pork sections and a great range of baby products – particularly food and formula. The large branch opposite Safa Park is open until 1am.

Park n Shop
Al Wasl Rd Al Safa 1 **04 394 5671**
Map **2 C5** Metro **Noor Bank**
A superb local supermarket for residents of Jumeira, Park n Shop has great prices and is worth a trip simply because it has the best bakery (famous for its birthday cakes, fresh goodies and seasonal treats) and butchery in the city. The butchery has a Christmas ordering service for your turkey and ham. There's also a surprising selection of treats from home that you might not find elsewhere. The Park n Shop Cash n Carry at Dubai Investments Park is huge, blissfully quiet, and has a loyalty scheme.

Spinneys
Nr Centrepoint Al Mankhool **04 351 1777**
spinneys-dubai.com
Map **2 L5** Metro **Al Karama**
With branches across Dubai, this high-end supermarket (with prices to match) has a great range of South African and Australian, as well as British and American items and a selection of Waitrose products. The freezer section and vegetarian options are both good, along with the deli counter. If you stay in town for Christmas you can order your seasonal goodies from here. Most branches have a pork section.

Union Co-operative Society
Nr Rashidiya Police Station Al Rashidiya **800 8889**
ucs.ae
Map **1 P11** Metro **Rashidiya**
It may lack the shine of other hypermarkets, but it's great for shaving a few dirhams off your grocery bill. The huge fruit and veg section is packed with farm-fresh produce at great prices, and it has a superb selection of Arabic cheeses, olives, and family size bargain packs. The Al Wasl Road branch is open 24 hours a day, and a new branch is due to open in Umm Suqeim in 2014.

Waitrose
The Dubai Mall Burj Khalifa **04 434 0700**
waitrose.com
Map **2 F7** Metro **Burj Khalifa/Dubai Mall**
This upmarket UK chain is well known for its premium range of British produce and gourmet goods, and this, along with the ease of shopping experience, is reflected in the price. It has a well-stocked deli filled with hot and cold selections of pre-made dishes and a great selection of baked goods, meat and cheese. There's a large, quiet branch in Umm Suqeim and several more around the city.

Delicatessens, Gourmet & Health Foods

If you have tastebuds that can only be satisfied by the best or healthiest ingredients, you'll find several stores dedicated to organic products and gourmet options. The main supermarkets also stock increasing varieties of speciality foods, including organic products and breads made from spelt or rye, and they all now carry products for diabetics.

The range of health food is improving; prices are generally high, but it is worth shopping around as costs vary. Nutrition Zone and Holland & Barrett have a good selection of vitamins, health supplements and detoxifying products and carry a range of health food, grains, gluten and wheat-free products, as well as some ecological household products.

Emirates Gourmet General Trading
Jumeira Plaza Jumeira 1 **04 349 3181**
emiratesgourmetdubai.com
Map **2 H4** Metro **Emirates Towers**
A favourite on the high-end deli scene. Shelves are stacked with a fine collection of speciality gourmet foods from France, Italy, Spain, Germany, Belgium, USA and Lebanon. There's condiments and olives, chocolates and chutneys. Brands include Stonewall Kitchen and there is also an enticing collection of seasonal goods for the Christmas, Thanksgiving or Easter shopping trip.

SHOPPING
PLACES TO SHOP

Jones The Grocer
Indigo Central 8, Nr Times Square, Shk Zayed Rd
Al Manara **04 346 6886**
jonesthegrocer.com
Map **1 T6** Metro **First Gulf Bank**
The Australian gourmet foodstore brings its artisan products to Dubai, with an extensive selection of deli items and fresh produce. It has an on-site bakery and cafe, and also offers a catering service. This is the perfect food emporium for connoisseurs looking to shop for a picnic basket or alfresco dining at home.

Market & Platters
Pinnacle Tower Marsa Dubai **04 450 4466**
marketandplatters.com
Map **1 M5** Metro **Dubai Marina**
This store sells platters of sushi, seafood and cheese, as well as beautifully presented fruit and vegetables, gourmet products and an extensive selection of fish and cheese.

Maybury Fresh Food Store
Ariyana Tower Marsa Dubai **04 340 0065**
facebook.com/MayburyStore
Map **1 L5** Metro **Dubai Marina**
A high-end store in a funky, urban space that stocks organic products, fresh halal meats, seafood, locally grown produce, cheeses, salads, freshly baked bread and fresh flowers.

Milk & Honey
Shoreline Bldg 10 Nakhlat Jumeira **04 432 8686**
milkandhoney.ae
Map **1 N3** Metro **Nakheel**
Open 24 hours a day and with a delivery service, this boutique supermarket has a range of organic products and everyday household essentials, with a focus on high-end brands and gourmet living.

Organic Foods & Cafe > p.339
The Village Jumeira 1 **04 338 2911**
organicfoodsandcafe.com
Map **2 G4** Metro **Emirates Towers**
Great for stocking up on fresh organic fruit, veg, meat, fish and bread. Weekly specials and 20% off events every third Saturday of the month make guilt-free grocery shopping far more affordable. The adjoining cafe serves food prepared with organic ingredients too. Also at Sheikh Zayed Road and the Greens.

Cakes & Breads
There's a fantastic choice of bakeries, including the Yamanote Japanese Bakery in Wasl Square, Belgian outlet Maison Mathis at Arabian Ranches, the Lebanese bakery Al Reef on Al Wasl Road, and Le Succes French Bakery & Pastry at MotorCity. And you're never more than a few metres away from a good cupcake with branches of Hummingbird Bakery, Magnolia and Kitsch Cupcakes across the emirate.

Farm Shops
As demand for organic and locally grown produce increases in Dubai, so does the number of shops offering these healthier options. Prices may be higher, but it's a real treat to be able to buy fresh and organic fruit and veg in the middle of the desert.

downtoearthorganic.ae
Have organic products and fresh produce delivered right to your door by this online store.

Greenheart Organic Farms
The Light Building, Arjan Al Barsha 2 **056 640 7060**
greenheartuae.com
Map **1 P11**
This farm shop in Arjan, Al Barsha 2, sells produce within hours of being harvested, and holds regular tasting events and demonstrations. Opening times are Monday, Wednesday and Saturday from 11.30am to 5pm, or deliveries can be ordered online.

Ripe
The Courtyard Al Qouz Ind. 1 **04 380 7602**
ripeme.com
Map **1 U6** Metro **Noor Bank**
Having served the Dubai community with fresh produce at its regular markets, Ripe's shop serves as a permanent base for fans.

Organic products are available

your organic supermarket

Eat Smart Eat Biodynamic

Organic foods & café
family run

SHEIKH ZAYED ROAD
Next to Oasis Centre

GREENS
Opp. Dubai Media City

THE VILLAGE
Jumeirah 1

- Fruit and Veg
- Fresh Dairy Products
- Fresh Meats
- Fresh Bread
- Groceries
- Body Care Products
- Cosmetics
- Food Supplements

15% OFF
Every 1st Sunday of the month

20% OFF
Every 3rd Saturday of the month & the Friday before

2000 AED IN SHOPPING VOUCHERS!
Send your name, mobile & email to:
marketingincharge@organicfoodsandcafe.com

HOME DELIVERY

Tel: 3382911, www.organicfoodsandcafe.com

organicfoodsandcafe   organicFoodUAE

SHOPPING
PLACES TO SHOP

Markets

Western-style markets are becoming more and more popular in Dubai and are usually based around crafts or gourmet food and are often seasonal. These are less daunting than the souks and a good place to find unique items and fresh produce.

The Fish Market and the Fruit & Vegetable Market, however, are pretty old school, and bustling with traders and restauranteurs picking up fresh produce.

Artisans of the Emirates (ARTE)
Times Square Center Al Qouz Ind. 1
arte.ae
Map **1 T6** Metro **Noor Bank**
Taking place fortnightly (alternating between Dubai Festival City Mall and Times Square Center) this is where you'll find all manner of individual and quirky products unlike anything you'll find in any of the bigger markets; from hand-printed cards or personalised artwork to bags, cushions and jewellery created by talented local designers.

Cultural Night Market
Safa Park Al Wasl 050 461 8888
greateventsdubai.com
Map **2 D5** Metro **Business Bay**
Providing an urban public space for local and international artists to develop and showcase their art, the Cultural Night Market offers music, paintings, sculptures, dance and theatre, as well as a world food market. There's a kids' corner, artistic market, books area and live performances in the park amphitheatre. Held every last Friday and Saturday of the month, 3pm to 11pm, September through to April. Admission costs Dhs.15 per person; free for children under 10.

Dubai Designer Market
The Beach Centre Jumeira 1 055 452 6030
dubaidesignermarket.com
Map **2 G4** Metro **Emirates Towers**
Thrifty fashionistas should head here for chic and boutique designer goods at affordable prices. Think rails of high-end brands like Gucci, Prada, and Chanel, as well as vintage items and collections by young, up and coming designers. The Market has a strict original brands and high-end goods only policy, so no fakes allowed! Every second Saturday of the month at the Beach Centre, Jumeira.

Dubai Flea Market
Safa Park Al Wasl 04 452 6030
dubai-fleamarket.com
Map **2 D5** Metro **Business Bay**
One man's junk is another man's treasure, and this is certainly true here. Winter sessions are at Safa Park on the first Saturday of the month. During the summer, the market takes place at Dubai World Trade Centre, on the first Friday of the month. From furniture and trinkets to clothes, toys and even household appliances, anything goes and you don't know what you might find.

The Farmers' Market
Emirates Towers Trade Center 2 04 427 9856
bakerandspiceme.com
Map **2 G6** Metro **Emirates Towers**
Taking place every Friday from 9am to 1pm during winter at Emirates Towers, The Farmers' Market On The Terrace sells local produce grown on UAE farms, as well as fresh bread and cakes baked by Baker & Spice and Sweet Connections Gluten Free Baking, plus more stalls packed with goodies. Produce is harvested just hours before the market and the farmers are on hand to answer any questions.

Fish Market
Nr Shindagha Tunnel Al Corniche 800 900
dm.gov.ae
Map **2 N4** Metro **Palm Deira**
To get the freshest fish for your evening meal, and to experience the vibrancy of this working market, head down early in the morning or late at night as the catch is coming in. There is an incredible range of seafood on display and the fish can be cleaned and gutted for you.

Fruit & Vegetable Market
Dubai – Hatta Rd Ras Al Khor Industrial 3
Map **2 K13** Metro **Rashidiya**
Located off Sheikh Mohammed bin Zayed Rd in Al Aweer, there is a huge variety of produce on offer that is usually fresher than in the supermarkets. Be sure to haggle; you can often tell if you have paid more than the trader thinks the goods are worth if they give you freebies. It is well signposted as you drive along the Dubai-Hatta Road and mornings are the best time to visit.

Ripe
The Courtyard Al Qouz Ind. 1 04 380 7602
ripeme.com
Map **1 U6** Metro **Noor Bank**
Ripe hosts a farmers' market every Saturday at The Courtyard, Al Qouz, and every Friday in Safa Park during the winter months, selling cardboard boxes packed with fresh local fruit and vegetables. Produce varies according to the season and can include anything from leafy, fragrant basil and irregular-sized courgettes to potatoes with the dirt still clinging to them. There are also stalls selling tasty treats such as locally made cheeses, olives and chutneys, as well as designer gifts and kitsch crafts. The Archive at Safa Park usually puts on accompanying live music.

SHOPPING
PLACES TO SHOP

Fish Market

Traditional items

Ripe Vegetable Market

341

Getting Started: 10 Shops to Set You Up

Whether you're waiting for your freight to arrive from overseas, or are staring at a big empty apartment, you'll need to turn your house into a home. Pretty much anything you'll ever need can be found in these convenient and affordable stores, and at the lowest prices in the city save some serious haggling at the souks. Delivery on larger items is usually free, too.

IKEA
Budget-friendly, well-designed furniture you can take straight home. Also stock up on bits for the house – from towels to tealights, cutlery to curtains.

Carrefour
Stock up on home appliances: toaster, kettle and fridge, and fill your kitchen cupboards with good international branded products as well.

Sharaf DG
Appliances, electronics and related accessories at very welcoming prices.

ACE Hardware > p.343
Everything you need for DIY around the house, plus garden furniture and plants, as well as outdoor equipment to get you ready for some exploring in the desert.

Home Centre > p.xi
Put the finishing touches on your new home with items from this classy but affordable range of essential homeware.

Centrepoint
This is a one-stop shop for several handy and affordable brands – clothe your kids, stock up on baby essentials and decorate the home.

LuLu Hypermarket
Great for all the household essentials – cleaning products and cheap necessities – as well as stocking up on tins and basics. The fruit and veg section is also brilliant.

Emax
A wide range of electronic brands to get your home entertainment sorted, from TVs and games consoles to wireless routers, plus a range of cameras to document your UAE adventures with.

Sports Direct
Prepare yourself for Dubai's outdoors and active lifestyle by stocking up on trainers, sportswear and all kinds of sports equipment.

dubizzle.com
Absolutely anything you can think of – from cars to furniture, someone will be selling theirs at a pre-owned price on this online expat institution.

Shop Online
Check out these local online stores and you won't even need to leave the house.

carrefouruae.com/webstore
tejuri.com
souq.com
alshop.com
ikea.com
dbbabies.com
geant-online.ae

Groceries
Chances are high that your local convenience store will deliver to your door, night and day. Pop inside and ask for a phone number, and you'll never need to nip out for milk again.

ACE
ONE STORE. MANY LIFESTYLES.

Thinking hardware? Think again.

There's certainly more to ACE than just a hardware store. From automotive accessories to kitchen appliances, camping gear to barbeques, outdoor furniture to paints and plants, gardening items to pet accessories. There's so much to choose from all under one roof. **ACE. One Store. Many Lifestyles.**

Dubai: Dubai Festival City, Tel: 800 ASK ACE (800 275 223), Sheikh Zayed Road, Tel: (04) 341 1906, Fax: (04) 341 7610, **Abu Dhabi:** Yas Island, Opposite IKEA, Tel: (02) 565 1945, Fax: (02) 565 1836, Mina Road, Tel: (02) 673 1665, Fax: (02) 673 0415, **Sharjah:** Al Wahda Street, Tel: (06) 537 1556, Fax: (06) 537 1575, Al Ain: Sultan Bin Zayed Road, Bawadi Mall, Tel: (03) 784 0561   e-mail: ace@alfuttaim.ae or www.al-futtaim.ae

An Al-Futtaim group company

www.aceuae.com

SHOPPING
PLACES TO SHOP

Souks

The souks are the traditional trading areas, the closest you'll get to an authentic, old world Arabian experience. In keeping with tradition, bargaining is expected and cash gives the best leverage.

The Gold, Spice and Textile Souks line either side of the creek, but parking is limited, so if possible it is better to go to these areas by taxi or, if you are visiting all three, park on one side of the creek and take an abra to the other side.

The modern souks tend to be more like malls with high-end shops and a nod to traditional architecture.

Al Fahidi Souk
Al Souk Al Kabeer 800 900
dm.gov.ae
Map **2 L4** Metro **Al Fahidi**

This heritage-themed souk in Al Fahidi is opening slowly, and at the time of going to print is only open on Saturdays from 10am until sunset. Built to resemble Naif Souk, it uses many traditional architectural cues.

Gold Souk
Baniyas Rd Al Ras
goldsouks.com
Map **2 M4** Metro **Al Ras**

This is Dubai's best-known souk and a must-do for every visitor. It's a good place to buy customised jewellery for unique souvenirs and gifts at a reasonable price. On the Deira side of the creek, the meandering lanes are lined with shops selling gold, silver, pearls and precious stones. These can be bought as they are or in a variety of settings so this is definitely a place to try your bargaining skills – but don't expect a massive discount. Gold is sold by weight according to the daily international price and so will be much the same as in the shops in malls – the price of the workmanship is where you will have more bargaining power. Most of the outlets are closed between 1pm and 4pm. The Gold Souk is always busy, and it is shaded.

Khan Murjan
Wafi Umm Hurair 2 04 3279795
Map **2 K7** Metro **Dubai Healthcare City**

For something a little different, head to Wafi's underground souk. Khan Murjan's magnificent stained glass ceiling (which stretches 64 metres) and long curved arches help make this an atmospheric place to shop. Over 150 stalls sell jewellery, antiques, Arabic perfume and souvenirs. It is particularly good if you wish to spice up your home with traditional arts and crafts; there are workshops where artisans can create various bits of arts and crafts on site. The open air marble courtyard in the centre houses the highly recommended Khan Murjan Arabic restaurant.

Naif Souk
Nr Naif Police Station Naif
Map **2 M4** Metro **Baniyas Square**

This souk in the heart of Deira re-opened in 2010, two years after the original burned down in a fire that destroyed most of the buildings. Before the inferno, this souk was a big draw for visitors and locals alike, and the new facilities – more modern, less rustic than the Naif of old – still bring crowds of shoppers and tourists back to look for bargains from the range of goods on sale.

Souk Al Bahar > p.345
Shk Zayed Rd Burj Khalifa 04 362 7011
soukalbahar.ae
Map **2 F6** Metro **Burj Khalifa/Dubai Mall**

Not exactly a souk in conventional terms, Souk Al Bahar in Downtown Dubai is an Arabian-style mall with many shops catering to tourists as well as a few international brands and the odd funky boutique. There are a number of useful outlets catering for residents including a Spinneys. Most folk head here for the views of the Burj Khalifa, Dubai Fountain and the fantastic range of eateries, cafes and bars.

Souk Madinat Jumeirah
Jumeira Rd Al Sufouh 1 04 366 8888
madinatjumeirah.com
Map **1 R5** Metro **Mall of the Emirates**

A recreation of a traditional souk complete with narrow alleyways, authentic architecture and motorised abras. The blend of outlets is unlike anywhere else in Dubai, with boutique shops, art galleries, souvenir stalls, and popular cafes, restaurants and bars. During the cooler months the doors and glass walls are opened to add an alfresco element and there is shisha on offer in the courtyard.

There are more than 20 waterfront cafes, bars and restaurants to choose from, including some of Dubai's hottest night spots, and you'll find Left Bank, Trader Vic's and BarZar to name a few. There's also the impressive Madinat Theatre which sees international and regional artists and theatre companies perform everything from ballet to comedy.

Spice Souk
Nr Gold Souk Al Ras
Map **2 M4** Metro **Al Ras**

The narrow streets and exotic aromas are a great way to get a feel for the way the city used to be. Vendors are usually happy to give advice on the types of spices and their uses, and the experience of buying from the Souk is more memorable than picking a packet off a shelf. You may even be able to pick up some saffron at a bargain price. The shops operate split shifts but, whether you visit in the morning or the evening, this is a bustling area of the city.

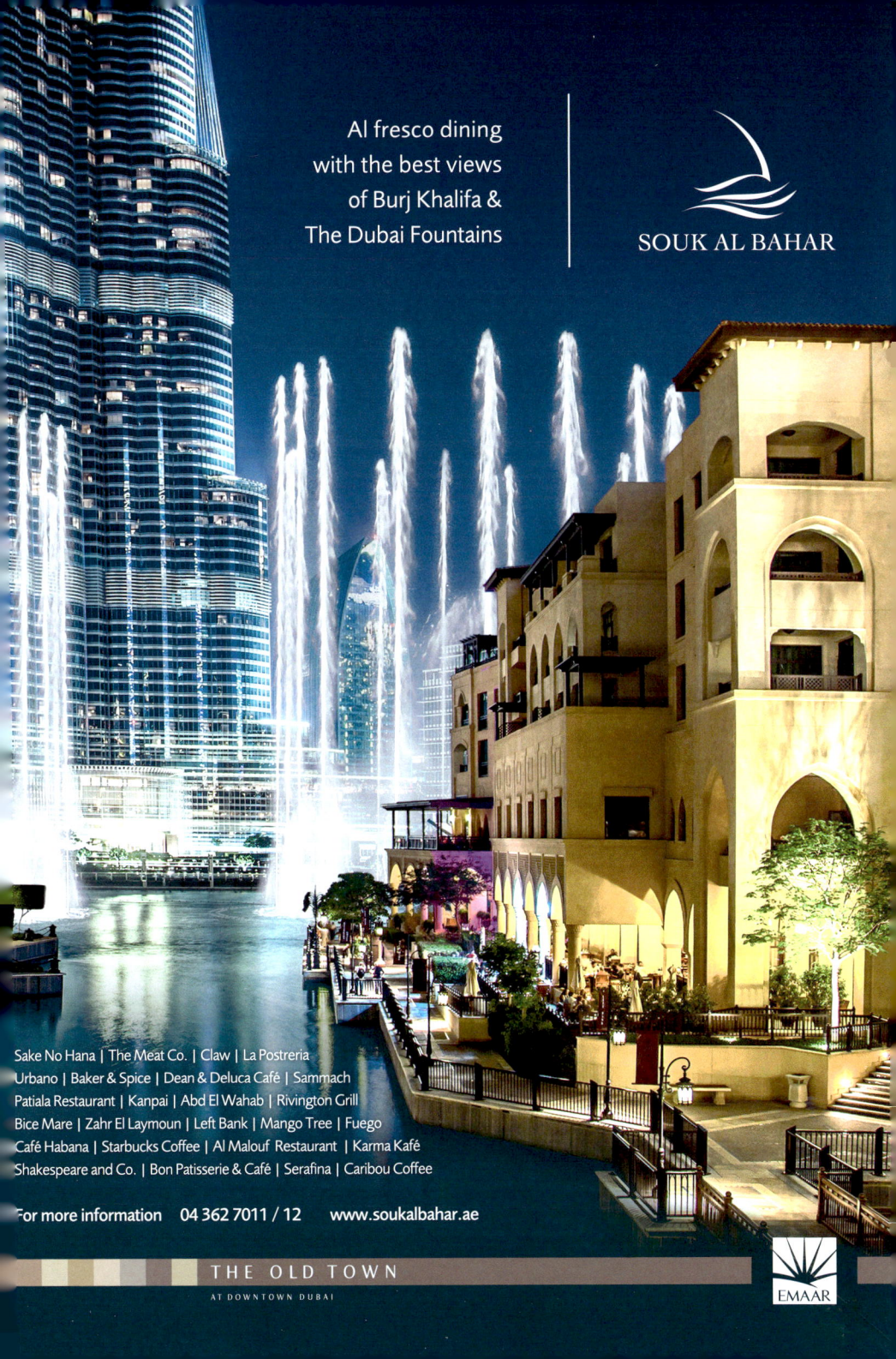

Al fresco dining with the best views of Burj Khalifa & The Dubai Fountains

SOUK AL BAHAR

Sake No Hana | The Meat Co. | Claw | La Postreria
Urbano | Baker & Spice | Dean & Deluca Café | Sammach
Patiala Restaurant | Kanpai | Abd El Wahab | Rivington Grill
Bice Mare | Zahr El Laymoun | Left Bank | Mango Tree | Fuego
Café Habana | Starbucks Coffee | Al Malouf Restaurant | Karma Kafé
Shakespeare and Co. | Bon Patisserie & Café | Serafina | Caribou Coffee

For more information   04 362 7011 / 12   www.soukalbahar.ae

THE OLD TOWN
AT DOWNTOWN DUBAI

EMAAR

SHOPPING
PLACES TO SHOP

Textile Souk
Nr Abra Station Al Souk Al Kabeer
Map **2 M4** Metro **Al Ras**
This souk in Bur Dubai is stocked with every fabric and colour imaginable. The textiles are imported from all over the world, with many of the more elaborate designs coming from the subcontinent and the Far East. There are silks and satins in an amazing array of colours and patterns, velvets and intricately embroidered fabrics. Prices here are somewhat negotiable, but it is worth having a look in a few shops before parting with your cash as they may have different stock and at better prices. The mornings tend to be a more relaxed time to browse.

Shopping Malls

Malls are not just places to shop; a huge mall culture exists here, and they are places to meet, eat and mingle. Many malls provide entertainment for people of all ages. With so much choice out there, malls make sure they can offer something unique to shoppers to draw the crowds. From one-of-a-kind attractions such as indoor skiing, and theme parks to unique shops, restaurants and bars, each mall has its own feel and its own pulling power. Most malls will have branches of the major banks, pharmacies and other services such as dry cleaning.

Special events are held during Dubai Shopping Festival, Dubai Summer Surprises and Ramadan, with entertainment for children, special offers and longer opening hours. These are peak shopping times and an evening in the larger malls at this time is not for the faint-hearted. Most of the malls have plenty of parking – often stretched to the limits at the weekends; all have taxi ranks (be warned that queues can be very long at chucking-out time on the weekends) and many are handy for bus and metro routes.

Al Ghurair Centre
Al Rigga Rd Al Muraqqabat **800 24327**
alghuraircentre.com
Map **2 N5** Metro **Union**
Housing an eight-screen Grand Cinemas, a Spinneys, and a good range of shops, this two-storey mall has the maze-like quality of a souk. There are a number of international brands, including Bhs, Book Corner and Mothercare, along with smaller boutiques. A major recent expansion has brought several new brands to the mall, including popular British supermarket fashion brand George, a branch of Marks & Spencer, Mango and Iconic, and the mall plans to have an ongoing programme of street theatre and other unique entertainment. There's also a Sparky's family entertainment centre with an ice rink, as well as rides that include an outdoor rollercoaster.

BurJuman
Shk Khalifa Bin Zayed St Al Mankhool **04 352 0222**
burjuman.com
Map **2 L5** Metro **Burjuman**
Renowned for its blend of designer and high-street brands, BurJuman attracts many a well-heeled shopper. There are famous brands such as Versace and Ralph Lauren, as well as some interesting smaller shops and New York department store Saks Fifth Avenue. Gap and Zara lead the way in everyday fashion. There are some independent music shops plus a branch of Virgin Megastore, while home stores include THE One. There is a Fitness First gym, and services include a pharmacy. Restaurants cater to all tastes, from Noodle House to Masala House, and the mall has direct access to the Dubai Metro. Major renovation and expansion works are currently underway and a section of the mall is closed until completion in mid 2014.

Deira City Centre
Al Ittihad Rd Port Saeed **04 295 1010**
deiracitycentre.com
Map **2 N7** Metro **Deira City Centre**
This popular mall attracts the most cosmopolitan crowd. Three floors offer a diverse range of shops where you can find anything from a postcard to a Persian carpet. There's a cinema, children's entertainment centre Magic Planet, with an eight-lane cosmic bowling arena, a jewellery court, a textiles court and an area dedicated to local furniture, gifts and souvenirs. It is all anchored by a huge Carrefour hypermarket, a Debenhams department store and Paris Gallery. Most of the high-street brands are represented, including New Look and River Island, plus a number of designer boutiques. The mall has two foodcourts, one serving mainly fast food, and one featuring several good sit-down restaurants such as Noodle House and Japengo. Deira City Centre Metro station offers easy access.

Dubai Festival City Mall
Crescent Drive Al Kheeran **800 33232**
festivalcentre.com
Map **2 M9** Metro **Emirates**
The biggest shopping draw here is Dubai's only IKEA store, but this waterfront destination features a number of useful retail outlets and plenty of alfresco restaurants, including Jamie's Italian and the hugely popular Hard Rock Cafe. There's a broad range of fashion, electronics and homeware outlets, and it is home to an enormous HyperPanda hypermarket, a large Plug-Ins, and the largest ACE store outside of North America, making it a great stop for setting up home. There is also a large modern gold souk where you can peruse gold from all over the world, and the monthly community ARTE craft market is worth a look.

SHOPPING
PLACES TO SHOP

BurJuman Mall

Festival City Mall

Al Ghurair Centre

askexplorer.com

SHOPPING
PLACES TO SHOP

The mall also features Brit favourite Marks & Spencer and designer stores like Marc By Marc Jacobs. You'll find a branch of the Dubai London Clinic here too, a pharmacy, banks and dry cleaners.

There is a Grand Cinemas and a 10 lane bowling alley, and plenty more for kids too, from Toys R Us to the Cool Times soft play area, which has an art zone.

The Dubai Mall
Financial Centre Rd Burj Khalifa 04 362 7500
thedubaimall.com
Map 2 F7 Metro Burj Khalifa/Dubai Mall
This colossus shopping centre is one of the largest in the world, and buzzes at weekends with the entire cross-section of Dubai society. The complex also houses an Olympic-size ice rink, an enormous aquarium and underwater zoo, a 22 screen cinema, indoor theme park SEGA Republic and unique children's 'edutainment' centre, KidZania.

Unique to The Dubai Mall are the regional flagship stores for New York department store Bloomingdale's, French department store Galeries Lafayette, and the world-renowned toy shop Hamleys. You'll find all of the haute couture designer brands along Fashion Avenue, as well as high-street favourites like Topshop and Forever 21, and a sprawling gold souk. There are branches of the major banks on the ground floor, a large Waitrose supermarket and a huge variety of fast food outlets, cafes and restaurants.

The fountain show beside the Burj Khalifa is a must-see, and starts at 6pm and runs every half hour.

For a complete contrast, cross the wooden bridge over the Burj Lake to Souk Al Bahar, offering a more relaxing stop after the onslaught of the mall.

Dubai Marina Mall > p.349
Off Shk Zayed Rd Marsa Dubai 04 436 1020
dubaimarinamall.com
Map 1 K5 Metro Jumeirah Lakes Towers
Located in Marsa Dubai's thriving community, and within walking distance of The Walk, Jumeirah Beach Residence, this manageably compact mall's outlets offer a mix of plush designer goods and high-street regulars. It offers Marina residents some good local, reasonably priced fashion outlets without having to venture far, but is worth a visit from further afield if you're this end of town.

Options include shops like New Look and Reiss, while kids' clothes and toys can be found at Mamas & Papas and Mothercare. There are banks, an exchange centre, opticians, a travel agency, a tailor and dry cleaner on site – all handy local amenities for local residents. The Waitrose supermarket is a huge draw for expats. Dining options range from the usual fast food suspects at the foodcourt to Carluccio's and Gourmet Burger Kitchen, while the connecting Address hotel has some upmarket venues.

A play area provides plenty of entertainment for kids, and you can drop them off while you shop, or alternatively there's a small offshoot of SEGA Republic by the cinema.

Dubai Outlet Mall
Dubai – Al Ain Rd Dubailand 04 423 4666
dubaioutletmall.com
In a city where the emphasis in on excess, it is refreshing (not only for the wallet) to find a mall dedicated to saving money. Dubai's first 'outlet' concept mall may be a way out of town (15 minutes down the Al Ain road) but it's worth the drive. Big discounts on major retailers and labels are available; think T-shirts for under Dhs.30 and Karama-esque prices for Marc Jacobs handbags.

High-street shops including Massimo Dutti, Giordano and Dune sit alongside designer names such as Tommy Hilfiger and DKNY, with city style and sports casual equally catered for. Pick up trainers from Asics, Adidas, Nike and Puma, reduced eyewear from Al Jaber or Magrabi, homewares from THE One and a range of electronics. There's some bargains to be had on trendy surf brands as well, including Billabong, Roxy and Quiksilver.

To keep the little ones happy there's US institution Chuck E Cheese serving up food and entertainment.

Ibn Battuta Mall
Off Shk Zayed Rd Jabal Ali 04 362 1900
ibnbattutamall.com
Map 1 G5 Metro Ibn Battuta
A theatre-like mall with whacky themed zones. There is a good range of mostly international stores and several anchor stores such as Debenhams and a huge Geant hypermarket. Shops are loosely grouped: China Court is dedicated to entertainment, with several restaurants (including the excellent Finz), a Fitness First gym and a large cinema; the IMAX screens regular blockbusters. The fashion conscious should head to Persia and India Courts for high street favourites such as H&M and Oasis. Persia Court is styled as the lifestyle area – when you get to Starbucks, look up to see the ceiling detail. Egypt Court is for sporty types; Andalusia Court covers life's necessities such as banking, dry cleaning, key cutting, and DVD and video rental.

The six zones of the mall are each based on a region that explorer Ibn Battuta visited in the 14th century. Guided tours that illuminate the mall's unusual features, such as the full-size replica of a Chinese Junk and Al Jazari's Elephant Clock, are available.

Food courts are located at either end of the mall, and there's a Fun City in Tunisia Court. It is an enjoyable mall to wander around, but its long, linear design means it can be a long way back if there's something you've missed.

DUBAI MARINA MALL

DUBAI MARINA MALL, SHOP & DINE WITH BEAUTIFUL VIEWS IN THE HEART OF THE MARINA

For more information
contact us on 04 436 1020
www.dubaimarinamall.com
dubaimarinamall
dubaimarinamall

SHOPPING
PLACES TO SHOP

Mall of the Emirates
Shk Zayed Rd Al Barsha 1 **04 409 9000**
malloftheemirates.com
Map **1 R6** Metro **Mall of the Emirates**
This lifestyle destination houses an indoor ski slope (Ski Dubai), a huge VOX Cinemas and the Dubai Community Theatre & Arts Centre. There are hundreds of outlets selling everything from forks to high fashion, and further expansion is under way. Label devotees should head to Via Rodeo and the Fashion Dome for designer labels like Burberry, Versace and Louis Vuitton. High-street fashion is covered with two H&M stores, Zara, the largest Dune store in the world, and much more.

The mall is anchored by Carrefour hypermarket, Dubai's largest branch of Debenhams, upmarket Harvey Nichols, and Centrepoint. Entertainment centre Magic Planet includes a bowling alley and a myriad of games and rides. Electronics stores are grouped handily into a corner, as are the homewares shops. A wide range of dining options encompass everything from the Swiss chalet feel of Apres to popular American eatery The Cheesecake Factory, as well as three separate foodcourts.

Mall Parking
Some malls, including Mall of the Emirates and Deira City Centre, charge for parking, but even at these it's free on weekends and public holidays, and for the first four hours on weekdays.

Mercato Shopping Mall
Jumeira Road Jumeira 1 **04 344 4161**
mercatoshoppingmall.com
Map **2 F4** Metro **Financial Centre**
The Renaissance-style architecture really makes this mall stand out and, once inside, the huge glass roof provides a lot of natural light, enhancing its Mediterranean feel.

The mall is anchored by Spinneys which has a dry cleaners, photo lab and music shop; a large Virgin Megastore (that has a decent book department); Laura Ashley Home, and Gap. There are also a few good options for kids such as Early Learning Centre, Toy Store Express and Armani Junior. It's a good stop for high-street brands, from Pull & Bear and Mango to Jack Wills.

There is a foodcourt and a number of cafes and restaurants, including Paul Patisserie, and American burger favourite Shake Shack. VOX Cinemas and a large Fun City play area should keep most of the family occupied. There is also a nail salon, hair salon and mother and baby room on the upper floor, in addition to ATMs, a money exchange and a key cutting and shoe repair shop.

Mirdif City Centre
Tripoli St Mirdif **04 602 3000**
mirdifcitycentre.com
Map **2 P12** Metro **Rashidiya**
This large and spacious mall is Mirdif's very own slice of upmarket retail action. Key anchor outlets include a large Carrefour, Debenhams, Emax and Centrepoint; there are some great home stores here too, including Home Centre, Pottery Barn and Crate & Barrel. High street fashion is comprehensive, with dozens of fashion outlets including Miss Selfridge, Forever 21 and Dorothy Perkins. There's a huge food court plus more upscale eateries such as MORE Cafe, Mango Tree Bistro and Butcher Shop & Grill.

Kids won't mind being dragged shopping here too; the VOX Cinemas houses 10 screens, and the Playnation centre has a number of fantastic attractions including a fun water play area called Aquaplay, footy-based Soccer Circus, a bowling alley, Little Explorers children's activity centre and even an indoor sky diving facility, iFLY Dubai.

Wafi Mall
Shk Rashid Rd Umm Hurair 2 **04 324 4555**
wafi.com
Map **2 L7** Metro **Dubai Healthcare City**
Wafi's Egyptian theme, designer stores and layout make this one of the more interesting malls to wander around, and it rarely feels busy. The distinctive building has three pyramids forming part of the roof and a large stained glass window. Two of the pyramids are decorated with stained glass, depicting Egyptian scenes – best viewed during daylight.

From jewellery to couture, the likes of Versace and Roberto Cavalli mix with well-known high-street shops like Oasis and a large branch of UK stalwart Marks & Spencer. THE One, a popular Dubai furniture store, has a branch here, as does Villeroy & Boch and Tanagra. For something different head to Khan Murjan, the mall's impressive underground souk.

There are a number of cafes and restaurants, including Biella and the highly recommended Khan Murjan Arabic restaurant, where you can enjoy your meal in an alfresco dining area. Children's play area Kids Connection keeps little ones very happy, and events include the Return of the Pharaohs light show and Movies Under the Stars screenings on the rooftop.

Wafi is also home to the exclusive Raffles Dubai hotel, with its Raffles Spa and Fire and Ice restaurant.

Appy Shopper
Several of the malls have developed their own apps, with information on which shops are there, useful navigation tools, and even offers and discounts. Visit the mall websites to find out more.

SHOPPING
PLACES TO SHOP

Mercato Mall

Mall of the Emirates

Mirdif City Centre

Traditional carpets

BUYERS' GUIDE

From antiques to technology, and from tools to toys, the aim of this section is to let you know what's out there and the best places to buy. It's by no means an exhaustive list, but is designed to help you find those items that, while in your home country you just know how to find, in a new city can be harder to figure out.

Hypermarkets such as Carrefour and LuLu are a good place to start, and ACE Hardware and IKEA are also great for the things you didn't even know you needed. We've referred to the main stores in each category, but many have branches all over the city. See askexplorer.com for a complete list of store locations.

Quick Reference

Alcohol	p.353	Garden & Pools	p.364	Pets	p.372
Arts & Crafts	p.353	Hardware & DIY	p.365	Second-Hand	p.374
Books, Music & DVDs	p.354	Jewellery	p.365	Soft Furnishings	p.374
Camera Equipment	p.358	Kids	p.366	Souvenirs	p.375
Car Accessories	p.358	Mother & Baby	p.368	Sports & Outdoor Equipment	p.376
Clothing & Shoes	p.359	Musical Instruments	p.369		
Electrical Goods	p.359	Parties	p.370	Textiles, Tailoring & Repairs	p.379
Furniture & Homewares	p.360	Perfumes & Cosmetics	p.372	Weddings	p.380

352   Dubai Explorer

SHOPPING
BUYERS' GUIDE

Alcohol

If you're over the age of 21 you can buy alcohol in Dubai's restaurants and licensed bars, and some sports clubs, for consumption on the premises. If you wish to drink at home you will need a liquor licence; how much you are permitted to buy is dependent on your monthly salary and Muslims are not allowed to apply.

Two companies operate liquor stores in Dubai: African + Eastern (A+E) and Maritime & Mercantile International (MMI). Both have branches in several locations around the city, the most handy being the ones near supermarkets. The selection is decent, and prices are not so bad: wine costs from around Dhs.35 and upwards; vodka from Dhs.60; whisky from Dhs.80; and beer from Dhs.4 to Dhs.8 per can or Dhs.100 to Dhs.135 per case. Alcohol is, however, subject to 30% tax on the marked price.

There is a good selection of alcohol available at the airport Duty Free. The alcohol available at the airport is similar in price to the shops in town, but you don't pay the tax.

There are also a number of 'hole in the wall' stores close to Dubai (in the northern emirates of Ajman, Ras Al Khaimah and Umm Al Quwain) that sell duty-free alcohol to members of the public, even if you don't have a licence. Prices are reasonable and there is no tax. You won't need to worry about being busted buying booze illegally, but you should be careful when driving home; it is the transporting of alcohol that could get you into trouble, especially if you are stopped within the borders of Sharjah, which is a 'dry' emirate. There have been reports of random police checks on vehicles driving from Ajman into Sharjah. Also, if you have an accident and you're found to have a boot full of liquor, your day could take a sudden turn for the worse.

African + Eastern > p.xiv, 45, 355
Spinneys Centre Al Safa 2 **04 394 2676**
africaneastern.com
Map **2 B5** Metro **Noor Bank**
With convenient locations across Dubai, a wide variety of products and regular promotions, A&E outlets remain a good place to purchase wine, spirits and beer. Its stores sell the typical brands and a few imports of Japanese and German beer.

Al Hamra Cellar
Al Hamra Village Ras Al Khaimah **07 244 7403**
mmidubai.com
Around an hour's drive from Dubai along Sheikh Mohammed bin Zayed Rd, this licence-free store stocks an amazing selection of beers, spirits and award-winning wines at fantastic tax-free prices – including wine specially selected by guru Oz Clarke.

Barracuda Beach Resort
Nr Dreamland Aqua Park, Khor Al Baida
Umm Al Quwain **06 768 1555**
barracuda.ae
A tax-free, licence-free booze emporium that is popular with Dubai's residents. There is a superb selection, including the regular brands of beer, wine and spirits.

Centaurus International
Ras Al Selaab Ras Al Khaimah **05 0654 9920**
centaurusint.info
Another licence-free 'hole in the wall' outlet that offers a good range of products. You can view its range of wine, beer and spirits on its online shop, and it also offers a delivery service.

Le Clos
Nr Gate 214 Dubai International Airport **04 220 3633**
leclos.net
Map **2 P8** Metro **Airport Terminal 3**
This exclusive store in Emirates Terminal 3 offers a premium selection of alcohol that can only be pre-ordered on departure and collected on arrival at the terminal. See the website for more details.

MMI
Trade Centre Rd Al Mankhool **04 352 3091**
mmidubai.com
Map **2 L5** Metro **Al Karama**
Similar to A&E, with a broad selection of international drink brands and some lesser known names. To get the best value for money, look for its special 'bin' with discounts on wine where you can select new or lesser known brands that are on promotion. Don't forget your liquor licence.

Arts & Crafts

A number of shops sell a good range of art and craft supplies, with everything from paints and crayons for children to top-quality oils available. Particularly good places to find materials are Bin Sougat Mall in Rashidiya and the Holiday Centre on Sheikh Zayed Road. For DIY picture framing, Rafi Frame Store, aka Al Warda Gallery, in Karama is the place to find the necessary equipment, including mountboards.

Craft Land
Town Centre Jumeirah Jumeira 1 **04 342 2237**
mycraftland.com
Map **2 F4** Metro **Burj Khalifa/Dubai Mall**
Supplies materials, machines, tools and gadgets for a host of needle crafts, including knitting, sewing, embroidery, quilting and crochet, and also offers classes, clinics and clubs for keen crafters.

askexplorer.com   353

SHOPPING
BUYERS' GUIDE

Creative Minds
Beach Centre Jumeira 1 **04 344 6628**
creativemindsdubai.com
Map **2 G4** Metro **Emirates Towers**
With stores in Al Barsha 1 (on Umm Suqeim Road) and at Beach Centre in Jumeira, Creative Minds is convenient for several areas of the city. Both stores stock a wide range of products, as well as school supplies and even fancy dress.

Emirates Trading Establishment
Villa 27, Nr Mercato Shopping Mall, Street 75B
Jumeira 1 **04 344 1052**
emirates-trading.com
Map **2 F4** Metro **Burj Khalifa/Dubai Mall**
Stocks everything from children's crayons to industrial spray booths and it is a supplier of Windsor & Newton and Daler-Rowney products.

White Star Bookshop (Wasco)
Beach Centre Jumeira 1 **04 342 2179**
Map **2 G4** Metro **Emirates Towers**
Stocks craft supplies that are suitable for children's projects and difficult to find elsewhere. Prices can be expensive for some speciality items, such as mosaic tiles, but art materials are reasonably priced.

ARTE Souk
Artisans of the Emirates (ARTE) occasionally sets up markets selling arts and crafts in Times Square Center and Dubai Festival City Mall. These stalls sell a range of items including photographs, jewellery and a variety of art. For more information on the stalls and market dates, visit arte.ae.

Books, Music & DVDs
You'll find both international bookstores and good local stores in Dubai. All malls feature at least one bookstore, and if you cannot find a publication, the larger stores let you place an order or enquire whether it is available in another branch. Dubai's transitory residents furnish the second-hand bookshops – you'll find a wide range of books, particularly fiction, many of which have only been read once. There are regular charity book sales, the most notable being the ones organised by Medecins Sans Frontieres (msf-me.org). They are held several times throughout the year, usually in the Dune Centre in Satwa. A small selection of books, DVDs and games sell in the supermarkets and hypermarkets.

Unless you have particularly obscure taste, you should find a satisfying collection of music in the city's supermarkets and record stores. Music and DVDs are generally more expensive than they are in other countries, but the advantage of Dubai's multicultural society is that you can open yourself up to new genres – Arabic dance music for example, is very popular. Everything has to go through the censor, so any music or DVDs deemed offensive will not be sold here, unless it can be edited to make it more acceptable. Retailers will order titles that are on the approved list for the UAE. Bollywood films are extremely popular and available in most shops.

Online shopping is an alternative if you can't find an item and you'll find more variety on sites like Amazon (amazon.com and amazon.co.uk), which delivers to the UAE. Delivery rates are cheaper from the UK site than the US site. Your package may be inspected by UAE customs. The UAE iTunes store sells a limited selection of music, TV shows, movies and iBooks, but you can log in to the UK or US sites for the extensive library – you'll need a UK or US registered credit card for these.

You can also buy guide books and photography books by Explorer in most of the bookstores listed below, or order online at askexplorer.com.

Movie Rentals
There are a few places where you can rent DVDs in the city; Spinneys stores often have rental sections where you can sign up. Some supermarkets have a self service DVD dispenser from Moviebank or Davina Box, where you pay to join and you are charged by the day – you simply return the DVD to the dispenser when you are finished. If DVDs are too old school for you, the On Demand services from OSN and du allow subscribers to rent movies and series through their cable or satellite receiver. See TV in Living in Dubai for more info.

Book Munch
Wasl Square Al Safa 1 **04 388 4006**
bookmunchcafe.com
Map **2 D5** Metro **Business Bay**
Dubai's first literary cafe houses a big collection of hand-picked titles that cater to all ages in addition to offering mouthwatering dishes for breakfast, lunch and dinner. You can peruse the titles while you eat, but be mindful of leaving the books in a saleable condition. Also hosts regular events for book lovers.

Book N Bean
ACE Hardware, Dubai Festival City Al Kheeran
04 232 6992
Map **2 M9** Metro **Emirates**
A good range of second-hand books from Dhs.25 – recent titles by best-selling authors, all in good condition. Return once read and you'll receive half your money back to put towards your next book.

AFRICAN + EASTERN STORES ARE ALL OVER TOWN!

With 13 conveniently-located African + Eastern stores all across the city, you will always find one in your neighbourhood.

And where there's African + Eastern, there's always an extensive portfolio of labels across ales, grape, malt and more from all over the world. Visit your nearest neighbourhood store for all the brands you love.

For more information call us on **800 CHEERS** (243377) or ask our staff in-store.

Al Wasl Road* · Arabian Ranches* · Bur Dubai* · Burj Views* · Deira* · Dubai Marina Mall*
Dubai Marina Walk* · Green Community** · Jumeirah* · Karama · Le Méridien Dubai** · Mirdif · TECOM*

Stores also open on Fridays from 2:00pm - 9:00pm
*Stores open Saturday to Thursday from 2:00pm - 9:00pm

www.africaneastern.com

african + eastern
INSPIRING GREAT BLENDS

SHOPPING
BUYERS' GUIDE

Book World
Nr Satwa Flower Shop Al Satwa 04 349 1914
Map 2 H5 Metro World Trade Centre
A literary paradise for all bookworms; browse an assortment of pre-loved titles and new books, as well as a fascinating collection of comics.

Books Kinokuniya
The Dubai Mall Burj Khalifa 04 434 0111
kinokuniya.com
Map 2 F7 Metro Burj Khalifa/Dubai Mall
The biggest bookshop in Dubai, this Japanese chain stocks a variety of international titles and a great selection of comics, as well as stationery, magazines and journals, and a fantastic range of childrens' books.

Booksplus
Dubai Festival City Mall Al Kheeran 04 232 5563
appareluae.com
Map 2 M9 Metro Emirates
A fairly comprehensive range of titles and international magazines are stocked at this small bookstore. This is a perfect place to pick up light reads and popular titles.

Bookworm
Park n Shop Al Safa 1 04 394 5770
Map 2 C5 Metro Noor Bank
A great store for inspiring kids to read with an extensive range of titles for very young kids up to young adults, plus educational books and a fun selection of toys and gifts.

Borders
Mall of the Emirates Al Barsha 1 04 341 5758
almaya.ae
Map 1 R6 Metro Mall of the Emirates
This US chain sells a vast variety of books and a fantastic selection of the latest international magazines. The store stocks a good range of Paperchase stationery items and a small gift range.

Culture & Co
Umm Hurair Rd Oud Metha 04 357 3603
culturecodubai.net
Map 2 L6 Metro Oud Metha
A great option for French speakers and readers, or students of the language, this bookshop in Oud Metha sells a good selection of French novels, guidebooks, magazines and papers.

Duflix Movies
Spinneys Centre Al Safa 2 04 394 0139
duflix.com
Map 2 B5 Metro Noor Bank
Stocks a good range of items, particularly BBC and children's titles, and also has a rental section.

House Of Prose
Dubai Garden Centre Al Qouz Industrial 3
04 344 9021
Map 1 S6 Metro First Gulf Bank
A huge collection of second-hand books; there's a great choice of English fiction for children and adults. Most of the stock is in excellent condition, and you may even find a new release.

Jashanmal Bookstores
Mall of the Emirates Al Barsha 1 04 340 6789
jashanmalbooks.com
Map 1 R6 Metro Mall of the Emirates
A wide-ranging selection, with international books and magazines. Head here during the sales and you can grab some really good bargains.

Magrudy's
Nr Jumeira Centre, Jumeira Rd Jumeira 1
04 344 4193
magrudy.com
Map 2 H4 Metro Emirates Towers
This local chain has a wide selection covering new releases, travel, fiction, children's books and much more. Outlets include a dedicated educational resource centre. There's an annual warehouse sale for discounted books, toys and gifts.

Ohm Records
Nr BurJuman Al Karama 04 397 3728
ohm-records.com
Map 2 L5 Metro Burjuman
Vinyl and electronic mixing fans should head to this speciality shop; you can buy processors and turntables, as well as record bags and accessories. Also stocks a range of mainstream DVDs and a few independent films.

The Old Library
DUCTAC, Mall of the Emirates Al Barsha 1
04 341 4777
theoldlibrary.ae
Map 1 R6 Metro Mall of the Emirates
Nestled within DUCTAC at Mall of the Emirates, this library has a collection of over 19,000 fiction and general reference books. There's also a selection of second-hand books for sale.

Virgin Megastore
Mall of the Emirates Al Barsha 1 04 341 4353
virginmegastore.me
Map 1 R6 Metro Mall of the Emirates
The widest selection of mainstream music is stocked at this store, as well as an excellent range of DVD box sets and an interesting selection of books related to music and popular culture. There's also a selection of quirky gifts and branded T-shirts.

356   Dubai Explorer

FOR LOVE OF THE WRITTEN WORD

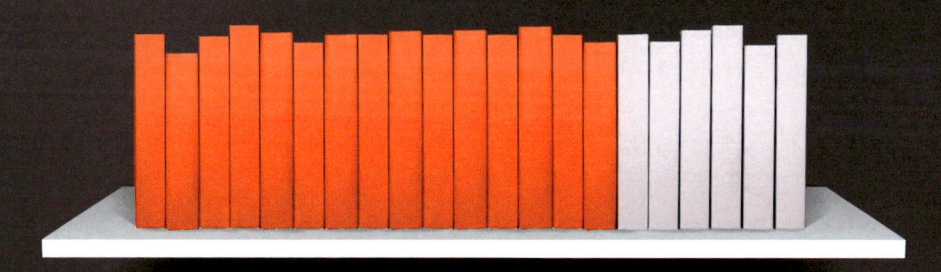

SHARJAH INTERNATIONAL BOOK FAIR

Loading of Knowledge....

#SIBF
sharjahbookfair.com

The **33**th Edition of the
Sharjah International Book Fair
5 - 15 November 2014, Sharjah Expo Centre

الشارقة عاصمة الثقافة الإسلامية
SHARJAH ISLAMIC CULTURE CAPITAL

20 14

@SICC2014   info@sicc.ae   www.sicc.ae

SHOPPING
BUYERS' GUIDE

Camera Equipment

From single-use cameras to darkroom equipment, photographers can usually find most things in Dubai. Prices vary between the larger outlets, where they are fixed, and the electronics shops of Bur Dubai. However, while you might be able to bag a bargain from the independent retailers using your superior powers of negotiation, you will ultimately get more protection buying from the larger outlets. The most important consideration, if you are buying the camera to take abroad, is to ensure your warranty is international; and don't just take the retailer's word for it, ask to read the warranty to make sure.

For second-hand equipment, gulfphotoplus.com (an essential site for all photography enthusiasts) has an equipment noticeboard, as well as being a great source of information.

Grand Stores
The Dubai Mall Burj Khalifa **04 339 8614**
grandstores.com
Map **2 F7** Metro **Burj Khalifa/Dubai Mall**
The main retailer for Nikon, Grand Stores also stocks Fuji, Canon and Mamiya. You can have your camera cleaned and repaired in its outlets, which can be found in several locations across Dubai.

MK Trading
Nr Twin Towers, Baniyas Rd Al Rigga **04 222 5745**
mktradingco.com
Map **2 N5** Metro **Union**
This store is the place to purchase Sigma cameras and lenses, as well as other leading brands; it also stocks a particularly good selection of filters. The store offers a repair facility.

National Store
Khansaheb Bldg, Al Fahidi St Al Souk Al Kabeer
04 353 4168
jksons.ae
Map **2 L4** Metro **Al Ghubaiba**
This store is a distributor of Canon products and you'll find a good selection of cameras, printers and camera accessories from the well-known brand. There are several branches of this store in Dubai.

Salam Studio & Stores
Wafi Umm Hurair 2 **04 704 8484**
salaminternational.com
Map **2 K7** Metro **Dubai Healthcare City**
Stocking a complete range of professional-grade camera and studio equipment, this department store is considered the most comprehensive photography store in the city. It carries Bronica, Leica, Minolta and Pentax, and there's a good selection of filters, tripods and studio equipment.

Car Accessories

Cars and their accessories are big business in Dubai, so you won't struggle to find the accessories you need. ACE Hardware and Carrefour have large departments selling everything from steering wheel covers to fridges that run off the car battery, and there is a wide selection of tools in larger stores and in the smaller shops in Satwa. Further out in Sharjah industrial area you'll find slightly cheaper outlets than in Dubai.

GPS systems are available from Picnico or mainstream shops like Plug-Ins and Sharaf DG. Car stereos are widely available, and are sold by most electronics shops, with some of the car dealerships stocking alternative models for their cars. To have them fitted, head either to the workshops of Rashidiya or Satwa, or AAA and the dealers – it should cost around Dhs.500 if you are providing all the parts.

Many car owners try to beat the heat by having their car windows tinted. The legal limit is 30% tint; if you get your windows tinted any darker you could be fined, and your car won't pass its annual inspection. Be aware though that company-owned cars are not allowed tinted windows. The options range from the Dhs.75 plastic film from the workshops in Satwa, to Dhs.1,300 to Dhs.1,500 at After Dark (covered by a 10-year warranty), and up to Dhs.5,000 at V-KOOL which is also covered by warranty, and its clear film is more heat resistant than the tinted one.

If you are just looking for some memorabilia, or if you simply love fast cars, Ferrari has stores selling memorabilia and accessories. Head to Al Qouz and Rashidiya to customise your car by increasing its performance – West Coast Customs (as featured on the MTV series Pimp My Ride) now has a showroom and workshop in Al Qouz.

AAA Service Center
Nr Honda Trading Enterprises Umm Ramoul
04 285 8989
aaadubai.com
Map **2 N9** Metro **Rashidiya**
Sells specialist sand tracks and heavy duty jacks and winches – if your car is fitted with a GPS system the company can rescue you from the most remote dune or wadi.

Yellow Hat
Times Square Center Al Qouz Industrial 1
04 341 8592
yellowhat.ae
Map **1 T6** Metro **Noor Bank**
A one-stop shop for car accessories, supplying everything from tyres and sound systems to engine tuning. Head here to pick up breakdown kits, steering wheels, air filters or alloy wheels. The store also offers car cleaning and servicing.

SHOPPING
BUYERS' GUIDE

Clothing & Shoes

You'll find no shortage of options when it comes to fashion in Dubai. For high-end brands and designer names, BurJuman is popular, as is Fashion Avenue and Level Shoe District at The Dubai Mall, and the Fashion Dome at Mall of the Emirates. Department stores like Saks Fifth Avenue, Harvey Nichols and Bloomingdale's stock a wide range of cutting-edge couture, and there are several boutiques dotted around Jumeira, such as Ayesha Depala Boutique and Boutique 1. TKD Lingerie at Town Centre Jumeirah stocks larger cup sizes that can be otherwise hard to find. Maktoum Road is lined with stores selling men's designer clothing, and there are also plenty of options inside the Twin Towers Mall in Deira.

For fashion that's less mainstream, head to stores like Kitsch, S*uce and Five Green for their eclectic mix of funky fashion. You can get beautiful hand-crafted fabrics and traditional Indian clothing at Fabindia on Al Mankhool Road, or Melangè in Jumeirah Plaza.

For high-street fashion head to any of the major malls, and many of the smaller ones, where you'll find pretty much all of the most popular international chains, such as Topshop, H&M, Forever 21, New Look, Pull & Bear and Mango.

For cut-price designer labels, Dubai Outlet Mall has all sorts of bargains, from designer to high street. Also check out My Ex Wardrobe (myexwardrobe.com) for pre-loved labels. The streets of Karama are crammed with designer fakes, ranging from cheap knock-offs to good quality copies.

All of the main hypermarkets stock affordable clothing and shoes, and Lamcy Plaza is a real bargain-hunter's mall – Mexx for Less, Peacocks and Factory Fashions are all excellent.

Shopping events such as Dubai Shopping Festival at the beginning of the year and Dubai Summer Surprises bring city-wide sweeping sales across all retail sectors; a great time to bag a discount.

Electrical Goods & Appliances

Whether you are setting up home or moving house, you'll have to spend some time looking for white goods. In Dubai, unfurnished really means unfurnished and you'll have to fork out for even the most standard items, like curtain rails for your windows. Unsurprisingly, there are plenty of places where you can buy goods and most international brands are sold here. Competition is high, so prices are reasonable and most dealers will offer warranties – some will offer a warranty extension for an extra year or two. You'll find a similar range of products in all of the electronics stores.

There are several stores dedicated to electronics and appliances in each of the larger malls and you'll find large sections in the hypermarkets, including Carrefour, Geant and HyperPanda, which stock a superb selection of goods from well-known brands (and some lesser known ones that also do the job) and usually offer a delivery and installation service. Everything from top-of-the-range high-definition televisions to games consoles, fridges and ovens to irons, water coolers and so on. It's worth waiting for the sales as there can be a noticeable drop in prices.

Bang & Olufsen and Bose offer a pricey, but undeniably stylish, range of goods for the home. You'll also find some high-end brands like Gaggenau on Jumeira Road and Miele at Trade Centre roundabout. For stylish kitchen appliances, head to Tavola, Bloomingdale's and Galeries Lafayette.

Many stores offer delivery and installation services, which take the hassle out of mounting a plasma screen or setting up your surround sound system.

Check that the warranty is valid internationally if you wish to take items back to your home country. Also check that the item will work in all areas of the world and whether you will have to pay any import duty if you return back home. Find out who will service the items if there are problems. For second-hand items, check the adverts placed on supermarket noticeboards and online classifieds, like dubizzle.com.

Al Ain Mall in Bur Dubai is dedicated to computer equipment, and several places do repairs and upgrades.

A Greener Future

The Change Initiative (thechangeinitiative.com) is a one-stop eco-store, offering environmentally-friendly and sustainable products. There's a range of household goods, appliances and building solutions that combine technology and good design, from ideas to improve insulation and lessen energy use, to eco-friendly furniture, paints and fashion accessories. Shop online or visit the store in Al Barsha 1, near the Ibis on Sheikh Zayed Rd.

ALSHOP
Burj Khalifa **800 257 467**
alshop.com Map **2 E7** Metro **Business Bay**
This online store is great for Apple products and the latest gadgets at competitive prices. Deliveries are prompt – usually within a few days, if not same day.

Better Life
Mall of the Emirates Al Barsha 1 **04 341 0716**
betterlifeuae.com
Map **1 R6** Metro **Mall of the Emirates**
This reliable store stocks the most popular brands, and its worth bartering for a discount if you're buying lots of items at once – good if you're setting up home.

SHOPPING
BUYERS' GUIDE

Dubai Audio
Nr Safestway, Shk Zayed Rd Al Wasl 04 343 1441
dubaiaudio.com
Map **2 E6** Metro **Business Bay**

A super stylish range of designer electronics from premium brands including Lexicon, Conrad Johnson and Linn. The range includes luxury home cinema and audio equipment and multi-room audio systems.

Jacky's Electronics
The Dubai Mall Burj Khalifa 04 434 0222
jackys.com
Map **2 F7** Metro **Burj Khalifa/Dubai Mall**

A wide range of electronics from well-known brands – particularly Sony products. The store offers home delivery and installation for some of its products as well as warranties and protection plans.

Jumbo Electronics
Al Mankhool 04 352 1323
jumbocorp.com
Map **2 L5** Metro **Al Fahidi**

A vast selection of popular entertainment brands, with good deals and helpful staff. A good place to head to if you are looking for Sony LCD televisions and home theatre systems.

Plug-Ins
Dubai Festival City Mall Al Kheeran 04 206 6777
pluginselectronix.com
Map **2 M9** Metro **Emirates**

A comprehensive range of electronics, including the latest products from Panasonic, Bose, Sony and LG.

Sharaf DG
Times Square Center Al Qouz Ind. 1
04 341 8060
sharafdg.com
Map **1 T6** Metro **Noor Bank**

A great first port of call because of its range of appliances and gadgets, from plasma TVs and laptop computers to mobile phones, washing machines, cookers and irons. Staff are helpful and prices are competitive, so you're sure to find what you're looking for. Also very good for camera equipment.

Furniture & Homewares

This is one of Dubai's most buoyant retail sectors; most tastes are catered for, from everyone's favourite Swedish flatpack store to unique ethnic pieces, to the latest designer concepts and specialist children's furniture stores.

The industrial area between interchanges three and four of Sheikh Zayed Road is home to a number of furniture warehouses, many of which sell pieces crafted from Indonesian teak. Their hot, dusty warehouses are not the most chic of all options, but prices are excellent and after a good polish the furniture looks fabulous. Genuine antiques are available but very rare (and therefore very expensive); including pieces from Oman and Yemen.

Most shopping areas will have at least one furniture store, and you'll be spoilt for choice in the larger malls. Dubai Festival City Mall has the city's only IKEA, as well as several other furniture and home accessories stores.

Jacky's Electronics

SHOPPING
BUYERS' GUIDE

Real investment pieces that you'll want to keep and take back home can be bought at Natuzzi (04 338 0777) in Al Qouz. For exotic designs, try Safita Trading Est (04 339 3230, Al Qouz) which stocks a range of exotic items from India and the Far East. For unusual designer items, head to THE One Fusion in Al Qouz. Another warehouse worth visiting is Dubai Antique Museum – an enormous treasure trove of furniture and quirky pieces, as well as souvenirs and lots more.

Panache Interiors (050 351 7100) offers design services and ready-made home accessories. BAFCO is the place to hit if you're looking for office furniture with added style.

The transient nature of some of Dubai's population results in an active second-hand furniture market. Items are advertised in the classified sections of the local newspapers and on websites like dubizzle.com, but supermarket noticeboards are the best source; this is also the place to find garage sales – you can get some real bargains.

BAFCO > p.209
Al Karama **04 335 0045**
bafco.com
Map **2 L6** Metro **Burjuman**
Originally known at 'the office furniture people', BAFCO are experts at creating stylish and practical workspaces for their customers.

Crate & Barrel
Mall of the Emirates Al Barsha 1 **04 399 0125**
crateandbarrel.com
Map **1 R6** Metro **Mall of the Emirates**
Contemporary, stylish and functional sums up the modern designs of this American home store. From classic to hip and trendy styles, furniture, home decor, gifts, or housewares – there is something for all tastes. Another outlet is located at Mirdif City Centre.

Home Centre > p.xi
Mall of the Emirates Al Barsha 1 **04 341 4441**
homecentrestores.com
Map **1 R6** Metro **Mall of the Emirates**
These large and inspiring stores are filled with a huge assortment of items and ideas. There are large ranges of bath towels, accessories, kitchenware in both traditional and modern styles. There's also plenty of furniture for the whole house.

Homes R Us
Mazaya Centre Al Wasl **04 321 3344**
www.homesrusgroup.com
Map **2 F6** Metro **Burj Khalifa/Dubai Mall**
A complete, one-stop lifestyle destination showcasing a wide range of home furniture, furnishings and accessories at reasonable prices. There are also stores at Ibn Battuta Mall and Arabian Centre, Mirdif.

IKEA
Dubai Festival City Mall Al Kheeran **04 203 7555**
ikea.com
Map **2 M9** Metro **Emirates**
This enormous showroom sells a great range of good value furniture and home accessories, suitable for most budgets; it stocks everything from Dhs.1 tealight holders to Dhs.20,000 kitchens. It's also good for reasonably priced kids' furniture.

THE One
Mall of the Emirates Al Barsha 1 **04 341 3777**
theoneplanet.com
Map **1 R6** Metro **Mall of the Emirates**
A favourite among the expat crowd because of its funky, modern style and good selection of home accessories. Partner store THE One Fusion in Al Qouz Industrial 1 stocks an imaginative range of quirky collectables and cool one-offs.

Pan Emirates
Umm Suqeim Rd Al Barsha 1 **04 383 0800**
panemirates.com
Map **1 R6** Metro **Mall of the Emirates**
A wide range of furniture and accessories, from stylish and modern to the more traditional, to some grander, more gaudy affairs. Also sells a small range of garden furniture. Also located at Ibn Battuta Mall.

Pottery Barn
Mirdif City Centre Mirdif **800 802**
potterybarn.me
Map **2 P12** Metro **Rashidiya**
An American giant that sells a good range of quality household furniture and accessories, and also has an in-store design studio where customers can get advice on their home furnishing needs and ideas. There's also a big branch at The Dubai Mall.

United Furniture > p.xv
Nr Oasis Centre Al Qouz 3 **04 338 9690**
unitedfurnitureco.com
Map **2 B6** Metro **Noor Bank**
A wide-ranging collection of home and office furniture and accessories. There's styles to suit international tastes, from the contemporary to the classic, and at affordable prices. Also features a variety of kids bedroom interiors.

Bloomingdale's The Dubai Mall, Burj Khalifa, 04 350 5333, *bloomingdales.com*
Debenhams Deira City Centre, Port Saeed, 04 294 0011, *debenhams.com*
Harvest Home Trading Jumeirah Centre, Jumeira 1, 04 342 0225
Tavola Spinneys Centre, Al Safa 2, 04 394 8150, *tavola.ae*

SHOPPING
BUYERS' GUIDE

Designer Furniture

BoConcept
Shk Zayed Rd Al Safa 2 **04 388 4522**
boconcept.ae
Map **2 A6** Metro **Noor Bank**
A varied selection of urban and contemporary, Danish designed and manufactured sofas, tables, chairs, beds and accessories all created for the design conscious, but without a price tag to match. The store also offers an interior decoration service.

IDdesign
Mall of the Emirates Al Barsha 1 **04 341 3434**
iddesignuae.com
Map **1 R6** Metro **Mall of the Emirates**
A selection of modern furniture for the home or office, and a decent range of outdoor furniture. The store also offers an interior design service, furniture re-upholstery, and custom-made curtains, pillows and other accessories. Other outlets are located at Mirdif City Centre and Al Khabaisi.

Aati Nr Karama Fish Market, Za'abeel Rd, Al Karama, 04 337 7825, *altayer.com*
Armani/Casa The Dubai Mall, Burj Khalifa, 04 339 8121, *armanicasa.com*
B&B Italia Mall of the Emirates, Al Barsha 1, 04 341 2445, *baituti.com*
B5 The Art Of Living Sidra Tower, Shk Zayed Rd, Al Sufouh 1, 04 447 3973, *b5living.com*
Ethan Allen The Dubai Mall, Burj Khalifa, 04 330 8871, *ethanallen.com*
Filini Nr Times Square Center, Al Qouz Ind. 1, 04 323 3636, *filini.com*
Hastens Dubai Sunset Mall, Jumeira 3, 04 380 9565, *hastensdubai.com*
Irony Home The Dubai Mall, Burj Khalifa, 04 434 0166, *ironyhomelifestyle.com*
Kart Furniture Villa 746, Jumeira Rd, Umm Suqeim 2, 04 348 8169, *kartdesign.net*
Muri Lunghi Italian Furniture Al Reem Residence, Umm Hurair Rd, Al Karama, 04 358 2341, *murilunghi.com*
Natuzzi Nr Bosh Service Centre, Al Qouz 3, 04 338 0777, *int.natuzzi.com*
Objekts Of Design Al Kuthban Bldg, Shk Zayed Rd, Al Qouz Ind. 1, 04 328 4300, *od.ae*
Roche Bobois Nr Sharaf DG Metro Station, Al Barsha 1, 04 399 0393, *roche-bobois.com*
Singways/Maison Decor Mall of the Emirates, Al Barsha 1, 04 340 9116, *singways.com*
Traffic 179 Umm Suqeim Rd, Al Qouz Ind. 4, 04 347 0209, *viatraffic.org*
Zen Interiors Essa Lutfi Bldg, Nr Sharaf DG Metro Station, Shk Zayed Rd, Al Barsha 1, 04 340 5050, *zeninteriors.net*

Wooden Furniture

Falaknaz – The Warehouse > *p.363*
Shk Zayed Rd Al Qouz 3 **04 328 5859**
falaknazthewarehouse.com
Map **2 A6** Metro **Noor Bank**
A big depot in Al Qouz, full to the brim with colonial-style teak home furniture and a good range of outdoor garden items. You can also have furniture custom-made by its factory in Indonesia.

Lucky's Furnitures & Handicrafts
2nd Street Sharjah **06 534 1937**
luckyfurnitureuae.com
This store in Sharjah is popular with expats seeking well-priced furniture. The range is vast, but the staff will happily explain the origin and design of the pieces, and can paint, varnish or make alterations.

Marina Exotic Home Interiors
Mall of the Emirates Al Barsha 1 **04 340 1112**
marinagulf.com
Map **1 R6** Metro **Mall of the Emirates**
Items here will add an exotic touch to your home and are generally more individual than you'll find at the usual furniture stores. You can pick up large wardrobes, tables, ornate chests and garden furniture. Other locations include Souk Al Bahar and The Walk at JBR.

Pinky Furniture
Nr Dubai American Academy Al Barsha 1
04 422 1720
pinkyfurnitureuae.com
Map **1 R7** Metro **Mall of the Emirates**
Much like Lucky's, Pinky has long been an expat favourite for traditional, hand-made Indian furniture. The new Barsha showroom saves customers the trip into Sharjah.

Kids

Kidz Inc
Nr ACE Hardware, Al Qouz Ind. 1 **04 328 5775**
kidzincdubai.com
Map **1 U6** Metro **Noor Bank**
This shop is the sole agent for Haba – its German, hand-made, wooden furniture doesn't come cheap but all pieces meet European and American safety standards and come with a warranty. Especially good is the range of themed beds (think pirate ships and flowery glades), with matching furniture and unique and inspirational accessories.

Bellini The Dubai Mall, Burj Khalifa, 04 325 3222
Indigo Living Oasis Centre, Al Qouz 1, 04 339 7705, *indigo-living.com*

THE WAREHOUSE

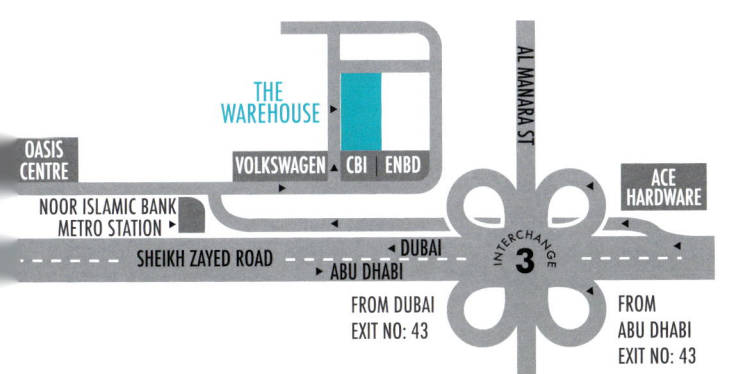

Falaknaz - The Warehouse (L.L.C.)

SHEIKH ZAYED RD.
SHOWROOM
04 328 5859

INDOOR & OUTDOOR FURNITURE | UMBRELLAS | LIGHTING | ACCESSORIES | SURPRISING ARTIFACTS |

www.falaknazthewarehouse.com

SHOPPING
BUYERS' GUIDE

Just Kidding Gold & Diamond Park,
Al Qouz Ind. 3, 04 341 3922, *justkidding-uae.com*
Laura Ashley The Dubai Mall, Burj Khalifa,
04 325 3245, *lauraashley.ae*
THE One Junior THE One Fusion, Al Qouz Ind. 1,
04 346 8977, *theone.com*
Pottery Barn Kids The Dubai Mall, Burj Khalifa,
04 325 3720, *potterybarnkids.me*

Art

Several galleries in Dubai sell traditional and contemporary art by Arabic and international artists, and there's an annual art fair called Art Dubai. You can also find information on art auctions, art fairs and gallery openings at artinthecity.com.

Souk Madinat Jumeirah has a large concentration of boutiques selling art, glass and photographs, both originals and reproductions. The style and subjects are diverse, from traditional to modern, Arabic to international. And Dubai's up-and-coming art district in Al Qouz is home to a variety of galleries.

Many galleries and showrooms have a framing service. There are some excellent framing shops on Plant Street in Satwa and in Karama – they can frame anything from prints to sports jerseys. You can also create your own art by transferring your photos onto canvas. There are a few stores that offer the service including Riot Studio (04 445 8488, riotstudio.com), as well as Portfolio (portfolio-uae.com) in Festival Centre and Mercato Shopping Mall.

MacKenzie Art

For an artistic touch, MacKenzie Art can hand paint gold, antique or modern flowers or cartoon characters onto your furniture. Commissioned canvases, murals and sculptures can also be created with your specific colour scheme in mind. Visit mackenzieart.com or call 04 341 9803 for further information.

Dubai Art
London **44 0208740 8708**
dubaiart.org
Specialises in commissions and bespoke art, from personal portraits to commercial paintings.

E-Walls Studio
API Business Suites, 403 Al Barsha 1 **04 399 4748**
ewalls-s.com
Map **1 P6** Metro **Dubai Internet City**
This local company designs fabulous wall stickers for the home and office. Check out beautiful and playful designs for the living room, bedroom, kitchen, bathroom and kids' room, or have your own customised. There are even designs for parties and celebrations. Delivery is available throughout the UAE.

Gallery One
Souk Madinat Jumeirah Al Sufouh 2 **04 368 6055**
g-1.com
Map **1 R5** Metro **Mall of the Emirates**
A selection of stylish photographs and canvas prints. Particularly good if you want images of the region.

The Majlis Gallery
Al Fahidi Historical Neighbourhood
Al Souk Al Kabeer **04 353 6233**
themajlisgallery.com
Map **2 M4** Metro **Al Fahidi**
A great venue for fine art, hand-made glass, pottery and other unusual pieces.

Boutique 1 Gallery The Walk at JBR, Marsa Dubai, 04 425 7888, *boutique1.com*
XVA Gallery Al Fahidi Historical Neighbourhood, Al Souk Al Kabeer, 04 353 5383, *xvagallery.com*

Outdoor

ACE Hardware >*p.343* Nr Times Square Center, Shk Zayed Rd, Al Qouz Ind. 1, 04 341 1906, *aceuae.com*
Ambar Garden Furniture Umm Suqeim Rd, Al Qouz Ind. 3, 04 323 2405, *ambargardenfurniture.com*
B&B Italia Mall of the Emirates, Al Barsha 1, 04 341 2445, *baituti.com*
Desert River Nr Times Square Center, Al Qouz Ind.1, 04 323 3636, *dcscrtriver.com*
Finasi Al Ittihad Rd, Al Khabaisi, 04 297 1777, *finasi.ae*
Haif Hospitality Furnishings Al Nasr Plaza, Oud Metha, 04 357 3221, *hhfuae.ae*
Nakkash Gallery Nr Indian Palace Restaurant, Shk Rashid Rd, Al Garhoud, 04 282 6767, *nakkashgallery.com*
Parasol Garden Furniture Umm Suqeim Rd, Al Qouz Ind. 4, 04 347 9003, *parasoldubai.com*
Rainbow Play Systems Dubai Investment Park 1, 050 450 7610, *rainbowplayuae.com*
Royal Gardenscape Nr ENOC Petrol Station, Al Qouz Ind.4, 04 340 0648, *royalgardenscape.com*
Soubra Tents & Awnings Nr Leader Sports, Al Khabaisi, 04 266 5347, *soubra-uae.ae*
Sultan Garden Center Nr Dubai Zoo, Jumeira 1, 04 344 5544, *sultangardencenter.com*

Gardens & Pools

Hardware retailers such as ACE Hardware stock a good range of outdoor furniture and gardening accessories, as do the major hypermarkets such as LuLu and Carrefour. IKEA has a good plants section and sells candles, watering cans and other useful items, and there are plenty of companies to call on for swimming pool installation and maintenance. Head to Plant Street in Satwa for all kinds of foliage and plant pots.

SHOPPING
BUYERS' GUIDE

Dubai Garden Centre
Nr Commercial Bank of Dubai Al Qouz Ind.3
04 340 0006
desertgroup.ae
Map **1 S6** Metro **First Gulf Bank**
A good bet for all your gardening needs, and also sells garden furniture.

Sultan Garden Center Nr Dubai Zoo, Jumeira 1, 04 344 5544, *sultangardencenter.com*

Hardware & DIY

With a number of companies offering handyman services, it may be easier and cheaper to find a 'man who can' rather than invest in the tools and materials you need for DIY jobs. If you'd rather do it yourself, there's a range of places to go, and the larger hypermarkets, such as Carrefour, often have a DIY section. There are numerous independent shops selling a broad range of items in Satwa, and Dragon Mart has a section for builder's merchants where you can find tiles, power tools and other hardware items.

ACE Hardware *> p.343*
Dubai Festival City Mall Al Kheeran **800 27 5223**
aceuae.com
Map **2 M9** Metro **Emirates**
DIY enthusiasts will find all the tools they need to get the job done. There's another large branch off Sheikh Zayed Rd, close to Times Square Center. Customised paints, glazes, electronic tools and hardware materials can also be found here, as well as some garden furniture and other household items.

Speedex
Nr Oasis Centre Al Qouz 1 **04 339 1929**
speedextools.com
Map **2 C6** Metro **Noor Bank**
Stocks comprehensive ranges of tools for everything from gardening to carpentry, along with all the nails, nuts, bolts and screws you may need.

Jewellery

Dubai is the world's leading re-exporter of gold and you'll find at least one jewellery shop in even the smallest malls, and large dedicated areas in the bigger malls. Gold is sold according to the international daily gold rate, so wherever you buy it there will be very little difference in the price of the actual metal. Where the price varies is in the workmanship that has gone into a particular piece.

While gold jewellery may be the most prevalent, silver, platinum, precious stones, gems and pearls are all sold, either separately or crafted into jewellery. Most outlets can make up a piece for you, working from a diagram or photograph. Just ensure that you are not obliged to buy it if it doesn't turn out quite how you had imagined. A pendant with your name spelled out in Arabic, or some jewellery crafted with black pearls, are traditional gifts. The Gold Souk in Deira is the best place to start in terms of choice, but some of the air-conditioned alternatives may be preferable in the summer, including the Gold & Diamond Park.

Many of the world's finest jewellers are represented in Saks Fifth Avenue's jewellery department, such as Cartier, Tiffany & Co, Graff and De Beers. For watches, whether it's a Rolex, Tag Heuer, Swatch or Timex, you'll find most models here. Costume jewellery and watches can be found in most department stores; there's a beautiful Swarovski range at Tanagra (04 324 2340), in Wafi. Several fashion stores also stock a small range of jewellery, and branches of Accessorize and Claire's Accessories can be found in many of the malls.

Al Fardan Jewels & Precious Stones Deira City Centre, Port Saeed, 04 295 3780, *alfardangroup.com*
Al Futtaim Jewellery Deira City Centre, Port Saeed, 04 295 2906, *watches.ae*
Damas The Dubai Mall, Burj Khalifa, 04 339 8846, *damasjewellery.com*
Golden Ring Jewellery Deira City Centre, Port Saeed, 04 295 0373
Liali Jewellery Mercato Shopping Mall , Jumeira 1, 04 344 5055, *lialijewellery.com*
Mansoor Jewellers Mall of the Emirates, Al Barsha 1, 04 341 1661

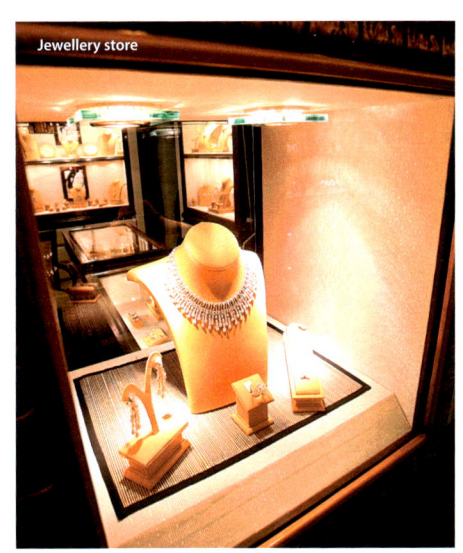

Jewellery store

SHOPPING
BUYERS' GUIDE

Paris Gallery Deira City Centre, Port Saeed,
04 295 5550, *parisgallery.com*
Prima Gold BurJuman, Al Mankhool, 04 355 1988,
primagold.co.th
Pure Gold Mercato Shopping Mall, Jumeira 1,
04 349 2400, *pugold.com*
Raymond Weil Deira City Centre, Port Saeed,
04 295 2906, *raymond-weil.com*
Saks Fifth Avenue BurJuman, Al Mankhool,
04 501 2700, *saksincorporated.com*
Tanagra Wafi, Umm Hurair 2, 04 324 2340,
chalhoub-group.com
Vhernier Jumeirah Emirates Towers, Trade Center 2,
04 354 4017, *vhernier.com*

All That Glitters

The Gold & Diamond Park (at junction four on Sheikh Zayed Road) has branches of many of the same shops as the Gold Souk in Deira, but in a calmer, air-conditioned atmosphere. You can still barter, and there is the added bonus of cafes to wait in while the jeweller makes any alterations. This is also a good spot to head for if you are looking for engagement or wedding rings and, like at the outlets in the souk, you are able to commission pieces. (goldanddiamondpark.com)

Kids

When it comes to clothing, there is plenty of choice, from high-end designer fashion to factory seconds from Sana. Many of the department stores have children's departments and, for real indulgence, The Dubai Mall has a section dedicated to premium brands such as Armani Junior.

School Supplies

Most schools will suggest a preferred supplier for its school uniforms, and Dar Al Tasmim Uniforms, Magrudy's and Zaks produce uniforms for many in Dubai. You can also buy generic uniforms from Marks & Spencer. Most hypermarkets stock a plethora of branded school bags and stationery items, especially in the 'back to school' promotions of summer, while Creative Minds stocks harder to find stationery and art materials that can come in useful for homework.

Creative Minds The Beach Centre, Jumeira 1,
04 344 6628, *creativemindsdubai.com*
Dar Al Tasmim Uniforms 04 285 9624, *ouruniform.com*
Magrudy's Nr Jumeira Centre, Jumeira 1,
04 344 4193, *magrudy.com*
Marks & Spencer The Dubai Mall, Burj Khalifa,
04 339 8890, *marksandspencerme.com*
Zaks Jumeira 1, 04 342 9828, *zaksstore.com*

Toys

As well as the major toy stores and kids' clothes shops, you'll find a wide range in the larger hypermarkets and supermarkets, including Park n Shop, as well as bookshops and places like Virgin Megastore.

IKEA and Kidz Inc in Al Qouz carry good quality toys that are built to last, whereas the little shops around Karama and Satwa are excellent for cheap toys that probably won't. Remember that not all toys conform to international safety standards and therefore should only be used under supervision.

Early Learning Centre
Wafi Umm Hurair 2 **04 324 2730**
elc.com
Map **2 K7** Metro **Dubai Healthcare City**
Stocks a good range of educational products and toys that stimulate play and imagination, and has a good reputation for the quality of its products, especially wooden toys. You'll also find inflatable pools, swimming jackets and arm bands. Plenty of locations include a large branch at Deira City Centre.

Hamleys
The Dubai Mall Burj Khalifa **04 339 8889**
hamleys.com
Map **2 F7** Metro **Burj Khalifa/Dubai Mall**
Hold on to your kids, this British store is well known for offering the best, and the biggest, variety of toys. There's a plethora of toys and games for pre-schoolers through to early teens.

The Toy Store
Mall of the Emirates Al Barsha 1 **04 341 2473**
mytoystore.com
Map **1 R6** Metro **Mall of the Emirates**
Recognisable by the large toy animals peering out of its store front, it's a great place to amaze kids. The Mall of the Emirates branch is large and filled with a broad variety of toys.

Toys R Us
Dubai Festival City Mall Al Kheeran **04 206 6568**
toysrusuae.com
Map **2 M9** Metro **Emirates**
This well-known emporium is guaranteed to get your little ones excited. The range is comprehensive so whatever you are looking for, from small toys and games to bikes, you're likely to find it.

Can't Find What You Need?

If you've scoured the city for a particular item and still not found it, log on to askexplorer.com and ask advice from your fellow expats. If we've missed your favourite store, log on and let us know why you love it.

Your Retail Therapy

Gold & Diamond Park
is the best destination for bargaining and buying jewellery. This specialty mall is a must on every tourist's list, with a wide selection of jewellery stores and manufacturing jewellers in a clean & air-conditioned environment.

EMAAR

مجمع الذهب والألماس
GOLD & DIAMOND PARK

www.goldanddiamondpark.com
Located on Sheikh Zayed Road - easy to get to by taxi or metro.
Sun to Thur: 10am–10pm   Fri: 4pm–10pm Tel: 04 347 7788 / 04 347 7574

SHOPPING
BUYERS' GUIDE

ZaZeeZou
Jumeirah Centre Jumeira 1 **04 344 0204**
harvesthomegroup.com/zaazeezou/
Map **2 H4** Metro **Emirates Towers**
A treasure trove of unique toys, nursery products and children's clothes from a range of independent brands, including Emma Bridgewater's children's crockery and wooden toys by French brand Moulin Roty.

Mother & Baby

Big business in Dubai, there are a multitude of shops selling baby paraphernalia, and many brands you'll know from your home country. You shouldn't have trouble finding nursery essentials like bottles, buggies, changing bags, clothes, cots, prams, rocking chairs and travel cots, and there are plenty of shops selling maternity ranges.

Supermarkets stock formula, nappies and wipes and many sell a good range of bottles and feeding equipment. Choithrams has the best selection of formulas, stocking popular UK brands SMA and Cow & Gate. Pharmacies sell baby essentials and some have breast pumps.

Safety 1st and Maxi Cosi car seats are widely available and should fit most cars; you can also rent car seats, buggies, strollers and other equipment from Rentacrib (rentacrib.ae) – if you hire a car seat its staff will fit it for you free of charge.

For clothing, The Dubai Mall has a very good selection of well-known stores that are grouped in one area on the top floor, and a range of high-end brands like Cacharel Paris and Burberry. Pablosky, Okaidi and Pumpkin Patch sell colourful and practical clothes.

Second-hand Stuff
Second-hand baby items are widely available in Dubai – you just need to know where to look. There are classifieds listings on dubizzle.com and expatwoman.com, and then of course there's always the supermarket noticeboards.

IKEA has a small range of nursery furniture such as cots, changing tables and bathtub, plus a selection of cot sheets and blankets and some baby-safe toys.

Many retailers have jumped on the maternity fashion bandwagon and now offer fashionable outfits for mums-to-be, including many high street stores, the main department stores and the popular baby shops. And you can shop online at blushandbloom.com and luxelittle.com for fashionable maternity lingerie, nightwear, dresses and 'mama and baby' twinsets. TKD Lingerie offers a pretty maternity range.

Storage bags for breast milk are widely available in Dubai (Playtex, Medela and Avent brands). Boppy breastfeeding pillows are available in Toys R Us, and Arabian Home Health Care (arabianhomecare.com), opposite Rashid Hospital, also stocks pillows for breastfeeding – ask for them when you go in.

Other essential accessories for pregnancy include a 'Bump Belt', a device that redirects your car seatbelt under your bump for protection, and which can be found in Mothercare and some Spinneys stores.

Babies R Us
Toys R Us Port Saeed **04 236 4166**
toysrusuae.com
Map **2 N7** Metro **Deira City Centre**
Usually found inside Toys R Us, stocks a wide range of products, from pushchairs to baby bottles, cots to travel accessories. The quality of the items is good and most conform to international safety standards.

Babyshop
Mall of the Emirates Al Barsha 1 **04 341 0604**
babyshopstores.com
Map **1 R6** Metro **Mall of the Emirates**
Sells low-cost baby clothing and essentials such as feeding items, clothing, toys and baby monitors. Its affordable newborn items come in value packs, and it's worth waiting for Babyshop's sales, held several times a year.

Blossom Mother & Child
The Dubai Mall Burj Khalifa **04 434 0103**
blossommotherandchild.com
Map **2 F7** Metro **Burj Khalifa/Dubai Mall**
A premium range of maternity items is sold at this store, all from well-known designers. The store also has a denim bar which features popular brands like J Brand Jeans and 7 For All Mankind, customised with the Blossom Band.

DbBabies
Town Centre Jumeirah Jumeira 1 **050 600 3199**
dubaibabies.com
Map **2 F4** Metro **Burj Khalifa/Dubai Mall**
This online boutique stocks a fabulous range of products including feeding essentials, slings and skincare products. There's also a good selection of gifts for baby showers and new parents. Offers free delivery within Dubai.

Goodbaby
Nr Abu Hail Centre Hor Al Lanz
04 397 5653
goodbabydubai.com
Map **2 Q6** Metro **Abu Hail**
A great store for key items like car seats and changing mats, and with a large selection of buggies from Maclaren, Quinny and Phil & Teds. The store also stocks stairguards, cots and engaging toys.

SHOPPING
BUYERS' GUIDE

Jenny Rose
Mall of the Emirates Al Barsha 1 **04 341 0577**
jennyrose.net
Map **1 R6** Metro **Mall of the Emirates**
Fashionable mums should head to this store for classy clothes for the day or night. Its collection is particularly suitable for Dubai's warm climate and you'll find a good assortment of dresses, sleeveless tops and comfortable trousers. It is a good place to find speciality items such as swimwear, lingerie and evening wear.

Just Kidding
Gold & Diamond Park Al Qouz Industrial 3
04 341 3922
justkidding-uae.com
Map **1 S6** Metro **First Gulf Bank**
Not for the budget conscious, with baby items, furniture and clothes from Europe, including Bugaboo buggies and Stokke high chairs. Also stocks interesting toys and a catalogue of maternity wear, gift sets and slings.

Mamas & Papas
Mercato Shopping Mall Jumeira 1 **04 344 0981**
mamasandpapas.com
Map **2 F4** Metro **Financial Centre**
A household name for well-designed, stylish products for babies and mums-to-be. The store stocks all you need from toys, car seats, pushchairs, cribs, nursery items and decorations to maternity clothes and feeding items.

Mothercare
The Dubai Mall Burj Khalifa **04 339 9812**
mothercare.com
Map **2 F7** Metro **Burj Khalifa/Dubai Mall**
A reliable place to shop for baby essentials, with a particularly good selection of clothes. Many of its larger stores stock breast pumps, cots, prams and car seats, and you can order items you've seen online or in a UK catalogue.

Mumzworld
04 449 3150
mumzworld.com
Has a huge range of products and is great for all those baby essentials, from walkers and playpens to clothing and skincare.

Organic Foods & Cafe > p.339
The Village Jumeira 1 **04 338 2911**
organicfoodsandcafe.com
Map **2 G4** Metro **Emirates Towers**
Sells a wide selection of natural and eco-friendly baby items, including biodegradable and terry cloth nappies, wooden toys, organic baby food and children's mattresses made from organic fibres.

Pregmamma
J3 Mall Al Manara **04 388 3993**
pregmamma.com
Map **1 U5** Metro **Noor Bank**
A complete maternity range for mums-to-be, all with a comfortable and fashionable touch. Shop in-store or order online.

Musical Instruments

There are some great specialist shops selling good quality musical instruments, as well as sheet music – and some offer lessons. Prices for pianos are considerably lower than elsewhere in the world. Sharaf DG, Carrefour, Geant and other large supermarkets stock basic keyboards and guitars, which are fine for beginners, as do some toy shops such as Toys R Us. Virgin Megastore also stocks a range of instruments.

Juli Music Center
Nr Mazaya Centre Trade Center 1 **04 321 2588**
Map **2 F6** Metro **Burj Khalifa/Dubai Mall**
This store on Sheikh Zayed Rd stocks a good range of instruments and can also arrange lessons for various instruments. Particularly useful is its 'hire before you buy' policy.

The Music Chamber
Times Square Center Al Qouz Ind. 1
04 346 8056
musicchamber.net
Map **1 T6** Metro **Noor Bank**
Sells instruments such as guitars, pianos and ouds, as well as sheet music, strings, tuners and many other accessories. Brands stocked include Godin, Seagull, Ritmuller, D'Addario, Jinbao and Oud Sekar.

The Music Institute
The Walk at JBR Marsa Dubai **04 424 3818**
tmi.ae
Map **1 K4** Metro **Dubai Marina**
A small range of items are stocked here such as digital pianos, guitars, violins and guitar accessories, but the range is primarily to support its students.

The Music Room
Majestic Hotel Tower Dubai Al Mankhool
04 501 2529
Map **2 L5** Metro **Al Fahidi**
Run by an experienced music teacher, this shop has the widest range of sheet music in Dubai. It stocks a range of instruments including clarinets, flutes, violins, trumpets and guitars, and their associated accessories. It is an agent for Steinway & Sons pianos, and also stocks Kawai grand, upright and digital pianos.

SHOPPING
BUYERS' GUIDE

Sadek Music
Souk Madinat Jumeirah Al Sufouh 2 **04 368 6570**
sadek-music.com
Map **1 R5** Metro **Mall of the Emirates**
Stocks an assortment of eastern and western instruments, including a good selection of guitars. The store offers a repair service and music lessons, and you can also rent a selection of its instruments.

Thomsun Music
Dubai Festival City Mall Al Kheeran **04 232 9900**
thomsunpuremusic.com
Map **2 M9** Metro **Emirates**
A wide range of mainly Yamaha instruments, from pianos to drum kits and guitars, and also sells mixing decks and equipment for digital music-making.

Thomsun Pure Music
Ibn Battuta Mall Jabal Ali 1 **04 366 9385**
thomsun.com
Map **1 G5** Metro **Ibn Battuta**
One of the largest distributors in the Middle East for Yamaha musical instruments, Thomsun offers a huge selection of grand pianos, keyboards, guitars, violins, percussion and wind instruments, plus accessories and home audio systems.

Turning Pointe Music
Bldg V23, Russia Cluster Warsan 1 **04 422 1592**
turningpointe.ae
Metro **Rashidiya**
Sells everything ranging from guitars and string instruments, through to keyboards and brass instruments, in addition to stands, cases, strings, picks and oils. Also leases instruments to students.

Zak Electronic & Musical Instruments
BurJuman Al Mankhool **04 336 8857**
zakelectronics.com
Map **2 L5** Metro **Burjuman**
This store carries grand pianos, keyboards, amplifiers and guitar accessories. You'll also find a good range of brands including Roland, Kawai and Fender.

Parties

Accessories
Party accessories are available in most supermarkets and toy shops but there are several specialist stores that stock everything for children's or adults' parties. Carrefour, Park n Shop and Toys R Us all sell themed party essentials, such as paper cups, gift bags, balloons and plates, and for certain occasions like Halloween and Easter, really get into the spirit of things, selling a range of costumes and accessories.

Fabric is inexpensive and it doesn't cost much to hire the services of a tailor, so you can easily have a costume made. See Textiles, Tailoring and Repairs for more information on where to go for this.

Balloon Lady
Jumeira Plaza Jumeira 1 **04 344 1062**
balloonladyme.com
Map **2 H4** Metro **Emirates Towers**
This store is the place to buy balloons and seasonal items; you can also hire bouncy castles and purchase costumes for special events. The store offers a balloon decoration service and can also customise balloons.

Mr Ben's Costume Closet
Al Ghazal Complex & Shopping Mall Al Bada' **04 346 3494**
mrbenscostumecloset.com
Map **2 J4** Metro **World Trade Centre**
The ultimate store for fancy dress outfits and accessories – available for adults and children to buy or rent. From character outfits to historical garbs, wigs to masks, there is an overwhelming choice of costumes to suit each and every occasion.

Party Centre > p.371
Nr Welcare Hospital Al Garhoud **04 283 1353**
mypartycentre.com
Map **2 N7** Metro **GGICO**
This enormous store stocks pretty much everything you will need, no matter what the occasion. This is a one-stop shop for decorations and party accessories, and it even sells children's fancy dress outfits. There's a second store at TECOM (04 453 3373).

Party Zone
The Dubai Mall Burj Khalifa **04 325 3443**
partyzone.ae
Map **2 F6** Metro **Burj Khalifa/Dubai Mall**
A good place for getting party supplies such as fancy dress outfits and themed table decorations.

Tickles & Giggles
The Walk at JBR Marsa Dubai **04 432 8681**
ticklesandgiggles.com
Map **1 K4** Metro **Jumeirah Lakes Towers**
A party zone for kids that also has a well-stocked party accessories store.

Celebration Cakes
Baskin Robbins Deira City Centre, Port Saeed, 04 295 1326, baskinrobbinsmea.com
Boulevard Gourmet Radisson Blu Hotel Dubai Deira Creek, Al Rigga, 04 222 7171, radissonblu.com/hotel-dubaideiracreek
Caesars Al Kuwait Rd, Al Raffa, 04 3259400, caesarsgroup.net

PARTY CENTRE
THE PARTY SUPERSTORE

LET'S GET THE PARTY STARTED!
PARTY CENTRE HAS THE LARGEST SECTION OF LICENSED CARTOON CHARACTERS, PARTY SUPPLIES, HOLIDAY PARTY MERCHANDISE, AND BALLOONS IN THE REGION. IT IS THE ONE STOP SHOP FOR YOUR PARTY.

GARHOUD 04 2831353   TECOM 04 4533373   AL RAHA 02 5565563   AL WAHDA 02 4459595

MYPARTYCENTRE.COM>>   f /My.Party.Centre   /Partycentre   /Partycentre   /MyPartyCentre

SHOPPING
BUYERS' GUIDE

Coco's Restaurant Deira City Centre, Port Saeed, 04 295 3777
French Bakery Interchange 1, Sheikh Zayed Rd, Al Satwa, 04 343 6444, *frenchbakery.ae*
Hey Sugar The Village, Jumeira 1, 04 344 8204
The House Of Cakes Block D-04, China Cluster Warsan 1, 04 420 6973, *houseofcakesdubai.com*
Park n Shop Al Safa Centre, Nr Jumeirah College, Al Safa 1, 04 338 8600

Perfumes & Cosmetics

This is big business here, from local scents like frankincense and oud, to the latest designer offerings. Local scents tend to be strong and spicy – you can often locate the stores by the smell of the incense they burn in their doorways.

Department stores such as Harvey Nichols, Saks Fifth Avenue, Bloomingdale's and Debenhams, as well as local chains such as Areej and Paris Gallery stock the most comprehensive ranges of international brand perfumes and cosmetics. Larger supermarkets and pharmacies stock skincare products and some makeup. Anti-allergenic ranges are available at some of the larger pharmacies. Most needs are covered but if yours aren't, specialist retailers often have online shopping facilities or you may find products available at your local beauty clinic. Glambox.me has an online cosmetics store, and also runs a service where, for a certain amount each month, they deliver a box of samples for you to try.

Prices for perfumes and cosmetics are similar to those in some other countries, although certain nationalities might find perfume is cheaper here than in their home country. There are no sales taxes, so there is rarely a difference between duty free and shopping mall prices.

Amouage
Deira City Centre Port Saeed 04 295 5550
amouage.com
Map **2 N7** Metro **Deira City Centre**
'The world's most valuable perfume,' Amouage is made in Oman. The luxurious brand has a standalone store at The Dubai Mall and is sold in Paris Gallery stores, as well as Dubai and Abu Dhabi Duty Free.

Bath & Body Works > *p.373*
Mirdif City Centre Mirdif 04 231 6751
facebook.com/bathandbodyworks
Map **2 P12** Metro **Rashidiya**
A one-stop shop for all things scented, this US-based store is present in several malls, including Mall of the Emirates and The Dubai Mall. All kinds of bath and beauty products are available here, including a men's range, and you can 'spray before you pay'.

Faces
BurJuman Al Mankhool 04 352 1441
faces-me.com
Map **2 L5** Metro **Burjuman**
All manner of lotions and potions are sold in this store. Get all of your monthly makeup, perfume and skincare buys here, from brands like Clarins, Lancome, Givenchy and Clinique. Main store locations include Mall of the Emirates and The Dubai Mall.

Paris Gallery
Ibn Battuta Mall Jabal Ali 1 04 368 5500
parisgallery.com
Map **1 G5** Metro **Ibn Battuta**
Although it stocks a wide selection of perfumes and cosmetics (and a good range of shoes, eyewear and jewellery), its stores never feel too busy, which allows plenty of freedom to browse. Outlets are located all over the city.

Boots Mall of the Emirates, Al Barsha 1, 04 340 6880, *me.boots.com*
L'Occitane The Dubai Mall, Burj Khalifa, 04 339 8148, *Loccitane-me.com*
Lush Mercato, Jumeira 1, 04 344 9334, *lush.com*
M.A.C Mall of the Emirates, Al Barsha 1, 04 409 8931, *maccosmetics.com*
Sephora Dubai Festival City Mall, Al Kheeran, 04 232 6023, *sephora.com*

Pets

Most supermarkets carry basic ranges of cat, dog, bird and fish food, although the choice is limited. If your pet has specific dietary requirements, many of the veterinary clinics carry specialist foods. There are pet shops dotted around the city which can supply most items you need for your pet, with Pet Land being well known for aquariums and Tetra products for fish keeping. While there are good pet shops, some can be a little depressing with animals kept in conditions that may make you feel uncomfortable. The pet shops along Plant Street in Satwa are notoriously the worst offenders and animals purchased there are often malnourished and diseased. On principal, it might be better to spend your money elsewhere. Below is a list of the better pet shops.

Pampered Pets
Dreams Tower 2, Nr Emaar Yacht Club Marsa Dubai 04 447 5330
pamperedpets.ae
Map **1 K5** Metro **Jumeirah Lakes Towers**
A range of couture pet beds and exclusive accessories and fashion for a pooch with a taste for the finer things in life.

Unlock the magic of midnight...forever

NEW! forever MIDNIGHT™

Exclusively at
Bath & Body Works

Store Locations
Dubai: Mall of the Emirates • The Dubai Mall • Mirdif City Centre • Deira City Centre • Ibn Battuta Mall
Abu Dhabi: Marina Mall • Bawabat Al Sharq Mall • Al Wahda Mall • Dalma Mall • World Trade Center Mall
Al Ain: Al Ain Mall • Bawadi Mall
Sharjah: Sahara Centre • Sharjah City Centre
Fujairah: Fujairah City Centre

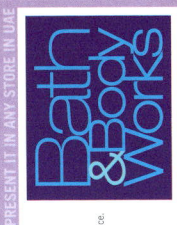

Customer Care: **800-74292 (SHAYA)**

FREE BODY LOTION WITH ANY PURCHASE!

TEAR OFF THIS STRIP AND PRESENT IT IN ANY STORE IN UAE

Bath & Body Works

Terms & Conditions:
- Offer valid until December 31, 2014.
1. Offer applies to any 8oz Body Lotion available in the store.
2. This voucher must be presented to the cashier at the time of purchase.
3. This voucher may only be redeemed once.
4. There is no cash equivalent for this voucher.
5. Offer redeemable at any Bath & Body Works stores in UAE.

EXP114

SHOPPING
BUYERS' GUIDE

Animal World Nr Jumeirah Centre, Jumeira, 04 344 4422
Glam Paws UAE 050 344 1984, *glam-paws.wix.com*
Paws & Claws Uptown Mirdiff, Mirdif, 04 288 4885, *pawsnclawspets.com*
Pet's Delight Arabian Ranches Centre, Wadi Al Safa 6, 04 361 8184, *pets-delight.com*
Petland Nr Health Mart, Shk Zayed Rd, Al Qouz 3, 04 380 4343, *petlanduae.com*
Petzone Nr Time Square Center, Al Qouz Ind. 1, 04 321 1424, *petzoneonline.com*
World of Pets Nr Dr Nicholas Clinic, Jumeira Rd, Jumeira 3, 04 395 5701, *worldofpetsme.com*

Second-hand

There is an extremely active second-hand market in Dubai, as people are always leaving, redecorating or downsizing, and need to get rid of their stuff. Supermarket noticeboards or noticeboards in apartment complexes are a great place to start, as many people post 'for sale' notices with pictures of all the items. Garage sales are also popular on Fridays and you'll notice signs going up in your neighbourhood from time to time.

For the Dhs.3 entry fee into Safa Park you can peruse the monthly flea market, and a car boot sale is held every Friday in the cooler winter months at the Autodrome which is free for shoppers. There are also a number of websites with classifieds sections; dubizzle.com is the main one, and expatwoman.com is another good one. Here you'll find absolutely anything, from appliances to furniture, cars and toys.

There are a number of second-hand shops, often linked to churches and special needs schools, but the opening hours can be somewhat eccentric. Second-hand bookshops such as Book World, House of Prose and Book & Bean buy books in good condition for 50% of the purchase price.

Al Noor Charity Thrift Shop
Al Barsha 1 **04 340 4844**
alnoorspneeds.ae
Map **1 R6** Metro **Mall of the Emirates**
Raises funds for the Al Noor School for Special Needs, and always welcomes donations of second-hand clothing in good condition.

Dubai Charity Centre
Nr Choithrams, Al Karama **04 337 8246**
Map **2 K6** Metro **Al Karama**
The biggest of the charity shops, this store supports the students who attend The Dubai Centre for Special Needs, and finances a number of places for those who are unable afford them. It stocks a good range of clothes, books and toys.

Holy Trinity Thrift Centre
Nr Dubai English Speaking School Oud Metha **04 337 8192**
holytrinitychurchdubai.org
Map **2 L7** Metro **Oud Metha**
Good for high-quality items and books in particular, and proceeds go towards a number of orphanages supported by the church. The shop gives you back 50% of what your items sell for.

Rashid Paediatric Therapy Centre
Nr Mall Of The Emirates Al Barsha 1 **04 340 0005**
rashidc.ae
Map **1 R6** Metro **Mall of the Emirates**
Has a decent range of items and raises money for projects at the centre.

Soft Furnishings

Carpets, Rugs & Curtains

Carpets are one of the region's signature items. The ones on sale here tend to be imported from Iran, Turkey, Pakistan and Central Asia. A carpet will vary in price depending on a number of factors such as its origin, the material used, the number of knots, and whether or not it is hand-made. The most expensive carpets are usually those hand-made with silk, in Iran.

Inspect carpets by turning them over – if the pattern is clearly depicted on the back and the knots are neat, the carpet is of higher quality than those that are indistinct. Try to do some research so that you have a basic idea of what you're looking for before you go, just in case you happen to meet an unscrupulous carpet dealer who could take advantage of your naivety.

Fortunately, carpet conmen are rare, and most will happily explain the differences between the rugs and share their extensive knowledge with you. If you ask the dealer, you can often garner some interesting information about the carpets and where they were made – for example, some carpets have family names sewn into the designs.

National Iranian Carpets has a section on its website (niccarpets.com) about the history and development of carpets from the various regions.

Ask to see a variety of carpets so that you can get a feel for the differences between hand-made or machine-made, silk, wool or blend carpets. Of course, asking may not be necessary, since carpet vendors will undoubtedly start unrolling carpets before you at a furious pace.

Carpets range in price from a few hundred dirhams to tens of thousands. It is always worth bargaining; make sure the seller knows you are not a tourist, and remain polite at all times to maximise the success of your haggling.

SHOPPING
BUYERS' GUIDE

Deira Tower on Al Nasr Square has a huge number of carpet outlets under one roof, and the Blue Souk in Sharjah also has a great range. If you happen to venture further out, the road to Hatta is lined with stalls selling carpets and the Friday Market in Fujairah is also a good place to pick them up.

Mall of the Emirates and The Dubai Mall have a selection of shops selling traditional carpets, as does Souk Al Bahar, but just bear in mind that prices will be steeper here.

Occasionally, you might get a travelling carpet seller ringing your doorbell – they usually drive around an area in a truck that is packed to the roof with carpets. The quality isn't great, and if you show the slightest bit of interest they'll keep coming back.

Invest in blackout curtains as the early morning light is very bright and will wake even the deepest sleeper.

Al Orooba Oriental Carpets BurJuman, Al Mankhool, 04 351 0919
Carpetland Pyramid Centre, Oud Metha, 04 337 7677, *aaf-me.com*
Mostafawi Al Karama, 04 334 9888
National Iranian Carpets Souk Madinat Jumeirah, Al Sufouh 1, 04 368 6003, *niccarpets.com*
The Orientalist Woven Art Jumeirah 1, 04 394 6989, *theorientalist.com*
Pride Of Kashmir Mall of the Emirates, Al Barsha 1, 04 341 4477, *prideofkashmir.com*
Qum Persian Carpets & Novelties Sheraton Dubai Creek Hotel & Towers, Al Rigga, 04 228 1848, *qumcarpets.com*
Dubai Blinds Silver Tower, Al Thanyah 5, 04 368 8759, *dubaiblinds.com*

Cute souvenirs

Souvenirs

From typical holiday trinkets to tasteful keepsakes, there is a huge range of souvenirs in Dubai. Many of the items are regional rather than local, and several are mass produced in India, Pakistan and Oman. You will find a good selection of traditional gifts like antique wooden wedding chests or pashminas, as well as the typical buys like fridge magnets, T-shirts and soft toys. Tourist hotspots like Souk Madinat Jumeirah and the major malls all have a variety of shops and stalls that sell a good selection, or head to the traditional souks around the Creek for a more authentic experience.

Camels feature heavily in souvenir shops; wooden carvings, camel pot stands and even carvings made from camel bones, and are great as novelty presents. Perhaps the tackiest souvenirs are plastic alarm clocks in the shape of a mosque – they only cost Dhs.10 and they wake you up with a loud call to prayer.

Coffee pots are symbols of Arabic hospitality and another popular souvenir item. Prices vary enormously from Dhs.100 for a brand new, shiny one, to several thousand dirhams for a genuine antique. Traditional silver items, such as the Arabic dagger (khanjar) and silver wedding jewellery, are excellent souvenirs, and are available both framed and unframed.

Wooden items are popular and representative of the region; trinket boxes (often with elaborate carvings or brass inlays) start from around Dhs.10. Elaborate Arabic doors and wedding chests, costing thousands, are also popular. The doors can be hung as art, or converted into tables or headboards.

While carpets are a good buy, it is worth doing some research before investing (see Soft Furnishings for more information). For a smaller, cheaper option, many shops sell woven coasters and camel bags, or you can buy a Persian carpet mouse pad.

You can hardly walk through a mall or shopping area without being offered a pashmina – they are available in an abundant range of colours and styles. Most are a cotton or silk mix and the ratio dictates the price. It is a good idea to check out a few shops before buying as prices vary and, as with most items, the more you buy the cheaper they are. For a decent quality pashmina, prices start from around Dhs.50. Shisha pipes make fun souvenirs and can be bought with various flavours of tobacco, such as apple or strawberry. Both functional and ornamental examples are on sale, prices start from around Dhs.75 in Carrefour.

Local scents, like oud and frankincense, make good gifts and are widely available in outlets such as Arabian Oud and Paris Gallery, while Amouage produces some of the world's most valuable perfumes, made with rare ingredients.

Explorer publishes a number of great, multi-language coffee table books, calendars and postcards

askexplorer.com **375**

SHOPPING
BUYERS' GUIDE

with stunning photos depicting the diversity of this vibrant city. Visit askexplorer.com to order copies.

Al Jaber Gallery
The Dubai Mall Burj Khalifa 04 339 8566
aljabergallery.ae
Map 2 F7 Metro Burj Khalifa/Dubai Mall
This eclectic store is good for a browse if you're short on inspiration. From tacky (plastic replicas of the Burj and 'I love Dubai' fridge magnets) to tasteful (colourfully painted mezze bowls and embroidered pashminas), it's a good spot to take out of town visitors.

Antique Museum
Nr Kanoo Int Paints Al Qouz Ind. 1 04 347 9935
fakihcollections.com
Map 1 U7 Metro Noor Bank
Upon entering this store's gilded doors, you'll be met by an eclectic maze of products. It has a large section devoted to teak Indian furniture and silver chests, plus a fantastic selection of token holiday tat, but you can also pick up pashminas, Omani silver boxes, Arabian lanterns and other traditional souvenirs.

The Sultani Lifestyle Gallerie
Souk Al Bahar Burj Khalifa 04 420 3676
Map 2 F6 Metro Burj Khalifa/Dubai Mall
Head here for good quality traditional souvenirs, carpets and exotic items from the region. The store also carries a good selection of postcards and elaborate home furnishings.

Sports & Outdoor Equipment

Dubai is a great place for a variety of sports, from common activities such as tennis, sailing, golf or football to exploring the great outdoors hiking or mountain biking – a popular pastime in the UAE, especially when the weather cools.

General sports shops are found all over the city and stock a good variety of items including rackets, swimming essentials or sports clothing. You can also find specialist sports shops that offer diving, sailing and desert sport equipment. Many of the major brand names have multiple outlets in Dubai, including Adidas, Nike and Timberland. You can also pick up a few basic items at Carrefour, especially camping gear and various accessories.

A growing range of camping and off-roading accessories is available at askexplorer.com, as well as several essential guides and apps to help you get the best of the great outdoors.

Clubs that organise specialist sports, such as Dubai Surfski Kayak Club (dskc.hu), can often be approached for equipment. Golf is extremely popular and clubs,

balls and bags are available in most sports shops. Golf House (04 434 0655) and the pro shops are the best places for decent kit.

ACE Hardware > p.343
Nr Times Square Center, Shk Zayed Rd
Al Qouz Ind. 1 04 341 1906
aceuae.com
Map 1 T6 Metro Noor Bank
You can buy all the basic equipment you need for a jaunt in the desert at this store, including tents, sleeping bags and cool boxes. The store also stocks a good range of hardware and accessories.

Adventure HQ
Times Square Center Al Qouz Ind. 1 04 346 6824
adventurehq.ae
Map 1 T6 Metro Noor Bank
An outdoor sport and camping specialist, you'll find everything here from tents, sleeping bags and hiking boots to full climbing gear, kayaks and paddleboards. There's a good range of Merida and BMC bikes, covering everything from mountain bikes to hybrids and high-end road racers, and it offers servicing and bike rental.

Decathlon Dubai
Mirdif City Centre Mirdif 04 283 9392
Map 2 P12 Metro Rashidiya
The French sporting giant has a cavernous Mirdif City Centre store. Covering everything from tracksuits and trainers to camping, climbing and equestrian gear, Decathlon has several of its own value brands as well as big name brands.

Go Sport
Ibn Battuta Mall Jabal Ali 1 04 368 5344
go-sport.com
Map 1 G5 Metro Ibn Battuta
The most comprehensive collection of sports goods, selling equipment for popular sports like running, basketball and tennis, and it also stocks cycling, camping and golfing gear. Has a large bike section and a workshop in its Mall of the Emirates store.

Intersport
Times Square Center Al Qouz Ind. 1 04 341 8214
intersport.ae
Map 1 T6 Metro Noor Bank
The world's largest sports retailer, these superstores cover football, rugby, basketball, running, racket sports, cycling, camping, watersports and more. You'll find all the major international labels, as well as services including footscan technology, racket stringing, jersey printing and bike maintenance/fitting. The concept store in Festival City has an outdoor activity and demo area.

SHOPPING
BUYERS' GUIDE

Knight Shot
Nr Mazaya Centre, Shk Zayed Rd Al Wasl
04 343 5678
knightshot.com
Map **2 F6** Metro **Burj Khalifa/Dubai Mall**
For fans of table sports, this is the must-know store in the UAE, selling everything from snooker, pool and table tennis tables (plus dartboards, table football and air hockey tables) to cues, bridges, chalk and apparel. Its experts can also re-tip your cues or service, clean and re-felt tables.

Lorna Jane
J3 Mall Al Manara **04 388 3006**
lornajane.com.au
Map **1 U5** Metro **Noor Bank**
Ladies will be pleased with the arrival of this Australian sportswear brand known for its bright, funky colours and flattering styles designed for various different sports, from running to yoga.

Picnico General Trading
Al Faraidooni Bldg, Shk Zayed Rd Al Barsha 1
04 395 1113
picnico.ae
Map **1 P6** Metro **Dubai Internet City**
An outdoor specialists, stocking a good range of Coleman and Campingaz equipment like cooler bags, tents and accessories. The store also stocks GPS systems, rock climbing gear and footwear. It has one of the largest ranges of hydration packs and it carries Dakine kitesurfing kit, sea kayaks, diving gear and angling equipment.

Stadium
Deira City Centre Port Saeed **04 295 0261**
Map **2 M7** Metro **Deira City Centre**
Along with sister store Studio R (located at BurJuman, Dubai Outlet Mall and Ibn Battuta Mall), Stadium sells brands that cater to those with an active lifestyle, with a range of well-known clothing labels and sports brands (Quiksilver, Adidas, New Balance and Speedo). It also stocks Teva, which make a range of practical sandals. Sales throughout the year see heavy discounts. Further outlets are located at The Dubai Mall and Dubai Marina Mall.

Sun & Sand Sports
Ibn Battuta Mall Jabal Ali 1 **04 366 9777**
sunandsandsports.com
Map **1 G5** Metro **Ibn Battuta**
One of the larger sports stores in the city with a good range of sportswear and home gym equipment, as well as a limited range of pool and snooker tables. Further branches are located at The Dubai Mall and Mirdif City Centre, and there's an outlet store in Al Qouz 3, behind the Gold & Diamond Park.

Adventure HQ

Timberland
The Dubai Mall Burj Khalifa **04 434 1291**
timberland.com
Map **2 F7** Metro **Burj Khalifa/Dubai Mall**
Get dressed for the great outdoors with this timeless collection of hiking boots, outdoor clothing and sporting products for men, women and children. Branches include Mall of the Emirates, Ibn Battuta Mall, Arabian Centre and Dubai Outlet Mall.

yApparel
Jumeirah Centre Jumeira 1 **04 344 4130**
yapparel.com
Map **2 H4** Metro **Emirates Towers**
Tucked away inside the Jumeirah Centre is this new, multi-brand yoga and fitness boutique apparel store – the first in the UAE that is solely dedicated to providing a range of high-quality athletic wear and accessories to the growing yoga and pilates community. Brands include Liquido and Wellicious.

Yas Sports
Nr Al Karama Bus Stand Al Karama **04 396 8009**
yassports.ae
Map **2 K6** Metro **Al Karama**
Although this store specialises in cricket equipment, it also stocks equipment for many other sports, including kit that can be harder to find. The store can also supply sports teams with personalised kits, and manage bulk orders.

Rage The Dubai Mall, Burj Khalifa, 04 434 1549, rage-shop.com
Golf House The Dubai Mall, Burj Khalifa, 04 434 0655

SHOPPING
BUYERS' GUIDE

Biking

For serious bikers, there are several shops selling specialist equipment and accessories, including BMXs, that are listed below. Many also do repairs. Joining a cycling club (see Clubs & Groups) can also help you find the bikes or accessories you need.

For the casual cyclist, various sports shops sell more basic models at reasonable prices. Children's bicycles are widely available in bike and sports shops, while the likes of Babyshop and Toys R Us have a range for tiny Bradley Wiggins wannabes, as do some hypermarkets, such as Carrefour. Both adults' and children's helmets are available at the main retailers. Supermarket noticeboards and online classifieds, such as dubizzle. com, are good places to look for second-hand bikes.

Probike
Shk Juma Bin Ahmed Al Maktoum Bldg Al Barsha 1
04 325 5705
probike.ae
Map **1 R6** Metro **Mall of the Emirates**
Run by biking enthusiasts, Probike stocks mountain, road and triathlon bikes for all levels, as well as shoes, helmets, apparel and components. Probike is the UAE dealer for Planet X bikes, which are renowned for their value for money. Both bike servicing and a professional fitting service are available and good road bikes can be rented by the day.

Ride Bike Shop
Mirdif City Centre Mirdif 04 284 0038
ridebikeshop.com
Map **2 P12** Metro **Rashidiya**
A good range of stock for both serious cyclists and those who just need something for recreational use, and staff will advise on the most suitable bike for your needs. The in-store workshops at both Mirdif City Centre and Sheikh Zayed Road branches offer a high standard of maintenance to ensure that you are constantly kept on your saddle. Brands include Topeak, Crank Brothers, WeThePeople Bike Company and CycleOps.

Wolfi's Bike Shop
Nr Oasis Centre, Shk Zayed Rd Al Qouz 3
04 339 4453
wbs.ae
Map **2 B6** Metro **Noor Bank**
For the cycling community, Wolfi's is more of an institution than simply a shop, although it is also the UAE's biggest dedicated cycle store, where you'll find everything from kids' and leisure bikes to hardcore carbon time trial machines, and plenty in between. The store specialises in top-end brands like Scott, Felt, Storck, Profile Design and Zipp, and staff are all passionate cyclists who are happy to assist. Bike fitting, servicing and bike hire are also available in-store.

The Cycle Hub MotorCity, Al Hebiah 1,
04 425 6555, thecyclehub.com
Kona Bikes Nr Rashid Hospital, Oud Metha,
04 335 0399, konabikeworld.com
Revolution Cycles Apex Atrium, MotorCity,
Al Hebiah 1, 04 369 7441
Trek Bike Shop Oud Metha, 04 335 0399, trekbike.ae

Boating

There's a cluster of marine equipment stores in Al Jaddaf, so it's a good place to head for all manner of boat related requirements, from fenders and ropes to upholstery services and anti-fouling services. There's also a few around Marsa Dubai, Deira and Al Qouz Industrial. Adventure HQ also sells a broad range of fishing equipment.

ACT Marine Marsa Dubai, 04 424 3191
Al Boom Marine Nr Coca Cola, Ras Al Khor,
04 289 4858, alboommarine.com
Al Hamur Marine & Sports Equipment Jumeira 1,
04 344 4468
Dubai Creek Marina Dubai Creek Golf & Yacht Club,
Port Saeed, 04 295 6000, dubaigolf.com

Diving

Al Boom Diving
Nr Iranian Hospital Jumeira 1 **04 342 2993**
alboomdiving.com
Map **2 H4** Metro **World Trade Centre**
The main outlet of the region's major diving company sells a good range of sub-aqua and watersports gear. All the main brands of technical scuba equipment can be found, including Technisub and GoPro, as well as kitesurfing equipment and beachwear.

The Dive Shop
Dubai Investment Park 1 **04 813 5474**
thediveshopdubai.com
Map **1 F9**
A small and friendly scuba dive shop selling snorkels, masks, regulators, fins and all other accessories.

Watersports

While sports shops such as Adventure HQ, Sun & Sand Sports and Intersport stock some gear, there are several stores dedicated to watersports equipment. Check dubizzle.com for second-hand equipment too.

Leisure Marine
The Walk at JBR Marsa Dubai **04 424 3133**
leisuremarine-me.com
Map **1 K4** Metro **Dubai Marina**
As well as larger boats, dinghies and kayaks, this store stocks a range of accessories from popular boating and watersports brands.

SHOPPING
BUYERS' GUIDE

Surf Shop Arabia
Nr Time Square Center, Al Manara Rd Al Qouz Ind. 1
04 379 1998
surfshopdubai.com
Map **1 U6** Metro **Noor Bank**
Has a range of new and used surfboards, as well as surfing products, stand up paddleboard (SUP) boards, kitesurfing gear and surf ski accessories. Boards can be custom made.

Textiles, Tailoring & Repairs

If you are looking for fabric, you have several options, including the Textile Souk near Al Fahidi Street, Satwa, or the shopping malls, most of which have at least one fabric outlet. Prices start from a few dirhams for a metre of basic cotton. The Textile Souk can get busy, but the sheer range of fabrics makes it worthwhile. There are several haberdashery shops in the same area should you wish to buy matching buttons, bows or cotton. Satwa Road has a good collection of general fabric stores and a few good haberdashers; Plant Street is the place to go for upholstery. IKEA and Fabindia also stock a range of vibrant fabrics that can be used for cushions, curtains or bedding.

Tailors can be found in most areas, but there is a concentration of stores in the Textile Souk, and on the main street in Satwa. For simple alterations and repairs, such as hemming, head to one of these areas and take your pick – for simple work, the general standard is fine. For anything more complex, the best way to select a tailor is by recommendation. A good tailor can make a garment from scratch, either from a photo or by copying an existing garment. It may take a few fitting sessions and alterations to get it just right, but it's worth the effort, and with tailoring services so cheap compared to other international cities, it's well worth getting some custom-made clothes while living in Dubai. Shirts usually start from Dhs.30 and suits from Dhs.500.

Deepak's Textiles
Nr Satwa Clinic Al Bada' **04 344 8836**
deepakstextiles.com
Map **2 H5** Metro **World Trade Centre**
Well-stocked with a fantastic range of fabrics – from casual denim to more glamorous silks, chiffons and pure linen. Also offers a tailoring service.

Dream Girl Tailors
Meena Bazaar Fashions Al Souq Al Kabeer
04 352 6463 dreamgirltailors.com
Map **2 L4** Metro **Al Fahidi**
Popular store that will take on all tailoring jobs from taking up trousers to making ball gowns.

Lobo Tailors
Nr Raymond's Al Souk Al Kabeer **04 352 3760**
Map **2 L4** Metro **Al Fahidi**
This is good for suits, which range from Dhs.1,500-2,500 including fabric and stitching.

Regal Textiles
Cosmos Lane, Meena Bazaar Al Souq Al Kabeer
04 359 6123 regaldubai.com
Map **2 L4** Metro **Al Fahidi**
Stocks a good selection of fabrics including French chiffon, printed silks, Swiss cotton and French lace.

Rivoli Textiles
Nr Mashreq Bank, Zabeel Rd Al Karama **04 335 0075**
rivoligroup.com
Map **2 L6** Metro **Al Karama**
This classy store has a broad range of fabrics and a personalised tailoring service. Its Satwa store caters to women, for a suit head to the Marsa Dubai branch.

Al Masroor Textiles Murshid Bazaar, 04 225 5343, *almasroorgroup.com*
Deepas Textile & Tailoring Nr Emirates Post Office, Al Bada', 04 349 9733, *deepastailoring.com*
Dream Boy Bur Dubai, 04 352 1840
Kachins Meena Bazaar, Al Souq Al Kabeer, 04 352 1386
Khamis Abdullah Trading & Embroidery
Al Rashidiya, 04 225 5940
Savile Row The Walk at JBR, Marsa Dubai, 04 423 3813, *savilerow.ae*
Stitches The Village, Jumeira 1, 04 342 1476
Whistle & Flute Nr Iranian Hospital, Al Satwa, 04 342 9259

Colourful garments

askexplorer.com

SHOPPING
BUYERS' GUIDE

Cobblers
Locksmiths in the city often offer a shoe repair service and you'll find stores in Satwa and Karama.

Minutes
Mall of the Emirates Al Barsha 1 **04 340 8281**
Map **1 R6** Metro **Mall of the Emirates**
Offers shoe repairs in addition to its key cutting service and it has outlets located in many of the main malls.

NDust Shoe Repairs
Nr LuLu Hypermarket Al Barsha 1 **04 325 5016**
ndustshoes.com
Map **1 R6** Metro **Mall of the Emirates**
Offers a handy collection and delivery service.

60 Second Lock & Shoe Repair Opp Ramada Hotel, Al Mankhool 04 355 2600
Al Fareed Shoes Musalla Road, Al Souq Al Kabeer, 04 359 2862

Weddings

For dresses, shoes and accessories, a good bet is Jumeira Road where you'll find several bridal stores, or for designer gowns head to Saks Fifth Avenue's bridal department, which stocks or can order the latest off-the-peg designer wedding gowns by Vera Wang and Reem Acra. The bride will need to attend a number of fittings, but alterations are done in-house and they are up to couture standards.

Some of the city's tailors are able to work from pictures to create your ideal dress; a traditional wedding dress will cost upwards of Dhs.2,000 (including tailoring and fabric), reaching in excess of Dhs.10,000 for a complex design and expensive fabric. It's a good idea for the bridesmaids' dresses, too.

For the groom, there are several shops where formal wear can be hired, including The Wedding Shop, Elegance and Formal Wear on 2nd December Street. Debenhams and Monsoon both sell girls' bridesmaids' dresses, and cater well to mothers of the bride and groom.

Magrudy's and Susan Walpole stock invitations, guest books and photo albums, while The Paper Room in The Dubai Mall has a particularly good range of stationery. Debenhams and THE One both offer wedding registry services.

As well as offering wedding venue and planning services, several of the city's hotels can be commissioned to make the wedding cake. Most of the city's florists can turn their hands to wedding bouquets and arrangements, with certain florists like Mamosa Flowers (mamoso.com) specialising in weddings. Discuss your requirements with them to find out what will be available.

Dresses

The Bridal Showroom
Jumeirah Business Center 2 Al Thanyah 5
04 457 9400
dubaibridalshowroom.com
Map **1 L5** Metro **Dubai Marina**
Consultants will help you find the perfect dress for your big day. Book an appointment to try on a range of gowns from designers including James Clifford and Sophia Tolli. There's also a stunning collection of bridal accessories, flower girl outfits and evening gowns.

Frost
Palm Strip Jumeira 1 **04 345 5690**
frostdubai.com
Map **2 H4** Metro **Emirates Towers**
Head here if you want contemporary wedding dresses from top US and European designers. The store has a great set-up for trying dresses on with exceptionally friendly staff. There's also a decent selection of evening gowns and bridesmaid dresses.

House Of Arushi
Villa 8, Jumeira Rd Jumeira 1 **04 344 2277**
Map **2 G4** Metro **Financial Centre**
Renowned as one of the best of several specialist bridal designers with workshops in Dubai. You can select the fabric yourself or it can be selected during the first meeting with the designer. Gowns take around one month to make, but as Arushi is so popular, there is often a waiting list.

Services

Studio Sol
055 101 2291
studiosol.me
These guys will consult with you on your wedding theme and design all of your stationery from scratch.

Amal & Amal
Jumeirah Centre Jumeira 1 **04 344 4671**
Map **2 H4** Metro **Emirates Towers**
Another bespoke wedding stationery service.

Cadorim
The Village Jumeira 1 **04 349 3333**
Map **2 H4** Metro **Emirates Towers**
Creates tailor-made favours and ring boxes.

The Wedding Shop
Jumeirah Centre Jumeira 1 **04 344 1618**
theweddingshop.ae
Map **2 H4** Metro **Emirates Towers**
A great place to get confetti, guest books and photo albums, not to mention a healthy dollop of inspiration.

Mackenzie Art

ART · MURALS · TROMPE L'OEIL · DECORATION

ENHANCE YOUR ENVIRONMENT

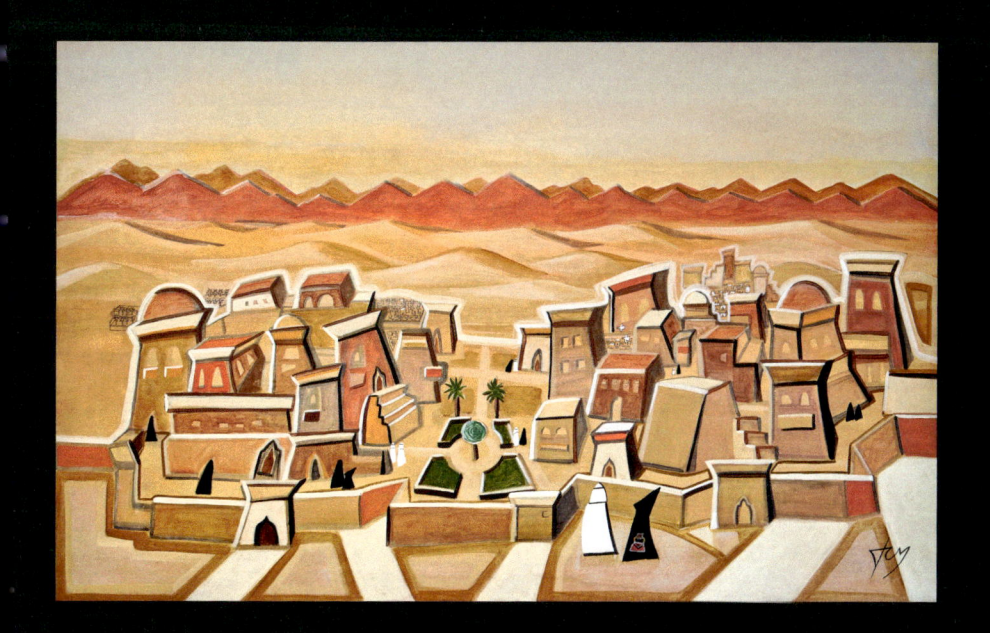

"From small to tall – we paint it all!"
Interior, exterior, walls and canvases – we provide personalised paintings for your homes, offices and projects

Tel.: +971 (4) 341 9803
www.mackenzieart.com

I WANT
DIFFERENT FLAVOURS EVERY NIGHT
PLEASE

You now have even more to choose from, all week long. So whether it is a yummy tasty meal, or drink with friends, join us for different themed night, every day.

Saturday: Pub Night at c.mondo from 6.30 to 10.30pm
Sunday: Latino Night at c.mondo from 6.30 to 10.30pm
Monday: Noodles Night at c.taste from 6.30 to 10.30pm
Tuesday: Burger Night at c.taste from 6.30 to 10.30pm
Wednesday: Tandoori Night at c.taste from 6.30 to 10.30pm
Thursday: Italian Night at c.taste from 6.30 to 10.30pm
Friday: Free-Flowing Brunch at c.taste from 12:30 to 4:00pm

For more information, please visit rotanatimes.com or call +971 (0)4 704 0000

*Price is inclusive of 10% municipality fee and 10% service charge

Hotels by Rotana

Barsha, P.O. Box 115060, Dubai, U.A.E
T: +971 (0)4 704 0000, F: +971 (0)4 3990111, centro.barsha@rotana.com
rotana.com

CENTRO
Barsha · Dubai

GOING OUT

Restaurants **385**
Cuisine Finder **386**
Cafes **416**
Bars, Pubs & Clubs **422**
Entertainment **435**
Staying In **439**

Al Mahara restaurant

GOING OUT

Everything you need to know about making the most of Dubai's great restaurants and nightlife.

Exploring the many entertainment options in Dubai is one of the best parts of living here. Whether you want to eat, party or stay overnight, this chapter will help guide you on your going out missions.

Dining & Dancing

The launch of numerous new hotels in Dubai over the last few years has seen the number of culinary treats on offer skyrocket. At one end of the spectrum, celebrity chefs, picturesque cocktail lounges and well-appointed clubs compete for your hard-earned dirhams. At the other end, bargain eateries, drink-deal bars and bang-for-your-buck brunches are there to help at the end of the month.

The licensing laws in Dubai mean that if you like a glass of grape with your meal, you will inevitably have to seek out a restaurant located within a hotel or leisure club. However, don't make the mistake of missing out on some of the culinary delights which can be found in non-licensed independent restaurants and cafes – you will find the bill is generally much more wallet-friendly, as a decent bottle of wine can often cost more than your whole meal.

When eating out in hotels, bear in mind that not only will your bottle of local water cost up to 10 times more than in the supermarket, you will also be stung with a 10% tourism fee, as well as a 10% service charge. Taxis are cheap and plentiful, so leave the car at home to avoid spending a night in the cells – the UAE has a zero-tolerance policy on drink driving. The legal drinking age is 21, and it's best to avoid getting staggeringly drunk; raucous behaviour is not tolerated and will land you in hot water. Clubs and bars close at about 1am, although some go on until 3am.

GOING OUT
RESTAURANTS

RESTAURANTS

While Dubai is well known for its high-end dining options, don't let first impressions deter you from giving some of the budget establishments around town a go. Food and drink outlets are subject to regular checks, so basic hygiene requirements are usually met; a good barometer is to choose an establishment which has a large number of hungry eaters wolfing down their dinner, so you know that the turnover of ingredients is high.

If you suffer from food allergies, don't assume that serving staff have understood your requirements, or that the menu will be suitably labelled.

Vegetarians are generally well catered for, as Dubai is home to a large population from the subcontinent who are vegetarian by religion. It's a good idea to confirm ingredients with staff, just in case meals which at first appear vegetarian may in fact have been cooked using animal fats. Arabic cuisine, although heavy on meat-based mains, offers a great range of mezze that are mostly vegetarian.

You will find that restaurants tend to fill up later in the evening, with the hip Lebanese crowd often not eating before 10pm at the weekends.

Wherever you're heading to dine, it's generally best to leave the flip-flops and shorts on the beach and trade up to smart trousers and shiny shoes – you may get some funny looks if you turn up looking like you've just rolled off your sun lounger.

New smoking laws are slowly being introduced and by mid-2014 smoking will not be allowed in any restaurant smaller than 1,000 square feet; those restaurants that do have smoking areas will have to limit the area to a maximum of 50% of the dining area. At the moment, smoking is banned in some restaurants and bars, but there are still many places where you can light up.

The following pages give you an all-round taster of restaurants in Dubai, whether you want alfresco dining, somewhere to take the kids, a romantic rendezvous, or a cheap and cheerful bite to eat before the cinema or night out on the town.

The Yellow Star
The yellow star highlights the Dubai gems that merit extra praise. It might be the atmosphere, the food, the cocktails, the music or the crowd, but any review that you see with the star attached is sure to be for somewhere that's a bit special.

Ramadan Timings
During Ramadan, opening and closing times of restaurants change considerably. Because eating and drinking in public is forbidden during daylight hours, many places only open after sunset, then keep going well into the early hours. Restaurants in some hotels remain open, but will be screened off from public view. Live entertainment is not allowed, so while some nightclubs remain open, all dance floors are closed.

Taxes & Service Charges
Look out for the small print on the bill and you may spot the words 'prices are subject to 10% service charge and 10% tourism fee'. This service charge is rather misleading as it isn't passed onto the staff, and there's no option to opt out if you're not happy with the service. If you do want to tip the waiting staff though, 10% is the norm – and try to give them cash if you can. Tourism tax is only levied in hotels.

Feast of Festivals
Dubai gastrophiles should look forward to the month of March as that's when the Taste of Dubai Festival hits the city. This three-day culinary tour de force sees Michelin-starred and celebrity chefs from restaurants across Dubai showcase their skills at Dubai Media City. Taste some signature dishes, enjoy a cookery class, participate in beverage tastings and see world-famous chefs share their secrets live on stage. See tasteofdubaifestival.com for more information.

In the UAE capital, Gourmet Abu Dhabi (gourmetabudhabi.ae) is a 10 day festival in February that showcases world renowned chefs and their culinary skills.

Cultural Meals
While it is possible to find pretty much any national cuisine you can imagine in the city, there are certain areas that cater best for those in search of some local flavour. Al Fahidi Historical Neighbourhood, formerly known as Bastakiya, is a great place to grab a bite to eat and soak up some culture.

This traditional part of the city is best experienced by strolling through the streets, visiting the museums and historical buildings, and dining at one of the many cafes – a culinary and cultural experience rolled into one. Alternatively, you can simply visit the Sheikh Mohammed Centre for Cultural Understanding. As well as organising tours of Jumeirah Mosque, the centre also hosts regular cultural meals to introduce visitors to the national cuisine, where you can chat to your local Emirati host about the culture and traditions.

The Department of Tourism & Commerce Marketing also works closely with the Emirates Culinary Guild (emirates-culinaryguild.com) and a few chefs to promote Emirati cuisine in Dubai.

GOING OUT
CUISINE FINDER

CUISINE FINDER

African
Tribes, Mall of the Emirates — p.416

Afternoon Tea
Arcadia, H Hotel — p.419
Hey Sugar, The Village — p.419
Karat, Address The Dubai Mall — p.419
Lobby Lounge, Ritz-Carlton Dubai — p.419
Lobby Lounge & Terrace, Ritz-Carlton DIFC — p.419
Mashrabiya Lounge, Fairmont The Palm — p.419
Plantation, Sofitel Jumeirah — p.419
Sahn Eddar, Burj Al Arab — p.420
Sultan's Lounge, Jumeirah Zabeel Saray — p.420

American
Applebee's, Shk Issa Tower — p.400
Caramel Restaurant & Lounge, DIFC — p.391
Cheesecake Factory, The, The Dubai Mall — p.412
Chili's, Nr Welcare Hospital — p.399
Claw BBQ, Souk Al Bahar — p.404
Cravin Cajun, Novotel Al Barsha — p.407
Gourmet Burger Kitchen, Mirdif City Centre — p.406
Johnny Rockets, Juma al Majid Center — p.400

Ketchup, Boulevard Plaza — p.406
Planet Hollywood, Wafi — p.401
Ruby Tuesday, The Dubai Mall — p.401
Shooters, JA Shooting Club — p.406

Argentinean
Gaucho, DIFC — p.403

Asian
Bamboo Lagoon, JW Marriott — p.407
Beachcombers, Jumeirah Beach Hotel — p.393
Eauzone, Arabian Court At One&Only Royal Mirage — p.391
Nomad, Jumeirah Creekside — p.393
Peppercrab, Grand Hyatt — p.401
Singapore Deli Restaurant, Nr BurJuman Centre — p.406

Brazilian
Fogo Vivo, JA Ocean View — p.414
Fogueira Restaurant & Lounge, Ramada Plaza — p.391

British
Ivy, The, The Boulevard At Jumeirah Emirates Towers — p.414
Reform Social & Grill, The, The Lakes Club — p.414
Rivington Grill, Souk Al Bahar — p.416

Buffet
Al Muna, Mina A'Salam — p.390
Meridien Village Terrace, Le Meridien — p.392
Senses, Mercure Gold — p.408
Spice Island, Crowne Plaza Deira — p.402

Cafe
1762, DIFC — p.418
Arabian Tea House, Al Fahidi Neighbourhood — p.420
Archive, The, Gate 5, Safa Park — p.416
Armani/Dubai Caffe, The Dubai Mall — p.417
Bagels & More, Marina Diamond 3 — p.418
Baker & Spice, Souk Al Bahar — p.416
Balance Cafe, Oasis Centre — p.418
Bert's Cafe, Una Bldg, Street 2 — p.418
Cafe Ceramique, Town Centre Jumeirah — p.420
Cafe Havana, Al Safa 2 — p.416
CafeM, Media One — p.408
Circle, Beach Park Plaza — p.417
Counter Culture, Marriott Harbour — p.416
Elements, Wafi — p.418
Fraiche, Swiss Tower, Y Cluster, JLT — p.416
Gerard's, Magrudy's — p.417
Jones The Grocer, Indigo Central 8 — p.418
Medley, Pullman Deira City Centre — p.418
Lime Tree Cafe & Kitchen, Jumeira Rd — p.420
Living Rooms Video Games Cafe, Dubai Festival City Mall — p.400

Celebrities restaurant

GOING OUT
CUISINE FINDER

Bamboo Lagoon

Madeleine Cafe & Boulangerie, The Dubai Mall	p.417
Maison Bagatelle, Shk Mohd Bin Rashid Blvd	p.416
Neos, The Address Downtown	p.411
One, THE, Jumeira Rd	p.420
Panini, Grand Hyatt	p.418
Shakespeare & Co, Al Attar Business Tower	p.420
Tea Junction, Nr Movenpick Hotel	p.420
Tom&Serg, 15A Street	p.419
Vienna Cafe, JW Marriott	p.417

Chinese

Ba, Fairmont The Palm	p.391
China Club, The, Radisson Blu Deira Creek	p.395
Hakkasan, Emirates Towers	p.411
Hong Loong, Sofitel The Palm	p.410
Noodle House, The, The Boulevard At Jumeirah Emirates Towers	p.414

Cuban

Cuba, Jumeirah Creekside	p.412
El Malecon, Dubai Marine Beach Resort	p.403

European

25°55° Cafe Bistro, Marina Yacht Club	p.392
A La Grand, Grand Excelsior	p.400
Celebrities, Palace At One&Only Royal Mirage	p.410
Embassy Dubai, Grosvenor House	p.410
Rhodes in Residence, Grosvenor House	p.397

Filipino

Max's Restaurant, Khalid Bin Al Waleed Rd	p.400
Tagpuan, Karama Shopping Centre	p.399

French

AOC, Sofitel Jumeirah	p.390
Bistro Domino, Ibis Deira City Centre	p.398
Bistro Madeleine, InterContinental Festival City	p.393
Imperium, Jumeirah Zabeel Saray	p.395
Reflets Par Pierre Gagnaire, InterContinental Festival City	p.397
Stay By Yannick Alleno, One&Only The Palm	p.398
Studio Du Chef, Sofitel The Palm	p.412

German

Brauhaus, Jumeira Rotana	p.412
Der Keller, Jumeirah Beach	p.404
Hofbrauhaus, JW Marriott	p.414

Greek

Elia, Majestic	p.391

Indian

Amala, Jumeirah Zabeel Saray	p.402
Antique Bazaar, Four Points Bur Dubai	p.407
Armani/Amal, Armani	p.402
Aryaas, Al Nakheel Bldg, Zabeel Rd	p.398

askexplorer.com

GOING OUT
CUISINE FINDER

Asha's, Wafi	p.402
Bombay, The, Marco Polo	p.398
Dhow Ka Aangan, Dhow Palace	p.407
Khazana, Al Nasr Leisureland	p.397
Nina, Arabian Court At One&Only Royal Mirage	p.403
Rupee Room, The, North Podium, Marina Walk	p.408
Signature By Sanjeev Kapoor, Melia	p.397

International

Academy, The, Creek Golf Club	p.408
Al Badia Golf Club By Intercontinental Dubai Festival City, Dubai Festival City	p.394
Al Qasr, Madinat Jumeirah	p.395
Apres, Mall of the Emirates	p.404
At.mosphere, Burj Khalifa	p.411
AZUR, Marriott Harbour	p.390
Bateaux Dubai, Nr British Embassy	p.409
Blades, Al Badia Golf Club	p.400
Bo House Cafe, The Walk at JBR	p.408
Boardwalk, The, Creek Golf Club	p.393
Channels, Media Rotana	p.398
Da Gama, Century Village	p.391
Deck, The, JA Ocean View	p.391
Epicure, Desert Palm	p.416
Farm, The, Nr Falcon City	p.400
Farriers, Meydan	p.395
Fazaris, The Address Downtown	p.410
Flow Kitchen, Fairmont The Palm	p.395
Japengo Cafe, Mall of the Emirates	p.406
Kris With A View, Park Regis Kris Kin	p.411
Mazina, Address Dubai Marina	p.395
MORE Cafe, The Dubai Mall	p.396
Nando's, Nr Four Points Sheraton	p.399
Nezesaussi Grill, Al Manzil	p.414
Observatory, The, Marriott Harbour	p.394
Orchid Restaurant, Ramada Downtown	p.401
Ranches Restaurant & Bar, Arabian Ranches Golf Club	p.401
Siddharta Lounge, Grosvenor House	p.411
Spectrum On One, Fairmont	p.396
Wavebreaker, Hilton Jumeirah	p.408
Yalumba, Le Meridien	p.396

Italian

BiCE, Hilton Jumeirah	p.412
BiCE Mare, Souk Al Bahar	p.409
Bussola, The Westin	p.393
Carluccio's, The Dubai Mall	p.404
Carnevale, Jumeirah Beach	p.400
Frankie's, Al Fattan Marine Tower	p.396
Jamie's Italian, Dubai Festival City Mall	p.396
Jazz@Pizza Express, Nr Movenpick JLT	p.407
La Veranda, Jumeirah Beach	p.400
Luciano's, Habtoor Grand	p.391
Medzo, Wafi	p.410
Mosaico, Emirates Towers	p.401
Olives, Palace At One&Only Royal Mirage	p.392
Ossigeno, Le Royal Meridien	p.410
Pax, Dusit Thani	p.399
Prego's, Media Rotana	p.414
Ronda Locatelli, Atlantis	p.397
Segreto, Madinat Jumeirah	p.404

Japanese

Armani/Hashi, Armani	p.409
Benihana, Amwaj Rotana	p.398
Bentoya Kitchen, Shk Zayed Rd	p.412
Honyaki, Souk Madinat	p.393
Icho Restaurant, Radisson Royal	p.411
Manga Sushi, Beach Park Plaza	p.403
Nobu, Atlantis, The Palm	p.397
Sushi, Grand Hyatt	p.408
Sushi Art, Marble Walk – Gate 5, DIFC	p.406
Wagamama, Al Fattan Marine Tower	p.408
Watatsumi, Le Meridien Mina Seyahi	p.392
YO! Sushi, Mirdif City Centre	p.407
Zuma, Gate Village	p.396

Korean

Mannaland Korean Restaurant, Al Mina Rd	p.399

Latin American

Pachanga, Hilton Jumeirah	p.403

Mediterranean

Al Muntaha, Burj Al Arab	p.403
Ewaan, The Palace Downtown	p.406
MED, The, Media One	p.395
Thyme Restaurant, JA Oasis Beach Tower	p.402
Villa Beach, Jumeirah Beach	p.394

Mexican

Cafe Habana, Al Bustan Rotana	p.412
El Chico Cafe, The Walk at JBR	p.406
Maria Bonita Taco Shop & Grill, Umm Al Sheif	p.406
Maya Modern Mexican Kitchen & Lounge, Le Royal Meridien	p.397

Middle Eastern

Al Basha, Habtoor Grand	p.407
Al Dahleez, Al Boom Tourist Village	p.402
Al Diwan, Metropolitan Palace	p.407
Al Koufa Restaurant, Nr Al Nasr Leisureland	p.407
Al Mansour Dhow, Radisson Blu Deira Creek	p.393
Al Safadi Restaurant, Shk Zayed Rd	p.398
Amaseena, Ritz-Carlton Dubai	p.409
Automatic, Beach Centre	p.398
Bastakiah Nights, Al Fahidi Neighbourhood	p.402
Wafi Gourmet, Wafi	p.408
Wild Peeta, Deira City Centre	p.409

GOING OUT
CUISINE FINDER

Moroccan
Almaz By Momo, Mall of the Emirates — p.404
Tagine, Palace At One&Only Royal Mirage — p.411

Pakistani
Ravi's, Nr Satwa R/A, Al Satwa Rd — p.414

Russian
Troyka, Ascot — p.408

Seafood
Al Bandar Restaurant, Heritage & Diving Villages — p.404
Al Mahara, Burj Al Arab — p.411
Aprons & Hammers, DIMC — p.390
Aquara, Marina Yacht Club — p.390
Asmak, Century Village — p.390
Beach Bar & Grill, Palace At One&Only Royal Mirage — p.393
Fish Market, Radisson Blu Deira Creek — p.403
Ossiano, Atlantis, The Palm — p.412
Pierchic, Al Qasr — p.412
Wheeler's, Gate Village — p.398

South American
Asado, The Palace Downtown — p.402
Beach House Cabana, Shoreline Apartments — p.393

Spanish
Al Hambra, Al Qasr — p.407
El Sur, The Westin — p.395

Sri Lankan
Chef Lanka, Nr LuLu Supermarket — p.399

Steakhouse
Butcher Shop & Grill, The, Mall of the Emirates — p.404
Center Cut, Ritz-Carlton DIFC — p.403
Meat Co, The, Souk Al Bahar — p.392
Porterhouse, Sofitel The Palm — p.410
Prime 68, JW Marriott Marquis — p.403
Rare Restaurant, Desert Palm — p.411
Seafire, Atlantis, The Palm — p.396

Thai
Blue Elephant, Al Bustan Rotana — p.402
Blue Rain, Ritz-Carlton DIFC — p.402
Lemongrass, Nr Lamcy Plaza — p.399
Pai Thai, Al Qasr — p.410
Royal Orchid, Dubai Festival City Mall — p.394
Smiling BKK, Al Wasl Rd — p.399
Thai Kitchen, The, Park Hyatt — p.396

Turkish
A La Turca Restaurant, Rixos The Palm — p.390

Vietnamese
Voi, Jumeirah Zabeel Saray — p.392

Yalumba

askexplorer.com

389

GOING OUT
RESTAURANTS

Alfresco

If the weather is cool enough, head outside onto a terrace or balcony for breakfast, lunch or dinner and you'll feel the vacation vibe flow over you.

A La Turca Restaurant   Turkish
Rixos The Palm Nakhlat Jumeira 04 4575 555
rixos.com
Map 1 P3 Metro Nakheel

Indulge in mouthwatering mezze and succulent kebabs at Rixos The Palm's all-day dining restaurant. It's predominantly a buffet concept that serves up the usual mix of Middle Eastern dishes, but also worth a try is the home made Turkish thin crust pizza. You'll need your appetite because it comes on a one metre-long platter! Outside there's a laidback, alfresco dining experience where gorgeous views of the cityscape create a lovely backdrop to your meal.

Al Muna   Buffet
Madinat Jumeirah, Al Sufouh 1 04 366 6730
jumeirah.com
Map 1 R4 Metro Mall of the Emirates

Al Muna offers an indulgent buffet of international cuisine, as well as a 24 hour a la carte menu catering to those who want a more personalised experience. Like every other venue in Madinat Jumeirah, it comes in a nice posh package with elegant decor and an inviting terrace to match. Book a table outside for the ever popular Friday brunch and you can observe the abras and dhows drift by along the water while you tuck in.

AOC   French
Sofitel Jumeirah JBR, Marsa Dubai 04 448 4848
sofitel-dubai-jumeirahbeach.com
Map 1 K4 Metro Jumeirah Lakes Towers

The staff are friendly and the venue, especially the terrace, is excellent but you should know that the a la carte menu serves up largely European main courses rather than anything authentically French. The wine list and desserts do their best to return a touch of 'ooh la la' to proceedings.

Aprons & Hammers   Seafood
DIMC Marsa Dubai 04 454 7097
apronsandhammers.com
Map 1 L4 Metro Dubai Marina

Soak up some incredible views on board this traditional dhow – from the dazzling skyscrapers of Marsa Dubai, to the Palm Jumeirah stretching out to sea. A visit here is a true must-do for seafood fans – armed with a wooden hammer and a giant bib, diners are served huge buckets of delicious crab and other fresh catch, and invited to get cracking.

Aquara   Seafood
Marina Yacht Club Marsa Dubai 04 362 7900
dubaimarinayachtclub.com
Map 1 K5 Metro Jumeirah Lakes Towers

Aquara is chic but understated, allowing the views of the marina's skyscrapers and million-dirham yachts to speak for themselves. It specialises in seafood, most of which is served with an Asian twist. Friday brunch is excellent – the centrepiece is the seafood bar with lobster, oysters, prawns, crab, clams, sushi and sashimi. A great terrace too.

Asmak   Seafood
Al Garhoud 04 282 5377
centuryvillage.ae
Map 2 N8 Metro GGICO

Asmak's simple, calm blue and white decor hides a quaint little place serving succulent seafood as well as a variety of hot and cold mezzes. The spicy garlic potatoes are a must-try but best avoided on any sort of romantic outing! Choose between indoor seating or alfresco dining on a beautiful wooden deck.

AZ.U.R   International
Marriott Harbour Marsa Dubai 04 319 4794
azur.dubaimarriottharbourhotel.com
Map 1 L5 Metro Dubai Marina

Boasting a fantastic wooden floored terrace with great views of the marina, AZ.U.R is a popular spot for outdoor dining during the cooler months. The restaurant offers a selection of Spanish, Moroccan, French and Italian inspired chicken, vegetarian, meat and seafood dishes. It's a child-friendly venue too, offering high chairs as well as a kids' menu.

GOING OUT
RESTAURANTS

Ba — Chinese
Fairmont The Palm Nakhlat Jumeira **04 457 3338**
dineatba.com
Map **1 N3** Metro **Nakheel**

Upstairs is a sumptuous lounge serving cocktails topped in gold leaf, while downstairs the vast oriental restaurant sprawls out onto a wonderfully situated terrace with sea views as far as Marsa Dubai. Chefs from all provinces of China showcase their unique skills in a range of Chinese cuisine.

Caramel Restaurant & Lounge — American
DIFC Zaa'beel 2 **04 425 6677**
caramelgroup.com
Map **2 G6** Metro **Financial Centre**

This is where those who work hard, come to play even harder. Stylish wooden furniture spills out from the bar on to the terrace, where trendy cabanas and warm lighting set the mood for stylish lounging. From the mac and cheese to the lobster tacos, expect high quality dishes with American flair. Dress to impress.

Da Gama — International
Al Garhoud **04 282 3636**
Map **2 N8** Metro **GGICO**

The Da Gama menu mixes traditional Portuguese dishes with Mexican favourites and Asian fusion options. Outside is for family dining, but inside is a nightclub style bar complete with dance floor. The tantalising selection of sweet and spicy delights includes edamame, Asian duck salad, miniature burgers, succulent steaks, mixed quesadillas and fajitas. The *espatada* skewers are Portuguese perfection.

The Deck — International
JA Ocean View JBR, Marsa Dubai **04 814 5590**
jaresortshotels.com
Map **1 J4** Metro **Jumeirah Lakes Towers**

Enjoy the panoramic views of The Deck, where the stylish yet relaxed seating area overlooks the Palm Jumeirah and a stunning infinity pool. A tempting selection of bar snacks are available throughout the day – and breakfast is served here too. But the real draw is the a la carte menu of Ocean-meets-Arabic gourmet fare, including authentic Arabic salad, Burrata Caprese, and mains of everything from baked gnocchi to fresh, juicy grilled salmon.

Eauzone — Asian
Al Sufouh 2 **04 399 9999**
oneandonlyresorts.com
Map **1 N5** Metro **Nakheel**

Dine beneath softly lit canopies overlooking a network of waterways for a truly romantic meal. This beachside restaurant has a casual ambience by day and a more stylish feel after sunset. The Thai and Japanese fusion dishes are best accompanied by an unusual sorbet such as chilli and raspberry, or some sake. Groups should try dining at the teppanyaki station, from Dhs.250 per head.

Elia — Greek
Majestic Al Mankhool **04 501 2529**
dubaimajestic.com
Map **2 L4** Metro **Al Fahidi**

Sit inside in the slightly over-air-conditioned dining area or, better still, out on the terrace, which manages to be serene despite its view looking out over Bur Dubai. The selection of Greek dishes is served with zesty olive oils, fluffy breads and includes succulent meatballs and moreish dolma.

Fogueira Restaurant & Lounge — Brazilian
Ramada Plaza Marsa Dubai **04 439 8888**
ramadaplazajbr.com
Map **1 K4** Metro **Jumeirah Lakes Towers**

An authentic Brazilian Churrascaria with daily live entertainment. It's a romantic setting and the terrace has a great view of Marsa Dubai and Palm Jumeirah. When you're ready to eat, turn your card green side up, and the passadores (meat waiters) will serve you. When you are satisfied, flip the disc to the red side.

Luciano's — Italian
Habtoor Grand Marsa Dubai **04 399 5000**
habtoorhotels.com
Map **1 L4** Metro **Dubai Marina**

Traditional and good-quality dishes from across Italy are served at this reasonably priced poolside restaurant, including seafood, meat and pasta. The portions are generous and the starters deserve a

askexplorer.com 391

GOING OUT
RESTAURANTS

special mention. The real stars of the show are the thin-crust pizzas. When the temperature permits, ask for a table outside underneath the fairy light bedecked palm trees.

The Meat Co Steakhouse
Downtown Dubai, Burj Khalifa **04 420 0737**
themeatco.com
Map **2 F6** Metro **Burj Khalifa/Dubai Mall**
While you're choosing the country you'd like your steak to come from, the cut, and how you want it prepared, enjoy the beautiful view of the Burj Khalifa from the terrace. You can't go wrong with anything on the Connoisseur's Choice menu. While it isn't cheap, many consider this one of the best steak joints in the city. There's also a branch at Souk Madinat Jumeirah (04 368 6040).

Meridien Village Terrace Buffet
Le Meridien Al Garhoud **04 702 2455**
meridienvillageterrace-dubai.com
Map **2 N8** Metro **Airport Terminal 1**
Set in the middle of Le Meridien's outdoor dining area, the huge buffet switches nightly between culinary themes including BBQ, Asian and Latino. Only open in winter, this is one of the best buffets in town. The Flames Band serenades diners throughout the evening, and keeps dancers on their feet after dinner.

Olives > p.175 Italian
The Palace At One&Only Royal Mirage Al Sufouh 2
04 399 9999
royalmirage.oneandonlyresorts.com
Map **1 M4** Metro **Nakheel**
There's an air of a riviera coastal cafe at Olives, with its dramatic archways, indoor foliage and white ceramic tiles, as well as a lovely outdoor terrace overlooking the gardens and pool. Pizzas and pastas are the highlight of the Mediterranean menu, but you shouldn't miss the braised lamb shank with roasted garlic salad and an orange rosemary jus – the chef's signature dish. Open for breakfast, lunch and dinner.

Voi Vietnamese
Jumeirah Zabeel Saray Nakhlat Jumeira **04 453 0444**
jumeirah.com
Map **1 L3** Metro **Nakheel**
The focus here is on upscale Vietnamese with French influences, using high quality fresh ingredients. Seafood dishes are particularly impressive and, if you are feeling adventurous, go for the chef's tasting menu. The atmosphere is as opulent as the food, with ornately designed ceilings and walls centred around a crystal chandelier, and the dramatic all-white dining room is straight out of a palatial French film set. Voi is especially suited to a romantic night out, as several candle-lit outdoor tables overlook the resort's grounds.

Watatsumi Japanese
Marsa Dubai **04 399 3373**
watatsumi.ae
Map **1 M4** Metro **Nakheel**
At Watatsumi, you'll find traditional Japanese dishes with a contemporary twist that take you on a culinary journey far beyond the usual sashimi and sushi.

The interior is opulent and the adjoining terrace has a funky vibe, lit by orange lanterns and kept buzzing by the sound of music from nearby Barasti bar. Ample greenery and a balmy sea breeze bring a tropical feel to the evening's festivities. Pair your dishes with Japanese-inspired cocktails or a choice of tasty (and potent) sakes.

Waterfront
Dubai has plenty of coastline which has spawned a clutch of very special beachfront restaurants. There's also a choice of eateries with marina and creek views.

25°55° Cafe Bistro European
Marina Yacht Club Marsa Dubai **04 362 7955**
dubaimarinayachtclub.com
Map **1 K5** Metro **Jumeirah Lakes Towers**
Whether you come to enjoy a pie and pint while watching the big match or for a must-have full-English breakfast after a big night out, this bistro/pub/yacht club restaurant will satisfy your hunger. It's not about the location – although the terrace affords a stunning view overlooking the marina – but rather about the hearty dishes and warm atmosphere.

Al Muntaha

GOING OUT
RESTAURANTS

Al Mansour Dhow — Middle Eastern
Radisson Blu Deira Creek Al Rigga **04 205 7433**
radissonblu.com
Map **2 M5** Metro **Union**
This two-hour creek trip features dinner aboard a traditional dhow operated by Radisson Blu. Great views, atmospheric oud music, a buffet of Middle Eastern and Indian food, and shisha make this a memorable evening. The ship sails at 8.30pm.

Al Muntaha — Mediterranean
Burj Al Arab Umm Suqeim 3 **04 301 7600**
jumeirah.com
Map **1 S4** Metro **Mall of the Emirates**
The breathtaking coastline view from the top of Burj Al Arab goes some way to excusing the grand yet eccentric decor. The Mediterranean menu, with its Atlantic lobster and sweetbread ravioli or 'wild sea bass three-ways', offers a fresh twist on simple flavours and ingredients.

Beach Bar & Grill > p.175 — Seafood
The Palace At One&Only Royal Mirage Al Sufouh 2 **04 399 9999**
royalmirage.oneandonlyresorts.com
Map **1 M4** Metro **Nakheel**
Seafood lovers must take a trip to this opulent, romantic beach bar. There are seafood platters to share, and surf and turf options for people who can't pick just one dish. The chef's recommendation is the cataplana of shellfish – clams, mussels, prawns, scallops and crabs with cooked beef chorizo, tomatoes, vegetables and fresh herbs.

Beach House Cabana — South American
Clubhouse Azraq, Shoreline Apartments Nakhlat Jumeira **04 361 8256**
emiratesleisureretail.com
Map **1 N4** Metro **Nakheel**
Perfect for a laidback evening with friends. Hot and cold tapas, hearty mains, reasonable prices and a good cocktail selection add to the convivial feel at this South American eatery. Devour peri-peri chicken stuffed with sun-blushed tomatoes, served with Mexican rice, or a Caribbean pumpkin and feta cheese salad. Once the sun goes down, salsa music entices diners onto the dancefloor.

Beachcombers — Asian
Jumeirah Beach Hotel Umm Suqeim 3 **04 406 8999**
jumeirah.com
Map **1 S4** Metro **First Gulf Bank**
This breezy shack has an idyllic location right on the beach with fantastic views of the Burj Al Arab from its deck terrace. Expect excellent far eastern buffets with live cooking stations for stir-fries and noodles. The Peking duck, curry hotpots and satay are highly recommended. Kids will love the ice cream machine, while you relax with a sundowner cocktail.

Bistro Madeleine — French
InterContinental Festival City Al Badia, Al Kheeran **04 701 1127**
diningdfc.com
Map **2 M9** Metro **Emirates**
Say au revoir to pretence with affordable, casual dining on the Festival City waterfront promenade. The bistro hits the mark with French classics such as duck confit, escargot and coq au vin. Dine a la carte or enjoy the weekday 'quick lunch' special, or terrific Thursday 'French Night' buffet.

The Boardwalk — International
Creek Golf Club Port Saeed **04 295 6000**
dubaigolf.com
Map **2 M7** Metro **Deira City Centre**
Boardwalk's water views are unmatched as it stands wooden stilts overlooking the creek. The menu features an array of generous and well-presented starters and mains including seafood and vegetarian options. The restaurant doesn't take reservations but you can grab a drink at QD's while you wait.

Bussola — Italian
The Westin Marsa Dubai **04 511 7136**
bussoladubai.com
Map **1 M4** Metro **Nakheel**
Adventurous, delicious Sicilian-influenced pizzas served alfresco on a terrace by the sea – Arabia doesn't get much more Mediterranean than this. Upstairs the open-air deck offers a relaxed atmosphere, with more formality and a fuller menu downstairs. The desserts are excellent whatever floor you're on and the food is certified by the Italian Cuisine Academy.

Honyaki — Japanese
Souk Madinat Al Sufouh 1 **04 366 6730**
jumeirah.com
Map **1 R4** Metro **Mall of the Emirates**
It would be easy for Honyaki to rely purely on its breathtaking views from the terrace overlooking the Madinat amphitheatre and Burj Al Arab, but this authentic Japanese restaurant goes further, preparing its miso, sashimi and maki with delightful twists. The mochi ice cream is a must.

Nomad — Asian
Jumeirah Creekside Al Garhoud **04 230 8571**
jumeirah.com
Map **2 M8** Metro **GGICO**
Set by Dubai Creek, Nomad has romantic waterside dining, cosy fireside lounging and an upbeat DJ. Starters include sushi and seafood tempura, and favourites such as nasi goreng and Singapore noodles complement a

askexplorer.com   393

GOING OUT
RESTAURANTS

number of a la carte meat and fish dishes. The venue also hosts an Asian tapas wine bar, New York-style deli, an Asian pool grill, and a dim sum trolley.

The Observatory International
Marriott Harbour Marsa Dubai **04 319 4795**
observatory.dubaimarriottharbourhotel.com
Map **1 L5** Metro **Dubai Marina**
It's all about the views at this atmospheric 52nd floor gastro-lounge. Spectacular 360° vistas over the marina and Palm Jumeirah accompany the concise (but tasty) menu with excellent cocktails. Come just before sunset then stay for the evening.

Royal Orchid Thai
Al Badia, Al Kheeran **04 232 8585**
theroyalorchid.com
Map **2 M9** Metro **Emirates**
Similar to its JBR counterpart, the Royal Orchid serves Thai, Chinese, and a few Mongolian dishes. The exterior is classically Thai inspired, with comfy loungers on the terrace decking. The inside is slightly too brightly lit to be romantic but great for a meal with friends.

Villa Beach Mediterranean
Jumeirah Beach Hotel Umm Suqeim 3 **04 406 8999**
jumeirah.com
Map **1 S4** Metro **First Gulf Bank**
With a prime location on the sand just a stone's throw from the Burj Al Arab, you can dine alfresco and appreciate the architectural wonder much more than if you were inside it. Villa Beach's simple wooden beach-hut decor has an almost Polynesian vibe although the menu is purely Mediterranean. This is a good choice for romantic reverie or to drop the jaws of out-of-towners. The service is swift and the dishes are presented with a finesse befitting the surroundings. The scenery doesn't come cheap, but the food is almost worth the price.

Brunch

A Friday ritual, all-you-can-eat (and drink) brunches are infamous in Dubai – you may struggle to find room for everything on offer.

Al Badia Golf Club By InterContinental Dubai Festival City International
Al Badia, Al Kheeran **04 601 0101**
albadiagolfclub.ae
Map **2 M10** Metro **Emirates**
Blades at Al Badia puts a Dubai spin on the traditional picnic and serves up a smorgasbord of delights in a casual, family-friendly brunch. Find a shady spot on the grassy lawns overlooking the golf course and lake, relax on the blanket around a low level table, and work your way through a heavily laden traditional wicker hamper; from the picnic staples of scotch eggs and pork pate to the more contemporary offerings of lentil crackers and fresh crab meat – it's a feast. Kids also get their own miniature hamper, packed with sandwiches, treats and mini pots of bubbles to pass the afternoon away. Leave room for the BBQ.

The Observatory

GOING OUT
RESTAURANTS

Al Qasr   International
Madinat Jumeirah Al Sufouh 1 04 366 8888
jumeirah.com
Map **1 R5** Metro **Mall of the Emirates**
The brunch at Al Qasr attracts the glitzier end of the brunching spectrum and has won numerous 'best brunch in Dubai' awards. Three ground floor restaurants offer an impressive array of delicately constructed dishes, which you can wash down with a deliciously dangerous mix of caipirinhas and mojitos. Face painting will keep children occupied.

Blurring The Boundaries
In the same vein as its counterparts in Istanbul, Amsterdam, Los Angeles, San Francisco and London, the ultra-cool Supperclub (04 451 1100, supperclub.com) offers more than just fine dining. This is a cultural experience, founded by artists, that also functions as a cocktail bar, club, gallery and performance art venue. You literally kick off your shoes and eat while lounging on a large white bed. The food and cocktails shout 'innovation', the vibe is relaxed, and you never know what kind of entertainment will appear next. Find it at Zabeel Saray, West Crescent, Palm Jumeirah. And of course, being the Palm, the sea is never far away.

The China Club   Chinese
Radisson Blu Deira Creek Al Rigga 04 205 7033
radissonblu.com
Map **2 M5** Metro **Union**
A chic space with subtle touches of authenticity tucked away in the Radisson Blu, the China Club serves up tasty recognisable favourites as well as new creations. The excellent Peking duck is theatrically carved tableside. It's also one of the best value Friday brunches – if you're not interested in sampling the house beverages or bubbly – with an all-you-can-eat deal for Dhs.140 per head excluding alcohol.

El Sur   Spanish
The Westin Marsa Dubai 04 399 7700
elsurdubai.com
Map **1 M5** Metro **Nakheel**
The Westin's newest dining spot serves up contemporary Spanish fare at a Saturday brunch that's perfect for ladies who lunch. Offering a more relaxed meal on a Mediterranean-style terrace, plates of tapas from traditional meats, breads and olives to calamari, paella and prawns, are all brought to the table. Order your main courses, choosing from a selection of Spanish-style fish, meat and vegetarian delights, and then squeeze in a taster of the delicious desserts. The all-inclusive menu also includes a rather upmarket choice of drinks and cocktails, including the restaurant's popular free-flowing sangria.

Farriers   International
Meydan Nadd Al Shiba 1 04 381 3111
meydanhotels.com
Map **2 E10** Metro **Business Bay**
Does Dubai really need another posh brunch? Yes, it does, if it's from the Meydan's stylish restaurant Farriers, with its free-flowing bubbly, live jazz and a kids' club. On other days, dine in the bright, airy interior or on the track-side terrace. Sample delicious signature dishes courtesy of vast interactive buffet stations. Once you're done, head for the hotel's Shiba bar, where brunchers can enjoy discount on drinks.

Flow Kitchen   International
Fairmont The Palm Nakhlat Jumeira 04 457 3457
fairmont.com
Map **1 N3** Metro **Nakheel**
An innovative brunch concept where waiters bring tasters to your table, such as the unique vegetable salad, crafted to look like a miniature garden complete with chocolate soil. You can also order classics such as eggs Benedict from the menu, and finish off your leisurely brunch with dessert. Kids will love the interactive juice bar.

Imperium   French
Jumeirah Zabeel Saray Nakhlat Jumeira 04 453 0444
jumeirah.com
Map **1 L3** Metro **Nakheel**
Located in the opulent and ever-impressive Jumeirah Zabeel Saray, the brunch at Imperium is an altogether refined affair. While the free flowing bubbly and mixed drinks are undoubtedly delicious, the emphasis here is firmly on the food, with a host of French-inspired dishes and a delicious selection of seafood. There's also a hot food and carving grill, as well as a tempting desserts station. One for those in search of a less rowdy, crowded weekend.

Mazina   International
The Address Dubai Marina Marsa Dubai 04 888 3444
theaddress.com
Map **1 K5** Metro **Dubai Marina**
The Saturday brunch at Mazina is perfect for families. Enjoy a long, hearty lunch while the young ones jump on the bouncy castle or get competitive on the Wii. Choose from never-ending salad options, dim sum, a variety of roasts, and a delicious array of desserts.

The MED   Mediterranean
Media One Al Sufouh 2 04 4271000
Map **1 M5** Metro **Nakheel**
On the eighth floor of Media City's latest hotspot, The MED serves up a fun, energetic and good value menu of Mediterranean classics, served with enough Gallic flare to reveal the chef's nationality. Head here on Fridays for a lively brunch.

GOING OUT
RESTAURANTS

MORE Cafe — International
The Dubai Mall Downtown Dubai, Burj Khalifa
04 339 8934
morecafe.biz
Map **2 F7** Metro **Burj Khalifa/Dubai Mall**
For an alcohol-free brunch and no Saturday hangover, head here. Its Gold and Diamond Park branches serve brunch from 11am-4pm for Dhs.95. The huge portions of home-made, wholesome food could set you up for a full day of swimming, cycling and other activities – all of which you will probably not get around to doing.

Seafire > *p.275* — Steakhouse
Atlantis Nakhlat Jumeira 04 426 2626
Map **1 N1** Metro **Nakheel**
Dinner at this friendly New York-style eatery starts with extravagant, delicious appetisers – just try to resist the succulent fillet or seafood grill. The Atlantis strip sirloin is one of the finest steaks you'll ever taste, and the sides are not to be missed. Seafire is mainly for beef lovers, but it does offer other meats as well as various vegetarian options.

Do You Drunch?
If you think brunch is simply a portmanteau of 'breakfast' and 'lunch', you clearly haven't been in Dubai that long. Here, 'brunch' has evolved one step further into 'drunch', an amalgamation of 'drinking' and 'brunch'. The act of 'drunching' is a hobby, a social skill, a weekend institution – the calorific glue that holds the weekend together. All for a set price. So raise your fork, pop your cork, and get stuck in.

Spectrum On One — International
Fairmont Trade Center 1 04 311 8316
Map **2 J5** Metro **World Trade Centre**
Divided into dishes from some of the world's most delicious regions – India, China, Thailand, Europe, Japan and Arabia – you need a good half hour to absorb the menu. The surroundings are spacious, with room for groups to mingle and a tucked-away bar. Spectrum On One also boasts a Thursday night 'Dupper' – dinner and supper, with free-flowing beverages and live entertainment.

The Thai Kitchen — Thai
Park Hyatt Port Saeed 04 317 2221
restaurants.dubai.hyatt.com
Map **2 M7** Metro **Deira City Centre**
The Thai Kitchen's menu might be on the small side but there's a decent range of Thai delicacies prepared to maximise the rich, authentic flavours. The decor is stylish and modern, portions are perfect for sharing and the Friday brunch, from 12.30pm to 4pm, is a delight – more refined than most.

Yalumba — International
Le Meridien Al Garhoud 04 702 2328
yalumba-dubai.com
Map **2 N8** Metro **Airport Terminal 1**
This Friday feast consists of a grand selection of seafood, international buffet options and desserts, complemented by four types of world-class champagne. At Dhs.499 per person, it certainly isn't the cheapest option; plus it is disappointing that the choice is not available for those who would prefer to dine sans alcohol. Diners can get quite rowdy after a drink or five.

Zuma — Japanese
Gate Village DIFC, Zaa'beel 2 04 425 5660
zumarestaurant.com
Map **2 G6** Metro **Financial Centre**
Despite being a perfect way to sample this sushi restaurant's legendary menu, the Zuma brunch is certainly not the place for you if you are looking for a smash and grab all-you-can-eat (and drink) affair. Dining is a combination of a la carte and buffet, and you are unlikely to end the afternoon having to trade up a clothing size. Delicate, stylish and sophisticated are the overwhelming themes in this trendy eatery.

Celebrity Chef
Big name celebrity chefs rub shoulders with Michelin-starred culinary giants in Dubai, including the likes of Marco Pierre White and Sanjeev Kapoor.

Frankie's — Italian
JBR, Marsa Dubai 04 399 4311
Map **1 K5** Metro **Jumeirah Lakes Towers**
Grab a vodka Martini and pizza in the bar at this stylish joint, co-owned by Frankie Dettori and Marco Pierre White, then head into the main restaurant for classic Italian dishes and new favourites such as duck ravioli. With its sultry interior, pianist and good quality Friday brunch, this is a classy establishment with a welcoming vibe.

Jamie's Italian — Italian
Al Badia, Al Kheeran 04 232 9969
jamieoliver.com
Map **2 L9** Metro **Emirates**
Unlike many celeb chefs before him, Jamie Oliver has opted not to chase after the big bucks, but has instead gone for the mid-range and family markets with Jamie's Italian. The restaurant is both chic and homely with a mezzanine level, a main dining room and a cosy terrace. The menu features some outstanding antipasti and a great selection of tasty traditional and innovative pastas. Newly opened at the end of 2013 is Jamie's Italian in Jumeirah Beach Hotel.

GOING OUT
RESTAURANTS

Khazana   Indian
Oud Metha **04 336 0061**
khazanadubai.com
Map **2 L6** Metro **Oud Metha**

Indian celebrity chef Sanjeev Kapoor's eatery specialises in cuisine from north India. Try the grilled tandoori seafood and gravy-based dishes, as well as the kebabs and Anglo-Indian novelties such as 'British raj railroad curry'.

Maya Modern Mexican Kitchen & Lounge   Mexican
Le Royal Meridien Marsa Dubai **04 316 5550**
richardsandoval.com/mayadubai
Map **1 L4** Metro **Dubai Marina**

Maya – from US chef Richard Sandoval – is a standout in Dubai. The food is a contemporary take on the dishes of rural Mexico. Forget fajitas. Dive into lobster with chilli chipotle or langoustine tacos. The *crepas con cajeta* is super sumptuous and the lovely terrace is perfect for margaritas.

Nobu > p.275   Japanese
Atlantis Nakhlat Jumeira **04 426 2626**
atlantisthepalm.com
Map **1 N1** Metro **Nakheel**

Nobuyuki Matsuhisa, the godfather of sushi, has upped the ante for Japanese food aficionados with his Dubai offering. You'll love the exceptional quality, attention to detail and huge menu of sushi, sashimi and tempura. Despite its reputation for exclusivity, Nobu is not restricted to celebrities – as long as you can get a reservation.

Reflets Par Pierre Gagnaire   French
InterContinental Festival City Al Badia, Al Kheeran **04 701 1127**
diningdfc.com
Map **2 L9** Metro **Emirates**

From the Michelin-starred grandfather of molecular gastronomy, Pierre Gagnaire, comes a magical, imaginative and highly conceptual dining experience incorporating French cuisine. Bold purple carpet and pink chandeliers along with floor-to-ceiling mirrors and white tablecloths are the backdrop to a menu that strives to be a work of art. The romantic waterfront setting is the perfect place to sample wines from the specialist cellar.

Rhodes In Residence   European
Grosvenor House Marsa Dubai **04 317 6000**
rhodesinresidence.com
Map **1 L5** Metro **Dubai Marina**

This elegant and refined restaurant focuses on the best of British cuisine in all its calorific glory. With the amuse bouche and petit fours (delightful twists on British fare such as tomato soup and scones) your meal will undoubtedly stretch long, especially as you'll need time to let all the delicious heavy dishes digest. Desserts are classically simple and taste divine.

Ronda Locatelli > p.275   Italian
Atlantis Nakhlat Jumeira **04 426 2626**
atlantisthepalm.com
Map **1 N1** Metro **Nakheel**

Giorgio Locatelli's cavernous restaurant can seat hundreds of diners in its raised alcoves or at tables surrounding a huge stone-built wood-fired oven. There's a charmingly rustic vibe and the casual menu offers a good range of authentic starters, pasta and mains, as well as a selection of small dishes that are perfect for sharing. A great comfort food venue with top quality dishes.

Signature By Sanjeev Kapoor   Indian
Melia Al Raffa **04 386 8111**
melia.com
Map **2 K4** Metro **Al Karama**

The aptly named Signature, Sanjeev Kapoor's latest Dubai restaurant, bears all the hallmarks of its progressive and eclectic chef, with traditional Indian dishes given an innovative makeover. Samosas and bhajis take a back seat to such modern delights as tandoori wasabi lobster, basil pepper hammour tikka, honey mustard chicken chat puffs or paneer tikka with asparagus fritters and avocado mousse. Main courses continue the trend. It's traditional but with a twist – so expect to find paneer cooked in a butternut pumpkin and tomato sauce, goat shanks simmered in kashmiri and chilli onion gravy, and mutton cubes fried in pepper. Every inch the fine dining restaurant.

Ronda Locatelli

askexplorer.com   397

GOING OUT
RESTAURANTS

STAY By Yannick Alleno — French
One&Only The Palm Nakhlat Jumeira 04 440 1030
Map **1 L3** Metro **Nakheel**

Yannick Alleno, with three Michelin stars to his name, has brought his contemporary French restaurant STAY to Dubai's dining scene. Located in the opulent One&Only The Palm, the emphasis is on impeccably selected ingredients cooked to perfection. Seasons dictate the menu but signature dishes are constant; the Black Angus beef fillet 'cafe de Paris' is recommended. Leave enough room for something sweet – the open Pastry Library allows you to participate in the dessert making process.

Drinking Water

Bottled water seems to rocket in price in the five-star venues, and if you ask for water you'll often be given an imported brand, costing up to Dhs.40 a bottle. You should specify 'local' water when ordering, but even then you can expect to pay Dhs.10 or Dhs.20 for a bottle of still water that costs less than Dhs.2 in the supermarket.

Wheeler's — Seafood
Gate Village Trade Center 2 04 386 0899
wheelersdubai.com
Map **2 G6** Metro **Financial Centre**

This trendy Marco Pierre White eatery serves perfect seafood and posh British nosh to happy post-work revellers in DIFC. With a buzzing, post-work drinks atmosphere, this is a good place to head with friends for a rowdy supper. There are some British classics, such as beer battered fish and triple cooked chips, as well as enough vegetarian and carnivorous options to keep most diners happy. But the menu here is mainly about seafood and, under the helm of the celebrity chef, it is guaranteed to delight.

Cheap & Cheerful

There's a huge mix of chain and independent restaurants in the city where two people eat well for less than Dhs.100 – perfect for a casual bite.

Al Safadi Restaurant — Middle Eastern
Al Kawakeb Bldg, Shk Zayed Rd Trade Center 2
04 343 5333
alsafadi.ae
Map **2 G5** Metro **Financial Centre**

Function rules over form at big and busy Al Safadi, but it's the high quality Arabic food that people come here for. Street-side tables are perfect for more relaxed dining, shisha and people watching. Another branch is on Al Rigga Road in Deira (04 227 9922).

Aryaas — Indian
Al Nakheel Bldg, Zabeel Rd Al Karama 04 335 5776
Map **2 L6** Metro **Al Karama**

This Indian chain has served excellent fare since 1959, and, despite its austere decor, the food is excellent. The house speciality is thali, small pots of different flavours into which you dip naan bread or rice. Around Dhs.15 will buy enough to fill you up for the day.

Automatic — Middle Eastern
Beach Centre Jumeira 1 04 349 4888
Map **2 G4** Metro **Emirates Towers**

This popular chain continues to serve high quality Arabic food in various locations in Dubai. The vast range of mezze is accompanied by mountainous portions of salad, and grilled meat, fish and kebabs. The atmosphere is minimalist but clean and bright, with family-friendly amenities and good service.

Benihana — Japanese
Amwaj Rotana JBR, Marsa Dubai 04 428 2000
rotana.com
Map **1 K4** Metro **Jumeirah Lakes Towers**

Dining at Benihana is a pleasure. The quality is excellent and the prices are great. The terrace is lovely, or sit at the teppanyaki grills where the chefs cook your food in front of you, with liberal amounts of cheeky banter and utensil trickery. Also available at Al Bustan Rotana (04 282 0000).

Bistro Domino — French
Ibis Deira City Centre Port Saeed 04 292 5000
ibishotel.com
Map **2 N7** Metro **Deira City Centre**

A hearty selection of dishes is served here that will leave you warm, satisfied and wishing you were tucking into your meal in a rustic chateau. The tempting menu is an authentic mix of typical French dishes (including deliciously buttery escargot) and fabulously rich desserts.

The Bombay — Indian
Marco Polo Al Muteena 04 272 0000
marcopolohotel.net
Map **2 P5** Metro **Salah Al Din**

The Bombay is an unassuming restaurant that packs quite a punch and is a favourite destination for Indian food lovers in the know. The dishes are well priced, generous and authentic, and the laid-back atmosphere lends itself to a convivial night out with friends.

Channels — International
TECOM, Al Thanyah 1 04 435 0201
rotana.com
Map **1 P6** Metro **Dubai Internet City**

This all-day diner makes up for rather drab surroundings and a flat atmosphere with its great

398   Dubai Explorer

GOING OUT
RESTAURANTS

value buffets four nights a week. The spread is staggering, the desserts in particular, and the price (from Dhs.179 including house drinks) makes it a great option for big groups.

Chef Lanka Sri Lankan
Nr LuLu Supermarket Al Karama **04 335 3050**
Map **2 L6** Metro **Al Karama**
This is a smart, clean, Sri Lankan restaurant with inexpensive, tasty food. The lunch buffet is just Dhs.8 and dinner costs Dhs.20. Alternatively, you can order a la carte for your desired spiciness. The excellent king fish curry and koththu roti (chopped roti bread stir-fried with chicken, leeks, tomatoes and carrots), come highly recommended.

Chili's > p.xii American
Nr Welcare Hospital Al Garhoud **04 282 8484**
chilisuae.com
Map **2 N7** Metro **GGICO**
Known all around the world and all over Dubai, Chili's delivers its winning formula for inexpensive, all-American tucker in generous portions and in family friendly surroundings. Takeaway and home delivery (600 561 112) are also available. See the website for locations throughout Dubai.

Street Food
Shawarma is a popular local snack consisting of rolled pita bread filled with lamb or chicken carved from a rotating spit, vegetables and tahina sauce. You'll see countless roadside stands offering shawarma for as little as Dhs.3 each, and they make a great alternative to the usual fast food staples. In residential areas, the small cluster of shops beside a mosque is often a good bet to find your local shawarma outlet. These cafes and stands usually sell other dishes, such as falafel (or *ta'amiya*), which are small savoury balls of deep-fried chickpeas, also sold separately or in a pita bread sandwich. Many offer freshly squeezed fruit juices for around Dhs.10. For a really unique version, check out Al Shera'a Fisheries Centre on Al Muraqqabat Road (04 227 1803) – the only place in town that offers fish shawarmas.

Lemongrass Thai
Nr Lamcy Plaza Oud Metha **04 334 2325**
lemongrassrestaurants.com
Map **2 K6** Metro **Oud Metha**
One of the better – and cheapest – Thai restaurants in Dubai, the menu at Lemongrass offers a typical range of decently executed Siamese dishes served in a casual dining atmosphere. There's no alcohol, but the fruity mocktails compensate. The setting is bright, inviting and comfortable, and the service unobtrusive. Also at Ibn Battuta Mall (04 368 5616).

Mannaland Korean Restaurant Korean
Al Mina Rd Madinat Dubai Al Melaheyah **04 345 1300**
Map **2 J4** Metro **Al Jafiliya**
A real find, for a truly unique Dubai dining experience, this Korean restaurant in Satwa offers traditional floor seating and excellent, authentic food cooked right there at your table. This is the place to try *kimchi* – a dish made of fermented vegetables, said to be a superfood. Wash it all down with a teapot of 'special brew'. Great value too.

Nando's International
Nr Four Points Sheraton Trade Center 1 **04 321 2000**
nandos.ae
Map **2 G6** Metro **Financial Centre**
Famous for its tasty flame-grilled chicken, Nando's has branches across the city, including The Dubai Mall, Greens and Novotel Suites Al Barsha. Delivering the same delicious Afro-Portuguese peri-peri chicken that is a trademark of Nando's across the world, it's a firm family favourite The good news is they even deliver too, so if you want your chicken to come to you, call for delivery on 600 542 525.

Pax Italian
Dusit Thani Trade Center 2 **04 343 3333**
dusit.com
Map **2 G6** Metro **Burj Khalifa/Dubai Mall**
Pax does traditional Italian dishes in less than traditional sizes to give punters a pick 'n' mix of tastes. The style is called bocconcini (little delicacies), and with appetisers starting at Dhs.15, and most mains costing less than Dhs.70, a hearty feed is not prohibitively expensive. There's also an extensive wine list.

Smiling BKK Thai
Al Wasl Rd Al Wasl **04 349 6677**
Map **2 E5** Metro **Burj Khalifa/Dubai Mall**
This outstanding Thai pad near Safa Park is a rare thing: great food topped with good humour and superb service. The cheekily named dishes are reasonable at around Dhs.30, but with gossip mag pages for place mats and theme nights such as 'sing for your supper', it's the spirit that sets Smiling BKK apart. Check out its Facebook page for details of the hilarious menu.

Tagpuan Filipino
Karama Complex Al Karama **04 337 3959**
Map **2 K6** Metro **Al Karama**
Tagpuan serves home-style Filipino cooking at great prices. The tiny tables inside this miniscule eatery fill up quickly, but the outside area on the terrace offers more space. Come here to try simple but tasty versions of Filipino home favourites including *adobong pusit* (squid), fried *tilapia* (fish) or *pinakbet* (mixed vegetables).

GOING OUT
RESTAURANTS

Family Friendly

Family is a huge part of Dubai life and many restaurants offer kids' menus, high chairs, changing facilities and child-friendly entertainment.

A La Grand   European
Grand Excelsior Al Barsha 1 **04 444 9999**
grandexcelsior.ae
Map **1 R7** Metro **Mall of the Emirates**
A La Grand offers a refined atmosphere; while it's not Michelin-starred stuff, the menu offers wholesome European food made using excellent ingredients and delivered to the table in a professional but friendly manner. The heartier meat-based mains are tasty and generous. The restaurant is open all day, has a good children's menu and also offers a good brunch.

Applebee's   American
Shk Issa Tower Trade Center 1 **04 343 7755**
applebees.com
Map **2 H6** Metro **Financial Centre**
This restaurant has everything you'd expect of the crowd-pleasing chain – friendly staff, a lively atmosphere and a familiar menu of kid-friendly favourites. It's easy to keep the whole clan with Applebee's huge portions of Tex-Mex fare, burgers, and other crowd pleasers. Wash it all down with an Oreo milkshake. The big screen TVs, and great kids' and dessert menus make this a winning choice for lunch or dinner.

Blades   International
Al Badia Golf Club Al Badia, Al Kheeran **04 601 0101**
albadiagolfclub.ae
Map **2 M10** Metro **Emirates**
Delicious Asian noodles, steaks and tasting platters feature prominently in this fine dining eatery that also makes children feel welcome with a healthy kids' menu and colouring books. Diners can look out over the golf course and its picturesque waterfalls, and during the cooler months adults can enjoy a shisha on the terrace. Excellent service for all ages and not a chicken nugget or plastic toy in sight.

Carnevale   Italian
Jumeirah Beach Hotel Umm Suqeim 3 **04 406 8999**
jumeirah.com
Map **1 S4** Metro **First Gulf Bank**
This family-friendly, award-winning Italian offers upmarket Italian food, swift service and views of the Burj Al Arab from the adjoining indoor terrace. Dishes include home-made fettuccine, served with garlic prawns, asparagus, tomato and fresh basil and other traditional favourites. Despite its exclusive, Venetian-themed interior, families and children are welcome and well catered for.

The Farm   International
Nr Falcon City Al Barari, Wadi Al Safa 3 **04 392 5660**
thefarmdubai.com
Map **2 A13**
Located within the new uber-luxurious Al Barari residential area, and hidden in an oasis of running water, frangipani trees and sprawling greenery, The Farm serves wholesome, tasty treats. From sensational seafood creations such as saffron shrimp curry and to marvellous meat feasts like rib eye steak and honey glazed duck, pretty much every palate is catered for.

Johnny Rockets   American
Juma Al Majid Center Jumeira 1 **04 344 7859**
johnnyrockets.com
Map **2 H4** Metro **Emirates Towers**
This 1950s inspired American diner, with its classic decor, red vinyl booths and jukeboxes, transforms a casual family meal into a novelty experience. Fresh burgers, great milkshakes, reasonable prices, and impromptu outpourings of dance to Staying Alive by friendly, bow-tied staff will brighten up anybody's evening. See the website for other locations.

La Veranda   Italian
Jumeirah Beach Hotel Umm Suqeim 3 **04 406 8999**
jumeirah.com
Map **1 S4** Metro **First Gulf Bank**
This cosy restaurant right on the beach serves large portions of inexpensive pizza, pasta and seafood with marina views. Children are well catered for with typical treats like burgers and fish fingers on the menu.

Living Rooms Video Games Cafe   Cafe
Al Badia, Al Kheeran **04 232 9291**
livingroomscafe.com
Map **2 M9** Metro **Emirates**
Gamers will love this: state-of-the-art video game systems and the latest games to play on Sony Playstation®, Nintendo Wii or Microsoft XBOX. Simply book one of the gaming rooms, plug in and battle it out with your friends as if you were in your own living room. For old school, pre-Playstation® fun, you can also play chess, Monopoly, Scrabble, Risk or dominos instead. Fizzy drinks and snacks are on the menu.

Max's Restaurant   Filipino
Khalid Bin Al Waleed Rd Al Karama **04 325 7797**
maxschicken.com
Map **2 L5** Metro **BurJuman**
This family-friendly diner is a firm favourite with the Filipino community and the food is plentiful and tasty. Max's serves up favourites such as fried chicken served with rice or kamote fries (yummy sweet potato fries). The menu also boasts traditional dishes such as kare-kare (oxtail and tripe stew) and lumpiang ubod (crab meat sauteed with fresh coconut).

GOING OUT
RESTAURANTS

Mosaico — Italian
Emirates Towers Trade Center 2 **04 319 8088**
jumeirah.com
Map **2 H6** Metro **Financial Centre**
Open 24 hours a day, Mosaico blends Italian flavours with Spanish flamboyance. The Mediterranean buffet incorporates freshly prepared tapas, pastas and pizzas made to order, and honey-drizzled profiteroles. There's a special combo menu for kids too.

Orchid Restaurant — International
Ramada Downtown Downtown Dubai, Burj Khalifa **04 330 7300**
ramadadowntowndubai.com
Map **2 F6** Metro **Burj Khalifa/Dubai Mall**
For diners looking to escape the shopping frenzy of The Dubai Mall, Orchid offers up international dishes from the hotel's in-room dining menu. Tucked away on the second floor, the restaurant has indoor and outdoor poolside seating – both with ample flat screen TVs. While not a destination in its own right, Orchid does give neighbourhood diners a good meal away from the crowds.

Peppercrab — Asian
Grand Hyatt Umm Hurair 2 **04 317 2222**
restaurants.dubai.hyatt.com
Map **2 L8** Metro **Dubai Healthcare City**
If you're looking for the ultimate Singaporean gastronomic experience, Peppercrab won't disappoint. You can even watch the chef in action in the kitchen. Order a smaller portion for children, who can enjoy the kids' club during the meal. The restaurant's famous chilli pepper crab remains a must-try and the wine selection is generous.

Planet Hollywood — American
Umm Hurair 2 **04 324 4777**
planethollywoodintl.com
Map **2 L7** Metro **Dubai Healthcare City**
With bright colours, lots of space and friendly staff, this is a popular place to take the kids. The menu features huge, American-style portions, a kids' menu, plus a Friday brunch with movies, toys and face painting.

Ranches Restaurant & Bar — International
Arabian Ranches, Wadi Al Safa 6 **04 360 7835**
arabianranchesgolfdubai.com
Map **1 Q13**
Ranches serves unpretentious fare in comfortable surroundings, with a focus on traditional British dishes. The outdoor terrace offers a more intimate dining experience overlooking the course. Tuesday is a popular quiz night, and there are themed buffets during the week.

Ruby Tuesday — American
The Dubai Mall Downtown Dubai, Burj Khalifa **04 434 1442**
binhendi.com
Map **2 F7** Metro **Burj Khalifa/Dubai Mall**
High quality Angus beef burgers and steaks are the speciality, and the affordable menu also includes ribs and seafood. There's a salad bar and kids' menu too.

Peppercrab

GOING OUT
RESTAURANTS

Spice Island — Buffet
Al Muteena **04 262 5555**
Map **2 P5** Metro **Abu Baker Al Siddique**
A trip to the Spice Island buffet is suitably informal and really good fun. Be entertained by a singing trio as you agonise over which cuisine you are going to choose. There's a choice of alcoholic and non-alcoholic packages, and the kids can hang out in the play area.

Thyme Restaurant — Mediterranean
JBR, Marsa Dubai **04 315 4200**
thethymerestaurant.com
Map **1 K4** Metro **Dubai Marina**
Think heavy wood, cast iron fittings, chalk boards, open kitchens and oversized wine glasses. This Mediterranean brasserie plays host to families, couples and groups of friends, all tucking in with gusto. There's even a kids' corner with Wii station and toys.

Hidden Gems
Perhaps not so much 'hidden' as less well-known or talked about on Dubai's dining circuit, these restaurants still deliver some fantastic dining options.

Al Dahleez — Middle Eastern
Umm Hurair 2 **04 324 3000**
alboom.ae
Map **2 L8** Metro **Al Jadaf**
This cavernous shisha cafe with juices and Arabic grills is always packed. Al Dahleez serves some of the best shisha in Dubai, and boasts an extensive menu. Its bizarre, faux-cavern interior is a great place to spend a few hours playing cards or backgammon. A great place for a dose of Emirati authenticity.

Amala — Indian
Jumeirah Zabeel Saray Nakhlat Jumeira **04 453 0444**
jumeirah.com
Map **1 L3** Metro **Nakheel**
This elegant restaurant serves authentic North Indian cuisine focusing on contemporary Mughalai curries, tandoori and biryani dishes. The service is attentive and the a la carte menu is great value for money.

Armani/Amal — Indian
Armani Downtown Dubai, Burj Khalifa **04 888 3888**
dubai.armanihotels.com
Map **2 F6** Metro **Burj Khalifa/Dubai Mall**
With its open kitchen and vaulted framework, this award-winning restaurant evokes a hip nightspot in a converted Indian marketplace. The high-end Indian cuisine is vibrant. Outside, the terrace is a magical spot with views of the Burj Khalifa tower and the perfect spot to watch the Dubai Fountain light show.

Asado — South American
The Palace Downtown Downtown Dubai, Burj Khalifa **04 888 3444**
theaddress.com
Map **2 F6** Metro **Burj Khalifa/Dubai Mall**
A combination of moody lighting, passionate music, and a meat lover's dream menu cement Asado's position as a steakhouse to be reckoned with. Excellent meat and an enormous wine selection, with terrace views of Burj Khalifa thrown in, make this Argentinean restaurant something special.

Asha's — Indian
Umm Hurair 2 **04 324 4100**
wafirestaurants.com
Map **2 L7** Metro **Dubai Healthcare City**
This is an atmospheric Indian eatery run by Indian superstar Asha Bhosle, who has clearly put a lot of love into this restaurant. Beautifully decorated, the quality of the atmospheric interior is equalled by the eclectic menu, which includes Indian classics, Asha's signature dishes, and some fusion choices. There are great cocktails too.

Bastakiah Nights — Middle Eastern
Al Fahidi Neighbourhood Al Souk Al Kabeer **04 353 7772**
bastakiah.com
Map **2 M4** Metro **Al Fahidi**
This is a magical place celebrating local cuisine and culture, and a good spot to take visitors. The venue offers a perfect amalgamation of great location and delectable food. Choose from the fixed menus or a la carte offerings – there's no alcohol on the menu, but you'd be a fool to let that put you off.

Blue Elephant — Thai
Al Bustan Rotana Al Garhoud **04 282 0000**
blueelephant.com/dubai
Map **2 N7** Metro **GGICO**
This stalwart of Dubai's Thai restaurant scene has changed little in its 15 years. If it isn't broke, why fix it? The food is excellent; Blue Elephant sticks to what it knows – pad thai, curries, and dim sum – plus adds more unusual options such as fresh lime sea bass.

Blue Rain — Thai
Ritz-Carlton DIFC Zaa'beel 2 **04 372 2323**
ritzcarlton.com
Map **2 G6** Metro **Financial Centre**
A spectacular waterfall on the building's exterior makes Blue Rain an impressive sight to behold. This fine-dining Thai restaurant offers dishes not found elsewhere in Dubai, priced from affordable to extravagant. A more unusual dish is red curry Wagyu beef – and everything is light, delicate and bursting with flavour.

GOING OUT
RESTAURANTS

Center Cut — Steakhouse
Ritz-Carlton DIFC Zaa'beel 2 **04 372 2222**
ritzcarlton.com
Map **2 G6** Metro **Financial Centre**

Center Cut's first impression of austerity is offset by friendly staff and an attractive menu. This is a meat-lover's paradise. Appetisers include salmon, scallops, foie gras and oysters but your main is all about meat. Choose from Australian or US cuts, add cocktails, wines, desserts and cheeses, and you're done.

El Malecon — Cuban
Dubai Marine Beach Resort Jumeira 1 **04 346 1111**
dxbmarine.com
Map **2 H4** Metro **World Trade Centre**

Graffiti-covered turquoise walls and low lighting create a sultry Cuban atmosphere that builds up during the evening, helped along by live music and salsa dancers. Big windows overlook the glowing Dubai Marine lagoon. Malecon's doors are constantly swinging; it's a great place to start or end the night with Cuban food and a superb drinks selection.

Fish Market — Seafood
Radisson Blu Deira Creek Al Rigga **04 222 7171**
radissonblu.com
Map **2 M5** Metro **Baniyas Square**

This novel restaurant lets diners pick raw ingredients from a large bank of fresh, raw seafood and vegetables. Choose anything from tiger prawns and Omani lobster to red snapper, and then request your cooking style preference. The food is not outstanding but the concept is entertaining.

Gaucho — Argentinean
DIFC Zaa'beel 2 **04 422 7898**
gauchorestaurants.co.uk
Map **2 G6** Metro **Financial Centre**

London favourite Gaucho is ultra-modern chic meets with cowhide upholstery. Upstairs is home to a lounge bar for informal dining, while downstairs is the restaurant. The service is impeccable, thanks to highly knowledgeable staff, and so is the food – try the Tira De Ancho, a spiral cut to share, slow grilled with chimchurri. A perfect dining experience.

Manga Sushi — Japanese
Jumeira 2 **04 342 8300**
mangasushi.ae
Map **2 D4** Metro **Business Bay**

As the name suggests, this Japanese eatery is all about Japan's cult comics, from the large screen showing Manga movies to the artworks on the walls. You may feel like you've drifted into Tokyo, where traditional fare has a modern edge.

Nina — Indian
Al Sufouh 2 **04 399 9999**
oneandonlyroyalmirage.com
Map **1 M4** Metro **Nakheel**

The refined menu includes roti and naan with savoury pickles and salads such as seared tuna with mustard cress and lime vinaigrette. The spinach kofta is exquisite, as are the tandoori prawns with lemon rice. Indian sauvignon blanc pairs with lighter dishes, while the shiraz matches meatier options.

Pachanga — Latin American
Hilton Jumeirah Marsa Dubai **04 318 2530**
hilton.com
Map **1 K4** Metro **Jumeirah Lakes Towers**

Pachanga's well-rounded menu of Latin American fare hails from Mexico to Argentina. On Tuesdays, the restaurant celebrates with a Brazilian-style Churrasco barbecue (from Dhs.195) with succulent beef, chicken and lamb served at your table. The peppered rib-eye is particularly tender. Still hungry? The buffet includes chorizo sausage and crispy breaded crab.

Prime 68 — Steakhouse
JW Marriott Marquis Business Bay **04 414 3000**
jwmarriottmarquisdubailife.com
Map **2 D6** Metro **Business Bay**

This boutique steakhouse serves up the most succulent steaks with some of the finest cuts you'll find in Dubai, from award-winning Australian full blood Wagyu to prime Black Angus beef. Combine that with breathtaking views from the 68th floor of the world's tallest, polished service and delicious desserts and you have one of the top fine dining experiences in the city.

GOING OUT
RESTAURANTS

Segreto Italian
Madinat Jumeirah Al Sufouh 1 **04 366 6730**
jumeirah.com
Map **1 R4** Metro **Mall of the Emirates**
Candle-lit lamps lead you through the many walkways of Madinat Jumeirah to this hidden gem. Start with a glass of prosecco on the terrace by the canal, then head into the stylish, modern interior for your meal. The food is aesthetically appealing, despite the fact that the portions seem to be aimed at a catwalk model. However, the traditional Italian flavours shine through in all dishes, from pasta to risotto.

Informal

There are times when all you want is carefree dining without the airs and graces, and where the food needs no dressing up. These restaurants provide just that.

Al Bandar Restaurant Seafood
Al Shindagha **04 393 9001**
alkoufa.com
Map **2 M4** Metro **Al Ghubaiba**
With an idyllic creekside location and good seafood, Al Bandar is the perfect venue to ease visitors into the Arabian dining experience. The restaurant caters for a dressed down clientele, making a pleasant change from the usual five-star hotels, so there's no need to throw on your coolest threads. The menu is good value, and the nearby resident camels make for excellent photo opportunities.

Almaz By Momo Moroccan
Mall of the Emirates Al Barsha 1 **04 409 8877**
altayer.com
Map **1 R6** Metro **Mall of the Emirates**
The subdued atmosphere inside this Moroccan restaurant inside Harvey Nichols is a refreshing contrast to the retail buzz outside. Take a break from shopping up a storm at the Mall of the Emirates with refreshing mocktails, tasty stews, tender lamb and fluffy couscous. Settle in and get stuck into the generous portions. You won't be going anywhere fast – the service is as laidback as the vibe.

Reem Al Bawadi

If it's Middle Eastern fare that you're craving, head for this Dubai institution. This atmospheric eatery serves traditional dishes at excellent prices as well as shisha. The Jumeira Road branch is by far the best, with its large outdoor garden, but there are also great spots in Downtown, Marsa Dubai and Sheikh Zayed Road. The falafel and hummus are possibly the best in town... and then there's the fluffy Arabic bread!

Apres International
Mall of the Emirates Al Barsha 1 **04 341 2575**
emiratesleisureretail.com
Map **1 R6** Metro **Mall of the Emirates**
This cosy eatery has a comfortable bar area and an unrivalled view of the Ski Dubai slopes. The menu offers wholesome fare including steaks, fondue and pizzas. During the day, it's great for families and, at night, the laidback vibe and cocktail list encourage chilled socialising.

The Butcher Shop & Grill Steakhouse
Mall of the Emirates Al Barsha 1 **04 347 1167**
thebutchershop-me.com
Map **1 R6** Metro **Mall of the Emirates**
This restaurant is all about steak, so pick your giant fillet, rump, T-bone, prime rib or rib-eye and tuck in. There's quality as well as quantity and, best of all, you can take home a few cuts from the in-house butcher's counter complete with cooking tips. Also located at The Walk, JBR and Mirdif City Centre.

Carluccio's Italian
Souk Al Bahar Downtown Dubai, Burj Khalifa **04 434 1320**
carluccios.com
Map **2 F7** Metro **Burj Khalifa/Dubai Mall**
From the hearty dishes to the shelves laden with cookery books and deli produce, Carluccio's is a slice of Italy. The alfresco dining are stylishly modern and the terrace has great views of Dubai Fountain. Serving breakfast, lunch and dinner, outlets are also open at Mirdif City Centre and Dubai Marina Mall.

Claw BBQ American
Souk Al Bahar Burj Khalifa **04 432 2300**
clawbbq.com
Map **2 F6** Metro **Burj Khalifa/Dubai Mall**
With its very own mechanical rodeo bull, drinks served in jam jars and lively decor, Claw BBQ guarantees an entertaining evening out. A casual bar-cum-diner vibe makes everyone feel comfortable, and the menu serves a gastronomic playground of American South delights. There's a terrace overlooking the Burj Khalifa and Dubai Fountain, so it'll impress visitors too.

Der Keller German
Jumeirah Beach Umm Suqeim 3 **04 406 8999**
jumeirah.com
Map **1 S4** Metro **First Gulf Bank**
In a cosy pseudo-subterranean setting with brick arches, wine barrels and solid oak furniture, Der Keller delivers fine German cuisine and imported beer. You'll find pretzels, schnitzels, frankfurters and fondue, as well as hearty meat dishes. Try to resist (if you can) as the fresh bread as the starters are as big as mains and the mains are bigger than Austria.

404 Dubai Explorer

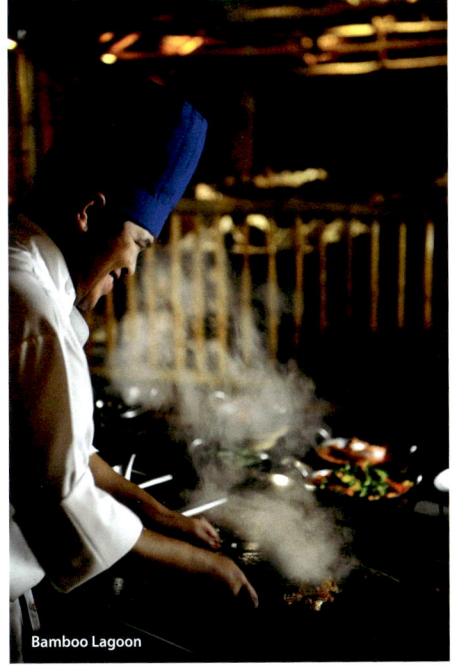

GOING OUT
RESTAURANTS

Apres

Bamboo Lagoon

Al Hambra

405

GOING OUT
RESTAURANTS

El Chico Cafe — Mexican
The Walk at JBR Marsa Dubai **04 423 3828**
elchico.com
Map **1 K4** Metro **Dubai Marina**
One of the most popular dining options on The Walk at JBR, this is proper Mexican overindulgence. Nachos dripping with cheese are dunked into the fresh guacamole for starters, while burritos, fajitas and enchiladas filled to bursting point make the best main courses, although spicy chicken and steaks are also on the menu. The restaurant is unlicensed but its location along the buzzing JBR is great for people-watching.

Ewaan — Mediterranean
The Palace Downtown Downtown Dubai, Burj Khalifa **04 888 3444**
theaddress.com
2 F6 Metro **Burj Khalifa/Dubai Mall**
Surrounding the palm-lined pool in the Arabian-themed Palace Hotel, the private cabanas at this shisha joint sit directly beneath the towering Burj Khalifa. Customers can stretch out on Arabic seating while a musician plays the oud and attentive staff serve up shisha and tasty mezze.

Gourmet Burger Kitchen — American
Mirdif **04 284 3955**
gbkinfo.com
Map **2 P12** Metro **Rashidiya**
This popular chain serves up a winning formula – good juicy meat, fresh produce, a diverse choice of toppings and sauces, and hearty portions of fries in trendy canteen-style settings. Burgers are made to order, and the delivery service has saved many a hungry couch potato. See the website for other locations around Dubai.

Japengo Cafe — International
Mall of the Emirates Al Barsha 1 **04 341 1671**
binhendi.com
Map **1 R6** Metro **Mall of the Emirates**
An impressive Japanese-western hybrid menu with top-notch food, in a neon bright, minimalist setting. The menu ticks all the boxes, ranging from sushi, rice and noodle classics such as nasi goreng to fish and chips, New York strip loin and Mexican taquitos. Other locations include Ibn Battuta, Mall of the Emirates, Palm Strip, Souk Madinat Jumeirah and Dubai Festival City.

Ketchup — American
Boulevard Plaza Burj Khalifa **04 363 8595**
ketchup.ae
Map **2 F6** Metro **Burj Khalifa/Dubai Mall**
The gimmick here is quite literally the ketchup – you are served five distinct kinds to work your way through, ranging from the sweetest, maple, through to BBQ, curry, Louisiana and then the spiciest (and rather tongue-tingling), chipotle. And to help you try these out, there are three kinds of fries: skinny, fat and sweet potato. It's a fun concept and the food is great!

Maria Bonita Taco Shop & Grill — Mexican
Nr Spinneys Centre Umm Suqeim 1 **04 395 4454**
mariabonitadubai.com
Map **2 B5** Metro **Noor Bank**
Maria Bonita stands out as a friendly, well-worn neighbourhood eatery serving traditional Mexican and Tex-Mex dishes that include flavoursome nachos, spicy quesadillas and meaty fajitas, served in a laidback atmosphere. Also at The Green Community (Casa Maria, 04 885 3188).

Shooters — American
Hessyan 1 **04 814 5604**
jaresortshotels.com
Metro **Jebel Ali**
A modern western saloon with denim-clad waiters, and surprisingly quiet despite the gunfire from the five floodlit shooting ranges below. The menu is simple but considered, mainly offering fish and steak dishes. King-sized prawns and lobster tails are firm favourites.

Fish & Chips
You may not find a 'chippy' on every street corner in Dubai, but if you're really hankering for some good old fish and chips there are a few choices at your disposal. The Fish & Chips Room at JBR is popular, as is the nearby Bob's Fish & Chips on the other side of the marina. Both stay open until the wee hours of the morning too. Mirdif Fish & Chips, 26C Street, near the mosque on 15 Street is a good option for Mirdif dwellers. The Irish Village, Barasti, The Boardwalk, the Dhow & Anchor and Apres all deserve a special mention for the quality of their fish and chips. MORE Cafe (morecafe.biz) also has excellent fish and spicy chunky chips.

Singapore Deli Restaurant — Asian
Nr BurJuman Centre Al Karama **04 396 6885**
Map **2 L5** Metro **BurJuman**
From bowls of steaming noodles to traditionally cooked nasi goreng, the authentic dishes available at Singapore Deli Restaurant are consistently excellent. The casual atmosphere and home-style cooking draws a large crowd of regular customers who come for a taste of home.

Sushi Art — Japanese
Marble Walk – Gate 5, DIFC Trade Center 2 **800 220**
sushiart.ae
Map **2 G6** Metro **Financial Centre**
The sushi here is inspired by award-winning chef Thierry Marx. Sushi Art is a lunchtime hub for DIFC

GOING OUT
RESTAURANTS

workers, but is usually pretty quiet in the evenings. The menu uses sustainably sourced fish, with some inspirational twists, such as the sea bream kiwi tartare.

YO! Sushi — Japanese
Mirdif **04 284 3995**
yosushi.com
Map **2 P12** Metro **Rashidiya**
Sushi addicts will enjoy both traditional and unconventional sushi here. Friendly staff explain the dishes on the conveyor belt, and the coloured plates indicate the price of each dish. Branches are also in Dubai Festival City, BurJuman, Dubai Marina Mall, The Dubai Mall and DIFC.

Live Music

If you fancy a bit of entertainment while you dine, then check out one of these venues below. There's everything from belly dancing to jazz and pianists.

Al Basha — Middle Eastern
Habtoor Grand Marsa Dubai **04 399 5000**
grandjumeirah.habtoorhotels.com
Map **1 L4** Metro **Dubai Marina**
Fine Lebanese food, with live music from 9.30pm. The set menus are wide-ranging; wafer-thin pita, cheese rolls and grilled meat start from Dhs.220 per person up to Dhs.350 with prawn and lobster. Dine on the terrace, and watch the belly dancers.

Al Diwan — Middle Eastern
Metropolitan Palace Al Muraqqabat **04 227 0000**
habtoorhotels.com
Map **2 N6** Metro **Al Rigga**
Enjoy traditional Lebanese food and belly dancing from 11pm at this cosy restaurant. The selection of wine, Montecristo cigars and Beluga caviar provide a special treat, but the hummus Al Diwan and the oriental mixed grill are not to be missed.

Al Hambra — Spanish
Al Qasr Al Sufouh 1 **04 366 6730**
jumeirah.com
Map **1 R5** Metro **Mall of the Emirates**
A mariachi duo sets the mood at this excellent if pricey Spanish venue. The seafood paella is a must, but there are also delicious tapas, rustic Spanish dishes and tasty vegetarian options.

Al Koufa Restaurant — Middle Eastern
Nr Al Nasr Leisureland Oud Metha **04 335 1511**
alkoufa.com
Map **2 L6** Metro **Oud Metha**
In true Arabic style, Al Koufa comes alive around 11pm. Enjoy a great atmosphere, delicious fruit juices

and excellent traditional Arabic food, including some lesser known and Emirati dishes, into the early hours. A charge of Dhs.30 covers the live performances.

Antique Bazaar — Indian
Four Points Bur Dubai Al Hamriya **04 397 7444**
antiquebazaar-dubai.com
Map **2 L5** Metro **BurJuman**
Antique Bazaar offers a full range of curried delights to an ever-present musical accompaniment. When in full swing, the live music show is a memorable cultural experience, but can detract from the great food. Arrive early for conversation, late to party.

Bamboo Lagoon — Asian
JW Marriott Al Muraqqabat **04 607 7977**
marriottdiningatjw.ae
Map **2 P6** Metro **Abu Baker Al Siddique**
Bamboo Lagoon's staggering range of exquisite fusion cuisine demands repeat visits. The bottomless buffet offers everything from sushi to curries and grills. At around 9pm a band takes to the stage and grass-skirted singers serenade diners with Polynesian tunes and entertaining covers.

Cravin Cajun — American
Novotel Al Barsha Al Barsha 1 **04 304 9000**
Map **1 Q6** Metro **Sharaf DG**
Don't be fooled by the smart but generic decor, the food here has bags of personality. Authentic Cajun cooking is whipped up by a chef from New Orleans, who serves up gumbo, jambalaya and other tasty dishes. A fabulous jazz band plays every night, and the location on Sheikh Zayed Road is very convenient.

Dhow Ka Aangan — Indian
Dhow Palace Al Mankhool **04 3599292**
dhowplacedubai.com
Map **2 L5** Metro **Al Karama**
Traditionally decorated in rich wood with many elaborate ornaments nailed to the walls, the atmosphere and live in-house music mingle well with the authentic food. Savour its range of biryanis, special curries and kebabs from the charcoal-smoked clay oven, plus excellent desserts.

Jazz@Pizza Express — Italian
Nr Movenpick JLT Al Thanyah 5 **04 441 6342**
pizzaexpressuae.com
Map **1 J5** Metro **Jumeirah Lakes Towers**
A pizza chain, but one with dignity, that also taps into the community music scene. The sleek, contemporary setting next to JLT's lake retains a cosy atmosphere, especially on Tuesday's open mic nights, when the venue is buzzing. Friday's brunch is also a great deal, with a steady stream of Pizza Express's tasty classics, a low key vibe and sultry jazz.

askexplorer.com   407

GOING OUT
RESTAURANTS

The Rupee Room — Indian
North Podium, Marina Walk Marsa Dubai 04 390 5755
therupeeroom.com
Map **1 K5** Metro **Jumeirah Lakes Towers**
Offers a wide selection of tasty north Indian dishes in relaxed surroundings. The glass-fronted kitchen allows you to keep an eye on the action and there is often a great trio of live musicians playing. There are a handful of tables outside offering marina views.

Senses — Buffet
Mercure Gold Madinat Dubai Al Melaheyah 04 301 9888
mercure.com
Map **2 J4** Metro **Al Jafiliya**
Senses offers a relaxing contrast to the bustle of nearby 2nd December Street. The a la carte menu offers pizzas and pastas and the modest buffet changes theme each evening, the most popular being the carvery night. Live music is played each evening, yet the restaurant remains family friendly and reasonably priced.

Troyka — Russian
Ascot Al Raffa 04 352 0900
ascothoteldubai.com
Map **2 L4** Metro **Al Fahidi**
Troyka conjures up a little of Russia's old world charm. The Tuesday night buffet is all-inclusive and comprises time-honoured Russian delicacies such as chicken Kiev and beef stroganoff. A band plays every night from 10.30pm and an extravagant, live Vegas-style cabaret begins at 11.30pm.

Quick Bites

When you don't have time to linger for hours over a meal but still want something tasty and satisfying, these are the places to go.

The Academy — International
Creek Golf Club Port Saeed 04 295 6000
dubaigolf.com
Map **2 M7** Metro **Deira City Centre**
A wide assortment of international appetisers, sandwiches, salads, main courses and beverages is available in this snack bar overlooking Dubai Creek's golf course; a cheerful colour scheme fits in well with the view of luscious greens and happy golfers.

Bo House Cafe — International
The Walk at JBR Marsa Dubai 04 429 8655
bohousecafe.com
Map **1 K4** Metro **Jumeirah Lakes Towers**
Home-cooked healthy food is the pride of this stylish and bohemian cafe. Inspired by travel, the all-day menu features breakfast, hearty Italian, tapas and Bo House burgers, as well as 'Mohemian' hummus and fattoush salad. The crepe station offers delicious chocolate and nutty desserts, while the 'health factory' offers personalised portion-controlled meals.

CafeM — Cafe
Media One Al Sufouh 2 04 427 1000
mediaonehotel.com
Map **1 M5** Metro **Nakheel**
Ideal for a business tete-a-tete during the day, CafeM takes on a bar atmosphere when the post-work crowd hits. From 7pm to 10pm on Sundays to Thursdays, enjoy unlimited wine and cheese for a bargain price. Great for a no-fuss night out with friends.

Sushi — Japanese
Grand Hyatt Umm Hurair 2 04 317 2222
restaurants.dubai.hyatt.com
Map **2 L8** Metro **Dubai Healthcare City**
Artfully prepared in the open kitchen of this petite venue, sushi and sashimi portions are served up delightfully and your bill is determined by the number of pieces you feel like indulging in. The careful preparation and the melt-in-your-mouth morsels are of high quality. The grill station is a new addition.

Wafi Gourmet — Middle Eastern
Umm Hurair 2 04 324 4433
wafigourmet.com
Map **2 L7** Metro **Dubai Healthcare City**
Deliciously prepared traditional Lebanese dishes, along with pastries, sweets, ice creams, exotic juices and hot drinks, make Wafi Gourmet a great sustenance stop when on a shopping spree. Make sure you browse the delicatessen and you're sure to leave with more bags than you arrived with.

Wagamama — Japanese
JBR, Marsa Dubai 04 399 5900
wagamama.ae
Map **1 K5** Metro **Jumeirah Lakes Towers**
Modelled on a traditional Japanese ramen bar with communal tables, Wagamama's streamlined design works well for a quick bite. Orders are immediately and freshly prepared. Also at Crowne Plaza and The Greens (though the Greens venue is not licensed to serve alcohol). Delivery is available.

Wavebreaker — International
Hilton Jumeirah Marsa Dubai 04 399 1111
www3.hilton.com
Map **1 K4** Metro **Jumeirah Lakes Towers**
A beach bar that serves snacks, light meals, barbecue grills and a variety of cocktails and mocktails. Enjoy juicy burgers, jumbo prawns or even lobster. Wavebreaker is perfect for a laidback afternoon, while at sunset, it's quiet, cool and the beach view is

GOING OUT
RESTAURANTS

stunning, making you want to linger for more than just one of their delicious sundowners.

Wild Peeta — Middle Eastern
Port Saeed **055 895 7272**
wildpeeta.com
Map **2 N7** Metro **Deira City Centre**

This Emirati-owned fusion shawarma restaurant created a buzz when it opened in 2009 thanks to its fresh, healthy shawarmas, salads and juices, served by some of the friendliest staff in Dubai. It's since become a popular, laidback haunt. The Moroccan salad and Thai shawarma are both highly recommended.

Romantic

If your aim is to sweep your date off his or her feet, these are the restaurants that go the extra mile to provide the perfect heartwarming setting for couples.

Amaseena — Middle Eastern
Ritz-Carlton Dubai Marsa Dubai **04 399 4000**
ritzcarlton.com
Map **1 L4** Metro **Dubai Marina**

With a torch-lit entrance, sounds of the oud, the aroma of shisha, and exotic belly dancing under the stars, a trip to Amaseena is a truly magical Arabian experience. The food – which takes the form of an all-you-can-eat Arabic buffet – is excellent, and you can sit in your own private majlis. The perfect setting for an unforgettable evening.

Armani/Hashi — Japanese
Armani Downtown Dubai, Burj Khalifa **04 888 3888**
dubai.armanihotels.com
Map **2 F6** Metro **Burj Khalifa/Dubai Mall**

Inside, the restaurant is beautifully elegant, but the prime seats are outside with the Burj Khalifa's sky-piercing spire above you and the romantic Dubai Fountain in front. The service is refreshingly down-to-earth, yet the food is as exquisite and out of the ordinary as the surroundings.

Bateaux Dubai — International
Nr British Embassy Al Hamriya **04 814 5553**
bateauxdubai.com
Map **2 M5** Metro **Baniyas Square**

This sleek, glass-topped vessel offers four-course fine dining from a varied international menu, with five-star surroundings to match. Intimate lighting, with cosy tables and splendid views of the city, make for a top pick for romance or a special tourist treat. A bubbly Friday brunch is also available.

BiCE Mare — Italian
Downtown Dubai, Burj Khalifa **04 423 0982**
bicemare.com
Map **2 F6** Metro **Burj Khalifa/Dubai Mall**

Sister to BiCE, the 'mare' signifies a seafood-dominated menu of delicious dishes that bring fish lovers back time and time again. Dine inside and be entertained by the sultry jazz hands of the resident pianist or, if the weather allows, take in the splendid Dubai Fountain show from the terrace.

Armani/Hashi

GOING OUT
RESTAURANTS

Celebrities > p.175   European
Palace At One&Only Royal Mirage Al Sufouh 2
04 399 9999
oneandonlyresorts.com
Map **1 M4** Metro **Nakheel**

Dine under crystal chandeliers at this elegant restaurant, which offers romantic views of softly lit gardens from tables peppered with rose petals and iridescent stones. The well-priced European menu contains dainty but filling dishes such as sea bass and baked rack of lamb, or try the tasting menu for a wider variety of options.

Embassy Dubai   European
Grosvenor House Marsa Dubai **04 317 6000**
grosvenorhouse-dubai.com
Map **1 L5** Metro **Dubai Marina**

This is a nightclub, restaurant, and champagne and vodka bar. The decor is opulent, with stunning views of Marsa Dubai. Fine dining appetisers include oysters, caviar (at Dhs.2,000 for 50g), and foie gras. It's not cheap – dinner is Dhs.500-600 per person without alcohol – but you won't be disappointed.

Embassy Dubai

Fazaris   International
The Address Downtown Downtown Dubai, Burj Khalifa **04 888 3444**
theaddress.com
Map **2 F7** Metro **Burj Khalifa/Dubai Mall**

With 12 pages of mouthwatering dishes from Japan, south-east Asia, India, Arabia and the Mediterranean, this is a menu that tries to cater for everyone. The inside is cavernous and bright, while outside is more romantic, with views of the Burj Khalifa.

Hong Loong   Chinese
Sofitel The Palm Nakhlat Jumeira **04 455 6600**
sofitel.com
Map **1 P1** Metro **Nakheel**

A delectable dining experience in a beautiful setting that transports you immediately to China. Specialities include traditional clay pot dishes and there's also delicious dim sum, seafood and meat dishes, along with veggie options and thought-provoking desserts. Staff are knowledgeable about the customs behind each dish. There's even a resident Tea Sommelier.

Medzo   Italian
Umm Hurair 2 **04 324 4100**
pyramidsrestaurantsatwafi.com
Map **2 L7** Metro **Dubai Healthcare City**

Back with a new look and a new, longer menu, Medzo still delivers the same splendid gastronomy. Elegant white mixes with chandeliers and dreamy drapes to create a more romantic atmosphere set to a soundtrack of soft piano. When the weather permits, the tree-shaded terrace completes the experience.

Ossigeno   Italian
Le Royal Meridien Marsa Dubai **04 399 5555**
lemeridien-minaseyahi.com
Map **1 L4** Metro **Dubai Marina**

Traditional Italian ingredients are fused with new flavours to create divine dishes. The emphasis is on sharing and there's a wide selection of antipasti as well as fish and meat dishes. Pizza and pasta lovers won't be disappointed either. A modern, relaxed and stylish vibe and impeccable service complete the package. Do not miss the desserts.

Pai Thai   Thai
Al Qasr Al Sufouh 1 **04 366 6730**
madinatjumeirah.com
Map **1 R5** Metro **Mall of the Emirates**

You'll have a night to remember at the stunning Pai Thai, from the abra boat ride to the restaurant to the nouvelle Thai cuisine. The outdoor seating offers delightful views across the canals, and the menu provides some exciting twists on familiar favourites.

Porterhouse   Steakhouse
Sofitel The Palm Nakhlat Jumeira **04 455 6677**
accorhotels.com
Map **1 P1** Metro **Nakheel**

Indisputably romantic with a wonderful outdoor terrace area overlooking Sofitel's pretty pools and palm trees. This is a place for steak aficionados looking to splash out on the best cuts money can buy – you'll find everything from purebred Wagyu to Black Angus, and the highlight is a prime Chateaubriand for two that's carved theatrically at your table.

GOING OUT
RESTAURANTS

Rare Restaurant — Steakhouse
Desert Palm Warsan 2 **04 323 8888**
desertpalm.peraquum.com
Metro **Rashidiya**

This tranquil tucked-away haven is a meat-lover's dream. Steaks, mostly 300 or 400 day grain-fed Australian beef, are the headline act, but grilled fish and seafood options as well as the corn-fed chicken will tempt the most ardent carnivores. The atmosphere is a relaxed sort of refinement and the green views offer a delicious respite from the desert. The wine list is lengthy, but manageable.

Siddharta Lounge — Asian
Grosvenor House Marsa Dubai **04 317 6000**
grosvenorhouse-dubai.com
Map **1 L5** Metro **Dubai Marina**

Soak up some rays during the day at this slick white venue with a beautifully lit pool terrace that's home to the glam crowd. In the evening chilled house music creates a lounge vibe, but ramps up a notch at 9pm when the DJ starts to play. The menu of 'Mediterrasian' flavours is innovative, as are the signature cocktails.

Tagine > p.175 — Moroccan
The Palace At One&Only Royal Mirage Al Sufouh 2 **04 399 999**
oneandonlyroyalmirage.com
Map **1 M4** Metro **Nakheel**

Duck down and enter through the tiny carved wooden doorway into a beautiful Moroccan den of embroidered hangings, glowing lanterns and sultry music. Providing a little taste of Marrakesh in the Middle East, the food here is deliciously authentic, and the meat dishes are so tender. The intimate cushioned booths are the best seats in the house.

Showstopper

In this land of make-believe and headline-grabbing mega projects it's only fitting that some of Dubai's restaurants put on a show to remember.

Al Mahara — Seafood
Burj Al Arab Umm Suqeim 3 **04 301 7600**
jumeirah.com
Map **1 S4** Metro **First Gulf Bank**

Al Mahara is more than just a restaurant – it's an experience. Your visit starts with a simulated submarine ride 'under the sea', arriving at an elegant restaurant curled around a huge aquarium. The fine dining menu is predominantly seafood – with gourmet delights such as Alaskan king crab and foie gras ravioli or poached Tsarskaya oysters – with prices to match. Gentlemen are required to wear a jacket.

At.mosphere — International
Downtown Dubai, Burj Khalifa 04 888 3444
atmosphereburjkhalifa.com
Map **2 F6** Metro **Burj Khalifa/Dubai Mall**

The wow factor at the world's highest restaurant goes beyond the stupendous views; the opulent dishes use premium ingredients and boast exquisite presentation (and prices). The Grill serves lunch and dinner and is the equal of any of the UAE's top restaurants. The Lounge opens from midday to 2am for drinks and snacks; it is also home to the highest high tea in the world.

Hakkasan — Chinese
Emirates Towers Trade Center 2 **04 384 8484**
hakkasan.com
Map **2 H6** Metro **Financial Centre**

Hakkasan shows how well a London restaurant can work in Dubai. Hakkasan favourites are on the menu such as crispy duck salad and stewed Wagyu beef. Mains such as the Pipa duck and sweet and sour pomegranate chicken – are best for sharing. Expensive, but as good as dining gets in Dubai.

Icho Restaurant — Japanese
Radisson Royal Trade Center 1 **04 308 0550**
radissonblu.com
Map **2 H5** Metro **Emirates Towers**

Given the luxury venue on the 49th floor, elevated standing of the chef and the high-end cuisine served here, Icho is surprisingly warm and welcoming. There's a relaxed atmosphere which is complemented by the jolly, yet professional staff, making Icho feel high class without being intimidating. This is a restaurant where even Japanese food aficionados can discover new flavours and textures in dishes that are nothing short of works of art.

Kris With A View — International
Park Regis Kris Kin Al Karama **04 377 1111**
kris.ae
Map **2 L5** Metro **Al Karama**

Dining on the top floor of the Park Regis Hotel gives you a unique vantage point over the city without paying the premium usually attached to lofty views. Enjoy dishes from across Asia, each prepared by a regional expert chef. Order dessert to be served at the adjacent wine bar, so you can enjoy live music and a great selection of wine.

Neos — Cafe
The Address Downtown Downtown Dubai, Burj Khalifa **04 436 7700**
Map **2 F7** Metro **Burj Khalifa/Dubai Mall**

Neos is the perfect place for that special occasion. Drag your eyes from the stunning skyline panorama to take in the extensive menu of cocktails and small bites.

askexplorer.com   411

GOING OUT
RESTAURANTS

Dress smart, sit back and enjoy the pianist in the glamorous bar. Reservations are recommended.

Ossiano > p.275   Seafood
Atlantis Nakhlat Jumeira **04 426 2626**
atlantisthepalm.com
Map **1 N1** Metro **Nakheel**
Famed Spanish chef Santi Santamaria serves up delicate Catalan-inspired seafood dishes at this impeccable eatery. Glistening chandeliers and floor-to-ceiling views of the Ambassador Lagoon aquarium provide a formal but romantic setting to enjoy the incredible and incredibly expensive fare – and you can watch 65,000 marine animals gliding by.

Pierchic   Seafood
Al Qasr Al Sufouh 1 **04 366 6730**
jumeirah.com
Map **1 R5** Metro **Mall of the Emirates**
Situated at the end of a long wooden pier that juts into the Arabian Gulf, Pierchic offers unobstructed views of the Burj Al Arab, which probably reflects in the heftier price tag. The superior seafood is meticulously presented and the wine menu reads like a sommelier's wish list. The sea surrounds on all sides, making this a unique dining location.

Studio Du Chef   French
Sofitel The Palm Nakhlat Jumeira **04 455 6677**
sofitel.com
Map **1 P1** Metro **Nakheel**
At Studio Du Chef, not only can you watch chefs conjure up modern gourmet French cuisine in the open kitchen – either round the table or on the screens dotted around the restaurant – but you can dine on some of the very best food to be served in Dubai. Select the Trust Your Chef menu and you will be served a superior five course menu of seafood, fish, *amuse bouche* and fine cuts of meat and desserts – each meticulously presented, delicately cooked, and expertly explained personally by the chef himself.

Taste Of Home

Part of being an expat means missing the friends, family and food that you leave behind. These eateries can take you back in a biteful.

Bentoya Kitchen   Japanese
Al Kawakeb Bldg, Shk Zayed Rd Trade Center 2 **04 343 0222**
bentoya.info
Map **2 G6** Metro **Financial Centre**
Bentoya's popularity with Dubai's Japanese expats vouches for the authenticity of its fresh, good quality maki, sushi and bento boxes. The teriyaki beef is particularly recommended. The compact, double storey restaurant is well priced and ideal for a casual bite.

BiCE   Italian
Hilton Jumeirah Marsa Dubai **04 318 2520**
hilton.com
Map **1 K4** Metro **Jumeirah Lakes Towers**
The old European feel of the place is a far cry from the trattoria-style bistro, but Italian is what this restaurant unashamedly is. Pizzas and pastas feature heavily, barely overshadowed by imaginative meat cuts and seafood. Or opt for fish from the trolley – prepared to order. Prices are fairly high but it's full all week.

Brauhaus   German
Jumeira Rotana Al Bada' **04 345 5888**
rotana.com
Map **2 J4** Metro **Al Jafiliya**
Join German expats and those after authentic Bavarian food and beer in this casual spot. The booths are the choice spot to enjoy substantial portions of well-cooked schnitzels, bratwursts and sauerkraut. Top it all off with one of the imported German bottled beers or draft ales.

Cafe Habana   Mexican
Souk Al Bahar Downtown Dubai **04 422 2620**
cafehabana.com
Map **2 F7** Metro **Burj Khalifa/Dubai Mall**
A menu that's small in size but big on flavour with all the Mexican staples thrown in, from huevos rancheros and nachos to quesadillas and burritos. The talk of the town though is the Mexican-style grilled cobs topped with cheese, lime and chili powder. The flair bar-tending and upbeat Cuban grooves add to the atmosphere – just how a Mexican joint should be.

The Cheesecake Factory   American
The Dubai Mall Downtown Dubai, Burj Khalifa **04 325 3521**
cheesecakefactory.com
Map **2 F7** Metro **Burj Khalifa/Dubai Mall**
Famed for its large portions, this American restaurant chain serves up eye-poppingly large portions of comfort food – from avocado rolls to the indulgent mac and cheese burger. And then there's the cheesecake; more than 40 different types. It's certainly not good for the waistline, but this is the place to come if you want to have your cake and eat it!

Cuba   Cuban
Jumeirah Creekside Al Garhoud **04 230 8459**
jumeirah.com
Map **2 M8** Metro **GGICO**
Ride the glass lift to the top floor and see the stunning roof terrace with panoramic city views, and then enjoy a taste of Cuba with infused rum

412   Dubai Explorer

Walk The Walk

Got the munchies? Head to The Walk, Dubai's latest place to be that's packed with a multitude of restaurants and cafes.

One of the most popular areas in Dubai for going out is The Walk, the 1.7km pedestrian-friendly boulevard that lies between the JBR residential development and the beach. You won't find any fine dining establishments here, but that's not the main draw; crowds come for the atmosphere and the relaxed, alfresco eating and drinking. It's one of the few parts of the city that feels like it was made for walking around.

During the cooler months, hundreds of people of all nationalities – families, friends, couples, tourists – stroll the strip before settling down at a table to sociably while the night away. There are dozens of cafes and restaurants on The Walk, serving up pretty much every popular cuisine available. If you can't decide what you're in the mood for, just go for a wander and you'll soon stumble upon something that takes your fancy.

Starting at the Dubai end of the strip, the first JBR court is Murjan. This is the more upmarket side of The Walk, where the designer boutiques and home accessory stores congregate. There's also a cluster of international dining options to choose from here: Da Shi Dai (Chinese); Umi Sushi (Japanese); Suvoroff (Russian); Scoozi (Italian-Japanese fusion); The Fish & Chip Room (British); and On The Border (Mexican). There's also a cigar lounge here, La Casa Del Habano, for a refined end to the evening.

The next court, Sadaf, has its main culinary treats tucked away up on the plaza level, including branches of the excellent Lebanese chain Automatic and the always-fun burger-and-shake joint Fuddruckers. Wedged among the JBR courts is Oasis Beach Tower, which contains some popular (and, unlike the JBR outlets, licensed) restaurants, including Frankie's, Wagamama and Trader Vic's Mai-Tai Lounge, all of which pretty much guarantee a lively evening. Next up come some of the newer offerings on The Walk, such as New Zealand's 'healthy' burger chain, Burger Fuel, and the popular Canadian coffee and donuts chain Tim Hortons.

JBR continues with Bahar and Rimal courts, which feature a great stretch of alfresco eating. Packed tables spread out onto the wide pavement, and it is perhaps The Walk's busiest section in the evenings and for leisurely weekend breakfasts. Highlights include Il Caffe Di Roma, Paul, Le Pain Quotidien, The Butcher Shop and Grill, Sukh Sagar and El Chico.

Things descend into more of a fast food frenzy by the time you reach Amwaj and Shams courts, with a selection of the usual suspects – Hardee's, Cinnabon, KFC, Pizza Hut, Figaro's Pizza – plus decent breakfast spot Coco's. If the endless options along The Walk are not enough to satisfy your appetite, there are plenty more cafes and restaurants by the water at Marina Walk, while the beachfront hotels – Amwaj Rotana, Sofitel, Habtoor Grand, Le Royal Meridien, Ritz-Carlton, Hilton and Sheraton – house a more upmarket selection of restaurants and bars.

GOING OUT
RESTAURANTS

beverages and an extensive selection of cigars. There's a selection of contemporary tapas to enjoy while seated on a plush couch by the pool, or private cabanas for an intimate escape.

Interactive Eating
If you like your dining interactive, then the stylishly modern Blue Flame restaurant at Jumeirah Creekside (04 230 8459) is the place to connect with. Step inside its 'cooking pod' and watch the chef prepare your meal while teaching you a whole range of tasty tricks, from preparation to plating. Up to five people can be hosted for cooking lessons in the pod too, which could make for a fun alternative for a day or evening out with friends.

Fogo Vivo   Brazilian
JA Ocean View JBR, Marsa Dubai **04 814 5590**
jaresortshotels.com
Map **1 J4** Metro **Jumeirah Lakes Towers**
Serving more than 10 different types of meat – many cooked 'live' in the open fire at the heart of the restaurant – this is a great place to come with family and friends. Novelties aplenty are delivered, with a Brazilian 'cowboy' carving a variety of grilled meats at the table. Inspired by the 'gaucho' style of cooking, this is a fun and interactive way to enjoy the wonderful flavours of Brazilian cuisine.

Hofbrauhaus   German
JW Marriott Al Muraqqabat **04 607 7588**
marriott.com
Map **2 P6** Metro **Abu Baker Al Siddique**
When it's hearty Bavarian food and hops that you're after, and dainty dishes just won't cut the mustard, head for Hofbrauhaus. From the tangy sauerkraut to the white sausage with sweet mustard, all rounded off with tasty strudel, everything on the menu here is top notch. Add in the great German beer, Bavarian garb for the fun-loving staff and accordion music, and you have a fun night out.

The Ivy   British
Trade Center 2 **04 319 8767**
theivy.ae
Map **2 H6** Metro **Emirates Towers**
If you've visited the Ivy's London sibling, you'll know exactly what to expect: ultra-fashionable interiors, impeccable service and, of course, great food. The restaurant serves predominantly British cuisine (think a high-end twist on traditional favourites like liver and crispy bacon and confit pork belly) but also adds in international dishes such as beef tataki and Scandinavian iced berries. Be sure to make a reservation as this is a busy and popular eatery.

Nezesaussi Grill   International
Al Manzil Downtown Dubai, Burj Khalifa **04 428 5888**
almanzilhotel.ae
Map **2 F7** Metro **Burj Khalifa/Dubai Mall**
Celebrating the sport and cuisine of the tri-nations, Nezesaussi is a popular sports bar, with its rugby paraphernalia and 13 big screens. Great food and a comprehensive menu appeals to more than just sports fans. Meaty mains include South African sausages, New Zealand lamb and Australian steaks.

The Noodle House   Chinese
Trade Center 2 **04 319 8088**
thenoodlehouse.com
Map **2 H6** Metro **Financial Centre**
A refreshingly relaxed affair, where you order by ticking your desired dishes on the notepads. The mouthwatering food is well priced, with big portions of soups, noodles and stir-fries served up in record speed. The modern decor, open kitchen and zingy cocktails add to the vibrant atmosphere. See the website for listings of other branches.

Prego's   Italian
TECOM, Al Thanyah 1 **04 435 0201**
rotana.com
Map **1 P6** Metro **Dubai Internet City**
Prego's takes one cuisine for its buffet – Italian – and specialises in it. From soups with shavings of parmesan and an antipasti station laden with marinated vegetables, to hearty pastas and pizzas for mains, the authentic dishes are all extremely satisfying and expertly prepared.

Ravi's   Pakistani
Nr Satwa R/A, Al Satwa Rd Al Satwa **04 331 5353**
Map **2 J5** Metro **World Trade Centre**
Ravi's has legendary status among western expats, and is one of the cheapest eateries in town. This 24-hour diner offers a range of Pakistani curried favourites and rice dishes. The prices are cheap at double the price and the dishes keep punters coming back for more. The venue is basic and dining is available inside or outside.

The Reform Social & Grill   British
The Lakes Club Al Thanyah 3 **04 454 2638**
reformsocialgrill.ae
Map **1 M6** Metro **Dubai Marina**
A cosy gastro-pub with top-notch old British favourites, great service and an alfresco terrace. Divine offerings include smoked salmon Scotch eggs with oats, asparagus and Hollandaise sauce; lamb cutlets with black truffles, wild mushrooms and beetroot; a selection of salads; catch of the day; and the 'Josper Charcoal Grill' where several cuts of Angus steak sizzle away with an optional addition of garlic snails.

GOING OUT
RESTAURANTS

Hofbrauhaus

Porterhouse

Armani/Amal

GOING OUT
CAFES

Rivington Grill — British
Downtown Dubai, Burj Khalifa **04 423 0903**
rivingtongrill.ae
Map **2 F6** Metro **Burj Khalifa/Dubai Mall**
Straight out of London, this intimate eatery brings the best in European cuisine. The meat is cooked to perfection, presented beautifully and served up with sides good enough to be mains. Watch the Dubai Fountain shows from the terrace and linger to enjoy the dessert menu. The Rivington Bar & Grill is now open at Souk Madinat Jumeirah, including a standalone bar on the second floor serving British cocktails and beers on tap with regular promotions.

Tribes — African
Mall of the Emirates Al Barsha 1 **04 395 0660**
tribesrestaurant.com
Map **1 R6** Metro **Mall of the Emirates**
The menu at this African eatery is as vast as the continent and features dishes from Morocco to South Africa. The friendly staff know their delicious menu inside out and they also have some notable musical talent to really ramp up the atmosphere. If you're planning a visit, be sure to bring your appetite.

CAFES

Breakfast

These popular cafes shine by providing some of the best eggs Benedict and continental breakfasts in town – and a mean cup of coffee too!

The Archive
Al Wasl **04 349 4033**
thearchive.ae
Map **2 D5** Metro **Business Bay**
A library and cafe, The Archive conjures up delicious and healthy breakfasts. It boasts a beautiful location next to the lake in Safa Park and has an outdoor terrace with unbeatable views. The cafe also runs a packed programme of cultural events and workshops.

Baker & Spice
Downtown Dubai, Burj Khalifa **04 425 2240**
bakerandspiceme.com
Map **2 F6** Metro **Burj Khalifa/Dubai Mall**
The menu here is based on organic ingredients sourced from local farmers, and changes daily. What is constant, however, is the carefully prepared 'home-cooked' flavour of every dish. If you're lucky, Barista Henji (a visual artist) will be on duty and maybe 'paint' the Burj Khalifa into the top of your cappuccino – if not, you can always see the record-breaking building itself from the terrace.

Cafe Havana
Spinneys Centre Al Safa 2 **04 394 1727**
binhendi.com
Map **2 B5** Metro **Noor Islamic Bank**
Dotted all over Dubai, this chain offers consistently good cafe-style food with a Middle Eastern twist. Filling breakfasts include French toast, pancakes, omelettes, fruit, croissants and full English fry-ups. Quality is high, prices reasonable and the service spot on. See website for branch listings.

Counter Culture
Marriott Harbour Marsa Dubai **04 319 4793**
counter-culture.dubaimarriottharbourhotel.com
Map **1 L5** Metro **Dubai Marina**
A tasty hot and cold breakfast buffet, fresh fruit juices, the sun shining on the terrace and a newspaper spread across the table… all weekends should start this way. The simple layout of this little gem is welcoming at any time of the day or night, and the food is deliciously unfussy. There's a wealth of choice and the friendliest of service.

Epicure
Desert Palm Warsan 2 **04 323 8888**
desertpalm.peraquum.com
Metro **Rashidiya**
This licensed gourmet deli serves freshly baked bread and pastries, fruit compotes, and cooked breakfasts while you gaze over the Desert Palm's swimming pool and polo fields or devour the day's newspapers. Lunch options and snacks are also available, along with juices and hot drinks.

Fraiche
Swiss Tower, Y Cluster, JLT Al Thanyah 5 **04 369 7821**
fraiche.ae
Map **1 L5** Metro **Dubai Marina**
A modern, light and airy bistro cafe serving breakfast through to evening meals. Diners enjoy views over JLT's lake, and the terrace overlooks a green, leafy area. There's also a fresh herb garden. Head over in the morning to try the Dhs.55 'craft your own a la carte breakfast', which lets you tailor-make your meal – served with coffee and fresh juice.

Maison Bagatelle
Shk Mohd Bin Rashid Blvd Downtown Dubai, Burj Khalifa **04 420 3442**
Map **2 F7** Metro **Burj Khalifa/Dubai Mall**
A fresh, vibrant and sophisticated cafe with reasonable prices and Parisian vibe, serving an array of breakfasts,

GOING OUT
CAFES

salads, crepes and evening meals of an exceptional standard. Think classic dishes with a luxury twist – burgers made with Wagyu beef and Gruyere cheese and mac and cheese served with truffles. Be sure to try the French pastries and specialist coffee menu. Floor-to-ceiling windows look out to the terrace and the queue of people eager to gain entry. There's also valet parking.

Game On!
There's a growing selection of cafes serving up a cappuccino with helping of board games and books. You can play chess and Trivial Pursuit on the comfy leather couches of Bert's Cafe in the Greens Village, or test your wits and patience in a game of Scrabble or Jenga at Tea Junction in Oud Metha. Teens will love the video gaming rooms at The Living Room Cafe at Festival City, where UNO and billiards are also on the menu. If you'd prefer to turn the pages of a book while savouring your morning eggs Benedict, then head to the reading cafes such as BookMunch in Wasl Square, The Archive in Safa Park or The Magazine Shop in DIFC – where there's a great selection of books and journals to peruse at your leisure.

Coffee Mornings
Dubai hasn't always been known for its cafe culture but the situation is improving, with more and more places to go and linger over a cup of coffee

Armani/Dubai Caffe
The Dubai Mall Downtown Dubai, Burj Khalifa
04 339 8396
thedubaimall.com
Map **2 F7** Metro **Burj Khalifa/Dubai Mall**
Classy Italian dishes are served up with the kind of flair you'd expect from this cafe's designer namesake, and the surroundings live up to the label too. It's all about moody reds and dark wood tones that create an ambience, which is at the same time welcoming and effortlessly stylish.

Circle
Jumeira 2 **04 342 8177**
circle-cafe.com
Map **2 D4** Metro **Business Bay**
A comfortable spot to chat over a coffee. Light, bright and gloriously feminine, the decor at Circle suits its menu of yummy bagels, salads, smoothies and puddings. Walls are lined with mirrors and quirky photos, and there's even a resident goldfish. Also at Dubai Media City (04 391 5170/1).

Gerard's
Jumeira 1 **04 344 3327**
Map **2 H4** Metro **World Trade Centre**
The courtyard setting gives this popular meeting spot and coffee house its unique traditional French atmosphere and, there's also a good selection of croissants, pastries and chocolate covered dates. Ideal for morning coffee, hot chocolate or afternoon tea. Takeaway trade is brisk.

Madeleine Cafe & Boulangerie
The Dubai Mall Downtown Dubai, Burj Khalifa
04 438 4335
madeleinecafe.com
Map **2 F7** Metro **Burj Khalifa/Dubai Mall**
This spacious, tucked-away cafe resembles a traditional Parisian restaurant. Wooden tables and chairs are accompanied by kitsch French ornaments. The menu offers casual French cuisine; sandwiches, soups and crepes, in hearty portions; try the freshly baked fairy cakes too. The pièce de résistance is the spectacular view of the Dubai Fountain show.

Vienna Cafe
JW Marriott Al Muraqqabat **04 607 7977**
marriottdiningatjw.ae
Map **2 N6** Metro **Al Rigga**
The wood panelling and delicate tablecloths are not readily associated with Deira, but the decor blends well with the grandeur of the JW Marriott hotel. There is a good selection of food, from light salads to steaks, but the real draw is people-watching while enjoying a good coffee. Order a slice of the home-made Baumkuchen and linger over a newspaper.

GOING OUT
CAFES

Working Lunch

Recommended for their central location, business facilities or quiet environment, these cafes are ideal for meetings, working lunches and personal workspace.

1762
DIFC Zaa'beel 2 **800 1762**
1762.ae
Map **2 G6** Metro **Financial Centre**
1762 has created a pleasant atmosphere to relax and enjoy the taste of artisan sandwiches, soups, salads and cakes. Its imaginative, deli-style menu features bursts of international flavours such as mango chilli chicken and wasabi labneh with salmon. And, as well as a daily changing variety of salads, quiche and soups, there are homemade pies, pastries and desserts of a gourmet standard.

Bagels & More
Marina Diamond 3 Marsa Dubai **04 430 8790**
bagelsandmore.com
Map **1 L5** Metro **Dubai Marina**
Take advantage of free wi-fi at this NYC-style deli and linger for ages over your morning bagel and coffee, or enjoy a hearty lunch outside on the terrace. The bagels come in a myriad of flavours and are crammed with a host of delicious fillings from lox to pastrami – this is as close as it gets to a genuine New York bagel experience on our sandy shores.

Balance Cafe
Al Quoz 1 **04 515 4051**
balance-wellness-centre.com
Map **2 C6** Metro **Noor Bank**
The menu features nutritionally balanced and tasty dishes inspired by Mediterranean, Indian and Japanese cooking. Choose between wraps, soups and sushi for light bites or opt for the heartier mains that include pasta, kebabs and barbecue grub. There's an emphasis on vegetarian dishes but meatier options like grilled prawns and lamb biryani are also available. Nutritional information is provided for all dishes and the prices are incredibly reasonable.

Bert's Cafe
The Greens, Al Thanyah 1 **04 361 9292**
bertsdxb.com
Map **1 N5** Metro **Dubai Internet City**
Love board games? Head to this healthy eatery to indulge your inner geek with some chess or Trivial Pursuit. Food-wise, the emphasis is on nutrition and you'll find scrumptious salads, soups and sandwiches alongside heartier dishes. Bright and breezy, this welcoming cafe also makes a perfect lunch-stop for workers in TECOM as well as a cosy breakfast spot to while away your time with coffee and newspapers.

Elements
Umm Hurair 2 **04 324 4252**
Map **2 L7** Metro **Dubai Healthcare City**
Vibrant yet stylish furniture and walls crammed with paintings give Elements the feel of an industrial art warehouse. Lunchtime is always a busy affair thanks to the bargain three-course buffet, while the shisha terrace fills up in the evenings as diners dig into sushi, tapas, pasta and Arabic dishes.

Jones The Grocer
Indigo Central 8 Al Manara **04 346 6886**
jonesthegrocer.com
Map **1 T6** Metro **First Gulf Bank**
This is more than a grocer – it's a Dubai institution: an emporium of homemade pastas, freshly baked breads, gourmet fresh and imported treats such as pestos and sweets, and a fromagerie of artisan cheeses. And that's just the deli. The urban chic cafe is not to be missed for breakfast or lunch and the bakery section is overflowing with fresh croissants. Unsurprisingly, it's packed on weekend mornings too. This is food as it should be – insanely good.

MAKE Business Hub
An urban cafe for the mobile worker, Make Business Hub (04 392 9216, makebusinesshub.com). offers a cool space where you can concentrate, and serves tasty nosh to keep the brain cells firing. Find it in the Marsa Dubai area in Al Fattan Office Tower – in between JLT and Dubai Marina Metro stations. It's open from 8am to 8pm (Saturday to Thursday) and 10am to 7pm (on Friday). Also hosts events to promote entrepreneurship, technology and design. Its Facebook page has more information.

Medley > p.xvi, IBC
Pullman Deira City Centre Port Saeed **04 294 1222**
pullmanhotels.com
Map **2 N7** Metro **Deira City Centre**
Warm yellow walls enclose beautifully appointed tables with fresh flowers and low lighting. The 'power lunch' at Medley, Sunday to Thursday, is always a hit with diners, who round off an excellent main with a winning dessert and satisfying beverages.

Panini
Grand Hyatt Umm Hurair 2 **04 317 2222**
restaurants.dubai.hyatt.com
Map **2 L8** Metro **Dubai Healthcare City**
Set among the tropical indoor 'rainforest' in the impressive lobby of the Grand Hyatt, complete with lush greenery and jungle mist, Panini is a good place to meet up with friends or business associates for a lunch on the run. The food is nothing special but it is very convenient.

418 Dubai Explorer

GOING OUT
CAFES

Tom&Serg
Al-Joud Centre Al Quoz **04 346 6886**
jonesthegrocer.com
Map **1 U6** Metro **Noor Bank**
The newest kid on the breakfast scene, Tom&Serge is a causing quite a stir. Popular with the grungy hipster crowd, the utilitarian warehouse setting is softened with quirky touches and a focus on good, tasty food. It's just what Dubai's been missing.

Afternoon Tea
The quintessentially British pastime of afternoon tea – with its quaint scones, finger sandwiches and china teacups – has found a welcome home in Dubai.

Arcadia
H Hotel Trade Center 1 **04 501 8888**
h-hotel.com
Map **2 J5** Metro **World Trade Centre**
The relaxing lobby lounge at the H Hotel is the perfect place to be ensconced with your scones. Start with a tower of sandwiches and a bottomless teapot, before moving on to scones and finally the patissier's platter.

Hey Sugar
Jumeira 1 **04 344 8204**
Map **2 H4** Metro **Emirates Towers**
Your first stop for an indulgent sugar rush – choose from the rainbow of delicious cupcakes, pair with a coffee or shake, and gorge yourself silly. Takeaway and delivery are available too.

Karat
The Address Dubai Mall Downtown Dubai, Burj Khalifa **04 888 3444**
theaddress.com
Map **2 F6** Metro **Burj Khalifa/Dubai Mall**
This is afternoon tea with serious style: settle on an opulent, high-backed leather seat and choose from 26 teas before the four-course feast arrives. Devonshire cream scones are followed by finger sandwiches, miniature cakes, pastries and Arabic sweets. It's vast by any standard and, at Dhs.125, it's one not to be missed.

Lobby Lounge
Ritz-Carlton Dubai Marsa Dubai **04 399 4000**
ritzcarlton.com
Map **1 L4** Metro **Dubai Marina**
Tea at the Ritz is an exquisite experience. Delicate finger sandwiches and dainty pastries, succulent scones with clotted cream and a selection of jams, a fabulously colonial selection of teas and the fine china are all deliciously regal. It feels exclusive, but everyone is welcome. Also try The Lobby Lounge & Terrace at DIFC – perfect for an informal business meeting.

Lobby Lounge & Terrace
Ritz-Carlton DIFC Zaa'beel 2 **04 372 2222**
ritzcarlton.com
Map **2 G6** Metro **Financial Centre**
Lofty ceilings and comfortable armchairs make for an informal business meeting. The Lobby Lounge & Terrace offers a traditional afternoon tea with raisin scones and English Wilkinson Jams. Try the comforting caffeine-free African amber tea with hibiscus and vanilla. High tea is 2pm to 5pm and costs Dhs.140.

Mashrabiya Lounge
Fairmont The Palm Nakhlat Jumeira **04 457 3457**
fairmont.com
Map **1 N3** Metro **Nakheel**
High ceilings, grand sofas and superb sea views from the terrace characterise this upscale venue. Afternoon tea includes sandwiches, scones and clotted cream, Eccles cakes, Bara Brith (speckled bread), and Battenberg cakes, plus homemade jams. Served between 12pm and 6pm, it costs Dhs.110 per person, or you can upgrade to include some bubbles.

Plantation
Sofitel Jumeirah JBR, Marsa Dubai **04 448 4848**
sofitel-dubai-jumeirahbeach.com
Map **1 K5** Metro **Jumeirah Lakes Towers**
A welcome change to stuffy alternatives, Plantation's light and airy surroundings have a 'modern colonial' feel. The conservatory makes a pleasingly relaxed setting for afternoon tea or a light bite. As the lights of JBR's towers start to glow, it becomes a relaxed lounge bar, perfect for a dapper drink or a neat nightcap.

Lobby Lounge

GOING OUT
CAFES

Sahn Eddar
Burj Al Arab Umm Suqeim 3 **04 301 7600**
jumeirah.com
Map **1 S4** Metro **Mall of the Emirates**

It may be an expensive cuppa, but this is the ultimate afternoon tea experience – as well as being the perfect way to see inside the Burj Al Arab, which requires a reservation in one of the hotel's restaurants or rooms. Your tea begins with a glass of bubbly and continues with course after course of dainty sandwiches and fine pastries. Sahn Eddar is on the first floor, but to make it really memorable, also go to the Skyview Bar to enjoy the stunning vistas.

Sultan's Lounge
Jumeirah Zabeel Saray Nakhlat Jumeirah **04 453 0444**
jumeirah.com
Map **1 L3** Metro **Nakheel**

The Sultan's Lounge is finely appointed for a Turkish-themed tea and coffee lounge. The English and Ottoman afternoon teas feature all manner of savoury and sweet treats with jam and cream and a wide variety of teas and coffees. Served with views of the beach and Palm Jumeirah.

Tea Junction
Nr Movenpick Hotel Oud Metha **04 357 6677**
teajunction.ae
Map **2 K7** Metro **Oud Metha**

A hip and arty hangout complete with board games and shisha. There are cosy sofas, big windows, free wi-fi and great music too. Diners can choose from a wide range of teas, mocktails and fresh fruit juices, as well as a generous selection of omelettes, crepes and healthy sandwiches.

Family Friendly

For a relaxed place to take the kids where they can run riot, order off a kiddie friendly menu, and be entertained – then look no further.

Arabian Tea House
Al Fahidi Historical Neighbourhood
Al Souk Al Kabeer **04 353 5071**
arabianteahouse.co
Map **2 M4** Metro **Al Fahidi**

Previously known as Basta Art Cafe, this courtyard cafe and gallery offers quiet sanctuary amid busy and atmospheric Al Fahidi Historical Neighbourhood (formerly known as Bastakiya). Visitors get to sit on majlis-style cushions or under a canopy while choosing from the menu of hearty breakfasts, healthy salads and tempting paninis. Its sister outlet at Arabian Ranches has a similarly rustic-chic atmosphere. Follow with a wander around the historical neighbourhood.

Cafe Ceramique
Jumeira 1 **04 344 7331**
cafeceramique.ae
Map **2 F4** Metro **Burj Khalifa/Dubai Mall**

Reserve this cafe for when you, or the kids, need to release your creativity. Choose an item and decorate it using paints and stencils – it will then be glazed for collection at a later date. The menu has light snacks, kids' choices and hot and cold drinks. It's also a popular place for children's parties. There's another branch in Festival Centre.

The Lime Tree Cafe & Kitchen
Nr Jumeirah Mosque Jumeira 1 **04 349 8498**
thelimetreecafe.com
Map **2 H4** Metro **World Trade Centre**

The Lime Tree Cafe & Kitchen is a true Dubai institution, and a great spot for breakfast with friends or a casual lunch. The menu nods towards Mediterranean cuisine, and features plenty of roast vegetables, halloumi cheese and grilled chicken paninis, as well as delicious salads, satay kebabs and quiches. Don't leave without sharing an enormous slice of the superlative carrot cake, which is widely thought to be the best of its kind in Dubai. There are good alfresco dining options too. Also at Ibn Batutta Mall, Al Qouz and Media City.

THE One
Jumeira Rd Jumeira 1 **04 345 6687**
theone.com
Map **2 H4** Metro **World Trade Centre**

Tucked away on the first floor of THE One furniture store, this funky cafe features an extensive and imaginative menu with high quality food, fresh juices and some astounding cakes. The all-day brunch menu includes creative dishes such as banana French toast (which the kids will love) as well as a zaatar and halloumi omelette. There's a good dedicated kids' menu to peruse too. A good spot for a family-friendly breakfast on the weekend.

Shakespeare & Co > p.421
Al Attar Business Tower Trade Center 2 **04 331 1757**
shakespeareandco.ae
Map **2 G6** Metro **Financial Centre**

With chic Victorian flair, an eclectic menu featuring cuisines from the US, Italy and the Middle East, and period-inspired decor, this ubiquitous chain offers more than just exquisite food and a relaxed atmosphere. Try the delicious smoothies, mocktails and hot and cold drinks and tuck into the home-made hand-wrapped chocolates and delicious French pastries. It's also a great option for a casual evening catch-up over fresh juices and shisha. Catering services are also available. There are branches all over the city – most having a dedicated kids' playroom.

Shakespeare and Co.
Café Restaurant - Catering - Pâtisserie - Chocolates

DUBAI

Souk Al Bahar
04 425 7971

Al Attar Business Tower
04 331 1757

Safa Center
04 394 1121

The Village
04 344 6228

Dubai Marina Mall
04 457 4199

Emirates Hills
04 360 8886

Dubai Mall
04 434 0195

Etihad Mall
04 284 3749

Arabian Ranches
04 447 0444

www.shakespeareandco.ae

GOING OUT
BARS, PUBS & CLUBS

BARS, PUBS & CLUBS

Whether you're looking for a quiet night munching on tapas and nursing a glass of red, or are dressed to take on the dance floor, you'll probably find a suitable venue amongst the ever-growing selection of nightspots on offer.

As with the restaurant scene, dress codes veer towards the smart rather than the casual. Large groups of gentlemen will have problems getting into most venues, so try and break up into mixed gender groups or couples. Some establishments have a shiny 'members only' sign on the door, which is generally ignored, but may be enforced on busy nights.

Although the drinking age is 21, you are well advised to take some form of ID even if you're well above the legal requirement. Arguing with the doorman is pointless and if you are refused entry due to your youthful glow, you will be left to make your way home alone. If you decide to book a table in a nightclub, expect to be subjected to a hefty minimum spend.

Club Rush
Got a 13-going-on-30 year old? Bored teens will love Club Rush at Atlantis – a teenage hang out with a mocktail and snack bar, chill out lounge, internet cafe, games room, dance floor and big sound system, and you'll love it too because it's supervised and alcohol free. Birthday parties with a DJ are also available (04 426 1365).

Happy Hour
Drinks can be expensive in Dubai, but thanks to the numerous happy hours around the city, you can enjoy a drink without emptying your bank account. It's not just bars desperate for custom that offer happy hour promotions – stylish joints such as The Observatory at the Marriott Harbour Hotel offer a three-hour Happy Hour daily; as does ICON Bar and Lounge, Radisson Blu, Media City. The usual start time is 5pm or 6pm, so don't forget to pencil in dinner to avoid that soul-crushing hangover the next day.

Safer Driver
If you've enjoyed a few drinks with dinner then leave the car and contact Safer Driver. You'll be breaking the law if you drive after even one drink, but this clever service means you avoid that and the hassle of picking up the car in the morning. Simply call 04 268 8797 and a driver will take you and your car home then be on his merry way. Be sure to book in advance.

Beach Bars & Sundowners
If your idea of the perfect night involves sea views with your sundowners, you've come to the right emirate. Take your pick of some of our favourites.

Under Age
The law in Dubai states that drinkers must be 21 or over. If you're lucky enough to look like you barely remember the 80s, make sure you carry some ID such as a passport or driving licence.

Barasti
Mina Seyahi **04 318 1313**
barastibeach.com
Map **1 M5** Metro **Nakheel**
Expats flock to this lively venue in flip-flops or their Friday finery. A tasty menu, combined with a sea view, big screens, live music and a friendly crowd make for a good night out. Entry is free all day, so you can spend the day on the beach and then head to the bar!

BidiBondi
Shoreline Apartments Nakhlat Jumeira **04 427 0515**
emiratesleisureretail.com
Map **1 N4** Metro **Nakheel**
Relaxed and informal, this Aussie bar on Palm Jumeirah has a beach diner feel. The menu offers hefty burgers, salads, bar snacks, breakfast and kids' specials alongside a range of cocktails, beers and wines.

The Jetty Lounge > p.175
One&Only Royal Mirage Al Sufouh 2 **04 399 9999**
royalmirage.oneandonlyresorts.com
Map **1 M5** Metro **Nakheel**
With awe-inspiring panoramas and chic beachside lounging, this is the perfect post-work hangout venue. After drinks you can jump aboard a private boat to the sister hotel, One&Only The Palm.

Koubba Bar
Al Qasr Al Sufouh 1 **04 366 6730**
jumeirah.com
Map **1 R5** Metro **Mall of the Emirates**
Stunning views of Dubai await you from the terrace of this sumptuous cocktail bar. Check out the Armoury Lounge, where you can indulge in Cuban cigars.

Meydan Beach
The Walk at JBR Marsa Dubai **04 433 3777**
meydanbeach.com
Map **1 K4** Metro **Jumeirah Lakes Towers**
Perfect beachfront setting boasting pools with floating loungers. Great range of drinks and live DJs from sunset. Also houses a gym, spa and salon.

GOING OUT
BARS, PUBS & CLUBS

The Jetty Lounge

Barasti

BidiBondi

GOING OUT
BARS, PUBS & CLUBS

Nasimi Beach > p.275
Atlantis Nakhlat Jumeira **04 426 2626**
atlantisthepalm.com
Map **1 N1** Metro **Nakheel**
Located in the shadow of Atlantis, Nasimi Beach boasts a relaxed vibe. The restaurant's select menu features expertly prepared seafood and meat dishes and, as evening becomes night, superstar DJs take to the decks and the glamour levels soar. Not cheap, but a great Dubai experience.

Sporting Action
The glitz and glamour of Dubai's bar scene is all very well, but sometimes you just want a joint where you can catch the big match and enjoy a pint with your mates. These venues are recommended for supping and spectating: Barasti, Boston Bar, Champions, Double Decker, Girders, Nezesaussi, and The Underground.

Cocktails
Serving both cocktails and mocktails, this selection of bars really knows how to mix it up – and you'll often enjoy a display of flair bartending too!

Balcony Bar
Shangri-La Dubai Trade Center 1 **04 405 2703**
shangri-la.com
Map **2 G6** Metro **Burj Khalifa/Dubai Mall**
Dark, masculine wooden panelling and black leather armchairs dominate this sophisticated cocktail bar. The drinks list is extensive, and each cocktail is artfully presented. For the extravagant pocket, there are some eye wateringly expensive champagnes and vintage whiskies, while teetotallers can choose from a basic selection of booze-free beverages.

Barzar
Souk Madinat Jumeirah Al Sufouh 1 **04 366 6730**
jumeirah.com
Map **1 R4** Metro **Mall of the Emirates**
This funky bar hits the balance between laidback cool and noisy revelry, with the added attraction of live bands. Eclectic drinks, such as beer cocktails, are paired with more traditional liquid offerings.

Dress Code
While many bars have a reasonably relaxed attitude towards dress code, some places will not allow you in if you are wearing shorts and sandals, while others require a collared shirt and have a 'no jeans or trainers' policy. In general, nightclubs are more strict, so dress to impress.

Cin Cin
Fairmont Trade Center 1 **04 311 8316**
fairmont.com
Map **2 J5** Metro **World Trade Centre**
With a stylish backdrop of warehouse-high wine shelves, and walls fashioned like falling water, it's easy to get carried away ordering imaginative cocktails and fine wines, but brace yourself for the bill – this is expense account territory.

Crossroads Cocktail Bar
Raffles Umm Hurair 2 **04 314 9888**
raffles.com
Map **2 K7** Metro **Dubai Healthcare City**
Home of the Dubai Sling, an imaginative mix of coriander, chilli, fig and lemon, and the drink of choice for surveying the nearby sparkling skyline. With extremely knowledgeable staff, well executed bar snacks and a dizzying choice of drinks, you won't mind paying above-average prices for the experience.

Left Bank
Downtown Dubai, Burj Khalifa **04 368 4501**
emiratesleisureretail.com
Map **2 F6** Metro **Burj Khalifa/Dubai Mall**
With its black wallpaper, deep red velvet booths and white leather couches, this bar feels like an exclusive spot in a cosmopolitan city. The stylish food and cocktails fit well with the swanky surroundings, and the 'small plates' menu begs to be explored with a cocktail in hand. Alternatively, order a sharing platter to sample as many dishes as possible. There's a more low-key version at Souk Madinat Jumeirah.

Left Bank

424 | Dubai Explorer

GOING OUT
BARS, PUBS & CLUBS

QD's
Creek Golf Club Port Saeed **04 295 6000**
dubaigolf.com
Map **2 M7** Metro **Deira City Centre**
Sitting so close to the water's edge that you can almost dip your toes into the creek, you can watch the passing abras as the sun sets over Sheikh Zayed Road from this charming and atmospheric locale. Elegant bar snacks accompany an excellent cocktail list and, as the night wears on, the live band keeps the shisha-smoking crowd entertained.

Sanctuary Pool Lounge
Sheraton Mall of the Emirates Al Barsha 1
04 377 2353
pullman-dubai.com
Map **1 R6** Metro **Mall of the Emirates**
Head to Sanctuary's poolside during the day to soak up some rays and enjoy relaxed light bites and cocktails with a fabulous view. At night, you can enjoy the chilled ambience with simple cuisine and cracking cocktails – or simply sit back and smoke a shisha pipe.

Sho Cho
Dubai Marine Beach Resort Jumeira 1 **04 346 1111**
sho-cho.com
Map **2 H4** Metro **World Trade Centre**
It may be a Japanese restaurant with delicate and imaginative dishes, but the huge terrace, not to mention the sunshine holiday vibe, is what attracts the beautiful clientele to this popular spot. The mix of house and trance music and a gorgeous view of the shoreline make this a must. And the cocktails add the perfect finishing touch.

Story Roof Top Lounge
Nr Zayed University Knowledge Village, Al Sufouh 2
04 365 9911
storydubai.com
Map **1 N5** Metro **Dubai Internet City**
An arty urban hangout with two rooftop terraces offering sweeping views from the Palm across to Jumeira. The bar is chic, yet bohemian, with funky, abstract Latin-American murals decorating the walls – a nod to the venue's passion for art. The varied cocktail menu will keep you occupied for hours.

Trader Vic's Mai Tai Lounge
Jumeirah Beach Residence Marsa Dubai **04 386 5646**
tradervics.com
Map **1 K4** Metro **Dubai Marina**
The livelier cousin of the Crowne Plaza and Madinat Jumeirah eateries (04 366 5346), this Tiki bar is decked out in Polynesian style. Mai Tai's totally tropical (and rather potent) cocktail list is accompanied by tasty, if expensive, bar snacks and the spacious dancefloor provides a clubby feel.

Veda Pavilion
Clubhouse Al Nafura, Shoreline Apartments
Nakhlat Jumeira **04 361 8845**
emiratesleisureretail.com
Map **1 N4** Metro **Nakheel**
Head to this chic yet comfortable bar after a day at the beach. The substantial drinks list (including delicious cocktails) and affordable far eastern inspired menu are suited to casual lunches, dinners with groups of friends, or just a lazy beer on the poolside terrace, with views of the Burj Al Arab and the Arabian Gulf.

Voda Bar
Jumeirah Zabeel Saray Nakhlat Jumeira **04 453 0444**
jumeirah.com
Map **1 L3** Metro **Nakheel**
Futuristic and minimalist, with a spacious floor plan that includes a handful of attractive white egg-shaped chairs and white leather sofas. There is a 15-page list of exotic Japanese inspired cocktails. The food served is specifically Japanese – beautifully presented and ideal for sharing. It's pricey, but the beauty of the bar and the delightful food ensure it is money well spent.

Ladies' Nights
Lucky ladies can go out almost any night of the week and enjoy free drinks. Of course, this isn't a charitable venture by Dubai's bar scene; where ladies are drinking, the men and their wallets inevitably follow. Tuesday is the biggest ladies' night with many bars and pubs offering at least two free drinks. The most legendary venues are Oeno and Healey's Bar & Terrace, while Boudoir and Blends are very lady friendly, with free bubbly or cocktails nearly every night of the week. Icon Bar is perfect for free post-work drinks straight from your office in Media City. In the interests of equality, the Media One Hotel is now hosting Madmen in Z:ONE on Mondays – where the boys get to enjoy two free drinks.

Pubs
These are the bars that do their best to focus more on beer, quiz nights and your favourite pub grub – and are all the more fun for it.

Dhow & Anchor
Jumeirah Beach Umm Suqeim 3 **04 406 8999**
jumeirah.com
Map **1 S4** Metro **Mall of the Emirates**
Dhow & Anchor's bar is a popular spot, particularly during happy hour and sporting events – try the outdoor terrace and enjoy glimpses of the Burj Al Arab. The menu includes terrific curries, pies, and fish and chips. There's a pub quiz on Tuesday night.

askexplorer.com 425

GOING OUT
BARS, PUBS & CLUBS

Double Decker
Al Murooj Rotana Trade Center 2 04 321 1111
rotana.com
Map **2 G6** Metro **Financial Centre**
Adorned with London transport memorabilia, this two-storey bar serves upmarket pub grub including plenty of stodgy choices and tasty sharing platters. It is packed on Fridays, with revellers attracted by its lively, bargain brunch. Weekly karaoke and ladies' nights plus plenty of big screen sports ensure there is something for everyone.

The Dubliner's
Le Meridien Al Garhoud 04 702 2307
diningatmeridiendubai.com
Map **2 N8** Metro **Airport Terminal 1**
Cosy and lively, this Irish pub has a weekly quiz, good music and plenty of screens for watching sports. The menu is full of fresh, tasty and reasonably priced dishes. Save room for the Bailey's cheesecake.

Fibber Magee's
Off Shk Zayed Rd Trade Center 1 04 332 2400
fibbersdubai.com
Map **2 H5** Metro **World Trade Centre**
Succeeding where many fail, Fibber's has the unpolished feel of a true pub. Televised sport, DJs, themed entertainment evenings (including the excellent Easy Tiger quiz on Tuesdays), great value promotions make it perennially popular.

Girders
JA Ocean View JBR, Marsa Dubai 04 814 5590
jaresortshotels.com
Map **1 K5** Metro **Jumeirah Lakes Towers**
A welcoming, traditional British pub that makes a nod to Scotland and Ireland with a Gaelic-themed menu. This is a place to come to enjoy the pub quiz, big-screen sporting action and a daily happy hour between 6pm and 10pm. From the modern steel furnishing to the cosy fireplace, this is the perfect spot to sample the well-stocked bar, hearty dishes such as the full Scottish breakfast and shepherd's pie, and a soak up the lively atmosphere. Get there early to bag a table on pub quiz night.

Quiz Night
If you want to test your brain power and knowledge of useless trivia then grab a group of mates and head to one of Dubai's many pub quiz nights. Try Boston Bar or Player's Lounge on Mondays, or Tuesdays at the Dhow & Anchor, Jumeirah Beach Hotel. If you don't mind fierce competition, give the quiz at the Arabian Ranches Golf Club a go, or enter the Girders quiz and enjoy some Scottish pub grub at the same time.

Harvester's Pub
Crowne Plaza Trade Center 1 04 331 1111
szrdining.com
Map **2 H5** Metro **Emirates Towers**
The decor at Harvester's is exactly what you would expect from a themed English pub, as in fact is the drinks menu. What you come here for though is the pub-style menu which is classically hearty and tasty, with a chicken tikka masala that would put many Indian restaurants to shame.

The Irish Village > p.427
Aviation Club Al Garhoud 04 282 4750
irishvillage.ae
Map **2 M8** Metro **GGICO**
Forget the city and enjoy a pint of the black stuff. This laidback Irish pub offers both indoor and alfresco seating, managing to create an authentic pub experience complete with a sprawling beer garden. There's a good selection of pub grub on offer that comes in generous portions and at a reasonable price, including freshly baked soda bread, Irish stew and Bailey's cheesecake, which is not to be missed! Keep an eye on the website for regular concerts and events.

McGettigan's Irish Pub
Bonnington JLT, Al Thanyah 5 04 356 0560
mcgettigansdubai.com
Map **1 K5** Metro **Jumeirah Lakes Towers**
This fairly cavernous bar is pretty rowdy all week. A far-cry from the old-fashioned 'Oirish t'bae sure' themed bar, there are plenty of stools, tables and nooks for drinkers and diners, with a menu that focuses on inexpensive but hearty fare over haute cuisine. Big matches are shown, the quiz is a hoot and there's regular live entertainment. The Guinness is well kept and well served, the Irish stew comes piping hot with a couple of doorstops of bread, and the singer kicks off with Dirty Old Town… what more could you want?

Nelson's
TECOM, Al Thanyah 1 04 435 0000
rotana.com
Map **1 P6** Metro **Dubai Internet City**
Pitch up to this unpretentious bar if you want to watch football, tuck into traditional English dishes and enjoy some British banter. The bar in the centre resembles a typical Victorian pub, and punters can settle into large armchairs, prop themselves up on bar stools, or cluster around wide-screen TVs.

Oak N Barrel
Grand Excelsior Al Barsha 1 04 444 9999
grandexcelsior.ae
Map **1 R7** Metro **Mall of the Emirates**
The deep leather chairs, mahogany bar counters and classical taps all add to the character of this traditional

The only real Irish experience in the heart of Dubai

Whether you decide to sit inside the traditional wooden pub or out on the terrace overlooking the garden and lake, let the music entertain you while sampling authentic meals served with a warm and friendly Irish smile – what better way of experiencing Ireland in Dubai!

WHAT'S ON BEST PUB FOOD 2002, 2003, 2004, 2005, 2009 & 2012
TIME OUT DUBAI NIGHTLIFE AWARDS - BEST LIVE MUSIC CONCERT 2011
TIME OUT NIGHTLIFE AWARDS - BEST MUSIC VENUE 2010 & 2011
WHAT'S ON 2012 - FAVOURITE BAR
TIME OUT 2012 - BEST PUB

The Irish Village Dubai

The Irish Village Dubai. Al Garhoud next to Dubai Tennis Stadium.
P.O. Box 55300, Dubai U.A.E. Tel: +971 4 2824700. www.theirishvillage.com   Visit us on:

GOING OUT
BARS, PUBS & CLUBS

English pub. Choose classic pub-style malt beverages or cocktails, or order a light meal while watching sports events. Regular events include the pub quiz every Sunday, Spare ribs & Steak Night, Friday Roast Lunch, a daily happy hour and promotional nights for ladies and teachers.

Warehouse
Le Meridien Al Garhoud **04 702 2560**
diningdubai.com
Map **2 N8** Metro **Airport Terminal 1**

Warehouse is a stylish and unusual addition to the old-school side of the creek because it houses several different themes: there is a beer bar and garden on the ground floor serving fish and chips and the like, while up the spiral staircase you'll find a dual-personality restaurant – half fine dining and half sushi – where the food is deliciously inventive. There is also an intimate nightclub should you want to continue the night.

The Whistler
JA Ocean View JBR, Marsa Dubai **04 814 5590**
jaresortshotels.com
Map **1 J4** Metro **Jumeirah Lakes Towers**

Wine, cheese and a whole lot of luxury are what you'll find when you walk into The Whistler. Located on the 25th floor, this is the place to admire Dubai's skyline and unwind. Let the sommelier advise you on the perfect pairing of fine cheese and wine, and enjoy a 'wine flight' – tasting a variety of red and white wines served using the popular Enomatic system. Live music from a saxophone player sets the mood perfectly.

Warehouse

Rooftop

Take advantage of balmy evenings with rooftop drinks under the stars. Sundowners overlooking the skyline of Dubai is a tough act to follow.

360 Hotel
Jumeirah Beach Umm Suqeim 3 **055 500 8518**
jumeirah.com
Map **1 S4** Metro **First Gulf Bank**

This two-tiered circular rooftop bar boasts all-round views of the Arabian Gulf and Burj Al Arab. House DJs spin at the weekends, and late afternoon loungers smoking shisha give way to scruffily chic stylistas sipping cocktails as the tempo rises. The bartenders here make a mean mojito, but for something sweeter, try the vanilla version. Open from 4pm and at weekends, arrive in time to catch the holiday snap-worthy sunset. It's the perfect place to take visitors for drinks but be sure to get your name on the guestlist through platinumlist.ae.

Cabana
The Address Dubai Mall Downtown Dubai, Burj Khalifa **04 888 3444**
theaddress.com
Map **2 F6** Metro **Burj Khalifa/Dubai Mall**

Cabana's Miami-cool pool bar and restaurant sit sweetly beneath the Burj Khalifa. Lounge on sunbeds and beanbags by the pool, or enjoy the privacy of a cabana as you enjoy the eclectic menu and chilled soundtrack. It's the perfect setting for cocktails, and Friday brunch is a lively occasion.

THE DEK On 8
Media One Al Sufouh 2 **04 427 1000**
mediaonehotel.com
Map **1 M5** Metro **Nakheel**

A popular post-work drinks spot, the bar takes on an alfresco club atmosphere at weekends with a resident DJ. Sip champagne and sample cocktails as you laze on white sofa beds and take in the stunning views of Marsa Dubai. The venue now hosts an indie rock night once or twice a month on Thursdays for those in search of something more down-to-earth.

Nawwara
JW Marriott Marquis Business Bay **04 414 3200**
jwmarriottmarquisdubai.com
Map **2 D6** Metro **Business Bay**

A glow of candlelight greets you when you enter this sublime setting. The feel is palatial without being intimidating – there's a vast lounge where a DJ plays post-dinner, and those not up for dancing can chill on the outdoor terrace with a shisha. The menu features hot and cold mezze and signature main dishes; all delicious and beautifully presented.

"That was the best restaurant I have been to in years.
Thank you James, Saeed and Zoe."

★★★★★ 5 Ratings

Find businesses reviewed and recommended by people just like you.
www.7DAYSinDubai.com/Directory

7DAYSin... Dubai

GOING OUT
BARS, PUBS & CLUBS

Rivington Bar & Terrace
Souk Madinat Jumeirah Al Sufouh 1 **04 366 6464**
rivingtongrill.ae
Map **1 R5** Metro **Mall of the Emirates**
With five outdoor terrace areas, and unobstructed views across the Dubai skyline, this is one of the finest spots to enjoy a cosy drink with friends. And with regular wine and cheese nights, happy hour deals, and a classic British menu of nibbles, it's hard to refuse.

The Rooftop Terrace & Sports Lounge > p.175
One&Only Royal Mirage Al Sufouh 2 **04 399 9999**
oneandonlyroyalmirage.com
Map **1 M4** Metro **Nakheel**
Rooftop is a hangout for the beautiful people, so expect to pay high prices for your tall drinks. That aside, views of The Palm are superb; cleverly placed Arabic cushion seats promote interaction between the clientele in one of the most chilled-out bars.

Shades
The Address Dubai Marina Marsa Dubai **04 377 2353**
theaddress.com
Map **1 K5** Metro **Dubai Marina**
For relaxed poolside dining with a delightfully spacious and breezy terrace, Shades manages to come up trumps. Located on the fourth floor of The Address Dubai Marina, Shades is divided into two sections; the first is on a raised-deck platform, equipped with glass tables and wicker chairs. The other is a pristine lounging area with large white comfy sofas, perfect for pre-dinner drinks or shisha. The new weekend a la carte BBQ special is stripped of all pretentiousness, leaving simple, delectable dishes. Try the delicious seafood platters offering succulent jumbo prawns, or the juicy lobster tail – both cooked to perfection without completely scorching the outside layers. Though it's a little pricey at around Dhs.160, the courteous service, wonderfully relaxing atmosphere and sublime food make it money well spent.

Tamanya Terrace
Radisson Blu Media City Al Sufouh 2 **04 366 9111**
radissonblu.com
Map **1 M5** Metro **Nakheel**
Tamanya treats its patrons to panoramic views of Media City, including iconic landmarks like the Burj Al Arab, The World and The Palm islands. The clientele is a good mix of tourists and expats and the resident DJ spins tunes from house and funk to sultry Latin grooves. Unlike some bars, the music is just loud enough to enjoy without having to scream in your mates' ears all night. There are typical bar snacks if you're peckish, while Tamanya boasts a very good selection of cocktails at very reasonable prices. Guests can also choose wines from the Certo menu if the particular wine they want is not on the bar's menu.

The Terrace
Media Rotana TECOM, Al Thanyah 1 **04 435 0000**
rotana.com
Map **1 P6** Metro **Dubai Internet City**
This rooftop bar is the perfect alfresco drinking spot, with the option of perching at the long bar or relaxing in the garden style furniture. Food is served during the day but after 5pm it is just drinks and shisha and the chill-out tunes of the resident DJ.

Karaoke Bars
Harry Ghatto's in Emirates Towers is a popular haunt, while the post-brunch karaoke sessions at Double Decker range from the sublime to the ridiculous. Also try Checkers Bar at the Majestic Hotel in Bur Dubai. For a unique night, try 'curryoke' at It's Mirchi in the Ramee Royal Hotel, Bur Dubai, which serves up Indian fare. On the other side of the creek, Kisaku is a good option, with private rooms for groups. Or sing your heart out at the Hibiki Music Lounge, a cosy karaoke lounge with three private rooms. For something a little more low-key (where you can also grab a tasty bite to eat), check out Kung Korean Restaurant and Karaoke in TECOM's Byblos Hotel.

Uptown Bar
Jumeirah Beach Hotel Umm Suqeim 3 **04 406 8999**
jumeirah.com
Map **1 S4** Metro **First Gulf Bank**
Uptown Bar certainly lives up to its name, offering both a stylish night out and incredible views from its location on the 24th floor of Jumeirah Beach Hotel. From its terrace you can enjoy stunning vistas of the Burj Al Arab and beyond, and the interior is classy enough – in a James Bond kind of way. An extensive menu of lip-smacking cocktails with price tags to match is complemented by tapas and bar snacks.

Vista Lounge
InterContinental Festival City Al Badia, Al Kheeran **04 701 1127**
diningdfc.com
Map **2 L9** Metro **Emirates**
With fabulous views over the creek from the relaxed terrace, a romantically lit piano bar and a modern cocktail bar, Vista is a welcome addition to the 'other side of the creek'. It also has a small food menu serving mainly sandwiches and salads.

Showstopper
Dubai has no shortage of party hotspots, and the following showstopping venues are the best places to throw on your swankiest threads and dress to impress.

GOING OUT
BARS, PUBS & CLUBS

Bahri Bar
Madinat Jumeirah Al Sufouh 1 **04 366 6730**
jumeirah.com
Map **1 R5** Metro **Mall of the Emirates**

This might just be the perfect bar: stunning views of the Burj Al Arab and the sparkling ocean beyond grace the spacious terrace while, inside, lavish but comfortable furnishings create an intimate atmosphere. A selection of delicious drinks and nibbles, plus live music at the weekends, complete a picture of perfection.

Buddha Bar
Grosvenor House Marsa Dubai **04 317 6000**
royaldiningcollection.com
Map **1 L5** Metro **Dubai Marina**

The domain of the stylish set, this half restaurant, half bar nightspot never fails to impress with moody lighting, a huge Buddha statue and marina views. If the waiter can hear you over the funky Buddha bar beats, then order a sublime cocktail and ask for recommendations from the south-east Asian menu.

Skyview Bar
Burj Al Arab Umm Suqeim 3 **04 301 7600**
jumeirah.com
Map **1 S4** Metro **First Gulf Bank**

A cocktail here can easily run into triple figures and you have to book well in advance – there's a minimum spend of Dhs.275 per person just to get in. But it is worth it for special occasions or to impress out-of-town visitors. The views are amazing, as you would expect. You can also take afternoon tea here.

XL Beach Club
Habtoor Grand Marsa Dubai **04 399 5000**
grandjumeirah.habtoorhotels.com
Map **1 L4** Metro **Dubai Marina**

With ample style and more than a pinch of decadence, XL Beach Club lives up to its grandiose name. Energetic beats and shimmering swimming pools set the scene, superstar DJs regularly spin the decks here and, once darkness falls, the chic outdoors venue plays host to some of the best parties in town. If you're feeling flash, splash out on one of the private cabanas.

Wine Bars & Cigar Lounges

For anyone who enjoys the finer things in life these stylish bars offer the very best selections of grape, cheeseboards and cigars.

The Agency
Trade Center 2 **04 319 8088**
jumeirah.com
Map **2 H6** Metro **Financial Centre**

At The Agency, the focus is firmly on what this popular venue does best: wine. There are 80 varieties of wine to test the palates of discerning oenophiles. These include a sommelier's selection and collection of Mondavi wines from California. Cheese platters and a selection of light bites are available, and the adjoining Rib Room has burgers. The Agency also offers Grape Academy and Blind Tasting events, as well as a daily happy hour from 5pm to 9pm.

Buddha Bar

GOING OUT
BARS, PUBS & CLUBS

CafeM
Media One Al Sufouh 2 **04 427 1000**
mediaonehotel.com
Map **1 M5** Metro **Nakheel**
Ideal for a business tete-a-tete during the day, CafeM takes on a bar atmosphere when the post-work crowd hits. From 7pm to 10pm, on Sundays to Thursdays, enjoy unlimited wine and cheese for a bargain price. Great for a no-fuss night out with friends.

Chinwaggery
Movenpick Jumeirah Beach JBR, Marsa Dubai
04 449 8888
moevenpick-hotels.com
Map **1 K4** Metro **Dubai Marina**
Derived from an English phrase to 'have a chin wag', meaning an informal talk or chat, Chinwaggery is the perfect venue for a casual get together or post-work wind down. Though its name may be British-inspired, Chinwaggery's decor and ambience takes its cue from across the Atlantic, New York style. The slick, elegant indoor lounge provides an intimate setting while an open air terrace, overlooking JBR, is ideal for group get-togethers during cooler months.

Chinwaggery

The Cigar Bar
Fairmont Trade Center 1 **04 311 8316**
fairmont.com/dubai
Map **2 H5** Metro **World Trade Centre**
A mid-town venue, the Cigar Bar boasts its own walk-in humidor in a swish country house setting. Sit back in soft leather armchairs and puff away your cares with a glass of your favourite cognac or whisky. The perfect end to a long day.

The Cigar Lounge
The Address Downtown Downtown Dubai, Burj Khalifa **04 436 8888**
theaddress.com
Map **2 F7** Metro **Burj Khalifa/Dubai Mall**
Whether for post-work cocktails or pre-dinner drinks, this is the spot. Take stunning views of the Burj Khalifa, add an extensive selection of cocktails, delicious cheeses, tapas and sweets, choice cigars and a chic atmosphere and mix with soothing jazz, and you've got a recipe for a venue where you'll want to pass the whole night.

Library Bar
Ritz-Carlton Dubai Marsa Dubai **04 399 4000**
ritzcarlton.com
Map **1 L4** Metro **Dubai Marina**
With its dark wood, comfy sofas and dimmed lighting, the Library Bar could be mistaken for a study in an English country house. The bar serves light bites, main meals, a good range of cocktails and, of course, top quality cigars.

No 5 Lounge & Bar
Ritz-Carlton DIFC Zaa'beel 2 **04 372 2323**
ritzcarlton.com
Map **2 G6** Metro **Financial Centre**
Not one for a raucous night out, this is a place to sip a nice malt whisky or expertly-prepared Martini while snacking on some of the poshest bar bites you'll find anywhere and listening to the smooth tunes of the resident DJ. Refined and ideal for an after-hours meeting or low-key catch-up.

Oeno Wine Bar
The Westin Marsa Dubai **04 399 4141**
westinminaseyahi.com
Map **1 M4** Metro **Nakheel**
Fine wine, more than 50 types of cheese and excellent service set Oeno apart. The decor is stylish and the wine wall, complete with library-style bookshelf ladder, adds a sense of decadence. Food is served tapas-style, and Tuesday nights bring three free glasses of sparkling wine for ladies from 7pm-11pm.

Oscar's Vine Society
Crowne Plaza Trade Center 1 **04 331 1111**
szrdining.com
Map **2 H5** Metro **Emirates Towers**
Wine cask tables, dim lighting and a warm welcome set the mood at Oscar's for indulging in full-bodied reds and ripe cheeses. Special dining offers throughout the week offer good value for great French dishes such as cassoulet and moules mariniere. Friendly bartenders and a 'cheese master' are happy to explain the selections.

GOING OUT
BARS, PUBS & CLUBS

Vantage
Sheraton Mall of the Emirates Al Barsha 1
04 377 2356
sheratondubaimalloftheemirates.com
Map **1 R6** Metro **Mall of the Emirates**
The plush, purple interior of this wine bar offers an opulent, but intimate, setting to sample an extensive wine and cocktail list, while the terrace affords sweeping coast views. Arabic snacks dominate the menu, which also features a classic cheese platter.

Vintage Cheese & Wine Bar
Umm Hurair 2 **04 324 4100**
pyramidsrestaurantsatwafi.com
Map **2 L7** Metro **Dubai Healthcare City**
Boasts an exclusive list of cold meat and cheese platters, costly vintages, burgundies and champagnes – but manages to retain the feel of a friendly local. The bar is small, so arrive early or very late to bag a sofa.

The Whistler
JA Ocean View JBR, Marsa Dubai **04 814 5590**
jaresortshotels.com
Map **1 J4** Metro **Jumeirah Lakes Towers**
Wine, cheese and a whole lot of luxury are what you'll find when you walk into The Whistler. Located on the 25th floor, this is the place to admire Dubai's skyline and unwind. Let the sommelier advise you on the perfect pairing of fine cheese and wine, and enjoy a 'wine flight' – tasting a variety of red and white wines served using the popular Enomatic system. Live music from a saxophone player sets the ambient mood perfectly.

Boudoir
Dubai Marine Beach Resort Jumeira 1 **04 345 5995**
myboudoir.com
Map **2 H4** Metro **World Trade Centre**
This exclusive spot has maintained its edge as the place to see and be seen for more than a decade. While it can be difficult to get into, once inside you'll be treated to a Parisian-style club with opulent fabrics, hypnotic tunes and moody lighting. The music varies through the week and there are drinks deals for ladies.

Cavalli Club
Fairmont Trade Center 1 **04 332 9260**
cavalliclubdubai.com
Map **2 H5** Metro **World Trade Centre**
Roberto Cavalli's leopard print and Swarovski encrusted nightspot is one of the city's places to be seen if you're part of the 'It' crowd. Earlier in the evening, the club serves up some good Mediterranean fare in its Italian restaurant. After that, move to the cocktail and cigar lounge, wine bar, or even the boutique shop.

Chameleon Club
Byblos TECOM, Al Thanyah 1 **050 113 5858**
chameleonclubdubai.com
Map **1 N6** Metro **Dubai Internet City**
Entry to this flashy and flamboyant club is via a red carpet that delivers you into an elevator to the penthouse level. You are greeted by a spectrum of neon lighting and a giant chameleon positioned over the bar with its tongue protruding across the dance floor. Although dining is an option, most patrons arrive from 11pm, in time for the techno to be turned up.

Nightlife Options
There is a whole host of clubs to boogie the night away in as well as a few places for impromptu dance routines. Classy venues on the club scene include the Cavalli Club at the Fairmont Dubai and Republique at The Address Dubai Mall. For something a little more down and dirty, check out Rock Bottom at the Regent Palace Hotel, Bur Dubai. For an eclectic music selection try Fridays at 360, which regularly hosts international DJs. For entry before 8pm on Fridays and Saturdays, you will need to get on the guest list at platinumlist.net.

Nightclubs
Dubai is one of the best (and safest cities) for partying; there are loads of clubs with local and international DJs. The city is famed for its swanky, high-class clubs, but there is also a more authentic side, with venues playing retro, indie rock and 80s and 90s tunes; and you can enter without sporting designer labels.

Cavalli Club

askexplorer.com

GOING OUT
BARS, PUBS & CLUBS

Chi@The Lodge
Oud Metha **04 337 9470**
chinightclubdubai.com
Map **2 L6** Metro **Oud Metha**

Best in the winter when the vast garden dancefloor is open, Chi@The Lodge is always busy with its three or four different rooms of contrasting music, lots of seating, large screens and VIP 'cabanas'. The regular fancy dress and themed nights are hugely popular as is the annual Rugby Sevens afterparty that takes place here. It's easy to get taxis outside, there's a shawarma stand in the car park and entrance is free before 10.30pm on most nights.

Kasbar > p.175
One&Only Royal Mirage Al Sufouh 2 **04 399 9999**
royalmirage.oneandonlyresorts.com
Map **1 M4** Metro **Nakheel**

Set over three vibrant floors, Kasbar combines the mystique and luxury of regal Arabia with the feel of an exclusive dance party. In keeping with the Arabian decor of the Royal Mirage, this is a sultry, candlelit nightclub perfect for liaisons, as well as dancing and chilling out.

Magnum
Ramada Jumeirah Al Hudaiba **04 702 7773**
ramadajumeirah.ae
Map **2 J4** Metro **Al Jafiliya**

From Edward Maya and Avicii to Ritchie Hawtin and Sven Vath, Magnum has all your favourite beats covered six days a week. During ladies night on a Tuesday, come in for tasty starters, receive free bubbly till midnight and relax in the trendy chic lounge to ultra-chill tunes. On Fridays, be sure to wear high tops or at least a comfortable pair of kicks, as DJ Nuthiya will have you breakdancing to rhythm and blues all night long. At Magnum they know Saturday usually means 'short changed' but not 'burnt out' so head down and receive 50% off on selected beverages and get footloose to the up-tempo beats pouring out of the speakers. Magnum also has an exclusive face card deal, which will knock 50% off your bill every time.

Rare The Place
TECOM, Al Thanyah 1 **055 505 7580**
Map **1 P6** Metro **Dubai Internet City**

One of TECOM's best kept secrets. Reminiscent of a drawing room from the Versailles Palace, Rare The Place is small but elegantly attired in baroque furnishings, and fuses old with new in a way that creates a unique theatrical atmosphere for guests to relax in and enjoy their night. Comprising three areas, Rare's main bar takes centre stage with two surrounding seating sections – a lounge space kitted out in comfy leather furniture, and a casual club area with dance floor. Operating as a bar/lounge in the evenings before turning into a fully lively nightclub after midnight, the venue offers nights suitable for everyone's taste – from house music to live jazz, and Arabic pop to R&B.

Rock Bottom
Regent Palace Al Karama **04 396 3888**
rameehotels.com
Map **2 L5** Metro **BurJuman**

Your experience at Rock Bottom, a real Dubai institution, depends on your time – or condition – of arrival. Early on in the evening, it draws a respectable-ish crowd enjoying the reasonably priced diner food or a game of pool, before undergoing a nightly transformation into the sweaty, heaving, hedonistic home of the legendary Bullfrog cocktail and a cracking cover band. So unique is its appeal, it seemed impossible to repeat elsewhere, but the second TECOM venue (04 450 0111) perfectly captured the spirit and the sweat.

Societe
Marina Byblos Hotel Marsa Dubai **050 3571126**
societe.ae
Map **1 K5** Metro **Jumeirah Lakes Towers**

You may wander into this nightspot and feel like you've crashed a wedding thanks to the unashamedly cheesy music from the 70s, 80s and 90s (as well as current tunes), but you won't feel like you shouldn't be there. Refreshingly unpretentious, this club attracts anyone who wants to have a good, old-fashioned boogie. The venue also hosts live performances and comedy nights.

Magnum

GOING OUT
ENTERTAINMENT

Submarine
Dhow Palace Al Mankhool **04 359 9992**
dhowplacedubai.com
Map **2 L5** Metro **Al Karama**
Submarine has filled a bit of the alternative dance void that exists in the city. It doesn't start to fill up until midnight, and the spaceship-meets-submarine decor might miss the mark, but Submarine's DJs will quickly remind you how diverse club music can be.

A Class Of Its Own
Cavalli 54, based on the legendary Studio 54, is a regular night at the Cavalli Club featuring classic hits from the 70s and 80s. Over the top details are introduced to the already lavish, crystal-decked club to help recreate the Studio 54 experience, from theatrics and backdrops, to retro-glam performers and dancers.

White Dubai
Meydan Nadd Al Shiba 1 **050 443 0933**
whitebeirut.com
Map **2 D10** Metro **Business Bay**
This achingly cool club is the Dubai version of its immensely popular sister-club in Beirut. Open since December 2013, it's quickly become the latest place to be seen. It's a must for lovers of electronic and house music thanks to the great guest performers and DJ line-ups, though be prepared to splash some cash as it's not the cheapest night out.

XL Beach Club
Habtoor Grand Marsa Dubai **04 399 5000**
grandjumeirah.habtoorhotels.com
Map **1 L4** Metro **Dubai Marina**
With ample style and more than a pinch of decadence, XL Beach Club lives up to its grandiose name. Private cabanas and a shimmering pool set the scene, superstar DJs regularly spin the decks here and, once darkness falls, the chic outdoors venue plays host to some of the best parties in town. Stylish crowds, an eye-popping drinks list and lively vibes complete the picture. And, although things don't get going till late, it's well worth the wait – this is partying under the stars at its finest.

Zinc
Crowne Plaza Trade Center 1 **04 331 1111**
szrdining.com
Map **2 H5** Metro **Emirates Towers**
The soundtrack to Zinc is modern, funky R&B, house and hip-hop, with Housexy (Ministry of Sound) and Kinky Malinki ferrying over their rostas of UK DJs. Design-wise, there are shiny flatscreens, lounge areas and glitzy mirrored walls, as well as a big dancefloor sectioned off by a mammoth bar.

ENTERTAINMENT

When you're not eating in fantastic restaurants, enjoying a spa or partaking in the numerous sporting activities around the city, then you may just find time to sample what else Dubai has to offer. Every year more events pop up, more venues are built and the decisions become even tougher. From film and music festivals to a comedy or quiz night – if you're bored in Dubai, then you're doing something wrong.

Cabaret
A recent growth in theatre and entertainment venues in Dubai has seen the launch of The Act (056 811 9900) at the Shangri-La Hotel, which aims to be the world's highest theatre on 42nd and 43rd floors. It's a version of venues already popular in Las Vegas and London and boasts international acts flying in from all over the world, as well as a Peruvian dining experience. It's not really theatre, but a hybrid of cabaret and a nightclub, with circus-like acts appearing throughout the night. After dinner, the tables are cleared and the expensively dressed crowd strut their stuff on the dancefloor.

The Lebanese crowd was delighted to welcome a home import in the form of Music Hall at Jumeirah Zabeel Saray on the Palm, a theatre club with varied acts. And Amsterdam's Supperclub is now also open at Jumeirah Zabeel Saray – an innovative, cutting edge venue with art, fine dining and entertainment.

Also new on the scene since the end of 2013 is Cafe de la Danse – an entertainment provider with dancers, musicians and theatrical acrobats (04 458 0762). Performers are available for corporate events, or can be seen at various venues around Dubai – see their website for up-to-date information (lecafedeladanse.com).

Cinema
If you've left the cinema feeling like you've somehow missed something, then it's likely you have. Nevertheless, censorship is less heavy handed than it used to be, when you might have been forgiven for wondering if Harry even met Sally, (although gratuitous violence is rarely cut). Freezing air conditioning, mobile phones, babies and general chattering is also likely to interfere with your movie experience. The big cinemas are located in the shopping malls, and most of the Hollywood and Bollywood blockbusters make it to Dubai screens.

askexplorer.com 435

GOING OUT
ENTERTAINMENT

Also, sound quality can be a little off and Arabic (and often French) subtitles cover the bottom of the screen. That said, it's a great place to cool off during summer. VOX Cinemas rents out screens for private use if you want it all to yourself; you can even play video games on the big screen.

The IMAX theatre at Meydan in Nadd Al Shiba shows all of the big 3D movies (as does the IMAX at Ibn Battuta Mall) as well as the occasional documentary.

Grand Cinemas Al Badia, Al Kheeran, 04 232 8523, *grandcinemas.com*
Grand Megaplex/IMAX Ibn Battuta, Jabal Ali 1, 04 366 9898, *grandcinemas.com*
Reel Cinemas Dubai Mall, Downtown Dubai, Burj Khalifa, 04 449 1988, *reelcinemas.ae*
VOX Cinemas MoE, Al Barsha 1, 04 341 4222, *voxcinemas.com*

Movies Under The Stars

During the temperate winter evenings, you can flop down onto a beanbag or comfy sun lounger and watch a movie under the night sky. Food and drinks are often available too. Try rooftop viewings at Wafi Mall every Sunday from October to the end of May for free; or on Fridays try The Address Montgomerie's Dive In Movies where you can tuck into popcorn, a tasty barbecue and other snacks as you relax on inflatable chairs – in the pool or on the deck. Movies & Munchies at Desert Palm (04 323 8888), or poolside movies at Dubai Polo & Equestrian Club (04 361 8111) are also worth checking out.

Alternative Screenings

While most of the cinema multiplexes only show big Hollywood movies, several bars and clubs put on screenings of older, foreign and independent films, usually early in the week and free of charge. The Scene Club is a monthly film club that screens international independent films, followed by a Q&A with the director or producer. These free screenings are held in Knowledge Village, and simply sign up to register for a seat (thesceneclub.com). It is also worth keeping an eye on the local press for details of one-off screenings at some of the city's more progressive art spaces, such as the jamjar and Shelter (shelter.ae).

Film Festival

Every October the Abu Dhabi Film Festival (ADFF) showcases Arabic and international film making talent. Films are shown in venues across the city, like Marina Mall or Emirates Palace, and film fans even get the chance to vote for their favourites and take part in question and answer sessions with the directors. Worth checking out if your movie appetite stretches beyond

Hollywood blockbusters. Then there's the Dubai International Film Festival, held every December, with screenings at cinemas across the emirate as well as outdoors in Burj Park and at Madinat Jumeirah.

The Fourth Dimension

4DX is a new style of movie watching that engages all five senses. Get moved about in seats with motion simulators, experience fog, rain, wind and even thunder and lightning, and sniff out the various scents that waft under your nose. Now showing at VOX cinemas at Mirdif City Centre and Deira City Centre.

Comedy

The comedy scene in Dubai is slowly growing and attracting a regular fanbase. To get involved, your best bet is to keep an eye on the Laughter Factory (thelaughterfactory.com) website for upcoming shows. Acts are imported from the UK and shows are usually held at Zinc at the Crowne Plaza, the Movenpick Hotel at JBR, and the Grand Millennium at TECOM. Also look out for monthly comedy shows staged by Punchline Comedy Club at Jumeirah Creekside Hotel.

There are also several one-off events featuring comedians from around the world, as well as local talent; some of these shows are organised by Dubomedy (dubomedy.com). Remember that a lot of comedy is regional, so unless you're familiar with the comedian's country, you might not get the joke.

Live Music

Dubai hosts a number of concerts each year, and it seems to be attracting bigger and bigger names. Past acts to play here include J-Lo, Kylie, Robbie Williams, Mariah Carey and Muse. These big name acts usually play at outdoor venues such as the Tennis Stadium, Dubai Autodrome, Dubai Festival City, Dubai World Trade Centre Arena, the amphitheatre at Media City or the Sevens Stadium. Smaller gigs with the likes of Bob Geldof, Texas and the Happy Mondays have been held at the Irish Village. Outdoor concerts tend to take place between November and April due to the weather.

Further afield, dance music events such as Creamfields are put on by Flash Entertainment at du Forum, while Beats on the Beach takes place around the Formula 1 weekend; a free concert on Abu Dhabi's Corniche beach that has seen Ludacris, Missy Elliott and Sean Kingston perform.

In terms of local bars that host live bands, Dubai is not as musically progressive as say, London, but there are a few choice venues around. The Fridge is

DUCTAC
DUBAI COMMUNITY THEATRE & ARTS CENTRE

- MUSIC
- DANCE
- MARKET
- THEATRE
- VISUAL ART
- COMEDY
- KIDS
- COMMUNITY
- EDUCATION

theatres . gallery . courses . workshops

Mall of the Emirates, Dubai
+971 4 3414 777
info@ductac.org   www.ductac.org

GOING OUT
ENTERTAINMENT

an alcohol-free venue in a converted warehouse in Al Qouz that has performances from local and expat artists; The Music Room in Bur Dubai has live bands and jam sessions; Barasti at Le Meridien Mina Seyahi Beach Resort & Marina has live guitar bands; and there's usually performances at The Irish Village in Garhoud. New to the scene is Freshly Ground Sounds, an initiative to create a community of independent acoustic musicians who play live across Dubai.

The Emirates Airline Dubai Jazz Festival
This popular event goes from strength to strength with past performers including The Script, James Morrison, James Blunt, Jools Holland and Macy Gray. The 2013 event attracted more than 55,000 fans over nine days with a mix of jazz, blues, funk, swing, acid, rock, contemporary, modern, and fusion. The venue is now at Festival Park in Dubai Festival City. To make an evening of it, take a picnic blanket, wrap up warm and explore the stalls before relaxing in front of the stage.

Sandance
Sandance is a hugely popular music festival held on Nasimi Beach at Atlantis, The Palm, with dazzling past acts including Rita Ora, Ellie Goulding, Stereophonics, Dizzee Rascal, Kaiser Chiefs, The Killers and Soul II Soul.
   Early birds can chill out on the beach as the sun goes down, before the party kicks off and hundreds of people are dancing in the sand. There are several live music acts as well as DJs and the night doesn't start to wind down until at least 2am. VIP tickets sell out fast.

Theatre
The First Group Theatre at Madinat Jumeirah and the theatres at DUCTAC are the city's main performance venues and between them offer a range of shows. There's also a good choice of child-friendly shows from The Gruffalo to We're Going On A Bear Hunt.
   The Dubai World Trade Centre Arena is adding more acts each year, with previous performances including Michael Jackson THE IMMORTAL World Tour show by Cirque du Soleil and Swan Lake. Keep an eye on small art spaces like Shelter (shelter.ae) and The Fridge (thefridgedubai.com) for one-off performances, as well as the American University in Dubai (AUD) Auditorium staging performances by student and community theatre groups.
   If you don't mind travelling to get your theatre fix, Abu Dhabi National Exhibition Centre (adnec.ae) has hosted large-scale productions such as Lord Of The Dance. The Act (theactdubai.com) in the Shangri-La Hotel on Sheikh Zayed Road teams an interesting performance calendar with a top-class Peruvian restaurant. Most tickets can be purchased at ticketmaster.ae or itp.net/tickets.

The Act
Shangri-La Dubai Trade Center 1 **056 811 9900**
theactdubai.com
Map **2 G6** Metro **Burj Khalifa/Dubai Mall**
Prepare to have your senses bombarded with a mix of frequently changing acts, innovative dining and expertly mixed cocktails. Past performers have

Emirates Airline Dubai Jazz Festival

438 Dubai Explorer

GOING OUT
STAYING IN

included dancers, acrobats and stars from America's Got Talent. The vibe becomes even more extravagant after the show when the DJ takes over.

Play The Part
Fancy getting into character on stage? Based in The Courtyard in Al Qouz 1, Drama Dubai is a theatre group with a 60-seat auditorium that offers improv, corporate training and adult workshops, as well as functioning as a casting agent (dramaworkshopsdubai.com). There's also Dubai Drama Group, a non-profit organisation that welcomes non-members to its workshops for a small fee. The group has been in existence for more than 25 years (dubaidramagroup.com). See Clubs & Groups for a list of drama groups across the emirate.

Dubai Community Theatre & Arts Centre > p.437
Mall of the Emirates Al Barsha 1 **04 341 4777**
ductac.org
Map **1 R6** Metro **Mall of the Emirates**
A cultural hub offering art classes for all ages. Decorative arts, drawing, painting, photography, sculpture and paper craft are just some of the wide variety of activities offered to help budding artists hone their creative talents. A variety of artist-led classes are held at the centre, and details are listed online and updated regularly. DUCTAC also has art galleries and studios for performance, comedy and dance. There's a cafe, art supplies shop and lending library. Open daily from 9am to 10pm and 2pm to 10pm on Fridays.

Dubai World Trade Centre
Shk Zayed Rd Trade Center 2 **04 332 1000**
dwtc.com
Map **2 J6** Metro **World Trade Centre**
Home to the enormous Trade Centre Arena and to smaller arenas inside, this is the go-to venue for large scale productions. Easily accessed by the metro (or there's ample parking if you drive), this indoor venue has an exciting programme of shows, comedy acts, concerts and events – and there's often a licensed bar and snacks available once you're inside too.

First Group Theatre
Souk Madinat Jumeirah Al Sufouh 1 **04 366 6546**
madinattheatre.com
Map **1 R5** Metro **Mall of the Emirates**
The theatre's 442-seat auditorium has witnessed an impressive list of performances over the years. From 'treading the boards' classics to musicals and innovative comedy shows, make sure you keep your eyes open for what's coming into town next, and chances are you won't be disappointed.

STAYING IN

Fun at home is well catered for in Dubai. No matter where in the city you are, you'll have access to all kinds of delivery services and ways to entertain without having to lift much more than a phone.

Home Delivery

It won't be long before you've assembled an impressive stash of flyers and delivery menus in a drawer of your otherwise under-utilised kitchen. Assuming you can actually convey your location to the restaurant in question, home delivery is a cheap and cheerful way to enjoy a night home with friends or in front of the TV. Fortunately, there are a number of websites that bring all of your favourite menus together – you can choose what type of cuisine you want, find out who delivers locally, make your order and, in some cases, even pay online. Try dubai.foodonclick.com, roomservice-uae.com, casseroleonline.com, thesecretchef.me and 24h.ae. Pretty much all restaurants will deliver, but here are a few of our favourites to get you started.

Black Canyon The Walk at JBR, Marsa Dubai, 04 423 1993, *salehbinlahejgroup.com*
Al Reef Lebanese Bakery Nr Union Co-op, Jumeira 3, 04 394 5200
Chez Sushi by Sho Cho Al Safa 1, 800 78744, *chezsushi.com*
KFC Dubai Mall, Downtown Dubai, Burj Khalifa, 04 339 8275, *kfc-arabia.com*
MORE Cafe Dubai Mall, Downtown Dubai, Burj Khalifa, 04 339 8934, *morecafe.biz*
The Noodle House Dubai Mall, Downtown Dubai, Burj Khalifa, 04 388 4825, *thenoodlehouse.com*
Subway Dubai Mall, Downtown Dubai, Burj Khalifa, 04 339 8808, *subwayarabia.com*

Parties

If you really want to push the boat out when entertaining at home, the companies listed below offer a complete party planning service, from event organisation to hiring performers and equipment rental. For a novel outdoor party idea, you can get your own shawarma stand set up in the garden, complete with shawarma maker, or hire an ice cream van from Desert Chill (desertchill.ae).

GOING OUT
STAYING IN

Caterers

There are several companies in Dubai that can do all the cooking, decorating and cleaning up, leaving you with more time to concentrate on your witty after-dinner anecdotes. Many restaurants, hotels, and clubs have catering departments, so pick your favourite and ask if they can help out.

Cheeky Little Events
04 388 6114
CheekyLittleEvents.com
Specialises in parties for children, from babies through to teenagers, as well as hen parties or baby showers are just as doable. Not only looks after the catering, but the entertainment and decorations too.

ChoCo'a
Nr Mall of the Emirates Al Barsha 1 04 340 9092
chocoa.ae
Map **1 R6** Metro **Mall of the Emirates**
ChoCo'a chefs offer a selection of cakes, pastries, Arabic delicacies and individually-designed speciality cakes and chocolate arrangements for birthdays, graduations, anniversaries and weddings.

Decorative Cakes
050 594 6708
decorativecakes.piczo.com
Perfect for kids' parties, weddings or just about any event that requires a cake, this company can create an edible masterpiece in any design you ask of them.

Dish Catering & Events
China Cluster, International City International City 1, Warsan 1 04 422 1613
dish.ae
With a promise to deliver 'food that steals the show', Dish caters modern cuisine for functions ranging from 20 to 700 people.

Dubaipartyqueen
HDS Tower JLT, Al Thanyah 5 04 348 9475
dubaipartyqueen.com
Map **1 K5** Metro **Jumeirah Lakes Towers**
From corporate shindigs to money-no-object weddings, this company can arrange parties for all occasions and age groups.

Flying Elephant > p.441
Shk Zayed Rd Al Qouz Ind. 1 04 347 9170
flyingelephantuae.com
Map **1 U6** Metro **Noor Bank**
This company has existed for more than 16 years and offers everything from theme decorations and catering to invitations and entertainment. Its Pink Elephant division specialises in organising kids' parties. It also organises corporate events.

Harlequin Marquees & Event Services
Nr Marlin Furniture Al Qouz Ind. 1 04 347 0110
harlequinmarquees.com
Map **1 U6** Metro **Noor Bank**
Everything you need for an outdoor event, including marquees, tables, chairs, and even outdoor AC units.

Indigo Entertainment
City Tower 1 Trade Center 1 04 331 8704
indigouae.com
Map **2 H5** Metro **Financial Centre**
Offers an array of solutions for private and corporate events, children's parties, and holiday camps.

Italian Chef At Home
04 444 3627
chefathomedubai.com
Prepares personalised menus for dinners and lunches, prepared and served in your own home – and the kitchen is always left spotless!

The Lime Tree Cafe & Kitchen
Nr Times Square Al Qouz Ind. 1 04 325 6325
thelimetreecafe.com
Map **1 U6** Metro **Noor Bank**
Lime Tree prepares customised catering for your event, from canapes to full-on gourmet.

Marta's Kitchen
Swiss Tower Al Thanyah 5 050 379 8002
martaskitchen.com
Map **1 L5** Metro **Dubai Marina**
Specialises in canape-based and buffet menus, from traditional food to more avant-garde gastronomy.

Open House
Nr Pyramid Bldg Al Karama 04 396 5481
Map **2 L5** Metro **Al Karama**
Catering service providing tasty Indian food, perfect for small to medium-sized parties.

Procat Catering Services
Al Khaleej Centre Al Raffa 04 885 9990
profms.com
Map **2 L4** Metro **Al Fahidi**
Large, professional catering outfit that is particularly suited to bigger catering jobs, such as large wedding parties or corporate catering gigs.

Sweet Connection – The Gluten Free Kitchen
Mayfair Bldg Dubai Investment Park 1 04 880 0656
sweetconnectiondubai.com
Map **1 G10**
Dedicated to developing recipes for coeliac disease sufferers and anyone who needs to follow a gluten-free diet: tasty breads, pizzas, cupcakes and biscuits.

flying elephant
EVENTS

MULTI AWARD WINNERS

DUBAI ONEHUNDRED SME / DUBAI SME
MEBA Awards WINNER - LEADERS
Lloyds TSB - BEST BUSINESS GROWTH WINNER - SME AWARDS - BEST SMALL BUSINESS
ADCB - SME ADVISOR MIDDLE EAST - WINNER - STAR OF BUSINESS MEDIA AWARD

Customized Fabrication • Themed Events • Festive Mall Decoration • Shop Window Display • Event Props and Decor

800-EVENTS (383687)   flyingelephant.ae

Love travel?

Wherever you love, we'll take you there.

Call **+971 4 316 6666** or visit **dnatatravel.com**
You can also email us at **holidays@dnatatravel.com**

dnata. we love travel

dnata
dnatatravel.com

OUT OF THE CITY

Abu Dhabi **445**
Al Ain **452**
Al Gharbia **454**
Ajman **457**
Fujairah **458**
Ras Al Khaimah **460**
Short Breaks From The UAE **466**
Sharjah **468**
Umm Al Quwain **471**
Oman **472**
Qatar **476**
Desert Resorts **480**

OUT OF THE CITY

Discover the desert dunes and wadi beds of Dubai – and then head off to explore six more emirates.

Sheikh Zayed Grand Mosque

Dubai may have everything from ski slopes and souks to boutiques and beaches, but there are six other emirates in the UAE and five other countries in the GCC, all of which warrant exploration.

All six other emirates – Abu Dhabi, Sharjah, Ras Al Khaimah, Umm Al Quwain, Ajman and Fujairah – are within a two-hour drive of the centre of Dubai (see overview map at rear). From the cultural grandiose of Sharjah to the Garden City of Al Ain in Abu Dhabi, each emirate has something different to offer, and each can be explored, at least in part, over a weekend.

The country's vast deserts and rugged mountains are equally accessible with a copy of the *UAE Off-Road Explorer*, and can be reached within a 45 minute drive of Dubai, if you need to escape civilisation for a while. Amongst these landscapes you'll find historic forts, pretty waterfalls and pools.

The neighbouring GCC countries of Oman, Saudi Arabia, Qatar, Bahrain and Kuwait are all less than 90 minutes' flight away. Oman is considered by many to be one of the most beautiful and culturally interesting countries in the region and it can easily be reached and explored by car – Muscat is just a four-hour drive from Dubai.

Door To Door

Driving from Dubai to Abu Dhabi or Al Ain takes an hour and a half; it's an hour and a quarter to Ras Al Khaimah; 35 minutes to Ajman; 45 minutes to Umm Al Quwain; around two hours to get to Fujairah; and only 20 minutes to Sharjah.

Low-cost carrier flydubai operates cheap flights to nearby countries like Oman, as do regional airlines like Emirates, Oman Air and Qatar Airways.

OUT OF THE CITY
ABU DHABI

ABU DHABI

Dubai may be the UAE's brashest member, but Abu Dhabi remains both the nation's capital and the richest of all the emirates, with a blossoming, burgeoning city to prove it. Recently, there has been a greater commitment to tourism, and mega-projects such as Yas Island with its Grand Prix racetrack and the development of the Desert Islands are proof of that.

The city is a series of islands, connected to the mainland by bridges. Each of the main islands is growing into its own destination, and each enjoys stunning views of the Gulf. The islands to the west of the city are popular with boating and watersports enthusiasts, and driving in that direction reveals kilometre upon kilometre of gorgeous open water and beaches.

The city is home to numerous internationally renowned hotels, shopping malls, heritage sites and souks, and is marketed as the cultural capital of the UAE with an annual jazz festival, a film festival, and a music and arts festival. Find out more from the Abu Dhabi Tourism and Culture Authority (adach.ae).

For more information and ideas for exploring Abu Dhabi, check out Explorer's *Abu Dhabi Visitors' Guide*, *Al Gharbia Visitors' Guide* or the *Abu Dhabi Residents' Guide* – order copies at askexplorer.com.

Attractions

Abu Dhabi Corniche
Corniche West St Abu Dhabi
visitabudhabi.ae

No trip to Abu Dhabi would be complete without spending some time on the Corniche, with its golden beaches and pleasant promenade. Of the six kilometres of parks, play areas and cafes, Family Park is a highlight, with leafy gardens, picnic areas and tree-lined walkways. Watch fishermen casting their lines into the Gulf and stop for lunch at Havana Cafe.

Al Forsan International Sports Resort
Khalifa City Abu Dhabi 02 556 8555
alforsan.com

The ultimate multi-sports hub, Al Forsan's superb cable-boarding facilities are well worth checking out. Similar to wakeboarding, you grab a cable instead of being pulled by a boat, and you can even try it on your knees if you're nervous. There is also paintballing, karting, horse riding, clay pigeon shooting and archery.

Emirates Park Zoo
Al Bahia Abu Dhabi 02501 0000
emiratesparkzoo.com

Both kids and adults are sure to enjoy a trip to this recently renovated zoo which houses more than 2,000 species of animals, including white tigers, blue monkeys and brown bears. The emphasis is on allowing you to get close to your favourite animals through touch and interaction; for example, at the Giraffe Cafe, visitors can feed the giraffes and zebras. Young visitors can even volunteer as a 'zoo keeper'.

Bird Watchers
The Abu Dhabi Falcon Hospital (02 575 5155, falconhospital.com) specialises in treating the region's falcons and various other species of birds. The hospital offers two-hour guided tours on weekdays that must be booked in advance.

Ferrari World Abu Dhabi
Yas Island Abu Dhabi 02 496 8000
ferrariworldabudhabi.com

Ferrari World Abu Dhabi is part F1 amusement park and part museum dedicated to the Italian supercar. There's plenty to keep kids entertained, as well as rides for teen and adult adrenaline junkies. One of the highlights is undoubtedly Formula Rossa – billed as the world's fastest rollercoaster, it reaches such high speeds (up to 240kph) that anyone adventurous enough to give it a go has to wear goggles.

Murjan Splash Park
Khalifa Park Abu Dhabi 050 878 1009
murjansplashpark.weebly.com

Located in the vast Khalifa Park, this attraction is the perfect destination for water babies with plenty of rides and games aimed at children aged three to 12. The highlight is an enormous water play climbing structure with tunnels, water guns and waterslides, and a giant tipping bucket. The Surf Wrangler is a surf board simulator, and for youngsters that don't fancy making a splash, there's the Lily Pad hop, a collection of four trampolines with harnesses.

Sheikh Zayed Grand Mosque
Shk Rashid Bin Saeed Al Maktoum St Abu Dhabi
02 419 1919
szgmc.ae

This stunning Abu Dhabi icon is a truly remarkable architectural feat, reminiscent of a sultan's palace from the Arabian Nights. Unlike most mosques in the UAE, it is open to non-Muslims and you can take guided tours throughout the day (except Friday mornings). It has a capacity for an astonishing 40,000 worshippers and the world's largest hand-woven Persian carpet.

The Entertainment Island

A handy guide to making the most of Yas Island's wet, wild and wonderful attractions.

Stay in style
Yas Island's six hotels are perfect for holidaymakers, event visitors or local residents looking for a staycation. After all, together the Yas Plaza's five hotels and the Yas Viceroy Abu Dhabi account for 22 of the island's restaurants and 12 of its bars – and that's not including lobby lounges.

Some of the most popular include Angar and Kazu at Yas Viceroy, Barouk at Crowne Plaza, and Fillini at Radisson Blu. Whether you're after fantastic value or something more high-end, every taste is catered for and each hotel has its own standout features; stunning views, brilliant pools or incredible design.

Get active
Regarded as one of the best courses in the world, Yas Links Golf course is a beautiful venue that offers serious golfers a real challenge, with a separate course where less confident golfers can hone their skills.

Yas Marina Circuit's driving experiences cater for your inner speed demon with everything from Aston Martin GT4s to Formula Yas 3000 single seaters. If you prefer to shun petrol power, run or cycle around the circuit on Tuesday evenings – for free!

On Yas Beach, Noukhada Adventure Company (noukhada.ae) has your watersports needs covered with windsurfing, sailing and kayaking.

Feel the rush
Ferrari World Abu Dhabi draws crowds from around the world with the lure of the 'world's fastest rollercoaster', the Formula Rossa. Head inside and you'll also have fun driving miniature cars, ogling world famous Ferraris and exploring a mini Italy.

Yas Waterworld makes for a fabulous family day out with kid-focused interactive games and the excellent Marah Fortress splash park. But 'big kids' can have fun too, lounging by the pool, relaxing in a private cabana or enjoying one of the park's adrenaline-pumping slides. Highlights include the heart-thumping Liwa Loop. Wet and wild fun at its best.

Shop 'til you drop
Shopping is currently limited to theme park stores, hotel shops, a pro shop at Yas Links and big hitters IKEA and ACE Hardware, but Yas Mall, due this year, is set to be the second largest mall in the UAE.

Party the night away
For the ultimate nightclub experience, head to either the super exclusive O1NE Yas Island – a purpose-built club from the team that created Beirut's world famous Sky Bar – or Rush, the party spot on Yas Viceroy's impressive circuit-crossing bridge.

FLASH Entertainment regularly brings world famous musical acts to perform at the island's du Arena. Madonna, Muse, Jay Z and a host of other pop, rock and dance talent have performed there. The smaller du Forum has a variety of fascinating entertainment throughout the year such as boxing events, Oktoberfest celebrations and science festivals for kids.

Dock, dine and discover
From US-inspired food at Stars 'n' Bars to funky alfresco tapas at Diabolito and fine dining at Cipriani and Aquarium, Yas Marina is one of the hottest food spots in town. To work up an appetite why not charter a boat for a tour of Abu Dhabi's waters from Azure Charters, or if you want to dock your own boat, berths can be had from Dhs.16,455 – which includes F1 passes, concert tickets and dining discounts. A great, relaxed place to hang out, eat or party.

Formula 1 weekend
Every November Yas Marina Circuit, and the whole of Yas Island, hosts the Abu Dhabi FIA Formula 1 World Championship. Huge yachts pour into the marina and the atmosphere is charged with excitement as helicopters buzz overhead. Even if you're not an F1 fan, the concerts, restaurant and bar events, and boat parties make for four days you don't want to miss. Past performers have included Muse and Depeche Mode.

Yas Express
A free bus, the Yas Express covers two circuits of the island. The Blue Route will ferry you between Yas Waterworld, Yas Plaza, Yas Viceroy, central Yas and Ferrari World Abu Dhabi/Yas Mall; the Red Route goes from Yas Plaza, to Yas Viceroy then on to Yas Marina and Yas Beach followed by Yas Links Golf Club. The free Saadiyat route leaves from St. Regis and Park Hyatt hotels on Saadiyat Island three times every morning with drop-offs at Yas Waterworld and Ferrari World. For timetables see yasisland.ae.

Explorer's Top 5

If you're visiting Yas Island, this checklist should help you make the most of your stay.

1. Watch the sun go down over Abu Dhabi at Yas Links Golf Club, either from the course or with a chilled drink on the terrace of Hickory's bar

2. Be courageous by braving Yas Waterworld's infamous Dawwama ride

3. Be even more courageous by taking the front seat of the Formula Rossa rollercoaster at Ferrari World Abu Dhabi

4. Take a kayak eco tour from Yas Beach to learn about Abu Dhabi's mangroves and sea life

5. Experience the Yas Marina Circuit with one of their driving experiences then head to Skylite at the top of the Yas Viceroy for an evening under the iconic canopy

Yas Waterworld

OUT OF THE CITY
ABU DHABI

Yas Waterworld Abu Dhabi > p.449
Yas Island Abu Dhabi **02 414 2000**
yaswaterworld.com
You could easily spend an entire day at this gargantuan water park on Yas Island, trying out the 43 rides, slides and attractions. Each one is handily categorised into one of four groups: Adrenaline Rush, Exciting Adventure, Moving and Grooving, or Young Fun, and there's something for everyone. For thrill seekers, the Liwa Loop – the first and only waterslide of its kind in the Middle East – is a near-vertical drop that shoots you through a winding loop at an incredible speed.

Emirates Palace Events
More than just a grand hotel, Emirates Palace is one of Abu Dhabi's top cultural and entertainment centres. It has staged major international concerts, including world-renowned pop artists like Coldplay and Elton John, and is a venue for the Abu Dhabi Festival, featuring classical orchestras and art installations. The hotel also hosts major art exhibitions, which have featured pieces from the likes of Pablo Picasso, and is part of the yearly Abu Dhabi Art Fair (abudhabiartfair.ae). Keep an eye on the Abu Dhabi Tourism website (abudhabitourism.ae) for details of upcoming events.

Hotels

Crowne Plaza Yas Island
Golf Plaza Yas Island West **02 656 3000**
ihg.com
Sitting right next to Yas Links Abu Dhabi golf course, this hotel has four excellent restaurants and two bars to tempt guests and visitors. For sports and leisure fans, it's just a short walk to both the Yas Marina Circuit and Yas Marina, as well as Yas Beach.

Eastern Mangroves Hotel & Spa By Anantara
Shk Zayed Rd Abu Dhabi **02 656 1000**
abu-dhabi.anantara.com
This is Anantara's first city-based hotel in the Middle East. The views are lush, green and skyscraper-free, thanks to the resort's enviable location alongside the mangroves. Some of the leisure activities include kayaking and sailing.

Emirates Palace
West Corniche Rd Abu Dhabi **02 690 9000**
kempinski.com
The lavish, $3bn Emirates Palace – arguably the world's most costly hotel – boasts 392 opulent rooms and suites, all decked out with the latest technology and sumptuous decor. Several outstanding food outlets offer 'seven-star' service (the afternoon tea is famed) and guests can enjoy the private beach, two amazing pools and indulgent treatments at the exclusive Anantara spa.

Fairmont Bab Al Bahr
Nr Al Maqtaa Bridge Abu Dhabi **02 654 3333**
fairmont.com
With its luxurious rooms, outdoor pools overlooking the creek, and stunning views of Sheikh Zayed Grand Mosque, it's no wonder that the Fairmont Bab Al Bahr is a much sought after Abu Dhabi destination. It also has some of the best dining and drinking spots in the city, and there are even more at the nearby Souk at Qaryat Al Beri complex.

St. Regis Saadiyat Island Resort
Saadiyat Beach Saadiyat Island **02 498 8888**
stregissaadiyatisland.com
A true beach resort that's quite unlike any other hotel in the UAE, the St. Regis looks more like a California retreat, with stunning colonial style rooms all offering views over the beautiful central pools, restaurants and private sandy beach (and one hole of the neighbouring Saadiyat Beach golf course). The restaurants alone are worth travelling for, and 55 and 5th The Grill is particularly recommended. The perfect place to escape the city, while being just a short drive away.

Westin Abu Dhabi Golf Resort & Spa
Abu Dhabi Golf Club Khalifa City
02 616 9999
westinabudhabigolfresort.com
A smart and peaceful resort located at Abu Dhabi Golf Club, with rooms overlooking the course. Its location on the mainland, away from the city centre, makes it a convenient option from the airport. There are plenty of amenities whether or not you plan to tee off, including two pools and a great spa. It's also home to the outrageous Bubbalicious Brunch at Fairways, a Moroccan restaurant and theme nights.

Yas Viceroy Abu Dhabi
Yas Marina Abu Dhabi **02 656 0000**
viceroyhotelsandresorts.com
This extraordinary hotel straddles the Formula 1 racetrack at Yas Marina Circuit and became an instant architectural classic and Abu Dhabi icon when it opened in 2009. The property is at once utterly modern but equally tactile, functional, sumptuous and welcoming. Rooms and suites all enjoy incredible views over the racetrack and surrounding Yas Island, and the restaurants are all individually worth a visit. The two rooftop pool bars are otherworldly locations, and the nightlife scene is renowned.

FEEL THE ACTION
Does he hit the target?
Or does she?
Live the ultimate water adventure
Book tickets online today at yaswaterworld.com
or call +971 2 414 2000. Open daily from 10am.
YAS ISLAND
Yas Waterworld
ABU DHABI

Abu Dhabi Art Scene

An ever-growing arts scene and the imminent arrival of world-class galleries will make Abu Dhabi a cultural hub for the UAE and beyond.

The art of the city
Saadiyat Island is already a special place; golden beaches stretching into the turquoise sea and top class dining venues, all only minutes from downtown Abu Dhabi. However, it's about to get a stroke of added artistic inspiration as it becomes host to the city's Cultural District. Aside from the Zayed National Museum and the Performing Arts Centre, both to be housed within stunning architecture, the globally recognised institutions of the Louvre and the Guggenheim will be represented, making Abu Dhabi, and the UAE, a focal point for the arts across the world.

Louvre Abu Dhabi
(Due to open: 2015)
The Louvre Abu Dhabi will be the first of the new museums to open, and construction is well underway behind its high walls. The building, designed by the legendary Jean Nouvel, will be an impressive landmark boasting a diameter of 180 metres, with a 7,000 tonne dome sat atop four pillars on a man-made platform. The area is dammed off, but before its opening in 2015 water will be flooded back to give it the feel of an island. The large dome will also let natural light through, dappling the public areas with sunshine.

Inside, the museum will present major objects from the fields of archaeology, fine arts and decorative arts, plus all regions, periods (including contemporary art) and the narrative of art history.

Guggenheim Abu Dhabi
(Due to open: 2017)
The fantastic Frank Gehry-designed architecture for the Guggenheim Abu Dhabi will be spectacular and create one of the most unusual buildings in the country. The 137,000 sq m museum will house a huge collection of modern and contemporary art, as well as special exhibitions from the Guggenheim Foundation's extensive collection. It will be built on the corner of the island stretching out to sea and will incorporate many traditional Arabic design cues.

Manarat Al Saadiyat
Home to a fascinating exhibition showing the future development of the island, Manarat Al Saadiyat is also a functioning gallery in its own right. The high ceilings and light, airy feel of this contemporary space create the perfect place to appreciate the sculptures, paintings and other works displayed in ever-changing exhibitions of local and international art.

Next to Manarat Al Saadiyat is the Norman Foster designed UAE Pavilion. The striking structure was first exhibited at the Shanghai World Expo 2010 then shipped to Saadiyat Island and re-erected. It's now a regular space for art and other exhibits.

Elsewhere in the city
There are a number of independent galleries around the city including the Salwa Zeidan Gallery (salwazeidangallery.com), that recently moved to Saadiyat Island, and Ghaf Gallery (ghafartgallery.com). The newly opened Etihad Modern Art Gallery in Al Bateen is an extension of the Etihad Antique Gallery (etihadgallery.com), both of which are now open to visitors. For something different, Abu Dhabi Pottery (abudhabipottery.com) showcases some fine ceramics and also holds classes. To find like-minded people to explore Abu Dhabi's art scene with, try groups like Abu Dhabi Art Squad (abudhabiartsquad.com).

Art work can also be found in many of the city's hotels, from classic antiquities at The Barakat Gallery in Emirates Palace, to contemporary work from international artists at places like the Lightbox in the Yas Viceroy. The Souk Qaryat Al Beri also houses Gallery One. Other hotels like the Rosewood, Fairmont Bab Al Bahr and the Jumeirah at Etihad Towers have all hosted one-off exhibitions too, so keep your eyes open for those as they crop up.

Abu Dhabi Art Hub
If you want to get more involved, the Abu Dhabi Art Hub (adah.ae) in Mussafah is the place to go. As well as having a gallery and holding affordable art fairs, it's also a working studio. Most months a small group of artists from a specific county is invited to live and work in the specially designed accommodation for residency artists. Not only do they each produce a series of works inspired by the region, but they also give classes and workshops to UAE residents, helping to spread their knowledge and techniques. ADAH also promotes traditional crafts and tries to help artists find new ways of incorporating them in contemporary pieces.

Super Saadiyat

The UAE is on track for a cultural awakening, the heart of which will undoubtedly be Saadiyat Island's Cultural District. With the Louvre Abu Dhabi, designed by Jean Nouvel, due to open in 2015, and the Frank Gehry-designed Guggenheim to follow, there'll be some seriously impressive exhibitions housed in soon-to-be iconic buildings. Zayed National Museum is another eagerly awaited centre that will soon find a home on Saadiyat. It's a refreshing and admirable investment by the capital, and puts Abu Dhabi firmly on the global map.

Zayed National Museum
(*image: Tourism Development & Investment Company*)

OUT OF THE CITY
AL AIN

AL AIN

Al Ain National Museum

Al Ain is Abu Dhabi emirate's second city and of great historical significance in the UAE. Its location on ancient trading routes between Oman and the Arabian Gulf rendered the oasis strategically important.

Commonly known as 'The Garden City', Al Ain features many oases and lovely patches of greenery for the public to enjoy. After a greening programme instigated by the late Sheikh Zayed, the seven natural oases are now set amid tree-lined streets and beautiful urban parks. Its unique history means that Al Ain is home to interesting sights and attractions, including the Hili Archaeological Garden and the Al Ain Palace Museum, although there are modern amusements too like Hili Fun City.

Just outside the city sits one of the largest mountains in the UAE, Jebel Hafeet, while the sand dunes of Bida Bint Saud are great to explore on camelback (Al Ain Golden Sands Camel Safaris runs tours that include transfers from Al Ain. Call 050 447 7268 for the details). Al Ain's archaeological and historical legacy is of such significance that the city was recently placed on the list of World Heritage Sites by UNESCO.

Attractions

Al Ain Camel & Livestock Souk
Nr Bawadi Mall, Zayed Bin Sultan St Al Ain
adach.ae
Conditions at the souk have improved dramatically with spacious pens for the animals and ample parking for visitors. A visit to the market is a fantastic way to mingle with locals and witness camel and goat trading taking place in the same way it has for centuries. Arrive early, preferably before 9am, to soak up the buzzing atmosphere.

Al Ain National Museum
Zayed Bin Sultan St Al Ain 03 764 1595
abudhabi.ae
The oldest museum in the UAE is divided into three main sections. The ethnography section focuses on traditional life, culture and pastimes and the archaeology section has examples of Stone Age, Bronze Age and Iron Age objects excavated from sites around Al Ain. The 'gifts' section hosts some weird and wonderful items that were presented to Sheikh Zayed by visiting dignitaries, including golden palm trees, ornamental camels and jewel-encrusted daggers.

Al Ain Oasis
Nr Al Ain Museum Al Ain 03 711 8208
visitabudhabi.ae
This impressive oasis in the heart of the city is filled with palm plantations, many of which are still working farms. You are welcome to wander through the plantations, but it's best to stick to the paved areas. The farms have plenty of working examples of *falaj*, the traditional irrigation system which has been used for centuries to tap into underground wells. There are eight different entrances, some of which have arched gates, and there is no entry fee.

Al Ain Palace Museum
Central District Al Ain 03 751 7755
abudhabi.ae
The museum was originally a palace belonging to Sheikh Zayed bin Sultan Al Nahyan, dating back to 1937. Now, it tells the story of its previous owner and his remarkable achievements turning the desert state into a wealthy, popular and thriving country. Guided tours are free and highly recommended, and the Emirati guides are proud and knowledgeable. You'll learn about Emirati traditions and culture in general, and gain a real sense of time and place. The museum is a lovely, quiet place to stroll around and explore.

Al Ain Zoo
Nhayyan Al Awwal St Al Ain 03 799 2000
alainzoo.ae
This zoo is not characterised by small cages and meagre wildlife displays. Instead, it feels much more like a safari park, with spacious enclosures spread

OUT OF THE CITY
AL AIN

across its 365 hectares interspersed with smaller exhibitions. Highlights include watching the hippos splash around in their 10m long ravine, catching a glimpse of the rare white lions in their enclosure, and getting up close to the giraffes at their feeding station. It's also an important conservation centre, with nearly 30% of the 180 species being on the endangered list.

Al Jahili Fort
Nr Central Public Gardens Al Ain 03 784 3996
abudhabi.ae
Al Jahili Fort is over 100 years old and one of the UAE's largest forts. Celebrated as the birthplace of the late Sheikh Zayed bin Sultan Al Nahyan, it is set in landscaped gardens and has been the stunning venue for a number of concerts during the Abu Dhabi Classics series (abudhabiclassics.com). The distinctive three-tiered fort appears on the UAE's Dhs.50 note.

Hili Archaeological Park
Nr Dubai Highway Al Ain 03 764 1595
abudhabi.ae
These landscaped gardens are home to a Bronze Age settlement (2,500-2,000BC), which was excavated and restored in 1995. Many of the artefacts found are displayed in Al Ain National Museum. Entry is Dhs.1.

Hili Fun City
Off Emirates St Al Ain 03 784 5542
hilifuncity.ae
This recently renovated, 22 hectare theme park offers you the best of both worlds: a theme park packed with rides and activities, and a scenic picnic spot for more relaxed get-togethers with friends. It's best to arrive early and make a day of it. There are more than 30 attractions, ranging from gentle rides for the little ones, such as the zebra-striped safari jeeps, to nail-biting, highflying rides for teens and adults, like the terrifying Sky Flyer that spins 360 degrees.

Jebel Hafeet
South of Al Ain
Among the highest peaks in the UAE, Jebel Hafeet towers over the border between Al Ain and Oman at an imposing 1,240 metres. It's an impressive backdrop to the city, and the winding road to the top is considered to be one of the world's best driving roads; head to the summit to be rewarded with fantastic views over Al Ain. Alternatively, if you're feeling active, the road is also a challenging cycle route.

Wadi Adventure
Off Al Ain Fayda Rd Al Ain 03 781 8422
wadiadventure.ae
A must for adrenaline junkies, this water park with a difference has white water rafting and kayaking runs, of more than a kilometre in length. A huge wave pool generates three-metre high breaks for surfing, or if water isn't your thing, the air park, zip line, climbing wall and canyon swing should keep your excitement levels high. There's a family swimming pool, man-made beach and a splash pool for little ones, making it a fantastic option for a family outing.

Hotels

Al Ain Rotana
Shk Zayed Rd Al Ain 03 754 5111
rotana.com
This city centre spot is a nightlife hub, thanks to six popular dining spots which include the lively Trader Vic's and the excellent Lebanese restaurant Min Zamaan. The rooms are attractive and spacious, and the pool and gardens are great for sunbathing.

Danat Al Ain Resort
Nr Khalid Bin Sultan & Al Salam Sts Al Ain
03 704 6000
danathotels.com
Well-known for being one of the UAE's best inland resorts, with its luxurious guestrooms and deluxe villas, landscaped gardens and swimming pools. There are plenty of family friendly facilities, while adults are sure to enjoy the luxury spa and the swim-up pool bar, as well as the Horse and Jockey Pub.

Green Mubazzarah Chalets
Nr Green Mubazzarah Park Al Ain 03 783 9555
Mubazzarah.150m.com
Situated among the lush and picturesque foothills of Jebel Hafeet, these fully-furnished two and three-bedroom chalets are ideal for enjoying the Green Mubazzarah natural springs and parkland.

Hilton Al Ain
Nr Khalid Bin Sultan & Zayed Bin Sultan Sts Al Ain
03 768 6666
hilton.com
Located near the heart of Al Ain, this ageing hotel is a key landmark and sits in lush, landscaped gardens that contain a nine-hole golf course, tennis and squash courts, a health club and a nice pool area. It is particularly convenient for visiting Al Ain Zoo. The Hiltonia Sports Bar and Paco's Bar are popular haunts.

Mercure Grand Jebel Hafeet
Al Ain 03 783 8888
mercure.com
This hotel's impressive location near the summit of Jebel Hafeet affords spectacular views of Al Ain. The rooms here are simple and comfortable, and there's plenty of fun to be had with three swimming pools to choose from, a waterslide and a mini-golf course.

OUT OF THE CITY
AL GHARBIA

AL GHARBIA

Al Gharbia is Abu Dhabi's Western Region – a vast 60,000 square kilometres or 60% of the total area of Abu Dhabi emirate and 51% of the UAE. Al Gharbia's natural resources such as palm trees, pearls, oil, gas and solar energy contribute 45% to the UAE's GDP. The region boasts the highest sand dunes in the world and 350km of coastline with beaches, rare wildlife, and beautiful desert islands such as Delma and Sir Bani Yas fast becoming popular tourist destinations.

Liwa

For most visitors to Al Gharbia, all roads lead to Liwa. On the way, you pass through tumbleweed towns such as Ghayathi (good for stocking up on authentic Bedouin souvenirs) and the regional capital Madinat Zayed. The land in this region holds evidence of life from ancient times; eight-million-year-old fossils have been found at Bu Ghar, while oases and the occasional farmstead are dotted throughout the region. Modern Bedouin criss-cross the interior with entire bungalows on the back of big-wheeled trucks.

Liwa Oasis is one of the largest oases on the Arabian Peninsula. This fertile crescent stretches for more than 150km and is home to the Bani Yas tribe, ancestors of the ruling family of Abu Dhabi. It's a quiet area, dotted with date plantations and small towns. Visitors go to see its ancient forts, traditional falconry, camel racing and trading, and because Liwa is the northern gate to the great desert.

It's at Liwa that you'll find the legendary sand dune known as 'Tel Moreeb', or the Hill of Terror, a 300m high slope which attracts only the most confident off-roaders. Prepare for the most adventurous desert driving – and incredible scenery – the UAE has to offer. For detailed routes and practical information, get a copy of Explorer's *UAE Off-Road*.

The Empty Quarter

The Rub Al Khali – also known as the Empty Quarter – spreads south from Liwa and is the biggest sand desert on the planet. It measures a mind-boggling 650,000 square kilometres and spreads over parts of Oman, Yemen, southern UAE and almost all of southern Saudi Arabia. Its dunes rise as high as 250m. The Rub Al Khali is one of the world's greatest attractions on an unsurpassed scale of majesty. It was historically regarded as the edge of civilisation by people living in the region. But there is an extraordinary beauty to this landscape, despite it being so harsh and inhospitable. Even today man has been able to make little mark on it. Desert driving in this area is more of an expedition than just a spot of dune bashing, so go prepared for the adventure of a lifetime. The opportunities for camping in the region are endless, and sleeping under the stars is a great way to experience the peace and tranquillity of the desert. Unless of course there's a sand storm.

The Pearl Coast

Drive west from Abu Dhabi and the first stop will be Mirfa, set up in the 1970s as a fishing port and pearling centre. Mirfa is quiet but may change once the Mirfa Corniche is developed under Abu Dhabi's 2030 regional plan. In the meantime the refurbished, 114 room Mirfa Hotel has breathed new life into the area. For now, the biggest draw to Mirfa remains the annual Al Gharbia Watersports Festival (algharbiafestivals.com), opposite the hotel. Crowds flock for a weekend of fireworks, competitive kitesurfing, wakeboarding and kayaking.

A hundred kilometres along the 'pearl coast' is Jebel Dhanna, another historic pearl diving destination. There are two hotels here on a great beach with clear, shallow sea and fantastic facilities that make for a great weekend getaway from Abu Dhabi. Nearby, Ruwais is a town built for ADNOC employees which holds little interest for visitors.

The last stop before the Saudi Arabia border is Sila, a true frontier town. There isn't much happening in Sila today but that may change when it's one of the regular stops of the proposed GCC railway network. Until then, if you're in Sila head down to the harbour for fresh fish from the Abu Dhabi Fishermen's Co-operative Society (02 673 0888). If a beach barbecue is on the menu, pick up extra provisions at Al Rahi Home Grocery next to the co-operative. Drive north, with the quarry-scarred embankment on your left, along the beach track, and find a spot away from the beach houses. This is one of the few spots along the coast where you can camp. Two headlands further west, you'll find an even more pristine spot with white sand, turquoise sea and bobbing pink flamingos.

Kitesurfing Mania

Every year, the world's best kitesurfers gather for the 10 day Al Gharbia Watersports Festival (algharbiafestivals.com) in Mirfa, which takes place in March.

Desert Islands

This eight-island, eco-tourism project involves the larger Sir Bani Yas and Delma islands, and the six uninhabited Discovery Islands.

Sir Bani Yas Island was once Sheikh Zayed's personal retreat and is becoming a noted wildlife reserve. The Desert Islands Resort & Spa By Anantara has received

MIRFA HOTEL
فندق المرفا

The Coastal Retreat

WATER SPORTS ACTIVITIES
- Jet Skiing
- Kayaking
- Wake Boarding

HOTEL FEATURES
- Newly renovated 114 rooms and suites
- Beach front
- Restaurant & Bars

For information and reservation
Tel : +971 2 8833030
Fax : +971 2 8836400
Email : rsvn@mirfahotel.com
Web : www.mirfahotel.com

An Oasis of Tranquility

LIWA HOTEL

LEISURE ACTIVITIES
- Camel Riding
- Quad Bike

HOTEL FEATURES:
- Ayurvedic Massage and Yoga
- 3 Bedrooms Private Villas
- Newly renovated rooms
- Restaurant and Bars

For information and reservation
T : +971 2 8822000
F : +971 2 8822830
E : rsvn@liwahotel.net
W : www.liwahotel.net

OUT OF THE CITY
AL GHARBIA

numerous accolades for eco-sensitive luxury, and its even more luxurious sister properties on the island – Al Yamm Villa Resort and Al Sahel Villa Resort – have beautiful self-contained units. Sir Bani Yas Island is 9km off the coast from Jebel Dhanna and offers safaris where you'll see a multitude of animals including giraffes, oryx and maybe even a hyena. There are also a few routes for mountain biking and the clear blue waters and creeks offer peaceful snorkelling and kayaking. Catch the ferry to the island or fly from Al Bateen Executive Airport.

Beyond Sir Bani Yas and 42km off the coast lies Delma Island, a two-hour ferry ride from Jebel Dhanna or a 45 minute flight from Abu Dhabi International Airport. Delma Island is only nine by six kilometres but until recently it was the most important island in the Gulf. With fertile land and more than 200 wells of fresh water it was a favourite stopping point for traders, fishermen and pearlers for thousands of years. Evidence of human habitation on the island dates back more than 7,000 years and even today it supports more than 4,000 locals whose livelihood is fishing and farming. The island's rich earth supports the cultivation of more than 20 varieties of African, Asian and European fruits.

The volcanic landscape literally sparkles and ospreys watch over the fields of ostrich, but even with car ferries plying the route from the mainland, the island's attractions are works in progress. The only accommodation is the Delma Motel (02 878 1222), or you can camp.

Hotels

Anantara Sir Bani Yas Island Al Yamm Villa Resort
Sir Bani Yas Island Ruwais **02 801 4200**
al-yamm.anantara.com

This special resort offers 30 five-star units in a serene location on the eastern shore of Sir Bani Yas Island, half of which are located on the beach and the other half in the tranquil mangroves. The rooms have beautiful views of the water, either the turquoise sea or the bird-filled lagoon. Two more properties owned by Anantara – Sir Bani Yas Island Al Sahel Villa Resort and Desert Islands Resort & Spa – also offer impeccable luxury and access to the island's wildlife reserve.

Danat Jebel Dhanna Resort
Jebel Dhanna Ruwais **02 801 2222**
jebeldhanna.danathotels.com

Sitting on 800 metres of private, picturesque beach, this undiscovered treat of a hotel offers 109 luxurious rooms and suites including six waterfront villas. It has a health club and a spa that includes beach massage huts and a nice pool area with swim-up bar.

Dhafra Beach Hotel
Jebel Dhanna Ruwais **02 801 2000**
danathotels.com

A very pleasant and reasonably priced hotel with a variety of rooms and suites to choose from, as well as a handful of dining options, a fitness centre with a sauna, and two swimming pools. A good option if heading west – you can even hire the late Sheikh Zayed's presidential suite for Dhs.3,000 per night.

Arabian Nights Under The Stars

An essential part of any Liwa adventure, camping in the desert is a truly unforgettable experience. The expanses of sand rolling into the distance at early dawn is quite magical. You can camp just about anywhere, so take any of the roads and tracks into the desert off the main road, but make sure that you drive far enough to find a peaceful spot. Try to get settled long before the sun goes down, for safety reasons and to allow you to enjoy the sunset. One particularly good area is on the road to Moreeb Hill passing the Liwa Resthouse. This minor, paved road heads into the desert for 11.5km, leading you into some of the best dunes, and crossing plenty of *sabkha* (salt) flats.

Liwa Hotel > p.455
Mezaira Liwa **02 882 2000**
almarfapearlhotels.com

With its raised location giving spectacular views of the Rub Al Khali (or Empty Quarter) desert, the green oasis and the neighbouring palace on the hilltop opposite, Liwa Hotel is a good option if you're not keen on camping but still want to enjoy the scenery. The hotel has spacious rooms and green, landscaped grounds with an attractive pool. There's also a choice of good dining options and evening venues.

Liwa Resthouse
Mezaira Liwa **02 882 2075**

A little past its prime, this guesthouse has been eclipsed by the nearby Liwa Hotel and its (mainly Arab) clientele includes visiting business travellers, government officials and families on holiday. Although pretty basic compared to local hotels, it is clean and functional, and the cheapest alternative to camping.

Mirfa Hotel
Abu Dhabi – Tarif Rd, Mirfa 02 883 3030
almarfapearlhotels.com

Located in the quiet town of Mirfa, 160 kilometres from Abu Dhabi, this hotel is perfect for a weekend break or as a stopover if you're driving to Saudi Arabia. The hotel has been renovated and now features 114 comfortable rooms and suites, and lush gardens as well as leisure facilities including two pools, floodlit tennis courts and a kids' playground.

OUT OF THE CITY
AJMAN

AJMAN

The smallest of the emirates, Ajman still has lots to offer travellers, including fine dining, luxury hotels and pristine beaches, with a few heritage attractions thrown in for good measure. It's a more relaxed emirate in all senses of the word; life has a slower pace, while dress codes are a bit more lenient and alcohol can be bought without a licence.

The emirate's star attraction, Ajman Museum, houses a variety of interesting displays in a restored fort that is well worth visiting, as much for the building as for its contents. The emirate's main souks are a reminder of days gone by, while the modern Ajman City Centre is home to shops, foodcourts and a cinema. The tiny emirate is known for being one of the largest boat building centres in the region; while mainly modern boats emerge from the yards these days, you may still catch a glimpse of a traditionally built wooden dhow sailing out to sea.

Attractions

Ajman Corniche
Corniche Road Ajman

Life in Ajman revolves around its pleasant seafront corniche, especially during the milder months. It is lined with cafes, shops, stalls, and there's a tidal pool for safe swimming. There are some excellent traditional restaurants, too. Try the seafood at Themar Al Bahar or the Middle Eastern cuisine at Attibrah.

Ajman Museum
Al Bustan Ajman **06 742 3824**

No trip to Ajman would be complete without a visit to the Ajman Museum. This attractive building is based inside a fort, thought to have originally been built during the late 18th century. The popular cultural attraction houses an astounding collection of artefacts and archaeological finds, including centuries-old manuscripts, weaponry and pottery.

Al Zorah Nature Reserve

This serene mangrove creek is teeming with wildlife, including a huge flock of flamingos. The area is currently under development but you can get a peek from the viewing deck on Al Zorah Street. The development will add more luxury resorts to the city, a golf course and a marina.

Attibrah
Corniche Road Ajman **06 744 8383**

A good option for sampling some authentic Emirati dishes with traditional local flavours. Go for the *gideesha* (a fragrant spiced fish dish) and some *harris biliyan* (a rich eggplant side dish), along with the usual Middle Eastern mezze spread.

Fish Market
Ajman

One of the best local fish markets in the country, head here early to see the day's catch being offloaded from fishing dhows and choose something fresh to have prepared and cooked onsite.

Hotels

Ajman Palace
Corniche Road Ajman **06 701 8888**
theajmanpalace.com

This gorgeous hotel may not serve alcohol (unusually for Ajman) but it's a relaxing place to spend time. Leisure facilities include an infinity pool, a private beach and a fully equipped spa and fitness centre.

Ajman Saray
Corniche Road Ajman **06 714 2222**
starwoodhotels.com

This brand new hotel from the Luxury Collection has its own private beach and brings a splash of glamour to Ajman. There are several restaurants, including a beach bar and grill.

Ajman Corniche

askexplorer.com 457

OUT OF THE CITY
FUJAIRAH

Kempinski
Corniche Road Ajman **06 714 5555**
kempinski.com
This beautiful five-star hotel offers the ultimate in luxury and hospitality. There's a stunning stretch of white sand beach overlooking the Arabian Gulf that's perfect for trying out watersports or simply soaking up the sun. You can even request to have a table set up in the surf for a romantic dinner for two. Be sure to sample the renowned Indian cuisine at the excellent Bukhara or the Italian fare at Sabella's.

Ramada Beach Hotel
Shk Humaid Bin Rashid Al Nuami St Ajman **06 742 9999**
ramadabeachajman.com
For a cheap and cheerful stay on the water's edge, this four-star hotel has a lot to offer. It has its own private beach where you can get spa treatments, and an enormous five-bedroom penthouse with its own Jacuzzi that can be rented at a very reasonable rate.

Lap of Luxury
Little Ajman is making big strides in the luxury travel stakes. While the Kempinski remains a hugely popular option for a weekend of pampering, the newly opened Ajman Saray brings more choice for a deluxe break, and a new offering from the Fairmont will open on the beachfront in 2014. Further luxury resorts are in development at the Al Zorah Nature Reserve.

FUJAIRAH

Fujairah may be less than a two-hour drive when travelling from Dubai, but the dramatic landscape of the east coast makes it feel like a different world. The journey itself takes you through the spectacular Hajar Mountains before arriving at this picturesque location along the Gulf of Oman. Fujairah city has seen little development compared to cities on the west coast, but the real draw here is the landscape. The mountains and wadis that stretch west of the coast contain some of the country's best and most accessible camping spots, and the beaches, reefs and villages that line the coast attract visitors from every emirate.

Dibba
Located at the northern-most point of the east coast, on the border with Musandam, Dibba is made up of three fishing villages. Unusually, each part comes under a different jurisdiction: Dibba Al Hisn is part of Sharjah, Dibba Al Fujairah is Fujairah and Dibba Bayah is Oman. The three Dibbas share an attractive bay, fishing communities, and excellent diving locations – from here you can arrange dhow trips to take you to unspoilt dive locations in Musandam. The Hajar Mountains, which run parallel to the east coast, provide a dramatic backdrop, rising in places to over 1,800 metres. There are good public beaches too, where your only company will be crabs and seagulls, and where seashell collectors may find a few treasures.

East Coast Made Easy
From Dubai, getting to the UAE's east coast takes anything from 30-90 minutes. For speed alone, take the Sharjah-Kalba Road and then the Sheikh Khalifa Highway. For a more scenic route through the mountains, take the E88 from Sharjah to Masafi, passing fruit sellers and local landmark the Friday Market, and then turn left to Dibba or right to Fujairah. If you're heading to Dibba outside of rush hour, it's usually quicker to head north on Sheikh Mohammed bin Zayed Road and take the truck road (at exit 119) across the country to the E87, which brings you to Dibba.

Fujairah City
A mix of old and new, its hillsides are dotted with ancient forts and watchtowers, which add an air of mystery and charm; most are undergoing restoration work. Fujairah is also a busy trading centre, with its modern container port and a thriving free zone attracting major companies from around the world. Off the coast, the seas and coral reefs are great for fishing, diving and watersports. It is a good place for birdwatching during the spring and autumn migrations as it's on the route from Africa to Central Asia. Since Fujairah is close to the mountains and many areas of natural beauty, it makes an excellent base from which to explore the countryside and discover stunning wadis, forts, waterfalls and even natural hot springs.

Kalba
Just to the south of Fujairah you'll find Kalba, which is renowned for its mangrove forest and golden beaches. Technically the town belongs to Sharjah, but it's a pretty fishing village that still manages to retain much of its historical charm. You can visit Bait Sheikh Saeed bin Hamed Al Qasimi, an old house dating back 100 years that's home to fascinating heritage displays and historical artefacts.

South of the town is the beautiful tidal estuary of Khor Kalba (*khor* is Arabic for creek), one of the oldest

OUT OF THE CITY
FUJAIRAH

mangrove forests in Arabia. It is home to a variety of wildlife not found anywhere else in the UAE. The mangroves in the estuary flourish thanks to a mix of seawater and freshwater from the mountains, but are now receding due to the excessive use of water from inland wells. For birdwatchers, the area is especially good during the spring and autumn migrations when rare species of bird can be spotted, including Sykes's warbler. It is also home to a rare subspecies of white collared kingfisher, which breeds here and in Oman, and nowhere else in the world. Canoe tours have been put on hold while conservation work is carried out, but check with Desert Rangers (04 357 2200) in case the tours have been re-opened to the public.

The road through the mountains linking Kalba to Hatta makes for an interesting alternative for returning towards Dubai or Abu Dhabi.

Attractions

Bidiyah Mosque
Bidiyah Fujairah
The site of the oldest mosque in the UAE, Bidiyah is one of the oldest settlements on the east coast and is believed to have been inhabited since 3,000BC. The mosque is made from gypsum, stone and mud bricks finished off with plaster, and is believed to date back to the middle of the 15th century. It is still used by worshippers for daily prayer, so non-Muslim visitors can't enter. Built next to a low hillside with several watchtowers on the ridge behind, the area is colourfully lit up at night.

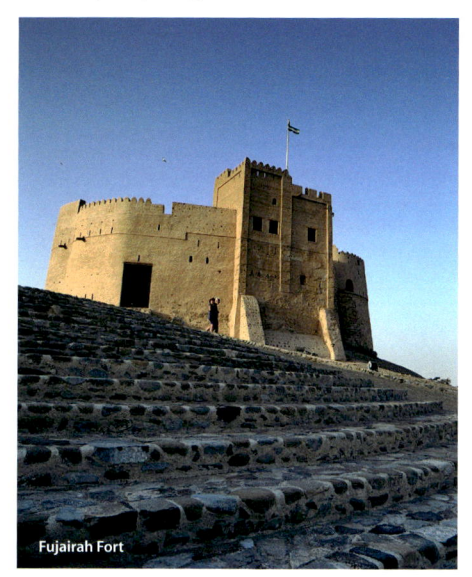

Fujairah Fort

Dibba Castle
Dibba Fujairah
Hidden away in the Omani part of Dibba (aka Daba), next to vast farms and plantations, Dibba Castle is an interesting place to have a walk around. Built over 180 years ago, it has been restored and, while there aren't a lot of artefacts on show, you can access all the rooms and climb up the towers, where you'll get views over the castle and its surroundings. It is signposted off the road past the UAE border check post.

Fujairah Fort
Nr Fujairah Heritage Village Fujairah
fujairahtourism.ae
The majestic Fujairah Fort is one of the oldest and most important in the emirate, as well as being among the most photographed. It's an impressive building located on a raised hilltop overlooking the city and just a few kilometres from the sea. Although you can't enter Fujairah Fort itself, the surrounding heritage buildings are open to the public, and the nearby remains of traditional houses are easily viewed.

Bull Butting
On Friday afternoons at around 4.30pm during winter, crowds gather close to the corniche to watch 'bull butting'. This ancient Portuguese sport consists of two huge bulls going head to head for several rounds, until after a few nudges and a bit of hoof bashing, a winner is determined. It's not as cruel or barbaric as other forms of bullfighting, but animal lovers may still want to avoid.

Fujairah Heritage Village
Nr Fujairah Fort Fujairah
fujmun.gov.ae
Situated just outside of Fujairah city, this purpose-built village takes you back in time to experience traditional life in the emirate. Walk around the village and see first-hand the realities of what traditional Bedouin life was like in the unforgiving desert climate. After a morning of cultural immersion, you can stay and relax in the sun, as there are two spring-fed swimming pools for men and women, and chalets that can be hired for the day.

Snoopy Island
Al Aqah Fujairah
Snoopy Island, so named because of its resemblance to the beloved comic book dog, is a popular snorkelling spot. The Sandy Beach Hotel & Resort's beach is a great launch pad (there's a small fee for non-guests to enter), as it's just a short swim away. Or, you can rent a kayak, as well as snorkelling gear. For the best visibility, go early; expect to be rewarded by an abundance of sea life including turtles and rays.

OUT OF THE CITY
RAS AL KHAIMAH

Hotels

Hilton Fujairah
Al Faseel St Fujairah 09 222 2411
hilton.com

Set at the north end of Fujairah's corniche, just a stone's throw from the foothills of the Hajar Mountains, this relaxing resort has all the facilities needed for a wonderful weekend away. If you get tired of lounging by the swimming pool, or activities like tennis, snooker, basketball or even watersports on the private beach, you could always explore the rugged splendour of the surrounding mountains. The hotel is great for families, and there is a safe play area to occupy the little ones.

Le Meridien Al Aqah
Dibba Fujairah 09 244 9000
lemeridien-alaqah.com

All of the rooms at Le Meridien Al Aqah have views over the Indian Ocean, and the grounds are covered by lush foliage. It is particularly geared up for families, with a kids' pool and outdoor and indoor play areas. There's an extensive spa and dive centre on site, as well as daily full or half-day fishing trips leaving from the beach. Entertainment options include a cinema, bars and restaurants serving a range of Thai, Indian and European cuisine.

Fujairah Rotana Resort & Spa – Al Aqah Beach
Al Aqah Beach, Dibba Rd Fujairah 09 244 9888
rotana.com

This resort puts its beachside location to good use, with each of the 250 guest rooms and suites boasting its own balcony with views over the sea. Some of the highlights of the hotel include its private beach, the swimming pool with pool bar and the indulgent spa offering plenty of pampering treatments. You can even opt to have a massage in a hut on the beach with an ocean view.

Sandy Beach Hotel
Dibba-Khorfakkan Rd Fujairah 09 244 5555
sandybm.com

Snoopy Island has long been recognised as one of the best diving spots in the United Arab Emirates, with an abundance of fish and even reef sharks. The island is right off the coast from the Sandy Beach Hotel, making it a firm favourite with UAE residents. Day trippers can purchase a day pass to the hotel to access the temperature-controlled pool, watersports and beach bar services. There is also a five-star PADI Dive Centre within the hotel that hires out diving and snorkelling gear for exploring the reefs around Snoopy Island, as well as offering courses for novices or those looking to improve their diving.

RAS AL KHAIMAH

Nature lovers, take note: Ras Al Khaimah boasts the best natural scenery in the UAE. With the stunning Hajar Mountains as its backdrop and the sparkling waters of the Arabian Gulf on its shore, the northernmost emirate is the perfect destination for an outdoor break with plenty of opportunities for camping, hiking and soaking up the sun. Several five-star hotels offer more for your dirham than you could expect to get in the bigger cities.

Ras Al Khaimah contains several archaeological sites, some dating back all the way to 3,000BC. Take the Al Ram road out of Al Nakheel district and towards the Hajar Mountains to discover some of the area's history, including the Dhayah Fort, Shimal Archaeological Site and Sheba's Palace. The bare ruins of the Dhayah Fort can be spotted from the road, but you might need a 4WD to access them.

The town is quiet, relaxing and a good starting point for exploring the surrounding mountains, visiting the ancient sites of Ghalilah and Shimal, the hot springs at Khatt, and the quirky local camel race track at Digdagga. Al Hamra Village, just south of the city, is a gorgeous development with its own mall (with a VOX Cinemas, restaurants, play centre and a supermarket), golf course, marina and five-star hotels.

Attractions

Al Hamra Golf Club
Al Hamra Village Ras Al Khaimah 07 244 7474
alhamragolf.com

Al Hamra Golf Course meanders around four interconnected open water lagoons that merge with the water of the Arabian Gulf. The club offers lessons for beginners, golf under the stars and a restaurant, sports bar and cafe, which is open to members and non-members alike.

The Haunted Village

Rumour has it that the residents of Jazirat Al Hamra saw spirits, or *djinn*, coming out of the sea and evacuated overnight in fear. This huge area of houses has been deserted for 40 years, and with hints of a bygone era, it is a fascinating, and somewhat creepy place to explore. Head north from Al Hamra Marina, take a u-turn at the pink pet shop, and turn right at the signpost to the archaeological park. Follow this road to the end.

Le MERIDIEN

DISCOVERY AWAITS

LE MERIDIEN
AL AQAH
BEACH RESORT
N 25° 30' E 56°21'
T +971 9 244 9000
lemeridien.com/fujairah

Explore the endless opportunities to unwind and relax in style at Le Méridien Al Aqah Beach Resort. Fujairah offers rich cultural traditions and contemporary luxury. Just 90 minutes from Dubai, you enjoy all of the seclusion and privacy your heart desires. The resort is only 50 kilometers from Fujairah City and within easy reach of the area's unique attractions, including ancient fjords, palm groves, hot springs, and historical landmarks.

All Sea view rooms • Room size starting from 48 sq meters • One of the largest swimming pools in the UAE • Water sports • Professional dive centre • Penguin Club • Teens Club • Choice of 9 restaurants & bars • Spa Al Aqah with Ayurvedic centre • Safaris and mountain excursions • Boat and dhow trips to Musandam • Chartered fishing trips

For more information or to make a reservation, please visit lemeridien.com/fujairah or call +971 9 244 9000 or email: reservation.lmaa@lemeridien.com

spg Starwood Preferred Guest

Le MERIDIEN | aloft | FOUR POINTS | WESTIN | THE LUXURY COLLECTION
W HOTELS | Sheraton | ST REGIS | element

©2012 Starwood Hotels & Resorts Worldwide, Inc. All Rights Reserved. Preferred Guest, SPG, Le Méridien and their logos are the trademarks of Starwood Hotels & Resorts Worldwide, Inc., or its affiliates.

OUT OF THE CITY
RAS AL KHAIMAH

Al Hamra Marina & Royal Yacht Club
Al Hamra Village Ras Al Khaimah 07 243 2274
alhamramarina.com
You can apply for membership to the club online, and daily membership is also available if you just want to visit for a short time. Facilities include a restaurant and there are charter boats.

Al Qawasim Corniche
Ras Al Khaimah 07 204 1111
rakftz.com
Ras Al Khaimah's Al Qawasim Corniche is a social hub that's lined with cafes. Enjoy the natural beauty of the mangroves and visit the Pearl Museum to learn about the emirate's pearling traditions, followed by a bit of local knowledge at the National Museum of Ras Al Khaimah. You can hire bikes for exploring the area. Round off your evening at Italian restaurant Pesto, followed by shisha on the rooftop terrace overlooking the serene mangroves.

Camel Racing
Around half an hour along Truck Road (turn left past Ras Al Khaimah Airport) is the camel race track at Digdagga, where local folk meet up early in the morning to compare and race their camels as they have done for centuries – albeit with robot jockeys atop the camels and the owners tearing around the course in their battered SUVs with horns blaring in encouragement. It's a brilliantly bonkers, wonderfully unapologetic slice of local life.

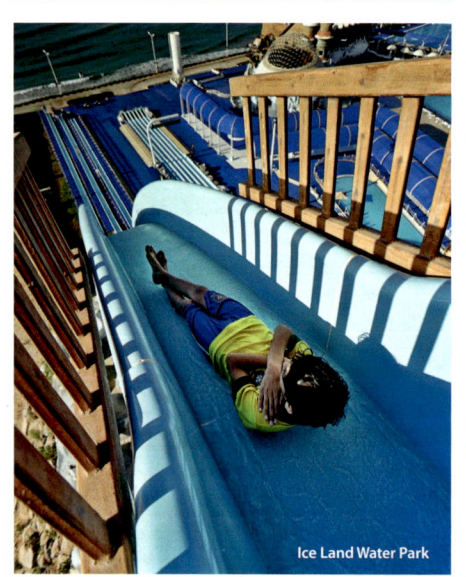

Bassata Desert Village
Ras Al Khaimah 055 993 8589
Experience traditional Arabian activities including a belly dancer, Egyptian tanoura, a henna lady, camel riding and dune bashing. The Arabic BBQ dinner at sunset is a great way to end the day.

Bedouin Oasis Desert Camp
Ras Al Khaimah 04 266 6020
arabianincentive.com
This camp provides visitors with the perfect opportunity to explore desert living. Using only traditional and natural materials the Bedouin Oasis Desert Camp is a step back to the days when tent roofs were originally made from goat hair and there was only fire or an antique gas light to provide heating and lighting.

Catamaran Freedom
Ras Al Khaimah 050 377 6613
facebook.com/Freedomtobesailing
'Freedom' cruises from Ras Al Khaimah Corniche and takes in the emirate's scenic coast. This is a good trip for group parties, romantic getaways or corporate excursions. Trips are tailored to individual requirements and can include swimming, snorkelling, fishing sunset dinners or champagne packages.

Ice Land Water Park
Al Jazeera, Al Hamra Ras Al Khaimah 07 206 7888
icelandwaterpark.com
With its ice-capped mountains and plastic penguins in the middle of a desert landscape, this polar-themed water park is certainly a sight to behold. Without a doubt, Ice Land is a magnet for tots and toddlers, who can't help but love the quirkiness of it all. There's Penguin Bay, an interactive play area that's home to the world's biggest rain dance pool and also Penguin Falls, the tallest man-made waterfall in the world.

Jazira Aviation Club
Jazirah Airport Ras Al Khaimah 07 244 6416
jac-uae.net
Enjoy scenic views of the desert, beach, sea and mountains from the air with light aircraft flights from Al Jazirah Aviation Club. There are short piloted flights in a variety of aircraft, or keen enthusiasts can embark on courses to gain their pilot's licence.

The Land of Pearls – Pearl Excursion
Ras Al Khaimah
rakpearls.com
The first of its kind in the UAE, this pearl farm produces more than 100,000 pearls each year. Your visit begins by learning how a pearl is cultivated and then you can have a go at opening an oyster. If the oyster contains a pearl, then you can keep it!

Ice Land Water Park

Find Adventure in Ras Al Khaimah

Located just 45 minutes from Dubai International Airport, Ras Al Khaimah offers a variety of entertainment and relaxation facilities including exclusive Hotels & Resorts, international cuisines and world-class spas, all at a great value for money. With a wide range of adventure and sports activities covering desert camps, golf courses, watersports and micro light aviation, the emirate of Ras Al Khaimah offers the ultimate outdoor experience.

www.rasalkhaimahtourism.com
www.Facebook.com/VisitRasAlKhaimah

Ras Al Khaimah
A RISING EMIRATE

OUT OF THE CITY
RAS AL KHAIMAH

Luxury hotels in Ras Al Khaimah

Prince Of Sea
Al Hamra Marina Ras Al Khaimah **055 120 5900**
Hop aboard this fabulous yacht for a daytime, sunset or dinner cruise. Depending on which excursion you choose, you could enjoy swimming in the Arabian Sea, snorkelling off the coast of Al Marjan Island (look out for the rare green turtles) or simply dining on delicious barbecued seafood as you watch the sun go down. The evening trips usually include a welcome drink, DJ music and a buffet dinner, as well as traditional Arabian entertainment such as belly dancing.

RAK Sailing Academy
Al Hamra Marina Ras Al Khaimah **056 352 4659**
raksailingacademy.com
Located in Al Hamra Marina, RAK Sailing Academy is open to sailing lovers every year from October to the end of April. The academy is equipped with dinghies, a catamaran and fixed keel sailing boats for juniors and seniors. Visitors are able to rent different types of boats either for relaxation or for training courses.

Ras Al Khaimah Country Club
Ras Al Khaimah **056 706 4884**
This newly opened equestrian club is already proving popular with local horse riding-enthusiasts and visitors from the UAE and abroad. As well as boasting superb equestrian facilities and expertly trained staff, there's also a restaurant and bar for lingering over a delicious meal or relaxing drink, and a large, scenic swimming pool for cooling off while you soak up some sun. Riding lessons and excursions are available to visitors of all ages and experiences. Contact info@rasalkhaimahtourism.com for more information.

Tower Links Golf Club
Ras Al Khaimah **07 227 8555**
towerlinks.com
One of Ras Al Khaimah's two 18 hole championship courses, Tower Links Golf Club is set in a beautiful mangrove reserve with the Hajar Mountains as a majestic backdrop. The club welcomes active and social members.

OUT OF THE CITY
RAS AL KHAIMAH

Hotels

Al Hamra Fort Hotel & Beach Resort
Al Jazeerah St Ras Al Khaimah 07 244 6666
alhamrabeachandgolfresort.hilton.com
With traditional Arabic architecture set among acres of lush gardens and a long strip of sandy beach, this hotel offers a peaceful getaway. A range of watersports and activities, including two floodlit golf courses and an onsite dive centre, will keep you entertained, as will the live entertainment concerts that take place on the beach. The themed eateries also offer a wide variety of international cuisines.

Stellar Cellar
Al Hamra Cellar, although owned by MMI (mmidubai.com), is a tax-free liquor store that is well worth the trip. You can take advantage of RAK's relaxed alcohol laws and browse a wide range of fine wines, spirits and beers at extremely competitive prices. Call 07 244 7403 for more info.

Al Hamra Residence
Al Jazerah St Ras Al Khaimah 07 206 7222
alhamraresorts.com
Located on a private beach in the Arabian Gulf, this five-star resort offers luxurious suites with fully equipped kitchenettes. The Sea Breeze restaurant serves traditional Arabic food, while guests can have a refreshing swim in the outdoor pool or enjoy the tennis court and fitness centre. The resort is just a five-minute drive from Al Hamra Golf Club.

Banyan Tree Ras Al Khaimah Beach
Al Hamra Village Ras Al Khaimah 07 206 7777
banyantree.com
The sister property of the gorgeous Banyan Tree Al Wadi (see Desert Resorts for more information), this stunning resort offers 32 beachfront villas built in the style of the Bedouin's tents – but far more luxurious. It's a lovely hideaway for some serious relaxation (each villa has its own plunge pool and comfy cabana), and it's also great for thrill seekers, with snorkelling, sailing and watersports all on offer.

Bin Majid Beach Resort
Al Jazeera Rd Ras Al Khaimah 07 244 6644
binmajid.com
Guests can relax and unwind along an 800m sandy beach at this affordable four-star hotel. As well as plenty of sports facilities for the active, including jet-skiing and parasailing, there is a great selection of licensed bars and restaurants serving Indian and international dishes. There's also a large pool with swim-up bar and a children's play area.

The Cove Rotana Resort
E11 Ras Al Khaimah 07 206 6000
rotana.com
This sprawling resort, comprising more than 200 rooms and 72 villas, has the feel of an old Mediterranean hill town, thanks to its location built into the hillsides overlooking the Arabian Gulf. The centrepiece is undoubtedly the lagoon that it is built around, which is protected from the sea by 600 metres of pristine beach.

Golden Tulip Khatt Springs Resort & Spa
Khatt Ras Al Khaimah 07 244 8777
goldentulipkhattsprings.com
Simple and subdued, Golden Tulip Khatt Springs Resort & Spa relies on mountain views, uninterrupted tranquillity and incredible spa packages to attract weekend visitors. Next to the hotel, you can take a dip in the public Khatt Hot Springs – piping hot water which, it is claimed, has curative powers. Men and women have separate pools and a variety of massages are also available. It's a good idea to visit the hot springs in the morning and avoid Fridays as it can get very busy with families.

Hilton Ras Al Khaimah Resort & Spa
Al Maareedh St Ras Al Khaimah 07 228 8844
hilton.com
With 1.5km of private, white sandy beach, six swimming pools, five-star service, loads of watersports on offer and some super fine dining options, you won't really need to leave. As well as rooms in the main building, there are 151 quaint villas with direct beach access, and for all that's on offer, it's actually rather good value.

Waldorf Astoria
Al Hamra Village Ras Al Khaimah 07 203 5555
waldorfastoria.com
An enormous hotel styled on an Arabian palace, the Waldorf Astoria is set on 350m of private beach and has various dining options, including the excellent Lexington Grill, as well as a cigar bar, spa, gym, and gorgeous pools. Following in the traditions of Waldorf Astoria hotels around the world, every inch of the place is beautifully designed but favouring elegance over ostentation, and each venue with its own style and story to tell.

New Hotels
Ras Al Khaimah's distinguished list of hotels will grow in 2014, with the opening of the Rixos Bab Al Bahr, Santorini Hotel, DoubleTree by Hilton Resort and Marjan Island Resort & Spa on the man-made Marjan island – RAK's answer to the Palm Jumeirah.

Short Breaks From The UAE

As much as we love living in the UAE, there are so many fantastic places to visit just a few hours away by plane. Here are just a few.

Dubai is an ideal base to explore the region. Fly in style with Emirates from Dubai or Etihad out of Abu Dhabi, or check the low-cost carriers for more budget-friendly travel. Air Arabia flies from Sharjah Airport and flydubai from Dubai Airport or Al Ain.

Cyprus
Flight time: *Four hours, five minutes (from Dubai) or four hours, 20 minutes (from Abu Dhabi)*
The three main towns, Larnaca, Limassol and Paphos, offer unique accommodation and leisure options, and the capital city Nicosia is great for shopping and nightlife. Drive up the mountains for crisp, cool air and awesome views, and explore the local villages.

India
Flight time: *Three to four hours*
Cruise the serene backwaters of Kerala and witness timeless rural life, or party on the beautiful beaches of Goa. Explore the vibrant city of New Delhi before catching the train around the Golden Triangle, taking in architectural marvel, the Taj Mahal, and the majestic palaces and forts of Rajasthan. And that's barely scratching the surface of this enormously diverse and colourful subcontinent.

Jordan
Flight time: *Three hours, 10 minutes*
Jordan's capital, Amman, will keep you busy for a few days, but heading south to Petra, the ancient city carved into solid rock canyons, is an absolute must. Stop at the Dead Sea to bathe in the mineral-rich black mud and test the buoyant waters. Be sure to head to Jerash, which has been continuously inhabited for 6,500 years, and visit holy sites, such as the brook where the baptism of Jesus Christ is said to have taken place.

Lebanon
Flight time: *Four hours, five minutes*
With its unique combination of snow and sun, Lebanon manages to be all things to all travellers. The mountains are ripe for outdoor adventure, the ancient ruins are fun to explore, the food is sublime – and then there's the nightlife. Dubbed the 'Paris of the Middle East', Beirut is considered by many to have the best clubs and bars in the region.

Sri Lanka
Flight time: *Four hours, 40 minutes*
An easily accessible paradise with rainforests, unspoilt beaches, well-populated game parks, great surf and gorgeous hotels offering exceptional rates. Have we got your attention yet? Add into the mix a charming blend of Buddhist, Hindu, Muslim, Christian and indigenous cultures, along with spicy, traditional curries, rotis and egg hoppers – and you have the ideal Sri Lankan holiday.

Seychelles
Flight time: *Four hours, 40 minutes*
Few travel destinations evoke the image of an island paradise as much as the Seychelles, and with good reason. Lush unexplored jungles, powdery white-sand beaches and an azure ocean teeming with marine life create the overall impression of a modern-day Eden. You can stay on 15 of the 115 islands scattered through the Indian Ocean, 1,600 kilometres east of Africa. The largest is Mahe, but the smaller Praslin and La Digue have much to offer too.

Maldives
Flight time: *Four hours, five minutes*
As one of the world's best destinations, if not the best, for diving and snorkelling, there are few places on earth where you can walk from a stunning beach straight into the ocean and see a lively coral reef a few feet below you. Time seems to slow down in the Maldives and spending a few days in awe of the ocean, relaxing in a hammock over impossibly pristine beaches, or sipping cocktails and dining on all-inclusive seafood buffets can certainly make for a dream holiday.

Kenya
Flight time: *Five hours, five minutes*
Here you'll find one of the highest concentrations of wild animals on the planet, including, of course, the Big Five. Witness an alpha lion stalk across the dusty plains in the dawn light, or a herd of elephants cross a crocodile-infested river under the hot African sun, or simply sip sundowners while the animal kingdom gathers at the watering hole below – head to Masai Mara National Reserve and you can experience all of that in just a few days.

Book It Online

Don't waste hours scouring the internet; whether you want to book an extravagant honeymoon to the Seychelles or a shoestring weekend break to Europe, dnata (dnatatravel.com) is a one-stop shop for hotels, flights and holiday packages. Book online or call 04 316 6666 – and sign up on the website for all the latest travel deals.

Explore Your Options

For more information on these and many more short-haul destinations out of Dubai, pick up a copy of Explorer's *Short Breaks From And Within The UAE*.

The Maldives

OUT OF THE CITY
SHARJAH

SHARJAH

Dubai's neighbouring emirate was named the cultural capital of the Arab world by UNESCO in 1998 and the Capital of Islamic Culture for 2014 by the Organisation of Islamic Conference, due to its well-preserved heritage area, an ever-evolving arts scene, some wonderful museums and a thriving cafe culture. Regular events such as the Sharjah Light Festival and Sharjah Biennial draw visitors from all over the UAE and beyond, and that's just the city – the emirate is home to some fantastic desert, including popular spots Big Red (a 90m high sand dune) and Fossil Rock, and a few enclaves over on the east coast.

For a sense of what the city is all about, head to Khalid Lagoon. At Al Majaz Waterfront you can choose from a cluster of restaurants to watch the nightly fountain show on the lagoon, take an abra ride, or check out the kids' play areas.

A wander further north brings you to the city's heritage and arts areas, currently being restored and developed under the Heart of Sharjah project, with one of the most impressive collections of museums and heritage sites in the region. Shoppers will have a blast too, searching for gifts in Sharjah's souks – Souk Al Arsah is a more authentic experience than those in the rest of the country, and with some canny bartering you could bag a bargain.

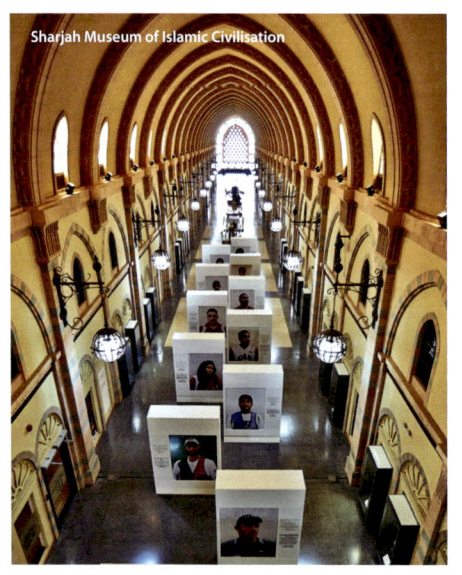

Sharjah Museum of Islamic Civilisation

Attractions

Adventureland > p.xvii
Sahara Centre Sharjah **06 531 6363**
adventureland-sharjah.com
Adventureland's recent revamp has made it a popular indoor attraction with a new jungle theme and 25 major thrill rides and attractions including a family fun train and a two-level indoor go-kart track.

Al Mahatta Museum
King Abdul Aziz St Sharjah **06 573 3079**
sharjahmuseums.ae
Home to the first airfield in the Gulf, opened in 1932, Sharjah played an important role as a primary stop-off point for the first commercial flights from Britain to India, and the museum looks at the impact this had on the traditional way of life in Sharjah and beyond. Four of the original propeller planes have been fully restored and are on display. Located behind Al Estiqlal Street, entry is Dhs.5 for adults and Dhs.10 for families.

Al Qasba
Nr Al Khan Lagoon Sharjah **06 556 0777**
alqasba.ae
Canal-side hub Al Qasba is packed with popular cafes and restaurants, and has some interesting attractions, such as Maraya Art Centre and the Eye of the Emirates observation wheel. Al Majaz Park is good for little ones; there are plenty of kids' play areas including a lovely splash park. Restaurants along the waterfront overlook Khalid Lagoon, where Sharjah's nightly answer to the Dubai Fountain is a colourful affair.

Al Tamimi Stables
Nr Al Zubair Municipality Bldg Sharjah **06 743 1122**
tamimistables.com
This private but friendly farm offers kids the chance to get up close to their favourite animals, from little mice to fluffy rabbits and even a friendly parrot. There's also pony rides, falcon shows, horse displays and guided nature trails, making for the perfect family day out.

Heart Of Sharjah
Nr Al Mareija & Corniche Sts
heartofsharjah.ae
The region's largest heritage project encompasses the heritage and arts areas and is dedicated to restoration and renovation; some of the traditional coral stone buildings date back more than 200 years. The narrow alleys and shady cobbled courtyards transport you to another era, and there are several fascinating museums. Check out Majlis Al Midfaa, an iconic round wind tower, as well as Sharjah Heritage Museum and Sharjah Art Museum, both of which use the unique and beautiful spaces of the area's traditional buildings. The 150 year-old Souk Al Arsah is located here too.

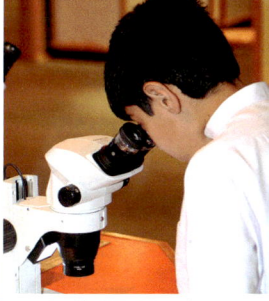

BEGIN YOUR JOURNEY OF DISCOVERY

@sharjahmuseums /SharjahMuseumsDept
@sharjahmuseums SharjahMuseums

www.SharjahMuseums.ae

الشارقة عاصمة الثقافة الإسلامية
SHARJAH ISLAMIC CULTURE CAPITAL

إدارة متاحف الشارقة
Sharjah Museums Department

OUT OF THE CITY
SHARJAH

Al Noor Mosque by Khalid Lagoon
(image: Sharjah Commerce & Tourism Development Authority)

Sharjah Art Museum
Sharjah Arts Area Sharjah **06 568 8222**
sharjahmuseums.ae
Permanent displays here include a personal collection of paintings and maps belonging to the ruler, HH Sheikh Dr Sultan bin Mohammad Al Qasimi, such as the fascinating work of several 18th century Orientalists, with oil paintings and watercolours depicting traditional life in the Arab world. Temporary exhibits include modern works by renowned international artists, especially during Sharjah Biennial, an important event on the international calendar.

Sharjah Classic Car Museum
Al Dhaid Rd Sharjah **06 558 0222**
sharjahmuseums.ae
This fantastic and well-curated museum is definitely worth a visit, whether or not you are 'into' cars. There's a large number of vehicles on display, all dating from 1979 or earlier. Many of the cars are from His Highness Sheikh Dr Sultan bin Mohammad Al Qasimi's personal collection, including a stunning 1934 Rolls Royce. Displays are quirky, fun and well presented – it's a great place to soak up some history and to impress any auto-enthusiasts.

Sharjah Desert Park
Al Dhaid Rd Sharjah **06 531 1501**
epaashj.com
Located just off the E611, this complex is worth heading to for its three animal-themed attractions. Arabia's Wildlife Centre is one of the UAE's best in terms of animal care and presentation, and home to a host of fascinating wildlife indigenous to the Arabian region, including the rare Arabian leopard. The Natural History & Botanical Museum features interactive displays on the relationships between man and the natural world in the UAE and beyond, while over at the Children's Farm petting zoo, you can feed some friendly camels, goats and more. The entrance fee, Dhs.15 for adults and Dhs.5 for children, covers all three attractions.

OUT OF THE CITY
UMM AL QUWAIN

UMM AL QUWAIN

Sharjah Discovery Centre
Al Dhaid Rd Sharjah **06 558 6577**
sharjahmuseums.ae
The Discovery Centre is divided into educational zones. The star attraction is Drive Town and its electric cars, where children learn the rules of the road.

Sharjah Golf & Shooting Club > p.vi-vii
Shk Mohammed Bin Zayed Rd Sharjah **06 548 7777**
golfandshootingshj.com
With golf, shooting, archery and paintball on the menu, there's enough to fill an whole weekend at this club. Once you're done with the activities, there's a choice of excellent restaurants.

Sharjah Museum of Islamic Civilization > p.469
Corniche St Sharjah **06 565 5455**
sharjahmuseums.ae
More than 5,000 artefacts from across the Arab world, all informatively displayed and housed in a beautiful building that was once a souk.

Hotels

Coral Beach Resort
Nr Al Muntazah & Al Nuamia Sts Sharjah **06 522 9999**
coral-international.com
With its own pristine sandy beach and a swimming pool with a waterslide, this is one hotel that's bound to keep the kids (and adults) happy. There's also a host of activities and sports facilities on offer, as well as a spa and hammam where you can wind down after a long day exploring the city. Be sure to try the excellent seafood at the restaurant Casa Samak during your stay or visit Al Bahar for their Sunday roast.

Hilton Sharjah
Corniche St Sharjah **06 519 2222**
hilton.com
A beautiful new art deco-styled resort which is located right on Khalid Lagoon and boasts some of the best facilities in the emirate. Enjoy succulent kebabs at the authentic Shiraz restaurant or indulge in a chilled mocktail on the pool terrace.

Radisson Blu Resort
Corniche St Sharjah **06 565 7777**
radissonblu.com
This reliably smart hotel chain has a five-star offering in a great location close to the city's historic centre and with its own beach. Facilities are plentiful and include temperature-controlled swimming pools, watersports, tennis courts, a spa and fitness centre, as well as several great dining options. .

A visit to Umm Al Quwain is a great way to see traditional Emirati life; fishing and date farming are still the main industries, as they have been for centuries. It has plenty of modern attractions too – its beach resorts are popular (and extremely affordable) hangout spots among UAE expats, and it was the first place in the country to offer skydiving (visit emiratesdropzone.webs.com for details).

The emirate has six forts, and a few old watchtowers surrounding the town. With plenty of mangroves and birdlife, the emirate's lagoon is a popular weekend spot for boat trips, windsurfing and other watersports. Another popular family activity is crab hunting at Flamingo Beach Resort. At nightfall, groups of hunters set off into the shallow mangrove waters with a guide, where they spear crabs, which are then barbecued and served on return to the resort.

Emirates Motorplex (motorplex.ae) hosts various motorsport events, including the Emirates Motocross Championship, and Dreamland Aqua Park is one of the most popular attractions. Barracuda Beach Resort is a favoured destination for Dubai residents, thanks to its well-stocked, duty-free liquor store.

Attractions

Dreamland Aqua Park > p.xiii
Al Rafaah Umm Al Quwain **06 768 1888**
dreamlanduae.com
This impressive water park is both huge and hugely popular. Perfect for a family day out, there are more than 30 rides, including four 'twisting dragons' that promise white knuckle thrills. There's also a lazy river and a play area if you're looking for something a little more relaxing, as well as a high-salinity floating pool. You can camp overnight, staying in one of the tents or huts provided. However, note that Fridays and public holidays are for families only.

Umm Al Quwain Marine Club
Nr Palm Beach Resort Umm Al Quwain **06 766 6644**
uaqmarineclub.com
This watersports centre takes advantage of the calm waters of the placid lagoon, which provides the perfect conditions for wakeboarding, as well as kayaking and stand up paddleboarding through the mangoves. All these and more are offered at competitive prices, and day members can use the pool and kids' play facilities.

OUT OF THE CITY
OMAN

Hotels

Barracuda Beach Resort
Nr Dreamland Aqua Park, Khor Al Baida
Umm Al Quwain **06 768 1555**
barracuda.ae

This comfortable, laidback resort is perfect for a short break or even a quick weekend getaway, especially as prices are very reasonable. There's a variety of rooms, but you might prefer one of the lagoon-side one-bedroom chalets, each of which accommodates up to five people. These are fitted out with kitchenettes and barbecues, which make them ideal for private overnight parties, and the hotel boasts a large pool and Jacuzzi too. You can also take advantage of the tax-free booze emporium while you're there, and there's a lovely gourmet shop opposite the liquor store that's worth a look before you head home.

Flamingo Beach Resort
Nr Horsehead R/A Umm Al Quwain **06 765 0000**
flamingoresort.ae

This cheap and cheerful hotel is perfect for nature lovers, as it's surrounded by a shallow lagoon and green islands that attract a variety of fauna, including visiting flamingos. The hotel organises a variety of excursions to keep guests entertained, including flamingo tours and deep sea fishing trips. Guests can also go on a night-time crab hunt – not an activity for the faint-hearted, you head out to the shallows with a guide (and a spear), and whatever you catch will be cooked for you back at the resort. There's a beach bar, cafe and dhow restaurant too.

Dreamland Aqua Park

OMAN

The most accessible country in the Gulf for Dubai residents, Oman is a peaceful and breathtaking place, with history, culture and spectacular scenery, from the southernmost city of Salalah to the quaint capital Muscat, and up to the Musandam Peninsula, which is separated from the main body of Oman by the UAE.

A flight from Dubai to Muscat takes about an hour but, when you factor in check-in times and clearing customs, it's not much quicker than driving – and you miss out on some stunning views en route.

Like the UAE, summers in Oman are incredibly hot and winters much milder, although southern Salalah is actually rather cool, wet and green during the summer.

Buraimi

This historical town nudges Al Ain from just over the Oman border; although the only problem getting from Al Ain to Buraimi is finding it, as there are almost no signs. If you're heading there in a UAE taxi, agree a price, as once they've crossed the border their meters may magically stop working. You don't need a visa but you will need your passport.

Find pottery, silver jewellery and woven crafts at Buraimi Souk, and check out the many forts. Al Khandaq Fort is 400 years old; it has been lovingly restored and offers great views from its battlements.

Musandam

The UAE's northern neighbour, Musandam is an isolated enclave belonging to Oman. The region is dominated by the same Hajar Mountains that run through the eastern UAE. As the peninsula juts into the Strait of Hormuz, it splits into a myriad of jagged, picturesque fjords. Spending a day exploring the fjords on a wooden dhow is a must for anyone. Most trips originate from the region's capital, Khasab. The marine life here is some of the best in region; set off from Dibba with your snorkel and explore the reef of corals around Dibba Island, where you are virtually guaranteed to spot a turtle, or take a dive trip to one of the many dive sites – at the Landing Craft you can explore a well preserved shipwreck – and see if you spot a whale shark.

Alternatively, you can access the famous Wadi Bih off-road route from Dibba and spend a weekend camping. See Explorer's *UAE Off-Road* for more information about the route.

472   Dubai Explorer

OUT OF THE CITY
OMAN

Marina Bandar Al Rowhda

Golden Tulip Resort
Mina Rd Dibba **968 2683 6654**
goldentulipdibba.com

In the foothills of the Hajar Mountains, the Golden Tulip Resort is on a private beach on the east coast of the Musandam Peninsula. It's a great base for snorkelling and diving, with a coral reef located just off the coast, and there's also the chance to go rock climbing and exploring the mountains from the resort. Facilities include a Jacuzzi, swimming pool with temperature control and a children's indoor play area.

Six Senses Zighy Bay
Zighy Bay, Musandam Daba **968 2673 5555**
sixsenses.com

Located in a secluded cove in Musandam, the resort has been designed in a rustic style and is made up of individual pool villas. Like all Six Senses resorts, the focus here is on relaxation. The spa treatments available are of the highest quality, and expertly prepared dinners can be enjoyed from either the comfort of your own villa or from the mountainside restaurant with breathtaking views of the bay.

Muscat

One of the most charismatic and visually striking capitals in the Middle East, once you've visited, you'll understand why many count Muscat as their favourite regional city. With beautiful beaches, lots of green spaces, a collection of great restaurants and cafes, and some fascinating museums, you'll need at least a few days to fully discover this clean and friendly city.

Rather than a bustling CBD characterised by countless skyscrapers, gridlocked traffic and smog, Muscat has many separate areas nestling between the low craggy mountains and the Indian Ocean. Visit the old town of Muscat or Mutrah, charming clusters of pretty whitewashed buildings sandwiched between rocky hills. The warren-like Mutrah Souk is one of the best markets in the region that's jam-packed with

askexplorer.com 473

OUT OF THE CITY
OMAN

Omani silver, frankincense, perfume oils and spices. The impressive Sultan Qaboos Grand Mosque held the record for the world's largest carpet and the world's largest chandelier, until Abu Dhabi's own Sheikh Zayed Grand Mosque raised the bar.

Exploring the city's majestic coastline is a must, and there are plenty of rocky coves for snorkelling and dive sites a short distance away. At Ras Al Jinz Turtle Reserve in Sur, south of Muscat, you can camp overnight and watch nesting turtles lumber up the beach to lay their eggs, and then, after a few hours' sleep, the mass of tiny hatchlings struggle out of their eggs and make their journey into the sea.

The Chedi Muscat
18th November St Muscat **968 2452 4400**
chedimuscat.com
This beautiful boutique hotel on the shore is famed for its clean lines, five-star luxury and an impressive sense of tranquillity – the stunning spa and outstanding restaurant don't hurt either. With an infinity pool, private beach and library, this is the perfect destination for a break from the city hustle and bustle, but perhaps isn't an ideal choice for families.

Crowne Plaza Muscat
Off Al Qurm St Muscat **968 2466 0660**
crowneplaza.com
This hotel boasts cliff top views over Al Qurum and the beach below. Many of the 200 guest rooms benefit from the striking vistas and several of the restaurants boast outdoor terraces. There's a large swimming pool, gym, spa and dolphin watching trips available, making it a great choice for those looking for relaxation and for visitors who want an action-packed break.

Oman Dive Center
Nr Qantab R/A, Al Jissah St Muscat
968 2482 4240
extradivers-worldwide.com
Just south of Muscat, a stay here is an amazing and sociable experience whether you're a diver or not. You can book a barasti hut (they are actually made of stone, with barasti covering) for an average of RO.66 (around Dhs.600) for two people, including breakfast and dinner.

Shangri-La's Barr Al Jissah Resort & Spa
Off Al Jissah St Muscat
968 2477 6666
shangri-la.com
With three hotels catering for families and luxury seekers, this is one of the most gorgeous resorts in the region. The hotels have several swimming pools and enough play areas to keep children occupied for days. The exclusive, six-star Al Husn is incredibly luxurious and perfect for a weekend of out-of-town pampering.

Salalah

Home to several museums and souks, Salalah – in the south of Oman on the Arabian Sea coast – is best known for its lush landscape and is especially attractive over the summer when it is cooled by the monsoon rains sweeping across the Indian Ocean. From June to September, when Dubai is hitting 50°C, Salalah is enjoying temperatures in the 20s. This climatic quirk has given the region an important place in the history books – it is one of the few places in the world that grows frankincense, and has been exporting it to kings and pharaohs for millennia. It's a fascinating, not to mention fragrant, place to visit – head to the Museum of the Frankincense Land to learn more, and then to Souk Al Hafah to pick up some quality samples. The climate also enables banana plantations and coconut groves to thrive, and fruit stalls line the roadsides giving the place a tropical feel far removed from the desert landscape of the UAE.

Salalah's wild and truly magnificent coastline ranges from wide, untouched beaches to towering jagged cliffs, and is home to the famous blowholes at Al Mughsayl. Thundering waves have eroded caverns underfoot and explode through openings in the rock, drenching the more adventurous visitors.

Taking an impossibly windy road that zigzags its way up a mountain ascent, while minding out for charging camels and wandering donkeys, brings you to the incredible picnic spot of Shaat. At 1,000m above sea level, it's a stomach-turning cliff top that drops straight down to the ocean. Salalah is a 1.5 hour flight from Dubai.

Hilton Salalah Resort
Sultan Qaboos St Salalah **968 2321 1234**
salalah.hilton.com
This attractive resort is set on the beach by the Arabian Sea, and has beachfront pools (with a waterslide and kids' area), a sea-view restaurant, a lively bar, tennis courts and a gym, and a dive centre. The rooms have balconies overlooking the water or the gardens. The Hilton is about 12 kilometres from the city centre, so it's as easy to explore Salalah as it is to escape the crowds.

Juweira Boutique Hotel
Salalah Beach Marina, Salalah **968 2323 9600**
juweirahotel.com
This relatively new hotel is on an inlet used by local fishermen. Each room has a terrace and overlooks the waterfront promenade, the fluffy cloud-capped mountains, the sea or the plentiful coconut trees that Salalah is famous for. Suites are spacious and light, a heavenly pool area has a bar and comfy sun loungers, and the seafood restaurant serves deliciously fresh Omani lobster.

OUT OF THE CITY
OMAN

Salalah

Ruwi neighbourhood of Muscat

The Chedi Muscat

OUT OF THE CITY
QATAR

Western Hajar

The Hajar Mountains stretch all the way down the east coast of Oman, right from the Musandam Peninsula. The most spectacular section is that of the Western Hajar, southwest and inland from Muscat, and is a must for outdoorsy weekend breakers.

Jebel Shams, the 'Mountain of the Sun' has a rugged terrain that is actually a fairly easy trek with several good camping locations. Below the summit, Wadi An Nakhur has some of the most stupendous views in the country as you drive through the 'Grand Canyon of Oman'. Sayq Plateau on top of Jebel Akhdar has beautiful mountain villages.

More popular spots for hiking include the amazing rock formations of Al Hoota Cave, the challenging but spectacular Snake Canyon (which involves some daring jumps into rock pools and a fair bit of swimming through ravines) and the pools of Wadi Al Abyad, just over an hour west of Muscat.

Nizwa

After driving deep into the Hajar Mountains, you'll find Nizwa, the largest city in Oman's interior. This oasis city offers fascinating sights and heritage, including the impressive 17th century Nizwa Fort, set amid a verdant spread of date palms. This fine citadel features a maze of rooms, doorways, terraces, narrow stairways and corridors; its most striking feature is its colossal central tower, soaring 35m above the fort. Nearby Jabrin Fort, notable for its ceiling decorations and secret passageways, is also worth a visit. Be sure to pick up some freshly made local *halwa* (a sweet dessert) at Nizwa Souk, and it's also a hotspot for souvenir shopping. From Nizwa you can also explore the mountains and hill towns that surround the city.

Sahab Hotel
Jabal Al Akhdar Nizwa 968 2542 9288
sahab-hotel.com
On the Sayq Plateau, 2,004m above sea level, this boutique hotel overlooks an incredible canyon and a village perched precariously on a cliff face. The surrounding gardens contain marine fossils dating back 270 million years. There are stunning sunrise and sunset views from the infinity pool, and from the hotel you can trek the mountains, have a go at goat herding with the locals, or stay up late to watch the stars.

Visas On Arrival

Most travellers to Oman will be issued a single entry visa on arrival for Dhs.50. Women may require a letter of no objection from their employer (if single) or husband (if married), while visitors to Dibba must pre-arrange their visa with their accommodation.

QATAR

Qatar once had a sleepy reputation, but things are changing fast. Development and investment in the country means it is becoming increasingly popular with visitors, especially UAE residents, as it is less than an hour's flight from Dubai.

With an attractive corniche, world-class museums and bustling cultural centres, the capital Doha makes a perfect weekend retreat, with the focus firmly on luxury travel and tourism. Away from the city, the Inland Sea (Khor Al Adaid) in the south of the country makes for a great day trip.

Qatar has a very hot summer and the best time to go is usually over the winter, between October and April. Explorer's *Qatar Visitors' Guide* has more details and includes a pull-out map.

FIFA 2022 World Cup

The choice of Qatar as host of the FIFA 2022 World Cup has been a controversial one, largely due to the intense heat of the Qatari summer and, most recently, the reported deaths of migrant workers who died whilst constructing the various stadiums around the country. FIFA still intends to go ahead with plans in Qatar, with the possibility of moving the tournament to the winter.

Attractions

Bir Zekreet
70km west of Doha
The beach destination of Bir Zekreet is one of Qatar's most popular spots for weekend warriors, and the desert landscape surrounding the city is a great place to spot the picturesque natural formations known as 'desert mushrooms'.

Katara Cultural Village
Off Lusail St Doha 974 4408 0000
katara.net
This is a unique development, bringing together all the artistic elements in Qatar including music, dance, theatre, photography, painting and sculpture. The site, which looks like a large village, allows artists to meet and collaborate on different projects. It is also open to the public with two concert halls designed for opera, ballet and large theatrical productions, an outdoor amphitheatre which holds 5,000 people, as well as galleries, workshops, cafes, restaurants and souks.

explorer

there's more to life...

YOUR INDISPENSABLE GUIDE TO QATAR

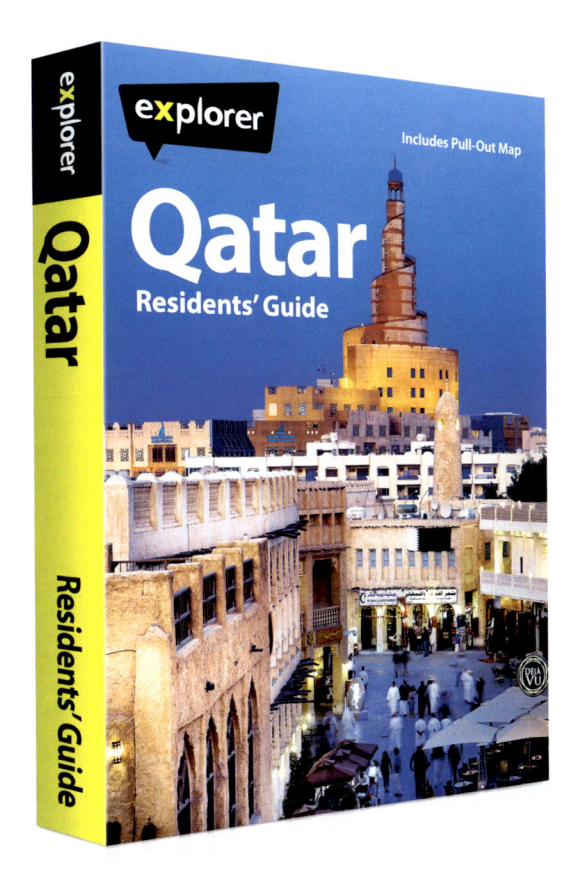

askexplorer.com/shop

askexplorer

OUT OF THE CITY
QATAR

Khor Al Adaid
80km south of Doha Doha
qatartourism.gov.qa

A popular day trip destination also known as the Inland Sea, Khor Al Adaid is a wide inlet which narrows in the centre and widens out to a large, seawater lake. It's surrounded by crescent-shaped dunes, and the border between Qatar and Saudi Arabia runs down the middle. Although strong currents make the narrows too dangerous for swimming, taking a dip around the shore is popular and safe. A number of tour companies organise trips to this spectacular landscape, either for a few hours or a full overnight camping stay. Other popular activities in the area include dune bashing, camel riding and sand skiing.

Mathaf – Arab Museum Of Modern Art
Education City Doha 974 4402 8855
mathaf.org.qa

Housed in a former school, redesigned by the French architect Jean-François Bodin, Mathaf holds its own impressive permanent collection and regularly welcomes other exhibitions. Education is central to the museum, and there's a great library full of resources, as well as a museum shop and relaxed, contemporary cafe space.

Museum of Islamic Art
The Corniche Doha 974 4422 4444
mia.org.qa

Culture vultures should not miss a trip to this iconic attraction on an island of reclaimed land just off the corniche. The masterful Islamic-influenced architecture is the work of IM Pei, the legendary architect responsible for the iconic pyramid of the Louvre in Paris. The museum houses a marvellous collection of temporary and permanent exhibitions showcased as a journey through time, countries and cultures, and the oldest pieces date from the ninth century. There's also a cafe and a 200 seat auditorium.

The Pearl Qatar
North of West Bay Doha
thepearlqatar.com

Doha's beloved Pearl is a stunning series of interconnected man-made islands that are perfect for a leisurely stroll, so much so that the area has been nicknamed the Arabian Riviera. One of the most popular areas is the island Porto Arabia, which boasts everything a visitor could possibly desire, from high-end shopping options to fine restaurants and cafes serving up international cuisine. Indeed, The Pearl Qatar is the perfect destination for foodies (alcohol is prohibited), who can indulge in everything from nouveau Mexican at Pampano to modern Japanese dishes at Megu. Perhaps best of all are the decadent treats on offer at Alison Nelson's Chocolate Bar.

Souk Waqif
Off Grand Hamad St Doha

The city's oldest market, Souk Waqif was renovated in 2004 using traditional building methods and materials. The resulting warren-like complex is now one of the most beautiful and authentic modern souks in the Gulf. The most refreshing aspect of the souk area is its dual purpose – tourists can easily stroll the narrow alleys in search of exotic wares and souvenirs while locals can purchase everything from fishing nets to pots and pans. Aside from the shops and restaurants, there is the Waqif Art Centre, which houses several small galleries and craft shops. Alternatively, simply find a cafe, order a Turkish coffee or sweet mint tea and some apple-scented shisha, and watch the world go by.

Hotels

Four Seasons
Al Corniche St Doha 974 4494 8888
fourseasons.com

One of the finest hotels in the city, the Four Seasons has an exclusive beach and marina, first-class service and excellent restaurants, including the classy Italian eatery Il Teatro.

Grand Hyatt Doha
West Bay Lagoon Doha 974 4448 1234
doha.grand.hyatt.com

The majority of rooms at this Doha institution enjoy stunning views of the Arabian Gulf, and guests can relax on an expansive 400m private beach or at the outdoor swimming pool. Be sure to indulge in a pampering treatment at the luxurious Jaula Spa.

La Cigale
60 Suhaim Bin Hamad St Doha 974 4428 8888
lacigalehotel.com

A short drive from the airport, La Cigale has a reputation for first-class hospitality and is an exclusive nightlife destination. It has five restaurants ranging from sushi to Mediterranean, a sleek gym and spa, city views from the Sky View Lounge on the 15th floor, and 225 rooms and suites from which to choose.

Movenpick Doha
Corniche Rd Doha 974 4429 1111
moevenpick-hotels.com

This modern hotel boasts breathtaking views of the corniche, where guests can enjoy a morning jog or afternoon stroll. Popular with business travellers, this boutique-style hotel also attracts tourists with its excellent restaurants and leisure facilities which include a swimming pool, whirlpool and steam bath. The hotel's location is convenient for the airport.

OUT OF THE CITY
QATAR

Museum of Islamic Art

Radisson Blu Doha
Nr C Ring Rd & Salwa Rd Doha
974 4428 1428
radissonblu.com
With plenty of restaurants, bars and lounges to enjoy, this is a staple of Doha's nightlife. Renovated in 2012, the hotel's draws include a large swimming pool and a wide variety of fitness facilities. There is a champagne bar, and an excellent seafood restaurant, Pier 12.

Ritz-Carlton Doha
West Bay Lagoon Doha **974 4484 8000**
ritzcarlton.com
The opulent Ritz-Carlton is a perfect stop-off if you're sailing in the region, with its 235 berth marina and clubhouse. All of the 374 rooms and suites have breathtaking views over the sea or marina. The beach club has a great selection of watersports and there's a lavish spa, plus a whopping nine restaurants – the delicious French-inspired seafood served at La Mer is particularly recommended.

Sharq Village & Spa
Ras Abu Abboud St Doha **974 4425 6666**
sharqvillage.com
Reminiscent of a traditional Qatari town, Sharq Village & Spa is another example of Qatar's insistence on spectacular architecture. The Six Senses Spa was constructed using traditional building techniques and the resort's restaurants are some of the finest in Doha. With pool or sea views from the 174 luxury suites and villas, this Ritz-Carlton managed resort makes for a perfect Qatari getaway.

W Doha
Off Diplomatic St Doha **974 4453 5000**
whoteldoha.com
Adding a touch of fun to Doha's rather conservative luxury hotel scene, the W hotel chain is known for its funky design and fabulous level and quality of individualised service. Every inch of the hotel is an exercise in architectural minimalism, and its central location makes exploring Doha easy.

Desert Resorts

Within a 45 minute drive of Dubai – and with a copy of Explorer's *UAE Off-Road* – the UAE's vast deserts can be easily accessed, should you need to escape civilisation for a while. A range of hotel accommodation options exist, from five-star luxury resorts, like Al Maha Desert Resort & Spa and the Banyan Tree, to less expensive resorts for those on a tighter budget.

Out in the desert, you can ride camels, dune buggies and horses. Many resorts have excellent spas, which are perfect for unwinding in these exotic, tranquil surroundings; some also have kids' clubs to keep the little ones equally as happy.

Arabian Nights

For a more authentic experience, check out Arabian Nights Village in Abu Dhabi. They run all sorts of unique desert activities for intrepid explorers, from camping under the stars to dune bashing. Plus, the delicious food, awesome entertainment and pristine pools provide plenty of luxury in the midst of your adventure.

Al Maha Desert Resort & Spa
Dubai – Al Ain Rd 04 832 9900
al-maha.com
Set within the 225 sq km Dubai Desert Conservation Reserve, with breathtaking views of picturesque dunes and rare wildlife, this luxury getaway was named as one of the best ecotourism models by National Geographic in 2008. Al Maha is designed to resemble a typical Bedouin camp, but conditions are anything but basic – each suite is beautifully crafted and has its own private pool and butler service. Activities include horse riding, camel trekking and falconry. There is also a superb spa.

Bab Al Shams Desert Resort & Spa > p.481
Nr Endurance Village Mugatrah 04 809 6100
meydanhotels.com/babalshams
This is a beautiful desert resort built in the style of a traditional Arabic fort.

Each of its 115 rooms is decorated with subtle yet stunning Arabian touches, and pristine desert dunes form the backdrop. The authentic, open-air, Arabic desert restaurant Al Hadheerah is highly recommended; during dinner guests are treated to an incredible heritage show.

There is also a kids' club, two large swimming pools (complete with swim-up bar), desert activities, falconry shows and lawn games on offer, as well as the luxurious and indulgent Satori Spa.

Banyan Tree Al Wadi
Al Mazraa Ras Al Khaimah 07 206 7777
banyantree.com
Built in traditional Arabian style and set within a wildlife conservation area in the impressive desert landscape of Wadi Khadeja, this stunning resort combines the wild beauty of its surroundings with exclusive luxury. Villas and luxury 'tents' each have a private pool and sundeck, and views of the desert, where oryx trip skittishly by.

Qasr Al Sarab Desert Resort By Anantara
Nr Liwa Al Gharbia 02 886 2088
qasralsarab.anantara.com
This hotel has a stunning location amid the giant dunes outside Liwa. Designed as an Arabic fort, the resort features enormous villas, each with its own private pool. Guests can enjoy a wide range of desert activities before relaxing in oversized bathtubs, dining on gourmet dishes and being pampered in the spa. Around three hours from Dubai, it's a truly peaceful escape from life.

Tilal Liwa
Liwa Al Gharbia 02 894 6111
danathotels.com
This affordable, four-star desert hideaway has a charming pool area and a range of rooms and suites which blend old and new design elements, and provide gorgeous views over the endless sands. Desert safaris in the dunes should be at the top of every visitor's itinerary.

This breathtaking mirage actually has a telephone number.

BAB AL SHAMS
DESERT RESORT & SPA

Experience your very own Arabian fairytale at the five star Bab Al Shams Desert Resort & Spa. Hidden from the city, this unique desert retreat boasts gourmet restaurants, breathtaking views, indulgent Satori Spa treatments and activities including sunset camel back safaris.

Bab Al Shams is located close to Dubai Endurance City, just 45 minutes from Dubai International Airport, yet a world away from the buzz of city life. Meandering walkways, shaded courtyards, sensational water features and relaxing rooftop lounges are cocooned by natural desert landscape, making Bab Al Shams one of the world's most serene settings.

Seamlessly blending rich Middle Eastern culture with every modern convenience and luxury you could dream of, Bab Al Shams is also ideal for meetings, conferences, product launches and team building activities.

For reservations or further information call +971 4 809 6100 or email BAS.info@meydanhotels.com
www.meydanhotels.com/babalshams

INDEX

#

1762	418
1847	176
25-55-Cafe Bistro	392
2nd December Street	262
3 Square	84
360 Bar & Lounge	262
360 Hotel	428
4 Walls Art Gallery	264
4X4 Garage	106
4X4 Motors	102
4Yacht Arabia	310
6 Sigma Financial Consultancy	116
60 Second Lock & Shoe Repair	380
7 DAYS, Al Sidra Media	
...ADVERT	429
7 Seas Divers	300
800 Doctor	
...ADVERT	xxv

A

A La Grand	400
A La Turca Restaurant	390
AAA Service Center	358
Aati	362
Abn Amro Bank	115
Abra	109
Absconding	210
Absolute Adventure	303
Abu Dhabi	445
Abu Dhabi Art	266, 448
Abu Dhabi Corniche	445
Abu Dhabi Desert Challenge	27
Abu Dhabi Falcon Hospital	445
Abu Dhabi Festival	448
Abu Dhabi FIA Formula 1 World Championship	29, 446
Abu Dhabi Film Festival	436
Abu Dhabi HSBC Golf Championship	286
Abu Dhabi International Motor Show	220
Abu Dhabi National Takaful Company	116
Abu Dhabi Tourism And Culture Authority	445
Abu Dhabi Vision 2030 Plan	3
Academic City	247
Academy, The	408
Accessories	370
Accidents & Emergencies	121
Accommodation	51
ACE Hardware	264, 342, 364, 376
...ADVERT	343
Ace Sports Academy	192
Acorn Movers	83
Act, The	435, 438
Act Marine	378
Active Sports Academy	157, 179, 190
Activities	294
Activities For Kids	152
Acuma Wealth Management	116
Addresses	51, 95

Adoption	151
Adventure HQ	298, 376
Adventureland	468
...ADVERT	xvii
Aerial Tours	312
Aerogulf Services	312
Aesthetica Clinic	140
Aetna Global Benefits (Middle East)	116
AFIA Insurance Brokerage Services LLC	93, 118
African Cuisine	386
African + Eastern	353
...ADVERT	xiv, 45, 355
Afridi & Angell	146
Afternoon Tea	386, 419
After-school Activities	153, 246
Agency, The	431
AGS Movers	83
...ADVERT	75
Air Arabia	112
Air France	112
Air Freight	83
Air India	112
Air Mauritius	112
Air Seychelles	112
Airlines	112
Ajman	
...Corniche	457
...Museum	457
....Palace	457
...Saray	457
Al Ahli Driving Center	99
Al Ahli Horse Riding Club	185
Al Ahmadiya School & Heritage House	269
Al Ain	296, 302, 303, 452
Al Ain Ahlia Insurance Company	118
Al Ain Camel & Livestock Souk	452
Al Ain National Museum	452
Al Ain Oasis	452
Al Ain Palace Museum	452
Al Ain Rotana	453
Al Ain Zoo	14, 276, 452
Al Badia Golf Club By InterContinental Dubai Festival City	285, 394
Al Bandar Restaurant	404
Al Baraha Hospital	124
Al Barsha	74, 328
...Mall	328
...Pond Park	282
Al Barsha Veterinary Clinic	160
Al Basha	407
Al Boom Diving	300, 310, 378
Al Boom Marine	378
Al Boom Tourist Village	310
Al Borj Medical Center	128
Al Bustan Residence Hotel Apartments	46
Al Bustan Rotana	316
Al Dahleez	402
Al Diwan	407
Al Diyafa Modern Medical Centre	122
Al Fahidi	270
...Fort	269
...Historical Neighbourhood	259, 269
...Souk	344

Al Fardan Exchange	114
...ADVERT	117
Al Fardan Jewels & Precious Stones	365
Al Fareed Shoes	380
Al Forsan International Sports Resort	305, 445
Al Furjan	76
Al Futtaim Automall	102
Al Futtaim Jewellery	365
Al Futtaim Logistics	83
...ADVERT	67
Al Futtaim Training Centre	299
Al Garhoud Private Hospital	124
Al Gharbia	454
Al Gharbia Watersports Festival	295, 454
Al Ghurair Centre	346
Al Hambra	407
Al Hamra Cellar	353, 465
Al Hamra Fort Hotel & Beach Resort	465
Al Hamra Golf Club	460
Al Hamra Marina & Royal Yacht Club	462
Al Hamra Residence	465
Al Hamur Marine & Sports Equipment	378
Al Hurr Falconry Services	276
Al Ittihad Park	263, 282
Al Jaber Gallery	376
Al Jaber Optical	140
Al Jahili Fort	453
Al Jazeera	90
Al Jazirah Aviation Club	199
Al Jiyad Stables	185
Al Khazna Insurance Company	118
Al Koufa Restaurant	407
Al Maha Desert Resort & Spa	480
Al Mahara	411
Al Mahatta Museum	468
Al Maktoum International Airport	10
Al Mallah	262
Al Mansour Dhow	393
Al Manzil	261
Al Manzil Downtown Dubai	316
Al Marsa Tours & Cargo	310
Al Masroor Textiles	379
Al Maya	336
Al Mizhar American Academy	233
Al Mousa Medical Centre	122
Al Muna	390
Al Muntaha	393
Al Murooj Rotana	316
Al Naboodah Automobiles	102
Al Nasr Leisureland	179, 284, 288
Al Noor Charity Thrift Shop	374
Al Noor Polyclinic	122
Al Noor Training Center For Children With Special Needs	245
Al Orooba Oriental Carpets	375
Al Qasba	468
Al Qasr	395

Al Qawasim Corniche	462
Al Qouz	264, 329
...Pond Park	282
Al Reef Lebanese Bakery	439
Al Saeedi Automotive Trading	106
Al Safadi Restaurant	398
Al Sahel Villa Resort	456
Al Sahra Desert Resort Equestrian Centre	185
Al Shalal	86
Al Shera'a Fisheries Centre	399
Al Shifa Al Khaleeji Medical Centre	128
Al Tamimi & Company	146
Al Tamimi Stables	276, 468
Al Tayer Motors	102
Al Waleed Palace Hotel Apartments	46
Al Wasl Cruising & Fishing	310
Al Wataniya Workshop	106
Al Yamm Villa Resort	456
Al Zahra Private Medical Centre	130
Alain & Milad	169
Alcohol	20, 465
Alfred's Insurance Market	118
All 4 Down Syndrome Dubai	245
All As One	218
All Day Mini Mart	336
All The Frills	146
Alliance Insurance	118
Allianz Se	118
Allied Diagnostics	128
Allied Pickfords	83
Almaz By Momo	404
Alpha Cleaning Services	90
Alpha Tours	308
Alphabet Street Nursery	229
Alserkal Avenue	264, 266
Alshop	359
Alternative Therapies	140
Amal & Amal	380
Amala	402
Amara Spa	172
Amaseena	409
Amaya Salon & Spa	169
Ambar Garden Furniture	364
Amber Clinics	122, 128
American Cuisine	386
American Academy Of Cosmetic Surgery Hospital	140
American Airlines	112
American Business Council Of Dubai & The Northern Emirates	216
American College Of Dubai	252
American Curriculum	233
American Dental Clinic	138
American Fitness	165
American Football	179
American Hospital Dubai	124, 132
...ADVERT	125
American International School	234
American School Of Dubai	234
American University In Dubai	248

482   Dubai Explorer

INDEX

American University Of Ras Al Khaimah	248
American University Of Sharjah	248
Amigos Balloons	312
Amity University	248
Amouage	372
Amusement Centres	273
Amwaj Rotana Jumeirah Beach Residence	316
Anantara Dubai The Palm	313
Anantara Sir Bani Yas Island Al Yamm Villa Resort	456
Angar	446
Angsana Spa Arabian Ranches	173
Animal World	374
Anna By Top Vision Optics	140
Antique Bazaar	407
Antique Furniture	264
Antique Museum	376
Antiques	267
AOC	390
Apartments	51
Apple Seeds	156
Applebee's	400
Apres	404
Aprons & Hammers	390
Aqua Sports Academy	190
Aquaplay	153, 273
Aquara	390
Aquaventure	263, 270, 274, 276, 313
Arab Business Club	216
Arab Emirate Dirham	3
Arab Orient Insurance Company	118
Arabia Outdoors	303
Arabia's Wildlife Centre And Children's Farm	276
Arabian Adventures	308
Arabian Center	333
Arabian Court	314
Arabian Divers & Sportfishing Charters	300
Arabian Nights Village	480
Arabian Oryx	14
Arabian Ranches	78
Arabian Ranches Golf Club	145, 285, 426
Arabian Tea House	420
Arabian Travel Market (ATM)	220
Arabic Cuisine	385
Arady Developers	58
Aramex	326
Arcadia	419
Archery	283, 310, 445
Archive, The	268, 416
Argentinean Cuisine	386
Arjaan By Rotana Dubai Media City	46
Armani Hotel Dubai	195, 316
Armani/Amal	402
Armani/Casa	262
Armani/Dubai Caffe	417
Armani/Hashi	409
Armani/Spa	173
Aroushi Beauty Salon	169
Art	364
Art & Culture	266
Art Couture	266
Art District	264
Art Dubai	27, 268, 325
Art Galleries	266
Art Labs	194
Art Marine	311
Artbus	267, 307
Arthur Murray Dance Centre	197
Artisans Of The Emirates (ARTE)	340, 354
Arts & Crafts	353
Artsawa	264, 266
Artspace	266
Aryaas	398
Asado	261, 402
Ascott Park Place Dubai	46
Asha's	402
Asian Cuisine	386
Asiana Hotel	316
Ask Explorer	177
Asmak	390
Assawan Spa & Health Club	173
Aster Medical Centre	122
At The Top	260, 270
At.mosphere	260, 411
Athena Charter Yacht	311
Atlanta Vision Clinic	140
Atlantis Dive Centre	300
Atlantis Tennis Academy	193
Atlantis, The Palm	145, 263, 313
...ADVERT	275
Atlas Star Medical Center	128
Attesting Certificates	33
Attibrah	457
Attractions	65, 80, 270, 445
Australian Business Council Dubai	216
Australian International Swim Schools (AISS)	190
...ADVERT	191
Austrian Airlines	112
Autodrome	286
Autolease Rent A Car	100
Automatic	398, 413
Automatic Licence Transfer	44
Automobile & Touring Club Of The UAE	187
Aviation Club, The	165, 283, 286, 290
Avis	100
AXA Insurance (Gulf)	93, 118, 295
...ADVERT	105
Ayyam Art Center	264
AZ.U.R	390

B

B&B Italia	362, 364
B/Attitude Spa	173
B5 The Art Of Living	362
Ba	391
Bab Al Shams Desert Resort & Spa	308, 480
...ADVERT	481
Babies R Us	368
Baby Land Nursery	229
Babyshop	368
Babysitting	152
BAC Middle East	207
Badminton	179
...Badeemonz Badminton Club Dubai	179
...Badmintown	179
BAFCO	361
...ADVERT	209
Bagels & More	418
Bahrain Air	112
Bahri Bar	431
Baker & Spice	416
Balance Cafe	418
...Cookery School	195
Balcony Bar	424
Ballet Centre	197
Balloon Adventures Emirates	312
...ADVERT	19
Balloon Flights	308
Balloon Lady	370
Bamboo Lagoon	407
Banana Boat	280
Bani Yas Tribe	454
Banks	114
Banyan Tree Al Wadi	296, 480
Banyan Tree Ras Al Khaimah Beach	465
Barakat Optical	140
Barasti	280, 422, 424
Barbers & Male Salons	170
Barclays	115
Baré Gents Salon	169
Bargaining	325
Barracuda Beach Resort	353, 472
Bars & Restaurants	65
Bars, Pubs & Clubs	422
Barzar	424
Baseball	179
Basketball	179
Basketball Academy Of Dubai	179
Baskin Robbins	370
Bassata Desert Village	462
Basta Art Cafe	420
Bastakiah Nights	402
Bastakiya	259, 269
Bateaux Dubai	145, 311, 409
Bath & Body Works	372
...ADVERT	373
Bayat Legal Services	146
Bayt.com	207
Beaches	278, 281
Beach Bar & Grill	393
Beach Bars & Sundowners	422
Beach Centre	331
Beach Clubs	280
Beach House Cabana	393
Beachcombers	393
Beaches	278
Beachfront Restaurants	392
Beats On The Beach	436
Beauty Salons & Nail Bars	168
Beauty World Middle East	220
Bedouin Oasis Desert Camp	462
Before You Arrive	33
Before You Leave	49
Belgium Medical Services	122
Belhasa Driving Center	99
Belhoul European Hospital	122
Belhoul Speciality Hospital	126
Bellini	362
Belly Dancing	197, 407
Benihana	398
Bentley	102
Bentoya Kitchen	412
Bert's Cafe	417, 418
Better Homes	52
Better Life	359
Bettercar Rentals	100
Bharat Thakurís Artistic Yoga	202
BiCE	412
BiCE Mare	409
Bidibondi	263, 422
Bidiyah Mosque	459
Big Boys Toys	220
Big Bus Tours	307
Big Five Exhibition	220
Bike-sharing	106
Biking	294, 378
Bikinis	278
Bilal Le Salon	169
Bilgidubai	48
Billiards	202, 417
Bin Majid Beach Resort	465
Bin Sougat Centre	333
Biolite Aesthetic Clinic	140
Bir Zekreet	476
Bird Watchers	445
Birdwatching	195
Births	150
Bistro Domino	398
Bistro Madeleine	393
Biterite	142
Black Canyon	439
Black Palace Beach	278
Blades	400
Blends	425
Blokarting	288
Bloomingdale's	334
Blossom Children's Nursery	225
Blossom Mother & Child	368
Blossom Village Nursery	157
Blue Elephant	402
Blue Flag	280
Blue Flame	195, 414
Blue Mart	336
Blue Rain	402
Bluewaters Island	262
Bo House Cafe	408
Board Games	417
Boarding Schools	233
Boardwalk, The	393
Boat Tours	310
Boating	294, 378
Bob's Fish & Chips	406
Boconcept	362
Bodylines Health & Fitness Centre	165
Bodysmart	142
Bombay, The	398
Bonnington Jumeirah Lakes Towers	316
Book N Bean	354
Book World	356
BookMunch	354, 417
Books Kinokuniya	356
Books, Music & DVDs	354
Booksplus	356
Bookworm	356
Boots The Chemist	372
Borders	356
Bosch Service Centre	106
Boston Bar	424, 426

askexplorer.com 483

INDEX

Bottled Water	398	Cabsat Mena	220	Center Cut	403	Clearance Certificate	86
Boudoir	313, 425, 433	Cadillac	102	Central Motors &		Cleopatra's Spa &	
Boulevard Bus Tour	307	Cadorim	380	Equipment	106	Wellness	165, 172, 298
Boulevard Gourmet	370	Caesars	370	Centre For Musical		Climbing	180, 296
Bourn Hall Clinic	134	Cafe Ceramique	194, 420	Arts	200, 201	Climbing Dubai	298
Boutique 1 Gallery	364	Cafe De La Danse	435	Centrepoint	335, 342	Clothing & Shoes	359
Bowling	283	Cafe Habana	412	Centro Barsha		Club Joumana	182, 305
Bowling City	284	Cafe Havana	416	...ADVERT	382	Club Rush At Atlantis	422
Boxing	179	CafeM	408, 432	Century Mall	330	Club Stretch	165, 202
Bradenton Preparatory		Cafes	386, 416	Ceroc Arabia	197	Clubs & Groups	178
Academy	234	Cakes & Breads	338	Chameleon Club	433	Cobblers	380
Brauhaus	412	California Chiropractic &		Champions	424	Cocktails	424
Brazilian Cuisine	386	Sports Medicine Center	135	Change Initiative, The	219, 359	Coco's	413
Breakfast	416	Calligraphy	267	Changing Jobs	210	Coco's Restaurant	372
Breast Cancer Arabia	218	Cambridge International		Channels	398	Code Men's Salon	169
Bridal Showroom, The	380	School Dubai	236	Charly Polyclinic	138	Codes & Prefixes	88
Bride Club ME	146	Camel Polo	308	Charterhouse Middle East	207	Coffee Mornings	417
Bride Show Dubai	220	Camel Racing	28, 286	Chauffeur Service	111	Colleges	247
Bridge	195	Camera Equipment	358	Checkers Bar	430	Collegiate American	
Bristol Middle East		Camille Albane	169	Checklist	33	School	234
Yacht Solution	305, 311	Camping	295, 296	Chedi Muscat	474	Color Nail Beauty Lounge	169
British Cuisine	386	Camping Essentials	297	Cheeky Little Events	440	Colosseum Muay Thai	
British Airways	112	Canadian Business Council	216	Cheeky Monkeys Playland	153	Health & Fitness Club 179, 186	
British Business Group	216	Canadian Chiropractic &		Cheerleading	179	Comedy	436
British Dental Clinic	138	Natural Health Centre	135	Cheesecake Factory	412	Commercial Bank Of Dubai	115
British Guides In		Canadian Specialist		Chef Lanka	399	Commit Chartered	
Foreign Countries	156	Hospital	122	Chelsea Tower Hotel		Accountants	218
British Medical Consulting		Canadian University		Apartments	46	Company Closure	212
Centre	128	Of Dubai	248	Cheques	115	Conrad Dubai	316
British Orchard Nursery	225	Cancelling Visas	49	Chess	195	Consultants & Chartered	
British University In Dubai	248	Canoeing & Kayaking	304	Chevrolet	102	Accountants	218
British Withdrawal	6	Capital City (UAE)	3	Chez Sushi By Sho Cho	439	Consumer Protection	
Brunch	394	Cars		Chez Toi	169	Department	326
BSAC 406 Wanderers		...Accessories	358	Chi@The Lodge	434	Consumer Rights Unit	326
Dive Club	301	...Breakdowns	98	Child's Play	296	Convenience Stores	336
Buddha Bar	431	...Buying A Car	100	Children's Bicycles	378	Cooking At Home	196
Budget Car & Van		...Driving In Dubai	96	Children's City	153, 273	Cooking Classes	195
Rental UAE	100	...Hiring A Car	99	Children's Garden, The	226	Cooper Health Clinic	134
...ADVERT	101	...Importing A Car	102	Chili's	399	Coral Beach Resort	471
Budget Hotels	46	...Insurance	104	Chill Salon	170	Core Fit	165
Buffets	386	...New Car Dealers	102	China Airlines	112	Cosmesurge	140
Bugatti	102	...Transferring Ownership	105	China Club	395	Cosmetics	372
Builders	91	Car Cemetery	300	Chinwaggery	432	Cosmetic Treatment &	
Building Blocks Nursery &		Car Hire Companies	100	Chiropractic Health &		Surgery	140
Child Enrichment Centre	226	Caractere Gents Saloon	170	Physio Polyclinic	135	Cost Of Living	38
Bur Dubai	80, 329	Caramel Restaurant &		Choco'a	440	Cottage Chic	84
Buraimi	296	Lounge	391	Choithrams	337	Counselling &	
Buraimi Souk	472	Carbon 12 Dubai	264	Christ Church Jebel Ali	49	Development Clinic	143
Burger Fuel	413	Carla K Styling	169	Chrysler	102	Counselling & Therapy	143
Burj Al Arab	262, 313	Carluccio's	404	Churchill	90	Counter Culture	416
Burj Al Arab Aquarium	14	Carnegie Mellon University		Cigar Bar, The	432	Country Code	4
Burj Daycare Nursery	226	...ADVERT	IFC	Cigar Lounge, The	260, 432	Country Profile	3
Burj Khalifa	8, 260	Carnevale	400	Cin Cin	424	Coupons	325
Burj Lake	260, 270	Carpetland	375	Cinema	435	Courtyard Playhouse	264
BurJuman	346	Carpets, Rugs & Curtains	374	...4DX	436	Courtyard, The	266, 439
Buses	110, 307	Carrefour	336, 342	...Alternative Screenings	436	Cove Rotana Resort	465
Business	214	Cartier	365	Cinnabon	413	Craft Land	194, 353
...Councils	216	Cash Points	114	Circle	417	Cranleigh Abu Dhabi	233
...Culture	214	Cass Business School City		Citibank	115	Crate & Barrel	361
...Hours	4	University London	249	City Profile	33	Cravin' Cajun	407
Business Domain Name	218	Catamaran Freedom	462	City School International	236	Creamfields	436
Bussola	393	Caterers	440	City Sky Maid Services	90	Creative Hands	194
Butcher Shop & Grill	404, 413	Cathay Pacific	112	Cityscape Abu Dhabi	220	Creative Minds	354, 366
Buying A Boat	295	Cavalli Club	433	Citywalk	331	Credit Cards	115
		Caving	296	Clarins Boutique	169	Creek	270
C		Cedars Jebel Ali		Clark Francis Tennis		...Creek Tours	259
		International Hospital	126	Academy	193, 246	Creek Hash House Harriers	184
Cabana	428	Celebration Cakes	370	Class 1 World Power		Creek Park	108, 273, 282
Cabaret	435	Celebrities	410	Boating Championship	295	Crescent Cosmetic	
Cable-boarding	305, 445	Celebrity Chefs	396	Classes	156	Medical Center	122
Caboodle Pamper		Cello Music & Ballet Centre	197	Claw BBQ	404	Cricket	180, 286
& Play	170, 176	Cement Barge	300	Clay Pigeon Shooting	445	Crime	20
		Centaurus International	353	Cleaners	90	Cross Fit	167

484   Dubai Explorer

INDEX

Crossroads Cocktail Bar	424	Deira & The Creek	259	Divorce	147	Dubai Bank	115
Crown Relocations	83	Deira International School	243	Djinn	460	Dubai Blinds	375
...ADVERTS	ii-iii, 35, 41,	Deira Private School	236	Dubai Kennels &		Dubai Bone & Joint Center	135
	85, 204, 237	Dek On 8, The	428	Cattery (DKC)		Dubai Bowling Centre	284
Crowne Fitness	165	Delhi Private School		...ADVERT	159	Dubai Bride Show	145
Crowne Plaza Dubai	316	Academy	243	DMCA	295	Dubai British School	236
Crowne Plaza Dubai Deira	321	Delicatessens, Gourmet &		dnata Travel Centre	467	Dubai Caledonian Society	48
Crowne Plaza Dubai		Health Foods	337	...ADVERT	442	Dubai Canal	263
Festival City	317	Deliveries & Shipping	326	Doctor On Call	122	Dubai Carpet Cleaning	90
Crowne Plaza Muscat	474	Delta Air Lines	112	Dodge	102	Dubai Celts GAA	184
Crowne Plaza Yas Island	448	Dentists	138	Doggies Palace	160	Dubai Centre For Special	
Cruise With Nakheel	311	Dental Center, The	138	Dogs	278	Needs	246
Cuadro Education Program	266	Dental Spa, The	138	Dolphin Bay	263, 276	Dubai Chamber Choir	202
Cuadro Fine Art Gallery	266	Dental Studio, The	138	Domestic Help	90	Dubai Chamber Orchestra	201
Cuba	412	Department Stores	334	Door Policy	433	Dubai Charity Centre	374
Cuisine Finder	386	Der Keller	404	Double Decker	424, 426, 430	Dubai Chess & Culture Club	195
Culligan International	86	Dermalase Clinic	142	Doubletree By Hilton		Dubai Classical Guitar	
Cultural Meals	385	Dermalogica	169	Resort	465	Orchestra	201
Cultural Night Market	340	Desert & Mountain Tours	307	Downtown		Dubai College	236
Culture	16	Desert Activities	298	Dubai	72, 108, 260, 270, 330	Dubai Community Health	
Culture & Co	356	Desert Adventures	308	DP World Tour		Centre	143
Cure, The	172	Desert Chill Ice		Championship	28, 286	Dubai Community Theatre	
Currency	3	Cream	153, 439	Dr Al Rustom's Medical &		& Arts Centre	194, 437, 439
Curriculum	230	...ADVERT	155	Day Care Surgery Centre	128	...ADVERT	437
Customs	33	Desert Driving	299	Dr Leila Soudah Clinic	134	Dubai Cosmetic Surgery	142
Cycle Hub, The	180, 378	Desert Equestrian Club	185	Dr Mahaveer Mehta		Dubai Creek	270
Cycle Safe Dubai	181	Desert Hash House Harriers	184	Skin Medical	128	Dubai Creek Golf	
Cycling	106	Desert Islands	454	Dr Michael's Dental Clinic	138	& Yacht Club	182, 260, 285
Cycling & Mountain Biking	180	Desert Islands Resort &		Dr Mohamed Al Zubaidy		Dubai Creek Marina	378
Cyprus	466	Spa By Anantara	454	Clinic	128	Dubai Creek Striders	189
Cyprus Airways	112	Desert Palm Riding School	185	Dr Taher H Khalil Clinic	128	Dubai Dawn Patrol	181
		Desert Ranch	276	Dragon Boat Events	295	Dubai Deira Creek	260
D		Desert		Dragon Boat Racing	181	Dubai Desert Classic	286
		Rangers	299, 303, 304, 308	Dragon Mart	333	Dubai Designer Market	340
Da Gama	391	Desert Resorts	480	Dragon Warriors Dubai	181	Dubai Diggers	181
Da Shi Dai	413	Desert River	364	Drama	199	Dubai Dolphinarium	273, 278
Dadabhai Travel	308	Desert Rose Tourism	308	Drama Dubai	199, 439	...ADVERT	279
Dali	266	Desert Safari	270	DRC Rent A Car	100	Dubai Drama Group	199, 439
Damac Properties	58	Desert Safari Abu Dhabi		Dream Boy	379	Dubai Driving Center	99
Daman National Health		& Dubai	308	Dream Explorer	308	Dubai Drums	201
Insurance Company	118	Desert Sport Diving Club	301	Dream Girl Tailors	379	Dubai Duty Free	
Damas	365	Desert Sport Services	156, 190	Dreamdays	288	...ADVERT	viii
Danat Al Ain Resort	453	Desert Springs	86	Dreamland Aqua Park	274, 471	Dubai Duty Free Tennis	
Danat Jebel Dhanna		Designer Furniture	362	...ADVERT	xiii	Championships	27, 286
Resort	456	DEWA	86	Dreamworks Spa &		Dubai English Speaking	
Dance	197, 384	...ADVERT	87	Massage	172	College	236
Dance Horizons 1	197	Deyaar	52	Dress Codes	422	Dubai English Speaking	
Danish Business Council		Deyaar Development PJSC		Dresses	380	School	236
Dubai	216	...ADVERT	53	Drink Driving	384	Dubai Evangelical Church	
Dar Al Marefa		Dhafra Beach Hotel	456	Drinking Water	86, 398	Centre	49
Private School	243	Dhow & Anchor	425, 426	Driving Licence	44	Dubai Exiles Rugby	
Dar Al Tasmim Uniforms	366	Dhow And Out	312	...Getting Your Licence	46	Football Club	188
Day Spas	174	Dhow Cruise	270	...International Driving		Dubai Exotic Limo	100
DbBabies	368	Dhow Ka Aangan	407	Permit	44	Dubai Eye	262
De Beers	365	Dhow Palace	321	...Learning To Drive	99	Dubai Festival City Dragon	
De Dietrich Cuisine		Dhow Wharfage	260	...Licence Transfers	96	Boat Festival	28
Academy	196	Diabetes &		Drs Nicolas & Asp	122, 138	Dubai Festival City Mall	346
De La Mer Day Spa	169, 174	Endocrine Center	128	Drunch	396	Dubai Fight Academy	180
Death		Diamondlease Car Rental	100	Dubai	12	Dubai Flea Market	340
...Death Certificates	147	Dibba	300, 458	Dubai Airshow	28	Dubai Flying Dragons	181
...Local Burial Or Cremation	148	Dibba Castle	459	Dubai Amateur Football		Dubai Football Academy	183
Debenhams	335	DIFC Gate Village	266	League	183	Dubai Fountain	260, 270
Debt	118	Dining & Dancing	384	Dubai American Academy	234	Dubai Garden Centre	93, 365
Decathlon Dubai	376	Dubai Investment Properties		Dubai Antique		Dubai Gardening Group	201
Deck, The	391	...ADVERT	322	Museum	264, 361	Dubai GEMS Private	
Decompression Sickness	302	Dirhams	3	Dubai Aquarium &		School	236
Decorative Cakes	440	Disco Dance Dubai	197	Underwater Zoo	260, 276	Dubai Gynaecology &	
Deepak's Textiles	379	Discovery Gardens	76	Dubai Archers	283	Fertility Centre	134
Deepa's Textile & Tailoring	379	Dish Catering & Events	440	Dubai Art	364	Dubai Harmony	202
Deira	80, 330	Divaz	311	Dubai Audio	360	Dubai Hockey Club	185
...City Centre	260, 346	Divers Down UAE	301	Dubai Autism Center	246	Dubai Holiday Camps	157
...Corniche	260	Dive Shop, The	378	Dubai Autodrome	187, 290	Dubai Hospital	124
		Diving	299, 378	...ADVERT	291		

askexplorer.com **485**

INDEX

Dubai Hurricanes Rugby
  Football Club 188
Dubai Ice Rink 260, 288
Dubai Insurance 295
Dubai International
  Academic City 247
Dubai International
  Academy 243
Dubai International Art
  Centre 194, 267
Dubai International Boat
  Show 27, 220
Dubai International
  Bowling Centre 284
Dubai International Film
  Festival 29, 436
Dubai International
  Horse Fair 220
Dubai International
  Marine Club 294, 306
Dubai Investments Park 330
Dubai Islamic Bank 115
Dubai Karate Centre 186
Dubai Kendo Club 186
Dubai Kennels & Cattery
  ...See also DKC 160
Dubai Kite Forum 304
Dubai Ladies Bridge Club 195
Dubai Ladies
  Club 165, 283, 290
Dubai Liners 197
Dubai Little League 179
Dubai London Clinic
  Dental Centre 138
Dubai London Specialty
  Hospital 122, 126, 128
Dubai Maids 90
Dubai
  Mall, The 260, 270, 276, 348
Dubai Marina 65, 270
Dubai Marina Mall 261, 348
  ...ADVERT 349
Dubai Marine
  Beach Resort 280, 313
Dubai Marriott Harbour 317
Dubai Media City 213
Dubai Medical Village 142
Dubai Mighty Camels Ice
  Hockey Club 186
Dubai Modern High
  School 244
Dubai Motocross
  Club (DMX) 187
Dubai MotorCity 78
Dubai Mountain
  Bikers UAE 181
Dubai Moving Image
  Museum 272
Dubai Mums Club 151
Dubai
  Museum 259, 269, 270, 272
Dubai Music School 200
Dubai Natural History
  Group 200
Dubai Netball League 188
Dubai Offshore Sailing
  Club 295, 306
Dubai Olympic
  Gymnastics Club 184
Dubai Outlet Mall 333, 348
Dubai Paddling School 306
Dubai Physiotherapy &
  Family Medicine Clinic 136

Dubai Polo & Equestrian
  Club 185, 188, 270, 286
Dubai Polo Gold Cup 27
Dubai Properties Group 58
Dubai Road Network 95
Dubai Road Runners 189
Dubai Roadsters 181
Dubai Sandstorms Ice
  Hockey Club 186
Dubai School Of Dental
  Medicine 139, 252
Dubai Schools
  Football League 183
Dubai Scrabble League 202
Dubai Shopping
  Festival 26, 260, 325
Dubai Singers 202
Dubai Ski Club 189
Dubai Sky Clinic 139
Dubai Snooker Club 202
Dubai Softball League 189
Dubai Sports City 77, 283
  ...ADVERT 256
Dubai Squash 190
Dubai St George's Society 48
Dubai Strata Law 58
Dubai Summer
  Surprises 28, 220,
  260, 326, 346
Dubai Surfski &
  Kayak Club 306
Dubai Tennis Academy 193
Dubai Toastmasters Club 48
Dubai Tourism & Travel
  Services 308
Dubai Turtle Rehabilitation
  Project 14
Dubai Women's Football
  Association 183
Dubai World Central 111
Dubai World Cup 27, 286
Dubai World Game Expo 29
Dubai World Trade
  Centre 261, 439
Dubai Zoo 276, 278
Dubailand 77, 330
Dubaipartyqueen 440
dubizzle 342
Dubliner's, The 426
Dubomedy 436
Duco Maritime 306
Duet Sports Club 193
Duflix Movies 356
Dugym Gymnastics
  Club 156, 184
Duke Of Edinburgh Award 246
Dukite 304
Dune Dinners 310
Dunes At Liwa 296
Dunlop 24H Endurance
  Series 286
Duplays 183, 188, 190, 193
Dusit Residence Dubai
  Marina 46
Dusit Thani 317
DVDs 354
DWC High School 234
  ...ADVERT 235

E

Early Learning Centre 366

Earning Potential 9
East Coast 303
Eastern Mangroves Hotel
  & Spa By Anantara 448
Easy Tour 307
Eauzone 391
Ebmas School Of Self
  Defense 186
Ecomaid Middle East 90
Economy 8
  ...Economic Diversification 9
Edge Hair & Beauty Salon 169
Education UK Exhibition 247
e-Gate 112
EK Volleyball Club 193
El Chico 413
El Chico Cafe 406
El Firulete BNF Dance
  Company Dubai 197
El Malecon 198, 403
El Mundo 311
El Sur 395
Elan Interiors 84
Electrical Goods &
  Appliances 359
Electricity & Water 86
Elements 418
Elia 391
Els Club, The 108, 285
Elyazia Beauty Center 169
Emaar Properties PJSC 58
Emax 342
Embassy Dubai 410
EMDI Institute Of Media &
  Communication 252
Emirates 112
Emirates Academy Of
  Hospitality Management 252
  ...ADVERT 253
Emirates Airline
  ...Dubai Jazz Festival 27, 438
  ...Dubai Rugby Sevens 29, 286
  ...Festival Of Literature 27
Emirates Badminton Club 179
Emirates Baptist Church
  International 49
Emirates Bird Records
  Committee 195
Emirates British Nursery 226
Emirates Culinary Guild 385
Emirates Decor & Furniture
  Directory 84
Emirates Diving
  Association 301
Emirates Driving
  Institute 99, 299
Emirates Environmental
  Group 200
Emirates Equestrian
  Centre 185
Emirates European
  Medical Centre 136
Emirates Flying School 199
Emirates Golf Club 26, 193, 285
Emirates Golf Federation 285
Emirates Gourmet
  General Trading 337
Emirates Grand Hotel 317
Emirates Hospital 126
Emirates Insurance
  Company 93, 118
Emirates International
  School – Jumeirah 244

Emirates International
  School – Meadows 244
Emirates Kart Zone 288
Emirates Living 70
Emirates Marine
  Environmental
  Group (EMEG) 14
Emirates Motor Sports
  Federation 187
Emirates NBD 115
Emirates Palace 448
Emirates Park Zoo 276, 445
Emirates Photography
  Club 201
Emirates Trading
  Establishment 354
Emirates Wildlife Society 14
Emirati Artists 267
Emirati Culture 269
Employment 207
  ...Contracts 208
  ...Visa 36
Empost 326
Empty Quarter 266, 302, 454
English National
  Curriculum 234
English Premier League 90
Engraving 267
Entertainment 435
Entrepreneurs 215
Environment 13, 199
Environmental Agency
  Abu Dhabi 14
Environmental Groups 219
Epicure 416
Ernst & Young 116
E-Smart Travel Estate Pack
  (E-Step) 60
Esmod Dubai 249
E-Sports 157, 298
Essentials Hair & Beauty
  Salon 169
Eternal Medspa 142
Etihad Airways 112
Etihad Mall 333
Etisalat Academy
  Recreation & Sports
  Complex 290
Etisalat Academy Sports
  & Leisure Club 283
Euroline Rent A Car 100
Euromed Clinic 142
European Cuisine 387
European PGA Tour 286
European Tour Omega
  Dubai Desert Classic 26, 285
European Tour's Race
  To Dubai 286
European University
  College 249, 252
European Veterinary
  Centre 160
Eurostar Rent A Car 100
Events & Exhibitions 26
Ewaan 406
E-Walls Studio 364
Excel Sports 190
Exhale 165, 203
Explorer Tours 306
Extreme Fun 273

486　　Dubai Explorer

INDEX

F

Faces	372
Fairmont	221
Fairmont Bab Al Bahr	448
Fairmont Dubai	317
Fairmont The Palm	313
Fakih IVF	134
Falaknaz – The Warehouse	362
...ADVERT	363
Falcon Museum & Heritage Sports Centre	272
Falcon Spring Drinking Water	86
Falconry	272
Familia De La Salsa	198
Family & Parenting	144
Family First Medical Center	122
Family Friendly Restaurants	400, 420
Family Law	146
Family Sponsored	208
Fantasy Kingdom	273
Farjam Collection	266
Farm, The	400
Farm Shops	338
Farmer's Market	264, 340
Farriers	395
Favourite Things	153
Fazaris	410
Federal National Council (FNC)	8
Feline Friends Dubai	218
Fellowship Of The Emirates	49
Fencing	182
Ferrari	102
Ferrari World Abu Dhabi	445
Fetal Medicine & Genetic Center	132
Fibber Magee's	426
Fidelity Fitness Club	165
Figaro's Pizza	413
Filini	362
Filipino Cuisine	387
Film Festivals	436
Film Screenings	267, 268
Finance	114
Financial Advisors	116
Finasi	364
Fines	97
First Aid Courses	152
First Group Theatre	438, 439
First Gulf Bank	115
First International Dance Studio	198
First Steps Nursery Dubai	229
First Things First	82
Fish & Chips	406
Fish & Chips Room	406, 413
Fish Keeping	372
Fish Market	260, 340, 403, 457
Fishing	182, 304
Fitness	164
Fitness First	165, 203
Fitness O2	165
Flamingo Beach Resort	472
Flamingos	457
Flooka	280
Flora & Fauna	13
Flow Kitchen	395
flydubai	112, 444
Flying	199
Flying Elephant	440
...ADVERT	441
Flying House	267
Fogo Vivo	414
Fogueira Restaurant & Lounge	391
Football	182, 286
Ford	102
Foremarke	238
Formula 1 Grand Prix	29, 286
Formula Rossa	445
Fossil Rock	296, 310
Foundation Stage	225
Fountain, The Dubai	260
Four Seasons	478
Fraiche	416
Framing	364
Franck Provost	169
Frankie's	396, 413
Frankincense	372
Free Zones	36, 212
....Choosing A Free Zone	213
...Setting Up In A Free Zone	215
Freediving UAE	301
Freelance Work	213
Freestyle Divers	301
French Cuisine	387
French Bakery	372
French Business Council Dubai & The Northern Emirates	216
French Ligue 1	90
Freshly Ground Sounds	438
Friday Polo	270
Fridays	433
Fridge, The	264, 436
Frost	380
Fruit & Vegetable Market	340
Fuddruckers	413
Fujairah	458
...City	458
...Fort	459
...Heritage Village	459
Fujairah Aviation Academy	312
Fujairah Rotana Resort & Spa – Al Aqah Beach	460
Full-day Safari	310
Fun City	170, 273
Funky Lanes Bowling Centre	284
Furniture & Homewares	360

G

Gaelic Games	184
Galadari Motor Driving Center	99
Galeries Lafayette	335
Galleria Ice Rink	288
Gallery Etemad	264
Gallery Isabelle Van Den Eynde	264
Gallery One	364
Garage Sales	374
Gardening	201
Gardens & Pools	92, 364
Gargash Insurance	118
Gas	86
Gate Village	266
Gaucho	403
Geant	336
GEMS International School Al Khail	244
GEMS Jumeirah Primary School	238
GEMS Modern Nursery	229
GEMS New Millennium School Al Khail	238
Gems Of Yoga	203
GEMS Royal Dubai School	238
GEMS Wellington Academy	238
GEMS Wellington International School	238
GEMS Wellington Primary School	238
GEMS Winchester School Dubai	238
GEMS World Academy Dubai	244
General Medical Care	122
General Medical Centre (GMC)	122, 142
...ADVERT	123
General Motors ...ADVERT	xviii-xix
Geography	4
Gerard's	417
German Cuisine	387
German Clinic	134
German Emirati Joint Council For Industry & Commerce	216
German Heart Centre Bremen	129
German Medical Center	129
Getting Around	94
Ghayathi	454
Giraffe Cafe	445
Girders	424, 426
Gitex Shopper	220
Gitex Technology Week	28, 220
Glam Paws UAE	374
Glamping	296
Global Village	330
Globaleye	116
Gloria Hotel	46
GMC Clinics	139
Go Sport	376
Goal Attained	165
Go-kart	468
Gold & Diamond Park	264, 329, 366
...ADVERT	367
Gold Salon	169
Gold Souk	259, 260, 330, 344
Golden Beach Nursery	226
Golden Falcon Karate Centre	187
Golden Fist Karate Club	187
Golden Mile	263
Golden Ring Jewellery	365
Golden Tulip Khatt Springs Resort & Spa	465
Golden Tulip Resort	473
Golf	284, 286
Golf House	377
Good Habits	142
Goodbaby	368
Gourmet Foods	337
Gourmet Burger Kitchen	406
Government	8
Government Healthcare	121
Government Hospitals	124
Graff	365
Grand Belle Vue Hotel	46
Grand Excelsior	317, 400
Grand Hyatt	317
Grand Hyatt Doha	478
Grand Hyatt Residence	46
Grand Optics	140
Grand Stores	358
Gratuity Payments	210
Greek Cuisine	387
Green Art Gallery	264
Green Car Rental	100
Green Community	78
Green Middle East	220
Green Mubazzarah Chalets	453
Greenfield Community School	244
Greenheart Organic Farms	338
Greens, The	70
Greenshield Insurance Brokers	93, 118
...ADVERT	107, 119
Grosvenor House	317
Guardian Life Management	116
Guggenheim Abu Dhabi	266, 450
Guinness World Records	5
Girl Guides	156, 246
Gulf Air	112
Gulf Bike Week	28
Gulf Education & Training Exhibition	220
Gulf Eye Center	140
Gulf For Good	218
Gulf Greetings General Trading LLC ...ADVERT	327
Gulf Montessori Nursery	229
Gulf Photo Plus	201, 264
Gulf Speciality Hospital	142
Gulf Star Sports	157
Gulf Ventures	308, 312
...ADVERT	309
Gymnastex	184
Gymnastics	179, 184
Gyms & Fitness Clubs	164

H

H Hotel	317
Habtoor Grand Beach	317
Haif Hospitality Furnishings	364
Hair Corridor	169
Hair Shop	169
Hair Station	169
Hair@Pyramids	169
Hairdressers	169
Hajar Mountains	4, 296, 302, 310
Hakkasan	411
Hamdan bin Mohammed Sports Complex	190
Hamilton Aquatics	192
Hamleys	366
Hamptons International	52
...ADVERT	57
Happy Hour	422
Hardee's	413
Hardware & Diy	365

askexplorer.com   487

INDEX

Harlequin Marquees & Event Services	440
Harley Owners Group Dubai Chapter	188
Harvester's Pub	426
Harvey Nichols	335
Hashing	184
Hastens Dubai	362
Hatta	296, 303
Hatta Pools Safari	310
Hawksbill Turtles	14
Hays Middle East	207
Health	120
Health Bay Clinic	132
Health Call	122
Health Card	43, 121
Health Care Medical Centre	129
Health Club, The	165
Health Factory	142
Health Foods	337
Health Psychology UAE	143
Health Supplements	337
Healthcare	65, 68, 70, 72, 74, 77, 81
Healthcare City	126
Healy Consultants	218
Heart Of Sharjah	468
Hello Kitty Beauty Spa	169, 170, 176
Heriot Watt University Dubai Campus	249
Heritage & Diving Villages	259, 269
Heritage Sites	268
Heroes Of The UAE	15
Hertz UAE	100
Hey Sugar	372, 419
Hibiki Music Lounge	430
High Tea	270
Higher Colleges Of Technology	250
Highland Dance Dubai	198
Hiking	302
Hili Archaeological Park	453
Hili Fun City	453
Hilton	261
...Al Ain	453
...Dubai Creek	260, 318
...Dubai Jumeirah Resort	318
...Fujairah	460
...Ras Al Khaimah Resort	465
...Salalah Resort	474
...Sharjah	471
Hiring A Car	99
Hiring A Nanny	151
History	6
HIV	42
HLB Hamt Chartered Accountants	218
Hobbies	194
Hockey	185
Hofbrauhaus	414
Holborn Assets	116
Holiday Calendar	232
Holiday Inn	321
Holy Trinity Church Dubai	49
Holy Trinity Thrift Centre	374
Home Centre	342, 361
...ADVERT	xi
Home Delivery	439
Home Grown Children's Eco Nursery	226
Home Help	90
Home Improvements	91
Home Insurance	93
Homes R Us	361
Homewares	360
Honda	102
Hong Loong	410
Honyaki	393
Hoofbeatz	185
Hope Montessori Nursery	229
Hopscotch Nursery	226
Horizon Kids Nursery	226
Horizon School	238
Horse Racing	286
Horse Riding	185
Hot-Cog Mountain Bike Club	181
Hotels	313, 448, 453, 457, 460, 465, 472, 478
Hotels & Serviced Apartments	46
Housing	50
...Buying A Home	56
...Buying Process	60
...House Hunting	56
...Residential Areas	64
House Of Arushi	380
House Of Cakes	372
House Of Cars	102, 106
...ADVERT	103
House Of Prose	356
Housekeeping Co	90
Housing	50
...Buying A Home	56
...Buying Process	60
...House Hunting	56
...Purchase Costs	60
Howdra	90
HSBC Bank Middle East	115
Hult International Business School	249
Human Relations Institute & Clinics	143
Hunar Gallery	267
Hundred Pilates Studio	166
Hyatt Regency	318
Hyatt Regency Dubai Golf Park	288
Hypermarkets	336
Hyperpanda	336

I

Ibn Battuta Mall	348
Icare Clinics	129
ICC Global Cricket Academy	180
Ice Hockey	186
Ice Land Water Park	274, 462
Ice Skating	288
Icho Restaurant	411
Icon Auto Garage	106
Icon Bar	425
Iddesign	362
iFLY Dubai	274, 292
IKEA	342, 361
Ikebana Sogetsu Group	194
Iko Instructors	304
Il Caff – Di Roma	413
IMAX	436
Immigration Department	36
Imperial Healthcare Institute	142
Imperium	395
Improv	439
In Shape Ladies Fitness Club	165
Inchcape Shipping Services	83
Independent Films	436
India	466
India Club	165, 179
Indian Academy, The	244
Indian Cuisine	387
Indian Business & Professional Council	216
Indigo Entertainment	440
Indigo Living	84, 362
Indoor Activities	153
Infinity Health Clinic	122
Informal Dining	404
Insportz Club	165
Insurance	104
...Companies	116
InterContinental Dubai Festival City	318
Interem	83
...ADVERT	73
Interior Decorating	91
Interior Design	84
International Cuisine	388
International Baccalaureate Programme	243
International Centre For Culinary Arts Dubai	196
International City	80
International Football Academy	183, 246
International Fund For Houbara Conservation (IFHC)	14
International House Dubai	254
...ADVERT	255
International Monetary Fund (IMF)	9
International Property Show	28
International Relations	13
International School Of Arts & Sciences	234
International Universities	248
Internet	23, 89
Intersport	376
Iranair	112
Iranian Business Council	216
Iranian Hospital	126
Irish Village	426, 438
...ADVERT	427
Irony Home	362
ISAHD (Insurance System for Advancing Healthcare in Dubai)	210
Isis The French Clinic	135
Islam	16
Islamic Mortgages	59
Italian Cuisine	388
Italian Business Council	216
Italian Chef At Home	440
Italian Serie A	90
It's Just Football	183
It's Mirchi	430
Ivy, The	414

J

J+A Gallery	267
J3 Mall	331
JA Jebel Ali Golf Resort	186, 278, 285, 290, 311
JA Oasis Beach Tower	46
JA Ocean View	318
JA Shooting Club	290
Jacky's Electronics	360
Jadis Interiors	84
Jaguar	102
jamjar, the	195, 201, 264, 267
James & Alex Dance Studios	198
Jamie's Italian	314, 396
Japan Airlines	112
Japanese Cuisine	388
Japengo Cafe	406
Jashanmal	335
Jashanmal Bookstores	356
Jazeera Airways	112
Jazira Aviation Club	462
Jazirat Al Hamra	460
Jazz	407
...Festival	27, 438
Jazz@Pizza Express	407
JBR	65
JBR Beach	278
Jebel Ali Equestrian Club	186
Jebel Ali Port	10
Jebel Ali Primary School	238
Jebel Hafeet	296, 302, 453
Jebel Yibir	3, 296
Jeep	102
Jen's Hair Studio	169
Jenny Rose	369
Jet Skis	280
Jetset	169
Jet-skiing	305
Jetty Lounge	422
Jewellery	365
Job Hunting	207
Johnny Rockets	400
Jointly Owned Property (JOP) Law	58
Jones The Grocer	196, 338, 418
Jordan	466
JTS Medical Centre	122
Juan Hair Salon	169
Juli Music Center	200, 369
Julian Hairdressing	170
Jumbo Electronics	360
Jumeira	68, 262
Jumeira & Umm Suqeim	331
Jumeira Baccalaureate School	244
Jumeirah Open Beach Running Track	108
Jumeira Plaza	332
Jumeirah Beach Hotel	262, 278, 314
Jumeirah Beach Park	262, 280
Jumeirah Beach Residence (JBR)	108, 261
Jumeirah Centre	332
Jumeirah College	240
Jumeirah Corniche	106, 262
Jumeirah Creekside	318

488   Dubai Explorer

INDEX

Jumeirah Emirates Towers 261, 318
Jumeirah English Speaking School 240
Jumeirah Golf Estates 77, 285
Jumeirah International Nursery School 226
Jumeirah Islands 70
Jumreirah Lake Towers (JLT) 65
Jumeirah Lakes Towers Park 282
Jumeirah Mosque 262, 269
Jumeirah Music Centre 200
Jumeirah Open Beach 262
Jumeirah Park 70
Jumeirah Sceirah 276
Jumeirah Veterinary Clinic 160
Jumeirah Zabeel Saray 263, 314
Just Kidding 364, 369
Juweira Boutique Hotel 474
JW Marriott Hotel Dubai 321
JW Marriott Marquis 318

K

K9 Friends 219
...ADVERT 161
Kachins 379
Kalba 458
Kalm Beauty 170
Kalm Grooming Lounge 176
Karachi Darbar 262
Karama 80, 329
Karama Complex 329
Karaoke Bars 430
Karat 419
Kart Furniture 362
Kartdrome 288
Karting 288
Kasbar 434
Katara Cultural Village 476
Kaya Skin Clinic 142
Kayak Hire 304
Kayaking 186, 280, 304
Kazu 446
Kebabs 390
Keith Nicholl Medical Centre 135
Kempinski 263, 318, 458
Kensington Nursery 228
Kenya 466
Ketchup 406
Key Government Figures 8
KFC 413, 439
Khalifa bin Zayed Al Nahyan Foundation 8
Khamis Abdullah Trading & Embroidery 379
Khan Murjan 344
Khanjar 375
Khasab 300
Khasab Travel & Tours 311
Khazana 397
KHDA Rankings 231
Khor Al Adaid 478
Kiddo Cuts 478
Kids 169, 170, 362, 366
Kids Connection 154
Kids Cuts 170
Kids Island Nursery 228
Kids Zone Nursery 228

Kidsfirst Medical Center 122, 135
Kids' Theatre Works 156
Kidville 156
Kidz Inc 362
Kidz Venture 154, 230
Kidzania 273
Kings' School Dubai 240
Kings' School Nad Al Sheba 240
Kisaku 430
Kite Beach 280, 304
Kite People 304
Kitesurfing 186, 295, 304
KLM Royal Dutch Airlines 112
Knight Shot 377
Knowledge & Human Development Authority (KHDA) 231
Knowledge Village 247
Kona Bikes 378
Korean Cuisine 388
Koubba Bar 422
KPMG 116
Kris With A View 411
Kuwait Airways 112

L

La Casa Del Habano 413
La Cigale 478
La Veranda 400
Labour Camps 50
Labour Card 36, 208
Ladies' Nights 425
Ladybird Nursery 230
Lama Tours 308
Lamcy Plaza 330
Landline
... Closing A Landline 88
Land Of Pearls – Pearl Excursion 462
Land Registry 60
Land Rover 102
Landmark Properties 52
Landscaping 92
Language 16, 17
Language Courses 254
Laserdrome Dubai 290
Last Man Stands Cricket League 180
Latifa Hospital 124, 132
Latin American Cuisine 388
Laughter Factory 436
Laundry Services 90
Laura Ashley 364
Lawrie Shabibi 264
Law 20
...If You're Arrested 22
...Smoking 385
Le Clos 353
Leisure Activities 283
Le Meridien Al Aqah 460
...ADVERT 461
Le Meridien Dubai 319
Le Meridien Mina Seyahi 278, 319
Le Pain Quotidien 413
Le Petit Palais 154
Le Royal Meridien 278
Le Royal Meridien Beach Resort 319

Leap Of Faith 270, 274
Lebanon 466
Left Bank 424
Legal System 22
Leisure Marine 378
Lemongrass 399
Lexus 102
Liali Jewellery 365
L'atelier Des Chefs 196
Liberty Automobiles 102
Libraries 249
Library Bar 432
Library, The Old 356
Licence To Drive 96
Lifco 336
Lifecare International 118
Lifeline Hospital 129
Lifeline Medical Centre Dubai Marina 122
Lifeworks Counselling & Development 143
Lightform 201
Lime Spa 176
Lime Tree Cafe & Kitchen 262, 264 420, 440
Lincoln 102
L'occitane 372
Liquor Licence 20, 44
...Applying For A Liquor Licence 46
Liquor Stores 44
Literature Festival 27
Little Discoverers Nursery 228
Little Explorers 154, 273
Little Explorers Edutainment Centre 274
Little Land Nursery & Montessori Centre 230
Little Musicians 200
Little Wonders Nursery 228
Live Music 407, 436
Live'ly (nutritional services) 142
Living Room Cafe 417
Living Rooms Video Games Cafe 400
Liwa 303, 454
...Dunes 296
Liwa Hotel 456
...ADVERT 455
Liwa Loop 274
Liwa Resthouse 456
Lobby Lounge 419
Lobby Lounge & Terrace 419
Lobo Tailors 379
Local Media 23
London Centre For Aesthetic Surgery 142
London School Of Fashion In Dubai 247
Lorna Jane 377
Lost Chambers Aquarium 263, 273, 278, 313
Lotus Educational Institute 252
Lotus Hotel Apartments & Spa Marina 46
Lotus Salon 170
Louvre Abu Dhabi 266, 450
Loyalty Cards 325
Luciano's 391
Lucky's Furnitures & Handicrafts 362
Lufthansa 112

LuLu Hypermarket 342, 336
Lunettes House Of Quality Optics 140
Lush 372
Lutfi Optical Centre 140
Luxury Spas 173

M

M.A.C 372
Mackenzie Art 364
...ADVERT 381
Madah 296
Madam 296
Madeleine Cafe & Boulangerie 417
Madina Mall 330
Madinat Jumeirah 262, 314, 344
Magazine Shop 417
Magic Planet 154, 274, 284
Magnum 434
Magrabi Optical 140
Magrudy's 356, 366
Mahdah 303
Maids & Cleaners 90
Maison Bagatelle 416
Maison De Joelle 169
Majlis Al Jinn Cave 296
Majlis Gallery 266, 267, 269, 364
Majlis Ghorfat Um Al Sheif 269
MAKE Business Hub 418
Making A Will 147
Maktoum Sailing Trophy 286
Malaysia Airlines 112
Malaysia Business Council 216
Maldives 466
Male Salons 170
Male Spas 176
Mall of the Emirates 350
Mall Walkers 109
Mamas & Papas 369
Mamzar Beach Park 260, 280
Man/Age 170, 176
Manchester Business School 249
Manchester Clinic 122
Manga Sushi 403
Mango Tree 260, 270
Mangrove 304
Mangroves 306
Manhattan Film Academy 199
Manipal University Dubai Campus 249
Mannaland Korean Restaurant 399
Manpower Middle East 207
Mansoor Jewellers 365
Marhaba Meet & Greet Service 34
Marhaba Service
...ADVERT 30
Maria Bonita Taco Shop & Grill 406
Maria Dowling 170
Mariam Express 300
Marina Exotic Home Interiors 362
Marina Walk 261, 331
Marine Equipment 378
Marjan Island 465

askexplorer.com 489

INDEX

Marjan Island Resort & Spa	465	Mercure Grand		Mountain Biking	180, 299	Nestle Waters Management	
Market & Platters	338	Jebel Hafeet	453	Mountain High		& Technology	86
Markets	340	Meridien Village Terrace	392	Middle East	296	Net Tours	308
Marks & Spencer	335, 366	Metlife Alico	118	Mountain Safari	310	Netball	188
Marriage	144	Metro	110	Movenpick Hotels		Netherlands Business	
Marsa Dubai	65, 261, 331	Mexican Cuisine	388	...Doha	478	Council	216
Marsa Dubai & JBR	65	Meydan, The	320	...Ibn Battuta Gate	320	Networking	216
Marta's Kitchen	440	Meydan Beach	281, 422	...Jumeirah Beach	320	Neuro Spinal Centre	130
Martial Arts	167, 186	MICE	220	Movies & Munchies	436	Neuro Spinal Hospital	127
Martini Rock	300	Michigan State University		Moving Services	83	Neuron	118
Mary Foot Spa	169	Dubai	249	Mr Ben's Costume		New Covenant Church	
Masafi	86	Middle East & Africa		Closet	331, 370	Dubai	49
Masdar City	5	Monitor	218	MSF		New Masters Art Gallery	267
Maserati	102	Middle East Airlines	112	...ADVERT	133	New York University	
Mashrabiya Lounge	419	Middle East Funeral		Mudo City	335	Abu Dhabi	250
Mashreq Bank	115	Services	147	Mulberry Tree Nursery	230	Newspapers	24
Maternity	130	Middle Eastern	388	Multi-sports	290	Nexus Insurance	93, 116, 118
...Fashion	368	Middlesex University		Mumcierge	151	Nezesaussi Grill	261, 414, 224
...Leave	210	Dubai	250	Mumzworld	369	Nightclubs	433
Mathaf – Arab Museum Of		Midland Cars	102	Murdoch University		Nike+ Run Club	189
Modern Art	478	Milk & Honey	338	International Study		Nina	403
Max Garage	106	Miller Hay	207	Centre Dubai	250	NMC Hospital	127
Max's Restaurant	400	...ADVERT	211	Muri Lunghi Italian		NMC Speciality Hospital	132
Maya Modern Mexican		Mina Seyahi		Furniture	362	No 5 Lounge & Bar	419
Kitchen & Lounge	397	Watersports Club	306	Murjan Splash Park	445	Nobu	196, 263, 397
Maybury Fresh Food Store	338	Mini Golf	288	Musandam	300, 310, 472	Nol Card	109
Mazina	395	Ministry Of Labour	36	Muscat	444, 473	Nomad	393
McGettigan Irish Football		Minutes	380	Museum Of Islamic Art	478	Nomad Ocean Adventures	301
Club	184	Miracle Garden	282	Museums	272	Noodle House	414, 439
McGettigan's Irish Pub	426	Miraj Islamic Art Centre	267	Mushrif Park	282	Noor Library Of Islamic Art	267
McLaren Dubai	102	Miral		Music	354	Nora Dance Group	197
Meat Co., The	392	...ADVERT	ix	Music Chamber, The	200, 369	Nord Anglia International	
Mecca	16	Mirdif	81, 108, 333	Music Groups	200	School Dubai	240
MED, The	395	Mirdif City Centre	350	Music Hall	435	...ADVERT	241
Medcare Hospital	126, 132	Mirdif Fish & Chips	406	Music Institute, The	200, 369	Northern Emirates	303
Medcare Medical		Mirdif Mums Dubai	151	Music Room	369, 438	Noukhada Adventure	
Centre	122, 126	Mirfa	295	Musical Instruments	369	Company	304, 446
Medcare Orthopaedics		Mirfa Hotel	456	MV Dara Wreck	300	NStyle Nail Lounge	169
& Spine Hospital	126	Mitera Clinic	134	My Gym UAE	156	Nurseries & Pre-schools	225
Medecins Sans		Mitsubishi Motors	102	My Nursery	228	Nutritionists & Slimming	142
Frontieres (MSF)	219	MK Fencing Academy	182				
Media One	319	MK Trading	358	**N**		**O**	
Media Rotana	319	MMI	353				
Medic Polyclinic	129	Mobile Banking	115	N Bar	169	O1NE Yas Island	446
Medical Test	42	Mobile Doctors	121	Naif Museum	272	Oak N Barrel	426
Medication	136	Mobile Phones	89	Naif Souk	344	Oasis Centre	329
Mediclinic		...Pre-paid Mobile	88	Nail Moda	169	Oasis Palm Tourism	308
...ADVERT	iv-v	...Registering A Sim Card	89	Nail Spa, The	169, 172	Oasis School	240
...Al Qusais	129	Mocktails	424	Nail Station	169	Oasis Water	86
...Al Sufouh	126, 129	Modern Cleaning Methods	90	Nail Zone	169	Oberoi, The	320
...Arabian Ranches	129	Modern Veterinary Clinic	160	Nails At Home	169	Objects & Elements	195
...Beach Road	129	Mohammad bin Rashid		Nakheel Properties	58	Objekts Of Design	362
...City Hospital	127, 132	School Of Government	254	Nakkash Gallery	364	Observatory, The	394
...Dubai Mall	122, 129	Mohammed bin Zayed Species		Nando's	399	Obstetrics & Gynaecology	132
...Ibn Battuta	129	Conservation Fund	14	Nannies		Ocean Active	182
...Meadows	129	Mojo	264	...Hiring A Nanny	151	OCEAN Independence	
...Mirdif	130	Molly Maid	90	Nappies	368	(yacht charters)	311
...Welcare Hospital	127, 132	Mondial (Dubai)	116	Nasco Karaoglan	118	Oceanair UAE	304
Mediclinic Middle East		Monorail	110, 263	Nasimi Beach	281, 424	Octane Garage	106
Mediterranean Cuisine	388	Montessori	229	Natalie Beauty Saloon JLT	169	Oeno Wine Bar	425, 432
Medley	418	Moorfields Eye Hospital	140	National Dress	18	Off-roading	303
Mednet UAE	118	...ADVERT	141	National General		Offroad-Zone	299, 303
Medzo	410	MORE Cafe	264, 396	Insurance Co.	93, 118	Offshore Accounts	118
Meem Gallery	267	Moroccan	388	National Groups	48	OHM Records	356
Melia Dubai	319	Mortgages	59	National Iranian Carpets	375	Old Dubai	80
Menasa	10	Mosaico	401	National Store	358	Old Town	260
Men's Health Clinic	130	Mostafawi	375	Natuzzi	362	Olives	392
Meraas Development	58	Mother & Baby Groups	151	Nawwara	428	Oman	472
Mercato Family Clinic	122	Mother & Child Fitness	165	NDust Shoe Repairs	380	Oman Air	112
Mercato Shopping		Mother, Baby & Child Show	29	Nelson's	426	Oman Dive Center	474
Mall	262, 350	Mothercare	369	Neos	260, 411	Oman Insurance Company	118
Mercedes-Benz	102	Motion Fitness Center	165				
		Motorsports	187, 286, 290				

490   Dubai Explorer

INDEX

On The Border
  (Mexican restaurant) 413
One&Only Royal
  Mirage 173, 314
  ...ADVERT 175
One&Only The Palm 263, 320
Online Banking 115
Online Forums 48
Online Services 44
Online Shopping 326
Opel 102
Open House 440
Opera Gallery 266
Opera House District 266
Optic Center 140
Opticians 139
Optivision 140
Orchestras & Bands 201
Orchid Restaurant 401
Organic 169, 416
Organic Foods & Cafe 338, 369
  ...ADVERT 339
Organic Glow Beauty
  Lounge 169
Orientalist Woven Art, The 375
Orient Tours 310
Original Fitness 165, 166
Orthopaedics 134
Orthosports Medical
  Center 136
Oscar's Vine Society 432
Ossiano 412
Ossigeno 410
Osteopathic Health Centre 136
  ...ADVERT 137
Oud 372
Outdoor Equipment 376
Outlet Mall 81
Overseas Births 150
Overseas Study 248
OX Interior Design 84

P

Pace E Luce 170
Pachanga 403
Pacific Ventures 52
  ...ADVERT 55
PADI 300
Paedriatrics 134
Pai Thai 410
Paintballing 290, 445
Pakistan Business
  Council Dubai 216
Pakistani Cuisine 389
Palace, The 261, 314
Palace Downtown
  Dubai, The 320
Palm Jumeirah 66, 263
Palm Strip 332
Pampered Pets 160, 372
Pan Emirates 361
Panacea Medical &
  Wellness Centre 130
Panini 418
Paper At Artisans
  Of The Emirates 195
Paper Lane 195
Parasol Garden Furniture 364
Parenting 144
Paris Gallery 366, 372

Paris Sorbonne University
  Abu Dhabi 250
Park Dental Centre 139
Park Hyatt
  Dubai 146, 260, 320
Park N Shop 337, 372
Park Regis Kris Kin 321
Parking 51, 96
  ...Fines 97
  ...Pre-paid Parking 97
Parks & Beaches 278, 281
Parsons Brinckerhoff 207
Parties 370, 439
Part-time Work 214
Party Centre 370
  ...ADVERT 371
Party Zone 370
Pashminas 375
Passport Photos 36
Pastels 169, 170
Patsi Collins Hair
  Beauty Nails 170
Paul 413
Pavilion Dive Centre 301
Pavilion Downtown
  Dubai 267
Pavilion Marina &
  Sports Club 165
Paws & Claws 374
Pax 399
Pearl Coast 454
Pearl Diving 269
Pearl Qatar, The 478
Peekaboo Creative
  Play Centre 154
Pensions 116
Peppercrab 401
Perfect Figure 142
Perfect Help, The 152
Perfect Shape Up
  Beauty Centre 172
Performing Arts Theatre 264
Perfumes & Cosmetics 372
Permit To Work 208
Personal Training 166
Pets 158, 372
  ...Kennels & Boarding 160
  ...Taking Your Pet Home 160
Pet Secure 93
Pet's Delight 374
Petland 374
Petrol Stations 99
Pets 158, 372
  ...Moving Your Pet 158
  ...Insurance 93
Petzone 374
Peugeot 102
Pharmacies 136
Physiotherapy 135
Pianists 407
PIC Middle East 116
Picasso 266
Picnico General Trading 377
Picturehouse, The 201
Pierchic 412
Pilates 165, 202
Pinky Furniture 362
Pizza Hut 413
Places Of Interest 259
Places Of Worship 49
Planet Hollywood 401
Planet Travel & Tourism 310
Planetarium 273

Plant Street 93, 263
Plantation 419
Platinum List 433
Play A Round
  @ Some Place Nice 154, 290
Player's Lounge 426
Playnation 274
Plug-ins 360
Police 22
Polo 188
Pool 202
Pools 92, 364
Popular Music Institute 200
Population 3
Pork 18
Port Rashid 260
Porterhouse 410
Poshpaws Kennels
  & Cattery 160
Positive Paws 160
Postal Services 89
  ...PO Boxes 215
Post-graduate Study 247
Post-paid Mobile 88
Pottery Barn 361
Pottery Barn Kids 364
Powerboat Racing 29
Pregmamma 369
Pregnancy
  ...Having A Baby 148
  ...Healthy Pregnancy 150
  ...Pregnant Out Of Wedlock 150
  ...Registering A Baby 149
  ...Water Births 150
Prego's 196, 414
Premier Habitat 52
Pride Of Kashmir 375
Prima Gold 366
Prima Performing Arts 198
Primary & Secondary
  Schools 232
Primavera Medical Centre 134
Prime 68 403
Prime Medical Center 130
  ...ADVERT 131
Prince Of Sea 464
Pristine Private School 240
Private Healthcare 121
Private Hospitals 124
Private Medical
  Insurance 124
Pro Art 268
Probation 208
Probike 378
Procat Catering Services 440
Property Maintenance 91
Property Prices 61
Property Search 50
Propertyfinder 52
Pub Grub 425
Public Holidays 26
Public Relations
  Officer (PRO) 36
Public Transport 109
Public Universities 250
Pubs 425
Pullman Deira City Centre 320
  ...ADVERT IBC, xvi
Punchline Comedy Club 436
Pure Gold 366
Pursuit Games 290

Q

Qantas 112
Qasr Al Sarab Desert
  Resort By Anantara 480
Qatar 476
Qatar Airways 112
Qatar General Insurance
  & Reinsurance Co. 118
QD's 425
Quad Biking 299
Quay Health Club 165
Quay Skillz Youth Facility 154
Queen Of Ice World
  (ice-skating school) 288
Quick Bites 408
Quiz Nights 426
Qum Persian Carpets
  & Novelties 375
Qusais 80

R

Radio 24
Radisson Blu 260, 321
  ...Doha 479
  ...Resort 471
  ...Royal 321
  ...Raffles 321
Raffles International
  School 228, 240
Raffles Spa 176
Raffles World Academy 245
Rage 377
Rage Bowl 292
Raifet N Shawe 187
Rail Network 112
Rainbow Play Systems 364
RAK Airways 112
RAK Bank 115
RAK Sailing Academy 464
Ram Trading Enterprises 102
Ramada Beach Hotel 458
Ramadan Timings 272, 385
Ranches Ladies 48
Ranches Restaurant & Bar 401
Rare Restaurant 411
Rare The Place 434
Ras Al Khaimah 296, 460
Ras Al Khaimah
  Country Club 464
Ras Al Khaimah Tourism
  Development Authority
  ...ADVERT 463
Ras Al Khor Wildlife
  Sanctuary 276
Ras Khumais 295
Rashid Hospital 124, 132
Rashid Paediatric
  Therapy Centre 246, 374
Ravi's 262, 414
Rawr Yoga 203
Raymond Weil 366
Ready Maids 90
Real Estate Agents 52
Real Estate Law 58
Real Pilates 166
Rebecca Treston
  Aesthetics At Euromed 142
Re-compression
  Chambers 302

askexplorer.com 491

INDEX

Record Breakers	313
Recovery Services	98
Recycling	15
Redtag	335
Redundancy	212
Reebok Running Club	189
Reef Mall	330
Reel Cinemas	260
Reem Al Bawadi	261, 404
Reem Automobiles	102
Reflection Hair & Beauty Centre	170
Reflets Par Pierre Gagnaire	397
Reform Social & Grill	414
Refunds, Exchanges & Consumer Rights	326
Regal Textiles	379
Regent International School	240
Regime Fitness	166
Registering A Vehicle	104
Religion	16
Relocation & Removal Companies	83
Renoir	266
Renting A Home	52
...Renewals & Rent Rises	56
...Residential Areas	64
...Sharing Accommodation	54
Repton School Dubai	233, 242
Republique	433
RERA (Real Estate Regulatory Agency)	52
Residence Spa At One&Only Royal Mirage	173
Residence Visas	36
Resident Identity Card	43
Restaurants	385
Revolution Cycles	378
Rhodes In Residence	397
Ride Bike Shop	378
Riding For The Disabled Association Of Dubai	186, 219, 246
Right Bite	143
Rights Lawyers, The	146
Rip Tides	278
Ripe	264, 338, 340
Rira Gallery	267
Ritmo De Havana	198
Ritz-Carlton	261
...Beach Club	280
...Doha	479
...Dubai	321
Riva Beach Club	263, 281
Rivington Bar & Terrace	430
Rivington Grill	270, 416
Rivoli Textiles	379
Rixos	
...Bab Al Bahr	465
...Royal Spa	173
...The Palm	281, 314
Road Signs	95
Road Tolls	97
Roche Bobois	362
Rochester Institute Of Technology	254
Rock Bottom	433, 434
Rococo	196
Romantic Dining	409
Ronda Locatelli	397
Rooftop Bars	428

Rooftop Terrace & Sports Lounge	430
Roots Salon	170
Rotana	321
Rotana Jet	112
Royal Air Maroc	112
Royal Brunei Airlines	112
Royal Enfield Dubai	188
Royal Gardenscape	364
Royal Jet	112
Royal Jordanian	112
Royal Orchid	394
RSA Insurance	93, 118
Rubbish Disposal	88
Ruby Tuesday	401
Rugby	188, 286
...Rugby Sevens	29, 286
Rupee Room, The	408
Ru'us Al Jibal Mountains	302
Running	189
Russian Cuisine	389
RYA Courses	306

S

Saab	102
Sadek Music	370
SAE Institute Dubai	202, 254
Safa Kindergarten Nursery	228
Safa Park	108, 268, 282
Safa School	242
Safer Driver	422
Saga World	267
Sahab Hotel	476
Sahn Eddar	270, 420
Sailing	189
Saks Fifth Avenue	335, 366
Saks Hair Salon	170
Salalah	474
Salam Studio & Stores	335, 358
Salaries	207
Saleh Bin Lahej Group	
...ADVERT	xii
Salik Tag	97
Salon Ink	170
Salsa Dubai	198
Salsali Private Museum	264
Sanctuary Pool Lounge	425
Sandance	438
Sandboarding	299
Sandy Beach Diving Centre	301
Sandy Beach Hotel	302, 460
Sansaya Clinic	139
Santa Fe Relocation Services	83
...ADVERT	69
Santorini Hotel	465
Saravana Bhavan	262
Saray Spa	174
Satori Spa	174
Satwa	68, 333
Saudi Arabian Airlines	112
Saudi German Hospital	127
Savage Garden	198
Savile Row	379
Scene Club, The	202, 436
School	
...Fees	231
...Lunches	232
...Regulator	232

...Selection	230
...Supplies	366
...Transfers	233
...Transport	232
School Transport Services LLC	232
Schools	65, 68, 70, 72, 74, 76, 80, 231
Scoozi	413
Scouts Association (British Scouting Overseas)	157
Scouts & Guides	156, 246
Scrabble	202
Scuba 2000	301
Scubatec Diving Center	301
Sea Freight	83
Sea Riders	306
Seafire Steakhouse	396
Seafood Dining	389
Sealife	14, 276
Seashells Nursery	228
Seawings	312
...ADVERT	xxvi
Secondary Schools	232
Second-hand Cars	100
Second-hand Goods	374
SEGA Republic	260, 273, 274
Segreto	404
Selecting A Nursery	225
Selling A Home	60
Senses	408
Sephora	372
Setting Up Home	82
Seven Dental Centre	139
Sewerage	86
Seychelles	466
Shades	430
Shakespeare & Co	420
...ADVERT	421
Shamaal International Surfski Race	306
Shangri-La	261, 321
Shangri-La's Barr Al Jissah Resort & Spa	474
Sharaf DG	342, 360
Shariah Law	144
Sharif Eye Center	140
Sharjah	468
Sharjah Art Museum	470
Sharjah Biennial	468
Sharjah Classic Car Museum	470
Sharjah Desert Park	470
Sharjah Discovery Centre	471
Sharjah Golf & Shooting Club	283, 292, 471
...ADVERT	vi-vii
Sharjah International Book Fair	
...ADVERT	357
Sharjah Light Festival	468
Sharjah Museum Of Islamic Civilization	471
Sharjah Museums	
...ADVERT	469
Sharjah Wanderers Sports Club	165
Sharjah Water Festival	295
Sharmila Dance Gala	29
Sharq Village & Spa	479
Sheesa Beach Dive Center	302, 311
Sheffield Private School	242

Sheikh Hamdan bin Rashid Al Maktoum	8
Sheikh Khalifa bin Zayed Al Nahyan	8
Sheikh Mohammed bin Rashid Boulevard	261
Sheikh Mohammed Centre For Cultural Understanding	16, 269, 385
...ADVERT	227
Sheikh Rashid bin Saeed Al Maktoum	6
Sheikh Saeed Al Maktoum House	259, 272
Sheikh Zayed Grand Mosque	6, 445
Sheikh Zayed Road	72
Shelter	202, 264, 436, 438
Sheraton	
...Dubai Creek	260
...Jumeirah Beach	278, 321
Shift Car Rental & Leasing	100
Shindagha	259, 272
Shipping	326
Shisha	20
Sho Cho	313, 425
Shooters	406
Shooting, Paintballing & Laser Games	290
Shopping	328, 334
...Buyers' Guide	352
...Events	325
...Malls	346
...Tours	307
...Districts	328
Shops	65, 68, 70, 72, 76, 80
Short Breaks From The UAE	466
Shuiqi Salon	170
Shuiqi Spa & Fitness	165, 174
Siddharta Lounge	411
Sightseeing Cruises	310
Signature By Sanjeev Kapoor	397
Silicon Oasis	81
Singapore Airlines	112
Singapore Business Council	216
Singapore Deli Restaurant	406
Singing	202
Single Parents	151
Singways/Maison Decor	362
Sir Bani Yas Island	454
Sisters Beauty Lounge	169, 170
Six Senses Zighy Bay	473
Skateparks	268, 292
Skating & Rollerblading	189
Ski Dubai	270, 292, 350
...ADVERT	293
Skiing	189, 292
Sky & Sea Adventures	306
Skydive Dubai	270, 292
Skydiving	292
Skype	89
Skyview Bar	270, 431
Slimming	142
Slim Spa	143
Small World Nursery	228
Smiling BKK	399
Snooker	202
Snoopy Island	14, 302, 459
Snorkelling	302

492   Dubai Explorer

INDEX

Socatots	184	Stand Up		T		Tips & Toes	169, 172
Soccer Circus Dubai	184	Paddleboarding (SUP)	304			Toll Gates	97
Social Circles UAE	48	Standard Chartered		Tagine	411	Tom&Serg	264, 419
Social Networks	48	Bank – Middle East	115	Tagpuan	399	Toni & Guy	170
Sociate	434	Standard Chartered		Talass Orthodontic &		Top Scores	231
Socotra Cormorant	14	Dubai Marathon	26	Dental Center	139	Top Style Hair Salon	170
Sofitel Jumeirah Beach	321	Star International School	242	Talise Fitness	165	Top Style Salon	170
Sofitel The Palm	314	Star International School		Talise Ottoman Spa	174	Total Arts	268
Softball	189	Mirdif	242	Talise Spa At Jumeirah		Tour Dubai	311
Softouch Spa	174	Star International School		Emirates Towers	174	Tourism	12
Solid Rock	198, 200	Umm Sheif	242	Talise Spa Madinat		Tours	307
Soolyman Sport Fishing	182	Stars 'N' Bars	446	Jumeirah	176	Tower Clinic	139
SOS Beauty Salon	170	Starting A Business	216	Tamanya Terrace	430	Tower Links Golf Club	464
Soubra Tents & Awnings	364	Stay By Yannick Alleno	398	Tanagra	366	Tower Of Neptune	270
Souk Al Bahar	260, 270, 344	Staycations	313	Tango Dubai	198	Town Centre Jumeirah	332
...ADVERT	345	Staying In	439	Tashkeel	268, 292	Toyota	102
Souk Madinat		Steakhouses	389	Taste Of Dubai Festival	385	Toys	366
Jumeirah	262, 344	Stitches	379	Tavola	196	Toy Store, The	366
Souk Waqif	478	STORALL	83	Tax	118	Toys R Us	366
Souks	270, 344	Story Roof Top Lounge	425	Taxes & Service Charges	385	Track Meydan Golf, The	288
South African Airways	112	Strata Law	58	Tax-free Shopping	34	Trade	12
South African Business		Street Food	399	Taxis	111	...Fairs	220
Council	216	Stride For Life	189	Tea Junction	417, 420	...Licence	215
South African Women's		Studio Du Chef	412	TECOM	74	Trader Vic's Mai Tai	
Association	48	Studio Sol	380	Ted Morgan Hair	170	Lounge	413, 425
South American Cuisine	389	Submarine	435	Tee & Putt Mini Golf	290	Traffic	362
Souvenirs	375	Subway	439	Tel Moreeb	454	...Accidents	98
Spa At The Palace		Sue Anderson		Telecommunications	88	...Fines	97
Downtown Dubai, The	174	Consultants	233	Telephone		...Offences	97
Spaces Spa & Salon	173	Sukh Sagar	413	...Installing A Landline	88	Transformations Institute	248
Spadunya Club	172	Sultan Garden		...International Dialling Code	4	Trek Bike Shop	378
Spanish Business Council	216	Center	364, 365	Television	24, 90	Trench & Associates	146
Spanish Cuisine	389	Sultani Lifestyle Gallerie	376	Temporary Accommodation	46	Triathlon	193
Spanish La Liga	90	Sultan's Lounge	420	Temporary Work Permits	208	Tribes	416
Spas	170	Summer Camps	157	Tenancy Contract	54	Tridubai	193
Speak Dating	48	Sun & Sand Sports	377	Tennis	192, 286	Troyka	408
Special Needs Education	245	Sundowners	422	Terrace, The	430	Trucial Coast	6
Special Needs Future		Sunset Beach	280	Terry Fox Run	28	Tuberculosis	42
Development Centre	246	Sunset Mall	332	Tertiary Education	247	Tunisair	112
Specialist Hospitals &		Supermarkets	337	Textile Souk	346	Turkish Cuisine	389
Clinics	128	Supertri	193	Textiles, Tailoring &		Turkish Airlines	112
Spectator Sports	286	Supperclub	395	Repairs	379	Turning Pointe Music	199, 370
Spectrum On One	396	Supreme Council	8	Thai Cuisine	389	Turtles	160, 304
Speedex	365	Surf Club	280	Thai Airways	112		
Speedo Swim Squads	192	Surf Dubai	306	Thai At The Blue Elephant	196	**U**	
Spice & Aroma	196	Surf School UAE	306	Thai Elite Spa	173		
Spice Island	321, 402	Surf Shop Arabia	379	Thai Kitchen, The	396	U Energy	165
Spice Souk	259, 330, 344	Surfers' Beach	280	The Address		UAE & Oman Rock	
Spicejet	112	Surfing	190, 305	...Downtown Dubai	314	Climbing & Outdoor	
Spinneys	337	Surfing Dubai	304	...Dubai Marina	197	Adventures	296
Spinneys Centre	332	Sushi	408	...Montgomerie Dubai	285	UAE Active	166
Splash Land	274	Sushi Art	406	THE One	262, 361, 420	UAE Calendar	26
Sports Clubs	179	Sustainability	14	THE One Junior	364	UAE English Soccer School	
Sports & Leisure		Suvoroff	413	Theatre	438	Of Excellence	184, 246
Activities	283	Swedish Business		Theme Parks	274	UAE Fencing Federation	182
Sports & Outdoor		Council	216	Thiptara	196	UAE Flag	3
Equipment	376	Swedish Dental Clinic	139	Third Line, The	264, 268	UAE Horseracing	29
Sports Direct	342	Sweet Connection – The		Thomsun Music	370	UAE Labour Law	210
Sports Fit	165	Gluten Free Kitchen	440	Thomsun Pure Music	370	UAE National Day	25
Sports Package	90	Swim School, Australian		Thrill Zone	292	UAE Underwater Explorer	300
Spring Dubai	165	International (AISS)	190	Thyme Restaurant	402	UEFA Champion's	
Squash	190	Swimming	190, 304	Tickles &		UIM F1 H2O World	90
Sri Lanka	466	Swimming Pools	93	Giggles	156, 170, 176, 370	Championship	295
Sri Lankan Cuisine	389	Swiss Business Council	216	Tiffany & Co	365	Ultimate Charter	311
SriLankan Airlines	112	Swiss Dental Clinic	139	Tilal Liwa	480	Umi Sushi	413
St Francis Of Assisi Church	49	Swiss International		Tilia & Finn	169	Umm Al Quwain	304, 471
St Mary's Catholic		Air Lines	112	Tim Hortons	413	Umm Al Quwain Marine	
Church Dubai	49	Switch Bowling Dubai	284	Timberland	377	Club	471
St Mary's Catholic High		Sword Dancing	269	Time Zone	3	Umm Suqeim	262
School	242	Symmetry Gym	165	Times Square Center	264, 329	Umm Suqeim Beach	280
St Regis Saadiyat		Synergy Fitness	165	Tinted Windows	100, 358	Umm Suqeim Park	283
Island Resort	448	Synquatics	192	Tiny Home Nursery	230	Underground, The	424
Stadium	377						

493

INDEX

UNESCO	468	VLCC Wellness	143	Wild Wadi's Swim		Zayed University	250
Union Co-operative		Voda Bar	425	Burj Al Arab	27	Zazeezou	368
Society	337	VOG Color Your Life	170	Wildlife & Sealife	14, 276	Zebra Crossing	154
Union National Bank	115	Voi	392	Wills	147	Zen Interiors	362
United Airlines	112	Volkswagen	102	Willow Children's Nursery	229	Zen Yoga	166, 203
United Furniture	361	Volleyball	193	Willow Stream Spa	313	Zinc	435
...ADVERT	xv	Voluntary & Charity Work	218	Wills	146	Zip Line	274
Universal American		Volvo	102	Winchester School	243	Zouari Hair Salon	170
School Dubai	234			Wine Bars & Cigar		Zulekha Hospital	127
Universities & Colleges	247			Lounges	431	Zuma	197, 396
University Of Wollongong		**W**		Wolfi's Bike Shop	378	Zurich Insurance	93
In Dubai	250			Women For Women		Zurich International Life	118
UOWD		W Doha	479	International	219		
...ADVERT	251	Wa International	84	Wonder Bus Tours	307		
Up & Running Integrated		Wadi Adventure	304, 306, 453	Wonderland	274		
Sports Medical Center	136	Wadi Bih	296	Wooridul Spine Centre	130		
Uptown Bar	430	Wadi Khab Al Shamis	296	Working Hours	4, 208		
Uptown Mirdiff	333	Wadi Sidr	296	Working Lunch	418		
Uptown MotorCity	331	Wafi Gourmet	408	World Expo 2020	10, 14		
Uptown Primary School	245	Wafi Mall	350	World Happiness Report	3		
Urban Male		Wagamama	408, 413	World Of Pets	160, 374		
Lounge (UML)	170, 176	Waitrose	337	World Records	5		
Urban Tails Pet Resort	160	Wakeboarding	280, 305, 445	WPF Dubai Women			
...ADVERT	163	Waldorf Astoria	465	Personal Training	166		
Used Car Dealers	102	Waldorf Astoria					
Useful Apps	23	Palm Jumeirah	321	**X**			
Useful Websites	24	Walk at JBR, The	261, 280, 331				
Utilities & Services	86	Walking	106	Xclusive Yachts Sport			
		Warehouse	428	Fishing & Yacht			
V		Wasl Square	332	Charter	182, 312		
		Watatsumi	392	XL Beach Club	431, 435		
		Water Supply	86	XVA Art Hotel	146		
Vaccinations &		Water Activities	304	XVA Gallery	259, 266, 268, 364		
Registration	122, 160	Water Buses	109				
Vantage	433	Water Parks	270, 274	**Y**			
Vasan Eye Care	140	Water Taxis	110, 259				
VCU Qatar		Watercooled	306				
...ADVERT	222	Waterfront	392	Y12	170		
Veda Pavilion	425	Watersports	193, 286, 378	Yalla! Bowling Lanes			
Vegetarian Cuisine	385	Watersports Centres	305	& Lounge	274, 284		
Vehicle Finance	102	Waterworld Yacht Rental	312	Yalumba	396		
Vehicle Inspection Test	104	Wavebreaker	408	YApparel	377		
Vehicle Repairs	104	Weather	4	Yas Island	445		
Version Francaise	169	Wedding Planners	144	...ADVERT	449		
Vets, Kennels & Boarding	160	Weddings	380	...Yas Links Golf	446		
Vhernier	366	...Ceremony	145	...Yas Mall	446		
Victory Heights Primary		...Services	380	...Yas Marina Circuit	446		
School	243	Wedding Shop, The	380	...Yas Viceroy Abu Dhabi	448		
Vienna Cafe	417	Well Of Life Church Dubai	49	...Yas Waterworld	274, 446, 448		
Vietnamese Cuisine	389	Well-being	168	Yas Sports	377		
Villa, The	78	West 14th At Oceana	263	Yateem Optician	140		
Villa 47	321	West Coast Customs	358	Yellow Brick Road Nursery	229		
Villa Beach	394	Western Hajar	476	Yellow Hat	358		
Village Mall	332	Westin Abu Dhabi Golf		Yo! Sushi	407		
Vintage Cheese &		Resort & Spa	448	Yoga & Pilates	165, 202		
Wine Bar	433	Westin Dubai Mina Seyahi		Yoga Room	203		
Virgin Atlantic	112	Beach Resort	146, 321	Yogalates Bliss	203		
Virgin Megastore	356	Westminster School	243	Youngsters Hair & Spa	170		
Virtuzone	213	Whatever Floats Your Boat	29				
Visas		Wheeler's	398	**Z**			
...Domestic Worker Visa	40	Where-To-Be-Born Index	8				
...Employment Visa	36	Whistle & Flute	379	Zabeel Park	283		
...Family Visa	40	Whistler, The	428, 433	Zak Electronic & Musical			
...Sponsoring Family		White Dubai	435	Instruments	370		
Members	40	White Star Bookshop		Zaks	366		
...Transferring A Visa	210	(Wasco)	354	Zanshinkan Aikido			
...Visa On Arrival	34	Wi-fi	89	Club Dubai	187		
...Visit Visa	34	Wild Peeta	409	Zayed National Museum	450		
Vision Express	140	Wild Wadi	262, 273, 276				
Vista Lounge	430	...ADVERT	x, 277				

494 Dubai Explorer

NOTES

Explorer Products

Residents' Guides

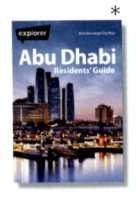

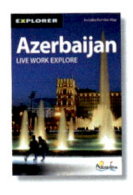

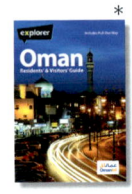

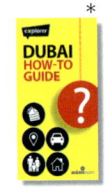

Visitors' Guides

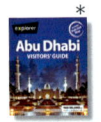

Photography Books & Calendars

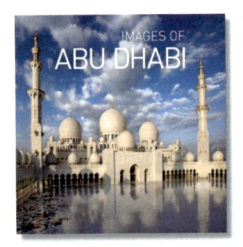

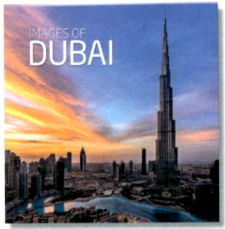

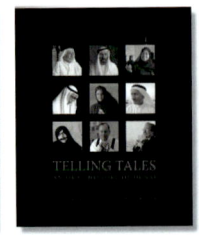

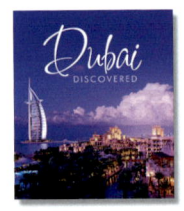

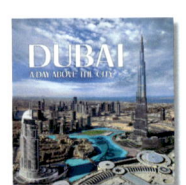

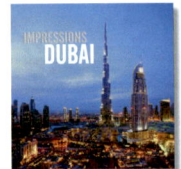

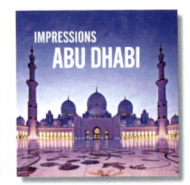

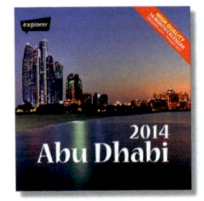

496 Dubai Explorer

Check out ask**explorer**.com

Maps

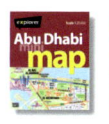

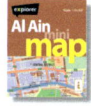

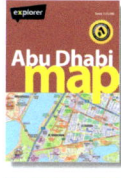

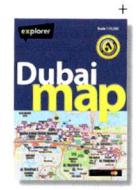

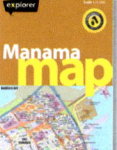

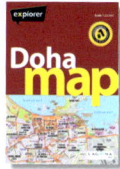

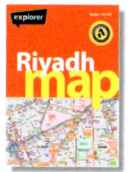

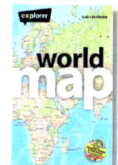

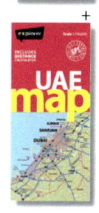

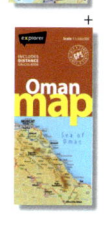

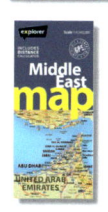

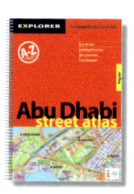

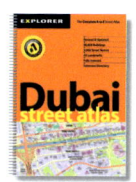

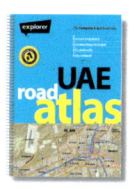

Adventure & Lifestyle Guides

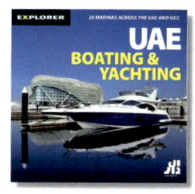

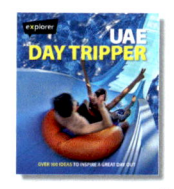

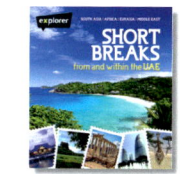

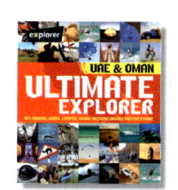

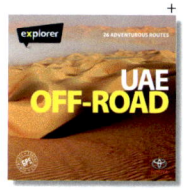

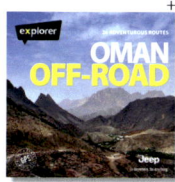

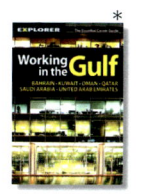

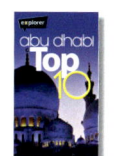

Apps & eBooks
+ Also available as applications. Visit askexplorer.com/apps.
* Now available in eBook format.
Visit askexplorer.com/shop or Amazon for a full product list.

UAE COUNTRY MAP

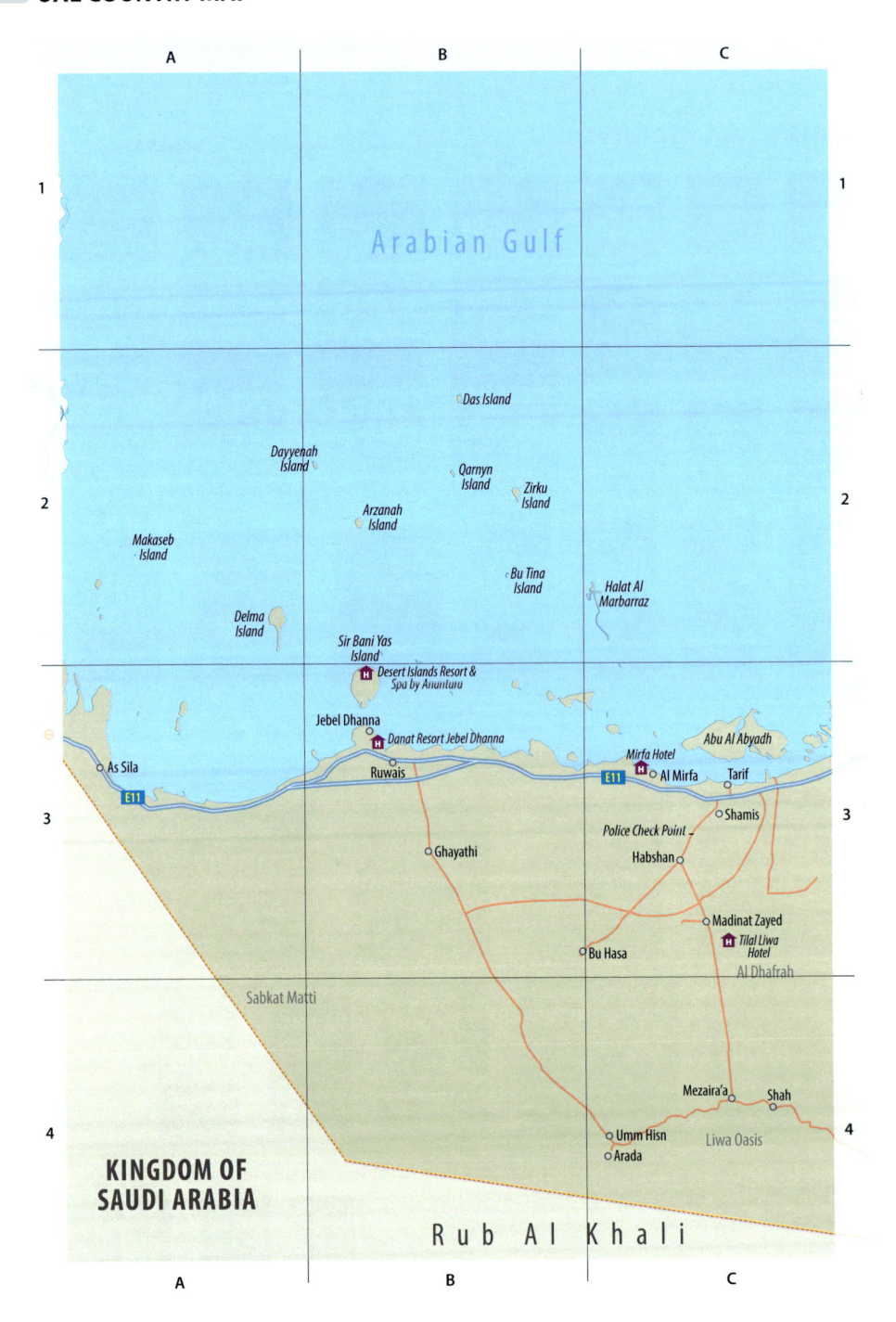

D
E
F
1
2
3
4
Shams
Musandam
OMAN
Gulf of Oman
Abu Musa
Rams
Ras Al Khaimah
E18
Jazirat
Al Hamra
Digdagga
Dibba
Umm Al Quwain
Al Rafaah
Aqah
Hamriya
E11
E311
E87
Ajman
E18
E89
E99
Sharjah
E55
Khor Fakkan
Deira
Al Dhaid
Manama
Madha
(Oman)
Masafi
E88
Nahwa (UAE)
Sir Bu Na'air Island
Dubai
Bithnah
Jumeira
Al Awir
Maleihah
E611
E89
Fujairah
Nadd Al Shiba
Jabal Ali
Lahbab
Kalba
JA Jebel Ali Golf
Resort & Spa
E55
E44
E77
Hatta Fort
Hotel
E311
Al Lusaili
Madam
Golden Tulip Al Jazira
Al Maha
Desert Resort
Bab Al Shams
Desert Resort
E66
Hatta
E11
Al Faqa
Al Shwaib
Shinas
E55
Al Haiyir
ABU DHABI
Sweihan
E20
Mahdah
E66
Musaffah
Mafraq
Bu Kesheishah
Baniyas
Al Ain
Buraimi
E22
Khatam
Rumaitha
Jebel
Hafeet
UNITED ARAB
EMIRATES
21
SULTANATE
OF OMAN
Al Wijan
Ramlat
Al Hamra
Al Qua'a
Al Humrah
Hamim
Qasr Al Sarab Desert
Resort by Anantara
N
0
50km
Umm Az Zamul
© Explorer Group Ltd. 2014
This map is not an authority on international and administrative boundaries
D
E
F

Useful Numbers

Embassies & Consulates

Australian Consulate	04 508 7100
Bahrain Embassy	02 665 7500
British Embassy	04 309 4444
Canadian Consulate	04 404 8444
Chinese Consulate	04 394 4733
Czech Embassy	02 678 2800
Danish Consulate	04 348 0877
Egyptian Consulate	04 397 1122
French Consulate	04 408 4900
German Consulate	04 349 8888
Indian Consulate	04 397 1222
Iranian Consulate	04 344 4717
Irish Embassy	02 495 8200
Italian Consulate	04 331 4167
Japanese Consulate	04 331 9191
Jordanian Consulate	04 397 0500
Kuwaiti Consulate	04 397 8000
Lebanese Consulate	04 397 7450
Malaysian Consulate	04 398 5843
Netherlands Consulate	04 440 7600
New Zealand Consulate	04 331 7500
Norwegian Consulate	04 382 3880
Omani Consulate	04 397 1000
Pakistani Consulate	04 397 0412
Philippine Consulate	04 220 7100
Qatar Consulate	04 396 0444
Russian Consulate	04 328 5347
Saudi Arabian Consulate	04 397 9777
Spanish Embassy	02 626 9544
South African Consulate	04 397 5222
Sri Lankan Consulate	04 398 6535
Swedish Embassy	02 417 8800
Swiss Consulate	04 329 0999
Thai Consulate	04 348 9550
US Consulate General	04 309 4000

Emergency Services

Ambulance	998/999
DEWA Emergency	991
Dubai Police Emergency	999
Fire Department	997

Police Services

Al Ameen (for neighbourhood problems)	800 4888
Department for Tourist Security	800 423
Dubai Police	04 609 9999
Dubai Police Information Line	800 7777

Directory

Dubai International Airport Help Desk	04 224 5555
Flight Information	04 216 6666
Baggage Services	04 224 5383
Directory Enquiries (du)	199
Directory Enquiries (Etisalat)	181
du Contact Centre (mobile enquiries)	
From mobile	155
From any phone	055 567 8155
du Contact Centre (home enquiries)	04 390 5555
Dubai Consumer Protection	600 54 5555
Dubai Municipality	800 900
Dubai Rent Committee	04 206 3456
Etisalat Customer Care	101
Etisalat Information	144
International Operator Assistance	100
Mobile Phone Code (du)	052/055
Mobile Phone Code (Etisalat)	050/056
Ministry Of Labour Hotline	800 665
National Center Of Meteorology & Seismology	02 222 7777
RTA Complaints Line	800 90 90
Salik	800 72545
Speaking Clock	141

Airlines

Aeroflot	04 222 2245
Air Arabia	06 508 8888
Air France	800 23823
Air India	04 227 6787
Air Mauritius	04 221 4455
Air New Zealand	04 335 9126
Air Seychelles	04 286 8008
Alitalia	04 282 6113
American Airlines	04 316 6116
Austrian Airlines	04 211 2538
Biman Bangladesh Airlines	04 2203 2029
British Airways	800 0441 3322
Cathay Pacific	04 204 2888
China Airlines	04 271 8555
CSA Czech Airlines	04 294 5666
Cyprus Airways	04 221 4455
Delta Airlines	04 397 0118
Egypt Air	04 230 6666
Emirates	600 555 555
Etihad Airways	04 407 2200
flydubai	04 231 1000
Gulf Air	04 271 6207
Iran Air	04 224 0200
Japan Airlines	04 217 7501
KLM Royal Dutch Airlines	800 556
Kuwait Airways	04 228 5896
Lufthansa	04 373 9100
Malaysia Airlines	04 325 4411
Middle East Airlines	04 223 7080
Oman Air	04 351 8080
Pakistan International Airlines	04 223 4888
Qantas	04 316 6652
Qatar Airways	04 231 9999
RAK Airways	04 294 5666
Royal Brunei Airlines	04 334 4884
Royal Jet Group	02 575 1777
Royal Jordanian	04 294 4288
Saudi Arabian Airlines	04 229 6227
Singapore Airlines	04 316 6888
Swiss Air	04 381 6100

Hospitals

American Hospital	04 377 6644
Cedars Jebel Ali Int'l Hospital	04 881 4000
Dubai Hospital	04 219 5000
Iranian Hospital	04 344 0250
Latifa Hospital	04 219 3000
Medcare Hospital	04 407 9111
Mediclinic City Hospital	04 435 9999
Mediclinic Welcare Hospital	04 282 7788
Neuro Spinal Hospital	04 342 0000
Rashid Hospital	04 219 2000

24 Hour Pharmacy

Life Pharmacy	04 344 1122
IBN Sina Pharmacy	04 355 6909
Yara Pharmacy	04 222 5503

Taxi Service

Al Arabia Taxi	04 285 5566
Cars Taxi	800 227 789
Dubai Taxis	04 208 0808
Metro Taxi	600 566000
National Taxi	600 543322

Car Rental

Autolease Rent-A-Car	04 282 6565
Avis	04 295 9899
Budget Car & Van Rental	800 2722
Diamondlease	04 885 2677
Dubai Exotic Limo	800 5466
EuroStar Rent-A-Car	04 266 1117
Hertz	800 437 89
Icon Car Rental	04 257 8228
National Car Rental	04 283 2020
Payless Car Rental	04 384 5526
Thrifty Car Rental	800 4694
United Car Rentals	04 285 7777

Road Service

Arabian Automobile Association (AAA)	800 4900
MESAR Roadside Assistance	050 204 5208

Dubai Residents' Guide – 18th Edition
Lead Editor Kirsty Tuxford
Section Editors Laura Coughlan, Lily Lawes, Stacey Siebritz, Andy Mills
Contributors Emma Bladen, Lisa Crowther, Heather Richardson
Proofread by Lidiya Baltova-Kalichuk
Data managed by Amapola Castillo, Suzzette S.Privado, Maria Luisa Reyes
Sales by Sabrina Ahmed, Bryan Aynes
Designed by Ieyad Charaf, Jayde Fernandes, Pete Maloney, M. Shakkeer
Maps by Noushad Madathil, Zainudheen Madathil, Dhanya Nellikkunnummal
Photographs by Henry Hilos, Hardy Mendrofa, Pete Maloney, Andy Mills, Victor Romero, Bart Wojcinski, Gary McGovern

PublishiPublishing
Chief Content Officer & Founder Alistair MacKenzie

Editorial
Managing Editor Carli Allan
Editors Laura Coughlan, Andy Mills, Kirsty Tuxford
Deputy Editors Lily Lawes, Stacey Siebritz
Production Coordinator Rahul Rajan
Editorial Assistant Amapola Castillo Baldo
Researchers Farida, Amrit Raj, Roja P, Praseena, Shahla Noura

Design & Photography
Creative Director Pete Maloney
Art Director Ieyad Charaf
Senior Designer Gary McGovern
Junior Designer M. Shakkeer
Layout Manager Jayde Fernandes
Cartography Manager Zain Madathil
Cartographers Noushad Madathil, Dhanya Nellikkunnummal, Ramla Kambravan, Shalu Sukumar
GIS Analyst Rafi KM, Hidayath Razi, Aslam
Photographer & Image Editor Hardy Mendrofa

Sales & Marketing
Director of Sales Peter Saxby
Media Sales Area Managers Sabrina Ahmed, Bryan Anes, Louise Burton, Matthew Whitbread, Laura Zuffova
Business Development Manager Pouneh Hafizi, Nischay Kaul
Corporate Sales Manager Zendi De Coning
Director of Marketing Lindsay West
Senior Marketing Executive Stuart L. Cunningham
Director of Retail Ivan Rodrigues
Retail Sales Coordinator Michelle Mascarenhas
Retail Sales Area Supervisors Ahmed Mainodin, Firos Khan
Retail Sales Merchandisers Johny Mathew, Shan Kumar
Retail Sales Drivers Shabsir Madathil, Najumudeen K.I., Sujeer Khan
Warehouse Assistant Mohamed Haji, Jithinraj M

Finance, HR & Administration
Accountant Cherry Enriquez
Accounts Assistants Sunil Suvarna, Jeanette Carino Enecillo
Administrative Assistant
Joy H. San Buenaventura
Reception Edelyn Isiderio
Public Relations Officer Rafi Jamal
Office Assistant Shafeer Ahamed
Office Manager – India Jithesh Kalathingal

IT & Digital Solutions
Digital Solutions Manager Derrick Pereira
Web Developer Mirza Ali Nasrullah
IT Manager R. Ajay
Database Programmer Pradeep T.P.

Contact Us
General Enquiries
We'd love to hear your thoughts and answer any questions you have about this book or any other Explorer product.
Contact us at **info@askexplorer.com**

Careers
If you fancy yourself as an Explorer, send your CV (stating the position you're interested in) to
jobs@askexplorer.com

Contract Publishing
For enquiries about Explorer's Contract Publishing arm and design services contact
contracts@askexplorer.com

Retail Sales
Our products are available in most good bookshops as well as online at askexplorer.com/shop or Amazon.
retail@askexplorer.com

PR & Marketing
For PR and marketing enquiries contact
marketing@askexplorer.com

Corporate Sales & Licensing
For bulk sales and customisation options, as well as licensing of this book or any Explorer product, contact
leads@askexplorer.com

Advertising & Sponsorship
For advertising and sponsorship, contact
sales@askexplorer.com

Explorer Publishing & Distribution
PO Box 34275, Dubai, United Arab Emirates
askexplorer.com

Phone: +971 (0)4 340 8805
Fax: +971 (0)4 340 8806